Letters of H. P. Lovecraft

LETTERS WITH DONALD AND HOWARD WANDREI AND TO EMIL PETAJA

Donald and Howard Wandrei, 3 July 1935. Courtesy David Rajchel.

H. P. LOVECRAFT

LETTERS WITH DONALD AND HOWARD WANDREI AND TO EMIL PETAJA

EDITED BY S. T. JOSHI AND DAVID E. SCHULTZ

Hippocampus Press

New York

Published by Hippocampus Press
P.O. Box 641, New York, NY 10156.
www.hippocampuspress.com

Cover design and Hippocampus Press logo by Anastasia Damianakos.
Cover production by Barbara Briggs Silbert.

First Edition
3 5 7 9 8 6 4 2

ISBN 978-1-61498-257-9

Contents

Donald Wandrei, Connie Colestock, and Howard Wandrei

*Donald Wandrei, H. P. Lovecraft, and Frank Belknap Long, Jr.,
in New York, 7 January 1934*

Introduction

Like many of us, Donald Wandrei (1908–1987) developed an affinity for weird fiction as a teenager. Also like many of us, for years he felt as if no one shared his literary and artistic tastes, except perhaps his younger brother Howard. Some time in late 1924, Donald wrote to Clark Ashton Smith (1893–1961), evidently hoping to purchase Smith's *The Star-Treader*. Wandrei had been a devoted reader of *Weird Tales* since its inception in March 1923, and he apparently expressed to Smith his fondness for some of the writers who made it distinctive, including H. P. Lovecraft (1890–1937). Smith, who had been corresponding with Lovecraft for several years, wrote Wandrei on 11 December 1924: "Lovecraft is great—his horror stories are totally unlike those of any one else."[1] Eventually Smith began writing to Lovecraft about his bright young correspondent. Smith's comments about Wandrei and his work piqued Lovecraft's interest, for he wrote to Smith, "This Wandrei must certainly be an interesting character, having the tastes he does; & I'm greatly interested to learn that it was my reference in the *Weird Tale*[s] 'Eyrie' which set him on your trail."[2] Surely he's welcome to see the two latest, & I shall be glad to hear from him if he returns them directly to me."[3]

Although Lovecraft and his work are mentioned several times in Smith's letters to Wandrei (not many of Wandrei's to Smith survive for this period), it would be two full years before Wandrei wrote to Lovecraft himself. In No-

---

1. CAS to DAW, 11 December 1924 (ms., Minnesota Historical Society).
2. HPL refers to his letter published in "The Eyrie," *WT* 2, No. 3 (October 1923): 82, in which he had mentioned "A friend of mine—Clark Ashton Smith, the California poet of horror, madness, and morbid beauty." DAW's account of the matter, written about thirty years after the fact, contains numerous errors: "In a 1926 issue, the magazine published a letter from Lovecraft highly praising the fantastic poetry of Clark Ashton Smith in a book titled *Ebony and Crystal*. I could find no record of this book or author at the St. Paul Public Library; and the St. Paul Book & Stationery could find no listing in any book index or catalogue. I then wrote to the editor of *Weird Tales,* inclosing a letter to be forwarded to H. P. Lovecraft, asking the name of the publisher and price of the Smith book. Lovecraft's letter to me was in reply to this request. His letter was of equal literary status with his stories, and gave me Clark Ashton Smith's address in Auburn, California. I immediately wrote to Smith, inclosing payment, and receiving a reply and the book, which enthralled me fully as much as Lovecraft's stories. A lifelong correspondence and friendship with both authors developed" (*DD* 369). HPL did not write of CAS's poetry, although by this time CAS had had three poems published in *WT*. Among other errors, DAW's account suggests that he became acquainted with HPL before he contacted CAS.
3. HPL to CAS, 29 October 1926 (*DS* 111).

vember 1926 Smith sub-lent manuscripts of two of Lovecraft's unpublished stories to Wandrei, instructing Wandrei to return them to Lovecraft directly. Wandrei did so the next month, thereupon initiating a correspondence that lasted till Lovecraft's death.

In Lovecraft's first letter to Wandrei—written two years to the day after Smith's first letter to him—he acknowledged that he and Smith had discussed Wandrei on occasion in their own letters. On one such occasion, having read some of Wandrei's manuscripts lent to him by Smith, Lovecraft wrote:

> The Wandrei manuscripts safely arrived today, & I am really quite enthusiastic about them. The author has a genuine grasp of the strange, & a verbal facility & richness which needs only practice to evolve into a powerful & compelling style. The cosmic pieces are perhaps the most distinctive, but all the others have qualities which it is impossible to praise too highly. 'The Chuckler' certainly is a hair-raiser deluxe! I hope Wandrei will keep up his writing, & am anxious to see more of his material.[4]

Wandrei had, of course, by this time published very little, aside from some items in the University of Minnesota's student literary magazine, the *Minnesota Quarterly;* but Wandrei's article on Smith, "The Emperor of Dreams," had, through the intervention of George Sterling, found its way into the *Overland Monthly* for December 1926, and Lovecraft welcomed its enthusiastic praise of Smith's poetry when he read the essay in manuscript:

> I was very glad to hear from you, & to receive the critique I have so long been anxious to see. The latter is really very just & acute in its analysis of your work, but as you say may meet editorial opposition because of its tone of youthful effervescence & colourful rhapsody. I imagine that Wandrei must be rather a young chap—though possessed of a fund of imagery & command of language which will serve him well when he has learnt the lessons of restraint & austerity of form which come with later life. I certainly wish he could get the review into print somewhere, though I know the process is none too easy. What is Wandrei, anyway? That is, what does he write, & what are his general literary bearings? I am interested in anyone as genuinely sensitive to the fantastic as he.[5]

As was often the case with their other correspondents, Lovecraft and Wandrei eagerly exchanged manuscripts. Many of Lovecraft's early stories had, at this time, appeared only in amateur journals or remained unpublished, and Wandrei must have asked in his nonextant letter of 4 December to see these items, or at least to learn whether Lovecraft had any tales that had not ap-

---

4. HPL to CAS, 17 January 1927 (*DS* 119). HPL was later less enthusiastic about "The Chuckler" (see letter 2n2).
5. HPL to CAS, 12 October 1926 (*DS* 109–10).

peared in *Weird Tales* or other commercial magazines. Wandrei himself was at this time primarily a poet and sent Lovecraft many of his early poems—not only those that ultimately appeared in his first book, *Ecstasy and Other Poems* (1928), but also some that were unpublished and whose whereabouts are not now known. It may seem surprising that Wandrei's book was published by an obscure printer/publisher in Athol, Mass., of all places, but in fact he was in good company, for W. Paul Cook published books by members of the Lovecraft circle: Samuel Loveman, *The Hermaphrodite: A Poem* (1926); Frank Belknap Long, Jr., *A Man from Genoa and Other Poems* (1926); John Ravenor Bullen, *White Fire* (January 1928; Lovecraft edited the late poet's book); *Ecstasy and Other Poems* (1928); Lovecraft, *The Shunned House* (1928; printed but not bound or distributed at the time); Loveman, *The Sphinx* (1944), and books by amateur associates of Lovecraft and Cook. Cook's one-shot magazine, the *Recluse* (1927), contained work by Lovecraft, Wandrei, Clark Ashton Smith, Loveman, and others in the circle.

Wandrei soon began sending Lovecraft his early prose work as well. Wandrei's taste for weird fiction had impelled him to collect many now scarce volumes of weird and early science fiction, with the purpose of compiling a comprehensive bibliography of the field. Lovecraft himself had an impressive library of weird fiction, collected over a lifetime of book-hunting in spite of his penury. It is interesting to note that there is relatively little overlap in the lists of weird books that each correspondent supplied in early letters. To be sure, such titans as Poe, Machen, Blackwood, and Bierce were well represented in both collections; but Wandrei appeared to have a penchant for what might nowadays be called "science fantasy" or "scientific romance"—the work of H. G. Wells, Garrett P. Serviss, and the like. And Wandrei had only a single volume of Lord Dunsany, in contrast to Lovecraft's far greater holdings of the Irish fantaisiste. Naturally enough, Lovecraft and Wandrei began lending their choice volumes to each other, with mutually beneficial results. In the short term, however, the benefit was far more on Lovecraft's side than Wandrei's.

Lovecraft was in the midst of completing his historical survey, "Supernatural Horror in Literature," written for the *Recluse*. By March 1927 it had reached the proof stage, and it was just then that Wandrei lent Lovecraft a key volume from his collection—F. Marion Crawford's *Wandering Ghosts* (1911). Lovecraft was so impressed with the collection (he had previously read only Crawford's "The Upper Berth" and one other story) that he made a hasty addition to the proofs of his essay to augment his discussion of Crawford. Another volume lent by Wandrei at this time, Charles Fort's *Book of the Damned* (1919), might have influenced "The Colour out of Space," which Lovecraft was writing at the time he read the Fort volume.

The two colleagues aided each other in many ways in a relationship that was almost symbiotic. Lovecraft, impressed with the cosmic vision of Wandrei's early tale, "The Twilight of Time," had praised it in a letter to *Weird Tales* editor Farnsworth Wright, who had previously rejected it. In late February 1927 Wandrei learned of its acceptance by Wright (who retitled it "The Red Brain"), and Lovecraft was convinced that his influence had something to do with Wright's change of heart. Wandrei sought to return the favor, but it would be some months before he could do so.

After completing his first year of college in the summer of 1927, Wandrei determined to head east—both to see Lovecraft and others on the East Coast and to gain a foothold in publishing by making contacts with authors, editors, and publishers in New York. He hitchhiked the entire trip, stopping in Chicago, New York, Providence, and elsewhere. On occasion he slept outside, even in the rain, when he could not find shelter. In Chicago he looked up Farnsworth Wright at the *Weird Tales* offices. His letters say nothing of what he did there, but as Wandrei later recalled:

> [. . .] I casually worked in a reference to a story, "The Call of Cthulhu," that Lovecraft was revising and finishing and which I thought was a wonderful tale. But I added that for some reason or other, Lovecraft had talked about submitting it to other magazines. I said I just couldn't understand why he was apparently planning to by-pass *Weird Tales* unless he was seeking to broaden his markets or widen his reading public. None of this was true, but I could see that my fanciful account took effect, in the way Wright began to fidget and show signs of agitation.[6]

As a result of this mild chicanery, Wright soon afterward asked to see "The Call of Cthulhu" again, and this time accepted it.

A few months later Lovecraft performed a simple act that would much later have momentous consequences for his own work and reputation: he put Wandrei in touch with fellow Midwesterner August Derleth, who had been corresponding with Lovecraft only since the summer of 1926. Clearly no one could then have imagined that these two young writers would in a dozen years become the founders of Arkham House, a publishing company formed for the sole purpose of preserving Lovecraft's work in hard covers.[7]

Wandrei, a twenty-year-old college student, effected a major shift in the nature of Lovecraft's poesy. He let Lovecraft read a series of weird poems he was writing—*Sonnets of the Midnight Hours*—intended for a future book that ultimately did not appear. Only ten of the poems were published in *Weird Tales*, where Lovecraft read them once again. The following year, Lovecraft undertook *Fungi from Yuggoth*, a sonnet sequence. It was somewhat similar in theme

---

6. DAW, "Lovecraft in Providence" (1959), *Ave atque Vale* 276.

7. Fortunately, the name Arkham House prevailed over such monstrosities as Derwan House, Wander House, Wander-Craft, Sac Prairie Sanctum, House of Dagon, Sign of Dagon, and others, all suggested by DAW.

to *Sonnets of the Midnight Hours*, nearly each sonnet being an individual vignette on a single fantastic theme. (*Weird Tales* published ten of Lovecraft's sonnets in a manner that mimicked the way Wandrei's sonnets were published.) But *Fungi from Yuggoth* represented a radical shift in Lovecraft's poetical composition. He maintained a fixed form, but his manner of expression was much looser, more natural, more nearly speech-like, for most of the poems are narrated in the first person.

Lovecraft clearly saw in Wandrei a distinctive mind and personality—far beyond the "fans" who would consume so much of his epistolary time in the 1930s. It was not merely their mutual love of weird fiction that immediately established a bond between the two writers; it was their sense of the *cosmic*, something Lovecraft knew was an extraordinarily rare trait, and one certainly lacking in Derleth, whom Lovecraft once called a "self-blinded earth-gazer."[8] In 1930 Lovecraft wrote to Smith: "You have it [the cosmic quality] yourself to a supreme degree, & so have Wandrei & Bernard Dwyer; but I'm hanged if I can carry the list any farther."[9] This quality is embodied not merely in so obvious a tale as "The Red Brain" but also in "Colossus" (*Astounding Stories*, January 1934) and "Colossus Eternal" (*Astounding Stories*, December 1934), which, however dated they may now seem, still retain the breathless thrill inspired by unthinkably vast cosmic spaces.

The origin of Wandrei's cosmic sensibility is not entirely clear, but it may have had some bearing on the misanthropy he exhibited in his early work and thought. Perhaps the contemplation of the immense gulfs of the cosmos caused Wandrei to regard the antics of the insignificant human race with a particularly jaundiced eye; the stultifying intellectual atmosphere of the Midwest may have had something to do with it as well. Lovecraft on occasion gently chided Wandrei for his misanthropy, maintaining that "indifferentism" was a more appropriate response on the part of the cosmic philosopher; but he could easily share Wandrei's sense of intellectual and imaginative isolation. Wandrei's admission, early in their correspondence, that the interest Lovecraft and Smith had shown in his early work provided much-needed encouragement must have been gratifying to Lovecraft:

> I am touched and profoundly grateful for the interest that you and C.A.S. take in my work. It has amazed me to find all at once two people who are interested when there has not been one in these five years that I have been practicising my apprenticeship. I don't care for the opinions of other people; ... but after a half-dozen years, I was coming to the conclusion that there were no dreamers in the world of today, none who ever rose above the mediocrity which is America, that it was useless, consequently, to write, and that I might as well enjoy my dreams as dreams without troubling to set them forth.

---

8. HPL to FBL, [27 February 1931] (*SL* 3.291).
9. HPL to CAS, 17 October 1930 (*DS* 248).

It must have been passages like this that revealed to Lovecraft how many values he shared with Wandrei. The fact that Lovecraft preserved nearly all of Wandrei's early letters—something he rarely did with his far-flung correspondence, both because he lacked the space in his cramped quarters and because most of the letters he received were frankly not worth preserving—is a testament to the high regard in which he held the Minnesota writer. It was Lovecraft who also put Wandrei in touch with W. Paul Cook, who printed Wandrei's first book.

The fact that, scarcely more than half a year after their acquaintance, Wandrei took the trouble to visit Lovecraft at his own expense must also have affected Lovecraft. The two and a half weeks that Wandrei spent in Providence are of course not discussed in the correspondence, but Wandrei has provided illuminating glimpses of that time in his two memoirs, "The Dweller in Darkness: Lovecraft, 1927" (1944) and "Lovecraft in Providence" (1959), and the affidavit he wrote for his later lawsuit against Arkham House.[10] Through Lovecraft, Wandrei became acquainted with Frank Belknap Long, Samuel Loveman, Bernard Austin Dwyer, W. Paul Cook, H. Warner Munn, and others of what came to be known as the "Lovecraft circle." Few of them became lifelong associates of the reclusive Wandrei, but Smith and Derleth remained so to the end. Wandrei's delight in travel (which waned in his later years, as he became more and more ensconced in his St. Paul home) also forged a close bond with Lovecraft, leading to Lovecraft's delightful comparison of YMCAs in various New England towns and the sending of a flurry of postcards when either correspondent was on the road; frequently these postcards would bear notes or signatures of other members of the "gang," becoming distinctive biographical documents in their own right.

By the early 1930s the correspondence had grown somewhat sporadic. Wandrei was at that time making vigorous efforts to establish himself in the pulp field, and was also shuttling back and forth between New York (where for a time he held a position in the advertising department of E. P. Dutton) and St. Paul, in an attempt to find the right environment for literary work. Before that, he published a second book of poetry—*Dark Odyssey* (1931)— through Webb Publishing Company of St. Paul, a firm specializing in agricultural publishing. He quickly shifted from weird fiction to science fantasy, recognizing that the latter was a more marketable product. His work became a fixture in *Astounding Stories,* although *Weird Tales* remained a steady haven for his purely weird work. Lovecraft looked upon Wandrei's later work with considerable reservation. Although having nothing but praise for this work in his letters to Wandrei himself, Lovecraft was less charitable in letters to others. In 1936, writing to C. L. Moore, he wrote cuttingly:

---

10. See D. H. Olson, "Of Donald Wandrei, August Derleth, and H. P. Lovecraft" (*DD* 369–80).

Whoever consents to aim for the tawdry effects demanded by commerce, is deliberately checking & perhaps permanently injuring his ability in an effort to achieve certain cheap results alien & antagonistic to literature. The literary ruin of brilliant figures like Long, Quinn, Price, Merritt, & Wandrei speaks for itself.[11]

Wandrei admitted that remarks like this, when he came upon them while compiling Lovecraft's *Selected Letters*, were markedly discouraging. He wrote to Derleth:

I am both depressed and annoyed by the dishearteningly low opinion that HPL had of me and of my work in recent years. I am newly reminded of this by a contemptuous reference in one of the Shea letters—'Wandrei thinks he's a regular devil—and so he is, but his associates in the wench-and-gin world are merely other well-born sensation-seekers like himself. He knows nothing of the elemental substance and struggle of life except on paper, and can have no idea of the emotions and tides of action taking form among the seething hordes of waterfront, factory, wheatfield, railway "rods", &.'

That is about as fantastic a picture of my New York existence as I can imagine. I am completely at loss to account for it, unless it developed from possible distortions and attempts to shock HPL by Belknap through letters; and from my own scant correspondence of recent years, combined with an almost fanatical reluctance to admit anyone to my private life. There is not one single statement of fact—or even of theory, so far as I can see—in the paragraph quoted. Oh well—it can't be of much interest to you, but it has powerfully shaken my faith in the validity of HPL's estimate of all other people whom he knew. I wish I had never seen the damned paragraph, since it will probably also demolish my readiness to accept any and all estimates of his which I may see hereafter, concerning Belknap, Loveman, Morton, you, Smith, and the others of the group. I'm beginning to think that the absence of human characterization and motivation in HPL's tales was due not only to a complete lack of interest in them but to a complete failure to understand them.[12]

On another occasion Wandrei wrote:

Yes, the Shea letters are certainly making me revise my opinion of Lovecraft's opinions. But if HPL thought commercialism had hooked me to the exclusion of all else, he must have had a weird concept of commercialism, because he read my second novel, that which I can hardly imagine anything less commercial, except the first novel. Or maybe my own definitions and understandings of meanings—in their strictly logical and philological significations—have undergone an insidious detrioration [*sic*] under the influence of that modern hydra. I can't say that the possibility worries me much. . . . If any basic distinction

11. HPL to C. L. Moore, [c. 20 October 1936] (*Letters to C. L. Moore* 183).

12. DAW to AWD, 5 May 1937 (ms., WHS). DAW quotes HPL to J. Vernon Shea, 13 March 1935 (*Letters to J. Vernon Shea . . .* 257).

were to be made between HPL's outlook and mine, I suppose it would be that in his writings he strove to depart farther and farther from objective reality, and that I try to get closer and closer.[13]

But Lovecraft's own increasingly antagonistic relationship to the pulp field, as well as repeated rejections of his work by book publishers in the 1930s, had much to do with his reaction. Farnsworth Wright's rejection of *At the Mountains of Madness* in the summer of 1931 resulted in Lovecraft's refusal to submit anything to *Weird Tales* for nearly five and a half years (although others, such as Derleth and Wandrei, occasionally submitted his stories without Lovecraft's knowledge or permission); and a string of bootless attempts to land collections of stories with publishers—Putnam's in 1931, Vanguard in 1932, Knopf in 1933, and Loring & Mussey in 1935—reduced Lovecraft to near-inarticulateness as a creative artist, and embittered him against the entire field of commercial writing, most notably pulp fiction. Fortunately Wandrei weathered the shock of Lovecraft's comments and went on to undertake the editing and proofreading of *The Outsider and Others* and Lovecraft's letters, although only ten of Lovecraft's letters to him appear in *Selected Letters*.

As Wandrei suggested, Lovecraft's response to two major literary projects undertaken by Wandrei in the early 1930s is perhaps reflective of his general attitude. When Wandrei sent *Dead Titans, Waken!* (the novel that later became *The Web of Easter Island*) to Lovecraft in early 1932, the latter made scrupulous comments, but emphasized the "disharmony in tone betwixt the popular 'action' style of the first half & the tense cosmicism of the second half": clearly, he preferred the latter to the former, and wished that Wandrei would rewrite the beginning to bring it more in line with the end. Wandrei, however, was in no mood to undertake major revision on the 50,000-word novel after arduously typing it, and after its rejection by one publisher he let it lie untouched for fifteen years, only to be published by the company he co-founded.

A year later, Wandrei finished another novel—an 80,000-word mainstream work, *Invisible Sun*. This was a very different proposition altogether: heavily autobiographical and with only a few touches of the weird or fantastic, *Invisible Sun* is a powerful psychological and character study that, in spite of occasional flaws in style and proportioning, reveals Wandrei grappling with serious literary, philosophical, and personal issues in a dynamic and imaginative way; parts of it embody some of his finest writing. The draft of the novel had come to Lovecraft from August Derleth, who, though no Puritan, had expressed violent disapprobation of it, chiefly on account of several sexually explicit passages. Surprisingly, given his general distaste for the whole subject of sex, Lovecraft rendered a much more favorable verdict on *Invisible Sun*,

---

13. DAW to AWD, 18 May 1937 (ms., WHS).

correctly seeing in it an attempt to treat these issues with the unflinching honesty they required. Lovecraft manifestly felt that in this novel Wandrei was making headway as a serious writer rather than a pulp hack; but Wandrei's inability to sell the novel, after a few half-hearted queries with publishers, caused him to resume his pulpsmithing.

We are fortunate to have the Lovecraft–Wandrei correspondence in as nearly complete a condition as it is. It appears that Wandrei preserved virtually every letter or postcard he received from Lovecraft. For Lovecraft's part, he preserved nearly all Wandrei's letters (aside from his first) for the first several years of their relationship, but, as their letters became relatively infrequent in the 1930s, did not keep Wandrei's missives consistently. (It is a bit harrowing to see that Wandrei's final letter is dated two days after Lovecraft's death on 15 March 1937—apparently the first letter Wandrei had written to Lovecraft in three months.) What is revealed in these letters—beyond the multitude of details about each author's life and work, discussions of classic and contemporary weird fiction, accounts of travels and of meeting mutual colleagues, and the progress of each author's literary work—is the parallel maturation of both Lovecraft and Wandrei over more than a decade of living and writing, and the close intellectual and imaginative bonds forged by common philosophical outlooks, common ties to their native regions, and, for a time, common literary aspirations. Although Wandrei visited Lovecraft twice in Providence—in 1927 and 1932—and met him briefly in New York on several occasions in the 1930s, their relationship was largely confined to paper; but despite its occasionally sporadic nature, it remained strong to the end. Lovecraft and Wandrei knew that they were members of a very small circle of cosmic visionaries, and that each required the encouragement of the other to maintain his unique perspective on literature and life.

Howard Elmer Wandrei (1909–1956), Donald's younger brother, was a late associate of Lovecraft. Howard had a turbulent youth, being arrested for burglary at the age of eighteen and spending three years in a reformatory. During that time, he developed into a brilliant and distinctive pictorial artist, chiefly in pen-and-ink work. He illustrated Donald's book of poetry, *Dark Odyssey* (1931), and then did some illustrations for the weird and science fiction pulps. He also took to writing, publishing detective, horror, and science fiction tales in the pulp magazines. Lovecraft met Wandrei for the first time in New York on 27 December 1933, and they corresponded sporadically thereafter. Lovecraft had a high regard for Wandrei's artwork: "he certainly has a vastly greater talent than anyone else in the gang. I was astonished at [the paintings'] sheer genius & maturity";[14] later, when he read some of Wandrei's stories, he was

---

14. HPL to Annie E. P. Gamwell, [28 December 1933]; *Letters to Family and Family Friends* 962.

also impressed: "I'm hang'd if I don't think the kid is, all apart from his pictorial genius, getting to be a better writer than big bwuvver!"[15] But from 1935 onward, to step out of the shadow cast by his brother Donald, Howard Wandrei prolifically wrote primarily detective fiction. He was not to earn fame as Howard Wandrei, for he published under many pseudonyms, including the transparent Howard Von Drey, and also Robert Coley, Robert A. Garron, Howard W. Graham, Ph.D., H. W. Guernsey, and H. F. Guernsey.

In the few surviving letters to Howard Wandrei, Lovecraft addresses him as "H. E.," but in gossipy comments in letters about the writers in his circle, Lovecraft typically referred to him as "Albrecht Dürer" (1471–1528)—the German painter and printmaker whom Howard admired. The reason for the epithet is that Howard had done a piece he gave the parodic title "Night, Death, and the Devil," named after Dürer's engraving "Knight, Death, and the Devil" (1513). Only one of eight surviving known letters by Lovecraft to Howard was transcribed by Arkham House for *Selected Letters*. It appears that the two did not correspond much. As a pulp writer, Wandrei needed to write to earn a living and so did not have much time for letters. Two of Wandrei's postcards are noteworthy. Both (of which only one survives—the other being a transcription by R. H. Barlow) are written in the most microscopic script imaginable, perhaps as a kind of retaliation for Lovecraft's own minutely written postcards.

Howard moved to New York in 1934. He married Connie Colestock in 1936 and they had one child, Suzanne, in 1941. The couple was divorced in 1946. Howard moved back to St. Paul in 1945 and lived there for the remainder of his life.

It was Howard who informed August Derleth about Lovecraft's death. On 16 March 1937, he addressed the matter tersely: "I suppose the tragic news of Lovecraft's death has reached you. The fact is a thing which one is not willing to believe." His letter was the first notice Derleth had received. In the ensuing weeks, he wrote Derleth informing him of R. H. Barlow's discussions with the New York gang. It was he who, along with brother Donald and Samuel Loveman, started a virulent smear campaign against Barlow. He "utterly detest[ed]" Barlow and stated that Barlow was "making himself Howard's literary executor," not knowing, or imagining, that Lovecraft had made the appointment himself. Barlow was perceived as operating contrarily to Donald Wandrei and August Derleth, who had been making plans to see that Lovecraft's work would get published in book form, one way or another. Howard Wandrei had been earmarked to do the cover art for Lovecraft's *Outsider and Others,* but he was stricken with pneumonia and so Virgil Finlay was selected to do the job.

---

15. HPL to R. H. Barlow, 20 April 1935; *OFF* 255.

Howard's later years were marked by continued writing and drawing, and also inventing, jewelry-making, and other pursuits. After a long illness, he died on 5 September 1956.

Emil Theodore Petaja (1915–2000; last name pronounced "Pet-EYE-ya") was, like so many other of Lovecraft's correspondents of the mid-1930s, a science fiction fan, a fledgling writer and poet, and a would-be publisher. He was the youngest of ten children in his family, his parents being of Finnish ancestry, residing in Milltown, Mont. The family once resided in an area known as "Hell Gate," a ghost town at the western end of the Missoula Valley in Missoula County. Lovecraft first knew of him from reading his brief articles in the *Fantasy Fan*. He came in touch with Lovecraft in late 1934, probably through *Weird Tales* or one of the young fanzine editors, and soon was sending Lovecraft examples of his work in various media. About his work, Lovecraft wrote: "Petaja, by the way, is a very clever artist himself, as attested by sketches he has sent me. He shewed me the sonnet dedicated jointly to C A S & me. His versatility is really unusual—violinist, artist, poet, & fiction writer."[16]

In accordance with his Finnish ancestry, Petaja displayed an interest in the Kalevala (a nineteenth-century epic based on Finnish folklore) and a love for the music of the great twentieth-century Finnish composer Jean Sibelius. In 1936, he self-published a chapbook of poems, *Brief Candle*, making copies on the mimeograph machine at Montana State University, where he was a student majoring in creative writing. The booklet contained illustrations by Petaja's new friend, Hannes Bok (1914–1964), whom he had met that same year. The chapbook marked the first book publication for each of them.

In two and one half years, Lovecraft wrote more than one hundred pages of letters to the young writer. The next year he proposed teaming with Duane W. Rimel to form a fan magazine, *The Fantaisiste's Mirror*, that would resume serializing Lovecraft's "Supernatural Horror in Literature" from the point it had left off in the defunct *Fantasy Fan*, but the magazine never materialized. However, Petaja and Rimel did collaborate on the piece "Weird Music." He and Lovecraft corresponded fairly frequently until the latter's death.

Petaja was somewhat late in turning over to Arkham House his letters from Lovecraft for transcription, first inquiring about the matter in March 1941. He told August Derleth he had twenty-eight to thirty letters and that he thought he may have lost several during numerous moves. (The John Hay Library has twenty-nine letters.) Arkham House transcribed only six letters, in part (Petaja had held back some letters he felt would be of little interest), and in the end published a selection from only one letter. He is mentioned only twice

---

16. HPL to Duane W. Rimel (28 January 1935), *Letters to F. Lee Baldwin, Duane W. Rimel, and Nils Frome*, 251.

in the entirety of *Selected Letters*. Thus, he is something of an unknown quantity in Lovecraftdom—at least in Lovecraft's published writings as of the 1960s and 1970s—though he was an active fan and his writing career spanned seven decades.

In later years Petaja contributed to *Amazing Stories* and *Weird Tales,* and wrote several science fiction and fantasy novels, some based upon Finnish legendry. He also worked as a commercial photographer, maintaining studios in San Francisco and Sausalito. He exhibited his photography and hand wrought copper at galleries in Sausalito in 1949. Petaja died in 2000.

—S. T. JOSHI
DAVID E. SCHULTZ

A Note on the Text

Virtually the entire correspondence of Lovecraft and Donald Wandrei is held at the John Hay Library, Brown University (Providence, R.I.). We are grateful to the library for permission to print the letters. Lovecraft's letters to Howard Wandrei derive primarily from the Arkham House transcripts, although some individual manuscripts and postcards were available. Howard Wandrei's letters to Lovecraft were obtained from George Smisor's microfilm of the papers of R. H. Barlow. Lovecraft's letters to Emil Petaja are also held at the John Hay Library. Several, unfortunately, suffered water damage over the years. In some cases we were able to fill in obliterated passages with text from the Arkham House transcripts, made before the letters were damaged. We are grateful to Lovecraft Holdings, LLC, for permission to publish the letters of H. P. Lovecraft; to Dwayne H. Olson for permission to publish the letters of Donald and Howard Wandrei and for providing photographs of them; and to Thomas Gladysz for permission to publish the works of Emil Petaja.

Colleagues who lent valuable assistance in various ways to the preparation of this volume include Steve Behrends, Scott Connors, Leslie Crabtree, Stefan Dziemianowicz, Kenneth W. Faig, Jr., Thomas Gladysz, Marcos Legaria, Donovan K. Loucks, M. Eileen McNamara, Steve Miller, Carol A. Montgomery, Christopher O'Brien, Charles D. O'Connor III, Dwayne H. Olson, Philip J. Rahman, and John H. Stanley, Christopher Geissler, and Karen Eberhart of the John Hay Library.

Abbreviations

AT	Lovecraft, *The Ancient Track: Complete Poetical Works* (2013)
BM	Wandrei et al., *Broken Mirrors* (1928)
C	Wandrei, *Colossus* (1989)
CB	Lovecraft, *Commonplace Book* (in *CE* 5.219–35; numbers refer to entries)
CE	Lovecraft, *Collected Essays* (2004–06; 5 vols.)
CF	Lovecraft, *Collected Fiction: A Variorum Edition* (2015–17; 4 vols.)

DD	Wandrei, *Don't Dream* (1997)
DO	Wandrei, *Dark Odyssey* (1931)
DS	Lovecraft and Smith, *Dawnward Spire, Lonely Hill* (2017)
DT	Wandrei, *Dark Titans, Waken! and Invisible Sun* (2011)
E	Wandrei, *Ecstasy and Other Poems* (1928)
EF	Wandrei, *The Eye and the Finger* (1944)
ES	Lovecraft and Derleth, *Essential Solitude* (2008)
FF	*Fantasy Fan*
LL	S. T. Joshi, comp., *Lovecraft's Library: A Catalogue* (rev. and enl.; Hippocampus Press, 2017) (numbers refer to entries)
LR	Cannon, *Lovecraft Remembered* (1998)
OFF	Lovecraft, *O Fortunate Floridian* (2007)
PM	Wandrei, *Poems for Midnight* (1964)
SH	Wandrei, *Strange Harvest* (1965)
SHL	Lovecraft, "Supernatural Horror in Literature"
SL	Lovecraft, *Selected Letters* (1965–76; 5 vols.)
ST	*Strange Tales of Mystery and Terror*
WT	*Weird Tales*
AHT	Arkham House transcripts of Lovecraft's letters
ALS	autograph letter, signed
AMS	autograph manuscript, signed
ANS	autograph note (e.g., postcard), signed
AMS	autograph manuscript
AWD	August W. Derleth
CAS	Clark Ashton Smith
DAW	Donald A. Wandrei
FBL	Frank Belknap Long
FW	Farnsworth Wright
HW	Howard Wandrei
JHL	John Hay Library, Brown University
NAPA	National Amateur Press Association
RHB	R. H. Barlow
RMB	Rulon-Miller Books, *Selections from the Archive of Donald Wandrei: Manuscripts, Letters, Printed Ephemera, and Original Art* (1994)
TLS	typed letter, signed
WHS	Wisconsin Historical Society, Madison

Donald Wandrei, sailing on White Bear Lake c. 1930–32

Letters of H. P. Lovecraft and Donald Wandrei

1926

[1]   [HPL to DAW] [ALS]

10 Barnes St.,
Providence, R.I.,
Decr. 11, 1926

Dear Mr. Wandrei:—

Having heard of you very often from Clark Ashton Smith, I was exceedingly pleased to receive yours of the 4th. & learn that you found some of my tales interesting. Of late my material has not been finding much favour with *Weird Tales,* so kindly opinions of such rejected items as "Cthulhu" are rather encouraging.[1] It is highly flattering to think that you deem that tale worth copying, & I shall certainly be glad to let you have the MS. again in the spring.

No—I have nothing appearing in magazines other than W.T., & am sorry you spent such a fruitless hour with the catalogues & indexes! The only non-W.T. stories I ever had published were in an abysmally wretched & now happily defunct periodical called *Home Brew,* (ugh!) but these two tales—serials—were written down to an impossible clientele by editorial mandate.[2] If you ever care to see any tales of mine which have not been published, I shall be glad to lend you the MSS. The following are all in manuscript—& all available for lending except one or two, of which the only copies are in the keeping of others.

Polaris	The Nameless City
Beyond the Wall of Sleep	The Quest of Iranon
The Doom that Came to Sarnath	The Other Gods
The Tree	The Lurking Fear (pub. Home Brew)
Celephaïs	The Shunned House
From Beyond	In the Vault
Nyarlathotep	Cool Air
Psychopompos (in rhyme)	The Silver Key
	The Strange High House in the Mist[3]

I am now writing a weird novel about Randolph Carter's adventures in dreamland,[4] but am not greatly impressed with the result so far. I fancy it will turn out to be more practice work than anything else.

Like you I have always been a devotee of weird & fantastic literature; Poe, Dunsany, Arthur Machen, & Algernon Blackwood being my particular idols. I read the Birkhead book on "The Tale of Terror", but found it exceedingly ill-proportioned & imaginatively unappreciative.[5] A history of weird fiction from your pen would certainly fill the proverbial long-felt want, & I hope to see it some day. I wrote a brief thing of the kind myself last winter & spring, but have not yet typed it because of new data unearthed—a whole long list of weird fiction at the Providence Public Library—which I intend to follow up when I have time.[6]

As to the hostility of the present age to fantastic work—I don't let it worry me much. Of course I'd appreciate the financial boon if I could sell my stuff widely, but apart from that I'm too much of a cynic to care whether the gaping populace like to read my junk or not. I write it for my own amusement, & two or three appreciative readers are perfectly sufficient to gratify my vanity.[7] Still—it really is a pity to have any one definite art form widely neglected, so I suppose I can sincerely join in a chorus of regret.

I read with much admiration your critique of C A S's work, & have ordered two copies of the Dec. *Overland* containing it.[8] My opinion of Smith is as enthusiastically favourable as yours, & I hope to see him more properly recognised some day. His poetry is marvellous, & his weird drawings & paintings are beyond description! I don't know of anyone else since Blake who has combined the two arts so well—though Beardsley might have done it had he lived.[9] Smith, by the way, tells me that you write weird material yourself, & has promised to forward me some things of yours. With every good wish, I am

Most cordially & sincerely yrs—

H P Lovecraft

Notes

1. At this time, HPL had had seventeen stories, three poems, five letters to the editor, and six other stories revised for clients published in *WT*. HPL was more successful placing stories in *WT* under the editorship of Edwin Baird (1923–24) than under that of FW (1924–40) in that Baird accepted HPL's submittals outright, whereas FW rejected many stories, of which he published only a few on second consideration. DAW came to read "The Call of Cthulhu" because CAS sub-loaned the ms. to him.

2. "Herbert West—Reanimator" and "The Lurking Fear."

3. FW rejected nearly all these works. "The Lurking Fear" had not been submitted to *WT* at this time because of its appearance in *Home Brew*. Most of these stories saw print in the mid-1930s in fan publications; a few eventually appeared in *WT*, most after HPL's death.

4. I.e., *The Dream-Quest of Unknown Kadath*, which remained unpublished in HPL's lifetime. Previous Carter stories included "The Statement of Randolph Carter" (1919), "The Unnamable" (1923), and "The Silver Key" (1926).

5. HPL read the book in November 1925 and relied on it heavily for the early chapters of SHL.

6. The last-minute additions were suggested by Howard Wolf, an early advocate of HPL's work. See "'Variety' Column" (*LR* 403–5).

7. Cf. "The Defense Remains Open!" (1921): "There are probably seven persons, in all, who really like my work; and they are enough. I should write even if I were the only patient reader, for my aim is merely self-expression" (*CE* 5.53).

8. "The Emperor of Dreams."

9. William Blake (1757–1827), British poet, artist, and mystic; Aubrey Beardsley (1872–1898), British artist and illustrator.

[2]   [DAW to HPL] [ALS]

1152 Portland Ave.,
St. Paul, Minn.
Dec. 20, 1926

Dear Mr. Lovecraft:

I was extremely pleased to hear from you. Since the publication of "Dagon"[1] I have watched closely for your tales, and sought any bits of information I might unearth, but they are few. Your letter made me happy—as if I had aspired to something I never could attain, and then found it suddenly within my reach.

I am eager to read all the mss. you name. I would ask to have them all at once, but I think this an imposition. I have a feeling that I shall regret to return them to you, and keep them longer than courtesy permits. If you are willing, then, I shall be more than glad to have the loan of half the mss. now, those in the first column—

Polaris
Beyond the Wall of Sleep
The Doom that Came to Sarnath
The Tree
Celephais
From Beyond
Nyarlathotep
Psychopompos
The Strange High House in the Mist

When I return them, I shall look for the eight others. It is with a great deal of anticipation and expectancy that I await the first. I have longed to read your unpublished tales ever since Clark said, in one of his letters, that some of your best work had been returned by Weird Tales.

I have just sent some of my own work to him; you are welcome to it if you wish. Most of the things I write are short, and few of them are really stories. But they may interest you; at least they are remote enough from the common life.

It gave me pleasure to know that you liked my critique of C.A.S. I have been surprised at his neglect by reviewers and critics, and searched in vain for appreciation of his poetry. I hope my essay will win him some notice, and, perhaps, more enthusiasts of his work. If it does, I shall be satisfied.

I should like to see your article or history of weird literature when you type it. So very little has been done in this field that any note on it is valuable. You are fortunate to obtain many such books in the Providence Public Library. I have a damnable time trying to find Gothic literature in the impossible libraries of St. Paul and Minneapolis. One great need at present is a bibliography of fantastic literature. A tentative project is to make a bibliography in three sections: the Gothic novel from Walpole to the present, the Gothic short story, and books in associated subjects, such as Witchcraft, occultism, and Demonology. If you ever make any kind of list in the field, let me see it; sometimes it is quite difficult to trace such books.

I wish you success with your novel, partly because, in that event, I shall have the pleasure of reading it. I began a novel once, but never got very far; I had it all planned out, so that there was nothing to do but write it, and thereupon lost interest in it. "The Chuckler", by the way, a brief tale in those I sent Clark, may interest you; it is partly a definite answer to "The Statement of Randolph Carter".[2] All I can say of my effort is that those who criticised the indefinite end of your story are to be pitied.[3]

Send me your mss. as soon as it is convenient to you. I am anxious to read them.

Cordially,
Donald Wandrei

Notes

1. "Dagon" was HPL's first appearance (save for a letter) in *WT*.

2. Concerning "The Chuckler" (not published until 1934), HPL wrote that "on reading it, I'd tend to say that it is not so much a *sequel* to 'Randolph Carter' as something *suggested* by that yarn. It disappointed me just a trifle" (HPL to Duane W. Rimel, 30 October 1934; *Letters to F. Lee Baldwin, Duane W. Rimel, and Nils Frome* 229), and "I don't think 'The Chuckler' is Wandrei at his best" (HPL to Duane W. Rimel, 19 November 1934; ibid. 235). DAW's story resembles HPL's only in that an underground denizen's voice is heard. In "The Chuckler," a policeman encounters a chuckling corpse that has thwarted a grave-robber, whereas in "The Statement of Randolph Carter," the underground dweller (not necessarily a corpse) is heard but not seen. DAW's story does not share in the indefinite character that he admired in HPL's story.

3. Howard Anderson wrote a letter to *WT* stating: "He [HPL] should go further into the story and explain the mystery." But another reader, Ward Motz, declared: "The best of this was that Mr. Lovecraft left something to the imagination" (*WT* 5, No. 4 [April 1925]: 165; in Joshi, *Weird Writer* 65).

[3]   [HPL to DAW] [ALS]

10 Barnes St.,

Providence, R.I.,

Dec. 24, 1926

My dear Mr. Wandrei:—

I am greatly flattered by your wish to read more of my tales, & take pleasure in sending under separate cover such items of the list you named as are now in my possession. "Polaris" & "Celephaïs" are lent to another correspondent,[1] & I will send them to you as soon as he returns them. Of "Nyarlathotep" I have no available copy, but will look it up in obscure files before long. At the same time, in looking over my stock of MSS., I find that I have no copies of "The Quest of Iranon", "Herbert West—Reanimator", or "The Shunned House"; but can send any of the others which you may desire. Remind me which ones are wanted when you are ready. Sooner or later "The Shunned House" may be privately printed in an amateur magazine,[2] while I intend sometime to make another copy of "Iranon" from the rough draught. Of those I am now mailing you, at least two are among my poorest work—"From Beyond" & "Beyond the Wall of Sleep". "The Strange High House in the Mist" is my newest completed piece, written last month. Of the MS. of "Psychopompos" I'll have to ask you to be very careful, since it is almost worn to powder. I abhor typing, so dread the job of doing this over again. Probably I'll confine my reconstructive efforts to the last page.[3] And incidentally—there's no especial hurry about the return of these things. Of most of them I have more or less seedy & illegible duplicates. Altogether, I hope that the tales may not disappoint you. They are perhaps *different* rather than *better* as compared with the material in *Weird Tales,* & certainly merit no place among the major achievements of weird fiction.

I shall read your tales with extreme interest when they arrive from C A S, & am especially eager to learn the hellish subterrene secrets revealed in "The Chuckler". It amuses me to note the demands for prosaic consistency, carefully explained endings, & such-like, which the clientele of *Weird Tales* occasionally makes. The editor is evidently influenced by them to some extent, since I note he is very timid about using really fantastic or imaginative material.

Smith recently sent me two *Overlands* with your critique, & I must commiserate you upon the typographical mauling which your text received! I had no idea that so famous a magazine could tolerate such slovenly printing, but find it is the rule throughout—Samuel *Loveman's* name, for instance, is consistently rendered as *"Tweman"!*[4] As to the lack of appreciation of Smith—it appears to me to be due to the peculiarly prosaic temper of the age, in which the very inmost essence of true imagination is discarded in favour of a purely intellectual standard. What critics really want at present is not actual art, but thinly disguised science & philosophy; & until they return to the proper standard of feeling & imagination there is no use expecting any intelligent treatment of fantasy from them. Their idea of fantasy is the sophisticated snickering of James Branch Cabell—& the only reason they half-tolerate Dunsany is that he also has his "smart" side; a side which I deem the one flaw in the homogeneous perfection of his ethereal genius. Poe could not even get a hearing on his own intrinsic merits today. Smith has had some recognition in his own part of the country, but not nearly so much as he deserves. Outside California very few critics have noticed him, & a review of his work written by a friend of mine—Alfred Galpin of Chicago—was rejected by fully a dozen reviews & magazines. I enclose a copy of the amateur magazine (which I edited) in which it finally appeared.[5] The association issuing this organ is in a very anaemic state just now, but in its heyday it fostered a number of writers whose work did not take well with the general literary world. Among these is Samuel Loveman, whose long classic poem "The Hermaphrodite" is just out as a book—as you will see by Sterling's review in the *Overland* containing your Smith critique.[6]

I have not yet followed up the list of weird fiction at the local public library, but hope to get time to do so before long. It will not, of course, be at all complete or comprehensive, for no one library has a very full array of Gothic or fantastic books; but it will help to piece out the data I have accumulated at other libraries. I doubt if the libraries in St. Paul & Minneapolis are much worse than the average. There is, for instance, no copy of "Melmoth the Wanderer" in either the New York or Brooklyn public library; although it is to be found in the libraries of Cleveland, Ohio, & Madison, Wisconsin.[7] Your plan for a weird bibliography is splendid, & I hope to see it carried into effect. Such a thing ought to include not only books but isolated tales in magazines as well; since some veritable masterpieces have never got beyond that form. Single tales in anthologies, also, (like Mrs. Charlotte Perkins Gilman's "Yellow Wall Paper" in Howells' collection) merit citation.[8] Speaking of weird stories—do you know "The House of Sounds" by M. P. Shiel?[9] It is a titanic isolated achievement by an obscure writer whose general run of stories is very mediocre. What you say of your novel reminds me of the fate of some of my unwritten short tales! With me, as probably with you, the chief pleasure of creation is the creative process itself; so that when I get a picture perfectly crystallised in my mind without writing a story I no longer have the urge to write it—the demand having been already been satisfied. In the case of the present novel, I left most of the incidents rather indeterminate; so that there is much of suspense & expectancy still remaining. On account of other duties it has been developing rather slowly of late, only 86 pages being now finished. Whether I shall ever bother to type it yet remains to be seen.

Hoping that the accompanying tales may not bore you excessively, & wishing you all the joys of the season, I remain

Most cordially & sincerely yours,

H P Lovecraft

Notes

1. This was AWD.

2. W. Paul Cook had intended since 1925 to publish "The Shunned House" in the *Recluse*. He later attempted to publish the story as a booklet, but it was never in fact published in HPL's lifetime. See letter 99.

3. AWD himself had already retyped the poem. See HPL to AWD, 19 November 1926: "How can I thank you sufficiently for that carbon of Psychopompos! I am flattered that you found the thing worth typing, & infinitely glad of the duplicate. That other copy wouldn't have survived many more trips—at least, its last page wouldn't!" (*ES* 50).

4. This persistent error occurs not in DAW's article, but in George Sterling's review of Loveman's *Hermaphrodite*. See n. 6.

5. "Consul Hasting" [pseud. of Alfred Galpin], "Echoes from Beyond Space," *United Amateur* 24, No. 1 (July 1925): 3–4. HPL also published a brief review of *Ebony and Crystal* in the amateur magazine *L'Alouette* 1, No. 1 (January 1924): 20–21.

6. George Sterling, "Rhymes and Reactions," *Overland Monthly* 84. No. 12 (December 1926): 395. It contains a short review of *The Hermaphrodite: A Poem* (1926).

7. The novel *Melmoth the Wanderer* (1820) by Charles Robert Maturin (1782?–1824) was the inspiration for the pun on DAW's name, Melmoth the Wandrei.

8. Charlotte Perkins Gilman (1850–1935), "The Yellow Wall Paper" (1892), in *The Great Modern American Stories,* ed. William Dean Howells (New York: Boni & Liveright, 1920). See HPL to AWD, 27 September 1926: "Howells . . . was old-womanishly opposed to the really gruesome & terrible. He made an absurd apology for including Mrs. Gilman's 'Yellow Wall Paper' in an anthology he edited" (*ES* 37).

9. See HPL to Edwin Baird of *WT* (c. October 1923; *Uncollected Letters* 7): "This is the most haunting thing I have read in a decade—a creeping horror and menace trickling down the centuries in a sub-Arctic island off the coast of Norway, where, amidst the sweep of daemon winds and the ceaseless din of hellish waves and cataracts, a vengeful dead man built a brazen tower of terror. It is vaguely like—yet infinitely unlike—'The Fall of the House of Usher'. I wish there were a way of getting republication rights from the publisher—for it would surely be a sensation in *Weird Tales*."

1927

[4]   [DAW to HPL] [ALS]

1152 Portland Ave.,

St. Paul, Minn.

Jan. 5, 1927.

Dear Mr. Lovecraft:

I am a little late, but I wish to thank you very much for the loan of the stories. I shall retain them a while longer, for I wish to copy "The Doom That Came to Sarnath" and "The Strange High House in the

Mist", if I can possibly find the time. These two in particular are the best of the group, and some of the finer of the tales you have written. I do not care so much for the others, but I hope you rewrite some day "From Beyond" and "Beyond the Wall of Sleep"; portions of them are beautifully done, but they are not up to your usual high standard in their entirety. I took the liberty of letting three close friends of mine read "The Doom That Came to Sarnath" and "The Strange High House in the Mist". The last tale pleased them immensely. One in particular, who both draws and writes, thought the story exquisitely done, and certain images—the mist rising from the sea, and the strange house on the sheer cliff—beautiful and unforgettable.

I shall try to copy the two as soon as possible, for I am anxious to read the others you have, but I want to reread them all before returning them. Like yourself, I detest typewriting, but I shall make as much haste as I can.

After reading my article in the "Overland", I can only commiserate myself and wish I could commit assault and battery on the magazine's linotype man. C.A.S. suggested hurling him from the San Francisco Ferry Building, but I think the punishment too mild. I can not understand how "The Overland Monthly" retains any kind of prestige with such miserable proof-reading. C.A.S. spoke of the idiotic "Tweman" mistake, and I even note Bret Harte's name on the front cover as "Brete"!

I was greatly interested in the magazine you sent. Galpin's was an eccentric review, and not nearly so sympathetic or well-handled as it might have been. But I should like to obtain a copy of the magazine, if any are available, or retain this one, if you have others. I read all the items with interest, especially those of Mr. Long and Mr. Loveman.[1] I am deeply indebted both to you and to Mr. Long for the inscribed copy of his book, "The Man From Genoa", and will watch for the appearance of other books by him. I found a number of things of his, poems and tales, in looking over my file of "Weird Tales" recently, and read all I had time to with liking for most. I have ordered a copy of Loveman's "Hermaphrodite" on the combined recommendations of you, C.A.S., and Sterling. Do you know any other such writers, either in connection with your magazine, or elsewhere? I have an extremely difficult time in obtaining both the names and the books of these writers of fantastic and beautiful prose and poetry, though they are almost the sole authors whose work I desire or read. If you know any others, I would appreciate their names. My own favourite prose authors are Poe, Machen, Dunsany, and Blackwood, besides yourself, with portions of other writers' work. I have three editions of Poe, one with the magnificent illustrations of Harry Clarke, some seventeen books by Blackwood, and a number of Machen's, including "The Hill of Dreams" in the blue paper edition. Some time ago I wrote a criticism of this last volume, which appeared in my university's literary magazine.[2] If I can discover a copy, I'll send you it, if you care to read it. I have always considered the book a great work of art and a masterpiece. The magazine is hard to obtain now, however.

I don't know "Yellow Wall Paper" except by hearsay, but I possess "The Pale Ape" which contains "The House of Sounds". As I remember, I sent for the book after seeing your mention of it in Weird Tales—another source of indebtedness to you. I have read other tales of Shiel, but never anything to compare with it. In some respects, it is like "The Fall of the House of Usher"; but what an achievement it is!

Your 86 pages sounds like a tremendous accomplishment to me. I have never written anything of length, because my mind and thoughts change so rapidly. That is, whenever I do try to write long work, I expand or change the tale so much that it is not coherent, or lose interest in it entirely. This will account largely for the brevity of the tales and fantasies that Clark now has. For the past year I have turned almost entirely to poetry. A very little prose and some thirty-five or forty poems are all I have done.

I had intended to include isolated tales and stories in magazines in the bibliography. Blackwood's printed a great many altogether, especially in the period 1815 to 1830. I have been able to pick up occasionally such items as Polidori's tale "The Vampyre" (1819), which seems to be the father of Stoker's "Dracula", and Le Fanu's anthology, "A Stable for Nightmares". I have never seen a copy of Maturin's work advertised for sale, but his "Melmoth the Wanderer" is in the library of the University of Minnesota, where I read it several years ago. This library, by the way, has some good things in it, including a set of Blackwood's, and many of the Gothic romances of the eighteenth and early nineteenth centuries. Some of the cheap, popular magazines have also printed tales of this kind. The Argosy and the All-Story have had many mediocre and a few good ones. The old Black Mask used to print them, and I picked up a magazine called "The All-Around" that printed in 1916 a story called "The Derelict",[3] which, after a poor beginning, turned into a horror-story that I remembered for a long time. Then there are such Utopian things as Parry's "The Scarlet Empire", Rousseau's "The Messiah of the Cylinder", and Wells' "The Time Machine". Bradshaw's "The Goddess of Atvatabar" is a queer volume. Of late, books like "The Street of Queer Houses" by Knowles, and "The Worm Ouroboros", by Eddison, have appeared from time to time.

Well! I hope I haven't bored you, but I find this a fascinating subject. It may take years, but I hope to see the bibliography published eventually in fairly complete and comprehensive form.

Thanking you again for the loan of the typescripts,

Most sincerely,

Donald Wandrei

Notes

1. FBL's contributions to the *United Amateur* of July 1925 include "Pirates and Hamadryades" (an essay on Samuel Loveman) (pp. 1–2) and two poems, "A Man from Genoa" (p. 4) and "From the Catullan Fount" (p. 7). The issue contained Loveman's short story, "The One Who Found Pity" (pp. 5–6).
2. "Arthur Machen and *The Hill of Dreams*."
3. William Hope Hodgson (1877–1918), "The Derelict," *All-Around* 11, No. 4 (February 1916): 79–95. The story was first published in the *Red Magazine* No. 88 (1 December 1912): 490–504, and is one of Hodgson's most frequently reprinted tales.

[5]   [HPL to DAW] [ALS]

10 Barnes St.,

Providence, R.I.,

Jany. 11, 1927

Dear Mr. Wandrei:—

I am glad to hear that you enjoyed the tales, & quite encouraged to see that your preferences coincide so closely with my own. Your wish to copy "Sarnath" & "High House" flatters me very highly! Take your time about it, for there is no demand for the MSS. elsewhere. Glad your drawing & writing acquaintance liked the "High House"—which is my most recent completed product.

The *Overland* is certainly a sorry piece of "pi", & I wonder at its continued ability to retain even a fraction of its ancient standing.[1] Intense local pride—so typical of California—& absence of local competition are doubtless responsible. Another magazine on the Pacific Coast would be a salutary spur to greater pains, & I hope the literary life of the region may some day warrant it.

The *United Amateur* which I sent was indeed for you to keep, as is also the earlier issue (with my critique of Long)[2] which I am now sending under separate cover. This amateur literary organisation did splendid work in its day, & I only wish it could secure enough enthusiastic adherents of the younger generation to redeem it from the decadence into which it has now fallen. It discovered & encouraged Loveman & Long in their respective periods, & would be doing similar service today but for a curious alienation of interests which prevents the youngsters from taking hold & keeping things going as we elders did in our time. If you feel sufficiently interested to consider joining & helping in the task of pulling the organisation out of the mud, you might write to one of the present officials for further information—preferably the Official Editor—Victor E. Bacon, 5932 Julian Ave., St. Louis, Mo. Bacon is a young & energetic chap—& with a dozen like him the society would be on its feet again!

Galpin was a great amateur in his day, but he has now deserted literature altogether in favour of music, having studied a year under Vincent D'Indy[3] at the Schola Cantorum in Paris. He has, in all probability, the most brilliant & highly evolved intellect of any person of my acquaintance; but lacks the emotional centralisation necessary to continuous employment in any one direction. He is only 25 years old, & teaches French in Northwestern University. He was born in Appleton, Wis., & is a graduate of the U. of Wisconsin.

I'm glad you've sent for "The Hermaphrodite", which is the most purely classical poem written in this generation. Loveman is an authentic genius, & has kept the Hellenic (or perhaps I should say *Hellenistic*)[4] spirit more perfectly than anyone else I know of. He belongs vividly & definitely to the colourful civilisation of Alexandria & Antioch. Long—25 years old—is a marvellous boy; not fully developed, but with infinite possibilities as a poet. No—I don't know just now of any other writers of comparable brilliancy in the amateur circle, but will surely notify you of any that I come across.

I can understand your difficulty in procuring fantastic material, & will let you know if my search at the library (which other matters forces me to postpone) reveals any unusual reservoir of unusual titles. I am not very diligent in research, & am probably far behind you in my knowledge of weird literature. My library, the bulk of which is inherited rather than acquired, is not rich in the bizarre; although I have most of Poe, Dunsany, & Machen. Of Blackwood, curiously enough, I have not a solitary item—but mean eventually to get one or two choice specimens, probably "The Listener", (with Blackwood's masterpiece, "The Willows") "John Silence", & "Incredible Adventures". Besides his really good things, Blackwood does write the most depressing flood of utter twaddle & puerility—& he has no instinctive sense of style at all. Whenever he achieves mastery in language it is naively & unconsciously, under the influence of some conception so utterly powerful that it virtually writes itself. Machen's "Hill of Dreams" is surely one of the memorable classics of this generation, both as to style & material. The Roman dream-existence is almost unique in literature, & the whole book abounds with a glamour & tense magic which nothing short of real genius can possess. I am really very eager to see your critique of "The Hill of Dreams", & will promise a safe & intact return in case you find a spare copy to lend me.

"The Yellow Wall Paper" is the sole fictional effort of the feminist & social worker Charlotte Perkins Gilman[5]—whom, by the way, my mother knew in youth.[6] It is a most insidiously potent tale of the aura of madness, & was included by William Dean Howells in his anthology of American Short Story masterpieces. The way to find it would be to look up the anthology in question—which oughtn't to be hard to identify, though I don't recall the exact title. "The House of Sounds" is the only first-rate story Shiel ever wrote; & it is significant to note that its final form is the second published version. In 1896 or thereabouts it appeared under another name (I forget what) in a collection called "Shapes In the Fire",[7] & clothed in a flashy, tinsel style characteristic of "the mauve decade". Then, ten years later, Shiel appears to have recognised its curiously mixed merits & defects, so that he eliminated the latter & salvaged the former, producing the perfected tale about which all good judges become so pardonably enthusiastic.

My novel, though it may represent industry & application, isn't likely to represent much more. Pressure of other things has delayed work on it lately, but I shall probably have it done—& running to 100-odd pages—in a month or so. The older I get, the longer my tales tend to run—so that today I hardly could write a brief bit like "Polaris" or "Nyarlathotep". I am anxiously awaiting those tales of yours which Smith has promised to forward me. I'd like to see your poetry also, & hope you have a few specimens available for lending. I can't write poetry, although I used to try it ten or fifteen years ago.

Your projected bibliography exceeds in scope anything of the kind which I had planned, & I certainly hope you will carry the plan through. I wish I could get hold of Polidori's "Vampyre" & something by Le Fanu. The latter has long been a familiar name to me, yet I have seen absolutely nothing of his.[8] In general, the libraries in the East seem very weak on Gothic romance. Yes—I know that the cheap magazines have often printed excellent weird bits, & recall many things in the old *All-Story;* which I have not seen, however, for years.[9] *The Black Cat* used to have some excellent fragments of the macabre.[10] I don't care for "Utopian" things like the early Wells, where social satire & didacticism weaken the force of fantastic narration. In my article I shall hit only the 'high spots'—leaving to you the more difficult & thankless task of a really inclusive & scholarly compilation. By the way—there's a finely developed *conte cruel,* "The Church Stove", in the current *Weird Tales.*[11]

With every good wish, & hoping to see some of your creative work soon, I remain

Most cordially & sincerely yrs—

H P Lovecraft

[*Enclosure:* United Amateur Press Association / Application for Membership.]

Notes

1. Bret Harte had founded the *Overland Monthly* in 1868. "Pi" is disordered type.

2. "The Work of Frank Belknap Long, Jr."

3. Vincent d'Indy (1851–1931), French composer, pupil of César Franck, founder and director of the Schola Cantorum, Paris (1911–31).

4. The Hellenistic era is the literary period of the 4th and 3rd centuries B.C.E., when such Alexandrian writers as Callimachus and Apollonius Rhodius introduced an irony and sophistication foreign to the literature of the classic Hellenic period of the 6th and 5th centuries B.C.E.

5. Actually, Gilman wrote a feminist utopian fantasy, *Herland* (1914), but it was first published only in 1979. Otherwise her work consisted of social and political criticism.

6. See HPL to AWD, 20 September 1935: "My mother knew her well—since as plain Charlotte Perkins she used to be governess in the home of some friends of ours. Later her first husband was the Providence artist Stetson. She always had an affected, eccentric streak of self-conscious intellectuality" (*ES* 708).

7. "The House of Sounds" initially appeared as "Vaila" in *Shapes in the Fire* (London: John Lane; Boston: Roberts Brothers, 1896).

8. HPL later acquired Le Fanu's *The House by the Churchyard* (1863), but did not care for it. Still later he read Le Fanu's "Green Tea" in Dorothy L. Sayers's *Omnibus of Crime* (1928), but his reaction was lukewarm: "I at last . . . have read 'Green Tea.' It is certainly better than anything else of Le Fanu's that I have ever seen, though I'd hardly put it in the Poe-Blackwood-Machen class" (HPL to CAS, [16 January 1932]; *DS* 342).

9. HPL had three letters to the editor published in the *All-Story* (8 February 1913, 7 March 1914, 15 August 1914), the first of which praises Irvin S. Cobb's "Fishhead."

10. See HPL to RHB, 14 April [1932]: "*The Black Cat* ran a high percentage of weird material around 1904 or so, when I first began to notice it" (*OFF* 29); and HPL to James F. Morton, 23 February 1936: "I used to buy that [*Black Cat*] reg'lar-like, & recall the swell weird stuff it had. That & the old *All-Story* were the first sources of contemporary weird material I ever stumbled on!" (*Letters to James F. Morton* 372).

11. G. Appleby Terrill, "The Church Stove at Raebrudafisk" (*WT*, February 1927).

[6]   [HPL to DAW] [ANS]

10 Barnes St.,
Providence, R.I.,
Jany. 17, 1927

Dear Mr. Wandrei:—

Your MSS. have just arrived from Smith; & truly, they are marvellous! I don't know when I've ever seen such authentically *cosmic* material—or a vision so genuinely sensitive to impressions from *outside!* The items relating to the death of the universe are infinitely powerful, while virtually all the others have touches of bizarre perspective which stamp them as emphatically "the real stuff". "The Chuckler" surely presents one form of the ultimate refinement of horror! In every piece is a pictorial sense which I can only compare to Smith's grotesque polarisations. A thousand congratulations upon your ability!

With your permission I shall return this material via Frank B. Long, who I am very certain will appreciate the tales profoundly.

Sincerely & admiringly—

H P Lovecraft

[7]   [DAW to HPL]

[Postmarked Saint Paul, Minn.,
26 January 1927]

[Envelope only.]

[8]   [HPL to DAW] [ALS]

10 Barnes St.,
Providence, R.I.,
Jany. 29, 1927

My dear Mr. Wandrei:—

I was very glad to learn that my opinion of your work formed an encouragement for you, & wish to reiterate the admiration—now fortified by a second perusal of the tales—which I hastened to express on the postal. Smith gave them very high praise when sending them to me, being especially fond of "The Door of [*sic*] the Room", the "Fragment of a Dream", "The Messengers", & "The Pursuers". Long also—to whom I sent the MSS.—is enthusiastic, & says: "Wandrei's work has a fine imaginative quality. 'The Twilight of Time' & the two Ambrose-Biercian *contes cruels* ('The Chuckler' & 'The Decomposer') are excellent, & technically above reproach. That *red brain* & the whirling cosmic dust! Yes—Wandrei has had glimpses . . . . *outside!* I shall return the tales promptly & safely. A thousand thanks for letting me see them."

I wouldn't destroy any of the tales, if I were you. Not that I don't think unsatisfactory work ought to be destroyed, for I've torn up reams of my own minor drivel; but that I don't think any of these particular specimens can be held to merit such a fate. Some are much better than others, it is true; but I think all are well above the limit of candidacy for oblivion. I have just mentioned you & your work to the editor of *Weird Tales*, & hope you will submit something to him. If he has any regard for my opinion—which he has often said that he has—your tales cannot fail to gain at least a careful reading; though of course absolute merit is by no means the standard of acceptance in a commercial publication catering to a more or less rabblish clientele. If you have any more work available, I am exceedingly anxious to see it—be it either prose or poetry. Any additions to the cosmic series will be hailed with wildest enthusiasm! The early date of some of your work is indeed interesting—& would surely never be suspected from the text itself. I began concocting weird stuff incredible ages ago, & have some infantile things ("The Mysterious Ship", "The Secret of the Grave", &c) written when I was eight. The earliest tale that I continue to take seriously—"The Beast in the Cave"[1]—was written at the age of fourteen; & even this will have to be revised extensively before it can be published. My style in those days was a pompous Johnsonese, for I am an antiquarian by nature, & never used to read a modern book if I could possibly find anything with long s's to take its place. I had the run of our old family library, & surely made yᵉ most of it! My "Beast in the Cave" starts out this way:

"The horrible conclusion which had gradually been obtruding itself upon my confused yet reluctant comprehension was now become an awful certainty. I was lost, hopelessly & irrevocably lost, in the vast & labyrinthine recesses of the Mammoth Cave."

Even now I have not wholly shed the intangible aura of my beloved eighteenth century, as many characteristic turns of style & diction attest. When I was eighteen I decided that my fiction was mostly trash, & destroyed all of it save "The Beast in the Cave" & "The Alchemist"—which though of later date was not so good. Poetry, science, & a thousand other interests then absorbed me for nine years, at the end of which time a friend (the same W. Paul Cook who published Long's & Loveman's books) saw some of my old stuff & urged me to begin again. I did—producing "Dagon" & "The Tomb" in 1917, "Polaris" in 1918, "Beyond the Wall of Sleep" in 1919, & thereafter grinding 'em out with some frequency. I have not noticed any tendency in myself to think in terms of less mystic & ethereal imagery as my years advance, hence from analogy would say that you need have no apprehensions about your own continuance of the exotic vein. Your teacher's reaction to "The Door to the Room" was certainly a sincere compliment! The pedagogic train are certainly naive creatures—I recall an incident in high school when a motherly old matron in the English department refused to believe that a theme of mine was not copied from something somewhere. Wishing to give the good soul a jolt, I blandly informed her that it was indeed taken verbatim from an article in a small rural weekly, & that I hoped no errors of transcription had occurred! Only when she shewed some signs of recovery did I add that the printed article was my own—a statement which I buttressed on the following day by exhibiting the cutting with my name in conspicuous type at the head.[2]

"Amateur Journalism" will most cordially welcome you whenever you are ready to join. As I think I warned you, it is now in a very depressed state; & you will find its output sadly uneven. But with the material it has, I can't help thinking that it holds within itself the possibilities of a renaissance, & that it will somehow manage to "come back" either through a consolidation of the two major associations or otherwise. Meanwhile I am anxious to see the Machen essay & the poems.

I know how difficult Le Fanu is to get. He is wholly absent from the Prov. Public Library, & although two or three of his titles are listed in the N.Y. Pub. Lib., I was never able to get hold of any of these. Polidori is likewise a rare bird—although everyone knows *about* him because of his connexion with the genesis of "Frankenstein".[3] I would indeed be ecstatically grateful for the loan of any of these volumes, & would promise their return in prime condition. It might save bother in frequent packing to send them two by two—beginning, say, with Polidori's "Vampyre" & Le Fanu's collection— "A Stable for Nightmares". I don't want to impose on you, though, if it would be the least trouble. In reciprocation I hope I can fill up some of your own weird-literary lacunae by the loan of volumes on my shelves—although my collection in that field is woefully meagre. I think I'll pause at this point & copy down the titles at hand—& if you note any which you've not been able to secure, it will give me pleasure to send them on immediately.

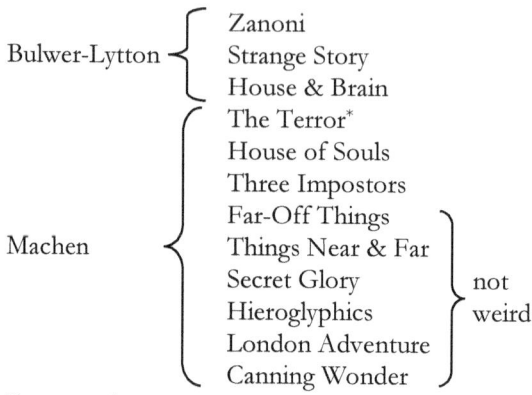

Bulwer-Lytton {
  Zanoni
  Strange Story
  House & Brain
}

Machen {
  The Terror*
  House of Souls
  Three Impostors
  Far-Off Things ⎫
  Things Near & Far ⎪
  Secret Glory   ⎬ not
  Hieroglyphics ⎪ weird
  London Adventure ⎪
  Canning Wonder ⎭
}

Poe complete
Bierce—Can Such Things Be?
Level—Tales of Mystery & Horror
Saintsbury (ed) Tales of Mystery†
Shiel—Prince Zaleski
Radcliffe—Udolpho
Benson‡—Visible & Invisible
Beckford Vathek
      Episodes of Vathek
Dunsany—all short tales & plays
      Chronicles of Rodriguez
      King of Elfland's Daughter
Fouque—Undine & other tales
Wells—1st Men in Moon
      Island of Dr. Moreau (in mag. instalments)
Moore—The Epicurean
Savile—Beyond the Great South Wall (not weird, but impossible adventure)
De Mille—MS. found in Copper Cylinder
Haggard—She
Shelley, Mrs.—Frankenstein
Gautier—Avatar
Mérimée—Venus of Ille

---

*in an old Century Magazine
†Extracts from Mrs. Radcliffe, Lewis, & Maturin
‡I also have his "Man Who Went Too Far" in one of the Haldeman-Julius Blue Books.

Verne   Earth to Moon
         20,000 Leag. under Sea
D'Aurevilly—Story Without a Name
Webster—Oracle of Baal
Lock & Key Library (which has some good weird things)

Hawthorne   { 7 Gables
             { Marble Faun
             { & short stories

This is about all I can think of, & even this list contains a lot of standard stuff which you no doubt either possess or can easily get at the library. I also have Emily Brontë's "Wuthering Heights", which is semi-weird, Lang's Arabian Nights, & various other things which I suppose are on the borderline of the extra-natural, though not really belonging to the spectral tradition. Altogether, my library is a very poor one so far as this province is concerned. I have not a thing, for example, by Algernon Blackwood. As to our relative familiarity with weird letters—I still think it very likely that you are in the lead; for although I am probably much older—36 being my accumulated store of winters—I am exceedingly indolent in pursuing any one theme, & have had long periods of alienation from the domain of the bizarre. In writing my outline of weird fiction I have had to set down dozens of titles which I know only by reputation—this being especially true of the early Gothick novel. The only real "Gothick" novels I've ever read are Walpole's "Castle of Otranto", Miss Reeve's "Old English Baron", Lewis's "Monk", Mrs. Shelley's "Franken-stein", & *parts* of "Melmoth". I've never had access to a complete "Melmoth" long enough to read it through. By the way—I *have* seen "Melmoth" for sale, but at a time when I was financially unable to invest. That was about a year ago, when the bookseller Meredith Janvier of Baltimore listed a 2-volume copy for $8.00. I've always regretted having had to pass up that bargain.[4] A few years ago I read two curious survivals of the Gothic spirit—written in the mid-Victorian period by George W. M. Reynolds—entitled "Wagner the Wehr-Wolf" & "Faust & the Demon". They have all the pomposity & involution of their type at its zenith! Have you read anything of Stoker's aside from "Dracula"? "The Jewel of Seven Stars" is pretty fair, but "The Lair of the White Worm" is absolutely the most amorphous & infantile mess I've ever seen between cloth covers; & that in spite of a magnificent idea which one would ordinarily deem well-nigh fool-proof.[5] Stoker was absolutely devoid of a sense of form, & could not write a coherent tale to save his life. Everything of his went through the hands of a re-writer, (except, perhaps, the "White Worm") & it is curious to note that one of our circle of amateur journalists—an old lady named Mrs. Miniter[6]—had a chance to revise the "Dracula" MS. (which was a fiendish mess!) before its publication, but turned it down be-cause Stoker refused to pay the price which the difficulty of the work impelled her to charge. Stoker had a brilliantly fantastic mind, but was unable to shape the images he created.

I'm glad you enjoyed the article on Long. Unfortunately his early work is scattered through amateur papers to such an extent that its recapture would be very difficult; but I'll try to locate some & lend or copy the text.[7] They are not so much in the actually weird tradition as in that of the French symbolists & decadents; but they are well worthy of perusal & admiration. If Loveman does not soon lend you a batch of his work, I will send you a great deal which I have on hand—albeit in MSS. of very doubtful neatness. I'll also send you a copy of his amateur magazine "The Saturnian" to keep—for I have an extra one, & can't think of any more deserving & appreciative custodian than yourself. Loveman is certainly a true artist, & in his translations he does more justice to Baudelaire than Arthur Symons has recently done.[8] I think, though, that Verlaine's vision is closer to his own than Baudelaire's. For a couple of years it was very pleasant to be in daily touch with Long & Loveman in New York—Long having always lived there, Loveman coming in Sept. 1924, & I in March 1924.[9] But after a time my dislike for the city became so great as to outweigh any amelioration which personal friendships might furnish—especially since the most vital part of the friendships can survive unimpaired in correspondence—so I came home in April 1926 to this ancient New England town that dreams on its hills at the head of the blue bay—the town where I was born, lived for 34 years of my life, & shall live all the rest of my life, *diis volentibus!*[10] Around Long & Loveman there is quite a little circle of literary enthusiasts—eight or nine men of various types & ages—who meet once a week at the homes of one or another of them.[11] These meetings form, on the whole, the pleasantest of all my memories of the metropolis, aside from the museums & one or two landscape or architectural effects.

My novel—or novelette, since it came only to 110 pages—is now finished, & I have given it the provisional title of "The Dream-Quest of Unknown Kadath".[12] I am not sure how well I like it, but you will certainly see it as soon as it is in typed form.[13] I dread the job of typing infinitely, & shan't attempt such a stretch of it unless I feel that the story is really worth bothering with. Meanwhile I am already at work on a new shorter tale, which I think will come well within the category of the poisonously horrible. It will be full of the colour of colonial Providence, having a kind of harking-back to a very singular man who came here in 1692 & refused to grow old. In a modern framework I am giving something of an impression of the old town as it stands today, full of the classic doorways & Georgian steeples & antique chimneys & gables & narrow glamorous ways climbing the steep hill east of the waterfront, which testify so colourfully to its centuries of continuous existence. You'll probably see this before you see the novel, & I shall surely try it on *Weird Tales*.[14] That magazine, I may remark, has just accepted another yarn of mine—"Pickman's Model"—which has an old Boston setting.

By the way—have you read any of the exotic ravings of Charles Fort, who thinks that all sorts of wonderful things exist in the air & outside visible space, & asserts that men of science are leagued in a conspiracy to keep us in ignorance of the true nature of the universe? I have heard of him for years, but never read his stuff—"The Book of the Damned" & "New Lands"—& now Long, who has just encountered this material, tells me that it is marvellously weird & imaginatively captivating. Fort appears to be a man of some culture & ability, far above the usual run of "flat-earthers" & kindred eccentrics.

With every good wish, & hoping soon to see more of your work, I remain

Most cordially & sincerely yrs—

H P Lovecraft

Notes

1. Final version written 21 April 1905.

2. HPL to Robert E. Howard, 25–29 March 1933: "I had handed in a theme entitled 'Can the Moon Be Reached by Man'? And something about it (gawd knows what) led her to question its originality. She said it sounded like a magazine article. Well—chance was with me that day, for I had the ammunition to stage a peach of a tableau. Did I deny the magazine-article charge? Not so! Instead, I calmly informed the lady that the theme was indeed a verbatim parallel of an article which had appeared in a rural weekly only a few days before. I felt sure, I said, that no one could possibly object to the parallelism! Indeed, I added—as the good soul's bewilderment became almost apoplectic—I would be glad to show her the printed article in question! Then, reaching in my pocket, I produced a badly printed cutting from a Rhode Island village paper (which would accept almost anything sent to it). Sure enough—here was the selfsame article. And mixed were the emotions of the honest Mrs. Blake when she perused the heading—CAN THE MOON BE REACHED BY MAN? BY H. P. LOVECRAFT" (*A Means to Freedom* 583). The article was published in a rural newspaper in Phenix, R.I., the *Pawtuxet Valley Gleaner,* for 12 October 1906. In this account to Howard, HPL does not mention that he brought the clipping to school the day following his confrontation with Mrs. Blake.

3. Polidori participated in a kind of ghost-writing contest that resulted in his *The Vampyre: A Tale* and Mary Shelley's *Frankenstein.* (Percy Bysshe Shelley and Lord Byron also participated.) Polidori plagiarized his story from an uncompleted fragment by Lord Byron.

4. HPL acquired his personal copy of *Melmoth the Wanderer* as a gift from W. Paul Cook in January 1933.

5. The idea being that of an enormous worm or dragon lurking beneath the vault of an ancient castle.

6. Edith (Dowe) Miniter (1869–1934), an amateur journalist and author of a professionally published novel, *Our Natupski Neighbors* (1916). This account of her involvement with *Dracula* has not been confirmed.

7. See FBL's *The Eye Above the Mantel* (West Hills, CA: Tsathoggua Press, 1995), reprinting four tales published in amateur journals.

8. Loveman published three numbers of *The Saturnian: A Journal of Art and Literature*: 1, No. 1 (June–July [1920]); 1, No. 2 (August–September [1920]); and 1, No. 3 (March 1922). HPL refers to Loveman's "Translations from Baudelaire" in No. 3.

9. HPL does not mention here (or anywhere in his letters to DAW) that he moved to New York as a consequence of his marriage to Sonia H. Greene.

10. "The gods being willing" (adaptation of the singular *deo volente*).

11. Dubbed the Kalem Club because most members' surnames started with the letters K, L, and M.

12. HPL's ms. of the novel lists seven potential titles.

13. HPL never typed the novel. He lent the ms. to RHB some time in 1935 for typing, but by December 1936 RHB had typed only approximately the first half.

14. The "shorter tale," another novel, was *The Case of Charles Dexter Ward*, which proved to be the longest of HPL's fictional works. HPL never prepared the work for publication.

[9]   [HPL to DAW] [ANS]

> [Postmarked Providence, R.I.,
> 3 February 1927]
> Monday

Your poems (plus my MSS.) came this morning, & I must hasten to congratulate you on the undoubtedly deep & authentic poetic spirit which animates all your verses.

"The Woodland Pool" is a moving & sombrely delightful garland of black blossoms, & it's quite difficult to select single items to praise, so essentially homogeneous & organically unified is the whole collection.

Here & there are technical immaturities—stiffly turned phrases & lines with essential prose rather than poetic content—but these are so insignificant beside the cypress-like beauty of the whole that one sees & mentions them only incidentally & casually.

I'll see that these come back safely in the end, & meanwhile I'm eager to see any more work which you may send. ¶ Thanks & best wishes—

> Most cordially yrs—
> H P Lovecraft

[10]   [DAW to HPL] [ALS]

> 1152 Portland Ave.,
> St. Paul, Minn.
> Feb. 7, 1927

Dear Mr. Lovecraft:

I returned your manuscripts last week, and thank you again for loaning them to me. The delay in returning them was due, as I said, to the fact that I made copies of "The Strange High House in the Mist", and "The Doom That Came to Sarnath". I hope you have received them by now, and in good condition. If you have them available, I should be glad to read the others you listed, that is:

> The Nameless City
> The Other Gods
> In the Vault
> Cool Air
> The Silver Key
> The Lurking Fear.

If you have had "Polaris" and "Celephais" returned to you, I should like them also; and if you ever make other copies of "The Quest of Iranon", "Herbert West—Reanimator", "The Shunned House", and "Nyarlathotep", be sure to let me read them. I have just bought the new "Weird Tales" and read "The White Ship". I think that is one of the best of your tales, for this reason: in most of your work hitherto, the element of utter horror has brooded over it and predominated; but here are beauty and horror both, and the craftsmanship, as usual, is on a level far above W.T. I congratulate you on W.T.'s acceptance of "Pickman's Model", but I confess I would rather have seen "The Call of Cthulhu" or "The Strange High House in the Mist" printed. I am quite eager to see your novel when you typewrite it; 110 pages is an appalling amount, though; if the work were mine, I doubt whether I could ever get courage enough to undertake typewriting it.

I sent you most of my poems when I returned your manuscripts. I hope some of them may please you. There are a few which I shall probably remove from the group, to make room for better. I have never shown them to anyone, except for six that Sterling read. They were "The Song of Oblivion"— which I liked very much and kept—"Mystical Quest", "The Witches' Sabbath", "Old Fantasy",—which he liked "for its beauty", and "Strange Flowers", which he said was too Swinburnian. Unfortunately, he was right, and I have therefore plucked the flowers. I haven't any particular favourites among them, though I prefer the dirges. The manuscript, you will notice, is in book form. I am going to try to get it published, when I write enough other poems to give it fair size. But I seem to have lost interest in poetry as a medium, of late, and perhaps I am on the point of returning to prose. You are welcome to keep the manuscript, or rather, typescript, as long as you wish.

I have no other manuscripts at present. I am sending you a copy of "The Minnesota Quarterly" with my essay on "The Hill of Dreams", which you can keep if you wish. I am enclosing with this letter the last two poems I have written. Other than these, all I have are a story, "The Shadow of a Nightmare", and a few short fantasies which I would have sent with the other prose things except that they weren't good enough. Another story of the cosmic group, which will be the second in it, is but partially completed; and I have never taken the trouble to typewrite the fragments of the novel, though they are short.[1]

You may be right about the environment. I am absolutely sick of the Twin Cities. I have lived here all my life—I will be 19 in two months—and hate this place and the people with all my heart. There isn't a person here with any imagination, nor is any encouragement of it offered. I may graduate from the University of Minnesota this spring; if I do, I shall thank God for a parting which, I believe, will be mutually appreciated by the U. and myself. I have a friend who lives in Hartford, Connecticut; he is driving east next June when school lets out, and regardless of whether I make enough honor points to graduate, I am going with him. New York is my destiny. All my tastes are literary, and as far as I can see, New York is the logical place. There certainly is nothing in this part of the country for people with such leanings. What I do after I arrive there is uncertain. If I obtain work I like, I'll stay; if I don't, I'll keep on going,—to London, or south along the seaboard and west to California. Whatever I do, it means escape; and it will be a long, long time before I have any desire to return to Minnesota.

I am sending you Polidori's "Vampyre", and the two Le Fanu books. You may use them as long as you wish, but you will have to use some care with Polidori's book, for it is in rather poor condition. I have examined the list of books you give with great interest; most of them I know, but there are some whose names and authors both are totally unfamiliar to me. These are: Webster: The Oracle of Baal; De Mille: Ms. found in Copper Cylinder; Moore: The Epicurean; and Savile: Beyond the Great South Wall. The first three of these, in particular, I should like to read, if it is not too much trouble to you. I have heard of *Prince Zaleski,* but have never seen it. The stories of Mérimée, Gautier, and D'Aurevilly you list, I haven't read; but they are available here. Fort's two books I read a couple of years ago. They are extremely interesting and miserably written. They consist largely of authentic records of phenomena inexplicable to science, for which Mr. Fort offers suggestions based on his revolutionary concept of the universe. I'll be glad to send you the two if you wish to read them. This seems like a good place to list the more or less weird books I possess.

Benson: Visible and Invisible
Blackwood: Jimbo
    Pan's Garden
    The Bright Messenger
    Julius Levallon
    The Empty House
    John Silence
    The Listener

The Wolves of God
The Wave
The Promise of Air
Tongues of Fire
Incredible Adventures
The Human Chord
Ten Minute Stories
Day and Night Stories
Bierce: Collected Works, 12 vols.
Bullet: The Street of the Eye
Capek: Krakatit
Crawford: Wandering Ghosts
Cummings: The Girl in the Golden Atom
Dickinson: True Tales of the Weird
Doyle: The Lost World
    The Poison Belt
Dunsany: The King of Elfland's Daughter
Eddison: The Worm Ouroboros
Egbert: The Sea Demons
Ferenczy: The Ants of Timothy Thümmel
Fish: The Wrists on the Door
Fort: Book of the Damned
    New Lands
Fox: The People on Other Planets
Frank: Chalk Face
Gernsback: Ralph 124C41+
Glasgow: The Shadowy Third
Haggard: Wisdom's Daughter
    The Witch's Head
Kitchell: The Earl of Hell
Knowles: The Street of Queer Houses
Le Fanu: All in the Dark
    Stable for Nightmares
Library of Imaginative Literature, 3 vols.[2]
Machen: The Terror
    The Great God Pan and The Inmost Light
    The Hill of Dreams (Blue Paper edition)
    The Shining Pyramid
    others not weird
Merritt: The Moon Pool
Nichols: Fantastica
O'Neill: Souls in Hell
Parry: The Scarlet Empire

Poe: complete
Plante: The Shadow of the Astral
Polidori: The Vampyre
Renard: New Bodies for Old
Robbins: Silent, White, and Beautiful
Rosny: The Giant Cat
Rudwin (collector): Devil Stories
Serviss: The Second Deluge
    The Moon Metal
Shelley: Frankenstein
Shiel: The Pale Ape
    The Lord of the Sea
Smith: Thus Far
Stockton: The Great Stone of Sardis
Stoker: Dracula
Train: The Man Who Rocked the Earth
Verne: Centre of the Earth
Wells: The Food of the Gods
    The Sea Lady
    Tales of Space and Time
    Thirty Strange Stories
    The Wonderful Visit
    The Island of Dr. Moreau
    The Time Machine
    The War in the Air
    Men Like Gods
    In the Days of the Comet
    When the Sleeper Wakes
    The First Men in the Moon
    The Country of the Blind
    The World Yet Free
    The War of the Worlds
Williams: The Thing in the Woods
Bradshaw: The Goddess of Atvatabar
Appleton's collection of ghost stories: 23 Tales
Patterson's collection: Weird Tales, 4 vols.
Howells collection: Shapes that Haunt the Dusk
Some stuff of Burroughs and Rohmer.
In magazines: Amazing Stories, complete.
    Weird Tales: all except 3 issues.
    Ghost Stories: First 6 numbers.

Fifty or sixty short stories and novels taken from various magazines.

I was not fortunate enough to inherit any books; my parents bought few, hence I have had to supply the deficiency myself. Many volumes that I ought to have are missing from the list because I have made it a custom to buy first the books not available at the libraries. I admire poetry of the fantastic more than prose, however, and I cherish such volumes as Smith's, Barnitz's "The Book of Jade", Thomson's "City of Dreadful Night", Saltus's "Shadows and Ideals", "Dreams After Sunset", "The Witch of En-Dor", and "The Baya-dere", Wilson's "The Undertaker's Garland", and others, as well as the work of poets like Swinburne, Keats, Shelley, Baudelaire, Beddoes, and Sterling. I really have little more than the nucleus of a library, but some day it may in-clude all the items I desire.

The early age at which you began writing is amazing, more so even than your vocabulary at fourteen. I was not so fortunate in having access to a good library, and can not help regretting my inability to obtain the finer and older books in my youth. I read an enormous number of books—from two hun-dred to four and five hundred a year—but most of this was trash. I discov-ered Poe and Verne when I was nine, acquired a definite taste for the weird and fantastic the next year—a development from an earlier passion for fairy-tales and legends—and have never lost this interest in Gothic literature. I have buried myself in book- and short-story indexes, pursued ghost stories through anthologies and forgotten collections, and gone over the stacks in the book-stores of the Twin Cities so often and minutely that I know them better than the proprietors do. I worked in the Public Library and Hill Reference Library for a year and a half,[3] and I verily believe I know every weird tale or novel of impossible adventure or pure fantasy that they possess, from "Tar-zan" to "Fantastics" and "The Hill of Dreams". Then, too, I carefully exam-ined all the booksellers' catalogues that were received, and took the titles of every book that might be of the imaginative school. But in spite of my efforts, I never succeeded in killing my taste for weird fiction, or reaching the point of satiation. Oddly enough, I wrote nothing until I was fifteen. Then I began five or six stories, none of which I finished or on which I wrote more than a few paragraphs; they are all in limbo now. I completed one story, "The Black Pool", which I keep as a curiosity; the manuscript is almost illegible, but the visible portions are nearly lurid enough to illuminate the rest. The next year, I entered the university, and began to write again, and produced "The Decom-positor", now "The Decomposer", "In the Hundred Billionth Aeon", now "The Twilight of Time", and "Beyond the Milky Way", which is pretty bad. I wrote at irregular intervals then until I was eighteen, when I decided to try poetry, and wrote "The Song of Autumn", and "The Corpse Speaks" (I think I changed the title of this to "In the Grave" in the typescript.) My previous attempts had produced two pieces of doggerel and three or four specimens of miserable stuff. Since then, I have written almost no prose (and perhaps no *poetry*), except the critique on Clark, the unfinished fragments of the novel, and the cosmic tale, and "The Green Flame".

Well! Perhaps I ought to say, Pax tecum! while you read my literary life; but this *is* an early age to begin my memoirs. The Greeks had a saying: Ὂν ὁι θεοι φιλουσιν, ἀποθνῇσκει νέος.[4] But the gods may be just as arbitrary with their challengers.

I have read only "Dracula" by Stoker, which certainly has enough flaws even though it was revised. Many of his things are still in print in England, published by Wm. Rider and Sons, London. It is significant that much more material in the Gothic field is published in England than here. I am reminded of this fact by a book I have just come upon, "Across the Zodiac",[5] which has never been published here, so far as I know.

I can not tell you how much I appreciate your mentioning my name to the editor of *Weird Tales,* and the kind things you and Smith and Long have said about the tales. The only person in the Twin Cities who cares at all for them is a professor at the U., Cortlandt Van Winkle, for whom I wrote "The Twilight of Time". But he likes the imaginative in spite of himself, and has endeavored to get me "to come down to earth". Ugh! He has a remarkable reading voice, deep and heavy, but very expressive; he read the story aloud, and I think one reason he liked it is that it suited his voice so well. Unconscious flattery is a subtle compliment of the ego to itself. I shall send some of them to Mr. Wright, though I am not sanguine about the outcome. "The Decomposer" and "The Twilight of Time" were returned by *Weird Tales* a year ago, though I am not certain whether they reached the editorial sanctum sanctorum. But there can be little harm, except to one's feelings, in trying.

I am anxious to see more of Long's and Loveman's work; if you succeed in finding any, I shall be more than glad to read it. I have read the *Saturnian* with great interest; Loveman's translations are unequal, but I like them on the whole. I have not seen Symons' renderings, but I understand that they are rather poor in many respects. I must thank you again for the copies of the *Saturnian* and *The United Amateur,* and for the loan of your mss.

Meanwhile, I am eager to read the rest of your tales. I hope you will send them as soon as possible, for I am anticipating them with pleasure.

Very sincerely,
Donald Wandrei

Notes

1. The second story referred to could be "On the Threshold of Eternity," a sequel to "The Twilight of Time" (i.e., "The Red Brain").

2. Unidentified.

3. In DAW's autobiographical novel *Invisible Sun* (1932–33), the main character Drew also holds a library job (see Chapter XIV).

4. "Whom the gods love dies young."

5. By Percy Greg.

[11]　[HPL to DAW] [ALS]

10 Barnes St.,

Providence, R.I.,

Feby. 10, 1927

Dear Mr. Wandrei:—

All the material duly came; & as you have no doubt learned from my postal, I was greatly delighted with the poems. While it was very hard to pick favourites from among them, I think that on the whole the strain most natural to you is that which dwells on the imminence of death & the worm—the authentic strain of Poe, if the comparison be not too hackneyed. Sterling's choices are very interesting to note—he evidently surveyed the material from the standpoint of the pure poet. I hope sincerely that you can get this material published, though that is a hard thing nowadays—bards as mature & experienced as Smith having great trouble in finding a publisher. Have you thought of writing Cook, who published the Long & Loveman books? He does excellent work, & you could discuss arrangements at length. Long's aunt financed his book, but Cook himself assumed the responsibility for Loveman's. The two poems you have just sent—"Lost Atlantis" & "The Cry of the Mad" impress me as splendid. If I were you, I would keep on with both poetry & prose, for you have much to say in each of these media. I am returning the poetic MS. with profound gratitude for the sight of it. The matter sent third-class will doubtless reach me soon, & I shall certainly peruse the Machen essay with keenest delight. Whenever you have the residual MSS. you mention—"Shadow of Nightmare" & the member of the cosmic group—in readiness, it would afford me great pleasure to see them. Also the fragments of the novel.

Under separate cover (& enclosed—for I've only just found "The Nameless City") I am sending all the tales you list—which comprise all that are in typed & available form. There is no hurry about their return, & I only hope they may not bore you. You will find both the pure horror & fantastic strains represented in this assortment—naturally I tend to veer betwixt the two, but professionally-minded persons urge me to stick to horror as the more marketable commodity. I am just now reacting against this advice, as you will see from "The Silver Key", which is recent. "The Lurking Fear" was done to order for a wretchedly sensational magazine four years ago—hence the mechanically shilling-shocker sub-climaxes at the end of each section. Some day I may rewrite it decently as a continuous unit. In "Polaris"—written in 1918—you will see how close I came to the Dunsany style before I ever heard of Dunsany. My discovery of D. took place in the autumn of 1919, & produced a profound effect upon me—you will see instant reflections in "The White Ship",

"Celephaïs", "The Other Gods", "The Doom that Came to Sarnath", &c. Pegāna only knows when I'll get my 110-page affair typed—& the same applies to the tale on which I'm now at work, (p. 58) & which may get to 75 pages or so before its natural & logical conclusion appears. It centres around Old Providence, & I shall call it either "The Case of Charles Dexter Ward," or "The Madness out of Time". Some may fancy there is too much descriptive & antiquarian matter in it—but I had to get it out of my system somehow!

As to the effect of environment on work—I forget exactly what I said in my former letter, but in any case I think an author strongly reflects his surroundings, & that he does best in founding his elements of incident & colour on a life & background to which he has a real & deep-seated relation. This may or may not be his native & childhood environment, but I think it is generally better so unless that setting be more than ordinarily devoid of vividness or dramatic possibilities. If the latter be the case, then I think the author would do well to choose a new setting with great care; keeping in mind both his own psychological tastes & requirements, & the general truth that life has more available literary values in such places as possess a visible & continuous linkage with their own sources & development, & a well-defined relation to some dominant stream of civilisation. This would really exclude any such cosmopolitan chaos as New York—which has no central identity or meaning, & no clean-cut relationship either to its own past or to anything else in particular—but of course I realise that different minds have different requirements, & that there are those who find in the intense surge of artificial life a certain stimulation which brings out what is already in them. But one ought to be warned in advance that all life in New York is purely artificial & affected—values are forced & arbitrary, mental fashions are capricious, pathological, or commercial rather than authentic, & literary activity & conversation are motivated by a shallow pose, a sophistical concealment of ignorance, & a morbidly charlatanic egotism & cheap assertiveness far removed from the solid aesthetic intensity which ought to underlie a life of art & letters. New York has, by force of sheer wealth & glitter & advertising, captured the *reputation* of a literary capital, but it is not a true one in the sense that Boston once was. The "aesthetes" of New York are less interested in art & beauty than in themselves; & their smart badinage & discussion savour much more of psychological exhibitionism & social gesture than of actual artistic insight, vision, & devotion. It is a case of inferior people trying to be conspicuous somehow, & choosing art as a form of ballyhoo more convenient & inexpensive than business or evangelism or sword-swallowing. Of the genuine flow of life, or the sincere recording of life & dreams which is literature, I can discern scarcely a trace. Whatever of value is produced there is merely the outcropping of things elsewhere nourished—except of course in the case of those few real native New Yorkers who survive in sadness from the dead & lovely old city that was; the gracious, glamorous elder New York of dignity & poise, which lies stark & horrible & ghoul-gnawed today beneath the foul claws of the mongrel & misshapen foreign colossus that gibbers & howls vulgarly & dreamlessly on its site. If you want to know what I think of New York, read "He". I was living there when I wrote it—& I had to get out of town to the quiet colonial shades of a New Jersey village in order to put it into coherent words.[1] No—New York is dead, & the brilliancy which so impresses one from outside is the phosphorescence of a maggoty corpse. There can be no normal American life or thought in a town full of twisted ratlike vermin from the ghetto & steerage of yesterday—a town where for block on block one can walk without seeing a single face which has any relation to the life & growth of the Nordic, Anglo-American stream of civilisation. It is not America—it is not even Europe—it is Asia & chaos & hell—the sort of stinking, amorphous hybridism which Juvenal noted in Rome when he wrote "Syrus Orontes in Tiberim defluxit."[2] I don't think America has any real literary capital today—although Chicago may tone down some day into the nearest approach to one. I've never been there, but from what I hear & from what correspondents say I believe there's at least more real artistic & intellectual vigour there than in New York. Philadelphia, too, may come back; for it has history & standards & taste & wealth, & more & more influential people will settle there as New York becomes increasingly impossible for a white man to live in. Philadelphia has the loveliest art museum & public library—not yet finished, however—in the world. Boston is passé, but despite its artistic anaemia its old traditional life flows graciously on with a degree of dignity & high level of taste & scholarship which make it an alluring place of residence. Old Beacon Hill in the sunset is yet something to behold & worship. On the whole, I think that of all large cities Boston & Philadelphia are the best to live in. In the far west I believe only San Francisco is really stimulating & aesthetically habitable. Southern California is a desert of boobs, Babbitts, & "realtors", & the Oregon & Washington regions are places of homes & commerce rather than of art. The South probably has some really good spots, but I don't know it. I found Washington delightful in a brief trip, & imagine that Baltimore, Richmond, Charleston, & New Orleans—especially the latter—all have the sort of background & historic richness to stimulate a sensitive imagination.[3] As for me—I have found from experience that Providence is the only place where I can be content. Here I was born, & here one-half of my ancestry has had its roots for nearly three centuries. The soil & the air are in my blood & cell-structure, & I have come to recognise myself as of the type that cannot live apart from its sources & background & historic reliquiae—in a word, the essential provincial as opposed to the cosmopolitan. In Providence are all the elements which appeal most poignantly to my spirit, with its joint love of beauty & antiquity.[4] The old town dreams on seven green hills at the head of its lovely blue bay, crowned by great domes & venerable steeples, & preserving unchanged a vast proportion of the narrow, winding hill streets, the peaked Colonial gables & gambrel roofs, the exquisitely carved classic doorways with double flights of iron-railed steps, & the stately Georgian mansions in their archaic walled gardens, which made it splendid & colourful at the time of the Revolution. Something of the stately old life lingers, too—for the residence section is on a precipitous hill which shoots up just east of the many-bridged river, & which has stemmed the creeping tide of cosmopolitan decadence. The old families & the old ideals still dominate, & there are little ways & customs on every hand which attest an unbroken evolution from colonial times, & an absolute, vital identity with the Gothic town of Roger Williams & the Georgian times of Stephen Hopkins.[5] Every night at nine, for example, the curfew still rings from the ancient steeple* of the First Baptist Church, which all my maternal ancestors attended. One comes to love all the old lanes & the old buildings—& what a wealth are still standing! The 1761 Colony House, the 1770 College Edifice, the 1773 Market House, the four old churches dating from betwixt 1775 & 1816,[6] the exquisite private homes with dates between 1770 & 1825, the smaller wooden houses in quaint hilly or labyrinthine rows dating from 1740 onward, & the vivid, glamorous waterfront with its rotting wharves & colonial warehouses & archaic lines of gambrel roofs & dark alleys with romantic names† & wondrous ship-chandleries & mysterious marine boarding-houses in ancient, lamplit, cobblestoned courts—that is Old Providence, the town that gave me birth & in which I have lived all but two of my thirty-six years. I am it, & it is I[7]—separation or disentanglement is impossible. You must *surely* see it when you come East—there is a fine & direct motor-coach service to Hartford, which you will find very convenient to patronise. Of course, it does not offer any brilliant opportunities for bizarre literary conversation; for it is very staid & traditional, & its aesthetic interests (which are many, & which include a fine museum system) run to music & pictorial art rather than to literature. But I have found from experience that for me, at least, it is better to do without actual conversation & depend on correspondence than to sacrifice this picturesque linkage with my own past & America's past in order to reside 'where poets most do congregate.'[8] A good nine-tenths of my best friends reside in New York from accident or necessity, & I thought three years ago that it was the logical place for me to settle—at least for several years. Accordingly I transferred my belongings thither in March 1924, & remained till April 1926, at the end of which time I found I absolutely could stand the beastly place no longer. It is true that I had the advantage of daily contact & conversation with those whom I know best & whose work lies along the same lines—Long, Morton, Kleiner, Loveman, & so on—but in spite of all this, & of the delightfully informal club which we formed to meet each week at the home of one member or another, the deadly

---

*1775—finest classic steeple in the United States
†Doubloon, Sovereign, Guilder, Bullion, &c. [No longer extant. ED.]

decadence, stridor, foreignism, & combined garishness & squalor of the parvenu & backgroundless metropolis became too much for me; so that I packed up & came home to "God's country" where one can see white men on the streets & behold about one the marks of gradual national unfolding & ancient tradition. Now, of course, I do not have frequent chances for the special literary conversation I then had—but after all, that formed but a small part of life. It is more important to live—to dream & to write—than to talk, & in New York I could not live. Everything I saw became unreal & two-dimensional, & everything I thought & did became trivial & devoid of meaning through lack of any points of reference belonging to any fabric of which I could conceivably form a part. I was stifled—poisoned—imprisoned in a nightmare—& now not even the threat of damnation could induce me to dwell in the accursed place again. It may be that younger, gayer souls than I can find something endurable in Manhattan. They are welcome to it. All I can say is that it is no place for a quiet, old-fashioned person strongly rooted in the past, & with an imagination depending on ancient, mellow things. During my last year there I did nothing but search out old neighbourhoods & quaint rural suburbs in an effort to find something to nourish my soul—something like venerable New England—a drowning man's straw. To give the devil his due, New York is a fine place to *visit*—but only to visit. Its tall buildings seen from a distance are an exquisite picture, & its museums, bookstalls, & general facilities are very convenient for occasional consultation. But to try to *live* there! May Pegāna's gods preserve me!

I don't know enough about the Middle West to judge the relative habitability of the Twin Cities, (my farthest west is Cleveland, where I visited Loveman in 1922 when he lived there) but I suppose they must lack much of the colour which older localities possess. Still, when they are one's native land, I fancy they must have a subtle place in one's imaginative life which a new spot could scarcely fill, even when offering such tangible advantages as finer scenery & more congenial associates. After all, they bred one—& that means much to many people. I only know one person who thoroughly & genuinely hates the Western town (Akron, Ohio) he left behind.[9] If I came from St. Paul, I'll wager I'd find my way back there in the end, as the place offering the maximum amount of fulfilment to the varied yearnings of my mind—but I know that in different individuals the several mental yearnings are differently proportioned. I think it would be a good idea for you to travel a bit about the country if you can practicably arrange it—seeing other towns & maturely testing the attractions they have to offer in competition with the imponderable anchors of one's native heath. But test them *well* before resigning the possibilities of an easy return. Sometimes even a sizeable trial isn't enough, so don't burn bridges behind. I had a gorgeous three-months' visit in New York before my residence there,[10] & was absolutely fascinated by the novel strangeness—& sightseeing—which appealed to my sense of wonder &

discovery. All this was magnificent—& offered no foretaste of the lethal ennui & disgust which supervened after I had come to know the damned place better than any published guide-book. If I had no particular linkage with Providence, & viewed the country impartially with the object of selecting a residence, I think I'd have hard work choosing between three general districts; each with an historic colour, a scenic beauty, & an ancient & dignified social background all its own—New England, Philadelphia, & the South. The quaint villages north of Boston on the Coast are incomparable—prototypes of my fictional *Arkham* & *Kingsport*.[11] Philadelphia is in a marvellous region— the glamour of the old town being well matched by the ancient stone-built villages (Germantown, for example) nearby, & the rapturous beauty of the Wissahickon Valley which stretches off to the northwest. The South, too, is rich in loveliness; although I have seen only the merest fringe—Washington, Alexandria, & some of the hills & vales & sleepy 'Co't-Haouse' or crossroads villages of the neighbouring Virginia countryside. Look them over, but don't pin yourself down till you have had an opportunity for some tall thinking & reflecting. Of course, I suppose that my own reactions are largely determined by the fact that I am more sensitive to *places* than to *people*. If I depended extensively on congenial discourse my problem would be complicated. Moreover, I am not really *literary* in the purest sense of the word. Books & authors, as such, do not interest me; since I want only what they transmit. It is beauty—the beauty of wonder, of antiquity, of landscape, of architecture, of horror, of light & shadow, line & contour, of mystic memory & hallowed tradition—that I worship, & I never think of talking about books when I can talk of the stars or the hills or the abbey towers of dim, far lands or the steep roofs that cluster on the slopes of archaic towns. That is why I have read so relatively little, & why *science* with its breathless mysteries & inconceivable vistas has so often crowded mere letters from my sphere of paramount interest. They do not talk much of these things in New York—but they surely do talk *books;* so that perhaps there are attractions after all for anyone whose taste inclines toward the media & mechanics of literature. Of that I can scarcely render a subjectively intelligent opinion.

I hope you can pardon all this elderly rambling, which must sound a bit odd to youth on the brink of life & adventure, with the long road to London ahead. What evokes it is the fact that I have so recently completed the cycle of home & metropolis & back home myself; a process which has so sharpened all my appreciations of intangible native things. I live in a vortex of relief since my Restoration; for after the vapid welter of New York even the least attribute of Providence has a nimbus of sanctity & ecstasy about it.

Let me thank you profoundly for the loan of the Polidori & Le Fanu books, which will doubtless arrive shortly. In return I am herewith mailing under separate cover the three you wish—"Oracle of Baal", "Copper Cylinder", & "Epicurean". I hope you won't be disappointed—the first two are cheapish popular things, & one of them—the Cylinder one—has that element of social satire which so wearies me in Wells. The last is a semi-classic of the Gothick period, but drearily dragged out & diluted by smug theology. I re-read "Baal" last fall, & was amused by its flatness as compared with the "kick" it gave me some thirty years ago when I read it as a small boy. Shiel's "Zaleski" isn't much good—& a young correspondent of mine who bought it this winter thinks himself rather badly cheated.[12] Shiel is atrociously uneven, & the only really first-rate thing he has ever turned out is that single marvel-lous "House of Sounds." I read your list of weird books with intense interest, & may plead for the loan of several after I return the present triad. The first I shall ask for is Fort's "Book of the Damned"—I can get "New Lands" at the local library. I know what the Fort books are like—the man must be a rather clever eccentric. Of the volumes you list, I have read only the following:

Benson—Vis. & Inv.	Poe—all
Blackwood—Jimbo	Rudwin—Dev. St.
J. Le V.	Serviss—2 Del
Emp. Ho.	M. Met
Lost Val.	Shelley—F's'n.
John Sil.	Shiel—Pale Ape
Listener	Ld of Sea
W. of G.	Stoker—Drac
Wave	Verne—Cent Earth
T of F	Wells—30 St. St.
Inc. Adv.	Isl. Dr. Mor.
10 m. St.	Time Mach
Day & Nt.	Days Com.
Bierce—Can Such &c.	1st Men in ☾
In the Midst	Country Bld.
Cummings—G. in G. A.	Williams—Thing in Woods
Doyle—L. Wld.	Rohmer—Brood of the Witch Queen
Poi. Blt.	Grey Face & others
Dunsany—K of E D	
Machen—all	
Merritt—Moon Pool	

Are any of the others conspicuously good? What are the tales in Crawford—Wandering Ghosts & Howells, Shapes that Haunt &c? And what W.T. issues do you lack? I have a complete file plus a few duplicates of those which con-tain my stuff. I have saved *Amazing Stories* up to this month, but am about to drop it. Too much original stuff of impossible quality. I bought three issues of *Ghost Stories* in the hope that it might develop into something—but after that, buenas noches! In the realm of poetry I fear my appreciation is deficient.

I love good verse, but it doesn't move me as do other forms of art such as weird prose or architecture. My library is nothing at all—about 1000 books, only a few of which are weird. I devote much shelf space to the antiquarian subjects which are taking a greater & greater proportion of my interests as I grow older, & also to the 'polite & elegant Letters' of the eighteenth century, a period for which I have an intense & singular predilection. I also cultivate the Graeco-Roman classics—Rome's shining majesty & power being one of my pet subjects. My early writing was perhaps unusual, but it tells against me rather than for me. When one reflects that at the age of seven I browsed among 18th century Difquifitions upon Correct Rhetorick and Poetick Numbers, & reeled off couplets of infantile verse with a date line of 1897,[13] one sees how slow & ineffective my development has been—for I am still, after thirty years, essentially an amateur, with far more plans for improvement than finished monuments of achievement. I never had much energy nor industry, & could never have digested the prodigious amount of literature which you have so conscientiously ploughed through. Like you, though, my love of the weird dates from fairy-tale days, my curve of taste running through Grimm, the Arabian Nights, Bulfinch's Age of Fable, the 17th & 18th century classical translations, POE, & everything I could conveniently find in the way of weirdness after that. My greatest single influence since Poe has been Dunsany, who dawned on me as late as 1919. I'd like to see your "Black Pool" some day—I wonder if it's as bad as my "Beast in the Cave!" Your style picked up more rapidly than mine—& at the same rate you will be well on Parnassus before long! I hope the editor of W.T. may prove receptive to future work of yours, & think him phenomenally stupid for rejecting "The Decomposer" & "The Twilight of Time"—if indeed he saw them. A young friend of mine in New York, Wilfred B. Talman, has just landed two—the first of which is a tale of diabolism entitled "Two Black Bottles".[14] Yes—I think the taste for weird fiction is stronger in England than here, & I am led to believe that in Germany it is stronger still. But even here it is not so utterly absent as it was ten or twenty years ago. Your vocally endowed professor must be quite a person—here's hoping you can write him something so sepulchrally resonant that he'll exalt it before all the world! I'd like to get him to read the last sentence of my "Randolph Carter"—"*You fool, Harley Warren is dead!*"[15] Only a contra-basso or a man with a bad throat cold ought to attempt that.

I am glad you enjoyed *The Saturnian*, & am sending under separate cover a fairly wide assortment of Loveman MSS. in varying stages of legibility. "The Sphinx" is a very ambitious attempt in the manner of Flaubert's "St. Antony", & I regret that I have not the conclusion of it. Most of the others are very short lyrics—many of them, I regret to say, in my most wretched & hasty style of penmanship; due to my having taken them down from the author's lips. Loveman is frightfully careless with his MSS., & many of his poems had absolutely vanished when I induced him to recall them from memory & recite them to me. These I took down as best I could—I wish I had better copies to lend.[16] The blue printed bookmark, & the copy of the United Amateur (which by the way contains a weird story by a fairly apt young beginner) with several Loveman items are for you to keep.[17] The rest, I regret to say, must be returned, though not in haste. These things are for the most part unpublished, & I certainly hope the author will some day make a book of them. As soon as I can find any, I'll send you some Long specimens.

With every good wish, & trusting that the unpremeditated longwindedness of the present epistle has not proved too acute a hardship for your patience, I remain

Most cordially & sincerely yours,
H P Lovecraft

P.S. [*on envelope:*] Printed matter has come. Abundant thanks. I see that Le Fanu collection has Fitz-James O'Brien's "What Was It"—have you been able to identify any others? Your essay on Machen is absolutely magnificent! I shall retain the magazine with extreme gratitude, & will lend it to Long & others. You envisage the malign spell of the book as few others of its readers seem to have done.

Have just read "The Vampyre". Pretty good for its period, but not up to "Frankenstein". Do you mind if I lend it to Long—who will safeguard its frail structure as punctiliously as I am myself doing? He has long been anxious to read it. Now for Le Fanu—who seems to have the cheerful, rambling style of the average Victorian. Let's hope he's blacker than he looks! Again I thank you sincerely for all these favours—& will return the books in prime condition.

Notes

1. HPL wrote "He" on 11 August 1925 in Scott Park, Elizabeth, NJ. Some of the descriptive passages about New York in this letter are adapted from the story.

2. "The Syrian [river] Orontes empties into the Tiber." Juvenal (D. Junius Juvenalis, 60?–140?), *Satires* 3.62. Juvenal's text reads: "Syrus in Tiberim defluxit Orontes."

3. HPL would later visit all these sites: Baltimore in 1928, Richmond in 1929, Charleston in 1930, New Orleans in 1932.

4. The following description of Providence is adapted from the opening pages of *The Case of Charles Dexter Ward*.

5. Roger Williams (1603?–1683), English colonist in New England and a proponent of religious liberty, was the founder of the colony of Rhode Island. Stephen Hopkins (1707–1785) was a prominent statesman and a colonial governor of Rhode Island; in his old age he signed the Declaration of Independence.

6. The Old State House (Colony House) was constructed at 150 Benefit Street in 1762, to replace the 1732 Colony House (then at 21 Meeting Street) that had burned in 1758 (see letter 16n10). A tower was added in 1850–51, another addition in 1867–68. The College Edifice (University Hall) on the Brown University Campus was erect-

ed in 1770. The four churches HPL refers to are the First Baptist Meeting House (1775) at 75 North Main Street (congregation founded by Roger Williams in 1638); Beneficent Congregational Church (1809) at 300 Weybosset Street; St. John's Episcopal Church (1810) at 271 North Main Street; First Unitarian Church (1816), 301 Benefit Street.

7. Cf. Robert Blake's utterance at the close of "The Haunter of the Dark" (1935), when his identity becomes fused with that of Nyarlathotep.

8. An adaptation of Shakespeare's "where merchants most do congregate" (*The Merchant of Venice* 1.3.49).

9. George Kirk was born in Akron (see *LR* 221).

10. August–October 1922.

11. HPL usually said that his Arkham was based on Salem and his Kingsport on Marblehead.

12. See HPL to AWD, 26 November 1926: "I feared you wouldn't find 'Zaleski' such a treasure, & am sorry you paid as much as $2.75 for it. You will not, however, be disappointed in 'The Pale Ape'" (*ES* 52). AWD intended for many years to publish Shiel's book, which eventually appeared as *Prince Zaleski and Cummings King Monk* (Sauk City, WI: Mycroft & Moran, 1977).

13. HPL's juvenile work "The Poem of Ulysses; or, The New Odyssey" dates to 1897.

14. See HPL to AWD, 6 October [1929]: "I'm rather pleased & amused to hear that Wright has been using 'Two Black Bottles' as a model, insomuch as I planned the entire action & denouement myself. Originally the thing was called 'Three Black Bottles', & had a vast amount of superfluous & loose-end material. I took it in hand & made a fresh synopsis—inventing the picture of the lumbering thing seen against the rising moon, as well as the evidences of disturbance from beneath in the parson's grave. I also invented the antecedent references—the background of diabolism & the origin of the hellish sexton. But I didn't do any of the writing—the phraseology is all Talman's" (*ES* 222). The second story referred to was probably "The Curse of Alabad and Ghinu and Aratza" (*WT*, February 1928).

15. The line actually reads: *"You fool, Warren is dead!"*

16. HPL's transcriptions of Loveman's poetry and some of Loveman's typescripts survive among HPL's papers at JHL.

17. Probably the *United Amateur* of May 1924. See also letter 12n1.

[12]   [DAW to HPL] [ALS]

1152 Portland Ave.,
St. Paul, Minn.
Feb. 28, 1927

Dear Mr. Lovecraft:

I am late in acknowledging receipt of your typescripts, Loveman's poems, and the books; I have been inexcusably busy the past few weeks and am rather appalled by the prodigious amount I must do in the near future. I have not been able to read the three books thoroughly, and can not tell which I shall like best. Some of the illustrations are interesting, though they are not quite works of art.

I have read your own tales with the greatest interest as usual, and will return them before long. I do not think they are so outstanding, so characteristic of your peculiar genius, as most of those in "Weird Tales", or the others I have read, but on the other hand, they are far above the common lot, especially in imagination. I shall have more to say about them and the books in my next letter, but I wish to thank you now—though belated—for their loan; they will have good care while they are in my hands.

I am very glad that you sent me the poems of Mr. Loveman, in whose work I am greatly interested. He wrote me a month ago that he was going to type some and send them to me, but he has apparently been too busy to do so. Those you send vary in merit; some are mediocre, but some are fine. "Bacchanale"[1] is to me the best; it has a certain fascination which I can not define; it is beautifully phrased, and lines of it keep running through my head. The poem is insidious; you may read it only once,—but it is a poem you don't forget. As for the "Sphinx"—I am critically incompetent before it. I can not give a passionless judgment of it, nor would I wish to do so. It is a superb piece of work—a work of pure beauty and craftsmanship. I have been enthralled and carried away by it, as much, and more, than "The Hermaphrodite" even. If you discover the ending, send me it by the fastest route. I was disappointed that I did not have the complete play, and I can scarcely wait for its publication. If you are in no hurry to receive these copies, let me keep them a while longer before returning them.

It is with the closest attention and most profound interest that I read all you had to say about New York, Providence, and other cities. I know absolutely nothing about any cities except St. Paul and Minneapolis. New York has been a magnet for me largely because the publishers and the literary market center there; and if I can not make a living by writing, I shall do so by allying myself with some publisher or other. People merely as people and conversation as the false literary product of so-called "intelligentsia" and pseudo-intellectuals have no interest for me. I hate sham and artificiality of every kind. Probably New York would evoke from me in time as bitter an indictment as yours. For some time I have been planning to write a particularly savage satire on the whole of our splendid civilization, and New York might be the cause of its fruition. I doubt whether I care for "book" conversation. I indulge in little of it here, and find besides, very few people who know anything about the fields in which I am interested. In all my life, which has been spent entirely in St. Paul, I have found only two people whom I cared enough about to make close personal friends of mine, and both I came to know at the university. One of them is a brilliant conversationalist, but "books" form only a small part of the things we discuss. Her tastes are literary and artistic; she is an aesthete, but a true aesthete; and she is unusually gifted with literary and artistic talent. She is an individualist, an eccentric, a romanticist. The other is an Icelander, equally sincere in all he does, romantic in appearance and thought, nonchalant in his attitude toward life, possessed of high intelligence and some literary gifts, and firm in his dislike of all artificiality. Though he doesn't know it, he has really been the anchor to which I have clung in my most despondent moods and some of them have been dangerous.[2] Hence it is that I say I should probably find no sudden appearance of an army of kindred spirits if I go to New York though possibly there are more than I believe. But I want to get away from the Twin Cities for awhile to a place where I can at least buy books if nothing else. I have never left St. Paul or Minneapolis except on two or three occasions, and then did not get more than two hundred miles away. I am bored to weariness by the cities, though Minneapolis is the worst. You may be right about my eventual return to them, however. I think that one reason I have written such weird and imaginative things is that the monotony of my environment has driven me to the opposite extreme as an escape; this is not entirely, but I am certain it is partly, the explanation. I should like to visit the other cities you name, but I am not certain whether I shall be financially able this summer, or have the time as yet. If I do not graduate this spring, I might as well come back next fall and get the process over with. The only deterrent of my going East is the possibility of getting some of my work published before my departure; this would remove one of the main reasons for my leaving. Which reminds me, I have just sold "The Twilight of Time," to "Weird Tales", which wants to publish it as "The Red Brain".[3] This is the same story that was returned last summer. I am confident that its acceptance was due to whatever you wrote the editor about my work. I wish to thank you again for all you have done for me, and to give you my lasting gratitude and appreciation of your assistance.

In the event that my present rather nebulous plans go through, I shall certainly visit Providence before completing the road to New York. Providence must be a lovely city. I have always had a passion for the sea that I do not know, and have wanted to live in some lonely or beautiful spot on the coast. The Twin Cities have neither tradition, background, picturesqueness, nor beauty. They are no place for an idealist, even one whose ideals are shattered. They are busy. They are manufacturing centers. They are dirty and smoky. The houses are mostly new, with no selection of any sort used in the crazy juxtaposition of Spanish patios with Colonial frame houses and charming brand new flats. The beautiful Mississippi which is a fine mud-brown color flows between the cities with various detestable things above it, in it, on it, and along it, including steel bridges, industrious factories, old logs and stumps, refuse and sewage, and other equally choice things. Minneapolis is a nice city with its streets all alphabetically arranged and neatly laid out, the whole unmarred in theory by a single trace of irregularity or antiquity. Unfortunately, the design has been spoiled in one place, or perhaps two, by some streets which have been disappointing enough to ramble about in a manner disapproved by the practical city fathers. There is a marvellous stockyard in South St. Paul, but this can be appreciated only when the wind is blowing right. There were some lakes, rather beautiful, foolishly enough, around the city; but the city council has been kind enough to remedy this defect by draining them for the water supply. The people are staid and conventional and mediocre, even at the university. I could have taught things of little or much importance to several professors and instructors I had at the university, but they were neither worth the trouble nor amenable to suggestion.

What is the "He" to which you refer? I should like to read it if you have a copy. I am very much interested in it, after the corrosive sublimate against New York in your last letter.

You are welcome to the loan of any books on the list which may strike your fancy, or in which you are interested. Ask for "The Book of the Damned" when you want it. F. Marion Crawford's "Wandering Ghosts" has some fine horror stories; it contains seven tales in all: "The Dead Smile", "The Screaming Skull", "Man Overboard!", "For the Blood is the Life", "The Upper Berth", "By the Waters of Paradise", and "The Doll's Ghost". "The Upper Berth", "The Dead Smile", and "For the Blood is the Life" were the best, as I recall. I have not read "Shapes That Haunt the Dusk", edited by W. D. Howells and H. M. Alden, but I think the contents are rather innocuous ghost stories. They are: "The Christmas Child", Georg Schock; "The White Sleep of Auber Hurn", Richard Rice; "In Tenebras", Howard Pyle; "The Little Room", Madalene Yale Wynne; "The Bringing of the Rose", Harriet Lewis Bradley; "Perdita", Hildegarde Hawthorne; "At La Glorieuse", M. E. M. Davis; "A Faded Scapular", F. D. Millet; "At the Hermitage", E. Levi Brown; and "The Reprisal", H. W. McVickar. Wells' book "Tales of Space and Time" has one fine story, "The Star". "The War of the Worlds" is rather famous but not so good as some of his other things. The four small books with the general title "Weird Tales" have some good stories here and there. Most of the other books, I can't recommend very strongly, but you can have them whenever you wish to read them. I have vainly tried to complete my file of "Weird Tales", and shall be profoundly grateful for the loan of the three issues I lack: May, June, and September, 1923. Have you by any chance a duplicate of the Dec.–Jan. issue, 1923–24, which contained your "Picture in the House"? I have a copy, but I loaned it once without discrimination, and received only the nucleus of it in return.

I am glad that you like the essay on Machen. "The Hill of Dreams" made a profound impression on me when I read it, a year ago and more, in the blue paper edition. You are welcome to lend the books to any of your friends who may appreciate them. I hope Long appreciates Polidori—I found the tale unusually interesting when I read it a couple of years ago, but I have not looked at it since. By the way, in looking through the bookstacks of the University library the other [day], I came across "The Supernatural in Modern English Fiction", by Dorothy Scarborough;[4] it does not seem to be especially good as a monograph but it mentions a great many books and tales which I do not know. I have also discovered at the U. a professor whose speciality is the eighteenth century and who is fond of Gothic literature. He says a French book on the subject has just been issued, under the title, I think, "Le Roman de Terreur".[5] I don't remember the author's name, but I'll find it out. The book apparently has not come into the library as yet; hence I can't say how good it is. I understand that a collection of eighteenth century Gothic tales is also to be issued, or has been, under a title something like, "The Pack of Autolycus".[6]

I'll type the most coherent and intelligible fragments of my novel sometime soon, if possible, and send you them, with the one bad story of mine still extant, "The Shadow of a Nightmare". I think the "Black Pool" was quite as bad and much worse than your own pristine attempts. Here are one or two of the less objectionable passages, as I have painfully deciphered them:

" . . . Suddenly the cavern widened on top and on the sides. A moment later, I was standing in a vast, gloomy cave, a great chamber whose sides I could not have seen except for one thing. I followed the wall to my right, and suddenly there loomed before me a series of upright white things. Oh God! In stately rows, reclining against the wall, were line after line of grinning skeletons. In the gloom and black darkness, I could see them standing before me in silent rows till they disappeared in the blackness, and bony feet clutched at the floor as if to hold their skeleton bodies erect, their fleshless arms hung limply down as if to steady themselves, their cavernous skulls reclined against the wall as if to aid the keeping of their position, and thus they kept their silent watch here and there or had fallen, and lay sprawled grotesquely on the floor. Here and there a tiny skeleton lay against the wall among the longer ones. And in that great semicircle they stared unseeingly straight ahead so that the stare of their grinning, empty, eye-sockets met on one thing, and that one thing was me."

. . . . . .

" . . . As he did so, a spasm of pain crossed his face, a facial contortion, and he began talking in a voice that rapidly rose to a scream, "I am dying, but what a death! I can feel the worms, the insidious maggots, crawling through my body, and I can feel the darkness, black, devouring darkness rushing toward me! Take 'em away! Take 'em away! They are gloating in the darkness! They are shaking with hideous glee! They are stretching their bony fingers at me! They are commanding the worms to devour me, and the worms are obeying! Blot them out, take their evil faces from me! They are killing me!" The old man shrieked maniacally. "Last night I saw them, and I screamed, and they went away! But now they only gloat, and command the worms!" A spasm of pain crossed his face and he gave a terrible scream. Then he lay there starkly, with his staring, glassy eyes fixed on me, while the cavern walls got his scream and threw it back and forth, raised it to an unearthly pitch, sent it cascading in a horrible, long-drawn out wail, and let it slowly die where it was whispered ghoulishly by countless stones.

"And then—in one moment all the horrors I had passed through were forgotten, were paled by the frightful thing that happened before my eyes. For as I watched it the old man's body began to swell! Slowly, then faster and faster, it grew and swelled like a bloated mushroom, and the skin turned a hideous black. Unable to move, unable to shake off the horror possessing me, I saw the body turn to a frightful, bloated shapeless mass, and then it split! In an instant, the split widened, separated into innumerable smaller cracks, and spread across the body showing through the rent clothes. Out of the split poured a stream of black, thick fluid. And in the horrible mess, I seemed to see wriggling, crawling things . . . . worms . . . . maggots."

I must be a personal friend of the devil; certainly my imagination has always been on speaking terms with the necessary lurid surroundings.

Before I end, let me express again my pleasure at the loan of your manuscripts and books and Loveman's poems, and let me thank you most profoundly and gratefully for them. For the receipt of one other thing, too, I am pleased and proud—the longest, the most interesting and fascinating letter I have received.

Most sincerely yours,
Donald Wandrei

Notes

1. Samuel Loveman, "Bacchanale," *United Amateur,* 23, No. 1 (May 1924): 1, dedicated to HPL.

2. The two individuals mentioned here are Barbara Fawcett Craigie and Hjalmar Björnson. In thinly disguised form they are two of the leading characters of DAW's autobiographical novel, *Invisible Sun* (see further letter 17).

3. HPL to CAS, 15 March 1927: "*Weird Tales* has just accepted his 'Twilight of Time', (which Wright wants to rename 'The Red Brain') which it had once before rejected, & I am almost flattering myself that a letter of mine in praise of Wandrei may have something to do with the change of attitude" (*DS* 125).

4. HPL did not read this book until late March 1932, when it was lent to him by J. Vernon Shea (HPL to J. V. Shea, 22 and 31 March 1932; *Letters to J. Vernon Shea . . .* 92, 95).

5. See letter 17n3.

6. Edited by Hyder Edward Rollins. The book reprints broadside ballads of strange occurrences from 1624 to 1693.

[13]   [HPL to DAW] [ALS]

10 Barnes St.,

Providence, R.I.,

March 13, 1927

My dear Mr. Wandrei:—

I received your highly interesting letter & am glad to find that the Loveman material sustained your expectations so well. It strikes a very high average, I believe, & "The Sphinx" is surely a triumph of riotous colour, musical cadence, & dramatic values. W. Paul Cook is thinking of making it the third in that series of thin books of which Long's poems & "The Hermaphrodite" are now extant. The missing part in my copy is not long, but is packed full of climactic strength. I have never possessed the ending, since the poem was written in instalments, & my copy antedates its completion. I have, however, asked Loveman himself to send you a copy as soon as he can find or make one; & this he has said he will do at the earliest possible moment.

As to cities, locales, & so on—of course I suppose the majority of publishing enterprises centre in New York, although professional connexions are woefully hard to obtain there. The number of persons seeking literary sustenance & finding nothing is so great that one surely cannot hail it as an author's El Dorado—but still, I presume the number of openings must be greater than elsewhere just now. Of the tone & atmosphere of New York I really can't find anything good to say, even in my most charitable mood, except that one may find two or three persons once in a long while who are worth speaking to—persons born elsewhere & not yet spoiled, or belonging (as young Long does) to an older New York which the present mongrel Babylon has wholly overridden. That's the odd thing—there used to be a delightful New York of tasteful old families living in prim rows of brownstone; but that has all gone now, & even the houses are rapidly disappearing in favour of great garish rabbit-warrens where strident, vulgar, metallic-souled people jazz out their cheap & traditionless lives. Surely you could not find a better inspiration for a satire against the flashy civilisation of the herd; for whatever is most contemptible in America as a whole, is certain to be emphasised in this metropolitan chaos. I have long thought of writing a savage satire on New York in imitation of Juvenal's third, as Johnson wrote his "London". Heaven knows there is material enough, & the parallel between modern New York & the decaying Rome of Domitian's time is really much more marked than that between London & Rome. If ever there was a modern Umbritius, it was when I returned to Providence after two years![1]

No—it isn't well to count too much on congenial personal friendships, for it is only by accident that a person of specialised tastes is likely to encounter another with outlook sufficiently similar to make any extensive exchange of thoughts profitable. I am a complete hermit at home, & was only slightly less so in New York, where Long, Morton, Loveman, & one or two others formed my sole roster of kindred spirits. As a general thing, I commune with places more than with people; & with the latter, do more corresponding than conversing. Your two university friends sound interesting—especially the Icelander, who comes from a land which has always fascinated me. The pastoral simplicity of that far idyllic land, peopled by one of the purest branches of the great Northern race of conquerors & so untouched by decadent civilisation that its language is an archaic one surviving from manlier times, has always had a tremendous power over my imagination; & I have often longed to catch a glimpse of its half-mystical jokulls & fjalls. I understand that there are great tracts in the interior never trodden by any human foot[2]—tracts whose stormy geologic history promises the most singular revelations, even if nothing quite so spectacular as that described in Verne's "Journey to the Centre of the Earth." The innate capacity of the race-stock seems to indicate a general level higher than that which the massed population of any other one nation has ever attained—the proportion of intellectual individuals being very high, & the literature exceedingly remarkable. Biology would seem to explain this, by shewing a population recruited from the most hardy & adventurous members of the most purely Nordic of all races, (Teutonic plus a slight Celtic mixture from the Irish Culdees preceding the Northmen) nourished by a social life untinged with decadence, & shielded from mongrelism by the isolation of the island. I would not be surprised if the Icelanders represented the finest racial material on the planet today—& I certainly hope they will retain something of an uncontaminated condition, & keep out of the general decadence into which the larger Western world has unmistakably begun to fall. It may be wise for their young men to study abroad for a while, but I hope they will plan for the development of their own culture rather than the assumption of any other. The one thing to be regretted, perhaps, is the limited aesthetic appeal of their topography—a topography which, notwithstanding strong claims on the sense of grandeur & mystery, would seem to lack much of the grace, richness, variety, colour, & gentle mellowness of more southerly scenes. I never met an Icelander, & rather envy you the opportunity for direct contact with such a fount of Northern unspoiledness—something which has so long captivated my fancy. To my mind, the only really beautiful life which the decaying world can hope to know in the years to come is that of the small, aloof nations with primitive simplicity & strong nationalistic self-consciousness; insular centres of ancient, intensely individual & tenaciously vital cultural impulses like Iceland or Ireland. These places are *still alive,* enjoying unbroken communion with the creative forces behind them, whereas the larger world is getting hopelessly standardised & mongrelised, with natural linkages broken, & the harmonious relation between local scene, population, & aesthetic expression wholly perverted, disrupted, & overridden.

I suppose that the Twin Cities must lack tradition & mellowness because of their newness & dominant industrialism, so fancy you are not unwise in wishing to see at least for a time a little more of the world. Every individual mind demands its own type of scene, & its own type of relation to that scene; & the only way to find out one's own needs when in doubt is to give the various types a trial. New York is surely an ideal book mart—& my old gang there can quickly put you in touch with the very heart of the bookstall mysteries; for George Kirk conducts a book shop, while Loveman is an important man in the large firm of booksellers, Dauber & Pine. Indeed, I saw so much of books while there that I have almost become bored with them! In time I hope you can make a round of the various interesting cities & regions of the country, for such diversified perceptions form a pleasant imaginative nourishment. Especially do I hope you will get to Providence, for I do not know of a lovelier place anywhere in the world. It is a city of steep hills & ancient winding ways & alluring vistas & old colonial roofs & carved doorways & graceful spires & domes; & some of the panoramas from the steep slopes are exquisite & breath-taking in their picturesque loveliness. If I can find some illustrated booklets which I had a short while ago I'll send you a glimpse or two of the ancient quaintness. My own present abode is only 3 doors from an old farmhouse of 200 years ago, long overtaken by the growing town, but still existing unchanged in its rustic yard, maintained in good condition by an artist. Then there are fine old public buildings & private mansions (one of the latter just around the corner from me) dating from 1760 onward[3]—& the churches are delightful. One of the latter—the ancestral church of my mother's family, in fact—was built in 1775 & has the finest Georgian steeple in America, built from the design of James Gibbs, architect of St.-Martin's-in-the-Fields, London. Others of our churches were built in 1808, 1809, & 1816.[4] In short, Providence is one of the few old American towns which remain like those of Europe—with individual vitality & colour, & with the marks of ancestry & unbroken growth upon them. Boston is another—very different from Providence, but equally true to itself, as is also Philadelphia, & as are undoubtedly many places in the South. Then one will likewise find in New England many towns still quainter & less changed because of slower progress—Newport, 30 miles south of here, Plymouth, Bristol, & the coast towns north of Boston such as Salem, Marblehead, Gloucester, Newburyport, & Portsmouth. This class of town does not merely shew the marks, relics, & atmosphere of the past—it actually remains very largely as it was before the Revolution. Newport has the same line of wharves with their ancient bordering warehouses, the same sea of gambrel-roofs on the hill with Trinity's white steeple (1726) crowning all, which the British & French armies saw in the old days when they successively occupied the town. (The luxurious parvenu millionaire part of Newport is wholly separate from the old town) Marblehead, with narrow curving alleys & tangles of incredibly ancient houses, is one of the most fascinating places in the world, & is the prototype of the imaginary "Kingsport" which I so often describe in my tales. The old towns I have mentioned, I know—Newport, Salem, Portsmouth, Bristol, & Marblehead well, Newburyport & Gloucester fairly, & Plymouth slightly. There are also others which I have visited with intense admiration & pleasure—Concord, Lexington, New London, New Bedford, & infinite small villages & rustic places in Rhode Island. This atmosphere is woven into the very tissue of my soul, & I could not live apart from it. Even so, there are many equally quaint places which I have *never seen*—Cape Cod with its old fishing towns, Nantucket—an island—with its incredible pre-Revolutionary survivals, Portland, Hartford, (more modern, of course, but probably with much background) & the region of the upper Connecticut Valley where ancient Deerfield & Hadley dream.[5] This Connecticut-Valley region has an architectural school all its own—examples of which I have of course seen only in museums.

My only remote trips from New England have been to Cleveland, (my farthest west) the Philadelphia region, & the Washington region. (my farthest south) Aside from that limited terrain, the world is still a terra incognita to me so far as personal sight is concerned—although if I had money I would certainly travel extensively. As you will see, Cleveland is the only place outside the archaic East that I have ever visited—I was there two weeks & three days in 1922. Oddly enough for an antiquarian, I liked the city very much, & found much of beauty & interest in it. The extreme drabness & "Babbitry" of the Middle West of which so many complain must lie still farther toward the setting sun. I think Chicago must be very tolerable, although it lacks background & is beginning to pick up "Greenwich Village" decadence in spots; & a friend in St. Louis (really an old town, founded in the 18th Century) finds much to admire in that municipality—an impartial opinion, since he is a Bostonian by boyhood environment. The places I most wish to see are Quebec, Annapolis,[6] Richmond, Charleston, St Augustine, & New Orleans. Each of these has a wealth of colour & a strong individuality, unless all books, pictures, & travellers lie. And of course I long to explore Europe some day—Old England, & the ancient towns of the Continent—Nuremburg, Ratsibon, Mt. St Michel, Chartres, all of Italy & some of Spain, Greece, Constantinople, & the dark mystery of fabled Ægyptus. Then I would like to see the Orient—fragile, exquisite Japan, brooding, immemorial China with its reticent wonder & barbaric refinements, & the black, portentous secrets of wind-swept Thibet with its blasphemous monasteries, diabolic hermits, & horrible forbidden citadels in the mountains. The Saracenic milieu, too, has allurement for one who has loved the Arabian nights—Cairo, Bagdad, Damascus, Mecca, & Samarcand— is there any line more haunting than that repeated burden spoken under the "burning moonlight" in the last act of James Elroy Flecker's "Hassan"—"We take the golden road to Samarcand"?[7] As for "He"—I thought you had seen that because it was printed in *Weird Tales* for last September, & it was my impression that you had read every recent number of that uncertain palladium of mystery. I enclose the tale, asking that you return it at your leisure. I don't know that it tells any more than the "hymn of hate" in my letter, but it summarises & symbolises my attitude after a fashion. As you will gather from the tale, there are still many antiquities remaining in New York. I made the most of these, & am almost willing to boast that my knowledge of colonial New York & environs exceeds that of any native of the place. These antiquities came to form my only psychological link with my normal atmosphere when I was living there, & I visited them so incessantly that I am today the one authentic human guidebook to such things. But they differ somewhat from New England antiquities, & did not fully satisfy my soul. Those having the Dutch influence are really very beautiful in their way, & I wish more of them were left. Everything old in New York is coming down tragically fast—whole long blocks of fascinating brick Georgian houses with pillared doorways of the London style (rare in New England) disappeared during the two years of my residence. I used to haunt the villages near by—some still untainted, & some coloured & engulfed in varying degree by the cancerously spreading metropolis. In fact, the place I lived for the first year was an overtaken village—Flatbush, with its ancient Dutch church & fascinating old churchyard whose stones bear inscriptions in the Dutch language. Slightly less engulfed than Flatbush is old Jamaica with its Georgian spires & quaint old houses. Still freer from the Gotham blight is Flushing, with its 1694 Quaker meeting-house & other houses as old as 1661. Then outside the city limits & *wholly* free from Manhattan atmosphere is lovely Hempstead, with old white cottages & belfried colonial church. This spot—together with the archaic town of Elizabeth (the Elizabethtown of Revolutionary fame) across the river in New Jersey—were my favourite refuges from New York miasma & alienage. Elizabethtown is a drowsy small city with many ancient buildings, & near it are some highly historic villages. At one of them—Springfield—occurred the famous Revolutionary battle wherein Parson Caldwell brought hymn-books from his church to give the troops gun-wadding, meanwhile shouting "Give 'em Watts, boys! Put Watts into 'em!" Now the troops thus supplied with psalmodic wadding were of peculiar interest to me, because they were my own home-colony troops—the 2nd Rhode Island regiment under Col. Israel Angell of North Providence! And fancy my delight when, upon examining the bronze tablet on Battle Bridge, I found it dedicated to Col. Angell himself, (and the very street I was born on—& lived on for 33 years—is Angell Street!) with an extract from Genl. Washington's letter to Gov. Greene of Rhode Island in praise of him & of his staunch Rhode Island men! That was a touch of home which indeed thrilled me in my exile![8] It was on a bench in a lovely park in Elizabethtown, close to a great yellow gambrel-roofed house built in 1760 & later inhabited by Gen. Winfield Scott, that I wrote "He." My disgust with New York had become so engulfing that I could no longer think or write there, so it was my habit to take my work in summer to this ancient town, which reminded me the least bit of Providence. There I vented my hatred & horror of Manhattan in the sketch which you will presently read—the final line about my return to New England being prophetic of what really did happen in the following spring. Glorious return! On the 17th of next month I shall celebrate its anniversary. The year has been a happy one, & today I scarcely realise that I have ever been away. When I was away life seemed unreal, phantasmagoric, & bi-dimensional; as if it were a dream out of which I might easily awake if I screamed loudly enough. Now the experience seems still more remote & insubstantial, as though it had never actually happened, but was something read of in a strange & fantastic volume. Most certainly, I have proved myself inseparably a Rhode-Islander!

Well—to wrench myself free of geography for a while—I am indeed glad that Wright has taken your "Twilight of Time". If my remarks to him had anything to do with it, I certainly feel gratified indeed; though as I told you, I don't think he has any too much enthusiasm for my work & opinions. The change of name he suggests is not a very bad one, & you might let him make it so long as the tale is to be published out of its natural sequence anyway. Later, when you issue the whole cycle in book form, you can make the necessary restorations.

Thanks enormously for your offer of loans. I will, if perfectly convenient to you, let you send on the following two whenever you like:

> "The Book of the Damned"—Fort
> "Wandering Ghosts"—Crawford.

I have read "The Upper Berth" & "By the Waters of Paradise", & liked the first as intensely as I was bored by the second. The others are still unknown to me, although I have heard a friend praise "For the Blood is the Life" very strongly. I suppose the "Screaming Skull" is based on the old type of family legend involving a skull handed down through generations & protesting when it is moved—like that at Wardley Hall. I have a book—given me last year—which relates a vast number of old castle legends & things of that sort. Would you care to borrow it? It is "Haunted Homes & Family Traditions of Great Britain", by John H. Ingram.[9] You are welcome to a sight of it if it would interest you. By the way—I've sent "The Vampyre" on to Long, who will return it directly to you. As soon as I read "All in the Dark" I'll return that, & the "Stable for Nightmares". Under separate cover I have sent you the three issues of *Weird Tales* which you mention not having seen. Unfortunately they are not duplicates, hence I will have to ask their ultimate return although there is not the slightest hurry involved. I regret also to say that I have not a duplicate of the damaged issue—my duplicates being all of the more recent issues.

Thanks tremendously for the names of those weird tale histories. I have just had to type mine—72 pages—without the proposed enlargement, since Cook sent out a hurry call for *Recluse* copy; but he says that later on he may arrange for re-publication, with additions, in book form.[10] As I typed the MS. I was strongly impressed with its essential mediocrity. I fear it will disappoint you when you see it in print, as you probably will in a couple of months. The job of typing was discouraging—I don't know how I'll ever do the 110-page novelette I did in midwinter, or the 147-page one which I have just finished! Cook, by the way, may use my "Shunned House" as the material for one of his thin blue-cloth books after he handles Loveman's "Sphinx".[11]

Your early work was certainly far from jejune in striking incident & situation—& really shews a marvellous imagination & literary sense despite the extravagance of immaturity. It easily beats my "Beast in the Cave". The idea of a body swelling like a black bladder also impressed Machen—do you recall the incident of the idiot boy in Prof. Gregg's study in "The Three Impostors"?

With every good wish, & hoping that you'll get around to Providence in time, I remain

Most cordially & sincerely yrs—
H P Lovecraft

Notes

1 Samuel Johnson (1709–1784) imitated Juvenal's third satire, about Rome, in his poem *London* (1738). Umbricius (not Umbritius) is the narrator of Juvenal's poem.

2. A common conceit in HPL's fiction and poetry; cf. "Hesperia" (1929): "ancient lore repeats / That human tread has never soiled these streets" (*AT* 85).

3. The most notable of these, the Thomas Lloyd Halsey House (c. 1800; brick front added c. 1825) at 140 Prospect, was the home of Charles Dexter Ward of HPL's *The Case of Charles Dexter Ward.*

4. See letter 11n6. HPL refers to the Beneficent Congregational Church (actually 1809), St. John's Episcopal Church (actually 1810), and the First Unitarian Church (1816).

5. HPL first visited Cape Cod in 1929, Nantucket in 1934, Portland (ME) in 1927, Hartford (CT) in 1931, and Deerfield (MA) in 1927.

6. HPL first visited Quebec in 1930, Annapolis in 1928.

7. See James Elroy Flecker (1884–1915), *Hassan* (1915), Act 5, sc. 2.

8. HPL refers to the battle of Springfield (23 June 1780) and to the minister Isaac Watts (1674–1748), known chiefly for his hymns.

9. The section in Ingram's book on "Wardley Hall" (pp. 602–6) tells the story of a skull at the castle that exacts vengeance upon anyone attempting to move, bury, or destroy it.

10. HPL often mentioned to correspondents that SHL might see eventual book publication from Cook's Recluse Press, and even kept a list of "Books to mention in new edition of weird article." However, the type for the *Recluse* appearance of SHL was scattered shortly after its publication, and Cook's plan to issue the essay as a book never materialized.

11. Cook did not publish *The Sphinx* until 1944, but he did publish *The Hermaphrodite* in 1926.

[14]   [HPL to DAW] [ANS]

[Postmarked Providence, R.I.,
16 March 1927]
Wednesday

Dear Mr. Wandrei:—

Glad to hear that the W.T. issues are welcome reading. If you've missed the recent September one (the one with my "He") I'll be glad to lend you that. I haven't bought the new (April) one yet—too busy to get down town.

Don't abandon your poetry! It is not as far *advanced* as your prose, but has the seeds of genius in it. Smith is enthusiastic over it—listen to what he says:

"I have an intuition that Wandrei may do something very fine in poetry if he keeps on. It is better, on the whole, for a poet not to be *too* precocious; & some of the greatest wrote very poor stuff at W's age. I find promise in some of these poems; & there is more than promise in many of the prose pieces."

So if you take Smith's advice—or mine—you will keep on with both prose & verse; comfortably assured that you have a chance of achieving very brilliant results in both. Only at a later stage—if ever—ought you to think of nourishing the one at the expense of the other.

With every good wish—
Sincerely yrs—
H P Lovecraft

[On front (no picture):] P.S. Would you like to contribute some of your very *best* (artistically, not commercially!) items—prose or verse—to the magazine which is going to print my weird fiction history?[1] No pay, but some dignity. The editor would like to see your work, of which I've spoken. Address—W. PAUL COOK, BOX 215, ATHOL, MASS.

Notes

1. *Recluse* No. 1 contains DAW's "A Fragment of a Dream" and "In the Grave."

[15]   [DAW to HPL] [ALS]

1152 Portland Ave.,
St. Paul, Minn.
March 21, 1927

Dear Mr. Lovecraft:

I am sending you today Fort's "Book of the Damned" and Crawford's "Wandering Ghosts". The second I think you will like, but I am not so certain of the first. At any rate, I hope its language doesn't infuriate you as much as it did me. It is at least interesting and unique, if not a literary masterpiece.

I am also returning your manuscripts with my deepest gratitude for the opportunity of reading them. There is nothing in the world which pleases me so much as new work from you and from C.A.S. I think I said in a previous letter that these tales were not so superbly characteristic of your weird genius as some of your other tales; but this is on the comparative basis of your own work, for the simple reason that, being in a class by themselves, they can hardly be compared with the work of ordinary authors. A few of them have traces of Dunsany, notably "Celephaïs" and "The Other Gods". Do they belong to the period when you say you discovered Dunsany? I liked best "The Nameless City", with "The Silver Key" and "Cool Air" next. "The Silver Key" interested me to begin with because of its connection with Randolph Carter. I am anxious to read his adventures in dreamland, and if you ever acquire the courage—which I probably wouldn't—to type the appallingly bulky manuscript, I would be delighted to read it. And I should like to see "The Lurking Fear" rewritten sometime with all traces and insidious reminders of "Home Brew" taken out. It is anticlimactic and rather lurid now, but a few changes, I think, are all that are necessary. Perhaps I am wrong—I do not know how you work—but it seems to me that it might be made into one of your better or best stories. I am profoundly grateful for the loan of these tales; if you have any others in your possession that I have not read, I should be eager to see them, whenever you find time for the drudgery of typing.

My honor is exonerated: I *have* read "He", and I am sorry that I put you to the trouble of sending it. My error came about in this fashion: some months ago, I went through my file of "Weird Tales" and indexed the copies for all your items, prose and poetry. Through some error, I missed the September number; hence when I referred to my list, I did not find the title "He" and concluded that it must be an unpublished manuscript. My memory for names and titles is none too good. I have reread the story now. For some reason, I derive an unusual and disproportionate amount of satisfaction in your pricking of the New York bubble. I really believe that people are afraid to say anything against the city. In the "provinces" of the United States, there is a growing distrust and antagonism to New York, which may become a powerful influence in this century; but from the city itself emanate only the most glowing accounts of its own greatness and rhapsodies in its praise. Nevertheless, I might be able to write even in New York. I am out of harmony with the only two cities I know, St. Paul and Minneapolis, and am bored by small towns of the sort you find in Minnesota; but I seem to be able to do my best when I am out of key with my setting, and hence, if the eastern city were sufficiently antagonistic, I could probably "survive" as far as writing is concerned, and writing is the only thing that matters to me.

I am touched and profoundly grateful for the interest that you and C.A.S. take in my work. It has amazed me to find all at once two people who are interested when there has not been one in these five or six years that I have been practising my apprenticeship. I don't care for the opinions of other people; I have written primarily for myself, and have not paid much attention to criticism; but after a half-dozen years, I was coming to the conclusion that there were no dreamers in the world of today, none who ever rose above the mediocrity which is America, that it was useless, consequently, to write, and that I might as well enjoy my dreams as dreams without troubling to set them forth. I have been despondent the past two or three years, when all the things I consider my best work thus far were written, and needlessly written as far as I could see; I had fits of depression, when even my best efforts seemed feeble, alternating with moments when I considered myself to be in a sphere beyond and above the herd, and my tales to have more lasting value than all the stuff that passes for literature in the dead days of the age of mechanism. A midwest university is a ghastly place for any one whose tastes and habits and ideas and writings are irregular or bizarre or in any way fantastic and original. My "Fragment of a Dream" is coming out in the next issue of the "Quarterly". I am quite well aware of the fact that I shall be considered insane. The head of our English department has remarked that he doesn't think the tale ought to be published in any literary magazine in the country. But we are publishing it, and the people be damned. I take a sardonic pleasure in doing what people don't expect me to do and writing things they don't like, and if they don't, I shall take greater pleasure in stuffing the same stories down their throats. You and Clark have restored to me the confidence that, in past, I had lost. But I doubt whether any one can ever make me think kindly of the human herd and horde. I hate people for what they are and for what they are not, for what they could have been and for what they never will be. I shall never flatter them to the extent of writing the stuff that they would read and enjoy.

You are more of a poet than you let me believe in one of your letters. Your own prose fantasies and tales would indicate this, without the additional help of your appreciation of "Hassan". I read the refrain in his "Collected Poems", a couple of years ago, and was simply carried away by its haunting beauty. I looked up the play immediately then and read the lines in their proper setting; they brought a sigh of regret from me when I had finished. There are some good things in his "Collected Poems", also, though I don't remember any titles except the two "Sonnets of Bathrolaire".

I am extremely pleased at the opportunity to read the three issues of "Weird Tales" which I lack, as I said on my card. For nearly three years I have been trying to buy or borrow them, but they are singularly scarce. You can imagine then how pleased I was that I finally had a chance to read them. I shall return them before very long; but I want to index them first as additions to my projected bibliography of Gothic literature. If Ingram's book is available, I shall be delighted to read it, providing it will not be too much trouble to send. I believe that it is a book I tried to get last year at our libraries, without success.

Together with your manuscripts I am sending two of mine, "The Woman at the Window" and "The Shadow of a Nightmare." The first is one I completed about a week ago; I think that it's fairly good, but it is weak in two or three spots. The other, I am afraid, is rather bad. It is a year or two old, and the last of my poor manuscripts still surviving, except for the juvenile "The Black Pool". You can read and return them at your leisure—but you won't need much leisure for the first and I hope you don't waste much on the second. Of late, I have again felt like writing; and if I only had more time, something worth while might make its appearance. As it is, I must make the best of the few hours I have; and sometimes I have deliberately taken them when I had other things to do. At your suggestion, I have sent several of my prose poems to Mr. Cook, and will send the verse when Smith returns the typescript. What is the name of his magazine? Again—I thank you from the bottom of my heart for your interest and encouragement. I should be pleased if Mr. Cook includes "The Shunned House" in his series. I like the format and the taste he shows in selecting material, and nothing would please me more than the sight of one of your own tales included in the group. I am eagerly awaiting the appearance of Loveman's "The Sphinx"; for that matter, I am going to keep an eye on all Mr. Cook's enterprises.

I hope you can find the views of Providence which you mention. I do not recall having ever seen a picture or photo of it, and am anxious to see some after your fascinating descriptions of its quaintness, a quality almost lacking in the Twin Cities, and other Mid-Western cities. I shall most certainly stop at Providence when I go east. I have an impression that I will like it. I have always wanted to live near the sea. I should like to live in some lonely spot where the roar of the wind and the roar of the sea are one and yet not one; where the crags rise tall and forbidding, and no man ever intrudes on the desolation; or else I should like to live on some warm island, where the waters murmur, and the winds whisper of immortal things, where the year is for ever spring, and the voice or foot of man for ever unknown, and peace and dream for ever deathless and for ever beautiful and enduring for ever.

Most cordially,
Donald Wandrei.

[16]   [HPL to DAW] [ALS]

10 Barnes St.,
Providence, R.I.,
March 27, 1927

Dear Mr. Wandrei:—

Your manuscripts delighted me exceedingly, & I found "The Woman At The Window" a particularly vivid & haunting prose-poem. The colour, music, & imagery hypnotise one completely, & transport one to red-litten realms beyond any star or nebula we know. I hope profoundly that you can place this to advantage, & am taking the liberty of forwarding the MS. to Long—whom I shall instruct to return it safely to you. "The Shadow of A Nightmare" is splendid, too, albeit in a less perfectly mature way. The basic theme—i.e., of the essential imperfection of all horror tales & the possibility of capturing some ultimate fright beyond fright—is one which has always fascinated me, so that I have many times been tempted to treat it fictionally. Just a breath of the idea is reflected in Bierce's story "The Suitable Surroundings", where an author says to his friend—"Bah! I have a manuscript in my pocket that would kill you!" If I were you I would keep this tale around for ultimate re-writing as I am keeping my "Lurking Fear". The possibilities are very great, & sooner or later some inspiration of perfection as to the working out of the idea will strike you. It is possible that the matter of the mad nation introduces an elaboration working against simplicity—which reminds me that this idea itself is really a master-stroke, & amply worthy of development as a separate tale. I think the MS. of utter horror might well be some tradition of pre-human antiquity, & allude to the terrestrial presence of some of those Outside Things so picturesquely suggested in "The Book of the Damned."[1] It might be well to hint that the secret of its horror concerns the relationship of man, or of life, or of the earth, or of all visible cosmic entity to infinity itself. It would be a good thing to have the MS. in English, & arrange to have the narrator catch a glimpse of a single passage—literally meaningless, but for some reason giving him a shock which will trouble him all the rest of his life. Your ingenuity can devise ways & means of effecting this whilst yet ensuring the safe killing-off of Marl & the destruction of the manuscript. The general impression to be left with the reader is one of hideous indefiniteness—stressing the fact that the essence of all supreme horror is doubt & indefiniteness. As one of Poe's characters says—"I shuddered the more thrillingly because I shuddered *knowing not why*."[2] But don't get the idea that the story isn't good just as it is. I found it, in truth, splendid; & I wish that you might "cash in" on it by placing it in *Weird Tales* in its present form before setting it aside for expert treatment. Incidentally—I am sure W.T. ought to like "The Woman At The Window". I am returning "The Shadow of a Nightmare" herewith—& while I think of it I must thank you for the compliment implied in the inclusion of my name among your cited horror-authors. I am giving Clark Ashton Smith such a mention—as you know—in my "Pickman's Model."[3] Yes—I can heartily congratulate you on both of these specimens; & hope to see more ere long. You have really caught that vague, elusive breath of the *Outside* which others not only cannot catch, but cannot even conceive as existing.

The books came safely, & I am infinitely grateful to you for their loan. My opinion of the relative merit of the Crawford tales coincides precisely with your own, & I have hastened to make an amendment to my article, admitting "For the Blood is the Life" & "The Dead Smile" as well as "The Upper Berth." The others didn't get at me so strongly, although the ending of that sea tale had its effective points. As to Fort—he is a fine author to skim, but an impossible one to read! What a fascinating jumble of rumours & travellers' tales he has assembled, & what a delicious set of conclusions he has drawn from them! He is distinctly above the average of such bizarre eccentrics, & seems well versed in philosophy though weak in science, psychology, & archaeology. I can understand why Long raved so violently about him, for there is truly a breathless sense of the unknown, the forbidden, & the mystic in his dreams of morbid, viscous worlds in the air, secret visits from other worlds & abysms of space, archaic cults on earth in touch with Beings from Beyond, & such like. It is a source-book full of imaginative provocation; & although the style is utterly hopeless, I think I shall muster up the patience to give "New Lands" the same sort of skimming I have given this. I shall send back these volumes with my sincerest thanks in reasonable season—including in the package that Ingram book of "Haunted Houses & Family Legends of Great Britain", which I shall be overjoyed to lend. You will find in that book more than one case of the "screaming skull" legend on which Crawford built his tale.

My MSS. came back safely, & I am glad they afforded you pleasure. Yes—"Celephaïs" & "The Other Gods" are reliques of my ultra-Dunsanian period; (1919–20) but "Polaris", despite apparent similarities, was written in 1918 before I had ever read a line of Dunsany's. I don't know when I'll ever get those novelettes typed, but I have just written another tale of the same length as "Cthulhu", which you shall see as soon as it is ready. This deals with a terror that came to earth on a meteor, & is called "The Colour out of Space." My history of weird fiction has now reached the proofreading stage, & ought to be out in a couple of months—although of course there will be many instalments of proofs to come before all 72 pages are in good shape. I shall be especially interested in your reception of this attempt, since you are yourself planning a larger work of the sort. Mine is the merest introduction to the subject, & I shall await in years to come the more definitive tome for which your bibliographical notes are a preparation. I'm glad the three W.T. back numbers proved a help—I haven't tried to keep track of any weird writing as low in quality as this, so that you won't find any popular-magazine idols in my sketch. There was no room for any but definitely literary figures. In a later & larger reprint in book form I might possibly mention A. Merritt, who has a touch of Outsideness despite a fatal willingness to compromise with the popular standard.[4]

So you had read "He" after all! Well—no harm done, for the cutting didn't take much postage to send. The story, to my mind, lacks balance & proportion; & I think I may some day break it up into two—using the introductory parts (the best, by far) in connexion with some plot & climax better calculated to live up to their possibilities. The later sections—about the old man & all that—could be used to far greater advantage in a story of very different character. I think a decade more will reveal a marked loss of caste on New York's part. No one of my background & sensitiveness can live in the town itself any more—& you will note an increasing proportion of its nominal inhabitants who commute from outlying semi-rural points where the air is a trifle fitter to breathe. It is getting worse & worse every year—vulgarity, decadence, & parvenu glitter—so that all its own self-advertising will not suffice much longer to spread the myth of its alleged attractiveness & mystery. It is good for just one thing—as a repository of books, data, museum material, & artistic facilities for people to visit when necessary—but as [a] place to live it is hopelessly passé. It is not a normal outgrowth of American life, but a feverish Asiatic cancer—a magnified ghetto wherein all marks of relation to the nation's history, traditions, & dominant cultural type are overwhelmingly submerged. Twenty or thirty years ago it must have been very delightful—I wish I had seen it then—but that phase is all submerged now, & in place of an American Paris or London or Vienna we have an Antioch or an Alexandria. For a real American metropolis, give me Boston or Philadelphia any day—there we have the true wonder of the large city with its mysterious vistas, yet without the fatal alienage & garish eccentricity which take a region altogether out of our type of civilisation & consequent sphere of personal interest. New York may have points of interest—but to an American that interest is as remote & detached as the interest one feels in Cairo or Benares or Peking.

I think I like to be more in harmony with my setting than you do, for my mind is a strongly geographic one. Scenery & architecture & general types affect me more than individual people & detailed conditions, & my ideal world is always more or less an outgrowth of the real world. In literature it wouldn't take much to transform me to a realist; for when out of my Dunsanian vein I love to build up my settings minutely & accurately from the New England landscape. You will see a marked touch of the ancient Yankee 'back country' in the new tale I shall shortly send you.[5] In a colourless or monotonous environment I should be hopelessly soul-starved—New York almost finished me, as it was! I find that I draw my prime contentment from beauty & mellowness as expressed in quaint town vistas & in the scenery of ancient farming & woodland regions. Continuous growth from the past is a sine qua non—in fact, I have long acknowledged *archaism* as the chief motivating force of my being. This is probably a decadent tendency—it was not so with the vigorous Renaissance spirits who took such a keen delight in the life around them—but if so is only natural in a decadent age whose vitality has been sapped through mechanisation & standardisation. Being as I am, my birth & lifelong residence in Providence have formed a marvellous streak of luck for me; since here I am given at least as much of my beloved antiquity & vividness as I could get anywhere in this age & nation. Of the surpassing beauty & quaintness of Providence there can be no doubt, as you will see from a glance over the items I have been saving for you. Three of these will reach you under separate cover, & I have just found a fourth which I am enclosing.[6]

My abode is just over the crest of the precipitous hill that rises east of the "river" or head of Narragansett Bay; & from a point not far from my door I can look dizzily out over all the clustered spires, domes, roofs, & skyscrapers of the lower town to the purple hills of the countryside beyond. Just around the corner is the great double-bayed Halsey Mansion built in 1801 & reputed to be haunted, (I will enclose a snapshot of this, & have also marked a picture of its classic late-Georgian porch occurring in one of the books I am sending) & only three doors away is a quaint little farmhouse & yard 200 years old, long overtaken by the town, & now preserved & inhabited by an appreciative artist. (I'll also send a photograph of this.) Strolling south along Prospect St. (laid out in 1772) from Barnes toward the ancient & stately college, (oldest building 1770) I can enjoy a sumptuous elder picture of old square brick mansions & smaller wooden houses with small Doric porches; all dreaming of the antique days, solid & exclusive amidst their generous yards & gardens. If I wish something still quainter, I can follow the line of Barnes St. (here called Jenckes) over the crest of the hill & down the precipitous slope to Congdon, which parallels Prospect like a ledge a third of the way toward the bottom, with all its easterly houses on high terraces. The small wooden houses average a greater age here, for it was up this hill that the growing town climbed; & here one may imbibe much of the colour of a thriving Colonial village. One may pause to sit on the benches of Prospect Terrace[7] (now in the course of an enlargement which will double its size) if one chooses—& one of my first memories is of the great westward sea of hazy roofs & domes & steeples & far hills which I saw one winter afternoon from that great railed embankment, all violet & mystic against a fevered, apocalyptic sunset of reds & golds & purples & curious greens. The vast marble dome of the State House (then under construction) stood out in massive silhouette, its crowning statue curiously haloed by a break in one of the tinted stratus clouds that barred the flaming sky. Then—craving older & older sights—one may tread gingerly down the vertical lower reaches of Jenckes St. with its bank walls & colonial gables to the shady Benefit St. corner, where before one is a wooden antique with an Ionic-pilastered pair of doorways, & beside one a prehistoric gambrel-roofer with bit of primal farmyard remaining, & the great Judge Durfee house with its fallen vestiges of Georgian grandeur.[8] It is getting to be a slum here; but the titan elms cast a restoring shadow over the place, & one is glad to stroll south past the long lines of pre-Revolutionary homes with their great central chimneys & classic portals. On the eastern side they are set high over basements with railed double flights of stone steps, & one can picture them as they were when the street (laid out in 1750) was new, & red heels & periwigs set off the painted pediments whose signs of wear are now becoming so sadly visible. Westward the hill drops almost as steeply—for the final third of its descent—as above, down the old "town street" that the founders laid out at the river's edge in 1636 along the line of an Indian trail. Here run innumerable little lanes with leaning, huddled houses of immense antiquity; & so like fantastic pictures do they seem, that it is long before one ventures to thread in person their archaic verticality. Then one continues south along Benefit St. past the iron fence of St. John's hidden churchyard (which Poe loved. He used to stop at the Mansion House—former Golden Ball—in this street, & his fiance Mrs. Whitman also lived there, in a house near the churchyard[9] still in excellent condition) & the rear of the 1761 Colony-House & the mouldering bulk of the Golden Ball Inn[10] where Washington & Lafayette stopped. At Meeting St.—the successive Gaol-Lane & King St. of other periods—one looks upward to the east & sees the arched flights of steps to which the highway had to resort in climbing the slope, & downward to the west, glimpsing the old brick colonial schoolhouse that smiles across the road at the ancient Sign of Shakespear's-Head where the Providence Gazette & Country-Journal (containing the freſheſt Advices, both Foreign & Domeſtick) was printed before the Revolution.[11] Then come the exquisite First Baptist Church of 1775, (that my ancestors attended, & one of my aunts still attends) with its matchless Gibbs steeple, (acknowledged the finest Colonial steeple in America—see pictures in accompanying matter) & the Georgian roofs & cupolas hovering by. (see pictures of "Old & New Providence" & "Providence Art Club &c" in the "Charm of Providence" booklet. My aunt lives in the old Truman Beckwith house[12] also shewn in that booklet) From this district southward the neighbourhood becomes much better, flowering at last into a matchless group of early mansions about George, Benevolet, Power, & Williams Sts., where the old slope holds unchanged the bits of walled garden & steep green lane* in which so many fragrant memories linger. But still the little ancient lanes lead off down the precipice to the west; spectral in their many-peaked archaism, & dipping to a riot of iridescent decay where the wicked old waterfront recalls its proud East India days amidst polyglot vice & squalor, rotting wharves & blear-eyed ship-chandleries, & such surviving alley names as Packet, Bullion, Gold, Silver, Coin, Doubloon, Sovereign, Guilder, Dollar, Dime, & Cent. Sometimes I venture down into this maelström of tottering houses, broken transoms, tumbling steps, twisted balustrades, swarthy faces, & nameless odours; winding from South Main to South Water, searching out the docks where the bay & sound steamers (from Newport, Block Island, New York, Baltimore, &c) still touch, & returning northward at this lower level past the steep-roofed 1816 warehouses & the broad square at the Great

---

*The presence of surviving bits of village & even rural scenery only a stone's throw from the heart of a large city is one of Providence's most unique characteristics, & is caused by the steepness of the great hill. I enclose a newspaper view especially illustrative of this. This cutting I'd like to see again, though you can keep all the other matter (and the poem) if you like.

Bridge, where 1773 Market House (see enclosed & accompanying matter) still stands firm on its ancient arches. In that square I pause to drink in the bewildering beauty of the old town as it rises on its eastward bluff, decked with its two Georgian spires & crowned by the vast new church dome as London is crowned by St. Paul's & Paris by the Pantheon. I like to reach this point in the late afternoon, when the slanting sunlight touches the Market House & the ancient hill roofs & belfries with gold, & throws magic around the dreaming wharves where Providence Indiamen used to ride at anchor. Just this week there is a genuine old-time sailing ship in port—a rare occurrence now—& I love the sight of its antique masts above the centuried warehouse roofs. We have not the open sea & wind-swept crags here—for those one must go to Newport or the Massachusetts north shore—but we do have all the wonder & glamour of bygone shipping & rich maritime memories. After a long look at this marine quaintness & sunset fascination, amidst which one grows almost dizzy with the elder charm of the sight, I like to scale the slope homeward in the dusk past the old white church & up the narrow precipitous ways where yellow gleams begin to peep out in small-paned windows & through fanlights set high over double flights of steps with curious wrought-iron railings. Old Providence! You certainly must see it when you come East, & if you report any particular quaintness & beauty at Hartford (which I've never seen) I must make a trip of exploration there. I hear that they have a fine late-Georgian State House—in fact, I saw a reproduction of it at the Philadelphia Sesquicentennial. When the weather gets warmer I mean to resume some of my antiquarian explorations, revisiting old places I know, & investigating several which I've either never seen or seen but once or twice. I must shew you *Newport* when you come, for that town is even closer than Providence to its antique state. It prospered earlier, and declined as Providence rose; hence represents a period of colonial architecture distinctly anterior to ours. You must also see the Boston region—especially Salem (my Arkham) and Marblehead. (my Kingsport) This sort of thing is really an inspiration—it gives one a background for the American civilisation, & supplies a sense of continuity with general life & history which must be woefully lacking in the west. Oh—by the way! I'll make one more enclosure, in the shape of a poem on Providence which I clipped from last Thursday's paper.[13] I'll ask you to return this sometime, though there's no haste about it.

Yes—it certainly is hard work finding anyone interested in the weird. I never encountered one till 1917, when I stumbled simultaneously on Cook & Loveman. Then, through Loveman, I got in touch with Smith; & had meanwhile come across Long. Through *Weird Tales* I encountered young August W. Derleth of Wisconsin (a U. of Wis. freshman 17 years old) & Bernard Dwyer of New York State; & through Smith I had the pleasure of making your acquaintance—this being the complete list of my Gothick circle to date. I write for my own edification exclusively, since it improves & crystallises my dreams to get them down on paper; & although I appreciate the kindly comment of the few who like my stuff, am not at all perturbed or disappointed because the majority are indifferent. By what standard could they be expected to be otherwise? It is this frank & cynical recognition of the inevitable limitations of people in general which makes me absolutely indifferent instead of actively hostile toward mankind. It can go to hell for all I care—but I'm not even interested enough to give it a push. It doesn't need me & I don't need it—it's only use is to build quaint cities for me to enjoy a century or two later! Incidentally—I was amused by the opinion which your English chief expressed regarding your "Fragment of a Dream". If you can get me a printed copy of that to keep I'll be eternally your debtor.

  With every good wish, & thanking you again for the loaned books, I remain

Most cordially & sincerely yours,
H P Lovecraft

[On envelope:] P.S. That magazine of Cook's will be called *The Recluse*. Glad you're contributing.

[Enclosures: Two photographs (of HPL's aunts?).]

Notes

1. HPL probably refers to Fort's chronicling of reports of a variety of strange celestial objects in chapters 20–26 of *The Book of the Damned*.

2. In "The Fall of the House of Usher," the narrator says "From the paintings over which his elaborate fancy brooded, and which grew, touch by touch, into vaguenesses at which I shuddered the more thrillingly, because I shuddered knowing not why;—from these paintings (vivid as their images now are before me) I would in vain endeavor to educe more than a small portion which should lie within the compass of merely written words" (*Collected Works of Edgar Allan Poe: Tales and Sketches*, ed. Thomas Ollive Mabbott [Cambridge, MA: Harvard University Press, 1978], 1.405).

3. See "Pickman's Model": "There was none of the exotic technique you see in Sidney Sime, none of the trans-Saturnian landscapes and lunar fungi that Clark Ashton Smith uses to freeze the blood" (*CF* 2.63).

4. HPL never did address the work of A. Merritt in later versions of SHL.

5. "The Colour out of Space," just completed in late March.

6. Steven J. Mariconda has pointed out that in the following passage, HPL quotes extensively from the text of his recent novel, *The Case of Charles Dexter Ward*, completed 1 March.

7. I.e., Prospect Terrace at roughly 70 Congdon Street.

8. Thomas Durfee (1721–1796), a longtime member of the General Court of Massachusetts. His house, the Joanna Barnes House (c. 1790–98), is located at 49 Benefit Street.

9. The John Reynolds House (c. 1785) at 88 Benefit Street.

10. Only the Golden Ball Inn Ell (1784 et seq.) stands today at 17–23 South Court Street. In HPL's time, the four-story Golden Ball Inn likely stood across from a stable (160 Benefit Street) adjacent to the Court House (150 Benefit Street). The main portion of the inn was demolished in 1941.

11. The Brick Schoolhouse (actually 1767), at 24 Meeting Street (formerly Gaol Lane), now the headquarters of the Providence Preservation Society. It is on the site of the former (1732) colony house at 21 Meeting Street opposite the John Carter House (Shakespear's Head; 1772).

12. The Truman Beckwith House (1826, John Holden Greene, architect; now the Providence Handicraft Club) at 42 College Street, only a few doors west of the final residence of HPL and his aunt Annie Gamwell at 66 College Street.

13. Marion A. Gleason, "Our Office Window," *Providence Journal* (24 March 1927): 14.

[17]   [DAW to HPL] [ALS]

1152 Portland Ave.,

St. Paul, Minn.

April 6, 1927

Dear Mr. Lovecraft:

I returned the three books you loaned me last week, and trust that you have received them in good condition by this time. I read them all carefully, though none of them has much of lasting value. The "Strange Manuscript" pleased me most, and was the most truly *Gothic* of the group in the 18th century sense of the word. Mr. de Mille writes like an amateur in places, like a fanatic in others, and occasionally like a drug-fiend. I wish I had read "The Oracle of Baal" when I was twelve. At that time, I would have been fascinated by the book, and enthralled by the story, whereas now it seems juvenile. "The Epicurean" made me feel what I can only describe as queasy; it belongs to an early nineteenth century school which employed a certain group of adjectives in the description of romantic or sentimental beauty, such adjectives, for example, as "beauteous orb", "radiant cheeks", and the like. It is an unfortunate truth that good words change in connotation, so that a fine and appropriate expression may lose caste or become artificial from decade to decade. I desire to express my heartiest thanks and appreciation of their loan; it is likely that I never would have discovered them if you had not been kind enough to send them.

I must also thank you for the pictures and cuttings of Providence that you sent. I have examined them with a great deal of interest, and see now why Providence means so much to you. As I said, I have never seen a picture of the city until now, and hence was the more eager to examine some views. I shall certainly visit Providence this summer, though I am afraid I shall have to content myself with a flying trip. What I'd like to do some day is to explore the whole Atlantic seaboard, especially in the New England states, perhaps for a year or two.

I am awaiting the arrival of your new tale and your history of weird fiction with a great deal of interest. I have just received a letter from Long in which he mentions and recommends "The Colour out of Space". The title itself is excellent and suggestive. Your industry appalls me at times. When I think of how many tales you have written, and how comparatively few I have completed, I am somewhat depressed. My muse is capricious; sometimes she only stays for a day, and sometimes doesn't come for a month. Of late, my mind has been in a turmoil with ideas and plots, but I have lacked the time to write. I have deliberately taken vacations from my studies now and then and written when I ought to be studying, but I am extremely tired of the university now. The longer I go, the more I dislike it. I have written two more poems in prose, at least one of which is fairly good, and which I shall send you soon. It is called "The Death of the Flowers". I don't like the other, which will be called "Black and Silver" or "Ebony and Silver", and am surprised at myself for writing it. I have also commenced the writing of a short story, the first in more than eight months. It will be rather long—for me—but I am not yet certain that it will be good. I'll type it and send you a copy when it's finished, or take it east with me if I do not finish it in time. I sent you a copy of the "Quarterly" containing "A Fragment of a Dream" with your books. I have eight or ten extra copies. Do you think Long or Loveman would care for one? I also have extra copies of a former issue containing "The Messengers" and "The Pursuers". If you want copies of this or the last issue, or know anyone who might care to read them, I shall be glad to send the issues. The last number, by the way, has a strangely beautiful poem in prose by Barbara Fawcett Craigie. I mentioned her in a former letter, I think, as one of the two friends I have made at the university, and out of all the hundreds of people I know there, one of the few with any real value. "La Dame" was written about two years ago, when "A Fragment of a Dream" was also written. She doesn't write so well now. Hjalmar Björnson—the Icelander—writes also, but in a rugged, saga-like fashion. He had a legend called "The Maiden Mengloth" in an old number of the "Quarterly"[1]—which, by the way, has published some extraordinary things for a college magazine; if I can find a copy in the Quarterly office, I'll send you one. He has written some unpublished things of a mystical sort, but I haven't copies myself. The best comment on "A Fragment of a Dream" came from Mrs. Craigie, who began reading the tale on a streetcar and couldn't finish it because it became too much for her! Her daughter was not quite so easily discouraged. "The Pen", an immature product of my younger brother, is better liked than "A Fragment" because it isn't so morbid. I am told by people who know that Minnesota is a more conventional university than any of the eastern ones, that nowhere in the east is one so entirely restricted as here. I'd like to see "The Door to the Room" appear in the Quarterly as my parting gift. It would make the faculty howl! Especially one delightful old soul who thought that "The Messengers" and "The Pursuers" were the *last word*, that the "Quarterly" *never* should have printed them! She teaches writing courses. Pity her students!

Who is Bernard Dwyer? I received a letter from him a week ago in which he mentioned my essay in the *Overland*, spoke highly of you, and asked to see some of my manuscripts. I sent him the prose, since the poetry was unavailable. I gathered that he was a devotee of the weird, and that he wrote and painted. This reminds me, have you ever seen the pictorial work of Smith? I have a few of his drawings and a splendid tapestry, but have never seen the large group which he possesses. He told me several months ago that he would let me see them sometime, but has apparently lacked the opportunity to prepare and send them. I am anxious to see them, both on account of those I have seen, and the mention of them in one issue of Loveman's "Saturnian".[2] The few I do know are magnificent and have made my impatience increase with the months.

I have just read Scarborough's "Supernatural in Modern English Fiction". It is a mediocre piece of work, but mentions a number of stories of more or less ephemeral value with which I was unacquainted. Alice M. Killen's "Le Roman Terrifiant" is a better piece of work. My French is none too good, but the book is easy reading. I have only had time to read the section on Lewis—I am doing a paper on him for the "Gothic professor" I mentioned before—but the book contains new material. There are several appendices, and bibliographies of various sorts. I picked up Hastings' "The City of Endless Night" and Stoker's "The Mystery of the Sea" in a second-hand bookstore last week. I haven't had time to read them, and shan't have for several months. The first seems to be of the social satire group, and probably wouldn't interest you. Stoker's book is a tome of five hundred pages whose value and interest are dubious. If you care to see either or both of these, let me know, and I'll send you them.

I doubt whether you could find much to interest you in St. Paul or Minneapolis. The people are white, at least,—they are largely Nordic of good stock—but the cities are both commercial, Minneapolis being more so. Their history scarcely goes before 1850, and the vestiges of age or history are very slight. The streets of St. Paul are narrow, and downtown their unusual narrowness tends to give an old-world illusion, what with cobblestones forming the pavement in places and rumbling carts clattering to the market on early summer days; but the illusion is dispelled by the ugly red-brick buildings which are too much in evidence, and which were of such popularity when St. Paul grew up. The steep bluffs along the Mississippi with many sandstone and limestone caverns are picturesqueful often, but factories or coal yards or some equal abomination are of too frequent occurrence and the river itself is so dangerously polluted that the university will not sanction shell-races as one of its sports. Typhoid and diphtheria are a constant menace to anyone in close association with the river. The only time I have enjoyed St. Paul is at night. I used to go out walking after midnight. The entire city is infinitely old and dead then, and the flaring gas lamps—now replaced by unfailing electric lights—stretched away in long and irregular lines, casting a spectral illumination on the narrow and deserted streets. The city was strangely quiet. I never met a person, and the black houses were unlighted and dead as the tomb. The sky is appalling on cold November nights. When there are no clouds, it sometimes takes on an intense blackness in which the stars gleam wan and frosty, dead in all the black immensity of the heavens. Some of the nights when I was fourteen and fifteen and sixteen were terrible. The city was necrophilic and age-old, and its inhabitants had passed away long ago. The pale light of the gas was corrupt and rotten, and the desolation and decay were of the grave. The stars were tired, weary of their own cold, incessant flame, white and morbid against the inkiness of space. The fearful and utter loneliness appalled me beyond measure, for my time-sense became lost, and it seemed as if all the world had died, and all the people vanished, so that I walked in horror amid the ruins of black emptiness. The skies here are strange. One of the most unusual occurred last spring and furnished the atmosphere for "The Messengers" and "The Pursuers". It was a sultry day, hot and dusty; great dust storms were sweeping over the prairies, and finally reached the Twin Cities. All that day, the air was so dusty that you could not see beyond a block; the sky smouldered, and the sun was suggested only by a dull and dark glow; everything was phantasmal in the pall, and the effect of that brooding, smoking sky with the sun a red and inflamed eye was depressing beyond measure. It was as if the heavens were burning, as if some great conflagration were raging beyond the obscuring dust-pall out in space.

Well! I have wandered somewhat. But perhaps, if for nothing else, I ought to thank Minnesota for the strange skies it has given me, and which I have used as atmosphere and setting for some of my tales.

Most cordially yours,
Donald Wandrei.

Notes

1. Hjalmar Björnson, "The Maiden Mengloth," *Minnesota Quarterly* 3, No. 2 (Winter 1926): 61–64.

2. "We hope, in our next number, to present our readers with an appreciation and appraisal of the poetry and drawings of Clark Ashton Smith, the young Californian." *Saturnian* 1, No. 1 (June–July [1920]): [8]. The piece was never published.

[18]   [HPL to DAW]   [ALS]

10 Barnes St.,
Providence, R.I.,
April 12, 1927.

My dear Mr. Wandrei:—

The returned books arrived safely, & I must thank you for the interesting number of the *Quarterly* enclosed with them. You are right, I think, as to the merits of the volumes—when I re-read "The Oracle of Baal" lately, after a lapse of some 25 years, it failed altogether to produce the impression of long ago. One must read these things young or not at all. I have not read the "Copper Cylinder" since that early period, & doubt whether I shall do so unless time hangs very heavily indeed upon my hands. Yes—Moore's "Epicurean" certainly has all the hackneyed rhetorical earmarks of early XIXth century Gothick composition. One must work back imaginatively into the period in order to restore to the florid words & phrases their original value. Being an extreme natural antiquarian myself, I have written much in that style—especially in verse—but this has only been part of a whole dream-life in the XVIIIth century, much like Lucian's Roman life in "The Hill of Dreams". Have you ever read Moore's poetic version of "The Epicurean"—which he did not finish, & which bore the title of "Alciphron"?—I discovered this long before I came upon the prose, & liked it infinitely better. It exerted a real influence over my imagination, as one may infer from my quotation in "The Nameless City". You can find it, I fancy, in almost any edition of Moore's collected poems.

I'm glad you enjoyed the Old Providence material, & hope you can arrange to spare at least two or three days in the venerable town during your Eastern sojourn. Over-night accomodations can easily be arranged here, & there are so many different things to see that any amount of time can be kept well occupied. You ought to take the boat trip to Newport & see at last the pounding open ocean as it beats against New England's stern & rock-bound coast—& of course the marvellously ancient town itself, with its multitudinous ante-Revolutionary landmarks. One ought to see Newport as soon as possible, for there are some detestable "civic improvement" plans which imperil the quaint narrowness of the main street & the incomparable colour & atmosphere of the ancient wharves.

What you say of St. Paul interests me very much, & I really think I'd prefer it to New York. You can't imagine the horror of being engulfed in a maelstrom of repulsive Orientals whose aberrant physiognomies & rat-like temperaments grate more & more on the sensibilities of an aesthetically impressionable person. New York represents such a stupendous ruin & decay—such a hideous replacement of virile & sound-heritaged stock by whipped, cringing, furtive dregs & offscourings—that I don't see how anyone can live long in it without sickening. The plebeian parts of our own New England

towns are bad enough with their jabbering Latins—but New York passes all
bounds. Only Dante could do it justice—one prays for a merciful earthquake
to end the blasphemous tragedy. St. Paul's narrow cobbled streets must certainly present some unusual nocturnal panoramas, & I can well imagine the
piquancy of your old-time walks. Providence, alas, has had electric lights since
the '80's, so that even as venerable a patriarch as I cannot look back to flickering gas except on a few side streets in the more sparsely settled residential
parts. New England, despite its residential quaintness, is woefully alert in mechanical progress; & had electric lights, trolley-cars, & many other modern
devices considerably before New York & the rest of the nation. We were
ahead even in the modern motor-coach system—for when I came home a
year ago New York had scarcely got used to interurban 'busses, yet Providence had a pandaemoniac terminal with lines reaching to every conceivable
point. The *sky* effects you mention must be alluring indeed, & I wish I might
some day see them. Your description has all the magic of fantasy & dream, &
I know that the original must be a highly striking phenomenon. We do not
always realise the important part played by atmospheric conditions in determining landscape & architectural values. The marvellous freshness & verdant
mystery of Old England's woods & meadows is due very largely to the omni-
present moisture & the solar effects of a very high latitude, whilst the vivid
tones of the Italian hills, lakes, & coast are no less dependent upon the sky.
New England, whose topography is probably more lovely in its quiet & reposeful diversity than that of any other region on the globe, has a magic all its
own from the combination of northern flora with the clear light of a latitude
relatively low. We have had, however, moments of strange & fantastic mystery sent down from the sky.* The "dark day" of May 19, 1780 (mentioned by
Whittier in his "Abraham Davenport") still lives in song & story, & a less famous one of Novr. 2, 1819 is recalled by antiquarians.[1] People not yet aged
can recall the famous "Yellow Day" of Sept. 6, 1881,[2] & I have myself seen
many strange illuminative anomalies which ought to be celebrated in weird
literature. Anent river pollution—I shall have to admit that Providence cannot claim much immunity. The broad cove, shewn in the *Netopian*[3] view of
the town a century ago, was a basin north of the Great Bridge into which
flowed two narrow & unnavigable streams—the Moshassuck from the north
& the Woonasquatucket from the west. This has now been filled up except
for a single channel to carry off the water of the two streams, & it must be
admitted that the waste of factories along both has done much to obscure the
originally aqueous character of the flowing fluid. Odours at certain hours
around the Great Bridge are not at all inviting, & the water has an oily, iridescent cast which has more than once moved me to weird reflections.[4] There is
not, however, anything dangerous or unsanitary in this pollution; & aside

---

*probably as a result of forest fires.

from its aesthetic drawbacks is harmful only in its destruction of the once-famous oyster beds of the upper bay. In that bay itself a new pollution has gradually crept—in the form of crude oil, since Providence is the greatest oil storage & distributing centre in the East. This, of course, is perfectly healthy—merely an olfactory nuisance—yet both this & the older factory pollution are steadily combated by sundry civic influences which will probably succeed, in the end, in forcing the manufacturers & oil companies to solve their waste problems in a less irresponsible way than merely dumping the stuff into the water. Providence sewage disposal is very scientific & effective, & the extension of the system to contiguous towns will still further improve the conditions. One good modern thing which you have in St. Paul, if postcards & folders err not, is your state capitol. A view of the rotunda now before me is certainly beautiful & impressive in the extreme, & I recall that the exterior is likewise very sightly & well-balanced. In this, Providence can offer you brisk competition, for our own pure marble State Capitol is one of the most famous & beautiful buildings in the United States. I may remark in passing that you will find the national Capitol at Washington a disappointment. It has been spoiled by wings, (as has the famous Boston state house) & is too much of a piecemeal affair to be really classic. In Rhode Island we have profited by the blunders of Washington & Boston, & have let our original marble triumph of thirty years ago severely alone. It is overcrowded, of course, but neighbouring houses are used to harbour the surplus departments, & work is already begun on a separate State Office Building of congruous architecture across the street. Thank God our legislators know enough to keep their hands off the exquisite creation of McKim, Mead, & White, with its perfect lines & ideal setting of balustraded marble terraces.[5]

The gang in N.Y. is so long in returning the carbon of my "Colour Out of Space" that I'm herewith sending the original MS.—of which I'll ask you to be very careful, since it is this copy which will invade the editorial premises of such magazines as I decide to approach. I hope it won't disappoint you—it is purely & simply an atmospheric study, & from the fictional standpoint is woefully lacking in climax. I have several new tales in mind—some potentially marketable, & others of too great bizarrerie for popular reception—but have just now been too busy for writing.[6] As to the amount I write—I am sure it isn't very great as compared with many other cases; & whatever credit for industry I might earn in composition, I lose through my ineradicable aversion from the process of typing. I doubt if any eye but mine will ever see the novelettes of the past winter! As a matter of fact, one begins to write voluminously when one has ceased to pay attention to the mechanical process of composition. My own periods of fecundity vary according to the amount of care I give to style. When I am feeling finical & fastidious, & critical as to commas, semicolons, & shades of etymological propriety, I find that I accomplish little. Results come when I forget everything about rhetoric & literature, & simply go ahead in roughneck fashion to imprison some dream or impression which has haunted me. That is why I have no undue veneration for books & the literary atmosphere. Words don't interest me—but bizarre & poignant impressions are the essence of my life. By the way—when the poet & critic Vincent Starrett of Chicago (who introduced the work of Machen to America) was last in New York he got in touch with our gang & saw some of my work. According to Long, he was very favourably disposed toward it—& yesterday I received a letter from him asking to see a more representative array. Naturally I am feeling highly flattered, & have just sent him a dozen tales illustrating different phases of my writing. I doubt if he will find them up to the classic standard, but at any rate it is encouraging to have the notice of one so well qualified to judge. As for your own writing—lud, Sir! but you have no reason to feel depressed! The inability to write at all times is something which you share with nearly every other writer (above the hack grade) under the sun—& so far as my own humble case counts, I can report many a day of blankness with ideas in my head & pen & paper in front of me; during which I have had to turn to something else & await the kindness of Fate in doling out a creative interval. At such times I often prepare skeletal synopses to preserve ideas & pictures which I am then unable to vivify in connected form. Every author must include waste time & infertile days in his calculations—using those periods for reading or excursions afield in search of new visual impressions. Today is a good case of this very thing with me. I have a notion I want to get in story form, but it simply doesn't shape itself this afternoon. Thus I have turned to correspondence, & if the present beastly wind goes down I shall take a walk through steep & ancient streets at sunset. Then tonight I shall try again. If it works, all right. If not, I'll get some revision done & wait for a still later mood. But under no circumstances will I try to write when the natural inclination & ability are not upon me. Concerning the university—I suppose it's dull enough, yet am sure that you will find its net effect beneficial. Imaginative minds are prone to one-sided development, & a standard curriculum holds one willy-nilly to a balanced perspective & normal orientation which one might not voluntarily acquire. I really regret that ill health kept me from attending college—the influence would have made me less of a freakish recluse than I am, & would have given me a contact with the world whereby my work might display a far richer background of realism than it does. Don't regret your university years. You are the better for them, & even as it is you are emerging from them far earlier than most youths succeed in doing. In general, I fancy you are right in assuming that eastern colleges are less stereotyped in thought than the smaller colleges of the west. However, such universities as Wisconsin & Chicago seem to be encouragingly in the vanguard. The worst of all are the smaller denominational colleges—my friend Galpin was almost driven to distraction by his home-town Lawrence

College of Appleton, Wis. (the "Methodist Seminary", as he called it) until he broke away & finished his education at U. of Wis. & U. of Chicago.

I'd like to see your new prose-poems when you get copies. Your *Quarterly* is really a splendid example of the collegiate magazine, & shews that there is no lack of fine material amongst the student body, whatever may be said of the faculty. I think, in truth, that there is far more general mental vigour in the west than in the east; & have often wished that the two sections could exchange populations—putting the hardy & undecayed western stock amidst the beauty & historic heritage of the east, & thus restoring to some extent the almost idyllic conditions of the colonial period. Yes—Long & Loveman would appreciate all the *Quarterlies* with your work which you can spare them. They both hold the most enthusiastic opinion of your abilities & promise, & will read any product of yours with the utmost appreciation. Let me add that I shall myself appreciate any further numbers you can spare—especially the one containing "The Messengers" & "The Pursuers". I have wished that I had permanent copies of these marvellous pieces. I'd also like to see the product of your Icelandic friend—I love the sagas of the frozen north, & wish there were some truth in the old belief that the Northmen visited Rhode Island in the 10th or 11th century. There is certainly genuine merit in the poem by Miss Craigie, & your brother's piece also shows very keen vision & promise. I trust that his development may parallel your own, perhaps producing a phenomenon something like that of the celebrated Edmond & Jules de Goncourt.[7] Yes—the *Quarterly* assumedly towers high amongst undergraduate publications, & I hope that before your graduation you will be able to incorporate "The Door to the Room" in its contents—whether or not the dear old lady instructor dies of the shock.

Bernard Dwyer is a very promising young artist, 29 years of age, who got in touch with me through the magazine *Weird Tales* after reading some of my stuff therein. He has a true appreciation of the fantastic, & will form a very worthy recipient for any original material you may care to send him. I have loaned him your Smith critique, as well as the *Quarterlies* with "The Hill of Dreams" & "Fragment of a Dream". His opinion of your work is very high, & I think you will find him a genuinely congenial correspondent. His coloured drawings shew every mark of growing genius, & if you would like to see an assortment of ten excellent specimens I will arrange for one to come your way. It has gone to Long, & he will forward it to Smith—& if you say the word I'll have C A S return it through you rather than directly to me. Dwyer lives in the country, but has spent much time in New York.

I enclose all the samples of Smith drawing now in my reachable possession. When I get my goods from storage in New York—which I am about to do after a year—I shall have a few more of the same kind to send; & there are one or two more now lent to others which you shall see. Unfortunately I have none of Smith's really ambitious pieces, but he has twice lent me consignments which have taken my breath away with their utter interplanetary strangeness & chromatic wonder. He is assuredly a master, & ought to be recognised as such some day. Loveman has a marvellous collection of earlier Smith material at his home in Cleveland, which I scanned with awe & admiration on my visit of five years ago. Smith promises to shew me more of his drawings shortly, & has said that he means to shew the same assortment to you. It is impossible to speak too highly of his genius as an exotic colourist.

I note your book observations with interest, & hope that some of the leads in the Scarborough & Killen volumes may prove profitable. I'd like to see your paper on Lewis—though I didn't find "The Monk" very thrilling except for the "Bleeding Nun" episode & one or two incantation scenes. I think Lewis stands immeasurably below Maturin. Let me know what you think of the Hastings & Stoker books when you read them—& maybe I'll ask for a loan later on. Stoker had creative genius but no sense of form. He couldn't write any decent connected novel without extensive help & revision. Have you ever seen that pitiful mess "The Lair of the White Worm"? Poor Bram makes a fizzle of a truly magnificent horror idea which I'd ordinarily consider almost fool-proof. Do you know his "Jewel of Seven Stars"? That is much better. I've just been reading Robert W. Chambers' forgotten horror "The King in Yellow", & find some magnificent atmosphere despite the floridity of the '90's which hangs about it. Also Elliott O'Donnell's "Sorcery Club"—an absolutely rotten & puerile crudity which is saved only by its ending & certain touches leading thereto. I'll let you see my history of weird fiction as soon as my carbon comes back.

Well—I must hustle if I expect to get the sunset. Hope you can see a Providence sunset yourself before many months are over!

With every good wish, & thanking you again for the *Quarterly*,

I remain

Most cordially & sincerely yrs—

H P Lovecraft

Notes

1. John Greenleaf Whittier (1807–1892), "Abraham Davenport" (1866), a poem about a Connecticut politician (1715–1789) who thought that the "dark day" was a sign that the Last Judgment was impending. The reference is similar to that of the "strange days" of HPL's "The Colour out of Space."

2. The *Providence Daily Journal* (Wednesday, 7 September 1881: 1) reported that the previous day, the atmosphere throughout New England was "pervaded with a yellowish light, which lends a strange appearance" to the landscape. Cf. "The Shunned House": "The blinding maelstrom of greenish-yellow vapour which surged tempestuously up from that hole as the floods of acid descended, will never leave my memory. All along the hill people tell of the yellow day, when virulent and horrible fumes arose

from the factory waste dumped in the Providence River, but I know how mistaken they are as to the source" (*CF* 1.478).

3. *The Netopian: A Monthly Magazine in the Interests of Friendly Business* was issued by Rhode Island Hospital Trust Company of Providence.

4. The Great Bridge spanned the Providence River, connecting downtown Providence with the East Side. In its day it was the widest river bridge in the world; however, recently much of it was removed to uncover more of the river. Cf. *CB* 15 (c. 1919): "Bridge & slimy black waters. Fungi—The Canal."

5. Charles Follen McKim (1847–1909), William Rutherford Mead (1846–1928), and Stanford White (1853–1906) of the celebrated architectural firm McKim, Mead & White designed the Rhode Island State House (1891–1904), at 90 Smith Street, overlooking downtown Providence. Their design influenced that of other state capitols in the 1890s and early 1900s.

6. HPL would not write another story until "The Dunwich Horror" in the summer of 1928.

7. Edmond (1822–1896) and Jules de Goncourt (1830–1870) were brothers who frequently collaborated on novels, monographs on art, and other works.

[19]   [DAW to HPL] [ALS]

1152 Portland Ave.,

St. Paul, Minn.

April 17—1927

Dear Mr. Lovecraft:

"The Colour out of Space" is a splendid piece of work. To my mind, it is one of the finest of your tales, and I sincerely hope you dispose of it to your best advantage. I had a touch of the "flu" when the tale arrived, and my eyes burned so that I could not read that day. But it is a tribute to you and your work that I read the story immediately regardless of the "flu" or my eyes. One of the best pictures in your entire work is that terrible scene toward the close when the well and the farm and the buildings shone with unnatural and awful phosphorescence. I do not find any of the flaws you mention; and I think that the climax is sufficient. A stronger climax might be brutally realistic; the indefinable horror that the tale leaves me is artistic in its effect.

I congratulate you on having drawn the attention of Mr. Starrett, and sincerely hope that something more will come of it. I did not know that he was interested in the weird, though I was aware of his interest in Machen, which, unfortunately, has not always been to the best advantage of Mr. Machen. Do you know his brochure, "Arthur Machen: Novelist of Ecstasy and Sin"? It contains much quoted material—which is often better than his own tributes—and has an unpleasant tone in places, but does more justice to the sorcerer of Wales than most reviews and most critics. This reminds me—I am proud to possess two letters from Mr. Machen which I received when he read my review in the "Quarterly". I am going to have my copy of "The Hill of Dreams"—which is a finely printed limited edition on blue linen paper—bound in adequate and artistic manner some day, and I'll have the letters inlaid. I have just removed everything I wrote at Minnesota from the theme file, and read it over. I noticed a curious fact. In three months—the summer I read "Ebony and Crystal" and "The Hill of Dreams"—my ideas underwent a complete revolution, and I walked to the opposite side of the fence, changing from a half-materialistic scientist to a romanticist and idealist and aesthete. I am surprised at the sudden and profound change. It is the difference between "The Decomposer" and "The Messengers". I have mailed you, by the way, the "Quarterly" containing "The Messengers" and "The Pursuers." I thought I had done this already when the issue came out, and regret my oversight. I haven't been to the university since Wednesday, and have thus had no opportunity to look up the issue containing Björnson's legend. I think there are some copies left and will send one in a day or two, or loan my own if that number is exhausted. The legend is interesting, though not of exceptional merit. As to the current number, I like Miss Craigie's prose poem so well that I am afraid its influence is only too obvious in "The Death of the Flowers". "The Pen" is full of immaturities, but Howard shows every sign of following my own development. I wish he would be original in his own way, but his tastes are akin to mine except that he has some talent in drawing whereas I can't even make a round dot! He is seventeen. I shall be celebrating my nineteenth birthday when this reaches you—it comes Wednesday—and on the whole, this has been the happiest year of my life. I can't say it has been happy, but, compared with other years, I have enjoyed myself more and accomplished more.

You have all the "Quarterlies" containing any of my work, since there are only three. I'll have some poems in the spring issue and will send you a copy when it appears.—I received my books, together with "Haunted Homes", a few days ago, and thank you for its loan. I have hastily run through it and think that I shall find it unusually interesting. I want to read it more carefully, however, and will keep it a week or ten days longer. I do not know Moore's "Alciphron", but I'll look it up at the U. library.

I have had a growing dislike of St. Paul in the last few years. Too many "civic" improvements are ruining the few qualities that give it atmosphere, and that made me like it at times. I do not believe there are any cobblestone streets left, though a few have old brick pavements. Ten years ago and even five years ago, electric lighting was confined to the business section and to a few of the main thoroughfares. We live in one of the best residential districts, but not until this winter did electric lights replace the picturesque and flaming gas-lamps that made a vivid impression on me years ago. Even the streets are being widened, and the oldest street in the city is being wrecked and rebuilt because it is dilapidated and old and not in keeping with an up-to-date commercial city. Nearly the entire city is properly illuminated now, and there is none of the mystery that I found when I walked the dark and obscure streets after midnight when I was still a youth. I can never explain what a wealth of atmosphere the feeble gas lamps gave, some of them yellow and some pale, and some flaming through broken mantles.[1] The motor traffic has greatly increased also, and the solitude I once found scarcely exists even at two or three o'clock in the morning. I walked down town this afternoon; it was a warm, spring day with a pleasant wind blowing. But the curious mediaeval atmosphere that St. Paul once possessed is vanishing. The city is built on the bluffs and terraces along the Mississippi; you can stand on the most fashionable street in the city at certain points and look across a lower section of St. Paul across the river which is intensely blue and lovely as it winds on in the distance, and still further to the bluffs and terraces miles away across the river, and even toward its open country beyond. It is a picturesque sight on clear days, and even when a haze hangs above the river valley. But the enchantment does not survive if one has occasion to cross the region he has surveyed, and this disillusionment has been growing on me in late years. The Capitol presents a fine appearance. It is many years since I was inside, but as I remember, it was not completed then, or needed repairing in one or two passageways. I have not paid much attention to buildings or homes here. I prefer vague effects and mystical impressions, but these are too often dispelled when the minutiae are examined. The atmospheric effects have been unusual in number and often extraordinary in their nature. Early in January a year ago, we had a fall of *red* snow.[2] I had an uneasy feeling, as if I were in a nightmare, when I went outside under the dull and leaden sky and saw the ground covered with a fine layer of reddish-brown snow. I forgot how the scientists accounted for the phenomenon—I think there were dust clouds an impossible distance away which were supposed to have drifted here in upper strata—but I was unusually sensitive since I had just finished reading "The Book of the Damned". I remember another night from my boyhood which I made use of in "Unto the End" and "The Twilight of Time" when I mention the heavens as being "deeply and darkly luminous." I do not remember the cause of the phenomenon, nor whether it was noticed by anyone else; but the stars were faint and the entire heavens seemed to be glowing with their own soft phosphorescence; and yet it was a luminosity that impressed me as being *dark,* as if the air itself were luminous in the skies and all the heavens behind them intensely black. I used to pay a great deal of attention to the skies; the riddle of the stars and the unfathomable mystery of the heavens held me "as one whom spells restrain";[3] and I was sometimes sick to depression with world-weariness when I had to turn my eyes away from the myriad of stars, cold and palely beautiful, shining with their deathless flame out in the gulfs of night, and return to earth. I have always had a longing for the unknown, for the great mystery of other stars and other realms and abysses beyond comprehension, for deliriums and ecstasies that can never be found on earth. I think that I shall be forever unsatisfied, living with men but vainly reaching toward infinitudes beyond my grasp, beauty and ideals that shall not be mine save in dreams.

I am glad that you liked "The Woman at the Window", which I just received from Long. I am enclosing another of these short "impressions", "The Death of the Flowers". It is probably the last I shall do for some time, since I am working on a short story and also have returned to work on the novel I began a year ago. I do not believe that I shall ever again be able to write a horror story. My work has become of so aesthetic a nature of late and beauty has become my ideal to such an extent that I think I shall enjoy the horror stories that you write and write so well rather than do them myself. I seem to lose interest in a field after I have written a few things in it and proved—to myself, at least—that I can do good work in it. My paper on Lewis won't be worth reading. The more of his work I read, the more I am bored by him and his crudities.

I have examined Smith's drawings with great interest. I have a profound admiration for those I have seen, and am impatient for the promised loan of a group. I shall be deeply grateful if I may see the others when you get them from storage. Some day, I hope to see Loveman's collection, as well as all that the artist himself has. I am going to devote a chapter of my novel to Smith, wherein the main character, who is an aesthete and romanticist, adorns one room completely with tapestries and paintings and drawings of Smith, and for years is dominated by their imaginative beauty. I should also be pleased to see the work of Mr. Dwyer. I'll be eternally grateful if you can arrange it.

I am returning herewith the drawings of Smith and your story, with my profound gratitude and thanks for their loan. I gave them both the best possible care, and hope that they will reach you in perfect condition.

I was cut short in my last letter. I meant to explain the genesis of "A Shadow of a Nightmare", but don't remember how much I said, or whether I had time to say anything or even thank you for your interest. You have really analysed the tale—it is already a union of three. The idea of a mad nation was originally separate, as well as the idea of a supreme horror story. The third idea was of something existing, either visibly or in memory, from incredibly ancient times. The end of the story is bodily removed from another that I wrote about two years ago, entitled "Beyond the Milky Way". It was a mess. I think it is destroyed now with some other inferior material which I gave a merited oblivion last fall. I have been unsatisfied with the tale as it is, and may attempt to improve it in time. I really believe the story is only second or third-rate, and is barely saved from a worse ranking by the basic ideas.

Let me thank you again for the interest you have shown in my work, an interest that I appreciate. Even so, it can hardly exceed my admiration for your horror stories. When I do critical work again, which may not be for a year or two, the first appreciation I write will be one I have long planned of you and your tales.

Most cordially,
Donald Wandrei

Notes

1. In DAW's science fiction story "Murray's Light" (in *SH* and *C*), small flickering lights of supernatural origin, caged within glass bulbs, are distributed across the country.
2. This phenomenon is cited in "The Monster from Nowhere," "Something from Above," and *Invisible Sun*.
3. CAS, "In Saturn," l. 6; in *Complete Poetry and Translations* (New York: Hippocampus Press, 2007–08), 1.176.

[20]   [HPL to DAW]   [ALS]

10 Barnes St.,
Providence, R.I.,
April 21, 1927

Dear Mr. Wandrei:—

First of all, let me wish you the traditionally numerous happy returns of that anniversary which made yesterday festive! It must be marvellous to be nineteen, & with all dreamland (to say nothing of so base a thing as the world) before one; & I trust you appreciate, amidst the inevitable ennui of the daily round, how great a boon & inspiration you have in the priceless quality of youth. Incidentally—accept my sympathy anent the touch of grippe; a thing which I lightly sampled a year ago, but which I have not yet had with full malignity.

I am glad that you found "The Colour Out of Space" acceptable, & feel much encouraged by this testimony to my continued freedom from senile decay. Every time I write a new tale I have a fear that mounting years may have begun to dull my fancy, hence am always glad when someone pronounces my recent effusions at least as good as the bulk of those which I wrote in my prime. I think I shall now try the "Colour" on the professional press—though I have not much hope of its acceptance. As to Starrett—if he likes my junk he could probably help a good deal with editors by speaking a good word for it; but I doubt if he will grow very enthusiastic. I recall his part in the American popularisation of Machen—& also a quarrel in which it seemed curiously hard to place the blame in view of the documentary evidence brought up on both sides. The bone of contention was the Covici-McGee edition of "The Shining Pyramid"—which Machen said he didn't authorise, but which Starrett said was accepted in good part by him until considerably after publication—& I hear that this feud is now happily extinct, with renewed amity reigning on both sides.[1] I am probably immune from such disharmonies, for I don't imagine Starrett will ever try to publish a book of my tales! Anyway, I shall be interested to hear what he has to say—I told him to take his time about reading the dozen specimens I sent. You are fortunate in hearing personally from Machen, & I don't blame you for wanting the letters bound up with your blue-paper "Hill of Dreams". I have never had direct correspondence with any eminent author—though a friend once sent Dunsany some verses I wrote about him, & received a kindly acknowledgment in Dunsany's well-known quill scrawl.[2] Speaking of the living great—have I asked you whether or not you've read the weird stories of the eminent antiquarian Montague Rhodes James? To me his power of evoking horror from the most prosaic scenes seems little short of prodigious, & I regard him as among the four or five greatest masters of the unreal now surviving.

I was greatly interested by your account of your literary mutation under the Smith-Machen influence; a mutation which reminds me of my own response to Dunsany when I discovered him in the fall of 1919. Prior to that time my excursions into the poetically fantastic had been very infrequent, but from then on the prose-poetic formed a steady element parallelling my more realistic horrors. I subsequently discovered Machen & Blackwood & De la Mare, but none of these has influenced me as Dunsany did. Perhaps this is because I am growing old, for after thirty we are not so impressionable as before; or perhaps it is because Dunsany's mood & attitude & fanciful dreamworld are so curiously like my own. (aside from my element of pure horror) At any rate, it is Dunsany who marks the only sudden & well-marked literary revolution I have had since the age of six, when Grecian tales displaced the Arabian Nights in my affection. I have, though, come to think of it, experienced long periods of reactions against all literature in favour of science. *Astronomy* has been a major subject with me, & for twelve years I wrote a monthly article on celestial phenomena for the local papers.[3] I still have the most profound respect for pure intellect—& am an absolute materialist & mechanist, believing the cosmos to be a purposeless & meaningless affair of endless cycles of alternate electronic condensation & dispersal—a thing without beginning, permanent direction, or ending, & consisting wholly of blind force operating according to fixed & eternal patterns inherent in entity. It is because I am a complete sceptic & cynic, recognising no such qualities as good or evil, beauty or ugliness, in the ultimate structure of the universe, that I insist on the artificial & traditional values of each particular cultural stream—proximate values which grew out of the race in question, & which are the sole available criteria for the members of that race & culture, though of course having no validity outside it. These backgrounds of tradition against which to scale the objects & events of experience are all that lend such objects & events the illusion of meaning, value, or dramatic interest in an ultimately purposeless cosmos—hence I preach & practice an extreme conservatism in art forms, society, & politics, as the only means of averting the ennui, despair, & confusion of a guideless & standardless struggle with unveiled chaos. There is no absolute right or wrong, upward or downward, or backward or forward—

and in order to gain the pleasurable contentment of a sense of harmonious orientation, we must measure all things by the system of feelings evolved by the primitive wonder & later surroundings of our especial line of forefathers. Only in this way can convincing points of reference—& thus landmarks of direction & standards of value—be established amidst the universal flux. If excess of intellect ever deprives us of the power of maintaining these illusions, we shall undergo a weary decadence beginning with radical experimentation & ending in a recrudescent savagery from which some new culture may or may not be born. I feel very strongly that we are now entering upon such a decadent phase—for spirit-wearying disillusion is everywhere discernible.

The *Quarterly* duly came, & I am delighted to have "The Messengers", "The Pursuers", & "The Song of Autumn" for permanent retention. Many thanks— & thanks also for the issue with your Icelander's saga if you find a copy to spare. The *Quarterly* really has some excellent things, & far surpasses most of the collegiate magazines I have seen. I don't believe a little emulation of yourself will hurt your brother's style. If his cast of fancy proves to be exactly identical, he will have had a good start in the right direction; & if it proves otherwise, he has plenty of time to build a new style around his own individual vision. In either case the practice in colourful prose & imaginative exercise will be good for him. I don't blame you for envying him his pictorial ability. Like you I unite a very sincere *wish* to draw with a most appalling incapacity.

The changes overtaking St. Paul are certainly discouraging in the extreme, & would drive me to exasperation if I had to witness them. It is bad enough here—with the main business section solid asphalt & with occasional street-widenings here & there—& I groan each time a colonial house disappears. But as compared with other places we are very conservative about our antiquities, & have saved many historic or picturesque buildings through popular clamour even at the very last moment before a threatened destruction. Moreover, most of our new construction follows local & traditional lines. The facade of the famous Joseph Brown house (1774—with cyma-curve pediment)[4] has been sedulously copied on a larger scale in one of our newest business blocks,[5] whilst the mammoth new court house will incorporate details taken from the old (1773) Market House[6] & bear a colonial belfry suggested by the ancient colony-house. (1761)[7] A new bank block now going up is a perfect specimen of Providence Georgian of the 1790 period,[8] & another bank has just expanded by annexing to itself two fine old Georgian houses—one on each side—& providing connective arcades & rear extensions of congruous design, in no way interfering with the street facades as architectural units.[9] What is not built in Georgian design is built in classic Graeco-Roman forms perfectly harmonious with it, so that Providence will always be a *traditional* city like old London, with the ancient architectural orders & a stately dome-crowned skyline instead of the freakish & garish modernism of New York & the mushroom towns of the West. The ultimate effect, with a multitude of

Georgian fronts varied by Vitruvian pediments & colonnades & Renaissance domes, will be strongly suggestive of eighteenth-century London—the London of Wren's St. Paul's & Chambers' Somerset House & Dance's Mansion House & Adam's Adelphi Terrace & Soane's Bank of England.[10] The hideous monstrosities of Victorian times are coming down with gratifying rapidity, the three worst eyesores all being condemned in the single year since my return home. Of really tall buildings we shall probably have only one, for the zoning laws are fairly rigid. That exception, which with its tower will probably amount to 26 stories, will have the effect of a lone cathedral or castle dominating the lower town but not reaching high enough to subordinate the crowning dome & spires of the hill.[11] As for gas-lamps—as I admitted, you beat me in having seen a town quite largely illuminated by them; but I can beat you in regard to the *kind* of gas-lamps I can recollect. For in my early days several of the obscurer lanes were still lit by the same diamond-globed *non-mantle* affairs which we had long before the Civil War! Just *two* of these, so far as I can deduce, now remain—that is, the external shells remain, though the archaic panes now shield incandescent electric bulbs. And one of these will go when the Victorian court house comes down. Up to the time of the late war Providence gas could be used in the old way as an illuminant without mantles. Then, however, the heavier hydrocarbon content was cut down in favour of a dominantly thermal content; & the universal use of Welsbach mantles made a return to the old standard inadvisable. Brooklyn N.Y. gas, however, retained its illuminant value as late as 1923; & I am told that the gas of Mt. Vernon N.Y. (where I've never stopped) even now clings to its primal carbonaceousness. The home of a highly Victorian old maid whom my aunt visited not so long ago in that town was completely dependent upon this deliciously nineteenth-century system of lighting—figured ground-glass globes & all; such as one now seldom sees except in pictures or museums, but which I recall so vividly from the naive, golden days of the 'nineties. Happy times! I can yet see the great glass chandeliers, & the ornate newel-post cluster with blue porcelain trimmings, which adorned the spacious rooms & hallways of the house where I was born & lived the first fourteen years of my life. These things, of course, were ugly & Victorian, & I don't pretend to class them with the graceful Georgian candelabra of still older houses; but they were linked so closely to my days of youth & pristine wonder that they will always have a breathless charm & affectionately associative value for me. What you say of the disillusion-filled vistas of St. Paul is probably true of most cities outside the really ancient area. It is certainly true of New York, whose faery & ethereal skyline demands distance & subdued light for its chief magic. One sees the same phenomenon, too, in the western & poorer parts of Providence—but one can enjoy them just as much from Prospect Terrace as if they were in truth the wondrous purple ways they seem. Which reminds me that a certain hill at the western edge of the town—Neutaconkanut Hill—gives a magnifi-

cent panorama of the whole urban & suburban area, outspread as impressively as London from the heights of Hampstead or Highgate. Like you I prefer
vague massed effects to details, & up to four years ago was astonishingly ignorant of architecture. Since then, however, I have felt the need of a little
analysis in order to choose new scenes from written descriptions & to describe my own favourite vistas in terms intelligible to others; so that I have
gradually absorbed considerable data on American colonial design, & can pick
out the high spots in classic & Renaissance architecture—though I am still
damnably weak on Gothic. My desire to know the principal forms is en-
hanced by a wish to visualise dramatically the various stages of history—when
I *think* 1725 I want to be able to *see* 1725; & to do that, I must know clearly
what types of building were then surviving, & what types were then being
built. Once I roughly block out my scene—knowing just what to include &
what to eliminate—I can drape it in as much mist & mysticism as I choose!
As time goes on, my taste for urban panoramic effects increases; till at the
present time I am really more sensitive to architecture than to any other art,
save only the weird wing of prose literature. The vistas I relish most are those
in which the sunset plays a transfiguring & glorifying part. Sometimes I stum-
ble accidentally on rare combinations of slope, curved street-line, roofs & gables & chimneys, & accessory details of verdure & background, which in the
magic of late afternoon assume a mystic majesty & exotic significance beyond
the power of words to describe. Absolutely nothing else in life now has the
power to move me so much; for in these momentary vistas there seem to
open before me bewildering avenues to all the wonders & lovelinesses I have
ever sought, & to all those gardens of eld whose memory trembles just beyond the rim of conscious recollection, yet close enough to lend to life all the
significance it possesses.[12] All that I live for is to recapture some fragment of
this hidden & just unreachable beauty; this beauty which is all of dream, yet
which I feel I have known closely & revelled in through long aeons before my
birth or the birth of this or any world.[13] There is somewhere, my fancy fabu-
lises, a marvellous city of ancient streets & hills & gardens & marble terraces,
wherein I once lived happy eternities, & to which I must return if ever I am
to have content. Its name & place I know not—save as reason tells me it has
neither name nor place, nor any existence at all—but every now & then there
flashes out some intimation of it in the travelled paths of men. Of this cryptic
& glorious city—this primal & archaic place of splendour in Atlantis or
Cockaigne or the Hesperides—many towns of earth hold vague & elusive
symbols that peep furtively out at certain moments, only to disappear again.
Providence is full of such symbols, & Boston has yielded gorgeous examples.
Salem & Newport & Marblehead are rich in them, & many spots in the country speak at evening in no dissimilar language. Old Philadelphia once gave me
stupefying glimpses at dawn, & even New York is not devoid of hints when
the night is young after a rain, & soft lamps flicker up one by one over the

shining wet asphalt as pink clearing rifts bar the sky & silhouette the fantastic western roofs across the lower end of Central Park where the fountain-studded & balustraded Plaza lies. In nearly every fresh haunt of antiquity I visit, I find fresh symbols of added poignancy; so that I seem to be driven onward to wider & wider explorations in the hope of coming again upon the terraced gardens I knew in the aeons before Time. This, in truth, is my aesthetic life, such as it is—the only life that is of any vitality or significance to me—& that life is none the less dominant because of the calm & amused & sceptical analysis my intelligence continually & cynically applies to it. It is so perfectly & utterly a life of dream that it leads to an almost Oriental inaction wherein vision is substituted for deed. Spring comes, & I resolve to go out & drench my soul in hyacinthine fields & waking woods & far incredible cities. I resolve—I call up those fields & woods & cities in my fancy—& lo! I have seen & experienced them! So I do not go out in bodily reality after all! It is the same with writing in many instances—though of course the sway of insubstantial dream is by no means so absolute as to keep me from taking many actual trips & penning many actual tales. I know that these trips & tales will never take me to the marvellous city of pre-cosmic memory, & I am probably rather glad of that knowledge, in that it secures for me an eternity of never-tarnished vision & never-sated quest through all the years of my consciousness. As in your case, the skies exert the utmost fascination upon me; nor is the weaving of wild dreams about their unplumbed deeps & their alien suns & worlds in the least hampered by the precise astronomical data which my scientific side demands. Indeed, there is nothing in the baldest truth about the sky which does not enhance rather than enfeeble one's awe at its fathomless & indescribable immensities. There is horror there, too—as some day I shall record in connexion with a voyage Randolph Carter once made into the abysses beyond human imagination. I have already told (in the novelette not yet typed) of Carter's terrible trip to the dark side of the moon—what took him thither, & by what means he was able to return to the plains of earth's dreamland beyond the Temple of Nasht & Kaman-Thah, & the Gate of Deeper Slumber, & the enchanted wood of the zoogs. Well! I must summon up the energy to type that damn thing! As to *red snow*—I certainly envy you your actual sight of it, for I have known it only in meteorological textbooks. The cause is a microscopic plant of great hardiness & wide though spasmodic & irregular diffusion, which can flourish & multiply under even arctic conditions. Under high magnification the organism reveals seven or 8 cells containing a red fluid which becomes *green* after long exposure to air & light. Sometimes this exposure under natural conditions gives rise to fields of green snow, though these are less commonly observed than red. It is easy for me to imagine how the phenomenon must look—yet I know I can scarcely have realised the thrill which comes from literally seeing it at first-hand. Possibly the instance you witnessed was unlike that encountered in the polar regions—the fact that the colour was reddish-*brown* would seem to favour the dust explanation locally advanced. Charles Fort, of course, would be ready with glib hypotheses—which reminds me that Wright says Fort is a close personal friend of the *Weird Tales* author Edmond Hamilton, to whom he has suggested several of the story plots appearing in the magazine. That "deeply & darkly luminous" sky must have been a prodigious stimulus to the weird fancy. Things of that sort are not to be looked for in New England's clear air; so that you really owe a great deal to your situation on the edge of those silent, cryptic prairies through which nocturnal Presences stalk in the hours when no man stirs.

"The Death of the Flowers" is very delightful, & represents an exercise in atmosphere & colouring which will stand you in good stead. I think it is an excellent thing to devote a certain part of one's development to the prose-poem, in which one may gain new levels of perfection in the graceful music of words & the delicate shadings of visual impression without having to maintain the tension of keeping an elaborate plot under control. Probably it is a mainly youthful form, which will later give way to something in which elements of motion & dynamic symmetry will work in conjunction with the setting & mood; but that is nothing at all against it. I think the present example is admirable, & would urge nothing save a general guarding against triteness of expression; such as references to a 'beauty that hurts' (a stock fixture of the 1890's) or conventionalised portraits suggesting Rossetti & the pre-Raphaelite brotherhood. I don't think the sketch shews any unauthorised borrowing from Miss Craigie's poem—although I haven't the latter at hand just now, the *Quarterly* being lent to Dwyer. I can sympathise with your reaction against horror in favour of sheer beauty, & shall be anxious to see the effect of this tendency on the novel & short story you are now handling. Your tastes will probably describe a rather wide cycle for a time, & finally crystallise into a sort of synthesis of favoured elements culled from all the ground you will have been over. Beauty will still be the desideratum, but it will perhaps be a subtler, deeper beauty less dependent upon the more obvious decorative forms. It will not neglect these forms, however, & will undoubtedly be of an ethereal & elusively imaginative rather than realistic cast.

I'll certainly send you every Smith drawing I can lay my hands on, & will see that some Dwyer drawings come your way as soon as possible. You'll have a new respect for Dwyer when you see the batch of ten large designs now going the rounds—Long to Smith, Smith to you. D. is now doing me a wood panel with "Faunus" on one side & "The Hill of Dreams" on the other. This you shall certainly see. And I am, of course, looking forward as eagerly as yourself to the new assortment which Smith promises to shew us. I shall read with interest your chapter on the modern Des Esseintes[14] with the Smith room—certainly C A S deserves as much exploitation as any of the earlier bizarre painters glorified by Huysmans.

I learn with interest of the composite origin of your "Shadow of Nightmare", & congratulate you on the able joining of the constituent elements. Speaking of tales *about* weird tales—I have just perused an especially glowing example in a virtually forgotten early book (1895) of the now degenerated Robert W. Chambers.[15] It is "The King in Yellow", (have you read it?)—a series of vaguely connected short tales having as a background a horrible book—abhorred & suppressed—whose perusal brings fright, madness, & spectral tragedy. There is a bit of *fin de siècle* affectation about the thing, but it's great for all that. The best tale is "The Yellow Sign", which introduces a silent & terrible churchyard watchman with a face like a puffy grave-worm's, & a weirdly hieroglyphed talisman which the dreaded book proves to be the nameless Yellow Sign handed down from primordial Carcosa; (note that Chambers gets this name from Bierce)[16] whereof the volume treats, & some nightmare memory of which seems to lurk latent & ominous at the back of all men's minds. But I won't spoil the story by telling you more—except that the hellish watchman has a thick muttering voice which fills the head "like thick oily smoke from a fat-rendering vat or an odour of noisome decay", & that when he gets into a fight with a boy, one of his fingers comes off in the boy's hand! I've borrowed the book from W. Paul Cook & am soon to sub-lend it to Long. If you'd like to 'get in on' the circuit I'm sure Cook wouldn't mind. Only the first five tales in the volume, as printed, belong to the real "King in Yellow" sequence.

Proofs of my weird-tale history continue to come, & I fancy Cook may use quite a generous section to start off with. I shall be eager to hear your opinion when you see it—of course there's nothing erudite about it, & it leaves vast areas of fertile ground lamentably uncovered.

Well—I fear I've dragged this missive out to boresome length! I think I'll go to Boston tomorrow to soak up colour—though I may content myself with *intending* to go, as I so often do! With every good wish,

Most cordially & sincerely yrs—
H P Lovecraft

Notes

1. The feud is chronicled in *Starrett vs. Machen: A Record of Discovery and Correspondence*, ed. Michael Murphy (St. Louis, MO: Autolycus Press, 1977).

2. Two of the poems Dunsany may have read (probably submitted by Alice Hamlet) were HPL's tributes "To Edward John Moreton Drax Plunkett, 18th Baron Dunsany" (*Tryout*, November 1919) and "On Reading Lord Dunsany's *Book of Wonder*" (*Silver Clarion*, March 1920).

3. HPL's astronomy columns appeared in the *Pawtuxet Valley Gleaner* (1906–08?), the *Providence Tribune* (1906–08), the [Providence] *Evening News* (1914–18), and the *Asheville* [NC] *Gazette-News* (1915). HPL published no astronomy articles during the period 1909–13.

4. Joseph Brown House (1774), 50 South Main Street, built and owned by Joseph Brown (1733–1785).

5. The Providence Gas Company (1924) at 100 Weybosset Street.

6. On Market Square.

7. I.e., the Old State House (1762), 150 Benefit Street. Rhode Island declared its independence from England in the Providence Colony House two months before the Declaration of Independence.

8. The Providence National Bank Building (1929) at 100 Westminster Street.

9. The People's Savings Bank (1913) at 27 North Main Street. See HPL to Maurice W. Moe, 5 August [1923]: "Betwixt 1820 and 1840 the Parthenon facade (in debas'd form) reign'd supreme; its chief Providence examples being the arcade, (1826) the Historical Society Building, Manning-Hall in Brown University, and several other publick structures, all still standing. (This tradition has just been reviv'd by the new home of the People's Bank, which was founded in the neo-Hellenic age of the twenties.)" *Letters to Maurice W. Moe and Others* 126.

10. St. Paul's Cathedral (1675–1708), built by Sir Christopher Wren (1632–1723); Somerset House (1775), built by Sir William Chambers (1726–1796); the Mansion House (1739–59), built by George Dance the Elder (1700–1768); Adelphi Terrace (1768–72), built by the Adam brothers, John (1721–1792), Robert (1728–1792), and James (1732–1794); the Bank of England (1788), built by Sir John Soane (1753–1837).

11. The Industrial National Bank Building (1928) at 55 Kennedy Plaza, a 26-story Art Deco skyscraper. Robert Blake observes the beacon atop the building in "The Haunter of the Dark."

12. See *Fungi from Yuggoth* (1929–30), especially "Continuity."

13. Cf. the sonnet "Recapture" (1929), incorporated into *Fungi from Yuggoth* in 1936.

14. The main character in J.-K. Huysmans's *À Rebours* (1884; *Against the Grain*).

15. At the time of this letter, Chambers was known primarily for his best-selling romances. *The King in Yellow* was lent to HPL by W. Paul Cook.

16. Ambrose Bierce, "An Inhabitant of Carcosa" (*San Francisco News Letter,* 25 December 1886), first collected in *Tales of Soldiers and Civilians* (1891), but later transferred to the revised edition of *Can Such Things Be?* (1910).

[21] [DAW to HPL] [ALS]

1152 Portland Ave.,

St. Paul, Minn.

May 1, 1927

Dear Mr. Lovecraft:

I have been so busy the past week with exams and other work at the university that I have scarcely had time even to be home. Hence I have had to content myself with reading your long and welcome letter two or three times instead of replying. But I rebel on the eve of being slaughtered by impossible questions from omniscient professors, and prefer to write this letter rather than to study tedious eighteenth century novels of incredible length and miraculous dullness.

I am glad that I shall have the pleasure of seeing Mr. Dwyer's work, and anticipate both his and Mr. Smith's. I have a profound respect and admiration, as you know, for Smith, and for other artists of the bizarre to a lesser extent. One of my greatest regrets is my inability to accomplish anything in this form of expression, but I have, at least, all the truer appreciation of the artists who can. I know two or three promising artists at the university and Minneapolis Art School; one of them is the Miss Craigie I have mentioned and who used to draw pictures of odd effect of imaginative quality; another is Donald Cordray, who has done some extraordinary fantastic and grotesque batik work in colour, as well as pencil and pen-and-ink drawings suggestive of Beardsley; he is nineteen, and an unknown, but has more genius than anyone else I have met; still another is Elizabeth Robbins, who is at her best in woodcuts; she has exotic elements of beauty in her work, but hasn't a great deal of originality. I obtain a good deal of pleasure in watching them draw, as they often do to while away an idle moment; I suppose it's an unconscious gratification by sympathy of my own desire and inability to paint and draw.

If you ever have the time and dogged determination to type the story of Randolph Carter's visit to the moon, I'd be glad of the privilege of seeing it, as well as any others you manage to type. I can appreciate your reluctance; I am making minor corrections on several of my tales, and must retype them all if I intend to take them with me when I go east. Weird Tales has done me the favor of accepting "The Shadow of a Nightmare" in preference to "The Door to the Room". I can understand though not entirely appreciate the editorial discrimination in favor of a public. I intend to stop in Chicago on my trip and call on Mr. Wright for a few minutes' conversation, if his duties will permit. Did I tell you that Cook is reprinting "A Fragment of a Dream" in the "Recluse"? The three stories in the cosmic group were to have been used, but Wright has the first on which the other two are based, and as a result, he could not print them. I wish you the best of luck, or I should say, merit, in disposing of "The Colour out of Space". It will add to your reputation when it appears.

I read your philosophic view of life with the greatest interest. Your emphasis on history inclines me to believe that you must be a fatalist. I am far from being a materialist, at least in writing; my friends tell me that I present anomalies in life, but I have no inclination to carry them into my tales. Until I was sixteen, I was deeply interested in science, but only as a basis for letting my imagination run wild. Even in history, I prefer vague effects, and when I imagine an age or period, I think of all its beauty and the fable connected with it, rather than the material aspects that characterized it. I have an innate dislike of scientific analysis, of matter of fact knowledge in tables and statistics which go with science and materialism and realism; I doubt whether I shall ever cease to be romantic in my tales. It is for this reason that I rarely attend the theater; and once deliberately enraged a number of "gallery gods" at the university by telling them that the drama was not a form of art! My own views of life still shift and change; and the flux has been so great in the last two years that I probably shall not attain a fixed principle for years to come, if ever. I have been romanticist, hedonist, epicure, fatalist, pessimist, scientist, rationalist, materialist, aesthete—the list is long and varied; new ideas and impressions continually run through my mind, but I belong to one principle only for a few weeks or a few months. Sometimes I return, but there is inevitable change. I think that I shall end as you suggest—with the element of beauty predominating. But the problem often has little concern for me; one can answer any question with, "What will it matter a thousand years from now?"

I should be very glad to see Mr. Chambers' book if I may have the loan. My opinion of him needs considerable change if he is to receive any respect from me, but the book may accomplish this. I am returning separately the three "Weird Tales" with my gratitude for the opportunity of examining them. And I am also returning the poems of Loveman with my profound and lasting thanks, as well as apologies for keeping them long past any reasonable time. I wanted to copy the "Sphinx" and one or two others, but have not had the opportunity. I enjoyed them greatly, and have taken a liking to the "Sphinx" such as I have accorded few other poems or works in prose. I shall not be satisfied until I own a copy. I think, if I were Loveman, I could be content with this one achievement though I lived to be a hundred.

Well! This letter is all too short and brief, but I have those damnable examinations, and rather than preserve an unexplained silence, I have taken "time off", as it were, to write.

> Most sincerely,
> Donald Wandrei

[22] [HPL to DAW] [ALS]

May 6, 1927

My dear Mr. Wandrei:—

You have my sympathy regarding examinations, & I trust you will soon be through them with the high ratings which I am somehow sure you deserve. They seem terrible while they last—yet look at the way Time heals things, so that grown-ups are voluntarily returning to the ancient yoke, & eagerly submitting themselves to questionnaires whose vogue is likely to rival the crossword's! Speaking of ordeals, though—if base physical pain may be accorded a place beside the torture of Apollonian thought, pray regard me as a fellow in misery! Hell—this ————— ————'d TOOTH! It was treated yesterday, but is conducting the weirdest conceivable experiments in bizarre sensation & grotesque facial remodelling! Boy, the oil of cloves! And believe me, there will be an emergency call on the accomplished Lewis Howe Kalloch, D.D.S., as soon as day breaks & the conventional world resumes its insipid round. Hell! Phlegethon! Tartarus! Abaddon! Gatun, Roosevelt, & all other Cyclopean dams, unite to do the situation justice!

You will see Dwyer's work in the course of its round—Long to Smith, Smith to Wandrei. I share your envy of those who can express themselves in line & form, & did not cease to aspire toward some slight mediocrity in that field till my absolute incapacity became very plain to me. The fellow-students you cite are surely to be congratulated—& perhaps they may some day coöperate with you by giving visible form to many of your verbal images. Teamwork betwixt author & artist is a rare blessing—Dunsany & Sime being as ideal a case as I know of in the present age.

Typing . . . . hades, let's change the subject! I am surely glad that Wright has taken "The Shadow of a Nightmare", & hope he'll acquire the accepting habit in your case. Last week I had a letter from Edwin Baird, *former* editor of *Weird Tales*, who says he is founding a new magazine open to all types of fiction, including "that manuscript which others have rejected." I've unloaded a good half-dozen Wright rejects on him, & am awaiting results. It occurs to me that you might try him—I forget his address, but you can get it from his present magazine *Real Detective Tales*, which is to be found on any news stand. You might call on Baird as well as Wright when in Chicago—both seem very good fellows, as most editors probably are when pried away from their stultifying responsibilities.

Yes—Cook spoke of your change in the *Recluse* item. In any case you will appear to advantage, & I trust some success will accrue from the announced policy of getting the magazine before responsible critics & reviewers. I am curious as to the make-up of the first issue, & wonder how much of my weird tale history will be printed. I finished the last set of galley-proofs last night, & hope I shan't have to wade through page-proofs—although of course I'd rather do that than have the text ruined by misprints. I can't forget that "Bow pale-che*c*ked to men's blas*h*phemies" in Loveman's "Hermaphrodite" after *five* careful proofreadings!

As to Chambers' early work—well, look at the enclosed rhapsody just evoked from my aesthetic young friend & adopted grandson Frank Belknap Long, Jun.! Yes—Bobby W. *has* changed! Another earlyish book of his—"In Search of the Unknown" (1904)—has faint residual echoes of the pristine strain despite the vitiation of a growing flippancy. But "The King in Yellow" is the book to read—or rather, the first five stories in it. God! You will never sleep again! *Have you found the Yellow Sign?* . . . . . . Grrrrh . . . . but wait till you see it! I am asking Cook to empower Long to sub-lend it to you as soon as possible—you to return it to Cook. You'll have a copy of Loveman's "Sphinx" for keeps when Cook issues it in book form. He is getting Smith to do some uncanny black & white drawings for it, & the result ought to be a truly notable synthesis.[1] Smith has already based some coloured abnormalities (now in Loveman's collection) on the earlier parts of it, which were written five or six years ago.

As for science & philosophy—I suppose I don't enjoy truth or research for its own sake, (Gawd knows I hate all diligent application, & would die rather than devote my life to the accurate observation & classification of arachnidae, or the study of variation amongst thallophytes!) but I do like the vistas opened up by certain lines of investigation & discovery. Of course I am a fatalist—who isn't? Can you imagine any cause of anything except the sum total of all antecedent & circumjacent things, which go back in turn along the path of limitless & unalterable cycles of linked energy? But we often have the illusion of freedom & cosmic adventure—& after all, nothing is more important than illusion. As to history—I surely don't visualise all events as mere matters of correct detail. I, too, prefer vague effects—but I want to know the properties in an ingrained, unconscious way, so that my picture may not contain grave flaws later to be exposed with shattering effect. As to the art element in drama—I'd hardly deny it *in toto*. Dialogue has genuinely aesthetic possibilities, & there are many impressions which can best be captured by its aid. I would not say that Shakespeare toiled in vain. My views of life are fairly constant, for they seem to me to be based on the only tangible evidence available. There is no value or purpose in anything—but since we need the illusion of these things we had better pretend to stick to the artificial system which heredity has foisted on us. That is all that can hold us strongly enough to give life the fixed points of reference needed to invest events & things with the semblance of direction & meaning. The enclosed (a private letter which the recipient insisted on my putting into impersonal form for printing—Gawd knows I'm no voluntary pamphleteer!)[2] gives my general view of the cosmos about as succinctly as anything can.

Hoping your teeth feel better than mine—

     Yr obt Servt

      H P L

Notes

1. Cook's publication of *The Sphinx* did not contain any drawings by CAS, but the drawings are still extant.
2. *The Materialist Today,* extracted from a letter to Walter J. Coates, the publisher.

[23] [DAW to HPL]

          [Postmarked St. Paul, Minn.,
             10 May 1927]

[Envelope only.]

[24] [DAW to HPL] [ALS]

1152 Portland Ave.,

St. Paul, Minn.

May 14, 1927

Dear Mr. Lovecraft:

I demand an accounting at sundown with pistol or rapier as you choose. You have the colossal gall to speak of toothache when for three months I have been living in a kind of blissfully idiotic coma trying to persuade myself that my dentist never did tell me I had three or four cavities on the most painful teeth which need filling. I rationalize the situation—I almost forget the teeth—lo and behold, Mr. H. P. Lovecraft lifts the exquisite pain out of his tales and stuffs it down my throat in reality! I ask you, is that the treatment of a gentleman? At thirty paces, zounds, and have at you!

If by any chance I should do so unnatural a thing as laugh when I am East, you would probably be dazzled by the sunlight reflected from the fillings I *may* have by then.

Your leaflet interested me, and that is saying a great deal because I have shied away from philosophy for lo, these many years. What struck me most was the one phrase "from nothing back to nothing". This has become my basic philosophy, the one to which I invariably return after long or short digressions as romanticist, epicure, etc.; for several years, I have been expressing this as "from nowhere into nothingness", and have used it as the basis for all my judgments, whether of art, literature, or life. I once said that every work of art that Man has produced began nowhere and ended nowhere. The statement may sound ridiculous—but think of all works of art you know, and see how many exceptions, in the ultimate, you are able to find. I am often accused of getting nowhere in my tales. What do I care? It is impossible really to "get anywhere"; and to proceed from Nowhere into Nothingness and to proceed beautifully leaving behind something which exists in itself and for itself is to me the summation, the highest form of Art. I have never concerned myself greatly with philosophy. Most of my life has been spent in splendid isolation, wherein I have taken my peculiar pleasure without paying much attention to the dictates or existence of human beings. I regard life as an unnecessary evil. We leave, as we enter, in mystery. The world knew nothing of us before we were. It proceeds without us while we are here. It forgets us when we are gone. "From Nowhere into Nothingness"—and what is the life of Man in the final judgment of Eternity? The present, which is the consequence of the past and the antecedent of the future, is after all the only time existing.—I shall yet end up as a materialist, I fear, with, "Eat, drink, and be merry for tomorrow we die." But my ideas change. In a week, a month, it may be, "There is no time save Eternity". I think I am guilty of playing with ideas sometimes. In my causeless and fruitless search for a meaning behind this visible phantasmagoria, I have found only a multiple meaninglessness.

And so, I toy with this or that conception, till I am suddenly struck by its frailty, whereupon I adopt a new philosophy or precept as readily as a chameleon a new color. In the long run, if anyone should ever have interest enough to analyse the ideas or statements in my writings he would in all likelihood discover flat and amazing contradictions in the work of different periods. There may be consistency of a sort; I don't know; but I am certain that there are queer antitheses. Until the last year or two, I had a comparatively fixed conception which lay behind all my tastes; but a growing chaos which may end in a lack of any definite theory is likely to be the most important flaw in my future work. That is, unless I make a rule of inconsistency. But again I ask, Of what importance will my mental perturbation be a thousand years from now?

Πρὸς Θεων![1] The more I think, the less I know. The result of my long meditations is usually that I do what I wish when I wish, but it is quite as easy to do so without going through a labyrinthine process of thought.

I finally returned your *Weird Tales* and the Loveman items, all of which I hope you have safely received by now. I offer again my apologies for keeping them an unconscionable length of time, and thank you most heartily for the extended loan. A thousand thanks also for the Baird tip and suggestion of calling on him. I have been revising some of my more imperfect tales, and retyping them, so that I shan't be able to submit anything for a few weeks. I'll call on him when I am in Chicago, however, especially if I have anything available for consideration by then. This reminds me, that some relatives of the student with whom I was going to ride East are coming for his graduation and will return with him. I am going alone then, and I intend to make the trip a lark and general escape from any sort of regulation. I'll leave after school closes for the summer, and "bum" my way to Chicago and thence eastward, by whatever rides I pick up. There will be much more zest and pleasure in this carefree method of sauntering across the countryside than I would get from the train or a straight auto trip from here to New York without stop. Besides, it will save me whatever the fare is—eighty or ninety dollars, I think. For once, thank God I'm young, unencumbered, and unbound by restraint. I don't need to keep any sort of pretense, and I can travel as I wish. I'll have to dispense with various conveniences since I won't have any too much money, but what do I care? I shall be absolute master of myself as far as financial limitations permit, and I shall gain a wealth of new impressions and new vistas. I intend to make for Providence first, however, and if it is possible, to spend a day or two there before descending on New York and becoming engulfed in its mysteries.

Has Loveman his Smith pictures in New York? If he has, he is likely to be worn to a shadow by me when I finally reach the city of blasphemies. I have seen just enough of the poet-artist's work to give me a burning desire to see everything else he has done. Smith is one of the most magnificent men of the century. Next year, I intend to reverse my direction and go to California, if I can manage, and see what he is like personally. I wish there were a publisher of sufficient intelligence, and appreciation, and financial backing, to issue a portfolio of his paintings. One of my regrets is that I was not blessed with enough hard metal to back Smith to the limit myself.

What did Starrett say about your tales? This reminds me for no particular reason that I am becoming highly interested in "The King in Yellow" especially after his diabolical letter.

As ever,
Donald Wandrei

P.S. My remark about drama was partly the result of a three-hour discussion I came in for from a remarkably intelligent club of students, to which I belong, at the U., the whole thing arising out of the "Fragment" in the *Quarterly*. I was thinking of actual performances, which bore me, since the companies are usually second or third-rate road casts when they reach the Twin Cities, and the plays are seldom the best. I enjoy many plays as literature. But, as far as I'm concerned, the drama does not interest me greatly because it so seldom does or can depict the things, especially the imaginative, which are my particular necessity and desire. Beddoes' "Death's Jest Book" is my favorite.

Notes

1. "By the gods!"

[25] [HPL to DAW] [ALS]

10 Barnes St.,
Providence, R.I.,
May 19, 1927.

My dear Mr Wandrei:—

Consider me as properly riddled with pistol balls or rapier thrusts for the innocently tactless allusion which I made—little knowing how tender a subject I was introducing! But since the harm is done, let me mend matters as best I may by assuring you that your coming ordeal is not at all likely to prove as formidable as you expect. It was so with me—I, too, had practiced long neglect despite many a subtle warning; but lo! when at last the sudden eruption of one molar Vesuvius forced me into the long-deferred dental siege, I found that there was almost a positive relief in having the decision made for me! The second treatment hit the spot & brought relief—& on the strength of this relief the whole epic of the other teeth has lost its aura of expectant dread. I have now had five sessions & am scheduled for another next Tuesday, yet am far more tranquil of soul than when the whole question formed a vague reef on the horizon ahead. Yes—I advise you to have the thing settled once & for all, & believe you will feel amply repaid by the resultant sense of completeness & liberation. And if you don't want to increase the albedo of your smile so extensively—take a tip from the effete East & have the filling done in a permanent *cement* as we always do here nowadays!

Rapidly ascending to cosmic matters—I am glad my printed letter on recurrent nothingness proved of interest to you, & am not surprised to learn that it represents an attitude you have occasionally shared. I can see its influence in much of your writing—as you can doubtless see it in mine; although most of my tales are so fragmentary in scope, & so bound up with favourite imaginative attitudes, (often diametrically opposed to my *intellectual* opinions) that I don't fancy they form a very good index to what I really think about infinity & eternity. Perhaps the sole reflection of my cynicism in my tales is my refusal to embody the conception of an upwardly progressing universe in shaping incidents & denouements. I do not cultivate mawkish sympathies for "right" against "wrong", or fancy that the forces of spirit have any great preferences in a similar direction; in this respect forming the exact antithesis of the somewhat sanctimonious Algernon Blackwood. I am likewise similar to yourself in not having my events move very definitely from point to point. Since my conception of the universe is one of cyclic flux, with no fixed progression in any one direction, it follows that my writings must lack all symbolisation of definite forward movement—being rather small sections of the general aimlessness & futility which I envisage around me. To me all notions of any meaning or purpose in the cosmos seem unutterably puerile; not only because such things would presuppose an inconceivable beginning & end, but because they are not sustained by even the slightest scrap of true evidence. I am not formally trained in philosophy, & have a very well-defined suspicion that many purely philosophic processes overstep themselves & their natural province in making large metaphysical claims unverifiable by science. Ideas have a dangerous tendency to elaborate themselves beyond all sound foundations, so that I have a much greater respect for the firmly grounded theories of a true observer & rigid reasoner like Haeckel,[1] than for the airier flights of mystics & idealists who use the unstable & illusion-ridden human emotions as bases for their beliefs. In nearly every case the doctrine of an idealist may be found faulty through its essential inclusion of some purely gratuitous assumption—such as the evolutionary trend (ignoring the de-volutionary) of our particular part of space, the existence of such abstract qualities as "right", "justice", &c, or the significance of intuition as opposed to reason. I consider all of these things absurd, derived as they clearly are from the natural mistakes of perspective incurred by a race confronting the unknown & slowly augmenting its pitiful modicum of knowledge. These beliefs are such natural consequences of man's terrestrial experience, that we might almost deduce them through pure biology & anthropology even if all traces of them were long extinct. And in the light of this obvious classification as inevitable delusive by-products of primitive thought, it seems to me wearily infantile to continue attaching anything more than a traditional or decorative significance to them. As a matter of fact, I am sceptical of almost everything which cannot be pretty well verified. I don't think we shall ever know much about the real cosmos, & I don't think it would do us much good if we did. That is why a fantastic cosmos of the imagination seems to me just as significant as any other. What infinity & eternity really are, it is quite impossible to guess from our small fragment. There is ground for a conjecture—& no more—that *pattern, rhythm, & regularity* play some part in the universal organisation, since we see these things repeated without apparent diminution in every type of quantitative organisation which we are able to observe; (i.e. proton-electron systems, solar systems, galactic systems, &c) but even this is pure theory, since we have no evidence of any kind as to the relation of this part of space & its laws to the whole or to any other part. The principle of *life* appears to be a very well-marked form of energy—as definite as heat or light—hence although we see it only on our globe, we may reasonably expect it to exist in such other places as possess somewhat similar conditions. But this applies only to the kind of space we know. Other parts may have other types of organisation, equally complex or perhaps more so, & differing widely from anything which we might recognise as life. I have often wished that I had the literary power to call up visions of some vast & remote realm of entity *beyond the universes of matter & energy;* where vivid interplays of unknown & inconceivable influences give vast & fabulous activity to dimensional areas that are not shapes, & to nuclei of complex rearrangement that are not minds. Like yours, my life has on the whole been a very isolated one, & I regard human beings only as incidents of landscape or architecture, or points of reference in the conception of symmetrical & interesting events. They are necessary to background & colouring except in pictures of the most difficult & cosmic sort, for it is easy to see that most of our images are in some way connected with them—with their heritage, attributes, & activities, or with our own undeniably human powers of perception & imagination. Thus my contempt for the species is tempered by a distinct recognition of its aesthetic importance, & by a definite conviction that its continuous stream of past history is all which has created for us our minds in their present form. Nothing but our organic heredity could possibly have moulded our reactions to the universe around us, so that everything we feel as a value, standard, fact, beauty, or source of interest is the result of our belonging not only to the primate genus of mammals & the human species of that genus, but to our particular race, culture, nationality, & social & family environment. Every man's world is a different world, & the events therein possess interest, pleasure, & significance only as correlated with the individual, family, social, national, cultural, & racial past of that man. There is no such thing as *freedom;* for the moment we shake off the relationships & allegiances which we have regarded as fetters, we lose all the contrasts & bearings which give pleasure & meaning to anything which we may do—thus floundering dully & aimlessly in a void where neither interest, satisfaction, direction, nor intelligibility can exist. Thus while recognising only pleasure as a logical end of life, I am an extreme conservative in maintaining that no real pleasure (as experienced in lasting form by an intelligent, sensitive, & cultivated man) can be obtained except through conformity to the traditional heritage of one's especial group. Secession destroys all meaning—or all of the emotional pattern which we call meaning—& leads to a listlessness, conflict, & chaos wherein grey futility & fruitless regret overbalance all the fancied rewards of independence & individualism. The rational Epicurean will always preserve a symmetrical relation to the fabric out of which he springs—not, of course, confining his thought, fancy, & expression to the commonplace; but making sensible concessions to his inherited emotions & childhood impressions in order to preserve his life as a unity & to back up his cerebral adventures with the stimulus & animating force of everything which Nature & experience have packed into his brain & cell-matter. In practice, I think that the effect of liberation is best secured through adventures of the pure intellect & the imagination. The basic emotions must stay more closely at home—or must at least derive their prime significance from old & tested memories—while one's actual deeds or conduct will always have a more satisfying artistic value when following out as faithfully as possible the hereditary ideals of the individual's particular group. When the group-ideals are essentially conflicting, as in those of our own civilisation, one's own natural feeling of preference between the opposed standards must determine one's choice. For example—I think most of our Christian sentiment of meekness & humility is altogether assumed, since it is an Oriental importation from a weak & decadent subject-people. Underneath all this we are proud & warlike freemen of the North—pagan sons of Alfadur, Woden, & Thor—& our natural ethic is the knight's haughty honour rather than the saint's cur-like turning of the other cheek. What we have gained from Christianity is a certain *colour* or aura surrounding one set of our natural impulses—a mediaeval, Gothic growth which has raised certain acts of gentleness among individuals to the level of accepted good manners. That much of our heritage is real & valid—but in mapping out a code we must not be deluded by legacies of mere words as distinguished from those legacies of real feeling which our biological as well as our outwardly cultural past sustains. We must disentangle the threads of Northern blood, acquired Graeco-Roman feeling, & imported & diluted Eastern mysticism which unite to form the existing Anglo-Saxon civilisation; &, correlating all these things with our own individual circumstances, try to decide what each of us is, & what he can best afford to do.

The *Weird Tales* & Loveman material arrived in safety, & there was no need for you to worry about the duration of the loan. I trust that when in Chicago you will personally strengthen your entree into the professional magazine world, & that Baird will prove as receptive toward your work as Wright is beginning to prove. He has just accepted two stories of Long's which

Wright previously rejected, but has not so far made any report on the six I sent him. Which reminds me that Robert Simpson of the *Mystery Magazine* (which I've never read, but about which a friend told me) has just rejected my "Call of Cthulhu".[2]

Your projected Eastern trip certainly has all the tang of spacious horizons, incredible adventures, & the mystery of unknown realms beyond the hills ahead! I certainly hope it can materialise as you wish, & without sufficient hardships to destroy its carefree charm. I would have enjoyed such things in youth, perhaps, but in those days was a semi-invalid—so that between the years of 1901 & 1920 I never spent a night except under my own roof. And now that health is slowly appearing, I am a bit middle-aged & set in habits for such irresponsible roving. I like the theory enormously—to knock about gloriously in a flannel shirt under mystical summer suns through ancient lands of wonder—but one has a hard time getting used to such things when one's 37th birthday is scheduled for the next 20th of August! I like visits to ancient places under moderately civilised conditions—as when I "did" archaic Philadelphia, stopping at the Y.M.C.A. nights. But I may come to haystacks yet—for Thoreau & I are products of the same New-England! Walking is an art in which my physique has let me indulge only during the last three years, but since 1924 I have been making more & more of a specialty of it. I love the brooding, cryptical hills north of Providence, where archaic vestiges linger & the voice of primal earth whispers darkly in the rocks. And as for beauty—nothing can surpass, in my limited experience, the awesome & immemorial majesty of the Wissahickon gorge or valley stretching northwest of Philadelphia, whose ancient & precipitous woodland wonders I explored to a full day's extent last September.

I certainly hope to see you here during your peregrinations, & am sure I can show you enough charm & antiquarian colour to keep your imagination busy for an indefinite time. Stopping accomodations will be easy to adjust—for there will be a good choice of quarters in this very house where we have rooms, a sedate, quiet place on the exact borderline betwixt the colonial hill & the Victorian regions over the crest. Providence is farther from you than N.Y. so far as formal bee-line transportation is concerned, but it is really on a line much north of the metropolis, so that your logical course would be to traverse (after leaving the Albany zone) the beautiful Berkshire country of Western Massachusetts; gradually working down toward Providence through Springfield or Worcester. It might be pleasant for you to include Athol, Mass. in your route, stopping to see that sterling patron of weird literature, W. Paul Cook. You can best envisage the situation through maps, & I trust that one of your few travelling encumbrances will be a good pocket atlas. I don't envy you your journey's end—New York—for I'm afraid you won't find that garish babel of the commonplace very replete with engulfing mysteries! If I were mapping out a route, I'd make for the Massachusetts seacoast, where some of the most myth-haunted & glamorous towns in America rear their ancient spires & gambrel roofs to the piercingly blue New England sky—a sky as fresh & vivid as that of Italy. Anyhow, you *MUST* see Newport. That will give you some idea of the earliest type of American colonial town even if you don't get up to the Mass. coast. I have always sensed a strong kinship between Newport & Salem—both representing the archaism of about the 1720 period whereas Providence represents that of 1760 or 1770 or 1780. And you ought certainly to see Boston, which is probably the most really civilised town in the United States. Its decay has been far less loathsome than that of New York, & when you see the quiet & spacious elegance of Commonwealth Ave. you will see something of the elder reposeful beauty which N.Y. has lost. Also, you will see a metropolis with a really traditional skyline of spires, domes, & slanting roofs—the nearest thing to London which America can produce. Of all *large* cities, I most admire Boston & Philadelphia. It's a toss-up which is the more interesting, but Boston undoubtedly has the present lead in mellow beauty. (Philadelphia, however, will be a dangerous rival when the splendid new classic museum & library get a little subdued by weathering, & the vegetation along the new parkway gets a little richer & fuller.) Boston is balanced & homogeneous—it is a richly cultivated old community with a dominant sense of taste & fitness. It knows beauty & it knows itself, & has not lost the elder secret of combining the two. Cambridge—the suburb containing Harvard College—is one of the loveliest & drowsiest & best-bred towns I have ever seen; shady & rambling & dream-filled & beautiful, with mossy brick sidewalks & glamorous ivied college buildings (dating from 1720 onward) & a type of hip-roofed colonial house peculiar to the region. Beyond it are sleepy Lexington & historic Concord—green, leafy towns of exquisite charm. Yes— on the whole anyone would be almost criminally foolish to make an eastern trip without seeing the Boston zone. If you can go, I can probably arrange to go along also as an antiquarian guide. After all this you can't help hating the dirt & drabness & vulgar stridor of New York—where even richness & elegance are dragged down by incongruity, tawdriness, & bad taste. In all the place there is just one really beautiful thing—the incomparable fairy *skyline* as glimpsed from the proper angle. The way to like N.Y. is to approach just near enough to drink this in, & then depart for ever without entering a muddle of prosaic slumness which belies every implication of wonder & mystery that the far-spied clustered pinnacles hold forth.

Loveman, I regret to say, has *not* his Smith collection in N.Y.—that galaxy of sinister marvels being securely stowed in his home in Cleveland, where his room is almost a museum of rare books, literary reliques, & ancient, curious, & exotic objets d'art. But you must see these things sometime & somehow! Smith is undoubtedly a great & unique figure inhabiting a strange interstellar zone whose very existence is unknown to most, & I certainly wish his wider celebrity could be effected. However—no author in the fantastic field, no matter how superlative in genius, could ever be a generally accepted pillar of letters. There simply aren't enough human beings of weird leanings alive to form an appreciative public of fame-producing size. About the drama—I see your point of view. Of course all commercial drama is wholly beneath notice, & I have been bored with it for the last decade, although I was an inveterate theatregoer in my youth. I don't think I especially care for the drama as a literary form—I am mostly for prose narration.

    With all good wishes, & hoping to see you this summer,
           Sincerely yrs
           H P Lovecraft

P.S. Not a word from Starrett about my tales.

P.P.S. Long has sent you "The King in Yellow" together with one or two other early Chambers books. I enclose his rhapsodic comment on a fresh horror which he is about to sub-lend me.

Notes

1. Ernst Haeckel (1834–1919), a highly noted biologist, zoologist, and anthropologist, author of *The Riddle of the Universe* (1899; English translation 1900).
2. In fact, it was Robert D. Sampson (1927–1992) of the short-lived pulp magazine *Mystery Stories* who rejected "The Call of Cthulhu."

[26]   [DAW to HPL] [ALS]

                       1152 Portland Ave.,
                         St. Paul, Minn.
                           May 21, 1927
Dear Mr. Lovecraft:
             I am a procrastinator. My teeth and my correspondence both languished the past week. I am taking care of the second now, but I fear that the first is in for some more languishing.

    I received "The King in Yellow" and "In Search of the Unknown" from Long. The first in particular with the five stories built around "The King in Yellow" is something that I can scarcely accredit to Chambers. I sat up reading it till late at night, or rather, early in the morning, when I received it. The suggestion—the implication—the artistry of the tales—oh, they are splendid in their restraint! The descriptions of Carcosa are sufficient to open out vast and haunted realms; there are some beautiful passages in the group, and yet, they are all the more powerful that they are meager. The poem given in the first tale and the passage of the play quoted at the beginning of the second are monstrous in their implication. Chambers' book is almost as poisonous as the unobtainable "King in Yellow" he imagined; he is more artistic and effective because he concealed or half-concealed where others would have elaborated. I can appreciate Long's enthusiasm, and share it. I read his rhapsody on "The Purple Cloud" with great interest. "The King in Yellow" lived up to its promise. If "The Purple Cloud" lives up to his enthusiasm equally, I shall be ready, I think, to let Long select books for me to read.

You must have wandered through inner realms frequently during your life. Like Smith, you have dived into your being deeper and deeper and drawn out regions illimitable and things unknown; and you have access to vast empires never defiled by human step, you pass along lethal shores of ancient seas and ruinous lands, you unveil sightless, soundless kingdoms for ever lost. When you return, you suggest the vision in a tale. I think that you will yet write the story of that "vast and remote realm of entity beyond the universes of matter and energy." It is a strange, wild conception; the attempt to write it will be a huge undertaking, but the result will be a tale of horror such as few can even guess.

I shall be on my way in three weeks according to my present plans. School closes Saturday, June 11, and I want to start at least by the following Friday. I shall probably pursue the northern course you suggest, and pass through Athol. But the route will depend in part on whatever "rides" I pick up, and I may of necessity be compelled to take the more direct route to New York. I am glad that I shall be so close to you when in Providence; and I most certainly will include Boston unless some cataclysm prevents. I have always enjoyed walking. I am far from being an "athlete" (I detest these animated bunches of muscle) but I have had good health, and anticipate finding a great deal of pleasure in my careless sauntering. As closely as I can reason, I shall be in New York only two or three weeks; this will not be long enough to impress me violently, but I do not wish to spend too much time in cities this summer.

I have another interesting bit of information to tell. I was to have been editor of the "Quarterly" next year; but the head of our English department disapproves of the nature of my work so much, and was so enraged by an editorial I wrote for the "Minnesota Daily", that he has turned thumbs down, and is cashiering the whole present and more or less rebellious board for next year. Will you excuse me while I go out in the back yard and weep crocodile tears?

(N.B. I am sorry, but just as I was ready, I thought of the editorial and the prof., and an unfortunate snicker spoiled my intention. Alas! Alas!—I inclose the editorial in question.)

I am returning "Haunted Homes" with my heartiest thanks for its loan. The ghosts in it are harmless for the most part, and, I believe, belong to the milder tastes of an older generation. This reminds me, I bought Dunsany's "The Charwoman's Shadow" and had it stolen the next day when I took it [to] the U. to lend it to a friend. The university is a charming place—from a distance.

Most sincerely,
Donald Wandrei

P.S. If Long is visiting you on July 15, I may run into him in Providence. That is about the time I should be there, unless I do not stop in Chicago. In that case, I may reach Providence a week or two earlier.

D W.

[Note appended by HPL:] how about it, young man? Get in touch with Wandrei on the subject

[27]   [HPL to DAW] [ALS]

10 Barnes St.,
Providence, R.I.,
June 2, 1927

My dear Mr. Wandrei:—

Well—be it on (or in) your own head if those teeth start trying to repay your neglect! Don't say you didn't have an old man's warning! My bill came from the dentist yesterday—but we won't talk about that. I'd hate to introduce any new discouraging element!

I knew you'd enjoy "The King in Yellow", & agree profoundly concerning its masterly restraint. Nothing can excel those vague, terrible *approaches* to a horror which the author dares not mention . . . . but just fancy such a tale in the hands of Farnsworth Wright's eager circle of readers! They would flood "The Eyrie" with protests! With Cook I agree that it's an eternal pity for Chambers ever to have been sidetracked from his early tendency.

"The Purple Cloud" is splendid—the first half being perhaps the most magnificent piece of connected fear, suspense, & cosmic corruption which I have ever seen. It lets down toward the end—but one can pardon anything for the sake of what has gone before. I shall tell Belknap to lend it to you when I send it back, unless your trip makes that date inapt. Possibly he had better keep it (it belongs to Cook) until you call in person at 823 West End Ave.

No—I'm afraid I'm not quite equal to the extra-cosmic novel which I'd so greatly like to see written. I know my own limitations, & the sort of book I want to read is far vaster in scope & depth than any sort which I could write! You may do it yourself some day, & if you do, I hope you will have C A S illustrate it. That would be a combination beyond all precedent & competition!

Your trip, I feel sure, will prove a most enviable adventure; & I am eager for that part of it which I can witness at first-hand. I shall expect postals from along the route telling of your progress, & hope that you can find my modest abode without difficulty when you reach this ancient & glamorous town. Incidentally, I had better furnish all the auxiliary data I can here & now—for your careful preservation or assiduous memorisation.

My telephone number is *DEXTER 9617*. Don't forget this, for you can't find it in the book; the instrument being in the name of Miss Reynolds,[1] in whose sedate Victorian retreat my aunt & I maintain our modest & limited households. To reach the house from the downtown district of Providence, where you will presumably land, heed the following simple directions; or you can telephone me, & I'll meet you downtown at some prominent point & pilot you safely.

(1) Look about you, & note the precipitous green hill with its white Georgian steeple & great church dome rising on the east.

(2) Ascend this hill by *College* or *Waterman Street*—to which anyone will guide you—turning to your left along *Prospect Street* when you attain the utmost summit.

(3) Walk northward along Prospect St., past the great Christian Science Church whose vast copper dome crowns the city's skyline. Keep on till you see, on a corner at your right, the trim white gable & picket-fence of a little old New England farmhouse; caught a century ago by the spreading town, but miraculously saved in pristine glory instead of perishing like most of its kind. It is now inhabited by an artist who appreciates its almost priceless quaintness. This is the corner of Barnes Street, down which you must turn—to your right. As you leave Prospect, you pass regretfully from the Georgian to the Victorian part of the town.

(4) 10 Barnes St. is the fourth house from Prospect, not counting the farm—& on the same side of the street (north) as the latter. It is a nondescript brown wooden house of the 1880 period—in mercy I will say no more, though it doubtless represented the very last word in architectural aesthetics to its builder . . . . . whose low-crowned derby, side-whiskers & moustache, high-cut vest & Ascot tie, low standing collar, short coat-lapels, bell-bottomed checked trousers, &c. &c. I can see painfully in my mind's eye. It is significant that a certain parallelism exists in cycles of architecture & costume. Well—after swallowing your artistic scruples, ring the bell & ask for me. I'll try to make you forget the exterior, although my shadowy & ancestrally-furnished den has a dreary number of Victorian pieces in its musty ensemble.

I certainly hope that your visit can be made to coincide with Belknap's, & shall urge him to get in touch with you at once on the subject. He is coming with his father & mother in their car, & at present expects to make July 15 the central date of the sojourn. Try to allow as much time here as you can, for I know your imagination (unused as you are to the physical sight of old houses & centuried streets) will find a gorgeous revelling-ground in the scenes I can show you—not only in Providence, but in Newport, Boston, Salem, & so on. We could go to Boston by 'bus, & stop over a night or two at the Y M C A if your antiquarian interest warrants it. Here's wishing you luck on the major hike Eastward—& I certainly hope you can work in Athol.

Commiserations on your editorial ill-fortune! I shall have a suitable set of tear-vases ready for your reception. Your editorial note arouses a very sympathetic response from me, since Pegāna did not bless my soul with a sophisticated musical taste. Ah, me—with what Gothick stupidity did I sit last

February with my aunt, whilst the Boston Symphony Orchestra vied valiantly with the riveters on the new Industrial Trust Co. Building—noon whistles & all—in the modernistic presentation of a somewhat extended symphony by one Igor Stravinsky![2]

Tough luck about "The Charwoman's Shadow"! I haven't read it yet, although I keep meaning to. No haste about "Haunted Houses"—tame stuff for a Machen addict, though there is a deep, underlying horror about the secret of *Glamis Castle*. Have you seen Sax Rohmer's use of this legend in "Brood of the Witch Queen"?[3]

Well—I must cease. I am utterly swamped & stifled with revisory work—although I'm going to break free of my desk to the extent of taking some of the stuff (in its pre-typing stage) out in the open this afternoon.

All best wishes—

Sincerely yrs—
H P Lovecraft

P.S. Since, after mastering the subjoined clue to the Providential labyrinth, you may wish some visual idea of the minotaur you will find at the centre, I'm enclosing the most flattering snap-shot of that animal which I can find at the moment. I'd appreciate a reciprocal kodak glimpse of yourself if you have any extra prints to spare at any time.

Notes

1. Florence F. Reynolds, HPL's landlady at 10 Barnes St.
2. The Boston Symphony Orchestra performed a program of Russian music in Boston on 8 February 1927 conducted by Serge Koussevitzky, consisting of Mussorgsky's prelude to the opera "Khovantchina"; Rimsky-Korsakoff's "Sadko"; Prokofieff's suite (op. 33) from the opera "The Love for Three Oranges"; Stravinsky's "Fire-Bird" suite (three movements); and Tchaikovsky's 4th Symphony in F minor (1st movement).
3. HPL had read the book in August 1926.

[28]   [DAW to HPL] [ANS]

[Postmarked St. Paul, Minn.,
13 June 1927]

Dear Mr. Lovecraft:

I meant to write last week but had an attack of acute conjunctivitis—alias "pink eye"—and now have finished final exams. Thank God! Just now I am chasing around town cleaning up various little matters attendant on my departure and have dropped in the P.O. I have mailed your book, which I had intended to send two weeks ago. Many thanks for the "snap" and the close directions. I shall memorize them and take the letter with me as well. I like the "snap", I haven't any of myself, but had some taken a few days ago which ought to be developed now. I will send one as soon as I receive them, together with a letter in a day or two. There will not be time to send "The Purple Cloud", but I shall most certainly read it when I reach the east. I hope I make connections with Long in Providence, though I can't tell definitely since I am not certain when I shall reach my goal. I have an excellent road map, and of the two good routes, my choice will partly depend on the route of the motorists who may—I hope—have mercy on me occasionally. I am going to include both Dwyer and Cook in my rambles before I leave the east, that is, if I come back. I am not particularly desirous of returning for many, many moons, but may need to. Boston interests me deeply, and I intend to include it. So you know the Y's! I am not acquainted with them, but will use them as stopping places quite often, I believe, on my trip, especially in the large cities like Chicago. Something inside me tells me I'll get more pleasure out of my roving than I have from anything else in a long, long time. I plan to leave Friday, but will write before them.

    Hasta mañana,
    Donald W.

[29] [DAW to HPL] [ALS]

          1152 Portland Ave.,
           St. Paul, Minn.
            June 17, 1927

Dear Mr. Lovecraft:

    I leave tomorrow for Chicago, and can not tell you how glad I am to be gone, on this the eve of my departure. I sent a hasty postcard a few days ago, but am doubtful whether this letter will be less hasty.

    Smith sent me your monograph, which I am herewith returning. It is a splendid piece of work. You have touched only the high spots as you intended, but you have done it and done it well. Yours is by far the best written review of the field that I have yet seen, and is infinitely superior to Birkhead and Scarborough, and even Killen. Yours is a personal as well as critical appreciation, and you have gained vastly thereby for you have not only given the data but made them vivid and supremely interesting. Your interpretations of Poe and Machen are the best single parts of the essay, and are brilliant examples of sane criticism, thorough understanding, and literary appreciation. You are most effective in Blackwood and Dunsany next, I should say. I enjoyed the reading of your survey as I seldom enjoy criticisms or literary reviews; you deserve the highest compliments for having done so excellent a monograph. I really have no unfavourable criticisms to make, save in a couple of minor points. One is that I think Verne should have brief mention. He really does not belong in the essay but has had vast influence. Another, but less tangible point, is one of influence. I believe that engravings and woodcuts had a great deal to do with the growth of Gothic literature, though I have never seen this point made. Many mediaeval books had horrible pictures, and witchcraft books in particular often had gruesome or fantastic pictures of spectres, ghouls, torture, and Satanic invocations of the witches' sabbath. Some of these books were enormously popular. "The Shepherd's Calendar"[1] ran through dozens of editions, and it had a great many Gothic woodcuts. The series of "The Dance of Death" or "Danse Macabre" was of great popularity from its first appearance in France and later in England. I don't know why this has never been pointed out as an influence. I may be exaggerating its importance, but I think it had a great deal of influence in preparing the popular mind and in suggesting ideas perhaps to some of the earlier Gothic writer and romanticists. The difficulty, of course, is to prove with incontrovertible facts that this was a valid influence. However, these are very minor objections indeed. I only hope that my attempt will be as good as yours; it can not possibly be better.

I have also received the Dwyer drawings. I was highly pleased at the opportunity of seeing them, and have carefully examined the group. I do not care for the pigeons or the boy ready to dive, but I think the other fantastic heads are marvellous. Dwyer has done fine work and has had extraordinary success in crayon, which is a very difficult medium. I sent him some charcoal paper, which is good for crayon work; I suppose artists' supplies are hard to get in W. Shokan, and would like to see his work on more durable paper. The portrait of the strange being is almost ruined.

I am inclosing the two snaps I promised with this letter. There was not room enough for all of me on one photo but the missing portion appears on the other. I think you will be able to tell me from my father and brother. Please don't be awed by my solemn aspect—it is not a perpetual mask.

I do not know when I shall reach Providence, but it will be within three weeks, I think. I shall go either of these routes: north, and down through Athol to Providence, or straight to New York for three days to a week, and then north through Providence, Boston, Athol, West Shokan, and back to New York for another couple of weeks or a month.

The prospective trip becomes more fascinating as the time for my going approaches. But I must get my things ready and attend to some more minor duties. I shall send you cards from along the route, but I shall be more satisfied when the spectre from the West appears in Providence.

> Sincerely,
> Donald Wandrei

Notes

1. Presumably *The Shepherd's Calendar* (1829), a collection of stories by James Hogg (1770–1835) containing some weird tales, although there is a volume of this title (1827) by the British poet John Clare (1793–1864).

[30] [DAW to HPL] [ANS]

[Postmarked Chicago, Ill.,
20 June 1927]

Dear Mr. Lovecraft:

Chicago. Unimpressed. Going on. The city is filthy. Came yesterday and am leaving today after I see Wright. Saw the Field Museum & Art Institute yesterday. The city is an eyesore to me already.

Sincerely,
Donald W.

[31] [DAW to HPL]

[Postmarked Fort Wayne, Ind.,
21 June 1927]

[Envelope only.]

[32] [DAW to HPL] [ANS]

[Postmarked Canton, Ohio,
23 June 1927]
Wooster, Ohio,
June 22, 1927

Dear Mr. Lovecraft:

I made only 200 miles or so today, but was again held up by rain; a young cloudburst almost struck here about seven p.m. I haven't cared for any except one or two of the smaller towns I have passed through, and none of the larger. For a long way out of Chicago, across all of Indiana and the western part of Ohio, the land was level with rarely a slope even and nothing that could be called a hill. But through the district surrounding Wooster and Marion, the countryside is idyllic with a myriad little hills sloping into each other, and clusters of trees sprinkled over their tops. I stood on one and looked away for miles and miles across many smaller slopes, and the mist in the air and the smell of clover lent a glamorous enchantment to the scene. I never before so acutely realized the physical basis of life, however, and long for one of my mother's excellent meals. I think I'll spend more time in Providence than in New York. A number of travelling salesmen have picked me up on the strength of two brief cases I am carrying, and I think I am unusually fortunate in general because I don't look like a bum. I have, as you will notice, got on the southern route, and will probably reach New York before Providence. But I am not so anxious to see it, after Chicago, and may spend only a couple of days before going in to Providence.

The farther away I get, the more fascinating St. Paul becomes.

Sincerely,
Donald W.

[33]   [DAW to HPL] [ANS]

[Postmarked Pittsburgh, Pa.,
26 June 1927]
Lancaster, Pa.
June 26

Dear Mr. Lovecraft:

I have missed several days but have been on the go from dawn till dusk or later, and have had no chance to write. Since I left Fort Wayne, I have travelled by way of Wooster, Lima, and Canton, Ohio, Pittsburgh, McConnelsburg, and Gettysburg, Pennsylvania. Pennsylvania has a lovely countryside, with its many hills and forests, its Alleghanies, and the long vistas from the tops of high peaks, when you can see for dozens of miles into the distance across the same beautiful country. I like this the best of those states through which I have passed. The rain pursued me, however, and I missed only one day. I slept on top the Alleghanies that night. Today, I got a lift from a couple who decided to tour Gettysburg. They asked me to go with them; I did, naturally, though the guide with his prattle irritated me.

I shall be in Providence in about ten days; I have come out on the southern route, and will stop in New York for a week.

My only regret on this trip, which has been a most enjoyable ramble in spite of difficulties, is that my mother wasn't with me to cook my meals. My taste is either too good or too bad for the stuff I got along my route.

Sincerely,
Donald Wandrei

[34]   [DAW to HPL] [ALS]

118 W. 73rd St.
New York, N.Y.
June 30, 1927

Dear Mr. Loveman:[*sic*]

I got on the Southern route and there I stayed perforce until I became so disgusted with the daily rain that on the approach of another deluge, I bought a ticket to Samarcand—or Babylon—from Lancaster, Pa. I arrived early Monday morning. I hunted for a room immediately and obtained this one, in a good neighborhood, for $6. I shall be here, however, only till Monday or a week from Monday.

I wish I had kept to the Northern route and reached Providence first. But my path was not entirely in my own hands, and I will, at any rate, reach Providence within ten or twelve days.

So far, I have been fascinated by the city, its immensity, and wealth, and speed. But, like you, I hate the people. I have been through good districts only as yet, but everywhere are mongrel anthropoid types, the scum of Europe and Asia. I can not imagine what the slums contain.

I went into the Dauber and Pine shop Tuesday and met Loveman. He took me to Long's apartment in the evening. I like them both and found them extremely pleasant. Before I left St. Paul, my father warned me to be disappointed in my correspondents, but the boomerang is on him. He is a disillusioned idealist, I believe. At any rate, I have thoroughly enjoyed both my tramp and the people I have met. Long leaves town today for an over the-Fourth trip, but I shall see Loveman in the meantime, and Long again when he returns, providing I stay two weeks.

I did little except buy books Monday and Tuesday. I must be a book-worm in the last analysis, because it is the bookstores for which I invariably search when I first visit a new city. I bought about two dozen, I should say, with the result that I will have to cut my trip to the middle of August. But I have obtained so much relief from the depression that continually followed me in the Twin Cities that I can return with impetus sufficient to last me a year or more. And I am not so sure that St. Paul will not take on a new glamour when I return after my ramble.

There is much to see here, too much for so short a visit as that to which I am limited. I shall undoubtedly have time only to receive the fascination of the city without its repulsive qualities. I visited the Metropolitan Museum yesterday and was enthralled beyond telling by the fabulously rich and marvellously beautiful collection of works of art therein contained. I have been up and down Fifth Avenue too, window shopping. These are the things that now spell for me the lure of New York. Perhaps if I were here for years, I would reach the rotten core, but now it is largely the resplendent surface that attracts me.

Long and Loveman have told me much about the old group. I wish I had known it. In particular, I'd like to have known Galpin, the renegade, as it were. Long introduced me to Kirk yesterday, and for the first time I saw a copy of Nora May French's poems.[1] Kirk wants four dollars, which is more than I can afford; but Loveman says he has two copies, and perhaps I can have one of his for less.

You must show me your novel, and everything else you have written, old or new, that I have not yet seen when I reach Providence. I am certain that I will like the city. The farther east I have come, the more I have liked the countryside and the towns. Long showed me an old 18th century district in lower Manhattan that had a charming antiquated aspect in spite of modern intrusions here and there.

The glamour of New York in the first few days is inconceivable. But whether it would last through a period of months or years, I can not say. I do know that I do not care to have much contact with the people.

     Sincerely,
     Donald Wandrei

Notes

1. Nora May French (1881–1907), *Poems* (San Francisco: Strange Co., 1910; *LL* 335).

[35] [HPL to DAW] [ANS]

[Postmarked Providence, R.I.,
30 June 1927]

Sir Wand'rer:—

Welcome East! I've been following all your messages with keen interest, & have four letters here for you. Did you take in colonial Philadelphia? Hope so! And isn't N.Y. a beastly mess? It won't be so bad while the gang is showing you around for the first time, though. I don't know whether this card will catch you or whether I'll see you first. Hope you're not missing any interesting sights in N.Y. If you're going to be there long I'll send you a list of things to see. But I guess Belknap & the rest can keep you busy for a while! Let me know when to expect you, & I'll try to have weather & scenery at their best. You won't know what old towns & fine landscapes are till you strike New England—unless you did some close looking in Pennsylvania. Was interested to hear of your Chicago experiences. Your earlier letter & returned MS. came safely—was glad to see the pleasing snapshots! Well—keep me posted ahead. Have you kept the directions & telephone number?

Expectantly—
H P L

[36] [HPL to DAW] [ALS]

10 Barnes St.,
Providence, R.I.,
July 1, 1927.

My dear Wandrei:—

I dropped you a card yesterday, after receiving the message which you, Kirk, & Long sent; but I now see that you won't get it till after the 4th, since I mailed it in Belknap's care. Let me therefore say here how much I appreciated your various bulletins en route, & how interested I was to hear of your *Weird Tales* call, your Chicago reaction, your growing appreciation of home & St. Paul, & your discerning recognition of the greater beauty of the eastern landscape! I'm sorry you missed old Philadelphia—which I thought you'd probably hit when I learned you were in Lancaster. That would have been a revelation of colourful archaism—though perhaps it would have required a good guide or guidebook to lead you to all of its choicest spots. And now I'm eagerly awaiting your advent to New England—which I think you'll find ahead of anything you've yet seen for general interest, historic &

architectural background, & scenic beauty. Let me know just when to expect you, & I'll have all the choicest sights on parade. We must certainly take in Newport & other outlying places, while Boston & environs absolutely cannot be missed. Boston will shew you what a first-rate city of elder America is like. I hope exceedingly that you can stay well over the 20th, since Long & his parents will be here the 21st & 22nd, (& possibly the 23d) & our portly fellow-gangster James F. Morton (whom you may see in N.Y.) expects to wander hither about the same time. If all could be in Providence at once, the combination surely would be festive! Meanwhile I am sending you the four letters which came here for you. They will keep you sufficiently in touch with home to ward off any nostalgia which might otherwise mar your programme.

And so you have taken the golden—or Pennsylvania—Road to Samarcand! Well—I suppose the poor old ruin is impressive at first sight, & can recall the delightful time I had on my first visit there—a five-day period in April, 1922. Of course, I had not the buoyancy of youth to lend magic to the scene; but even so, I was touched by the size & opulence & strangeness & mystery of the place. I can still recall bits of that first impression—the towers of Manhattan rising violet & magical from the sea against an apocalyptic sunset, the glister of early evening lamps on the wet pavement of Madison Square, the balustraded pomp of the Plaza at 5th Ave. & 59th St, with the white-blossomed boughs of Central Park limned delicately against the shadowy line of distant & fantastic roofs, the Alexandrian luxury of 5th Ave., with the costly wares of exotic Phœnician sea-traders in the windows, the daemonic glare of the haunted night, when the dusk presses like a low roof upon the chaos & nightmare of Broadway, the wonder of Prospect Park (Bklyn) at dusk, when the red west silhouettes strange terraces & pagoda roofs, & bronze lions crouch cryptic beside the marble quays of templed lakelets, the bewildering wealth of the museums, & the Dantean horror of slum byways in midnight blackness—yes, it was all great while it lasted, but I could never recall it again. Like Sardathrion, dream-city of Pegāna's gods, it has fallen by the sword of Time.[1] It is a place I once saw in a vision, but could never find again. The actuality, nowadays, does nothing but weary & disgust me, as one is wearied & disgusted by a noble ruin wherein one finds Death & the Plague & the spawn of unknown sorcery from the nether pits. To get the charm I once got from New York I have to visit Philadelphia or Boston. Boston has never lost the spell & sense of opulent witchery which it always exerted on me. New York, however, is still new & fresh to you, & I hope you'll make the most of it. I am herewith sending you a little guidebook (free duplicate—it's published by a chain of hotels) which I've found superior to any other in directing one to places of real charm & background & interest. I advise you to *miss nothing described therein,* for the items are very carefully selected, & are made easy of access by a series of excellent key-maps.¶ Besides this, of course, you had better get a Standard or Rand-McNally guidebook & see anything mentioned there which may appeal to you. As for this little brown book—I advise you to *read it through first*, & then formulate trips according to time & convenience. Some of the old houses will give you a faint foretaste of what you are to see in New England. Don't miss the following:

**   Fraunce's [*sic*] Tavern
     Planter's Hotel (where Poe stopped when he landed from Phila.)
*   Poe Cottage in Fordham (East Side Subway to Kingsbridge Rd.— walk E.)
     St. Paul's & Trinity
     City Hall—1812—fine late Georgian bldg. by McComb
     St. Mark's in the Bouwerie
     Greenwich Village (Milligan & Patchin Places, Gay St., Minetta St., Sheridan Sq., Charlton St, Grove St., &c.)
*   Jumel Mansion (West Side Subway to 157 st—walk E. & ask directions)
*   Dyckman Cottage (farmhouse of Dutch style—1783. West S. Sub. to 207th St., walk W. & S.)
*   Van Cortlandt Mansion (W. Side Subway to end of line)
*   Lefferts Cottage in Flatbush (B.M.T. subway to Prospect Park Sta.)
†   Old Flatbush Church (B.M.T. Subway to Church Ave—walk toward steeple you see on emerging)

Of modern things you ought surely to see the following:

Metropolitan Museum (don't miss the *American Wing* with colonial antiques)—study this in detail as a preparation for New England. A PROVIDENCE man arranged it! Note especially the THREE PERIODS represented.

American Museum of Natl. History

Hispanic Museum   B'way & 156th St. All in a group. See
Am. Indian Museum   them the day you visit the Jumel
Spanish chapel   mansion. W. side Sub. to 157th St.

Brooklyn Museum & *Japanese Garden* adjoining (walk from Lefferts Cottage or take *Interborough* subway to Bklyn Museum station)

Bronx Park Zoölogical Garden (Bronx subway to end of line—180th St)

View of Lower Manhattan from Bklyn. end of Manhattan Bridge.

Night view of Lwr. M'ht'n from Columbia Heights, Bklyn. (preferably from rear windows of house where Loveman lives)

View from top of Woolworth Bldg.

Public Library

Museum of N.Y. Historical Society*** (77th St. & Central Pk. W. Near Am. Museum—& near your lodgings)

Old French Cloister—(W. Side Sub. to 181st St. Walk W. to Ft. Wash'n Ave., then N. to cloister.)

Columbia College—Morningside Hts.—St John the Divine

The Battery—Aquarium (housed in 1812 fort)—Waterfront‡

@ The open sea (from S. Shore of Long Island. B M T subway to Brighton Beach or Coney Island)

College of City of New York—St Nicholas Hts—(good *Gothic* quadrangle in effective cliff setting)

The Grange, home of Alexander Hamilton. (Amsterdam Av. surface car to 135th St.)

Harlem negro district (sinister & fascinating—not a white face for blocks—Lenox Ave. subway to 125th St—walk N.)

Ghetto (most of N.Y., damn it all! but in particular, the pushcart region of hideous & colourful squalor east of the Bowery. Walk E. along Grand St.)

Chinatown (walk along Park Row from City Hall, turn into Mott St. at Chatham Sq.)

Soldiers' Monument, Riverside Dr. (copy, choragic monument of Lysicrates in Athens) Also Grant's Tomb

Prospect Park Plaza, Bklyn. (Roman arch & columns) (near Lefferts Cottage & Bklyn. Museum) (explore the park, too—Vale of Cashmere &c)

Grand Central Station—Original train of 1831 on rails in balcony

Penn. Station—architecture—copy of Baths of Caracalla.

*	closes 5 P.M.
**	closes 4 P.M.
†	edifice 1796—site much older. Ancient churchyard with stones in Dutch language
***	not only antiquarian material but valuable art objects, especially Renaissance paintings. A great Titian—the Martyrdom of St Lawrence—in basement.
‡	The best waterfront stretch is South St.—up the east shore from the Battery
@	you expressed a wish to see this, but since most of our New England seaports are at the head of deep bays, you'll only see it twice here—at Newport & Marblehead.
****	Unless they've torn it up for the extension of 6th Ave. Whole blocks of splendid colonial houses, especially in Varick St., have vanished since my first sight of N.Y. I'm glad I saw it when I did.

You will find the most typical bit of Colonial New York in *Charlton St.,***** Greenwich Village. This (although really early 19ᵗʰ century) looks exactly as the whole of residential New York did in the 18ᵗʰ century. Note the *special type of colonial doorway*—small columns flanking door, pair of engaged columns beyond, rectangular transom with traury, &c. Also general lines of N.Y. colonial house—brick, slant roof with dormers, symmetrically placed door & windows, high stoop with iron-railed steps— You will not find this type in New England, our 18ᵗʰ century architecture being entirely different & our colonial doorways having enormously greater variety & richness. (cf. booklet I sent you) So far as I know, there is only *one* pillared doorway of the N.Y. colonial type in Providence, & very few in Boston. Our types have semicircular or elliptical fanlights & highly diverse & individualised carving. Flat pilasters are more common here than are the New Yorkish columns.

As for N.Y. *suburbs*—if you want to study in composite detail the manner in which the cancerously spreading town engulfs an adjacent village, visit the following specimens: all *originally* much alike, but each representing a different degree of absorption.

1. Williamsburg—*wholly engulfed*. Brooklyn side Wmsbg. Bridge. Continuous with Bklyn.
2. Flatbush—*almost engulfed*. B M T subway to Parkside or Church Ave. Apartments & N.Y. type of Bldgs., but a few signs of village separatism like the old churchyard.
3. Jamaica—*half engulfed*. B.M.T. B'way-Bklyn Subway (change at Canal St. to end of line.) Jamaica still has many fine old village houses & colonial churches. Village atmosphere lingers perceptibly. Visit old King Mansion in Park near W. edge of village. There is *half-open* country between Jamaica & N.Y.
4. Flushing—*about to be engulfed*. Take Queensboro subway at Public Library or Grand Central—train for *Corona*, unless the extension to Flushing itself is done. Here is a village almost untouched by the city. Visit old Bowne house, 1661, Quaker Meeting-House, 1694, note many quaint & ancient streets. There is open country betwixt this place & N.Y., but the extension of the elevated with 5¢ fare will ruin it.
5. Hempstead—*wholly free of the metropolis*. Take subway-elevated to Jamaica, change to street-car for Hempstead. Here you have a perfectly untainted colonial village of the Long Island type, with ancient church & churchyard. English settled, but with N.Y. architectural details not found in New England. Quaint white houses—a foretaste of what you'll see in R.I. & Mass. Wide belt of open country separates this place from N.Y.

This cycle—Hempstead, Flushing, Jamaica, Flatbush, & Williamsburg— really shows very clearly the way N.Y. devours an adjacent town. You can omit *Williamsburg* if you like, since Greenwich Village is just as good a sample of the last stage of the process. Other former villages are Chelsea, Bowery Village, Bloomingdale, (where Belknap lives) Yorkville, &c. Another good suburb to visit is *Yonkers*, a city on the north rim of N.Y., beyond Van Cortlandt Park. Quaint & hilly. Don't miss the ancient Philipse Manor, now a colonial museum. The city of Elizabeth, N.J., is also a fine colonial survival. It & its suburbs have important Revolutionary associations. Take ferry to Staten Island, car to Elizabeth Ferry, cross, & ride or walk into town. Staten Island itself is full of quaint ancient villages. Note especially *Stapleton*, (S. of N.Y. ferry) & *Port Richmond*, on way to Elizabeth ferry. Port Richmond has a fine colonial church & churchyard. Car from Elizabeth goes to Springfield N.J.—famous battle scene with original buildings still standing. (Parson Caldwell episode—his church still intact & in use) Very quaint fishing village can be seen by taking the Jamaica subway-elevated, getting off at *Crescent St.*, & taking the municipal 'bus south to the *Old Mill*. Ask Loveman about this. Loveman can also shew you many quaint effects all around N. Y. which he & I have discovered. Don't fail to walk the full extent of Riverside Drive—all the way to its descent at Dyckman St.—noting fine castellated effects north of 181st St. Also walk full extent of Fort Washington Ave. For good views, take Ft. George 'bus to end of line—walking down hill & returning via West Side Subway at Dyckman St. Also take East Side subway to N.Y. Univ. Station & visit University Heights with its Hall of Fame. Fine view. Also walk across High Bridge, which Poe loved. If you have time, take a boat trip up the Hudson as far as Newburgh & back. The palisade & mountain landscapes are superb, & Newburgh itself is a marvellously quaint town, perched on steep terraces above the river. As for natural scenery—take the West Side Subway to 207th st. (where you go for the Dyckman Cottage) & walk due west to the Hudson, where the splendid woodlands of Inwood Park are encountered. You'll hardly believe you're on Manhattan Island! Note the great old tulip tree under which Henry Hudson is said to have treated with the Indians. If you leave the park on the Dyckman St. side, you might take the ferry across to the palisade region of New Jersey & absorb a bit of scenery. If you do, don't fail to ascend the palisades for the view. But perhaps you won't have time for all this. At any rate, I won't bore you with any more guidebook stuff! One thing, though. In coming from N.Y. to New England, don't patronise train or boat if you can help it. In those vehicles you miss all the charm of transition, & sacrifice some magnificent Connecticut scenery. Come over the old Boston Post Road via New Haven & New London—by motor coach if you don't decide to hoof & hitch. Note the lovely little white-steepled villages & green hills with rambling stone walls which mark your emergence from the N.Y. region & your advent to the ancient, beautiful, & distinctive realm of New England. Note places like Guilford & Madison as you pass through, & give the old colonial town of New London as much of an exploration as you can. I think New Haven—seat of Yale—is good too, but I never had a chance to stop there. Note also *Mystic*—on this side of New London. Quaint hilly streets, &c. You will enter R.I. at *Westerly*, but won't see our best scenery on the way to Prov. I'll shew you that (N. of the town) later. When you enter Providence note the lovely effect of the ancient green hill on the east; the (1775) great white steeple limned against it, the great copper dome crowning it, & the numerous pleasant roofs & belfries peeping through the verdure. Telephone up to me—*Dexter 9617*—& decide whether you want to thread the labyrinth alone or have a guide come & get you. I'm enclosing a pamphlet with some general Providence "dope". Keep it—& we'll get a fresh one when you arrive. It's issued every week.

I'm glad you've connected up with "the gang", & can imagine the conversations on congenial themes with Belknap & Loveman. Don't crow too soon, though, in writing to your father about your correspondents. When you strike Providence your sceptical parent's deepest disillusions will be upheld, for there is surely no person more disappointing & uninteresting to meet face-to-face than I. I'm relying wholly on the scenery & antiquities of New England to keep you from utter ennui!

Your bookshop revels are not hard to understand, for I recall how vastly impressed I was five years ago with the second-hand literary facilities of the New Alexandria. This is the one respect in which N.Y. does not disappoint; for there are undoubtedly more chances of getting any particular book one wants than there are anywhere else. Great bazaars like 4th Ave. & 59th St. certainly hold a potent lure; & my shelves bear more than one evidence of the extent to which I fell for their insidious temptations. However, I must admit that toward the last of my two-year exile I became weary even of these attractions. I am not, as I have said, a bibliophile; but merely one who uses a very few books now & then to evoke certain colourful imaginative pictures. When N.Y. had so asphyxiated my soul that I could not evoke the pictures by any device whatsoever, I ceased to value all books—for they were no longer able to serve me. But a few months back home were enough to restore my usual attitude, & I am now just as frequent a haunter of shops as I used to be. Indeed, the whole N.Y. story has become such a distant dream that I scarcely realise I've ever been away from Providence. We have some splendid book shops in Providence, (also Boston—which has two districts almost comparable to N.Y.'s marts) & I fear you will part with many a shilling at Eddy's, the Old Corner, Gregory's, Tyson's, & so on. When we get to Boston, you'll have to let me guard your pocketbook for you—I can picture you on Cornhill, or in Ashburton Place! By the way— just before you struck N.Y., Loveman sold Morton a fine copy of "Melmoth, the Wanderer" for $6.75 from the Dauber & Pine stock!

On the whole, I think your trip will be of great psychological & imaginative benefit to you—& I'll wager you'll like St. Paul the better for it! It's a great thing to get a sense of space & perspective—& to discover that the people in the alluring cities just beyond the hill aren't any less stupid & commonplace than the people in one's own town. The myth of a cultural centre disappears as soon as one travels & investigates—even Boston is a legend & a memory so far as active intellectual life is concerned, though of course it bears the deep & satisfying marks of a great tradition & a high, reposeful, & artistic level of taste & thought. I'm glad you saw the Metropolitan Museum. See it again—for it is undoubtedly the greatest single thing in New York. Later on I'll shew you the Boston Museum of Fine Arts, wherein you'll find many an object to enchant you. Providence, too, has an excellent set of museums—the main art museum being in a new building completed little more than a year ago. In the Metropolitan I received my main "kick" by getting inside the *Pantheon* model, holding my eyes down to the floor level, & forgetting the scale of relative magnitude enough to produce the illusion of being in the real edifice itself. Try it—if you love Rome a sixteenth as much as I do, you'll never forget it! It made me strike consular & senatorial & imperial attitudes, & orate with all the Latin I know! I also revelled in the new Wing K—the Roman garden with the statues. A certain austere head of a tight-lipped old Republican Roman is as much of a favourite of mine as that effeminately pretty Antinoüs-type Hellenic head in the corridor is a favourite of Loveman's.

Yes—it's a pity you never met Galpin, whose resemblance to yourself has impressed everyone in the 'gang' who has seen either of you or your picture. I'm going to take the liberty of enclosing Long's card about you, wherein your Galpinian similarity is stressed. Alfredus was a great boy—& I don't believe I've ever struck a human intellect more subtle, restless, & unerringly & instantaneously acquisitive than his. I discovered him in 1917, just before his sixteenth birthday, & watched him grow up into a blasé, disillusioned & cynical philosopher-aesthete. Then, just as I expected him to become a critic & professional scholar, he suddenly turned to *music*—& was lost to the world of thought. He is now, as you are doubtless aware, a French instructor at Northwestern University—though with ambitions focussed solely on a future as pianist & composer. I think I sent you his critique of Clark Ashton Smith. For a time I hoped he'd succeed in helping C A S to a wider recognition. I'll never forget the idyllic three weeks in 1922[2] when Galpin & I visited Loveman in Cleveland. Novel sights, crisp discussions, & the piquant charm of a pleasant city new to two out of the three of us brought back my youth for a time—for though I was 32 years old, it formed my first long trip, ill-health having prevented travel when I was a young man. I'll shew you snapshots of Galpin when you get here—which reminds me to thank you very sincerely for those of yourself which you sent. They delighted me exceedingly—& I noticed at once the Galpinian aspect which Long, Kirk, & Loveman were so quick to remark.

Nora May French seems quite an attribute of first trips to New York! On my first visit in 1922 I picked up a copy for 75¢ at a shop in Vesey St.—an old book district now wholly devoid of such emporia. I was told then that it was a vast bargain, & I doubt if even Loveman can quote you quite such a figure on his duplicate!

As to my novelettes—I don't know how in Pegāna's name you'll ever get their contents unless I read 'em aloud! You may think my ordinary penmanship is bad—but you ought to see the undecipherably interlined & corrected scrawls which form the rough draughts of my formal literary compositions! When I take pains with words, I do it in earnest—& the result surely appears in my scribbled pages. However, I think I have one or two printed tales which you haven't seen—& one MS. short enough to read aloud. This reminds me, by the way, that *Amazing Stories* has actually accepted my "Colour Out of Space"! The magazine certainly lived up to its name so far as I am concerned, for I really hadn't the remotest idea the thing would 'land'. I guess the pseudo-scientific camouflage near the beginning was what turned the trick.

Your pre-embarkation letter was very interesting, & I was very glad to hear that you found something of merit in my long article—which came back in perfect safety. Only one page was gone, so you missed nothing but the usual flowery finale. As you see, my effort is merely a sort of preface to the subject—& I look to you to compile the really scholarly critical & bibliographical volume which the field demands. As to Verne—I couldn't recall him as definitely weird enough to hold a niche in a strictly high-spot survey, though no doubt his influence told. The matter of old woodcuts is certainly of the highest interest, & I wish I had touched upon the subject. The same influences—culminating in the plague—shaped the pictures, as shaped the current of literature; & it would undoubtedly be well if someone were to trace the interdependence of the two streams. Surely a public fed on gruesome visual images would be more than ready for kindred imaginative titillation from another source. The version as you saw it contains many errors due to fatigue (erroneously repeated words, infelicitous combinations, & so on) which I eliminated in the proofs. I was also able to insert into the latter a paragraph on the Crawford material you lent me, as well as a good-sized passage anent Chambers' "King in Yellow". I was just too late with Shiel's "Purple Cloud".

Glad you liked the Dwyer drawings. Not up to the Smith standard by many a mile, but marvellously promising for all that. He'll appreciate the paper—& I hope you can get to call on him on your return trip. By the way—I appreciated very much the copy of your *Quarterly* with your poems & the Icelandic article.[3] You have been a mainstay of the enterprise, & it is really amusing that you were not appointed to the editorship for the following year. Magna est stupiditas, et praevalebit![4]

Well—I won't consume any more of your valuable sightseeing time. Time enough to chatter when you reach these agrestic shores. I know you'll like New England, & hope you can arrange for an ample period of scenic & antiquarian assimilation. The weather has been so rotten during June that it ought to give us a good July for outdoor excursions—at any rate, let us put aside our cynicism long enough to hope for the best! Keep me informed of experiences & prospects by postcard bulletins, & I shall be eagerly on the watch. Looking forward, then, to the 10th, I will subscribe myself as

Y^r most humble ob^t Servt

H P L

[P.S.] ¶ This book is for you to keep. Take it home as a souvenir of Antioch–Alexandria.

Notes

1. HPL refers to Lord Dunsany's "Time and the Gods" (originally published as "The Lament of the Gods for Sardathrion"), in *Time and the Gods* (1906).
2. 30 July–15 August 1922.
3. Hjalmar Björnson, "The Twilight Age of Icelandic Literature," *Minnesota Quarterly* 4, No. 3 (Spring 1927): 1–24. The issue also contained DAW's "Song of Oblivion," "Lost Atlantis," "Chant to the Dead," and "The Challenger."
4. "Great is stupidity, and it will prevail!"—a parody of *Magna est veritas* [truth] *et prae-valebit.*

[37]   [HPL to DAW] [ANS]

[Postmarked Providence, R.I.,
5 July 1927]
Tuesday

Dear W:—

Hope all is still glittering & glorious in Antioch! A sizeable package from your mother has just arrived here, & I'm forwarding another letter which came in the morning mail. Anything arriving after tomorrow I'll hold rather than forward.

An upstairs room in this house will be all ready whenever you arrive. Hope you can stay a couple of weeks or more. On the 21st. Long & his parents will be here, & the landlady has just arranged to let them also have a couple of rooms at #10—which will certainly provide quite a conclave under one roof!

Just had a note from Wright. Your call had a wholesome effect on him, for he asks to have another look at "Cthulhu"![1] He liked you very much.

Also have an *Overland* with Smith's article on Sterling.[2] I'm keeping it for you to see—your name is mentioned in an article on Sterling by the editor![3]

Well—enjoy Babylon while it's fresh!

Y^r obt Servt

H P L

Notes

1. On his way to Providence to visit HPL, DAW stopped at the *WT* offices in Chicago and personally urged FW to reconsider publishing "The Call of Cthulhu." HPL heard from FW before DAW reached Providence. See DAW, "Lovecraft in Providence" (*LR* 314–15).

2. CAS, "George Sterling—An Appreciation," *Overland Monthly* 85, No. 3 (March 1927): 79–80.

3. B. Virginia Lee, "Justice," *Overland Monthly* 85, No. 3 (March 1927): 74: "The morning of the tragedy he called the Overland office and asked to see proof of articles which he had been instrumental in obtaining for the December issue [including] an article on Clark Ashton Smith by D. A. Wandrei whom Sterling asked in one of his last directions on Overland copy to be mentioned as Donald A. Wanderei. [*sic*] He further gave the address in Minnesota to send the extra copies to the author. George, fulfilling a mission." The tragedy referred to was Sterling's suicide.

[38]   [DAW to HPL] [ALS]

118 West 73rd St.,

New York, N.Y.

July 6, 1927

Dear Mr. Lovecraft:

I was pleased to receive your letter yesterday, the card later at Long's, and the letters from home. A thousand thanks for sending them on; they weren't very important, but they were pleasant reading.

Some of the points you mention, I have already seen; many I won't have time to see; and a few don't attract me. To tell the truth, I have a growing aversion to the city; the people sicken me, and I am fast losing the glamour that caught me the first week. I went out to Coney Island the Fourth, but in the middle of the afternoon, I came to hate even the thought of association with the vast mob of beastly faces, and went back to my room. I enjoyed the sight of the open sea, but that was all.

I have been having a splendid holiday here under the auspices of Loveman, Long, Kirk and Co. I went to one "poet's" night thing in the Village with Loveman, at which we were both bored, and to another with Kirk, where the poetry and the people were even worse. Loveman read me the end of "The Sphinx" one night at his home. I wish he weren't so darned indifferent about publishing his work. He showed me a number of poems, too, and they were the best find I have made in a year. They were lyric in passion, lyric in ecstasy and with lyric beauty, and they had melody and music and the splendour of the deathless Greek as you never find them in the work of modern poets. I dined at Long's apartment last night, and had the most pleasant evening since I left home. He read me many of his poems which have been written since "A Man from Genoa", and showed me a portrait of Galpin. I am amazed by the number of things that both Long and Loveman have written—Long with a deskful of mss., and Loveman with enough poems for three volumes besides "The Sphinx". I am afraid that I will make a poor addition to this group as far as results go. If I had to live in New York, I believe it would mark my passing as a writer; I sometimes think I have passed anyway, but I simply could not and can not write here. I have had the impulse, the desire several nights, but the noise irritates me, and the city is oppressive. I am used to quiet when I write, and doubt whether I could become hardened to the noise. At any rate, I shall be glad to leave Monday and start for Providence. I should arrive Tuesday at the latest, or perhaps late Monday if I get an early start, which is doubtful.

I have read the "Purple Cloud," which Long loaned me. The first half of the book is by far the better. But I prefer "The House of Sounds" to the novel.

Congratulations on having sold "The Colour out of Space". I wish it had been W.T., because Amazing Stories pays poorly, and is not going so well as its backers believed it would. But it will probably extend your audience by some thousands.

This is a short letter, but I am surprised that I have time to write any kind of note. I am to lunch with Long in an hour, after which we shall visit the Poe cottage.[1]

I am *not* 75 inches high. That is a deliberate perversion of truth which you may visibly refute on the impending arrival of the Wanderer. I shall write again if I can, but if I don't, adios till next Tuesday.

With disillusion,
Donald Wanderer.

Notes

1. The Poe Cottage, in Fordham, NY. A visit to the cottage by HPL, FBL, and Morton is captured in a famous photograph taken there in September 1922 by Paul Livingston Keil.

[39]   [HPL to DAW]   [ANS]

[Postmarked Providence, R.I.,
7 July 1927]
Thursday

Dear W:—

Well, so Alexandria has begun to drag as soon as all this! You'll like Providence, I feel sure, & I'll certainly be on the watch Monday night or Tuesday. I'm sending another letter which came for you.

I thought the gang would see you didn't lack for entertainment. Loveman is a poet of the highest quality, & I only wish he could get the recognition he deserves. Cook is going to publish "The Sphinx" with a drawing by C A S. Long is a great boy—he'll certainly come out somewhere. You must stay here till his visit & get another sight of him on Providence soil. Interested to hear that you've seen the photograph of your immortal prototype Galpinius the Great.

Hope you'll like Poe's Cottage. I'll shew you some more associations of Poe's here. So *Amazing Stories* is languishing, eh? Too bad—I knew nothing about it. Glad you've seen "The Purple Cloud". That early part is priceless! ¶ Sincerely yrs

H P L

P.S. Your visit to Wright bore fruit! He's just asked to see "Cthulhu" again! I also sent him "Silver Key" & "Strange High House." He praises you greatly.

[40]   [Samuel Loveman, Frank Belknap Long, and DAW to HPL] [ANS]
[Postmarked New York, N.Y.,
9 July 1927]
Hello H.P.L. I wish I could join the pilgrimage to Providence. Selah! Sam

---

Thanks for the 10023 pages of travellogue—letter will follow. Wandrei has viewed the skyline at last, and was decidedly impressed by it. As ever, Francis

---

Won't arrive till Tues., perhaps Wed. I am enjoying N.Y. again by ignoring the people. The things I liked best: 1, Loveman's poems; 2, Long, Loveman, Kirk, & Co.; 3, skyline from Staten; 4, the Metropolitan treasure house. Adios.—I prepare to become a Wanderer again.—Donald.

[41]   [DAW to HPL] [ANS]
118 West 73rd St.,
New York, N.Y
July 10, 1927
Dear Mr. Lovecraft:

This is my last day in Babylon. I have had a marvellous time here in spite of my ephemeral consciousness and hatred of the people some days ago. Sam & Belknap have made my stay far more pleasant than it might otherwise have been. Sam is genial, and loveable, and boyish; and a poet of the first class whose lyrics have taken my citadel by storm. And Belknap is great—I have spent so many royal hours with him in quest of this and that and taking in sights that I profoundly regret not knowing him years ago. When all is said and done, the best that Babylon offered me was Belknap and Sam. Had I known a few such men in the Twin Cities, you couldn't have paid me to leave St. Paul. I have received a wealth of impressions and the deepest satisfaction from my rambles eastward; not in years have I so thoroughly enjoyed myself. I'll be back some day, next year, I hope.

Many thanks for everything—the list of places to see, of which I took in as much as possible, the street guide, information on Providence, letters from home, etc. I think I'll be able to stay two weeks—let us hope my cash is of a sedentary disposition! I anticipate Providence and Boston in particular. The sight of the sea from Coney Island was a source of high romance and both an allaying and arousing of my old longing for an hour. I wait again such a moment. But why pick out isolated memories? There are many such, and what I have already gained from my wandering will carry me for months or perhaps years in St. Paul.

I am leaving about noon Monday; hence I won't arrive till Tuesday evening, at least. I like the thought of taking the trail again; you may yet see me as a lifelong vagabond, for I seem to have the wanderlust, and I enjoy tramping the road. Dreams that I had long ago are coming true; yet their realisation is like a greater dream.

Selah for Providence! I'll be your second great-great-great grandson! As ever,

Donald W.

P.S. Glad of Wright's request. Hope you land "The Call", which I had no time to copy this spring. It's one of your best. The Sterling item is interesting. Hold it till my arrival—I'd like to see it. You, Morton, Belknap, and myself under one roof will be great!

D. W.

Wandrei visited Lovecraft in Providence from 12 to 29 July.

[42]   [DAW to HPL]   [ANS]

Athol, Mass.

July 31, 1927

Dear Necrophilist:

I had no trouble getting here; I picked a ride of about 10 miles a few minutes after we separated, stepped out of the car into another which was just behind, and reached Worcester by four stages before noon. I walked about a mile and a half altogether, to get out of Woonsocket, but that was all. Culinarius met me at one minute from the appointed hour—some timing! I've had a splendid time here with Munn & Cook, and am as sorry to leave as I have been the rest of your gang from N.Y. to Providence. It rained all day, but I hope for the best tomorrow.

I got Sam's "Faun" from Cook.[1] Blessings on thee, oh Culinarius! I also got the "Vagrant" in its massive grandeur.[2] Cook, by the way, has a wife who certainly lives up to her name. But I suppose I shouldn't bore you with the disgusting details of how much I have consumed while here.

If any mail should come the next two days or so, send it to Dwyer, but after Wed., to my home in St. Paul.

One of the best things in the "Vagrant" is a weird and unexpectedly good poem "Nathicana" by someone I never heard of, though it might be yours.[3] Look it up.

The Wanderer.

Notes

1. Samuel Loveman, "The Faun" [a story], *Vagrant* No. 12 (December 1919): 4–12; rpt. *Leaves* No. 2 (1938): 102–6.
2. DAW refers to the 300-page final issue of the *Vagrant*, planned for release in 1923 but published in Spring 1927 (see n. 3).
3. "Albert Frederick Willie" [i.e., HPL and Alfred Galpin], "Nathicana," *Vagrant* [Spring 1927]: 61–64.

[43] [HPL to DAW] [ALS]

Tuesday
[2 August 1927]

My dear Wanderer:—

I was highly pleased to learn from your card that you not only had good luck with lifts, but have found the Culinary table an acceptable substitute for Jake's![1] Your sessions with the Vagrant & the Werewolf are easy to depict in imagination, & I only regret that I could not have participated in them. Glad you have the "Faun" & the monster *Vagrant*. As to that "Nathicana"—I thought I told you all about that while you were here, though possibly it was Mortonius to whom I shed the enlightenment. It is a *joke* concocted by Galpin & myself in the old days—a parody on those stylistic excesses which really have no basic meaning. We tried it on Tryout, but the old fox saw through it & wouldn't print it. Then we let Cook have it, frankly admitting its spoofing nature but urging him to print it notwithstanding, to see how many critics would "bite". The name of the "author" is a Galpinian synthesis—Al(bert) fred(erick)—& "Willie" is a variant of Willy, which is Galpin's mother's maiden name. This reminds me that I heard from Galpin this morning—first time since Christmas. He is still at 1652 Jonquil Terrace, Chicago, (Apt. 1) & if you'd like to take a chance on seeing the young rascal you might drop him a card in advance—telling him that you're a new member of the old gang, & his logical successor as representative of the cosmos & the middle west! Incidentally—my letter to Belknap has come back—it having reached Belgrade Lakes just too late. I'll have to include it in the next batch when the Child telegraphs me another temporary address.

Well, I suppose you're at West Shokan now; & I certainly envy you your personal conversations with Dwyer. I shall have to try hiking around there some day—but for the present give him my regards & regrets. Enclosed is a critique of C A S's work in Berkeley, which ought to interest both you & Don Bernardo. I'll enclose Smith's letter, too, if I get it answered before mailing this. I'd like that back—& the critique as well after you've shown it to Dwyer. As you see, your advent home will mark the circulation of some Smith material which you, Dwyer, the N.Y. gang, & I will all have an opportunity of viewing. The critique seems to me very excellent & appreciative—one of the few really comprehending utterances of the sort. And speaking of professional acumen—after due deliberation & grave consultation with E. Hoffmann Price, Wright has very properly rejected my "Strange High House in the Mist," as not sufficiently clear for the acute minds of his highly intelligent readers. Oh, yes—I am also forwarding a letter of Smith's to you, which I trust you may receive in time.

I had a good outing Friday despite some showers, & repeated the event the next day. Since then, however, the weather has been too dubious for excursions. I've finished one revision job, thank Pegāna, but another still stares me in the face. As for the Bullen posthumous poems—Freer thought Cook's price was *too small,* & has sent a cheque for 500 bucks with a request for a more elegant job![2] He doesn't care what he does with his money! Well—I'll do my best to see that he gets something exquisite to the point of decadence! ¶ Have a good time & keep me posted!
    Yr obt Grandsire,
     Theobaldus

[On envelope:] P.S. The card from West Shokan just arrived. Greetings to you both, boys! Grandpa will have to hobble along that way before long! Belknap's party are at Lake George, N.Y.—they cut out Canada because of a typhoid epidemic—& I shall suggest that they take in West Shokan if they can arrange it. Shall answer Pickman's letter shortly, & return the Pyle drawings. Word from both Pickman & Wanderer will be welcome—but don't let the latter spoil his vacation by spending 3 hours on a paragraph!

Heard from young August W. Derleth today. He's quite interested in my account of The Wanderer, & hopes the latter won't forget him if he passes through Sauk City, Wis. en route home.

Notes

1. Jake's was a diner in a depressed section of Providence that provided ample portions for a low price.
2. HPL edited the posthumously published collection of the poetry of John Ravenor Bullen (1886–1927), *White Fire* (Athol, MA: The Recluse Press, 1927 [actually published January 1928]), financed by the wealthy Archibald Freer of Chicago. Cook's

presswork and binding make *White Fire* one of the finest amateur publications ever produced.

[44]   [DAW to HPL] [ALS]

West Shokan, N.Y.

August 3, 1927

Dear Necrophilist:

The last stage of my trip has been reached, and early tomorrow I shall take the long trail home. Dwyer is as congenial as all the gang on the road through Athol, Providence, New York, and Chicago; and so, my trip ends as it began, with relief from monotony and the greatest pleasure in making the personal acquaintance of my correspondents. All I regret is the fifty dollars or so that I spent in books—I could have stayed a month longer with you in Providence on the sum. But I'll be back sooner or later—and the bookstores will probably receive further contributions.

I have filled Dwyer with accounts of Providence and the very ancient master of ceremonies who presides at the Black Mass. He is eager to visit Providence in order to meet you, and I shouldn't be surprised if he made the trip within a year. You will find him, I fear me, much more congenial and less assertive than the obelisk that deserted Providence last week. He is a stalwart, impressive figure, taller than I by an inch, and weighing over two hundred pounds! His mind is of a slow type which requires several readings to digest a given work, but which never relinquishes that work or any part of it when it is once absorbed. He has a deep, pleasant voice, and has, like Loveman and Long, a good deal of the eternal child in him, not in a disparaging sense, but as many artists remain perpetually young. You can not help liking him. As you might expect, the neighbors in this small group of houses which really do not form a village can not understand his work. He has a very lonely seclusion in winter, a loneliness which is broken only by the letters of you, Smith, and myself. He needs some encouragement and appreciation in order to draw, but has found so little here that his output is small. He lives with his parents in a little farmhouse near the edge of the Ashokan reservoir which gives New York City its water. They are in modest circumstances, but as generous and courteous as the farmers of my own Middle West.

I have spoken to Dwyer about the drawings I returned to him by mistake, and he has promised to send them back to you before long. Just now he is at work on a new drawing of some sort, and I am taking the interval to write. Dwyer has a lot of time; the encouragement you, Smith, and I have given him has been an incentive. There are defects in his pictures, especially in his figures; but practice is what he needs to correct these, and practice is what he was not getting since he found no understanding among the farmers of the region.

I think I told you in our card that I made the trip here from Athol in fourteen hours. It was very misty when I started out at seven o'clock, and I feared there would be another day of rain like Sunday. But it cleared up about nine o'clock. I got several short lifts, and at twelve hailed a ride that carried me into Albany some time after three, after a ride of eighty miles or so. I ate a quick meal at a one-arm joint and started out. To keep up the tradition, it began raining again just as I reached the outskirts of the city. I was so disgusted that I walked a mile further, halted under an immense tree, and was almost immediately given a gratuitous ride to Catskill by a genial man who first took his wife home and then drove me out of town in order to set me on the right road. Then I hailed a car; an affable Jew was driving to Saugerties, about forty miles from West Shokan. He was a travelling salesman and visits St. Paul once a year. We reached Saugerties about half-past six, and since he had nothing to do that evening, he decided he might as well go out joy-riding in the general direction of West Shokan. He insisted on buying me dinner, gave me a cigar, and then drove down to West Shokan and to the very door of Dwyer's home! I certainly have had great luck over much of the territory covered on my trip. As closely as I can estimate, I made about two hundred miles Monday; at that rate, I shall be home in a week, rain or shine. With the experience I have picked up, I may be able to keep up such a pace.

Have just received a letter from home with some bad news. I'll have to leave early tomorrow, though I had intended to stay till Monday.

As ever,
The Wanderer

[45]   [DAW to HPL]   [ANS]

[Postmarked Ashtabula, Ohio,
6 August 1927]
Ashtabula, Ohio,
Aug. 6, 1927.

Dear Necrophilist:

It's noon now; hence, I ought to cover many more miles today. Thursday I made 240 miles, from W. Sh. to Syracuse. Slept out and got rained on about 4 A.M. Friday I made 160 miles, Syracuse to Buffalo, but walked twenty or thirty miles. It was one of my toughest days. Slept outside Buffalo last night and almost froze, besides getting dew-damp. I've made 150 miles today already and ought to get a good deal beyond Cleveland. I'm making fast time, but the closer home I get, the faster I wish it.

I think I'll lay off somewhere tomorrow and sleep all day. I'm fatigued about as much as I can stand now.

The Wanderer

[46]   [HPL to DAW] [ALS]

Saturday, Aug. 6, 1927

My dear Wanderer:—

I was exceedingly glad to receive your letter, but sorry to learn that your stay at West Shokan had to be curtailed. I hope the news from home was bad only in the most trivial & ephemeral sense, & that you'll be able to stop in Chicago to see Wright as you had planned. This reminds me that—as I've told you in a letter which Dwyer will doubtless forward to St. Paul—Wright finally turned down "The Strange High House in the Mist" as not sufficiently simple & obvious for his enlightened readers. Over against this, however, permit me to announce that "The Colour Out of Space" appears in the current *Amazing Stories*. They sent me two copies of the magazine, but I am still awaiting my cheque.

I am indeed glad that Dwyer turned out to be as attractive as his letters, & wish you could have remained longer at his agrestic villa. If only you hadn't squandered all your substance on mere typographical trifles, you might yet be basking in Providentian or Atholic or Shokanese glades—a thing you'll certainly have to do next year!

Thanks for infecting Don Bernardo with the virtues of Rhode-Island diabolism—& here's hoping it taints him sufficiently to set him on the eastward road. Shokan & Providence are really pretty much on a straight line, & all Dwyer would have to do would be to cross the Hudson at Poughkeepsie, then make successively for Hartford & Providence. Your description of him interested me greatly, & I fancy he must indeed be one of the pleasantest & most likeable of characters. He has spoken of his slowness of assimilation—which perhaps argues a correspondingly vital realisation of what he does assimilate. I have often wondered if the brain of the average modern scholar is not too crowded with mere details to prevent the vivid enjoyment of any one of them. That, I think, used to be the trouble with Galpin (from whom, by the way, I heard last week for the first time since Christmas) until he took to music & cast intellectualism overboard. I suppose Dwyer's life as an isolated farmer must be more or less lonely, but trust he will develop to an increasing degree those inward artistic resources which can make him independent of the world & of mankind. I wrote him a long letter two or three days ago, with some data on New England superstition which he wanted; & shall certainly do my part toward banishing any mental solitude which may tend to discourage his productivity. Thanks exceedingly for setting the crayon drawings in my direction again—they are remarkable things, & I shall be prodigiously glad to welcome them back. Did he shew you the wood panel with "The Hill of Dreams" & "Faunus" which he is doing for me? My expectations concerning this are very high! I wish he could get his things exhibited somewhere as Smith has done—you will see how well that Berkeley exhibition turned out when you read your forwarded mail.

I learn with great interest of your trip from Athol, & am sorry the Nemesis of wet weather still pursued you. Did you see much of Albany? And if so, what did you think of it? I have never beheld the place except when riding to & from Cleveland in 1922. If I recall aright, the train passed through on a sort of elevated viaduct. The town is an old Dutch one, & must have many antiquities. You were very fortunate in your encounter with the Phœnician trader, & he deserves a vote of thanks for the hospitality & transportation his caravan provided. And a dinner (equal to Jake's?) & cigar into the bargain! Two-hundred miles a day is certainly good progress, & I wouldn't be surprised if you saw the twinkling lights of St. Paul almost as soon as this epistle will. Let me know when to send the express package . . . . . which reminds me, uncomfortably enough, that I haven't yet sent Mortonius' rocks! But I'm relieved of one responsibility—Cook doesn't want his old raincoat, & bids me throw it away!

Cook & Munn, by the way, may get down here next week—perhaps giving me a ride back to Athol with them. I shall be glad to traverse the belt of country & see Cook's hangout, although I don't fancy Athol itself is a very quaint or alluring village. I shall have a good deal of business with Cook during the coming months, for that man in Chicago is in deadly earnest about the Bullen book. When I quoted him Cook's price he said it was *too small*, & sent a cheque for *$500.00* with a request that we use it up in increasing the luxurious appearance of the volume! The result will probably be a 6 × 9 format, with 10-point type & tasteful binding—but I must hustle to get the thing edited. I dread the task, with unperformed revision eternally jogging my elbow, but this is one thing I can't delay about.

Another gratuitous job of mine has been digging up data for a treatise on poetry which a friend of mine—the ex-amateur Maurice W. Moe of Milwaukee, now in Madison* helping a U. of Wis. professor edit a series of high-school classics—is gradually completing.[1] He wanted specimens of bad rhymes—& also triple & quadruple rhymes—from the great poets, [I could only find one quadruple—*eligible* & *intelligible* in Byron's "Don Juan"] & wanted to know whether he was justified in calling the heroic dactylic hexameter the dominant metre of classical antiquity. I told him, as regards the latter, that I didn't think he was; since the hexameter ruled only in epic, didactic, & satirical poetry. All the great dramas were in iambic trimeter, (plus lyric choral measures) whilst the amount of ancient work in the elegiac couplet, & various other non-heroic forms, includes an actual numerical majority of the poetic titans; such as Archilocus, Theognis, Tyrtaeus, Anacreon, Alcaeus, Sappho, Simonides, Alcman, Stesichorus, Pindar, Callimachus, Catullus, Propertius, Tibullus, Horace, Ovid, Martial, & so on. Rome made more of the hexameter than Greece, largely on account of the great satirists; but neither in Greece

---

*at the Y.M.C.A., & he confesses there are *mice* in his room—although he's the original Y fan

nor Rome did the heroic dactyl bulk as largely as the heroic iambic pentameter bulks with us. Another thing Moe wanted me to do was to think up a pentameter line *all in spondees*. That was a tough job, for I don't think it *can* be done with any perfection. What I finally concocted was

— — — — — — — — — —

Thus with / weak wings / that thrush / seeks out / far lands

Well—now that your journey is a completed unit, I trust you can look back on it with undivided pleasure. I'll wager little old St. Paul doesn't look half so bad, now that you have a good perspective from which to view it!

Hoping to hear from you—

Yr most obt

Necrophilistine

Notes

1. Maurice W. Moe, *Doorways to Poetry* (unpublished; apparently nonextant).

[47]   [DAW to HPL] [ANS]

[Postmarked Fremont, Ohio,
8 August 1927]
Fremont, Ohio
August 7, 1927

Dear Necrophilist:

It's about 10 p.m. now and I'm writing from the village p.o. which I discovered while hunting a place to rest after a two-hour cloudburst. I got wet a few miles beyond Cleveland last night, and have covered only a hundred miles or so today. I intended to stop and sleep, but I got several lifts while walking the road this morning and afternoon in search of a good spot, and accepted them, naturally. I slept in the Dover jail last night. No, I was not arrested. I was almost exhausted when I got that far, and couldn't take a step further. I asked the sergeant if I could sleep there. He looked me over, asked my source and destination, and then gave me a bunk and cell. The door was left open so I could "escape" if I wanted to. I ate off and on today. It's a pleasant habit that you ought to cultivate. About three blocks from this p.o. is a place that's almost as good as Jake's. For thirty-five cents, I got two large pork chops, a scoop of potatoes and gravy, bread and butter, coffee, and lemon tapioca pudding. I'm going back before I leave Fremont! You can send the package I left any time that you happen to be going by the express office, but don't go on purpose. With good luck, I'll be in St. Paul early Wednesday morning. Thursday is the latest possible date for my arrival, I think, and hope. I intend to cut my return Chicago trip to a short visit with Wright and Sprenger.[1] When I reach the Saintly City whose greatest catastrophe occurred in April, 1908,[2] I shall eat the first day and sleep the second. Gods! Won't that be an event for the historians!

I have sixty-three cents to get to Chicago on. Here is hoping. Carramba! Sacre bleu! Προς τον θεον!

Melmoth II

Notes

1. William R. Sprenger, secretary-treasurer of *WT*.
2. I.e., DAW's birth.

[48]   [HPL to DAW] [ALS]

August 9[, 1927]

My dear Wanderer:—

Your recent bulletin arrived yesterday—& my aunt is quite worried about your sleeping out in the cold & damp! I hope you took that all-day rest in some warm, dry place—though gawd knows the weather hereabouts hasn't given us much dryness! Better economise cash a bit less, & health a bit more, on the next trip. Still—youth is a resilient affair, & I dare say you're able to throw off fatigue with one good rest, & never feel the difference. I judge that you didn't stop much in Cleveland—although the art museum there is well worth exploring—& wonder how much attention you're giving Chicago. Galpin has just written that he'd be delighted to see you—but I can't catch you to transmit his message & telephone number in time! He was highly enthusiastic over C A S's French poems, which I sent him, & has almost recanted his former recantation of Smitholatry! He furnished some notes on erroneous Gallic usage which C A S will value very highly when I send them to him.

As for me—I am nearly rushed to bedlam by accumulated unperformed work! The Bullen volume is more of a job than I thought. But even so, I'm going to snatch one vacation, & go to Athol with Cook & Munn after their promised second visit this coming week-end. Being then somewhere near the ancient Deerfield region, where flourishes a local school of colonial architecture which I've never seen, I shall make my return trip a leisurely & exploratory one—perhaps trying out your mode of solicited transportation in preparation for heavier trips. Belknap will also probably pass through Athol during some part of his migrations, but I don't yet know whether his stay will coincide with mine.

Had quite a letter from Talman yesterday—& he wasn't in the least offended by my "Wyvern" criticism.[1] In fact, he was so grateful that he has just offered to draw me a book-plate (he's a decorative artist of no small capacity in an amateur way) with my coat-of-arms or any other design I may choose.[2] I shall let him—although I suppose a person as non-bibliophilic as I doesn't deserve to have such a thing as a book-plate! Talman, by the way, proposes a new member for our correspondent gang—an English professor in Johns

Hopkins Univ. who likes the weird & is about to try something on W.T. I am about to write him—his name & present habitat being Paul Mobray Wheeler,[3] 494 Orchard St., Englewood, N.J. Oh, yes—& speaking of correspondents— honest old McNeil of Brooklyn has just asked me to send you his regards. He liked you very much, & was sorry you couldn't stay longer when you & Belknap called on him.

I don't blame you for your increased desire for speed as you approach home! After all, there's no place like it; & I've not a doubt but that you'll find new charms in St. Paul's Providence-like precipices & uniquely cosmic sky-effects. Speaking of the cosmic—I've just read Wells' "War of the Worlds" *for the first time* in *Amazing Stories*,[4] & deem it the best thing of H. G.'s which I've ever seen. He really visualises his situations—& does them justice. This tale is obviously the prototype of scores of inferior imitations. Well—I hope to hear presently of your safe arrival!

Yr obt Grandsire—

The Necrophilistine

Notes

1. It does not appear that Talman's story "The Wyvern" was ever revised or published.

2. Talman eventually drew the celebrated book plate depicting a typical old Providence doorway with fan carving.

3. HPL eventually sent some of his stories to Wheeler for perusal. Wheeler had nothing published in *WT*.

4. Wells's *The War of the Worlds* (1898) appeared in *Amazing Stories* for August and September 1927.

[49]   [DAW to HPL] [AN]

[Postmarked Saint Paul, Minn.,
11 August 1927]
Tuesday, 8 A.M.

Home!

[50]   [HPL to DAW] [ANS][1]

[Postmarked Providence, R.I.,
11 August 1927]

Well—which is best, gaol or 10 Barnes? You're determined to run the gamut of life! Glad you've found the equivalent of Jake's—here's hoping you load up with enough fuel to make up for the fatigue! Don't get so tired next time—economise on the food & take it easier other ways! Hope you'll have a good time in Chicago—& wish you could have had word from me in time to make the call on Galpin. Did I say that Belknap expects to be back in N.Y. by the 15th? That being the case, I shan't be able to see him in Athol if I go there next week-end. Apparently they aren't going in the direction of West Shokan. ¶ Well—I hope you'll have good lifts on the final homeward stretch. I can imagine the unrestrained orgy of nourishment & dormitation which will follow your return—& hope that during the latter half you'll have pleasant dreams of the East. I'll send the express package on my next trip downtown—would to Pegāna the Mortonian material could be sent as easily!— Νεκρόφιλος

Notes

1. *Front:* The Shepard Cafeteria, 122–124–126 Mathewson Street, Providence, R.I.

[51]   [DAW to HPL] [ALS]

1152 Portland Ave.,

St. Paul, Minn.

Aug. 12, 1927

Dear Necrophilist:

I have finally reached home after a furious dash across half the continent. The last time I wrote, I think, was at Fremont, Ohio, when looking for a place to roost. I almost decided to try the jail there, but it was three or four blocks from the p.o., and when I began to walk, it began to rain. I sat in a kind of alcove made by a double flight of steps that sheltered a stone ledge adjutting the sidewalk, and waited for the rain to stop. I dozed off, and when I awoke the rain had stopped, but while I was trying to get up enough energy to walk to the station, I aroused again, and kept this up all night, said "all night" being from midnight to four a.m., which was my average night's rest on the home trail. I reached Toledo by 7:30 a.m. in rain, and ate breakfast at a place like Jacque's but serving an even lower clientele where you can get a bowl of soup, sausage or one of three other meats, coffee, a jelly roll, bread and butter, potatoes and gravy, for **fifteen** cents! When I was about forty miles beyond Toledo, I got picked up by three kids of sixteen or so who were heading West on two motorcycles. I rode in the sidecar of one. We broke down two or three times with chain trouble, and were held up by rain in the evening; hence, we didn't make the 250 or 300 miles to Chicago till the next afternoon. But when we went, we went! The kids were fine drivers; we sailed down the streets of Chicago at 30 to 60 miles per hour during the rush hour! From a distance, we looked like motorcycle cops, because the first machine, the one I was in, was a Harley-Davidson. We all wore goggles and we had the cutouts open; and some of the traffic policemen held up traffic while we roared down Michigan Boulevard! I got in Chicago too late to see Wright and Sprenger, and I hadn't the address of Galpin (your letter with his address awaited me at home), and much as I regretted missing him, I decided to keep on, since I would have to stop overnight, and would also lose most of the next day. Hence, my stay was very brief, though I carried away a more pleasant impression than the first time I saw it. The eastern districts were the most hideous that I saw in any city on my whole trip, but I ate a light lunch at some downtown one-arm joint where I had the finest apple pie since I left St. Paul; this atoned in part for the city's deformities. I took a train home on the end of my trip, since the roads through Wisconsin have little traffic and are none too good, and reached home about 8:00 o'clock Tuesday, no Wednesday morning. It was good to be back! The city looked marvellously fair in the chilly dawn. The news from home was bad in only a minor sense, but I couldn't waste much time on the return.

Thus endeth the Odyssey of a summer hobo!

Derleth, of course, I missed by taking the train across Wisconsin, but I'll get in touch with him this fall. I am swamped with miscellaneous work and odds and ends, not the least of which is getting the meals and taking care of the family while my mother is away. I am sorry I missed Wright, also. So he turned down "The Strange High House"? Too bad—this, of course, immediately damns the literary merit of the story; you ought to be ashamed of yourself for being so presumptuous, and might just as well throw the story away since it is utterly valueless if "Weird Tales" rejects it. Let this be a lesson to you not to be so bold with our front-rank publications!

Are you sure that "Nathicana" is the poem whose genesis you explained to me? As I remember, the "joke" poem was in another magazine, had an introduction and conclusion, and was in heroic couplets.[1] But if "Nathicana" is the poem, I think it defeats its purpose. It is a rare and curious kind of literary freak, a satire too good, so that, instead of parodying, it passes as, the original. Dwyer and I both like it very much. I have just read it again, and even with your explanation in mind do not find the satire.

Many thanks for the chance to read Cas.'s letter and the critique of the exhibition. I have just written him, and the drawings as a result will probably start their journey pretty soon. I am returning them herewith.

I spent most of my first two days home unpacking the books I bought and arranging them. My father bought me a new bookcase the day before I returned; it holds about three hundred books on its five shelves, but already there is less than one vacant shelf! I must get after Kirk though; he didn't send on one of the books I most wanted. I hope he hasn't put it back on his shelves and sold it.

Congratulations—financial—and commiserations—temporal—on your accumulating work! But if it were mine, I think I'd "ditch" it all and ramble up to Athol and over to West Shokan. It was nice of your aunt to think of my health; but sleeping out did no harm except make me chilly for the time being. I've always had good health, though I'm not precisely a Hercules.

I'm already looking forward to another trip to Providence and the Master of Ceremonies.

With piece, and pie—
The Wanderer at Rest.

Notes

1. DAW refers to "The Poe-et's Nightmare" (1916), in which a blank-verse section is surrounded by rhyming heroic couplets.

[52]   [HPL and W. Paul Cook to DAW] [ANS][1]

[Postmarked Providence, R.I.,
14 August 1927]

Welcome home! I'll bet St. Paul looked good to you! Did you see Wright in Chicago? I suppose this is one of your first home days of waking, after the day of eating & the one of sleeping. Does it seem as cosy as gaol? As you see, the conclaves keep up. We ate at Jake's last night, & now we're going down to Maxfield's to punish the 28.[2] Art envious? Yr obt Necrophilistine

---

"Neither Brute nor Human"[3]

W P Cook

Moe says that C A S has a fine notice by George Sterling in the new Braith-waite annual[4]

[P.S.] Belknap is back in N.Y. after a somewhat abbreviated trip.

[P.P.S.] Starrett has written in praise of my tales. He likes "Arthur Jermyn" best.

Notes

1. *Front:* Bird's-Eye View Showing New Union Station, Providence, R.I.
2. HPL refers to the ice cream parlor run by Charles R. Maxfield, Sr. (1879–1949), and his wife, Julia A. Maxfield. It featured up to 32 different flavors of ice cream.
3. Edgar Allan Poe, "The Bells" (1849), l. 87.
4. George Sterling, "The Poetry of the Pacific Coast," in *Anthology of Magazine Verse for 1926*, ed. William Stanley Braithwaite (Boston: B. J. Brimmer Co., 1926), 84–103; CAS is mentioned on p. 100.

[53]   [HPL to DAW] [ANS][1]

[Postmarked Worcester, Mass.,
19 August 1927]

Well—who's the Wanderer now? Like you, I'm meeting Cook here at 2 P.M.—ahoy for Athol, DEERFIELD, &c &c. May take side trip by myself later—Portland, &c. Mediocre weather, but will hope for luck. Will answer your letter shortly.

Yr obt Grandpa

Notes

1. Souvenir folder of Worcester, MA.

[54] [HPL and W. Paul Cook to DAW] [ANS][1]

[Postmarked Deerfield, Mass.,
22 August. 1927]

Necrophilous wandering! I'll bet I'm getting three times as big a kick out of the Swift & Deerfield valleys as you did! Deerfield is the summit of my earthly ambition—I've just gone broke on postcards! Cook is an ideal host, & I like Athol immensely. Tomorrow we may see a bit of New Hampshire.
Yr obt Grandfather—Theobaldus

Theobald sure seems to be enjoying himself. Have blown in $5.00 on post cards! Cook

Notes

1. *Front:* [No text; picture of tree.]

[55] [HPL to DAW] [ALS]

[Postmarked Athol, Mass.,
24 August 1927]
Home address—
10 Barnes St.,
Providence, R.I.,
August 23, 1927.

Dear Melmoth:—

As you have been made aware by recent messages, your laconic univerbal card & interesting final travelogue reached me in the midst of a surprising prolongation of my social season! I was indeed delighted to hear of your safe return, & hope the express package reached you without disaster. Just now I am still sampling the Athol hospitality of which you had such a brief taste—though I have had only one glimpse of Munn, who was called away Friday night because of the accidental death of a friend in Pennsylvania. I shall see him again tonight, however. Tomorrow I hit the lone trail again—

probably in the direction of Boston rather than Providence, since I want to work in the Portland trip if possible before going home.

In general, my Odyssey has probably been too traditional & antiquarian to be of much interest to you. On Saturday Cook took me on the same Amherst-Deerfield side trip which he gave you, & I certainly appreciated it to the last exquisite drop. Then Sunday we went on the Lake Sunapee excursion which rain cut short in your case. This time the skies were lenient, & we had an excellent journey involving a digression into Vermont, whose soil I had never previously trod. At Brattleboro we paused to call on the amateur poet Arthur Goodenough, & I was certainly glad to see this beloved veteran of the cause. Goodenough is a typical old-time rustic of a pattern almost extinct today. He has never seen a city of any size, & seldom goes even to the adjacent small town of Brattleboro. In speech, dress, & manner he reflects an admirable though vanished phase of American life—& you will smile when you see the archaic Prince Albert[1] he insisted on donning when Cook took his photograph with a new camera bought especially for the occasion. His stately courtesy & hospitality are worthy of the 17th century to which he intellectually belongs, & I was touched by the courtly grace with which he gave me a copy of his new book of poems.[2] He dwells in a peaked, unpainted farmhouse 150 years old, set with unconscious art on a hillside in the loveliest bit of unspoiled New England country I have ever seen.[3] I fear that the bard does not fully appreciate his setting, since he has never lived away from it & therefore lacks standards of comparison. North of Brattleboro we encountered a very wide detour, & were forced deeply inland from the Connecticut River. This gave me a better sight of the typical Vermont country with its quaint covered bridges & undecayed crossroads hamlets than I would otherwise have secured,[4] & I was very grateful for a circumstance which was merely provoking to Cook. We finally reached Lake Sunapee & returned through a less picturesque country, but I shall never forget my ample first sight of Vermont. Yesterday I took my writing materials to a high hill northwest of Athol, from which I obtained the finest rural vista I have ever seen in my life, with Mt. Monadnock in the distance. Today is rainy, but tomorrow I think I'll start onward rain or shine. I want to be home by Saturday night, since Munn is coming down on Sunday.

Your record of adventure west of Cleveland is indeed an exciting chapter. That night of drowsing probably sounds more comfortable than it was—& I hope it didn't give you any rheumatiz' in the j'ints! As for the Fremont meal—I shall have to concede that Jake's is quite definitely outclassed! But guard your weight! I'm down to *142* now, by the best Athol scales. Your wild ride through Chicago has epic material in it—& I truly envy you the experience. Too bad, though, that you couldn't get in touch with Galpin.

About "Nathicana"—it surely is the satire I mean, & is wholly distinct from the other verse with "joke" framework of heroics which I read to you in

Providence. I'm sorry if it fell short of its purpose—but that is no doubt a frequent circumstance with burlesque of the sort. It is hard to give just the right touch of humour in mimicking the emptiness of certain kinds of stereotyped & meaningless fantasy.

Cook is coming on well with *The Recluse*, & will probably have it done in a few days—all but the cover. Meanwhile our travail on the Bullen book continues. All the main text is now in type, but the preface is yet to be whipped into shape.[5] The arrangement & details are all provided for, & we are now debating on things like the binding, colour, &c. Out of all the poems submitted, only 40 were good enough to include. These I have arranged by subject in four classes.

Well—I trust St. Paul is getting reasonably familiar to you again, & that you're all ready for the second Providence jaunt next year!

Yr obt

Necrophilist

Notes

1. I.e., a long, double-breasted frock coat, named after Prince Albert (1819–1861), husband of Queen Victoria.
2. Arthur Goodenough (1871–1936). The book probably was *Songs of Four Decades* (Athol, MA: W. Paul Cook, 1927).
3. The house served as partial inspiration for the home of Henry Wentworth Akeley in "The Whisperer in Darkness" (1930).
4. HPL wrote about this visit in "Vermont—A First Impression."
5. To do this, HPL needed to revise his essay "The Poetry of John Ravenor Bullen" (*United Amateur* 25, No. 1 [September 1925]: 1–3, 6), in part to reflect the fact that Bullen was now deceased.

[56]   [HPL, H. Warner Munn, and W. Paul Cook to DAW] [ANS][1]

[Postmarked Athol, Mass.,
24 August 1927]

Took the Lake Sunapee trip & saw Arthur Goodenough at Brattleboro. Pity you couldn't work it in when you were here. Now to cut across the coast & do some colonial seaports before going home. I hope you appreciated the scenic loveliness of this hill country—it is truly an orgy of landscape magnificence.

More later—Yr obt Necrophilos

H. Warner Munn

Why didn't we think of this post card stunt when you were here.

Cook

Notes

1. *Front:* Petersham Road, Athol, Mass.

[57]   [HPL to DAW]   [ANS][1]

[Postmarked Boston, Mass.,
25 August 1927]

Well, young man—your necrophilous Grandpa is back in Boston with a ticket for Portland, Maine, in his pocket! It's a great life—sing ho for the open road! Ride from Athol was splendid—extending through northern Mass. towns I had never seen. Had dinner this evening at our memorable headquarters, the Excellent Lunch—across from the Y.M.C.A. I'm slowly repaying them for their hospitality of last month. And—odd tho' it may seem after the debatable accomodations of July—I am stopping at the Y. Got a queer kind of inner room for *$1.00*—which is much better than could be done elsewhere. I hate low-grade hotels. Will drop you cards from suitable points later on. Hope the weather will be decent! Mean to stop & see Tryout Smith in Haverhill before I'm through.

Yr obt Grandpa

Notes

1. *Front:* The Handmaid of the Lord. From a Painting by John S. Sargent, in the Boston Public Library.

[58]   [HPL to DAW]   [ANS—Envelope only]

[Postmarked Portland, Me.,
26 August 1927]

[On envelope:] From one Y to another! In the Portland one tonight—& this is a *bird!* Just finished, spick & span, *Georgian architecture,* cheerful rooms, & solicitously courteous chap at the desk. Believe me, son, it doesn't do to knock all Y's without a hearing! ¶ Glorious day for the coach trip. Portland is not nearly as colonial as Providence, & looks just as citified, although it's only ⅓ as large. Very fascinating from its marine colour—I went up that ancient tower (1807) shown on one of these cards, & had the maritime vista of my life! Have done the whole town & visited the colonial suburb of Stroudwater. Shall do the two Longfellow houses tomorrow—also visit Yarmouth, a quaint & ancient fishing village which will form my farthest north. The White Mts. are visible from here—had Mt. Washington pointed out to me. On Saturday I swing down to Portsmouth, Newburyport, & Haverhill. Maybe home Sunday, maybe not. It's a great life!

Yr obt & necrophilous
Grandpa

[59]   [HPL to DAW] [ANS][1]

[Postmarked Portland, Me.,
26 August 1927]

Ultima Thule! I'll get no farther north than this. *But* . . . I've about decided to stay over & take a $3.20 White Mt. excursion Sunday!

Yr necrophagous
Grandpa

Notes

1. *Front:* Memorial Hall, Yarmouth, Me.

[60]   [HPL to DAW] [ANS][1]

[Postmarked Bretton Woods, N.H.,
27 August 1927]

Got to White Mts a day ahead of schedule as planned. Ascended Mt. Washington, but find mountains slightly lacking in subtlety.

More anon.
Yr obt
Necrophilist

P.S. Glimpsed The Other Gods!

Notes

1. *Front:* The Flume, Franconia Notch, White Mountains, N. H.

[61]   [HPL to DAW] [ANS][1]

[Postmarked Bangor and Boston
29 August 1927]

Slowly edging homeward! Good old Portsmouth hasn't changed in the four years since I saw it last.[2] Most colonial city in America! Now for Newburyport!

Yr obt
Necrophilist

Notes

1. *Front:* Doorway of Pierce Mansion, Erected 1799, Court Street and Haymarket Square, Portsmouth. N H.
2. Actually, HPL was last there in November 1924.

[62]   [HPL to DAW] [ANS]¹

[Postmarked Newburyport, Mass.,
30 August 1927]

And the old man wanders on! This is a great town—a study in colourful decadence. The business section remains exactly as it was rebuilt in 1812 & 1813 after the great fire of 1811. They don't even have bright lights! Am stopping at a Y which would sustain your opinion as well as the Portland one sustained mine! Whole blocks here remain as they were before the Revolution—same houses, unpaved, & no sidewalks. These districts, like the corresponding ones in Portsmouth, are now slums.

Yr obt
Necro.

Notes

1. *Front:* Bird's-Eye View of Newburyport and Harbor, Newburyport, Mass.

[63]   [HPL to DAW] [ANS]1

[Postmarked Haverhill, Mass.,
31 August 1927]

Haverhill is really a metropolis—looks the part, though only 60,000 population. Have called on my honest old friend Tryout Smith & am now looking for routes to colonial Ipswich & Gloucester. The local Y is the kind you know!

Yr obt
Necro.

Notes

1. *Front:* Merrimack Street, Looking East, Haverhill, Mass.

[64]   [HPL to DAW] [AN]

[Postmarked Gloucester, Mass.,
1 September 1927]

[Souvenir Folder of Gloucester, Mass.] Still wandering! Gloucester is great, & I'm doing it with much greater minuteness than five years ago. You'd go wild over the cliffs at Magnolia, near here—in fact, I told you about them in July.

[65] [DAW to HPL] [ALS]

1152 Portland Ave.,

St. Paul, Minn.

Sept. 2, 1927

Dear Necrophilist:

How I envy you that extended tour through old Smith's paintings have just come. [*sic*] They are

MAGNIFICENT!

MAGNIFICENT!!

MAGNIFICENT!!!

beyond anything I dreamed of or expected! They are breath-taking in their cosmic sweep and the terrible implication of worlds of beauty and horror and fantastic dream! They are perfect in their delineation of inconceivable vistas and fragmentary supremely lovely and stupendous and cosmic landscapes! They are masterpieces of glittering and terrific and morbidly-decadent colour-contrasts! In their sheer and superb rendering of those wondrous and remote and unknown realms of imagination, of horror, of phantasmal splendour and monstrous glory and sinister suggestion which few men are ever permitted to hold in memory and fewer still to depict, they exceed and go beyond anything I know in all the interminable dessicated [*sic*] rubbish-heap of conventional-ized European and American painting with the possible exception of Kay Nielsen, Odilon Redon, and perhaps Harry Clarke.[1] It is impossible to ex-press an adequate appreciation of them! It is impossible to hint at even a tithe of their overwhelming appalling decadent beauty! They are as haunting as those uttermost abysses of frenzy and nightmare-born terror and unparalleled weird loveliness which Smith has woven into his poems, as those incredible and nameless gulfs which are never penetrated save by the dope-addict in his most colossal and remote space-and-time-destroying flights of the disembod-ied memory! Their beauty is a marvellous, an intolerable, an enthralling and rapturous representation in strange melancholy and fearful colour of the most alien ultra-cosmic dreamlands and hypnotic spheres of weirdly wildly exotic vistas and nocturnal borderlands of sleep! [Wavy line across page]

Will write as soon as I can sanely.

Donald

Notes

1. DAW refers to the artists Kai Nielsen (Danish; 1882–1924), Odilon Redon (French; 1840–1916), and Harry Clarke (British; 1890–1931).

[66] [HPL to DAW] [ANS][1]

[Postmarked Gloucester, Mass.,
2 September 1927]

Don't you wish you were sitting on these cliffs in a glorious blaze of Saturnian sunlight as I am?

Yr obt

Necro.

Notes

1. *Front:* Along the Shore, Magnolia, Mass.

[67] [HPL to DAW] [ANS][1]

[Postmarked Marblehead, Mass.,
3 September 1927]

Nearing home at last! Marblehead can't be beat!

Yr obt

Necro.

Notes

1. *Front:* A Quaint Old Street in Marblehead, Mass.

[68] [HPL to DAW] [ANS][1]

[Postmarked Providence, R.I.,
7 September 1927]

Say—d'ye know—I really believe you rather like those Smith pictures! Incidentally, I'll confess to no slight curiosity about the material which could
prompt such nobly poetick flights, & shall be no reluctant recipient when you
can bring yourself to send it on to me. No spoofing—C A S has seen terrible
objects, vistas, & worlds which no one ever saw before or will ever see in future—except through his mediation. He's the real goods, & I surely wish he
could get the recognition he deserves. ¶ Am reaping the whirlwind after my
scenic & architectural spree. My gawd—what piles of work! Not a second to
breathe! Just finished preface & second proofs of Bullen book—thank heav'n
that's moving along! Drop a line when you can regain your breath—& don't
feel afraid to jar the old man's nerves with the sight of those pictures when
you can spare 'em.

Yr obt Grandpa

Notes

1. *Front:* University Hall and Manning Hall, Brown University.

[69]   [DAW to HPL] [ALS]

1152 Portland Ave.,
St. Paul, Minn.
Sept. 8, 1927

Dear Νεκρο—

I dimly remember starting a letter to you last week which was scattered to the winds in its genesis. Permit me to rectify the dissolution by present atonement.

That was a glorious trip of yours! I would have given all my hopes of heaven and more valuable gifts if I could only have accompanied you on your wanderings along the New England coast. I have carefully preserved all the cards and folders, for they represent an Odyssey which I hope I can some day accomplish myself. The sea-views of Magnolia and to a lesser extent the other coastal towns are magnificent, and I particularly appreciated a picture of the quaint old street in Marblehead which, among others, we rambled on last July. I have visually been following you with the aid of the numerous cards and have tried and partially succeeded mentally to get part of the great pleasure you derived from the actuality. I had plenty of leisure in which to dream of your idyllic holiday, since I have done little save write letters, scribble verse, and scrape varnish from floors since I returned. May the gods be as generous to me in the near future!

Our mutual friend in [*sic*] a general farrago and holocaust in his Oct. issue which included among other things the omission of Smith's "Saturnienne" and a prose filler left out 26 lines of "The Red Brain" from various places by some incomprehensible method of deletion.[1] For no particular reason, this reminds me that I have time now and will copy that short tale of yours if you will send it on.

I didn't mean that "Nathicana" was a failure when I criticised it. Both Dwyer and I took a great liking to it, but we prefer to take it at its face value rather than to dive beneath and find the burlesque. If the matter ever became controversial, I could put up a strong argument to prove that N. was *not* a burlesque! At any rate, I like it, and that is as much as you can say for any literary attempt.

A curious fact came to my attention some days ago: in a hinterland region between St. Paul and Minneapolis, I discovered drug-stores that *do* sell coffee and sandwiches! Whether they are a recent efflorescence or of established pedigree, I can not say. They may easily have existed for years since I never saw or rather examined the region before.

The express package came all right. Many thanks again for taking the trouble, but you should have sent it collect as I directed. May Midas be at the bottom of your purse if you prepay the Mortonius mountains! Have you resigned yourself to your fate as yet and attacked the colossus?

I hope the Bullen book is worth the time and labour that you are putting on it, as well as Cook, to say nothing of its sponsor's cash! I have succeeded in rushing arrangements for a book of my own poems, and expect to send the ms. on to Cook in a week or two.

That Cook is a marvellous host I know from experience! But so are all you Easterners. I was warned to expect frigidity and barriers in the East. My disappointment was great—but not painful! It would give me great satisfaction if all my similar expectations met with a similar pleasant frustration! (N.b. Can an expectation be *frustrated?*)

You taught me one thing, at least, during my sojourn—how to write letters with greater facility. This one required less than an hour.

I will repack and ship on the Smith paintings, in a week or so when I have feasted on them, not enough, but as much as I feel I can without holding them too long. I had a lot of things to say in this letter; but all that has entered my mind the past five days is S M I T H. If I can recapture them from nebulosity, I will include them in a later specimen of my choice handwriting!

Your obedient,
Great-Great-Great, not
so great, grandson.

Notes

1. HPL's "Pickman's Model" and DAW's "The Red Brain" appeared in the October 1927 *WT*. CAS's "The Saturnienne" appeared in the December 1927 issue.

[70]   [HPL to DAW] [ALS]

Home—Septr. 11[, 1927]

Dear Melmoth:—

I was glad to receive yours of the 8th, & to learn that you found something of interest in my small-scale Odyssey even after your own extensive performance in that line. Mine was a highly specialised journey, with very definite objects in view; & I can truthfully say that it was a success in every way. I certainly got my money's worth in quaintness & scenery, & am already looking forward to a next-year's pilgrimage which shall cover the Cape Cod & South-of-Boston region as this one covered the terrain north of Boston. My record of Y M C A's is as follows:

Boston—medium to poor
Portland—immaculate, artistic, & magnificent
Portsmouth—closed on Sunday so had to patronise the Kearsage House
Newburyport—rather seedy & run-down
Haverhill—rotten! no central bldg.—scattered over a group of Victorian houses
Gloucester—very fair

The things you would have liked the best are the sea-cliffs & the White Mountains. I don't know whether or not you've ever seen real mountains—I had not, hence the spectacle of these celebrated peaks was to me especially impressive. The slopes rose sheer & forbidding as the train stole among them, & as clouds touched the summits I could well imagine the habitancy of strange & Clarcashtonic shapes in those unfrequented altitudes. The view ascending Mt Washington was beyond imagination—& when near the summit clouds gathered below, leaving one lone & cosmic on the barren pinnacle, across which swept furious winds that are not of earth.

The monthly offering of our noble colleague, Farnsworth Wrong, esq., is indeed getting worse & worse. I don't know a duller number than the present one—"The Red Brain" being its sole redeeming feature. The novelette—"The Dark Lore"—is a continuous mess of almost unprecedented amorphousness & puerility, whilst "The Bride of Osiris"[1] is on a par with the Nick Carter Weekly of ancient but unclassical memory. Too bad I didn't warn you about Farnie's deleting habit. I brought him up short at the very outset, when he practiced it on "The Festival", & he's been a good boy ever since so far as I'm concerned. "Print intact or return" was the pointed ultimatum which I issued in 1924, & since then I've had nothing to complain of.[2] Incidentally—I am enclosing that "Iranon" effusion, which strikes me in retrospect as drearily mawkish. Copy it as thou wilt—but don't say I advised you to do it, or ask me my opinion of your taste in doing it! As to poor old "Nathicana"—so far as I'm concerned, the reader may take it any way he jolly well pleases, but I don't commend the critical sense which can't spot the obviously (& intentionally) mechanical & conventionally literary nature of the droningly repeated images. The object was the demonstrate how essentially *empty* this form of composition is when divorced from at least the elements of intellectual content, & if the demonstration didn't work, it isn't my fault. That kind of stuff could be listlessly ground out by the yard without any thought, effort, or even attention, & would sound just the same. Words—words—words!

Congratulations to the Municipal Dioscuri on getting some real drug stores at last! The best way to test their status—i.e., whether established or novel—is to watch the other Æsculapian emporia of the region, & see whether or not the quasi-restaurantic gesture spreads. If it does—as I think it will—then you may justly regard the practice as an innovation. Customs like that, no matter how local their origin, generally spread in the end over all the wide expanse of our neatly standardised civilisation; so that it is only a question of time as to when the St Paulist & Minneapolitan will snatch his breakfast across the soda-fountain. The cafeteria arose as a strictly Californian institution—but gawd, look at it now! Everything spreads—you'll even have a Jake's some day!

As to that Mortonian freight shipment . . . . why the hell did you have to mention such a thing??!!!?? Grrrrr . . . yaahhh . . . Now just for spite I'm going to talk about *dental work!* When are you going to have all that nice extraction done, & the plates filled, & the bridge-work begun? Fine prospect! .... & that's the way I feel when I glance at the tall paper bags in the northwest corner . . . . . . here, give me air! I feel strangely faint & oppressed. Speaking of burthens—the Bullen book is *not* worth the time & labour, but must be done all the same. I've just read second galley proofs on the main text, & sent Cook the preface. This means that additional proofreading will be my only further concern with it. I'm glad to hear that your book of poems is taking form, & will read one set of the proofs if you like—the Old Man has a sort of eagle gaze for blunders. Cook will give you a good job—& I hope that the sales end may come up to all your expectations.

I'm glad that the East & its denizens pleasantly disappointed you. You can't believe popular conceptions of various regions & types—individuals are individuals, & only the flabby & colourless take on the general rhythms. According to legend, all you Westerners ought to be loud-voiced, progressive hustlers, with souls attuned only to real-estate values & chamber-of-commerce overtones—& yet, where did C A S & Loveman & Galpinius & half a hundred others, not excepting the Wanderer, originate? It's a complex world!

That case of Needham vandalism looks melancholy—though to tell the truth the doomed structure doesn't look very colonial to me. In fact, I never heard of it & don't know what it is! I wish the destroyer luck with his new house! Enclosed is a winter view of Marblehead (please return) giving an idea of my own first sight of it on Dec. 17, 1922. It is really much finer than in summer.

Glad my lessons in rapid epistolary composition are taking effect—& wish I could double or treble my own speed amidst the accumulated masses of mail with which I'm now coping! I am on the watch for that Smith material, & hope that it may inspire my sluggish old brain at least a tenth as much as it seems to have inspired your nimble young one! And when you can recapture other ideas, let's here them! ¶ With profoundest assurances of a cordial continuance of my most distinguished consideration, I am, sir, Ever y^r most obt

Avus Necrophilus.[3]

[*Enclosure:* Clipping from *Providence Journal* (10 September 1927): "And Now the One Arm Lunch Goes In for Higher Education"] See what our influence did to Jake

[*Enclosure:* "White Mountain Excursions"]

Notes

1. *WT,* October 1927: Nictzin Dyalhis, "The Dark Lore"; Otis Adelbert Kline, "The Bride of Osiris" (3 of 3).

2. The ultimatum actually was issued upon HPL's initial submittal of his stories in late summer 1923: "If the tale cannot be printed as written, down to the very last semicolon and comma, it must gratefully accept rejection." HPL, Letter to the Editor, *WT* 2, No. 2 (September 1923): 81–82; *Uncollected Letters* 4–5.

3. "Avus" is Latin for ancestor, father, or grandfather (avunculus = a maternal uncle).

[71]   [HPL to DAW] [ANS][1]

[Postmarked Providence, R.I.,
19 September 1927]

Thanks! A millionfold, thanks! Now I shall have to try it on Wright! ¶ And incidentally—as you value your aesthetic soul, don't fail to read "The Worm Ouroboros", by E. R. Eddison, within 24 hours!!! Art? Phantasy? Prose-poetry? Look & see! Man, what a style! Cook lent it to me, & if you can't get it in St. Paul I know he wouldn't mind my sub-lending his copy. How about it? Other loaned books I've been reading are:

Goat-Song, by Franz Werfel
New Lands—by Charles Fort
The Slayer of Souls—by Robt W Chambers
The Three Eyes—by Maurice LeBlanc
Atlantida—by Pierre Benoit
The World's Desire—Haggard & Lang.
Yr obt
Νεκρο

Notes

1. *Front:* University Hall and Manning Hall, Brown University.

[72]   [HPL and Wilfred Blanch Talman to DAW] [ANS][1]

[Postmarked Providence, R.I.,
24 September 1927]

Greetings from the latest conclave—& meet the guy *who discovered Jake's!!!* We dined there last night, & shall do so again tonight. The chicken gumbo was great!

Yr obt Νεκρόφιλος

I wonder why our dear friend H P L doesn't insist upon the original spelling of Jacque's—since he so often is particular in that way?

Wilfred Blanch Talman

[Marginal note by HPL:] I consider pronunciation the more important linguistic element

Notes

1. *Front:* College St. to Market Sq. Showing Hospital Trust and Chamber of Commerce, Providence, R. I.

[73] [HPL to DAW] [ALS]

Tuesday
[September 27, 1927]

Majestick Melmoth:—

Well—THEY HAVE COME! Ugh—wggghhh—nggrrrrh—— Planets reel in space—cosmic dust rattles on the panes of magic casements—SOUNDS trickle in through unfathom'd deeps from realms whose whereabouts I dare not name . . . . I reel, I faint . . . . . But more anon. I'll be interested to know which ones are your presumptive property, & hope they'll be treated well. Incidentally, though, the gang must not be blamed for the state of the Dwyer drawings. They were almost as bad when the artist sent them to me, & he apologised very profusely for their tattered form. Subsequent damage is really no more than legitimate wear & tear. I'll send on the Clericashtoniana in the original package with proper insurance, & can vouch that they will leave my hands in prime condition.

Yes—I went over "Iranon" & corrected whatever stenographic slips there were—though there really weren't many. I can never cease to be grateful for your kindness in preparing the copy—it's more than I'd do for any guy living! I haven't yet sent it to Bre'r Farnsworth—as I read it again it strikes me as not particularly weird . . . . . though that is as much for it as against it, to judge from a good part of the material in "weird" tales.

Shall be interested to watch the progress of your book. The Bullen volume is taking shape finely, so that all the work ahead of me in that job is repeated proofreading. Everything is in type, & all details are decided on. I'll try to get you a copy—as a curiosity.

So you've read "Ouroboros"! Didn't you find it magnificently poetic? The "Mercurian" setting was of course a mere surface gesture, the tale itself being preëminently terrestrial, with mediaeval wonder as the keynote. Some of the pictures are unforgettable—I can still see Koshtra Pivrarcha[1] towering up snow-clad & mysterious . . . . . and God! Those *Mantichores!* . . . . take 'em away! . . . . I've just sub-lent the book to Belknap. Let me know how you like "The Sorcerer's Apprentice",[2] of which I've heard a great deal. I had an idea that it was a study in abnormal psychology rather than in supernatural horror.

I presume you received the joint card from me & from the discoverer of "Jake's". He blew in Friday morning—staying with another local friend—& I saw a good deal of him between that time & last night, when he left on the New York boat. He duly apologised to swarthy Domingo for his epistolary neglect, & is fully restored to good standing at the classic counter! He is getting to be more & more of an artist, & is about to design me a bookplate with some Providence colonial matter as its motif. Heraldry is also his hobby, & he drew out some fine coats-of-arms from verbal descriptions in my family records.

Just received a new story from Belknap, of which *I* am the "hero"! It is the most *cosmically* hideous thing he has yet written, & I hope Wright will accept it. The title is "The Space-Eaters."[3]

All best wishes for Satan's reign—

Yr obt
ΝΕΚΡΟΦΙΛΟΣ

P.S. Belknap writes that Loveman has been in the hospital for 2 weeks at Cleveland after being struck by a motor. Whole vacation spoilt! But he's recovering & will be back on the job in a week.

[*Enclosure:* Postcard (Water Front showing Sky Scrapers by Night, Providence, R. I.); no writing on back.]

Notes

1. A mountain in *The Worm Ouroboros*.
2. By Hanns Heinz Ewers.
3. FBL, "The Space-Eaters" (*WT,* July 1928).

[74]   [DAW to HPL] [ALS]

1152 Portland Ave.,
St. Paul, Minn.
Oct. 2, 1927

Dear Necrophilist:

I am now suffering from an attack of schoolitis from which I fear I shall not recover till next spring. I had been making good progress on my novels, but now they will have to languish until the Master of Ceremonies again has leisure to summon the infernal powers.

"Taprobana" and "The Desert Oasis" are the two pictures that I shall purchase now. Later on, if I am wealthy enough, I intend to take "The Den of the Cockatrice", "Dreamland", and some of the tapestries. I'd like to get the entire group, but that is a paradisal dream which is not likely to be realised.

I got the heartbreaking card you and Talman sent from Jake's, and dreamed of eating colossal amounts of epicurean food. My meals come at eccentric intervals now when they come at all, and I have many a time wished that a branch would be established at the University.

Yours truly is learning how to dance. I intend to "take in" the senior prom and a couple of sorority formals this year and have as good a time as possible this last year.

I think Cook is setting my book up, though I haven't seen any proofs as yet. I am assured of all the local publicity I want, on the University Daily as well as the Twin City papers. My father has told some of his friends about the book and has already taken orders for delivery on publication!

Loveman was certainly unfortunate. I wrote him several weeks ago but he didn't answer the letter, and I'll write again this afternoon.

I'd be very glad to get a copy of the Bullen book. I'm curious to see what you've been slaving over. I like the postcard of Providence at night. I have made two efforts to find you some good postals of St. Paul but haven't had any success yet. The art doesn't seem to be nearly as highly developed here.

Have you heard from Mortonius? And how are your two aunts? Remember me to them—I have pleasant memories of my stay.

I'd like to read Belknap's new tale if it's available for loan. What is his new address?

> Yours for the return of His Satanic
> Majesty,
> The Sorcerer's Apprentice.

[P.S.] Have the gang return Smith's pictures to me first.

[75]   [HPL to DAW]   [ALS]

> 10 Barnes St.,
> Providence, R.I.,
> Octr. 7, 1927

Dear Melmoth:—

I am glad to hear that you are occupied with pleasant scholastic concernments, & fancy your novels will not permanently suffer from the interruption. You are young enough to be exempt from the need of hurrying matters—bless my soul, but what a prodigious expanse of years you children have before you!

Well—I have duly digested the Clericashtoniana, & lament the poverty which prevents me from making heavy investments therein. Your ebullient reaction to this material was surely not unjustified, & I would undoubtedly rhapsodise in a precisely similar strain if I were as young & full of energy! The choice of pictures you have made seems to shew a very intelligent discrimination—for it is in those poisonous nightmares of lush & polychromatic vegetation that the daemon Klarkash-Ton reveals one of his most poignant & potent moods. The paintings on black cloth have a charm all their own—& before long I shall certainly write a story with a morbid hero whose study boasts extensive hangings of that sort. Behind such unwholesome arras almost any blasphemy might well hatch! I have now re-crated this material for shipment to Dwyer, & am transmitting to him by mail the same forwarding instructions—$200.00 valuation, &c—which you transmitted to me. I will, as you request, tell Little Belknap to return the shipment to you instead of to Klarkash-Ton. That young decadent's new address, by the way, is *230 West 97th St.*—at the SE corner of Broadway. I hate to see poor old 823 in the wrecker's hands—it was the one spot in all the accursed desert of New York which seemed something like home. How Felis will ever survive the change I'm sure I don't know! I returned Belknap's tale to him with a few critical comments, & am sure he'll be glad to lend it to you if it isn't already sent off to Brother Farnsworth. I rather think Wright will accept it, for there is enough "action" in it to satisfy the avidly gaping throng of Quinn fans & Dyalhis hounds. Speaking of Farnie's alleged magazine—the latest number sustains its best traditions of inexpensive vacuity, there being just one tale worthy of the perusal of a civilised being—"The Shadows", by Henry S. Whitehead. F. W. informs me that Whitehead is a clergyman. He is certainly well-informed & cultivated, & knows the Danish West Indies like a book. You will also find in the current issue a story by Manly Wellman[1]—a friend & fellow-student of Talman's at Columbia—which wouldn't be outrageously bad if it weren't deplorably trite.

Speaking of Talman—his visit here was highly enjoyable, & he led me back to Jake's for the first time since your departure! Swarthy Domingo was very cordial, & magnanimously forgave his once steady patron for his epistolary neglect. Incidentally—Talman enlightened me concerning the identity of "Jake". It seems that there is a real person by this name—Adam Jacques—who actually pronounces his own patronymick *Jakes*. This is the big boss—& you may be able to recall him as the somewhat thick-set man with a moustache—the only one behind the counter to sport such an hirsute adornment. Domingo, however, is the life of the place. He, & he only, has the true quality of temperament or individual personality.

Well, well! So you're learning how to trip about to the sev'n-string'd lyre & the oaten pipe; to hoof it with Pan, & the dryads, & the nimble fauns, & disport with light-toed nymphs in beechen shades & o'er the flowery meads. Flaming youth! Now you can plunge into the wild student life of our time & write a sophisticated novel like the youth Wright told us about—fortunate swain, thus early to conquer an art whose rhythmick intricacies your Grandpa Theobald never sought to storm. Revel whilst you may—youth is fleeing—& the wreaths of ivy & myrtle soon fade. Which reminds me of the original words of the old drinking-song "To Anacreon in Heav'n" from which Mr. Key took the air for his fairly well-known hit, "The Star-Spangled Banner."

> To *Anacreon* in Heav'n, where he ſate in full Glee,
> A few Sons of Harmony ſent a Petition,

That he their Infpirer and Patron wou'd be,
    When this Anfwer arriv'd from the jolly old *Grecian:*
      Voice, Fiddle, and Flute,
      No longer be mute,
          I'll lent ye my Name
          And infpire ye to boot;
And befides, I'll inftruct ye like me to entwine
The Myrtle of *Venus* with *Bacchus's* Vine!

I shall be interested to follow the progress of your book, & am glad the prospects for its sale are so bright. Be sure to put me down for one of the earliest copies, whatever the price! Let us hope that it will net you such an handsome profit that a second collection will be quickly forthcoming—that, & a volume of your tales, which I am exceeding anxious to behold. You shall see the Bullen volume when it's done—it has now reached the stage of page proofs, & Cook is supplying a fine running-head in Old English type. We certainly intend to give Freer his money's worth, & I anticipate a finished result marked not only with quiet mechanical elegance, but with perfect typographical accuracy as well.

Loveman, I'm sure, will be glad to hear from you. I suppose he must be back in N Y by this time, though I've had no direct word. Let us hope his recovery is thorough, & that he'll be more careful next time! Glad the postcard was interesting—I think I'll send you quite a little collection of local views shortly, for I've seen a number of very decent ones lately. Here's a harbour view—not openly maritime enough to tantalise your inland, fresh-water soul, yet sufficiently colourful to evoke memories of the Newport trips. We took the boat on the left-hand shore, just this side of where the bridge shews in the picture.

Mortonius? DAMN those *minerals!* Yes—I've heard from him, & he's proving quite a model of tolerant forbearance. I've just had a local grocery send him two dozen cans of a kind of prepared coffee which he can't get around N Y any more. He sure is an epicure! Enclosed, by the way, is an article on hitch-hiking which may give you some pointers for next summer's travels. This much is certain—you simply must get some swank, baggy plus-fours, & stock up on the small-talk of baseball, politics, & home-brewing! ¶ With regards & compliments from both aunts & from my insignificant self, I have yᵉ honour to remain, Sir,
    Yr most morbid, blasphemous, & necrophagous Servt
      Grandpa Theobald

[*Enclosure:* Postcard (Providence River Looking Toward Narragansett Bay, Providence, R. I.); no writing on back.]

[*Enclosure:* "Hail the Hitch-Hiker! Is He Guest or Pest?" *Providence Sunday Journal* (2 October 1927).]

Notes

1. *WT,* November 1927: Henry S. Whitehead, "The Shadows"; Manly Wade Wellman, "Back to the Beast."

[76]   [DAW to HPL] [ALS]

> 1152 Portland Ave.,
> St. Paul, Minn.
> Oct. 17, 1927

Dear Necrophilist and Ghost-Eater:

I lament my inability to answer letters within a reasonable time. Though I read yours with keen pleasure, I seem to fall farther and farther behind. Shades of the U. of M.! I have just cancelled one course, but still it seems that I never have any time for my personal interests any more. Oh well, studies be damned. I'd rather write letters.

The article on hiking brought on nostalgia for other lands. Shame on you for making me lose interest in this my native city said the villain as a tear trickled down his whiskers. But seriously, there won't be any summer travels for me next year unless my finances undergo a phenomenal change. Buying Cas's pictures was as fatal to my purse as not buying would have been to my thoughts. At present, I am impatiently waiting for the return of the group so that I can extract the two which will adorn the walls of my room.

I have read "The Recluse" and your article with much pleasure. I am taking an honors course in "The Gothic Novel" at the U. and since your article is so opportune, am using it with Birkhead and Killen as my sources. I showed the article to one of my professors who is incidentally head of the English Department and is interested in this side-track of literature. He is writing to Cook for a copy in order to have your essay. I think this issue of "The Recluse" is going to be valuable some day, for it contains work of every member of the gang.[1]

I have changed my mind and don't think I'll go to any dances. I have learned how, know what a dance is, and have acquired all the sensations. To attend a dance would really be an anticlimax. I therefore intend to stop now, this being the most subtly artistic moment.

Did you give my respects to Jake? Fie on you, you know you should have!

If you ever dare to make such an insinuation concerning my book again, I will do something desperate. You will of course receive one of the first copies, which I shall be glad and proud to send you.

The enterprising Mr. Derleth has done himself the great honor of writing to me. By the ancestors of my descendants! I certainly am getting some fine training in rapid composition! My intentions of answering Mr. Derleth have not yet materialized but probably will in an off-moment tomorrow.

As soon as I have a chance, or rather can find one, I intend to raid a postcard station for you. My stars, but the people here must never use post-cards!

As for "Weird Tales"—I can't speak with authority. It's more than a year since I read an issue completely. I merely scan the title page for your name, Cas's, or Long's, and cease thereafter. Mr. Wright is an agreeable person; but he has the most horrible—and not in the sense in which it should be!—judgment when it comes to stories.

Alas, I must finish the gushy Mrs. Radcliffe's "Romance of the Forest" tonight, or at least the second volume. I'd like to have seen that woman cry!

           Yours in Skulls and Scarlet,
             Diabolus

Notes

1. Contributors included Walter J. Coates, CAS, DAW, Arthur H. Goodenough, HPL, Vrest Orton, H. Warner Munn, FBL, and Samuel Loveman.

[77]   [HPL to DAW] [ALS]

                             Saturday
                       [October 22, 1927]

My dear Melmoth:—

          Commiserations on the chronological congestion! Here's hoping your cancellation will give you at least an approximation of a breathing-spell. I can sympathise quite comprehendingly just now, for piled-up revision has annihilated all my sense of repose. Only this week have I managed to burrow upward to within a faint twilight distance of the world of freedom & sunshine.

Sorry the hike article proved tantalising—when it comes to a choice of rival sources of imaginative nourishment, one has to do some close figuring; but I'll trust your judgment to pick the thing that will really hit the spot most satisfyingly. Knowing your particular attunedness to the Clericashtonic landscape, I fancy you're wise in choosing as you are doing—but I can only hope that the sale of your book of poems will give you such an unexpectedly large surplus that you can take your trip & have your paintings too. The paintings, by the way, were sent on their carefully crated & conscientiously insured way to Dwyer last Monday. I trust he has them by now, & feel sure that he will exercise all proper caution in handling them & shipping them on to Little Belknap. He will want plenty of time to assimilate them, but I trust your patience can be fortified by the consoling thought that, once they return to you, at least two of them will nevermore depart. I hope Klarkash-Ton is knocking a bit off the quoted prices as affixed to the various specimens. He ought to appreciate your sincere admiration to that extent. I recall that he sold Belknap a splendid specimen for only five dollars a year or so ago. Did the youngster shew it to you in N.Y.?

Glad *The Recluse* reached you safely. It seems to have made a very decided hit wherever it has gone, & Dwyer & Orton indulge in fervid rhetoric about it. Dwyer thinks you are the purest fantaisiste of us all—& I wouldn't be surprised if he were right. He also thinks Orton's cover is a great achievement despite its occasional amateurishness of perspective; seeing in it the workings of an authentic if not highly developed or disciplined imagination, & a sympathetic comprehension of the Gothic spirit of his idol Albrecht Dürer. Too bad you didn't meet Orton in N.Y. He's something of a flighty, unplaceable cuss, but a damn good fellow for all that. The notice paid to my lowly article by your English professor flatters me tremendously—as does also your use of it as source material in the course you mention. Speaking of Gothic source material—Cook has just lent me a brand new book by one *Eino Railo* (never heard of him before) which for thoroughness throws Birkhead altogether into the shade—although its scope is even narrower. The title of this exhaustive tome is "The Haunted Castle: A Study of the Elements of English Romanticism",[1] & it surely leaves nothing to the imagination regarding the historical & scientific origins of the stock figures of early horror fiction. My only grave objection to it is that it makes *Lewis* an outstanding focal point, giving him an eminence which I don't think he deserves. *Maturin* is the big guy—with all due respects to Little Mat the Monk. I'll sub-lend you this book before returning it to Cook if you'd like to see it. Seems to fit in especially well with your present course. Other books lent by Cook are Dr. Thacher's celebrated "Ghosts & Superstitions", (Boston 1831) Yardley's "Supernatural in Romantic Fiction", & Vaughan's "Hours with the Mystics." I'd like to see the Killen & Scarborough volumes some time.

So you're *not* going to be a rhythmical rounder & Charleston-hound after all! Well—old M. Tullius remarked several centuries ago that "Nemo fere saltat sobrius, nisi forte insanit".[2] But one hates to think of all that potential sophistication going to waste. How are you ever going to compete with Michael Arlen & F. Scott Fitzgerald in chronicling the emotional life of the smart & the mundane?

Talman & I, in spirit, surely transmitted your sincerest regards to Jake & Domingo. Cook was here last Saturday & Sunday, but somehow harboured the least bit of reluctance toward lining up to the counter betwixt nigger stevedores & Salvation-Army derelicts—hence fell back on the Guernsey—that place we all ate with the Longs when they first hit town. And Sunday morn (Jake being closed) we breakfasted at the Waldorf . . . . or rather, *a* Waldorf, since they dot the town with neighbourly numerousness. I must get a super-meal at Jake's some day soon, just for old times' sake!

Glad Derleth got in touch with you. He's really a very nice kid—just about your age, though only in his second year at the U. of Wis. He is not a genius, but he is a terrifically earnest reader & fictional aspirant; & you'll have plenty to talk about the moment he gives you an inkling of his dizzying procession of bibliophilic purchases. He seems to be forming a very sound taste, though one less cosmic & exotic than your own. "The Red Brain" appealed to him greatly, & I think you will find in him a highly admiring reader for everything of yours. You may shortly hear from another & more picturesque character in the person of a young vagabond Frenchman named Jean Reçois, whom Loveman lately discovered & recommended to my notice. This sprightly wanderer—a devotee of the weird & terrific—has been in America five years, but writes English with the idiomatic ease of a born Yankee. He is at present a denizen of Greenwich Village, but will undoubtedly move on sooner or later. He has fictional aspirations, but I've not as yet seen any samples of his work. Since he says he comes from the daemon-haunted South of France, I'm sending him "Psychopompos" to air my sympathetic knowledge of "old Auvergne, where schools were poor & few, & peasants fancy'd what they scarcely knew".

Your reading programme as regards W.T. is that of a man of sense & discrimination. Wright, though, isn't such an ass as you'd think from his editorial dicta. He knows—at least, I assume that he knows—what junk he prints, but chooses it on the basis of its proved appeal to the brachycephalic longshoremen & coal-heavers who form his clientele & scrawl "fan letters" to the Eyrie with their stubby pencils & ruled five-cent pads. I think he works intelligently—as a sound business man—doing what he's paid to do, & steadily building up the magazine as a paying proposition in competition with the Macfadden enterprises & kindred humilifrontal rivals.

Well—I'll be grateful for the Paulist postcards when they do come, & trust that their deliberation spells discrimination. You're lucky to get hold of "The Romance of the Forest"—the only Radcliffian oeuvre which I've never seen in toto is "Udolpho", now being lent to Dwyer. Yes—her gentle melancholy is certainly both romantic & hydraulic!

     Yr obt Grandfather
     Νεκρόφιλος

P.S. I've just discharged the melancholy duty of writing an elegy upon our good old fellow-amateur Mr. Hoag,[3] who died last Monday at the age of 96 as the result of a fall. I feel quite desolated by the loss of this gentle & kindly link with the past—he made me think of my own grandfather, who died when I was 14.[4] Had it not been for the accident, I am certain that Mr. Hoag would have far exceeded the century-mark.

Notes

1. By Eino Railo, a Finnish scholar.
2. "Scarcely any sober person dances, unless by chance he is insane." From Cicero's oration *Pro Murena* 13.
3. "Ave atque Vale: To Jonathan E. Hoag, Esq.: February 10, 1831–October 17th, 1927."
4. Whipple Van Buren Phillips (1833–1904), HPL's maternal grandfather.

[78] [DAW to HPL] [ALS]

1152 Portland Ave.,
St. Paul, Minn.,
Oct. 31, 1927

Dear Necrophilist:

As usual, I was much pleased to receive your letter; and as usual, I am late in answering. I must plead the hydra-headed U. whose damnable habit of bobbing into view does not at all suit my plans for disposing of my time. This past week has been a veritable nightmare which began with my studying like a demon for a midquarter exam., continued with my "cutting" classes, including the exam., for two days, progressed with more furious efforts to make up what I missed, and came to a beautiful end in a searching investigation into the life of Heliogabalus[1] which I have been carrying on for my own amusement.

I have not yet seen "The Haunted Castle", but the U. library is ordering it for my special benefit in my Gothic Novel course. The same library is also ordering another new book which I think deals with the field. Unfortunately, I don't own either Killen or Scarborough, having read both at the U. library. Scarborough's is rather badly done, and Killen's has never been translated into English so far as I know. Hers is a very fine work though, and is the best I know on the early Gothic writers. Her book deals only with Walpole, Lewis, Radcliffe, Reeve, and Maturin, with chapters on influence and parodies, and several excellent bibliographies.

I certainly am getting fed up on lachrymose Anne. I have read "The Romance of the Forest", "The Sicilian Romance", and "The Mysteries of Udolpho", and have yet to read "The Italian". I am omitting "The Castles of Athlin and Dunbayne" and her unfinished work,[2] though they are available at the U. library. This library is rather rich in Gothic material of the early school, though it possesses only "Melmoth" of Maturin and not his "Fatal Revenge".

I can't see myself getting rich over this first book. I *am* fairly confident of breaking even, but that is all I expect. My German teacher, I have just discovered, is critic for the Minneapolis Tribune, and has offered to review the book when it appears. Somehow, I have lost interest in the project and am seriously considering destruction of the issue without letting any copies get out. All that deters me is the fact that I shall have excellent uses for whatever percentage of the money invested in the book I may get back.

I have been reading and studying almost continuously for four days, except for one memorable afternoon when I saw the fantastic film "Metropolis",[3] and am more tired than I've been in a long while. My paper on Lewis has at last come back to my hands, and if you still care to take a glance at it, I'll send it along.

It seems to me that I had some other things to say, but my brain isn't functioning much or well at present.

Hasta mañana!

> Your faithful apprentice,
> Heliogabalus

Notes

1. Heliogabalus (or Elagabalus), Emperor of Rome (218–22 C.E.), known for his decadence and lasciviousness.
2. I.e., the posthumously published *Gaston de Blondeville*.
3. *Metropolis* (UFA, 1926), directed by Fritz Lang; starring Alfred Abel, Gustav Frolich, Rudolf Klein-Rogge, and Brigitte Helm.

[79] [HPL to DAW] [ALS]

> [Postmarked Providence, R.I.,
> 3 November 1927]
> Thursday

Dear Melmoth:—

I was very glad to hear from you, & am properly sympathetic regarding the chronological interferences of the university. I suffer an analogous & even less endurable pest in the form of revisory activities—lately so abundant that little work of my own has been accomplished. So you are busy delving into the shady past of that insufferable young Asiatic Varius Avitus Bassianus! Ugh! There are few persons I loathe more than that cursed little Syrian rat! Somebody wrote a book about him a few years ago—trying to whitewash him,[1] I believe—& I have a vague idea that Belknap either owns or has owned it. You might ask him about it. Those loathsome days after Septimius Severus, when the mixed blood & fading art of the dying empire began to foreshadow the end openly & visibly, have a curious & melancholy parallelism with the present stage of history. We are nearing that point—although the reign of Commodus is perhaps a little closer analogue to this particular instant.

I have myself been carried back to Roman times by my recent perusal of James Rhoades' Æneid,[2] a translation never before read by me, & more faithful to P. Maro than any other version I have ever seen—including that of my late uncle Dr. Clark,[3] which did not attain publication. This Virgilian diversion, together with the spectral thoughts incident to All Hallows' Eve with its Witch-Sabbaths on the hills, produced in me last Monday night a Roman dream of such supernal clearness & vividness, & such titanic adumbrations of hidden horror, that I verily believe I shall some day employ it in fiction. Roman dreams were no uncommon features of my youth—I used to follow the Divine Julius all over Gallia as a Tribunus Militum o'nights—but I had so long ceased to experience them, that the present one impressed me with extraordinary force.[4]

It was a flaming sunset or late afternoon in the tiny provincial town of Pompelo, at the foot of the Pyrenees in Hispania Citerior. The year must have been in the late republic, for the province was still ruled by a senatorial proconsul instead of a praetorian legate of the Augustus, & the day was the first before the Kalends of November. The hills rose scarlet & gold to the north of the little town, & the westering sun shone ruddily & mystically on the crude new stone & plaster buildings of the dusty forum & the wooden walls of the circus some distance to the east. Groups of citizens—broad-browed Roman colonists & coarse-haired Romanised natives, together with obvious hybrids of the two strains, alike clad in cheap woollen togas—& sprinklings of helmeted legionaries & coarse-mantled, black-bearded tribesmen of the circumambient Vascones—all thronged the few paved streets & forum; moved by some vague & ill-defined uneasiness. I myself had just alighted from a litter, which the Illyrian bearers seemed to have brought in some haste from Calagurris, across the Iberus to the southward. It appeared that I was a provincial quaestor named L. Caelius Rufus, & that I had been summoned by the proconsul, P. Scribonius Libo, who had come from Tarraco some days before. The soldiers were the fifth cohort of the XIIth legion, under the military tribune Sex. Asellius; & the legatus of the whole legion, Cn. Balbutius, had also come from Calagurris, where the permanent station was. The cause of the conference was a horror that brooded on the hills. All the townsfolk were frightened, & had begged the presence of a cohort from Calagurris. It was the Terrible Season of the autumn, & the wild people in the mountains were preparing for the frightful ceremonies which only rumour told of in the towns. They were the very old folk who dwelt higher up in the hills & spoke a choppy language which the Vascones could not understand. One seldom saw them; but a few times a year they sent down little yellow squint-eyed messengers (who looked like Scythians) to trade with the merchants by means of gestures, & every spring & autumn they held the infamous rites on the peaks, their howlings & altar-fires throwing terror into the villages. Always the same—the night before the Kalends of Maius & the night before the Kalends of November. Townsfolk would disappear just before these nights, & never be heard of again. And there were whispers that the native shepherds & farmers were not ill-disposed toward the very old folk—that more than one thatched hut was vacant before midnight on the two hideous Sabbaths. This year the horror was very great, for the people knew that the wrath of the very old folk was upon Pompelo. Three months previously five of the little squint-eyed traders had come down from the hills, & in a market brawl three of them had been killed. The remaining two had gone back wordlessly to their mountains—*and this autumn not a single villager had disappeared.* There was a menace in this immunity. It was not like the very old folk to spare their victims at the Sabbath. It was too good to be normal, & the villagers were afraid. For many nights there had been a hollow drumming on the hills, & at last the aedile Tib. Annaeus Stilpo (half native in blood) had sent to Balbutius at Calagurris for a cohort to stamp out the Sabbath on the terrible night. Balbutius had carelessly refused, on the ground that the villagers' fears were empty, & that the loathsome rites of hill folk were of no concern to the Roman People unless our own citizens were menaced. I, however, who seemed to be a close friend of Balbutius, had disagreed with him; averring that I had studied deeply in the black forbidden lore, & that I believed the very old folk capable of visiting almost any nameless doom upon the town, which after all was a Roman settlement & contained a great number of our citizens. The complaining aedile's own mother Helvia was a pure Roman, the daughter of M. Helvius Cinna, who had come over with Scipio's army. Accordingly I had sent a slave—a nimble little Greek called Antipater—to the proconsul with letters, & Scribonius had heeded my plea & ordered Balbutius to send his fifth cohort, under Asellius, to Pompelo; entering the hills at dusk on the eve of November's Kalends & stamping out whatever nameless orgies he might find—bringing such prisoners as he might take to Tarraco for the next propraetor's court. Balbutius, however, had protested, so that more correspondence had ensued. I had written so much to the proconsul that he had become gravely interested, & had resolved to make a personal inquiry into the horror. He had at length proceeded to Pompelo with his lictors & attendants; there hearing enough rumours to be greatly impressed & disturbed, & standing firmly by his order for the Sabbath's extirpation. Desirous of conferring with one who had studied the subject, he ordered me to accompany Asellius' cohort—& Balbutius had also come along to press his adverse advice, for he honestly believed that drastic military action would stir up a dangerous sentiment of unrest among the Vascones both tribal & settled. So here we all were in the mystic sunset of the autumn hills—old Scribonius Libo in his toga praetexta, the golden light glancing on his shiny bald head & wrinkled hawk face, Balbutius with his gleaming helmet & breastplate, blue-shaven lips compressed in conscientiously dogged opposition, young Asellius with his polished greaves & superior sneer, & the curious throng of townsfolk, legionaries, tribesmen, peasants, lictors, slaves, & attendants. I myself seemed to wear a common toga, & to have no especially distinguishing characteristic.

And everywhere horror brooded. The town & country folk scarcely dared speak aloud, & the men of Libo's entourage, who had been there nearly a week, seemed to have caught something of the nameless dread. Old Scribonius himself looked very grave, & the sharp voices of us later comers seemed to hold something of curious inappropriateness, as in a place of death or the temple of some mystic god. We entered the praetorium & held grave converse. Balbutius pressed his objections, & was sustained by Asellius, who appeared to hold all the natives in extreme contempt while at the same time deeming it inadvisable to excite them. Both soldiers maintained that we could better afford to antagonise the minority of colonists & civilised natives by inaction, than to antagonise a probable majority of tribesmen & cottagers by stamping out the dread rites. I, on the other hand, renewed my demand for action, & offered to accompany the cohort on any expedition it might undertake. I pointed out that the barbarous Vascones were at best turbulent & uncertain, so that skirmishes with them were inevitable sooner or later whichever course we might take; that they had not in the past proved dangerous adversaries to our legions, & that it would ill become the representatives of the Roman People to suffer barbarians to interfere with a course which the justice & prestige of the Republic demanded. That, on the other hand, the successful administration of a province depended primarily upon the safety & good-will of the civilised element in whose hands the local machinery of commerce & prosperity reposed, & in whose veins a large mixture of our own Italian blood coursed. These, though in numbers they might form a minority, were the stable element whose constancy might be relied on, & whose coöperation would most firmly bind the province to the Imperium of the Senate & the Roman People. It was at once a duty & an advantage to afford them the protection due to Roman citizens; even (& here I shot a sarcastic look at Balbutius & Asellius) at the expense of a little trouble & activity, & of a slight interruption of the draught-playing & cock-fighting at the camp in Calagurris. That the danger to the town and inhabitants of Pompelo was a real one, I could not from my studies doubt. I had read many scrolls out of Syria & Ægyptus, & the cryptic towns of Etruria, & had talked at length with the bloodthirsty priest of Diana Aricina in his temple in the woods bordering Lacus Nemorensis. There were shocking dooms that might be called out of the hills on the Sabbaths; dooms which ought not to exist within the territories of the Roman People; & to permit orgies of the kind known to prevail at Sabbaths would be but little in consonance with the customs of those whose forefathers, A. Postumius being consul, had executed so many Roman citizens for the practice of the Bacchanalia—a matter kept ever in memory by the Senatus Consultum de Bacchanalibus, graven upon bronze & set open to every eye. Checked in time, before the progress of the rites might evoke anything with which the iron of a Roman pilum might not be able to deal, the Sabbath would not be too much for the powers of a single cohort. Only participants need be apprehended, & the sparing of a great number of mere spectators would considerably lessen the resentment which any of the sympathising country folk might feel. In short, both principle & policy demanded stern action; & I could not doubt but that Publius Scribonius, bearing in mind the dignity & obligations of the Roman People, would adhere to his plan of despatching the cohort, me accompanying, despite such objections as Balbutius & Asellius—speaking indeed more like provincials than Romans— might see fit to offer & multiply. The slanting sun was now very low, & the whole town seemed draped in an unreal & malign glamour. Then P. Scribonius the proconsul signified his approval of my words, & stationed me with the cohort in the provisional capacity of a centurio primipilus; Balbutius & Asellius assenting, the former with better grace than the latter. As twilight fell on the wild autumnal slopes, a measured, hideous beating of strange drums floated down from afar in terrible rhythm. Some few of the legionarii shewed timidity, but sharp commands brought them into line, & the whole cohort was soon drawn up on the open plain east of the circus. Libo himself, as well as Balbutius, insisted on accompanying the cohort; but great difficulty was suffered in getting a native guide to point out the paths up the mountain. Finally a young man named Vercellius, the son of pure Roman parents, agreed to take us at least past the foothills. We began to march in the new dusk, with the thin silvern sickle of a young moon trembling over the woods on our left. That which disquieted us most was *the fact that the Sabbath was to be held at all.* Reports of the coming cohort must have reached the hills, & even the lack of a final decision could not make the rumour less alarming—yet there were the sinister drums as of yore, as if the celebrants had some peculiar reason to be indifferent whether or not the forces of the Roman People marched against them. The sound grew louder as we entered a rising gap in the hills, steep wooded banks enclosing us narrowly on either side, & displaying curiously fantastic tree-trunks in the light of our bobbing torches. All were afoot save Libo, Balbutius, Asellius, two or three of the centuriones, & myself, & at length the way became so steep & narrow that those who had horses were forced to leave them; a squad of ten men being left to guard them, though robber bands were not likely to be abroad on such a night of terror. Once in a while it seemed as though we detected a skulking form in the woods nearby, & after a half-hour's climb the steepness & narrowness of the way made the advance of so great a body of men—over 300, all told—exceedingly cumbrous & difficult. Then with utter & horrifying suddenness we heard a frightful sound from below. It was from the tethered horses—they had *screamed* . . . . not neighed, but *screamed* . . . . . . & there was no light down there, nor the sound of any human thing, to shew why they had done so. At the same moment bonfires blazed out on all the peaks ahead, so that terror seemed to lurk equally before & behind us. Looking for the young Vercellius, our guide, we found only a crumpled heap weltering in a pool of blood. In his hand was a short sword snatched from the belt of D. Vibulanus, a subcenturio, & on his face was such a look of terror that the stoutest veterans turned pale at the sight. He had killed himself when the horses screamed . . . . he, who had been born & lived all his life in that region, & knew what men whispered about the hills. All the torches now began to dim, & the cries of frightened legionaries mingled with the unceasing screams of the tethered horses. The air grew perceptibly colder, more suddenly so than is usual at November's brink, & seemed stirred by terrible undulations which I could not help connecting with the beating of huge wings. The whole cohort now remained at a standstill, & as the torches faded I watched what I thought were fantastic shadows outlined in the sky by the spectral luminosity of the Via Lactea as it flowed through Perseus, Cassiopeia, Cepheus, & Cygnus. Then suddenly all the stars were blotted from the sky—even bright Deneb & Vega ahead, & the lone Altair & Fomalhaut behind us. And as the torches died out altogether, there remained above that stricken & shrieking cohort only the noxious & horrible altar-flames on the towering peaks; hellish & red, & now silhouetting the mad, leaping, & colossal forms of such nameless beasts as had never a Phrygian priest or Campanian grandam whispered of in the wildest of furtive tales. And above the nighted screaming of men & horses that daemoniac drumming rose to louder pitch, whilst an ice-cold wind of shocking sentience & deliberateness swept down from those forbidden heights & coiled about each man separately, till all the cohort was struggling & screaming in the dark, as if acting out the fate of Laocoön & his sons. Only old Scribonius Libo seemed resigned. He uttered words amidst the screaming, & they echo still in my ears. *"Malitia vetus—malitia vetus est . . . . . venit . . . . tandem venit. . . ."*[5]

And then I waked. It was the most vivid dream in years, drawing upon wells of the subconscious long untouched & forgotten. Of the fate of that cohort no record exists, but the town at least was saved—for encyclopaedias tell of the survival of Pompelo to this day, under the modern Spanish name of Pampelona. I shall have to look up Pampelona in some guidebook or travel volume, & see what its ancient tales & superstitions may be. But I shall never go near it on the night of All Hallows'—the night before the Kalends of November. In the genial summer it would be interesting to dig in those archaic hills, & to search a certain pass for the long-buried & encrusted eagles of a certain forgotten cohort.

I'm glad your scholastic pull is sufficient to get "The Haunted Castle" into the college library. It cost Cook $6.50, but is well worth the money. The author appears to be a Finn, though intimately acquainted with the English literary tradition. Hope the other new book will turn out well—though I can't understand why everybody harps on the early Gothic novel & neglects the much finer & more finished work of such real masters as Blackwood & Machen. Of the Goths, only Maturin had the sense of unholy *outsideness* developed to any considerable degree—you couldn't bribe me to swallow all the sobbing Radcliffery which your course is forcing upon you. The few selections in an anthology by George Saintsbury are all I want—though I have read Udolpho through. (Just now, by the way, I've lent it to Dwyer.) By the way—I didn't know the posthumous "Gaston de Blondeville" was *unfinished.* That it is very poor, however, all critics seem to agree. It is monstrously hard to get hold of the Gothic novels either in Providence or N.Y. The American Charles Brockden Brown is almost a myth—known only through second or third hand reports. Kirk gave me "Udolpho" & Morton lent me "The Monk"—which wearied me insufferably. I haven't read all of Melmoth yet—having gained what knowledge I have by piecing together the extracts found in sundry anthologies. Morton owns a copy now, & I'm going to ask him for the loan of it as soon as I summon up the energy to send him those min . . . . O Gawd! let's keep to the main subject . . . . I feel faint! Well, anyway, I'd like to see your essay on Lewis. He was rather a disappointment to me, nothing in The Monk giving me any particular kick except the episode of the Bleeding Nun, so that I was rather surprised at the amount of space accorded him by Railo. I soon saw, however, that Railo distinguishes him for historical reasons only; freely admitting the superiority of Maturin in weaving a malign tension & background of imminent terror.

Glad to hear that the critical influence of one of your preceptors is likely to increase the public notice of your coming book. Don't lose interest to such an extent that you'll lose money—& keep a few copies as a speculation. Think of Poe's "Tamerlane" & Hawthorne's "Fanshawe"![6] Be *damned careful* about the proofs—& don't let Cook put it on the press till you have had an *absolutely perfect* set of proofs in your hands. I'm nearly distracted over a blunder in the Bullen book which resulted from premature printing. Cook says he did not understand that another set of proofs was to be sent—& I suppose he's right—but I thought I had made myself clear enough. At any rate, I shall insist on a reprint of the affected sheet, even though I have to shoulder the entire cost personally.

Young Derleth mentioned that "Metropolis" film, & I guess I'll go to see it unless the notices escape me. I never attend the cinema nowadays except when dragged there by somebody who hasn't any better way of killing time . . . . in the almost two years since my return to Providence I've only been twice. Derleth, however, assures me that this production is genuinely fantastic & worthy of beholding. The last film I really enjoyed was "The Thief of Bagdad",[7] with its Dunsanian setting.

Well, O Divine Antoninus Elagabalus, I suppose I must now leave you to your Eastern infamies for a time. Don't let your tires skid in the gold dust strewing St. Paul's Via Sacra, or let your Syrian rites & luxuries get too thick for the long-suffering praetorians to stand. Be good to your cousin Alexander—there's a boy with the real Roman spirit, even if he is a bit short on real Roman blood. Ho, hum . . . . what times these be . . . . . we live, yet two centuries & a half ago M. Porcius Cato the Younger bumped himself off because he saw the end of our virtuous Respublica! Watch your step, boy, for there's a snoopy pair of half-Greeks hanging around to do ya doit on paper, & in another century a poor fish yet unborn will take a whack at ya in alleged Latin. The fierce white light that beats upon a throne, & all that! The local weather has been delightfully warm, & I took a hike last Saturday through a rustic realm I hadn't visited in 20 years. I was pleasantly surprised to find the choicest spot of all—a waterfall & wooded river valley—restored to pristine quiet after a period of considerable decay & vulgarisation. Another trip like that would make me an optimist! ¶ Yrs for Gothick Supremacy—

C. IVLIVS. VERVS. MAXIMINVS.

Notes

1. There was no biography of Heliogabalus following J. Stuart Hay's *The Amazing Emperor: Heliogabalus* (1911) until the 1950s. HPL is either thinking of that work or of *Heliogabalus* (1920), a play by H. L. Mencken and George Jean Nathan.

2. HPL owned at least four editions of Virgil (P. Vergilius Maro) (70–19 B.C.E.), though not James Rhoades's translation of *The Aeneid* in *The Poems of Virgil* (London: Oxford University Press, 1921).

3. Dr. Franklin Chase Clark (1847–1915), husband of HPL's aunt Lillian.

4. The following dream-account was published as "The Very Old Folk," *Scienti-Snaps* 3, No. 3 (Summer 1940): 4–8.

5. "The old evil . . . it is the old evil . . . it comes . . . it comes at last. . . ." HPL also chronicled this dream in letters to Bernard Austin Dwyer (see *Letters to Maurice W. Moe and Others* 466) and to FBL (who used it virtually verbatim in his novel *The Horror from the Hills*).

6. Poe's *Tamerlane and Other Poems* (1827) was published at the author's own expense and sold very poorly. *Fanshawe* (1828) was Hawthorne's first novel. He attempted to buy back all copies of the book and destroy them. Both volumes are among the rarest titles in American literature.

7. *The Thief of Bagdad* (United Artists, 1924), directed by Raoul Walsh; starring Douglas Fairbanks, Snitz Edwards, Charles Belcher, and Julanne Johnston. Some of the dialogue and scene descriptions were written by George Sterling.

[80]   [DAW to HPL] [ALS]

1152 Portland Ave.,
St. Paul, Minn.
Nov. 20, 1927.

Dear Necrophilist:

I must again beg indulgence for my delay. A couple of hectic weeks were climaxed today by homage to Morpheus till 3 p.m. Gratia Dei!

This forthcoming week will be deadly, but I hope to survive.

Your Roman dream exerts a great fascination upon me. It must have been remarkably vivid and of most unusual power. My dreams have never that I can remember offered so much in an evening, nor has there ever been a trace of the Grecian or Roman in them. I envy you the dream and its dormant capabilities; should you ever employ it for literary purposes, be assured that I shall vividly devour the result. One of the most envious features of the dream that impressed me was the importance of details; usually, dreams consist of dominant, general impressions, but yours was built up of minutiae which established the regnant atmosphere. May the gods be as generous toward me some night! In the past two years, I have been singularly free from nocturnal afflictions, pleasant or otherwise; though occasionally my brow rests lightly. One of these times came a week ago; but I can remember absolutely nothing of the dream except that it consisted of fitful nightmares.

The Bullen misprint is unfortunate. I hope it was possible to correct the error before any extra expense or great delay was incurred. As yet, even the first proofs of my book have not reached me, and the delay is beginning to cause me some worry.

The library has acquired two copies of "The Haunted Castle" one of which is now resting before me for examination. Mrs. Radcliffe is disposed of, for good, for ever, and completely. As for her posthumous work—it may be complete. I haven't read it, but have a vague impression of reading somewhere that it was not finished. My memory or the reference here is as likely to be at fault as not, but I haven't enough interest in the lady to correct the point by a further examination of her work. "The Italian" is the best of her novels. Schedoni, the villain, is the most convincing of all her characters, and there is one long scene before the Inquisition which is perhaps more dramatic and terrific than any other of hers. The essay on Lewis was mailed out a week ago. Neither it nor Lewis amounted to a great deal.

Edna St. Vincent Millay lectures here Saturday. I shall hear the lady, out of curiosity rather than actual interest in her or her work.

Have you heard from any members of the "gang" recently? Smith is the only one I have heard from in the past month. The others seem to have gone into hibernation or seclusion for the winter. Has Dwyer reported on Smith's paintings?

Like yourself, I haven't done much writing lately. Since school began, I have written but a dozen poems, one prose fantasy, and six or eight thousand words on another novel. Wish I had more time to write; the mood comes to me frequently, but studies or interruptions of various kinds usually prevent its fruition.

Auf wiedersehen!

[ornament] THE WANDERER [ornament] [written vertically]

[81] [HPL to DAW] [ALS]

Friday
[25 November 1927]

Dear Melmoth:—

Pray accept my sincerest sympathy anent the season's demands upon your time & energy! I have myself been more than commonly
opprest by sundry duties of late, & am even more heavily threaten'd for the
immediate future. To parallel your Morphean achievement of last Sunday, I
can cite my own performance of last night—when, gorged with a Thanksgiving feast of the utmost peril to my 140-lb standard, I was overcome by
drowsiness at 5 p.m., & continu'd in a somnolent state till ten this morning!
My dreams occasionally approach'd the phantastical in character, tho' falling
somewhat short of coherence. One scene is especially stamp'd upon my recollection—that of a dank, fœtid, reed-choak'd marsh under a grey autumn
sky, with a rugged cliff of lichen-crusted stone rising to the north. Impell'd by
some obscure quest, I ascended a rift or cleft in this beetling precipice, noting
as I did so the black mouths of many fearsome burrows extending from both
walls into the depths of the stony plateau. At several points the paſsage was
roof'd over by the choaking of the upper parts of the narrow fiſsure; these
places being exceeding dark, & forbidding the perception of such burrows as
may have existed there. In one such dark space I felt conscious of a singular
accession of fright, as if some subtile & bodileſs emanation from the abyſs
were ingulphing my spirit; but the blackneſs was too great for me to perceive
the source of my alarm. At length I emerg'd upon a table-land of moſs-grown
rock & scanty soil, lit up by a faint moonlight which had replac'd the expiring
orb of day. Casting my eyes about, I beheld no living object; but was sensible
of a very peculiar stirring far below me, amongst the whispering rushes of the
pestilential swamp I had lately quitted. After walking for some distance, I encounter'd the rusty tracks of a street-railway, & the worm-eaten poles which
still held the limp & sagging trolley wire. Following this line, I soon came upon a yellow, vestibuled car numbered 1852—of a plain, double-trucked type
common from 1900 to 1910. It was untenanted, but evidently ready to start;
the trolley being on the wire & the air-brake pump now & then throbbing
beneath the floor. I boarded it & looked vainly about for the light switch—
noting as I did so the absence of controller handle which implied the brief
absence of the motorman. Then I sat down in one of the cross seats toward
the middle, awaiting the arrival of the crew & the starting of the vehicle. Presently I heard a swishing in the sparse grass toward the left, & saw the dark
forms of two men looming up in the moonlight. They had the regulation caps
of a railway company, & I could not doubt but that they were the conductor
& motorman. Then one of them *sniffed* with singular sharpness, & raised his
face to howl at the moon. The other dropped on all fours to run toward the
car. I leaped up at once & raced madly out of that car & away across endless

leagues of plateau till exhaustion waked me—doing this not because the conductor had dropped on all-fours, but because the face of the motorman was a mere white cone tapering to one blood-red tentacle.[1] Yes—as you see, the Old Gentleman is by no means a stranger to unusual dreams; tho' very few have sufficient substance to serve as literary material. Details are often far stronger than general impressions, so that I am apt to recall an isolated name or incident even when the continuous setting has altogether vanisht. The Roman dream, of course, was exceptional in its scope, vividness, & mnemonick persistence; though in my youth I dreamed nearly every night of Rome or the flash of the republick's aquilae & vexilla against the barbarick sunsets of far frontiers. Rome & its power have always exercised the most phenomenal sway over my imagination & personality, notwithstanding my willing concession of aesthetick & intellectual superiority to the Grecian world. It is absolutely impossible for me to envisage the ancient world except from a Roman point of view; & I feel as fierce & natural a patriotism for the conquering republick of the Tiber, in its own age, as I do for the English civilisation in this age. The decadence of the Empire fills me with as great a melancholy as the present decay of the western world, & I am forced into the paradox of resenting, in the antique time, the incursions & achievements of my own Northern ancestors; whose present heritage I am so avidly eager to see defended against all rivals! In other words, when I think myself back to a point antedating the organised national existence of my own blood-ancestors, I instinctively gravitate to Rome as *my country*, instead of following the Saxon tribes into their original northern woods. My admiration for the warlike virtue & glorious virility of the blond tribesmen does not diminish; but somehow my immediate *sense of personal identity* seems transferred to the Seven Hills—which acquire for me, prior to 450 A.D., that atmosphere of centricity & quality of a fundamental seat of vision which for later ages belong to London & Providence. *Behind Rome* I find it impossible to project my personality. The primordially archaick world of Gnossus, Memphis, Thebes, Nineveh, & Babylon exists only on paper for me. Psychologically I am either a Roman or an Englishman, with no possibility of imaginative expansion.

I perused your Lewis essay with keenest interest, & am returning herewith. Much in it was new to me—I really had no idea of the *extent* of Monk's narrative peculations! Glad you have "The Haunted Castle" before you. One thing in it gave me a sense of importance—the place where Railo says he has never been able to consult a copy of Moore's "Zeluco". Well—*I own "Zeluco"*—albeit in a cheap form bound up with a lot of other early material.[2] Dwyer is just forming the acquaintance of our gushing friend Mrs. Radcliffe through my copy of "Udolpho", & expresses the opinion that she is unsurpassed in imparting horror to a frowning castle landscape. Cook is going to lend me "The Italian" shortly.

The Bullen misprinting has cost Cook much cash, me much labour, &

you much delay in your book! Vae nobis omnibus![3] We can just about get the de luxe copies to Freer by Christmas—the bulk of the edition can't make it. Your own volume is all in type, but Cook is sparing you the trouble by reading the earlier proofs—with the grosser errors—himself. You'll get the page proofs shortly. Of the gang, only Dwyer, Morton, & honest old McNeil have been vocal in my direction lately. Dwyer is ecstatic about the Smith work—especially the "Dreamland" illustration—& has sent the shipment safely on to Belknap. **And I have sent off Morton's minerals![4]**

I'd like to see such of your recent work as is at once portable & conveniently available. I'm wholly unproductive nowadays. Incidentally—Derleth tells me a *new weird magazine* has been founded—*Tales of Magic and Mystery,* edited by Walter Gibson, 931 Drexel Bldg., Phila. ¶ Yr obt Grandsire—Νεκρόφιλος

P.S. Speaking of *lectures*—I heard a really engrossing one last Monday night—vide cutting.[5] I had no idea so much classic mythology still survived in Greece under thin disguises. The peasants worship the old gods at their old shrines under saints' names, & there is still a belief in satyrs, nymphs, Charon, the Fates, &c. &c.

[*Enclosure:* "Former British Ambassador to Italy Lectures," from unidentified newspaper.]

Notes

1. The text of this dream, expanded by J. Chapman Miske, was published in Miske's *Bizarre* (January 1941) as "The Thing in the Moonlight" by HPL. (Miske also published "The Very Old Folk" in *Scienti-Snaps*.) The "story," sometimes dated to 1934 because Miske's text contained a reference to HPL's final address, is now known to be spurious based on Miske's own testimony.
2. The Gothic novel *Zeluco* (1789) by Dr. John Moore (1729–1802) was included in a compilation entitled *The British Novelist* (London: J. Limbird, 1823–32).
3. "Woe to us all!"
4. HPL had been rather tardy in shipping various long-promised mineral specimens from a local Providence quarry to his friend James F. Morton, curator of the Paterson (NJ) Museum.
5. HPL heard Sir Rennell Rodd speak on survivals of classic myth in modern Greek folklore.

[82]   [DAW to HPL] [ALS]

1152 Portland Ave.,
St. Paul, Minn.
Dec. 10, 1927

Dear Necrophilist:

Accept my heartiest congratulations on the ejection of the

Morton mountains! Would that my molar inconveniences were as easily corrected! Alas, I fear me the holidays have naught but the drill to offer, and the
school grind will merely be changed to a dental grind!

Your dream fascinated me, for it contained the elements that I tried to put
in the "Door to the Room". There is the "outside" suggestion, the essence of
utmost horror in that picture of the motorman with the cone-like face. Such
terrific anomalies and paradoxes and contrasts of common reality and abysmal terror were once nightly visitations of my childhood, but it is long since
they last occurred. Your dream suggested to me another story of "The Door"
type, but from a different angle, which I hope to write soon.[1] I sha'n't borrow
from your dream; may your own pen crystallize it as soon as possible! You
ought to spend more of your energy in creative efforts rather than in revisory
work; you don't write nearly enough to satisfy my omnivorous appetite for
your tastes! I am herewith returning "To Zara", which Dwyer sent me. In
memory of "Nathicana", I read it with a grain of salt, but believed in it on re-
reading. Hope I'm not being led astray again! Some lines I think are worthy
Poe, though I don't like the last few lines. When was it written?[2]

My recent writings aren't typed, but when school ends for the Fall, in a
week, I'll type and send on the last fantasy and a number of poems. Which
reminds me, I finally got a set of proofs and returned them with corrections.
Too bad they were delayed so long; the book probably won't appear till February or later, so far as I am able to tell. As for the Bullen book—you probably will heave a deep sigh of relief when it is finished and out of the way!

The Smith paintings came back yesterday, and I proudly abstracted two
which are now mine forever. I shall pore over them for some time before I
return the collection to Smith.

I am heartily sick of Mrs. Radcliffe. My professor insisted on having a
paper, though, so I am amusing myself with a sizzling, sarcastic survey of her
characters.

The lecture by Sir Rennell Rodd would probably have held much interest
to me. I am very sorry I missed it. Sir Rennell was no inconsiderable poet
when he was young, and I am pleased to own a copy of his "Rose-leaf and
Apple-leaf" which contains some very fine poems, small as it is. I heard Edna
St. Vincent Millay two weeks ago. She was disappointing, and did not even
read her best work. Last week I heard William Beebe give a most interesting
lecture, illustrated with slides and moving pictures, on "Under Tropic Seas".[3]

It has been devilishly cold here the past week. We had a bad blizzard, and
it was ten to twenty below for three days. I froze an ear but luckily discovered
it before it became serious. I do not like cold, and the more contact I have
the less I like it. I'd like to purchase a little South Sea Island and eat lotus the
rest of my life.

Did you see the last group of poems I typed? I sent them to Smith.
When I last heard of them, months ago, he was sending them to Long, thence

to go to you, Dwyer, and back to me. But Long hasn't acknowledged either them or a book I loaned him. Is he lazy, or offended at something I've done?

As ever,

The Wanderer (frozen).

Notes

1. The story may never have been completed. However, the central image of "Fantastic Sculpture," one of his *Sonnets of the Midnight Hours*—a figure whose head is "a tuft of slender tentacles"—resembles the coachman of HPL's dream.

2. "To Zara: Inscribed to Miss Sarah Longhurst—June 1829," as by "Edgar Allan Poe."

3. William Beebe (1877–1962), American naturalist and author. The lecture is presumably an abstract of his volume, *Beneath Tropic Seas* (1928). See HPL to Lillian D. Clark, [9 April 1929]: "Our session was highly congenial, & we soon adjourned to the Am. Museum of Nat. Hist., where we saw a marvellously arranged exhibit of the strange & sinister deep sea fishes discovered by William Beebe on his Arcturus expedition." *Letters to Family and Family Friends* 747.

[83]   [HPL to DAW] [ANS]

[Postmarked Providence, R.I.,
17 December 1927]

[Kindest remembrances and
Sincere good wishes for
Christmas and the New Year]

Πάππος Νεκρόφιλος

[84]   [HPL to DAW] [ALS]

Decr. 19[, 1927]

Dear Melmoth:—

I'll tell the world I'm to be congratulated! In revenge for my labour, I think of all the trouble Mortonius is going to have unpacking, classifying, & distributing his rocky booty. Poor devil! He has to cope not only with this shipment from me, but with three or four other consignments of even greater size from other points of the compass! Well—let us hope that both you & he may weather your respective trials with fortitude! What a cycle of exchange is kept up betwixt nature & the laboratories of man! Here is Mortonius wrenching mineral matter away from nature—& you having mineral matter planted where it ought to be in your natural œconomy! Such is the essential justice of the universe, whose evidences make us confident of the loving oversight & governance of an all-wise Father!

I'm glad my second recent dream proved of interest—no other of equal vividness & coherence has appeared since, & I am getting quite lonely for horror! I congratulate you upon having shared such glimpses of monstrous "outsideness", & hope that—like me—you may be treated to some choice vestigial specimens in later life. When we grow old, the feelings & images of our early childhood return to us with a freshness & intensity scarcely to be conceived of in young manhood or middle life. Pray give my vision all the literary use you can find for it—since I'd delight in seeing it artistically crystallised, yet have not a moment to perform the task myself. The dream I *may* work on when—or if ever—I get the time, is the *Roman* one lately related to you. Its details & names will have to be greatly changed, & I shall introduce a motivating framework & modern sequel to furnish the necessary elements of fictional plot & climax.

"To Zara" is one of the concoctions of my hoax-&-parody period, & was written in about half an hour in Belknap's presence in August 1922, in the hospitable living-room of that noble pile at 823 West End Ave. which is to-day—eheu!—but a gaping hole in the ground. It was the product of a discussion on some of Poe's stylistic mannerisms in verse—& I think one of the lines was suggested by Belknap, though I can't recall which. We sent it to your marvellous prodigy-prototype Alfred Galpin, & it deceived him to the extent of making him think it was taken from the minor work of some actual poet—he guessed Arthur O'Shaughnessy,[1] a favourite of Belknap's at the time. I tried to get it published in the amateur journals,[2] but no one would take it—so here it is, neglected & forgotten, & the world dreams not of what it might have known.

I want to see your new writings—and—hurrah!—I *have* seen your later poems at last! Belknap sent them along a couple of weeks ago, his delay having been due to an attack of influenza from which he is now quite recovered. You'll hear from him presently—& I will duly send the material onward to Dwyer. Needless to say, I found in the poems a prodigious fascination—so much, indeed, that I may yet base some prose tales on some of them, with the poems quoted at the head as mottos. I hope they will appear in your book—for I surely must have such things as "Sonnets of the Midnight Hours", "Red", "Ultimate Horror", (wgggllhh . . . . rrrrlhh . . Yog-Sothoth, Nug, & Yeb![3]) "Valerian", &c. &c. for my permanent collection. Your technique is improving rapidly—more & more of mature swing & phrasing appears—so that I would now hesitate to advise you as exclusively toward prose fantasy as I did a year ago. Develop the two streams side by side as Poe did—for you certainly, if I am not too old to have an opinion of my own, possess genius of the most authentic sort in both lines.

Glad you have the Klarkash-Ton monstrosities again—& gord! how I envy you the permanent detentions your plutocracy permits you to make! Belknap shewed them to the gang—& culled the following exquisite symposium of cultivated Babbitry:

Rheinhart Kleiner:

> Well, if woods were really like that I wouldn't take any more hikes with the Paterson Ramblers. Honestly, Belknap, I think Smith is crazy.

Belknap:

> But Poe . . . . .

Kleiner:

> I never saw anything in Poe. His poems suggest the ravings of a madman.

Wilfred B. Talman:

> I don't see anything weird in these drawings, Belknap. Gosh! who cares about the coasts of Saturn?

James Ferdinand Morton: [with his inimitable air of long-suffering patience]

> Well, these drawings are no worse than the things he expected us to praise last year!

Everett McNeil: [bridling & bristling, & with a quaver of defensiveness]

> Well, I like Poe as well as anyone here, but you can't expect me to admire the work of a man who doesn't know how to draw. If he didn't title them you wouldn't even know what they were about! Does *that* [pointing] look like a tree?

Such is the world of today! Is it a wonder that very few fantaisistes survive to such a ripe old age as mine?

Your Radcliffian satiation is scarcely an encouraging emotion to confront me as I stand on the brink of "The Italian" & "The Romance of the Forest"—lent me by Cook—but I do not think I shall let it deter me from at least a skimming. The author of a standard treatise on supernatural horror in literature ought to read—as a matter of duty—one or two of the volumes he has analysed & appraised so sagely. You & Dwyer can work up an interesting controversy about the sombre & sentimental Mother Anne, for "Udolpho" has made him a shouting Radcliffe-fan of the first & foremost order. He is, of course, right so far as the sheer weaving of vague, terrible impressions of cyclopean mystery & imminent nightmare is concerned; & we ought not to let the peterings-out or the salt lakes of "poetic" sensibility deter us from giving credit where credit is due. I'd like to read your sizzlingly sarcastic survey when it's available—& incidentally, both that & the "Monk" critique ought to be published. What's become of the good old *Minnesota Quarterly* under its safe & sane new management?

I'm sure you'd have enjoyed the Rodd lecture. I have not seen his poetry—but he read one poem on Greece which gives me a highly favourable idea of his style & attainments. He won, his local introducer reminded us, the Newdigate Prize whilst at Oxford. More recently I attended a lecture by Canon Fellowes of Windsor, from which I learned much that was new to me about early

English music.[4] I knew, in a general way, that our pre-Cromwellian past was far from being as unmusical as our present; but I certainly did not realise how fully Elizabethan England competed with the Continent in musical supremacy, or how essential a part of a gentleman's education a performing knowledge of music used to be. I haven't attended any lectures since—for cold weather is upon us, & I have gone into hibernation! William Beebe is going to give his address here, but I shall not be among those present. And I doubt if I'd go far to hear the estimable Miss Millay even on a mild day.

Your remarks on temperature back up some reports which my aunt has been getting from distant kinsfolk in Washburn, Wisconsin—wherever that is.[5] Brrrrrrrr!!!!! It is *never* more than 2 or 3 below in Providence, & seldom below 10 or 20 above—but I'll inform the empyrean that's plenty cold for your Grandpa, & then some! What I want is a plantation in Jamaica to inhabit during the winter—& I don't mean Jamaica Plain, Mass., nor Jamaica, N.Y., either! Commiserations on the ear—& thank Pegāna you saved it in time. One so sensitive to echoes from beyond space ought certainly to have all his ears kept in good order. Let the Kleiners & Talmans & Mortons & McNeils get all the freezing!

Glad you got your proofs from Cook—but too bad about the delay in the appearance of the volume. I'm getting fidgety about the promised Christmas delivery of the Bullen book. Cook hasn't dropped a line since his personal visit two weeks ago yesterday, & the Chicago "angel" has just been urbanely wondering when it's coming along. Only the 24 de luxe leather copies can possibly be delivered on that date—& if W. Paulus falls down even on these, I shall become quite embittered with all the world. On the whole—& using the most fundamental standards of comparison—I think this damn business almost dethrones the Morton minerals from their general nuisance championship! As I was telling Cook—it's a vivid test of my sincere regard for the late John Ravenor Bullen that I'm still able to surround his memory with fond veneration.

Speaking of jobs, though—my latest revisory grind is about as bad as anything I've yet struck. It is supposed to be fiction—at least, the author has furnished only internal evidence to the contrary—& the task is to make the world believe it is other than unmotivated chaos.[6] The perpetrator is an apparently learned but eccentric old cuss named Adolph Danziger de Castro, who knew Ambrose Bierce in the old days, (George Sterling says their acquaintance terminated with Bierce's breaking a cane over Adolph's head!) & who suggested the plot of "The Monk & the Hangman's Daughter".[7] Just now he has got some newspaper publicity through a new report of Bierce's death, & he wants to capitalise it by reissuing some of his old alleged tales. He also wants to discuss the revision of a forthcoming book of Bierce reminiscences[8]—for which purpose, sociable old soul, he purposes paying a visit to Providence! He claims to know 16 languages—which may explain where some of the knowledge which ought to have gone into English has leaked to. Loveman gave him my name—I hope he won't be a sharp guy to deal with financially, as Loveman thoughtfully warns me.

Oh, yes—& I must mention my latest source of hauteur & egotism! Listen to what I got in my morning's mail—with a Switzerland stamp & postmark, addressed in care of *Amazing Stories*, & by that institution forward to me:

> Hôtel Fleur-de-Lys,
> Gruyères, Switzerland.
> Nov. 29, 1927.
>
> Dear Sir:—
>   I should be grateful if you would send me a brief biographical note for inclusion in "The Best Short Stories."
>   Faithfully yours,
>   Edward J. O'Brien
> H. P. Lovecraft, Esq.[9]

Well, what the hell! Do you suppose he is going to use "The Colour Out of Space" in his anthology, or just mention it? I don't know enough about the makeup of the book to recall whether or not he uses biographical notes when he doesn't reprint the tales concerned.[10] But anyway, it's near enough to "big time stuff" to tickle an old man's vanity. I no longer speak to common folk! Anthologies, by the way, are right in my line. I've just received the 3d. of the Selwyn & Blount "Not at Night" series with my "Horror at Red Hook" as the last story in the book. This is my first—if not my last—appearance between cloth covers.[11] Wright still talks of that collection of my tales,[12] but I don't take much stock in expansive discourse. He's just rejected "The Quest of Iranon" with high disdain[13]—& to think you put in good labour typing that thing!

And so it goes. Don't let the dentist tackle any more teeth than he has to, & keep them covered by a stiff upper lip! Think of the Bullen book & the de Castro revision when he's doing his worst. And drown the worry in boar's head & plum pudding—or turkey & mince pie—a week hence: for which festive occasion, as well as for the ensuing Kalends of Ianuarius, pray accept my best wishes & blessings.

Πάππος Νεκρόφιλοσ

P.S. Oh, by the way. I got a letter from Vincent Starrett about my *Recluse* article. He spoke quite flatteringly of it, & slipped me some tips for weird reading on which I shall eventually act.

[P.P.S.] Have just read "The Weird o' It" by Clive Pemberton (mediocre) & "The Street of Queer Houses" & "Here & Otherwhere" by Vernon Knowles. This stuff is rather sissified, but has some powerful fantastic bits here & there.

Notes

1. Arthur William O'Shaughnessy (1844–1881), British poet.

2. "To Zara" remained unpublished in HPL's lifetime.

3. This is the first known mention of "Nug and Yeb" in HPL's writings, probably contemporaneous with the citation in HPL's revision of Adolphe de Castro's "The Last Test" (1927; *CF* 4.96).

4. Edmund H. Fellowes (1870–1951), a leading British musicologist, especially of the Elizabethan era.

5. On the southwestern shore of Lake Superior, about 160 miles from St. Paul.

6. HPL was revising "The Last Test," by Adolphe de Castro.

7. *The Monk and the Hangman's Daughter* was written in German by Richard Voss, translated into English by Danziger, and revised by Bierce. HPL, though enjoying the novel declared, "It is not a weird tale" (*SL* 5.69).

8. *Portrait of Ambrose Bierce* (New York: Century Co., 1929). HPL ultimately refused to work on the project, and FBL revised the book, adding a preface.

9. The card is extant among HPL's papers at JHL.

10. "The Colour out of Space" was cited as a three-star story on the "Roll of Honor" in Edward J. O'Brien (1890–1941), *The Best Short Stories of 1928 and the Yearbook of the American Short Story* (New York: Dodd, Mead, 1928). The story itself was not reprinted, but HPL's "[Biographical Notice]" appeared on p. 324.

11. Actually *The Collected Poems of Jonathan E. Hoag* (1923) contains an introduction and several poems by HPL.

12. FW's proposed collection, which HPL wished to call *The Outsider and Other Stories,* never appeared, but Arkham House published a collection with that title in 1939.

13. FW published the story after HPL's death.

1928

[85]   [DAW to HPL] [ALS]

1152 Portland Ave.,
St. Paul, Minn.
Jan. 15, 1928

Dear Νεκρόφιλοσ:

        I owe you a world of apologies for my delay in answering your letter, but it was unavoidable. My young brother got himself into a terrible mess of trouble,[1] and I even had to miss the first week of school. Now with things running smoothly again and six cavities filled with beautiful new gold or gold crowns or porcelain, I feel somewhat at peace with the world. I sent Cook the last proof yesterday marked "O.K.", hence my book ought to appear within the next month. Most of the poems you saw recently were too late for inclusion except "Valerian", "Nightmare", and "Red", which obtained entry. The sonnets I will use in a second book to be called "The Midnight Hours."[2] Which reminds me, I sent Dwyer some more of the "nightmare" poems, and two fantasies to be forwarded to you, Long, and Smith. The past two weeks, I have gone on another poetic spree, and will forward the results, which include about six more of the nightmare sonnets, before long. How did the Bullen book turn out?

I just got my essay on Mrs. Radcliffe back and herewith enclose it. Send it to Cook when you finish it.[3] *The Quarterly* is extant but put out its worst issue this fall, the entire magazine unrelieved by any symptoms of intelligence or signs of literary talent or value.

Smith's paintings will begin their homeward journey tomorrow, minus two. The comments you sent gave me a good laugh, and an appreciation of my own superiority to the criticisers.

The long-announced "Cthulhu" at last appeared, and I read it again with the same pleasure it gave me last spring. I do hope you find or take time as soon as possible to pursue purely artistic paths. If I were in your place, I think that last revision would cause me to "ditch" all such work and write for writing's sake or starve. I confidently expect to do both after I graduate.

I am glad you find evidence of improvement in the poems. For some unknown reason, I suddenly obtained a surprising ease and facility in writing last August, just after my return. At present, my time is turned to my first and greatest "talent"—buying books. I have added three of Machen's in the past week to my collection, besides some more expensive volumes whose illustrations caught my fancy. The only excuse I have to offer is the inducement of large reductions in price; and anyway, I'd rather have a lot of books than a lot of rocks (I almost said minerals, but there are plenty of those in my teeth now).

Congratulations on the O'Brien card, and may it mean all it would seem to! Henceforth, I shall feel as if I were addressing one of the superior deities when I write you. If O'Brien uses "The Colour out of Space", I shall have about fifty thousand percent more confidence in him. Your inclusion in the last "Not at Night" volume also gave me great pleasure, but you should have been there before with "The Outsider" or one of your more important tales than "The Horror at Red Hook".

You are entirely welcome and free to use any of the poems for prospective tales in any way you see fit. I shall feel highly flattered! In any event, I look forward with eagerness to new stories from your pen, and regret the many months that have produced none. If it's any inducement to you, I'll type your new tales for you, since I have classes at school only Tuesday and Thursday afternoons this quarter and thus have also much spare time.

With the Humble Apologies of One of the
Lesser Deities,
Melmoth.

Notes

1. Howard Wandrei was arrested and served time in prison for his participation in a series of burglaries.
2. The proposed *The Midnight Hours* never appeared. DAW's second collection of poems, *Dark Odyssey*, did not contain any of his *Sonnets of the Midnight Hours*, which ultimately were collected in *Poems for Midnight* (1964).
3. "The Lilies, Perfume-Bottles, and Some-Will-O'-the-Wisps."

[86]   [HPL to DAW] [ALS]

Friday
[20 January 1928]

Προσφιλιὰ Μὲλμοθ:—[1]

Many thanks for the generous envelope-full, all of which I have perused with appropriate interest & gratitude. The Radcliffian study is surely a masterpiece of wit & erudition, & gave both my aunt & myself a wholesome plenitude of mirth. Dwyer, I fear, would feel shocked at this irreverent treatment of a lady whose power in manipulating the mechanics of terror has so excited his admiration; but I am sure you do the alleged characters as more or less than justice. Cook will be delighted with it—& I hope you are according him permission to use this, as well as the Lewis essay,[2] in the second number of *The Recluse*. The good scholastic marks appended to the MS. did not escape my notice, & I can only say that I deem them abundantly well-deserved. I learn with regret of the *Minnesota Quarterly's* decadence. Sic transit gloria mundi!

The views of St. Paul were highly welcome, & I surely congratulate you upon your habitancy of so pleasing a hill town. That is—provided you are inured to the *temperatures!* I am still shaking from my exposure on January 2 to what is for me extreme cold—+14°—& when I consider how trifling this figure would seem in Minnesota, I thank heaven that fortune has cast me in a less rigorous realm of hyperborean frigor! We have had no snow as yet—& it is at this moment raining.

I'm glad the grinders are all properly repaired, & trust that a calm season of study & literary productivity may repay you for all the anxieties of the past month. I am eagerly awaiting the book, & wish you could have held the press long enough to slip in a few more items of the batch which captivated me so emphatically. I now eagerly await the fresh lot which is to come my way, & hope that your Aonian 'bender' will not cease till you have perpetrated a still ampler array of phantasmagoric blasphemies from outer space. Most certainly, your poems display a progress of the most decided sort; as I believe everyone who has watched your output for any considerable time will agree. It is really quite possible that your trip had something to do with the augmented burst of inspiration; for there is no doubt but what radical changes of scene, a stimulated sense of adventure, & a vivid succession of new & unfamiliar impressions operate marvellously toward a sharpening of the creative sense. You must surely try the experiment again next summer—hence beware of dissipating all your substance for ephemeral trifles like books! I don't blame you for any Machen acquisitions—unless you've sunk good money in that tedious "Canning Wonder"[3]—but pray go easy on the mere bindings & illustrations & first editions & such essentially un-literary fripperies! If you could dig your acquisitions out of the hills free of charge as Mortonius does, there might be some excuse for irresponsible collecting. But when it comes down to hard cash, I must say that sheer bibliophily impresses me as a super-luxury before which many more solid things ought to be placed!

I can imagine the reluctance with which you are parting with the paintings of Klarkash-Ton, the Lemurian sorcerer. The poor old gang certainly did stage quite a comedy over them—& the proportion of appreciative & unappreciative minds in this group is a pretty fair reflection of the corresponding proportion in the critical world at large. There's no doubt but that a sensitiveness to the fantastic is a rare special sense—a mental excrescence approaching positive abnormality—so that one can't blame the honest souls who remain stolid in the face of poignant strangeness & cryptic beauty. Their attainments in the general intellectual & aesthetic field are often brilliant, so that they are highly congenial when one can meet them on their own ground—minerals with Morton, vers de société with Kleiner, genealogy with Talman, boys' books & Victorian uprightness with honest old Mac, & so on. Still, it is fortunate when one can find a few genuine fellow-fantaisistes with whom to discuss one's special interests! Speaking of fantastic art—not long ago I received an inquiry from Vincent Starrett concerning that apocalyptically thunderous & darkly weird precursor of Doré—John Martin (1789–1854)—who won such popularity in the 1820's. Starrett had heard of him only by name; but I was fortunately able to supply considerable information, having seen excellent collections of his engravings on two occasions.[4]

Glad to hear that "Cthulhu" wears well with you. I'd like to get a chance to grind out some more junk—especially a story which my fancy has woven about that Roman dream I described to you—& perhaps I shall stage some sort of revolution after I get through with the execrable story-revision now weighing me down. It depends largely on what that old goof Danziger-de Castro wants to do about his volume of Bierce reminiscences. The Bullen book, despite all troubles, came out magnificently; & Cook has reluctantly agreed to attend to the marketing & distribution. It will cost $2.00 at retail & $1.50 wholesale—cloth of soft grey colour, paper labels, 86 pp 6 × 9 on art paper, with genuine photographic frontispiece in sepia on impressed panel. So far as I can see, there are absolutely no typographical errors. I am helping Cook send out the complimentary & review copies, & shall try to place it in a few bookstalls—& have Kirk & Loveman list it in their catalogues. The special leather gift edition—dark green stamped with gold—is a veritable bibliophile's dream of austere sumptuousness! I shall pass my duplicate around among the gang, so that you'll see it eventually. Each copy cost Cook $6.50 at wholesale for the binding alone, so that it's really a $10.00 or $15.00 item.

About O'Brien—I looked at one of his annuals the other day with analytical eye, hence can say with prosaic assurance that he is *not* about to reprint "The Colour Out of Space". Very few tales are used, whilst the biographical catalogue of authors is so long that inclusion is really not much of a distinction. It means just a word or two in an alphabetical list—pleasant enough, but nothing to get excited over. As for that 'Not at Night'—that's a mere lowbrow hash of absolutely no taste or significance. Aesthetically speaking, it doesn't exist. Thanks for the typing offer—but beware lest I put your magnanimity to the test some day!

Yrs for churchyards & Witches' Sabbaths—

Πάππος Νεκρόφιλος

P.S. Are you sure that Ellena really & finally turns out to be Schedoni's daughter? I haven't read "The Italian" yet, but it seems to me Saintsbury & Railo mention a second twist which shows the momentarily supposed relationship to be erroneous after all.

[P.]P.S. The new magazine *Tales of Magic & Mystery* has just accepted my story "Cool Air".[5]

Notes

1. "Dear Melmoth."

2. Evidently "The Monk, the Monk, and the Monk."

3. *The Canning Wonder* is a nonfiction account of the mysterious disappearance of Elizabeth Canning in 1753.

4. See HPL to Vincent Starrett, 10 January 1928; *Letters to Maurice W. Moe and Others* 527–30). HPL's source of information was *Encyclopaedia Britannica* (9th ed. [1896]; *LL* 318).

5. The magazine rejected seven other tales from HPL before taking "Cool Air," which it published in its final issue.

[87]   [DAW to HPL] [ALS]

1152 Portland Ave.,

St. Paul, Minn.

Jan. 31, 1928

Dear Νεκρόφιλος:

May the elder demons be praised that their tremendous labors over one Bullen at last bear fruit! My first enfant terrible hath not yet made its appearance. I wait. But meanwhile, the poetic impulse languishes again and I dabble in this and that. Wright has just taken eleven of the nightmare sonnets, to run as a series, one or two a month, under a standing head. I'm to send another to make an even dozen—he rejected one.[1]

It pleases me that you found both interest and mirth in my Radcliffian tour de force. I had much inward amusement in writing it. You are correct about the twist at the end which changes Schedoni's status, but as I remember—your copy being the original and only extant materialization of the essay—I simply used the scene at the shore as much to illustrate one of the most gripping moments in the book. I shan't bother to insert the explanation as finally given unless Cook sends the ms. back, in which case I might doctor it for future publication. I like some of Mrs. Radcliffe's gloomy descriptions—this is what Dwyer also admires—but her characters are impossible. Of late, I have read Godwin's "Caleb Williams" and "St. Leon", the first a great relief after a prolonged siege of lachrymose Ann, the second a great bore except in the last part.

St. Paul hasn't seemed to me old in any sense since I came back. I doubt whether you would find much to interest you for more than a day or two, and I know the climate would congeal you! It's been a mild winter so far—only four or five blizzards, (I froze my ears four times already), and the coldest day was just twenty below. I forget the record, though I know it's something over forty below, reached many years ago. At present, there is a strong wind whipping the snow along and whistling past the windows; it is getting colder, and I suppose we'll have a storm or heavy drifts by morning.

So you looked up O'Brien? I wasn't sure about my statements, since I haven't had the courage or the stupidity to go through one of his compilations for several years, but my memory of them did not contain any wild enthusiasms.

My nights have been troubled with evil dreams again. I don't know why this should be, but it's perhaps a combination of circumstances. I do not relish them, and most emphatically would be glad to dispense with their presence. It is all right to put them into sonnets and imagine them, but to live them is a bit too much even for me. Fortunately—or unfortunately for literary purposes!—the details have been unusually fugitive, and I retain but vague impressions of the spectral shapes that throng the chambers of sleep.

ow are those two delightful aunts whom I saw too briefly last summer? I would that I might take a similar idyllic, purposeless, carefree wandering for the rest of my life, but I fear that the hand of Mammon is about to fall on me in some guise. I must live, but I have not noticed any mad rush on the part of the world to give me the wherewithal. Who knows? Perhaps I may be assembling autos—or selling cheese—or writing inspiration verse and stories of the Great Outdoors—or milking cows a year hence!

Alas, the days of yesteryear!

Your humble slave of the Pen, Nightmares, and Gold,

Μέλμοθ

Notes

1. *WT* published twelve of DAW's sonnets between May 1928 and March 1929.

[88]   [HPL to DAW] [ALS]

Feby 15[, 1928]

Dear Melmoth:—

I was glad to receive yours of the 31st ult., & to hear of Wright's acceptance of the nightmare sonnets. They are indeed splendid—both those in the MS. Belknap forwarded, & in another which Dwyer passed along. I shall await their printed appearance with interest, & hope still later to see them all incorporated in a single book under the present title. I likewise read with interest the prose-poems "The Purple Land" & "The Lost Moon", both of which have a rich colouring & hypnotic cadence which appeals to me exceedingly. I'm sending this material on to Belknap.

I think Cook has retained your Radcliffe essay for publication, but the insertion of a single word—*supposed*—before the word *discovery* would clear up the Schedoni matter admirably. The essay itself is unalloyedly delicious. I've not yet had time to read "The Italian" or "The Romance of the Forest", but thanks to Cook's patience there's no hurry about returning the book. I've read "Caleb Williams", but never had a chance to get hold of "St. Leon", which I wrote up in my essay from hearsay alone. Apparently I haven't missed very much. Not long ago Cook lent me one of the minor Radcliffe imitations—"The Horrors of Oakendale Abbey" (1797)[1]—whose utter & all-pervading inanity shews how easy it is to sink below even the worst Radcliffe level. It has all of Mother Ann's insipidity, without possessing the least jot of her landscape & situation-weaving strength. Other things I've read lately are "Lazarus", a fine study in hallucination by one Henri Beraud, of which Belknap made me a present, & "Witch Wood", a very new novel by John Buchan. This latter treats of the hellish witch-cult as operating in Scotland in 1644–1646; & has an atmosphere of brooding terror hung about the black wood Melanudrigill, & the village ingulf'd by that wood, which atones amply for the tone of insipid romanticism which so popular a hack as Buchan cannot escape here & there. The actual supernatural is only faintly suggested, but this is done so well toward the end of the book that I think I'd include it in any future edition of my article. Other new books I want to read are "The Dark Chamber" by Leonard Cline, "The Place Called Dagon" (New England witch-horror) by Herbert S. Gorman, & "The Blessing of Pan" by Lord Dunsany. Belknap has just loaned me that James Hogg book you said you didn't care for, & also a novel, "The Barge of Haunted Lives" by J. Aubrey Tyson, which I read in the *All-Story* in 1905 or so—long before you were born!

I haven't had much time for reading, though, since revision has pressed heavily upon me. This Adolph Danziger-de Castro is a curious old cuss, & he's lately been airing a good deal of his controversy over the authorship of "The Monk & the Hangman's Daughter". Bierce, in his preface, claims most of the credit for the existing text; saying that de Castro merely gave him a crude translation from the German of Richard Voss[2] to be worked over completely. From this dictum de Castro violently dissents; declaring that on the contrary all the bulk of the authorship is his own, & that Bierce's revision was of only the most superficial sort. He has produced a letter of Bierce's in which old Ambrose declares his preference for de Castro's share of the work over his own; & on the strength of this the present publishers (A. & C. Boni) have agreed to insert a statement by de Castro in future editions. De C. has been generous enough to make me a present of a nice fresh copy of the book—with Bierce's original preface carefully torn out, & the new statement pasted in. My personal opinion is that Bierce & de Castro are both presumptuous in their claims. The great strength of the book is in its brooding local atmosphere & geographical colouring, a feature so marked that I cannot but think the existing images were fashioned by one who had known & studied the actual region described. In other words, the real author must be one who is both an artist & a German. Now de Castro is a German but not an artist, whilst Bierce was an artist but not a German. This, to my mind, leaves Voss—so lightly passed over by the later handlers of his plot—as the one really responsible for the dominant merits of the book. Do you know anything about him? Bierce, in the preface, shews knowledge of other work of his, & expresses much admiration for it. In de Castro's just-finished book of Bierce memoirs—which I may get the job of revising—I note (from a table of contents he submitted) that this controversy will bulk rather large toward the end. It will interest me to see what the old duffer will have to say in such detail!

I fear the colonial east has spoilt for you the appreciation of St. Paul antiquities; but perhaps some morning in the small hours, when you get down among the brick buildings & remember the gas lamps, you may recapture a bit of the primal thrill. As for *weather* . . . . well, I don't wonder that most of you Minnesota & Wisconsin boys are bright & healthy! With those temperatures, all the unsound or decadent stock must surely be killed off before it gets to be five years old. All hail the survival of the fittest! But let's not talk about such things. It makes me feel cold—though the room temperature just now is 80°, with a gentle rain tapping at the windows & laving a non-niveous terrain.

I'm sorry your nightmares are so disconcertingly realistic of late—bless my soul, but you *earn* those sonnets! I've had some strange nocturnal visions—confusing time & space in very fantastic ways—but nothing like a real nightmare for a couple of months. It's a long way from the palmy "nightgaunt" days of 1896,[3] when as a child of six I was actually afraid to fall asleep, & would vainly use every expedient to keep awake.

Both aunts, I'm glad to say, are flourishing. Would that they & I might see you again next summer . . . . . think of the sea-cliffs, & the hilly green shade of the rock-studded woods of old New England! Try to keep Mammon & his werewolves at bay till autumn, at least—or if you must become a cheese salesman, for Pete's sake pick out an Eastern territory. I'll give you an order—for as you may have noticed, I'm prodigiously addicted to cheese! But *don't* write "inspirational verse!" Anything else . . . . but that—no, *no* . . . . not *that*![4] ¶ Hoping to see your book before long, & to hear more directly when the chance comes, I am ever yʳ most obt Servt—

ΝΕΚΡΟΦΙΛΟΣ

P.S. Bullen book sells for 2 fish retail—1.50 wholesale. Makes a fine appearance! I've been sending out review copies one by one, but haven't heard of any results. Haven't had a line from Cook in a devil of a while—I guess he's hustling up on the final details of your book.

Notes

1. Attributed to a Mrs. Carver; it dates to 1799.
2. Richard Voss (1851–1918) was a prolific author of novels, stories, and plays. *the Monk and the Hangman's Daughter* first appeared as *Die Mönch des Berchtesgaden* in *Vom Fels zum Meer* 1 (1890–91): 193–200, 297–304, 412–18; published in book form in 1891. His novel *Zwei Menschen* (1911) was a bestseller.
3. See *SL* 1.35, and also the sonnet "Night-Gaunts."
4. HPL himself had revised such verse for his client David V. Bush.

[89]   [DAW to HPL] [ALS]

1152 Portland Ave.,
St. Paul, Minn.
Feb. 24, 1928

Dear Necrophilist:

        I shall look forward with considerable interest to De Castro's memoirs, though an innate distrust of literary claimants makes me skeptical of the value of his assertions. I know nothing about Voss, and never heard of him or saw his name except in connection with "The Monk and the Hangman's Daughter."

What do you think of Hogg's book? I owe Belknap an apology which I shall shortly make. His support of the book made me look it up again recently; and upon going through, I discovered that I had *not* read it. I *did* get as far as George Colman's adventure in the fog; but for some now-forgotten reason, stopped there. My opinion of it has been practically reversed now that I have read it, though I am not nearly so enthusiastic over it as he was last summer. Lately I have read Shelley's "Zastrozzi" and "St. Irvyne", both wretched stuff, Mrs. Shelley's "Frankenstein" and Polidori's "Vampyre", both which I had read before, Jane Austen's "Northanger Abbey", Peacock's "Nightmare Abbey", and Barrett's satire "The Heroine", which is a beautiful take-off on the Gothic novel at its worst, and quite as good as most of the best! I am now preparing to re-read "Melmoth", and shall conclude this quarter's reading with Bulwer-Lytton's "Zanoni".

My book hasn't arrived as yet. The delay is causing me a great deal of worry, for unless it comes within two or three weeks, it will be difficult to market it properly until next fall.

Would that I could rove Eastward again this summer! I feel as if I were "petering out" again and would welcome the stimulation of such rambling. Probably I shall be forced to remain here and commence the odious task of earning money, for a mouse could not live comfortably on what I have thus far received by writing. The biggest mistake my ancestors made was in not founding a family fortune!

I have amused myself the past few days by collecting all mss., typed or scribbled, from my drawers and desk, and destroying such as offended my critical eye. About thirty poems and a half-dozen prose items were happily obliterated, with perhaps a dozen more still to go. There is much joy among the Muses!

> With the hope of soon reincarnating
> Melmoth the Wanderer.

[90]   [HPL to DAW] [ALS]

> 10 Barnes St.,
> Providence, R.I.
> Feby. 29, 1928.

Dear Melmoth:—

The enclosed will help to explain Cook's silence regarding your book. It is certainly damnable luck to have such a delay at a time when the question of successful marketing is at stake, but I really fancy that poor Culinarius is not to be blamed. I can sympathise acutely with his fragile health, since I was a semi-invalid myself when I was young; & I know him well enough to swear that he would certainly have had your job delivered on the dot as per agreement if it had been in any way within the bounds of human possibility. This letter indicates that he is beginning to get about again, so results will doubtless be manifest in the near future. I haven't had a real letter from him since the middle of January—only pencil-scrawled envelopes relaying requests for review copies of the Bullen book . . . . of which my stock of 26 copies has just become exhausted.

I am inclined to share the saline admixture with which you will peruse the de Castro Bierce memoirs; for as you say, people with special claims view facts & events through an atmosphere of oddly refractive & polarising properties. The old codger seems harmless & affable enough—but he has an axe to grind. You will note George Sterling's none too favourable reference to him in the preface to the Modern Library edition of "In the Midst of Life". It would really be worth while—just to satisfy one's curiosity—to try to look up Prof. Richard Voss of Heidelberg. Surely some authority on German literature ought to know of him; for Bierce's praise of some of his work seems to me a sufficient assurance that he is not only not a myth, but a novelist of sufficient importance to be translated into English. (since Bierce was not a master of German) Whoever limned the geographic setting & constructed the plot of "The Monk & the Hangman's Daughter" was an artist of high calibre. Bierce has virtually stated that the plot is not his. I, personally, would be willing to take oath from a knowledge of his crude constructional ability & absolute lack of colour-sense, that neither plot nor atmosphere are de Castro's. And so I am damn curious about Voss! Meanwhile I've got a fine free book out of the matter—which Cook, as you'll see by the enclosed, assures me is quite a "collector's item."

I shall tell Belknap—unless indeed you have already done so—of your revised opinion of "Memoirs of a Justify'd Sinner". As for me—eheu! Revisory servitude has bowed me to the dust of illiteracy, so that I have not had time to peruse a deodamnate thing since Buchan's "Witch Wood", of which I think I told you. But I'm really glad to know your improved estimate of the Ettrick Shepherd[1] before reading his chef d'oeuvre; since it is always more comfortable to approach a pleasure which all qualified connoisseurs recommend, than to tackle one anent which expert opinion is divided. My sense of expectancy, thus sharpened, gives a keener zest to the whole proceeding. I shall be careful to tell you my own reaction in full detail when I do get to the long-awaited assimilation of the debated volume.

I can well imagine the inanity of "Zastrozzi" & "St Ervyne", [*sic*] & do not imagine that I shall ever go to the length of perusing them unless somebody sticks them under my very nose as Cook did "The Horrors of Oakendale Abbey." I haven't read "Northanger Abbey" in years, (when I did read it in youth I rather *resented* it!) & have never seen the Barrett & Peacock volumes. You really ought to read "Oakendale" as a literary curiosity. It represents the Radcliffe tradition sunk to its nadir in the hands of a cheap popular scribbler. I didn't care much for "Zanoni"—except in the few invocation scenes & in the general conception of the "Dweller of the Threshold"—though I did find much power in the "Strange Story."

I'm sorry indeed that you feel yourself "going stale" again, & wish that you might devise some means of rebuffing want just long enough to work in one good jaunt over ancient Novanglian byways. Think of what a well-chosen banquet at Jake's would do for your soul! Good old Jake's! I haven't been there myself since your visit, except twice when young Talman (its discoverer) was here last September. I shall certainly take a wild spree somewhither next summer—probably the Cape Cod & general South-of-Boston region, of which I am astonishingly ignorant considering its relative proximity to Providence. And I must see *Newburyport* again. Have you heard of the new clown mayor of that archaick & colonial municipality, whose antics are convulsing the sedate press of the East?[2] Another trip which I may work in is one to Vermont to see Walter J. Coates. Cook may give me a lift on that expedition in his Whippet.[3] I'm not sure yet whether I'll ever have the nerve & adventurousness to try a genuine 'hitch-hike' in the manner so successfully practiced by you.

I hope your literary destruction hasn't overshot the mark & annihilated anything which ought to be preserved! I conducted a similar holocaust when I was eighteen; sparing, of all my prose fiction, only the two tales of "The Alchemist" & "The Beast in the Cave." Of my newer stories I have repudiated & destroyed only two so far.

Providence is going to get a distinguished Poe scholar next autumn, when Prof. Thomas O. Mabbott, now of Northwestern, comes to Brown Univ. I shall meet him, for my adopted grandchild Galpin—your lank seven-foot prototype—knows him well, & will suggest his looking up the aged Poe-mad hermit on the ancient hill.[4] ¶ And so it goes. Hoping that a stampede sale of your book may make you financially independent & ensure you another trip to these seaboard colonies, I am, Sir, ever

Yr moſt oblig'd & obᵗ

Necrophilus Avus.

Notes

1. The epithet of James Hogg.

2. Andrew Jackson ("Bossy") Gillis was inducted mayor of Newburyport in January 1928. A former sailor, Gillis had several minor troubles with the police, including parking in a restricted area. In general, Gillis conducted himself in a flamboyant and undignified manner.

3. HPL did visit Vermont in 1928 but only on 10–24 June, following a six-week stay in Brooklyn.

4. HPL never met Thomas Ollive Mabbott (1898–1968), later editor of Poe's *Collected Works* (Harvard University Press). Mabbott was familiar with HPL's work, acknowledging HPL as determining the source for Yaanek in Poe's "Ulalume" and accurately summarizing the plot of "The Fall of the House of Usher." For a time Mabbott owned some of HPL's letters to Richard Ely Morse.

[91]   [DAW to HPL] [ALS]

1152 Portland Ave.,

St. Paul, Minn.

Mar. 11, 1928

Dear Νεκρόοφιλος:

I sympathize with Cook—he told me last summer that there were times when the health both of him and his wife was bad. The explanation of the delay has put me at rest, at least so far as the mere explanation goes, though I can't help feeling worried about a timely appearance of the edition. I may appear in another book before Cook's comes out; four other students at Minnesota and myself have formed an honorary literary society for men, and are publishing a book of our work to justify our existence. The volume should be out within a month. The edition is limited to fifty copies—ten apiece—so I shall not have enough copies to go around. However, I'll send one around the circle when it appears—probably start with Derleth or you and end up with Smith. The book is being printed on handmade paper with colored end-papers and a black-and-gold decorative binding. It has woodcuts by Henkora—the leading Twin City artist—and is to be signed by each of us and by the artist. Truly, it is a sumptuous work of art! This magnificent creation is as yet untitled, but will probably come out as "The Esoteric Muse". The expense would be heavy were there not five of us to share the cost, and if the father of one of us did not own a press where we can have the type set free.[1]

The general likeness of the picture to Cook is unusual. I wonder what the "gang" will say of it.

Wright just sent me proofs of the nightmare sonnets, and I made several changes. The first two will appear in the next issue—evidently the other story of mine which he has is not to appear for some months still. I wish he would publish the crime and get it off my mind for good and all.[2]

"Zanoni" had a number of poetic passages, the most striking, I think, being "The Dweller on the Threshold", but the style was frequently atrocious and the method simply abominable. The story was too long, moreover. I shall finish my course in the spring with the Gothic novel in America, which phase I know least. Bierce and Poe I am thoroughly acquainted with, but I have read nothing of Charles Brockden Brown and very little of Hawthorne.

I would gladly hike East or almost anywhere this summer but fear I shall have opportunity to get no further than Chicago. At present, what I most desire and need most is financial independence; that state, though the process of acquisition is not likely to savour of Paradise, would permit me to do as I wished; a pleasant ideal which can rarely be performed or carried out on a flat wallet! My ancestors neglected to build a family fortune; a slight mistake which I can not forgive them!

I was fairly careful in fuelling my literary fire; though I included my first youthful attempt of importance from which I quoted to you last year, and my other youthful hangovers, with various poems and trifles that were partially or completely failures. One was a long poem that Sterling liked but thought too Swinburnian. It was and went!

Sadly yours,
Melmoth (retired).

P.S. I'll look up "Voss" in the U. library.

Notes

1. The book was published as *Broken Mirrors*. The volume was illustrated by Leo August Henkora (1893–1954), a Viennese-born artist who settled in Minneapolis in 1920.
2. The next story by DAW to appear in *WT* was "Shadow of a Nightmare" (May 1929).

[92]   [HPL to DAW] [ALS]

March XVI[, 1928]

Dear Melmoth:—

Yes—both the Cooks have always been in very dubious health, & this present indisposition is evidently quite considerable. I haven't heard from W P C since answering the letter which I sent you—& I really must write again, inquiring how all the household is. It is surely provoking in the extreme that this illness comes at such an inopportune time for your book. Let us hope, though, that the volume can be successfully marketed despite the chronological derangement—as its merit must surely entitle it to be. Meanwhile I trust your newer venture may materialise successfully. The de luxeness of your extremely limited edition is quite awe-inspiring, & I am sure that all the recipients of the passed-around copy will exercise a properly reverential care in handling it. I only hope that all the other contributors may attain a literary standard as high as that which you will set—the club itself is no doubt a highly congenial organisation, & I trust it may continue to exist beyond the undergraduate days of its members.

Glad you've had a chance to give your sonnets their utmost, ultimate polish. Wright seems to have taken to the proof habit all of a sudden—he lately sent me proofs of that wretched "Lurking Fear" which he is reprinting.

And—good boy—he is offering to forego some of his ultra-modern spelling (*fantom—domicil—*&c) because of a wearily humorous protest which I idly affixed to a margin. I shall watch for the sonnets with interest as they appear. As yet, I've had no time to read the current issue; but see that our friend Munn is represented. Also, you are mentioned in the Eyrie in a complimentary way.[1] I hope he'll give your story a good setting when it finally appears.

What you say of "Zanoni" largely follows my own opinion. "A Strange Story", written twenty years later, is much better as a novel; though its length is even greater. I've never seen an American Gothic novel either, my knowledge of Charles Brockden Brown being confined to such parts of "Wieland" as appear in the Lock & Key Library. Our local libraries know him not.

I'll be interested to hear what you learn about Herr Professor Doktor Richard Voss. Old Danziger-de Castro is now in touch with Belknap, & that little imp has just revised his memoirs of Bierce *absolutely free of charge,* in return for the privilege of prefixing a signed preface![2] Belknap thinks it will bear him onward toward fame to be thus visibly connected with a work likely to become a standard source-authority for future Bierce biographers. Well—if the little divvle wants to do work for nothing, I wish him all the fame the process can bring him!

> Say, ſhall my little Barque attendant ſail,
> Purſue the Triumph, and partake the Gale?[3]

It seems that de Castro has written a great deal of more or less solid material, besides serving the government in several important capacities—consular & otherwise. Belknap says he is 62 years old, stout, & genial. Speaking of *stoutness,* though, (I'm now *139)* I've just sent Belknap a cutting of an interview with the latest musical visitor to American soil—Prince Joachim of Prussia.[4] The Prince remarks, among other things, that *"a gentleman does not get fat!"*

I am sorry that delicious early tale went into the hecatomb. Why, oh, why didn't you send it to me instead? I would have preserved it reverentially beside my own "Beast in the Cave"! Of late revision has absolutely annihilated me, but I got one job (writing a weird tale from synoptic notes) which gave me quite an opportunity to practice up on my old creative processes. As a result, if you see a story in W.T. called "The Curse of Yig", you will know that all of the writing & most of the plot are mine.[5] My only reading since "Witch Wood" has been "The Dark Chamber" by Leonard Cline, & this is *an absolutely magnificent work of art!* Poetry—song—& the ultimate quintessence of atmospheric morbidity & horror. It rambles unfortunately in its effort to build up a dense miasma of unwholesomeness & madness, but even the divagations are authentic art. And the main stream is superb—the terrible quest of a scholar back through the corridors of memory, personal *& ancestral.* Ugh! The strange *odour* .... & that hellish hound Tod, that bays in the night .... *Don't* *miss it!* Now the books I want to read are Dunsany's "Blessing of Pan", Gorman's "Place Called Dagon", (although Belknap says it is rather mediocre) Priestley's "Old Dark House", & Merritt's "Seven Footprints to Satan".

I must certainly hold it reprehensibly negligent of your forbears not to have founded a fortune—at least, enough of an one to give you an annual aestival tour of proper length & diversity! Why don't you go in for aviation like your illustrious fellow-Minnesotan?⁶ You're just the right build, & if you got hold of a good Spirit of St. Paul you could whizz all over the country, breakfasting with Clark Ashton Smith, lunching at home, & taking dinner at Jake's with me! Think it over!

Hopefully yrs—
Grandpa Necro.

P.S. Have you seen C A S's new literal Baudelaire translations? I like them exceedingly. Prose is the only way to get the exact shades of meaning & colour in the original.⁷

Notes

1. H. Warner Munn, "The Chain" (*WT,* April 1928). A reader, L. Lindsay, made a passing comment to "the vast thought-pictures of Donald Wandrei" (p. 436).

2. FBL's preface to Adolphe de Castro's *Portrait of Ambrose Bierce* is signed "Belknap Long."

3. Alexander Pope, *An Essay on Man,* 4.385–86.

4. Joachim Albrecht (1876–1939), Prince of Prussia, conducted the New York Symphony Orchestra on 13 March 1928.

5. Zealia Brown Reed received $45 for "The Curse of Yig," which HPL ghostwrote from her notes for a fee of $20.

6. Charles Lindbergh (1902–1974), although born in Detroit, graduated from high school in Little Falls, MN, in 1918. He set a record in transatlantic flight when he flew *The Spirit of St. Louis* from Long Island to Paris on 20–21 May 1927.

7. CAS translated Baudelaire's *Les Fleurs du mal* almost in its entirety. He first translated the poems into literal English prose, then recast most of them into verse. Some were published in his column in the *Auburn Journal* and in *Sandalwood.* The entire text is now published in CAS's *Complete Poetry and Translations,* Volume 3 (Hippocampus Press, 2007).

[93] [DAW to HPL] [ALS]

1152 Portland Ave.,
St. Paul, Minn.
March 25, 1928

Dear Necrophilist:

I haven't had time to do much with Voss, largely because my knowledge of German is very slight. A great many of his books are available in German at the University library, and at the Minneapolis library. When I have time, I'll go through these and try to find the original of "The Monk and the Hangman's Daughter". I can find only one biographical note, and that an exceedingly brief one in a German literary biographical dictionary. I had no German-English dictionary at hand, and was unable to translate it at sight. I shall take my dictionary over to the school library this week, and enclose a translation in my next letter. As for Belknap—wooh, and oof! I don't think he has accomplished anything except take a check away from you. His signed preface won't help him much for three valid reasons: first, signed prefaces in general mean very little nowadays even in the case of well-known or famous authors (Sterling's to "Ebony and Crystal" and Cabell's to "The Worm Ouroboros", for instance); second, Belknap is not well known enough to cause a reader to investigate beyond vaguely asking, "Who is he? Don't think I recall his name—probably not worth while looking up"; third, De Castro is not likely to find widespread interest in his volume. Bierce is known only to the initiate; and such are not certain to place credence in his account since Bierce can not refute it, and has already given his own explanation. Even so, granting that these things do not come to pass and that I am pessimistic, the squabble will seem petty to intelligent people. Bierce's reputation rests on "Can Such Things be" and "In the Midst of Life" largely. It is unlikely that the world will pay great attention to bickering over a translated book.

At last I can say that I too have the fundamental necessity of a Gentleman! Blessings on the Prince!

I would have sent my youthful masterpiece to you if I had only thought in time that you might be interested in it. However, it was written in a pencil-scrawl on cheap and faded scratch-paper. Several of the seventeen or so leaves were worn out, thumbed to fuzz, or so yellowed as to be wholly illegible. Hence, the loss was already partial when I made it complete. I got rid of about thirty more mss. last week—mostly freshman and sophomore themes I took from my theme file at the U. and decided were valueless.

My book received another set-back when the St. Paul Dispatch stopped its literary column last week.

And now to enter the last three months of my sojourn at the University of Minnesota—may they be brief, and sweet!

Melmoth

[On envelope in HPL's hand:]
Blackwood—"Dance of Death"
Lincoln MacVeagh—Dial Press
$2.00

[94] [HPL to DAW] [ALS]

April 5[, 1928]

Dear Melmoth:—

Don't waste too much time on the Voss quest—but it would be amusing to come on the real prototype of the M & H D just about the time that old de Castro blossoms forth with the bulky memoirs wherein his claim against Bierce bulks so large! There would be material for a good article by somebody who could read the German volume & collate it carefully with the Bierce–Danziger text. As for the memoirs themselves—alas! they are again set back to the raw material stage. Belknap did not take any job away from his old grandpa—he refused to consider it till old 'Dolph stated positively that he could not have the work done by anybody on any cash basis whatsoever. But behold & lament! Though the job *is* done, yet it *isn't*—for since the revision no less than three publishers have rejected the MS. on the ground that the style is still too crude, & the material still too ill-proportioned! I thought that Belknap must have made a rather light job of it when he said that he did that whole long *book* MS. in only *two days*—& lo! that is just about what did happen! Now old 'Dolph is looking for a regular recasting in the slow, extensive, & painfully conscientious manner of Grandpa Nekrophilos—indeed, a suggestion from the third & latest rejecting publisher has led him to consider a radical change of plan, & an abandonment of the memoir style for a regular biographical treatise in the third person. This, of course, means a radical text-upheaval which really amounts to *collaboration* rather than revision. But—eheu!—though his ideas are bigger, his purse most infelicitously isn't; so that he plaintively announces himself as 'bewildered, & at a loss how, where, & to whom to turn'. He hems & haws & alludes delicately to the 'almost certain' profits of the biography if it can be properly formulated & launched—placing the likely receipts most alluringly at about *$50,000.00.* [Fancy!] What he is leading up to is undoubtedly a proposition for me to do the work on a speculative basis—i.e., for a certain percentage of the possible royalties—but right here is where Grandpa pauses for sombre reflection! As a piece of work—*rightly* done—it would be a staggering all-summer asphyxiation; cutting off alike my immediately remunerative revision, & any possible original fiction I might wish to write. In exchange for this sacrifice I would have a *double* gamble, with *two* exceedingly doubtful spots—(a) whether any publisher would take the damn thing after all, & (b) whether, being published, it would really drag in enough to make a collaborator's percentage anything more than a joke. Yes—the old gentleman will be very deliberate! Moreover—I don't know how big a percentage a collaborator really ought to ask. And yet, at that, there's certainly great stuff in the book; real source material that no future Bierce student (if such the coming years may hold) can afford to overlook. Belknap went wild over it—eating up every word so avidly that he didn't see any mistakes at all until he started to go over it a second time with critical pencil in hand—& I shall be glad to get a chance to read the MS. myself. Old 'Dolph still talks of making a stage-coach trip to Providence—& I shall certainly receive him with civility if he does. But in my opinion he'd better stick to Belknap—who is right on the ground for personal consultation, & who is willing to toil for fame alone—as his collaborator; telling him just how extensive he wants the changes, & giving him plenty of time to make a really thorough job. In recompense he ought to include the Child's name on the title-page—"Ambrose Bierce: By Adolphe de Castro & Frank Belknap Long, Jun." Just how much fame it would bring Belknap remains to be seen. The book is no mere controversial item—it's a long string of general Bierce reminiscences—& now that a triple rejection has chastened him, Old 'Dolph would probably be willing to cut down the M & H D episode till it occupied a less disproportionate space in his whole oeuvre.

By this time you've undoubtedly heard from Cook anent your own book, & are aware of the relapse which came so near to finishing him but happily didn't. He's probably getting the volume bound & labelled now, & you may receive it any time. What a damn shame that the local lit colyum— best possible review source—stopped just at the most inopportune moment! It sure is a helluva world! Incidentally—the Bullen book is having an unexpected *sale* in Canada, so that a *second edition* may be called for.[1] My gawd! *More* of that ———————'d proofreading which made my autumn a nightmare & cast a shadow over the early Yuletide season!

Yes—I would surely have appreciated that infantile hell-raiser of yours; & no matter what its condition would have accomplished its recension with all the sympathetic insight & exhaustive particularity of a Leipzig pundit. What a priceless gem of biographical material has been lost to some future de Castro, whose reminiscences of "Donald Wandrei As I Knew Him" will be the literary sensation of 1978! Speaking of books—young Derleth is broadcasting the advice for everybody to invest $2.00 in Algernon Blackwood's new collection—"The Dance of Death"—published by Lincoln MacVeagh, The Dial Press. For my part, I'd rather have some of Algy's old ones; but those who dote bibliophilically on "modern firsts" may take the advice for what it is worth. ¶ And so it goes. Best of luck with all your ventures—book, studies, & everything! ¶ Yr obt Grandsire

Νεκρόφιλος

Notes

1. Money was advanced to Cook for the second edition, but it never appeared, although proofs were prepared.

[95] [HPL to DAW] [ANS]¹

[Postmarked Providence, R.I.,
17 April 1928]

Thanks & congratulations!!! I feel like rushing down & telling all the boys at Jake's!!! It makes a splendid appearance, & I had no idea that Cook was using a large-sized page. I haven't heard from him lately, & am glad to see by this indirect evidence that his recovery is continuing. Now I hope the publicity & sale will be decently satisfactory despite the regrettable delay. Yes—the volume is truly a fascinating item, & I think you ought to be grateful to W P C for turning out such a tasteful job—delay or no delay! Let me know what favourable reviews you get.

Yr obt Πάππος Νεκρόφιλος

P.S. I've broken hibernation & begun the spring hiking season. Walked 16 miles through idyllic countryside Easter Sunday—from the village of Esmond, R.I. to Woonsocket.

P.P.S. This skyscraper (over) is where you saw the aching void opposite the Arcade.

Notes

1. *Front:* New Industrial Trust Building, Providence, R.I.

[96] [HPL to DAW] [ANS]¹

[Postmarked Brooklyn, N.Y.,
7 May 1928]

Dear Melmoth:—

Well, Sir, your Grandpa Necrophilos is again more or less of a wanderer, though not an especially willing one this time. Necessity has forced me to be in the N.Y. region for a month or so, & I am making the best of it by sojourning in the oasis of Flatbush, which still remains more or less of a white man's town with single wooden houses, green lawns, &c. &c. If writing within the next 3 weeks or so, address me at *395 East 16th St., Brooklyn, N.Y.*² ¶ Have seen all the gang, & find them flourishing. They all admire "Ecstasy" tremendously. Have been on some great motor trips with the Longs. ¶ Dwyer may come down to Brooklyn during my stay, & I may take a trip up the Hudson to see him. He & honest old Mac are getting to be first-rate correspondents! ¶ Before I go home I expect to make a trip southward in quest of colonial antiquities. Shall touch Philadelphia, Washington, Annapolis, Alexandria, & possibly Richmond & Williamsburg, Va. ¶ Sorry you're so rushed, but I'm about the same. Have seen old de Castro, & find that he has the Voss book in the original. He is a queer old reprobate, & I doubt if he & I can strike any bargain in the matter of Bierce book revision.

Yr obt Grandpa Nekro

Notes

1. *Front:* Soldiers and Sailors Arch, Brooklyn, N. Y.
2. The "necessity" (never specified in the letters to DAW) was the demand by HPL's wife Sonia that he stay with her while she set up a hat shop in Brooklyn.

[97]   [HPL and James F. Morton to DAW] [ANS][1]

[Postmarked Paterson, N.J.,
12 May 1928]

Well—Grandpa Necrophilos is still keeping up the Melmoth stuff! Hope all three of us can get together in Providence this coming summer—what ho for beef stew at Jake's & 37½ varieties of frozen milk at Maxfield's!

—Πάππος Νεκρόφιλος

A lover of life adds his humble greetings.

James F. Morton.

Notes

1. *Front:* Garret Rock, Paterson, N. J.

[98]   [HPL and W. Paul Cook to DAW] [ANS][1]

[Postmarked Brattleboro, Vt.,
West Brattleboro Station,
18 June 1928]

Say, who's Melmoth now? Your aged Grandpa is still on the wing—visiting in Vermont, & expecting to take in Athol, West Shokan, & then some! See you later—Πάππος Νεκρόφιλος

You say you are getting fat! You should see me! Cook

Notes

1. *Front:* Camels Hump in the Green Mts. of Vermont.

[99]   [HPL to DAW] [ALS]

For the moment—
℅ W. Paul Cook,
Box 215,
Athol, Mass.
Tuesday, June 26, 1928

Dear Ex-Melmoth:—

Well—as you see, I am still on the move; taking the taste of N.Y. out of my mouth by means of extensive & intensive delvings in the sub-soil of my native New England! I spent two weeks in absolute rusticity—with a friend who has taken a Vermont farmhouse for the summer—& now I am indulging in the moderate urbanism of good old Athol. Vermont is an unbelievably un-spoiled piece of early-American terrain—it really brings the 18th & early 19th centuries back with phenomenal forcefulness. The scenery—endless wild domed hills & hanging woods & mysterious brooklets that tumble & gurgle through forest ravines—is worthy of Machen's Gwent country, & if I do not use it some day in fiction, then I am gone to seed in truth! It certainly put my attire out of business with its temptations to briery & swampy woodland rambles & arduous mountain-climbs. I had to buy a new suit yesterday in Athol! I climbed every peak of any eminence, in a radius of five miles, & had some stupendous vistas of distant hills & windings of the Connecticut. I shall be in Athol a few days, & then shall either go home (strange place! I wonder if I still recall the way?) or go to see Dwyer in West Shokan. Tonight Cook & I are going over to Munn's place to inspect his weird library. Are you not green with bitter envy? Just at this moment I am sitting beside a country road half way up the hill toward the Sentinel Elm.[1] The day is warm & ideal—welcome enough after a week of rotten weather.

I am indeed glad to hear of your stimulating activities, & congratulate you upon the various honours you have received. The editorship of the daily must really be quite a distinction—& I am glad the electorate had the good sense to confer it where it was best deserved. It pleases me, too, to hear that "Ecstasy" has taken so well. Cook tells me that you are planning an expurgated edition, which I am sure will command an even wider circle of admirers.

Your graduation no doubt causes you to heave deep sighs of relief at a long-wished escape from ennui. Now I trust that you may be able to establish some remunerative affiliation which may not prove too confining & repug-nant. I wish you could manage an eastern hike this summer. Belknap still cherishes the hope that you may be able to get around these parts, & I pray that his optimism may be justified. The reason you have not heard from him regarding "Ecstasy" is that he is devastatingly busy with *revision*. He has begun to emulate his Grandpa Nekrophilos in the matter of literary tinkering, & has found himself quite swamped with orders.

Speaking of tinkering—I have not yet come to any satisfactory terms with old de Castro, & doubt if I ever shall. He proved a cursed nuisance in N.Y.—pestering me continually with useless calls both telephonic & personal. He seems unwilling to pay anything in advance, & until he does that he will not secure any coöperation from me. Incidentally—he sold Wright (for $175.00) the story I revised for him last winter.[2] He wants Cook to get out a new edition of "The Monk & the Hangman's Daughter"; with additional matter translated from Voss's original, & with the plates which appeared in the first edition.

Cook is now printing "The Shunned House"—I saw the presses working on it last night when I called at the Transcript office.[3] Here is a sample sheet just to prove that I am right! You'll certainly be remembered when the very first batch of copies is sent out—although Cook & I may feel tempted to 'hold out on you' just to bring you to New England on that aeroplane excursion! By the way—believe it or not, that damned Bullen book is developing an actual *sale*, & going into a *second edition!* I read proofs of the latter last week. Good gawd—shall I ever be rid of it? It seems aeons ago that I read—in your presence, by the way—the letter which fastened the task upon me!

> Yr aged & obt
> Grandpa Melmoth III.

P.S. You didn't enclose the reviews which your letter led me to expect within.

[*Enclosure:* Sample sheet of The Shunned House.]

Notes

1. This locale may have inspired Sentinel Hill in "The Dunwich Horror."
2. HPL was paid only $16.00 for his work on "The Last Test."
3. W. Paul Cook printed sheets of HPL's *The Shunned House* but never bound or distributed them.

[100] [HPL to DAW] [ANS][1]

> [Postmarked Springfield, Mass.,
> 7 July 1928]

Still in circulation! Visited a week in North Wilbraham, & am now working north through Springfield, Holyoke, Northampton, & Greenfield for the Mohawk Trail & Albany. Hope you can get east before autumn!

> Yr obt Grandpa Melmoth

Notes

1. *Front:* The Gilbert Homestead, Eastern States Exposition, Springfield, Mass.

[101] [HPL to DAW] [ANS][1]

[Postmarked Philadelphia, Pa.,
11 July 1928]

Back to the colonial! Am doing Philadelphia, & will Melmoth it onward to Baltimore this afternoon. You can't tell me that antiquarian travel isn't better than authorship!

Yr obt Πάππος Νεκρόφιλος

Notes

1. *Front:* Carpenters' Hall, Philadelphia, Pa.

[102] [HPL to DAW] [ANS][1]

[Postmarked Baltimore, Md.,
12 July 1928]

Have just been to the grave of Edgar Allan Poe, in Westminster Presbyterian Churchyard. It is at once a melancholy & inspiring spot—I feel like writing verse about it! This afternoon I am going to Annapolis, & tonight I shall reach Washington. Am nearly broke, but have saved aside my fare home. Hope to see you in N Y shortly. Yr obt Melmoth III

Notes

1. *Front:* Mansion House, Druid Hill Park, Baltimore, Md.

[103] [HPL to DAW] [ANS][1]

[Postmarked Annapolis, Md.,
13 July 1928]

Have found Annapolis a second Marblehead!
I gasp with reverence in the presence of surviving antiquity!

Shakily thine,
ΠΑΠΠΟΣ ΝΕΚΡΟΦΙΛΟΣ

Notes

1. *Front:* The Chase Mansion, Annapolis, Md.

[104] [HPL to DAW] [ANS][1]

[Postmarked Alexandria, Va.,
13 July 1928]

God Save the King!

Wallowing in the colonial past—& Sunday I'm going to see the *Endless Caves*² at New Market, Va. Am asking my aunt to send more cash—just about broke, but happy withal.

See you soon.

Melmoth III

Notes

1. *Front:* King Street from Royal Street, Alexandria, Va.

2. I.e., the Endless Caverns near New Market, VA. See "Observations on Several Parts of America" (1928; *CE* 4.29–29). HPL called it his "first glimpse of the marvellous underground world."

[105] [HPL to DAW] [ANS]¹

[Postmarked Havre de Grace, Md.,
15 July 1928]

On the road back—still gasping with awe over the *Endless Caverns*. Will be in N Y Tuesday morning—to get in touch with me telephone Belknap. Hope we can all get together.

Yr obt

Melmoth

Notes

1. *Front:* Hotel Bayou, Havre de Grace, Md. Finest Hotel on Chesapeake Bay / 60 Rooms. Wm. Pinkney West, Manager. Modern. Fireproof. 60 Baths.

[106] [HPL to DAW] [ANS]¹

[Postmarked Providence, R.I.,
18 July 1928]

Sorry you couldn't get over to Belknap's yesterday. Didn't you receive my card from Havre-de-Grace, or have you actually landed the job that is to make you a millionaire overnight? ¶ Well, I'm home at last! Had word last evening that my elder aunt's health required my presence for errand-performing & so on, so omitted the Connecticut sightseeing & took a night train for these Plantations. Just blew in—& may or may not breakfast at Jake's. Hope you can get around to these parts in due course of time. ¶ And you *must* see the *Endless Caverns!!* Did you get the booklet I sent? It's the sight of a lifetime! Your imagination would run riot! Good luck—

Yr obt Grandsire

Melmoth

Notes

1. *Front:* Banjotti Memorial Fountain, Providence, R. I.

[107] [HPL to DAW] [ANS][1]

[Postmarked Providence, R.I.,
25 July 1928]

Delighted to hear from you, though sorry the Providential prospects are not bright. Why didn't you come over to McNeil's last week when you heard Belknap & I had gone? We left word for you to be told where we were, in case you called up, & were half expecting you to join us over at the good old boy's. Didn't you remember Mac's address? ¶ Belknap & his family called here last Monday on their way to Cape Cod. I don't believe it will be practicable for me to make the Marblehead trip at present, for I am more or less needed hereabouts till my aunt's health is better. ¶ Glad you looked up Morton. He spoke of meeting you & liking you very much. He had word that Cook has traded his slum-cottage for a 100-acre farm in the wild country east of Athol. I'll wager he'll have an interesting place when next we visit him! ¶ Hope you'll have an interesting sail to repay you for the yacht-painting. If you get as far as Newport or Providence let me know, & I'll meet you at the wharf. ¶ I am as busy as hades settling down again & reading back numbers of accumulated papers & magazines. My correspondence is a hopeless mess beyond recall! Best wishes to Red Hook.
Yr obt
Νεκρὸ

Notes

1. *Front:* College St. to Market Sq. Showing Hospital Trust and Chamber of Commerce, Providence, R. I.

[108] [HPL to DAW] [ANS][1]

[Postmarked Providence, R.I.,
31 July 1928]
July 31

Dear Melmoth:—

New Haven, eh? Too bad you didn't come the rest of the way to Providence! I trust Munn has by this time looked you up. He was here yesterday, & we had a very pleasant session—went down to Eddy's Bookstore[2] & nosed around until he found an old story by Camille Flammarion in some 1893 *Cosmopolitans*.[3] We didn't eat at Jake's because there was no free space to park Munn's car near there! Late in the afternoon I undertook to guide Munn on his way to N Y, & rode with him as far as East Greenwich, coming back by omnibus & trolley. ¶ My aunt is somewhat better, but it will be quite a while before she can dispense with the nurse or be in any way active. Lumbago is very slow in mending. ¶ Congratulations upon your coming escape from Red Hook—here's hoping it won't prove a jump from frying-pan to fire. If you want a really restful environment you'll have to move farther away from Manhattan rather than closer to it. The only really habitable spots in Greater N.Y. are remote overtaken villages like Flatbush, Jamaica, or Flushing, or the rural reaches of Staten Island. ¶ I hope I can get to see Dwyer this autumn. It depends partly on my aunt's health, & partly on Cook's ability & inclination to convey me in his car. ¶ Wright has just accepted "The Silver Key" (which he once rejected) for $70.00. Pretty good, I'll say! Regards to Munn if you see him. Are you taking in all the sights of N.Y., antiquarian & otherwise?

  Yr obt
   Νεκρὸ

Notes

1. *Front:* First Baptist Church, Providence, R. I.
2. Eddy's Book Store at 260 Weybosset St., owned by Arthur A. Eddy.
3. Camille Flammarion (1842–1925), "Omega: The Last Days of the World," *Cosmopolitan* 14, No. 6 (April 1893): 744–67; 15, No. 1 (May 1893): 15–35; 15, No. 2 (June 1893): 185–203; 15, No. 3 (July 1893): 311–28; 15, No. 4 (August 1893): 457–72.

[109] [DAW to HPL] [ALS]

      43–45 42nd St.,
      Long Island City, N.Y.
      Sept. 27, 1928

Dear Necrophilos:

   As you can see, I have fled far from Red Hook and the curse that contaminates it. I am sure that it, and it alone, was responsible for my depression and evil luck. Here perhaps I can escape its sinister influence sufficiently to garner in a host of those shekels which have thus far eluded me.

   And what have you been doing this past Summer either in the way of vacation or the summoning up of abyssal monstrosities? My own Summer has been productive of little.

   I have seen Vrest Orton several times, and Kirk and Loveman rather frequently. Belknap was away a considerable portion of the time, but I saw him a couple of days ago.

   I received a letter to-day from Machen, in which he mentioned your article and its hold on him.[11]

   My second book of poems has started its weary and what will be, I fear, lengthy travels. It has already fared forth to two publishers and fared back with distressing promptness.

What ho! I'm young, and who the Devil cares? There's gold in them there hills; and Avalon lies over the horizon; anything may happen to me, and I hope everything does.

Domiciled,
Melmoth

Notes

1. In a letter to AWD [6 January 1928; *ES* 124], HPL requested that AWD provide to W. Paul Cook the addresses of various living authors mentioned in SHL so that copies of its appearance in the *Recluse* could be mailed to them. We know with certainty that Machen, Blackwood, and M. R. James read the essay.

[110] [HPL to DAW] [ALS]

Sunday
[30 September 1928]

Dear Melmoth:—

I was very glad to hear from you, & to learn that you have escaped from Red Hook's tentacles at last. But the pull of the noxious place is insidious & far-reaching, & it has now enmeshed *another* of our struggling brotherhood—no less a dignitary than young Wilfred B. Talman, discoverer of *Jake's,* who now holds forth at 46 Garden Place. Have you met this pleasing youth? He is at present connected with the New York Times.

I trust that you will encounter success in the trifling matter of drachma-lassoing, though you must of course realise that spectacular fortunes are not to be made exactly overnight. Anything steady & promising is to be welcomed at first, even though it may not possess those dazzling qualities dreamed of by those who have envisaged the metropolis as a place of gold-paved streets. In sober truth, large & sudden fortunes are seldom if ever made save by those possessed of special commercial attributes—& a born aesthete is about the last person to have such natural tendencies.

Good luck with your new book! You will have great difficulty in placing verse material with professional publishers, but of course it *might* land through some single chance amidst an hundred. If not, I trust you will submit the MS. for Recluse issuance by our noble friend & colleague W P C—who has just moved to a 170-acre farm east of Athol. Is this volume the collected "Sonnets of the Midnight Hours?" I am very anxious to have a complete collection of your weird poetry in book form.

I note with much interest the exhibition catalogue in which your brother so prominently figures, & congratulate him upon his attainments & recognition. The sample on the cover surely displays a talent of the keenest intensity—a really Beardsleian vision & method. Is he in New York himself, or merely represented by his work? I envy anyone who can draw, with a verdant, mordant envy! My tastes are running more & more to landscape & architectural effects as distinguished from literature, yet I lack the least talent in the one logical medium for their expression.

My own recent days have been devoid of events, save such as local explorations have supplied. I have been to the Quinsnicket woods many times, taking my work or reading to the top of that high rock which you doubtless recall, & have also made many Machen-like voyages of discovery through strange Providence streets—including whole neighbourhoods whose very existence I had never suspected before. It is astonishing how many obscure & labyrinthine nooks & corners may lurk in even a small city, absolutely unknown to most lifetime inhabitants until chance or deliberate exploration brings them to light. One of my recent discoveries is a typical country lane less than ¼ mile from this house—a narrow path with ancient tottering gambrel-roofed houses that runs diagonally up the hill above the Charles St. factory district. From one point along it one can obtain a marvellously unique view of the citadel-like summit of Smith's Hill across the valley, with marble-domed State House & Gothic-towered St. Patrick's church in a magic juxtaposition suggesting the skyward apex of some Renaissance hill town in the Old World. When I came upon it in

the glamorous blaze of sunset I paused almost breathless with admiration, & could not resist attempting a crude sketch in my note book. The above embellishment is intended to give an idea of what it is like. Better make another trip to Providence & let me shew you some of its cryptic wonders!

I have written one story since seeing you—a 48-page affair called "The Dunwich Horror". The MS. is being passed around, & when our friend C A S returns it I'll send it to you. Incidentally—I'm interested to hear that Machen has seen my article.

In odd moments I have read a number of weird & almost weird books—including the "Romance of the Forest" & "Italian" of your friend Mrs. Radcliffe. Others are Arthur Ransome's "Elixir of Life", Mrs. H. D. Everett's "The Death Mask", H. R. Wakefield's "They Return at Evening", Buchan's "Runagates Club", (in which 3 out of the 12 tales are weird) & the French & Asquith ghost anthologies.[1] I am now reading Le Fanu's "House by the Churchyard."

With best wishes for your fame, fortune, & artistic creativeness, I remain

Yr most ob^t Servt

Νεϰϱόφιλος

[*Enclosure:* "R. I. Youth Claims 'Bumming' Record," clipping from *Providence Evening Bulletin* (?).]

Notes

1. HPL refers to Joseph Lewis French's *Ghosts, Grim and Gentle* and Cynthia Asquith's *The Ghost Book*. All the volumes cited here, except the French anthology, were mentioned in the revised version of SHL.

[111] [DAW to HPL] [ALS]

43–45 42nd St.,

Long Island City, N.Y.

Nov. 19, 1928

Dear Necrophilos:

I have criminal feelings at my epistolary negligence, which has in part been due to my unsettled condition. At the present moment, I am working in the advertising department of E. P. Dutton & Co., while waiting the long promised and overdue book of yours à la Cook. I also await with anticipatory pleasure a new tale of yours which Belknap says is to appear in W.T. The which, by the way, purchased my short story about emeralds[1] and wherein I am running next month a small ad on the troublesome Ecstasy.

If this letter is totally illegible, ascribe it to a burn on my finger resulting from an attempt to do my own ironing!

I received a short letter from Smith recently, but otherwise have not heard from any member of the gang in a long time, except Orton whom I frequently see. I like him a great deal, and to him is due the credit for my present position.

The muse has visited me infrequently; a few poetical attempts are the total of my last six months' work. Some sort of transition is taking place; and the end—who knows? I shall worry about that when it has definitely taken place.

I hope some day to revisit Providence, and not too far in the future. But much depends on the wayward grace of Lady Fortune.

Melmoth

Notes

1. "The Green Flame."

[112] [HPL to DAW] [ALS]

10 Barnes St.,
Providence, R.I.,
Novr. 23, 1928

Dear Melmoth:—

Congratulations on your new Dutton affiliation! Now for Pete's sake try to see that the books of our honest old friend McNeil are decently advertised! Your firm, Sir, has been damn'd remiss in pushing good old Mac's sales; & I shall look for better things now that you are at—or near—the helm. Make "The Shadow of the Iroquois" go over big for the Christmas trade, & pave the way for a big publicity campaign for "The Shores of Adventure" next year. Seriously, you ought to go around & see Mac one of these days. You know where to find him—457 Fifth St., Bklyn. Take an Interborough train to Bergen St. or a B.M.T. Brighton train to 7th Ave., & then take a 7th Ave. surface car & alight at Fifth St. Mac would be delighted to see you—& as fellow Duttonians you two would have a great deal to talk over.

Commiserations on your finger burn! I know what such things are like, for in the year 1907 I nearly lost the 3d finger of my right hand through a phosphorus burn sustained in my chemical laboratory. I had to type all my letters, but learned how to sign my name & make odd notations with my left hand. The damn thing was months in healing.

About "The Shunned House"—Cook is the guy to ask, not me! He bought a farm east of Athol this autumn, & began moving out to it; but found that he couldn't get the heating installed in time for cold weather. Therefore he has had to take rooms in Athol for the winter. All this moving turmoil has played havoc with his schedule, so that we must forgive him for any instances of apparent negligence. I expect him down here at least once before winter. We plan to make a raid on Eddy's bookstore!

Yes—Derleth told me of Wright's purchase of your once-rejected tale. Congrats! The readers took tremendously to your "Red Brain"—letters in praise of it have been appearing continuously since its publication. Guided by them, Wright will always be hospitable toward your material now. Hope the advt. of "Ecstasy" brings results. Belknap & I didn't net many returns from our revision advt. in W.T.[1] My new tale "The Dunwich Horror" sold for $240.00, the largest cheque I've yet had promised. In the next W.T. you will find "The Silver Key", which sold for $70.00. "The Call of Cthulhu" is to be reprinted in an anthology edited by one T. Everett Harré, 32 W. 73d. St., N.Y. City. Ever hear of that bird? O'Brien's "Best Short Stories of 1928" is now out, & I am told that my biography runs to 18 lines—although I haven't seen it yet. I suppose vanity will force me to buy the thing sooner or later!

You ought to get more in touch with the gang. I suppose you know that Dwyer has taken a position in Kingston, & is now to be addressed at 177 Green St. there. Glad you see Orton frequently—he's a delightful chap. Belknap tells me that you were much excited by a modern furniture exhibition which you & he went to see.

So your literary art is undergoing a transition? Don't desert the weird if you can help it! I'd hate to see you becoming a Sherwood Anderson or F. Scott Fitzgerald or T. S. Eliot!

You surely must get around to Providence soon. I enclose a catalogue of an art exhibition which threw me into a joint ecstasy of admiration & envy. Oh, boy! Maybe Peck didn't capture the very soul of Old Providence!

Well—don't get too metropolitan!

Πάππος Νεκρόφιλος

P.S. I hope to get to Boston net week to see the new wing of decorative arts at the museum. From all accounts, it will make the Metropolitan's American Wing a back number!

[*Enclosure:* "Catalogue of an Exhibition of Drawings and Etchings: 'Glimpses of Providence and Vicinity' by Henry J. Peck.[2] November 7 to 18, 1928. Providence Art Club, 11 Thomas Street."]

Notes

1. FBL and HPL placed the following ad in the August 1928 issue of *WT:*

Frank Belknap Long, Jr.——H. P. Lovecraft

Critical and advisory service for writers of prose and verse; literary revision in all degrees of extensiveness.

Address

Frank B. Long, Jr., 230 West 97th St., New York, N.Y.

2. Henry J. Peck (1880–1964), illustrator and landscape artist who lived on College Hill just below HPL and his aunt.

[113] [HPL to DAW] [ANS]

[Postmarked Providence, R.I.,
21 December 1928]

[May your Christmas be a Merry one
your New Year Bright and Prosperous]
Πάππος Νεκρόφιλος
1928.

1929

[114] [HPL and Samuel Loveman to DAW] [ANS][1]

[Postmarked Boston, Mass.,
4 January 1929]

Ave, young Melmoth! Behold the convention! We've been treading the ground which you'll recall from a year & a half ago—& glimpsed the Excellent Lunch (opposite the Y) from a car window this afternoon.[2] Tomorrow we behold Salem & Marblehead, & I myself shall stay over in Boston till Sunday & see the new period wing at the Museum. Trust you're not painting the Manhattan skyline too violent a shade of crimson! Get around New Englandward when you can.

Yr obt Servt Πάππος Νεκρόφιλος

What you need is a taste of the sanity of Boston. N.Y.C. really doesn't exist in the Berkleyan sense. Neither did I until I came here.

Frater   Sam

Notes

1. *Front:* Old South Church and Washington Street, Boston, Mass.
2. Possibly alluded to in "The Shadow over Innsmouth" as the Ideal Lunch (although said to be in Newburyport) (*CF* 3.169).

[115] [DAW to HPL] [ALS]

[E. P. DUTTON & CO., INC.
PUBLISHERS
286–302 FOURTH AVENUE
NEW YORK, N.Y.]

Jan. 13, 1929

Dear Necrophilos:

My sins are many, and likewise my excuses. May you forgive the first and accept the second! Work—more work—and still more work—plus flu.

I owe you innumerable thanks for your flattering comment to Mr. Harré. I have met him, am giving him what assistance I can, and find him a delightful personality.

So you have initiated Sam? Well well! You will make every New Yorker a new Englander if you keep up the good work. I frequently hanker for trees and a cliff, but do not see how I can quench my thirst for quite some time. Very shortly I must go through the contortions of moving, and thereafter it will still be work and more work.

I look forward to reading your latest story. Belknap says it's a masterpiece. How is the revision bureau? And the more worthy creative sanctum? My own muse is in a state of suspended animation.

> Resurrected,
> Melmoth

[116] [HPL to DAW] [ALS]

Jany 16, 1929

Dear Melmoth:—

I was very glad to receive your bulletin & to learn that you are still flourishing, though sorry to hear you are about to face the ordeal of moving again. Still, I fancy you are not so heavily weighted down with household goods that the ordeal will possess its gravest aspects. Let me know your new address when you have one.

Glad to know that you continue to assist the genial Harré in his anthological labours. Is he going to include your "Red Brain"? I told him he ought to. No doubt he has mentioned his acceptance of Belknap's "Space-Eaters". At first Belknap had other plans for this tale, but I persuaded him to let Harré have it, since the latter did not wish to accept any other in its stead.[1]

Sorry you've been so overburthened with work, & that influenza has added to your trials. I myself have been laid up with a hellish cold ever since my return from Boston, but its resemblance to my typical colds of the past convinces me that it is not connected with the prevailing pandemic.

Yes, indeed, I have gone far toward making a Yankee of our friend Samuelus—though the Greek rooms at the Museum of Fine Arts (which you will recall in connexion with a rainstorm & the Excellent Lunch) tended to cause a relapse into Hellenism. The Lovemanic trip was all too brief, but I managed to shew my guest something of colonial Providence by night, several of Boston's antiquarian high spots, & the selected cream of Salem's & Marblehead's glamorous reliquiae. You can't imagine how much greater the charm of Marblehead is in winter, when the streets are wholly free from the throng of urban vacationists. It is only then that the real, ancient life of the village comes to the surface & dominates the atmosphere. I stayed in Boston a day longer than Loveman, & did the new period wing of the Museum—a display of decorative & architectural art far surpassing the American Wing at the Metropolitan. It was no disappointment—though I had been looking forward to an inspection ever since it opened on the 22nd of November. You certainly must get around to ancient Novanglia next summer. New York is a prison, from which one simply must have occasional escapes.

Hope you've been doing your share toward keeping the disintegrating gang together. Call up Riverside 3465 & get in touch with Belknap some of these days—the youngster seems rather lonely of late, judging from his recent epistles. And don't neglect nice old Mac, either. Now you're a Dutton magnate, you must help to see that his books receive better advertising! Mortonius' hall of minerals opened on Jany. 10—the result of conscientious digging & still more conscientious classifying. Better drop around to Paterson & see the finished result of the quarrying you witnessed here in 1927! ¶ Sorry your productivity is at a low mark. So is mine—though I expect improvement later in the year.

With best of wishes—

Yr most obt

Πάππος Νεκρόφιλος.

[*Enclosure:* Postcard (*Front:* Old Town House, Built 1727. Marblehead, Mass.); no writing on back.]

Notes

1. Harré in fact published no story by FBL in *Beware After Dark!*

[117] [HPL to DAW] [ANS][1]

[Postmarked Yonkers, N.Y.,

8 April 1929]

Hail, Melmoth! I've allowed Orton to inveigle me into a brief metropolitan eclipse, so here I sit in the Rowfant at my favourite pastime of card-addressing! Hope we can get together before I return to civilisation 2 weeks hence—drop me a line in care of Orton. Did you make the charge of address foreshadow'd in your last note? I saw your tale in the new W.T.—good stuff![2] Write some more like it!

Yr obt

Πάππος Νεκρόφιλος

LATER—Have shewn the Dyckman & Van Cortlandt houses to Orton for the first time. Get in touch with me & have your antiquarian education completed!—Grandpa

Notes

1. *Front:* The Woolworth Building. New York City.
2. "The Shadow of a Nightmare."

[118] [HPL to DAW] [ANS][1]

[Postmarked Washington, D.C.,
2 May 1929]

Hail, Melmoth! Once again an old gent tries to steal your stuff & walk off with the migratory record! ¶ It's good to be out of N Y again—Washington is like a bath after a fall in the coal-bin! It is glorious *summer* here—gorgeously green & golden, with skies of a blue unknown to the north. No question—Wash'n is absolutely my favourite city outside New England. And now I'm about to deliver into the real old South—Fredericksburg, Richmond, Jamestown, Yorktown, Williamsburg, &c. Real historic stuff! This will come close to being the best of my trips. Hope I'll have cash enough left to shoot up the Hudson & see Dwyer on my return trip! ¶ Belknap & I saw Mac yesterday, & he seems vastly improved. Drop in the hospital & see him when you can. He needs good cheer as well as good diet! ¶ Hope you'll have a good trip to St Paul—give my regards to the sky!
Yr obt Servt
ΝΕΚΡΟΦΙΛΟΣ ΠΑΠΠΟΣ

Notes

1. *Front:* The Lee Mansion, Arlington, Va.

[119] [HPL to DAW] [ANS][1]

[Postmarked Richmond, Va.,
2 May 1929]

Don't you wish you were here?
The *Original* Melmoth.

Notes

1. *Front:* The Edgar Allen [*sic*] Poe Shrine (Oldest House in Richmond).

[120] [HPL to DAW] [ANS][1]

[Postmarked Philadelphia, Pa.,
9 May 1929]

Richmond, Williamsburg, Jamestown, Yorktown, Fredericksburg, Washington, & now Old Philadelphia again. Who's Melmoth now? Don't know as I can stop as I re-pass through N Y—may shoot right up Hudson to see Dwyer. And how's Mac? Incidentally—you ought to see the Cyclopean *Easter Island* images in the Smithsonian Museum at Washington! Regards—
Yr obt
Πάππος Νεκρόφιλος

Notes

1. *Front:* William Penn House, Fairmount Park, Philadelphia, Pa.

[121] [Bernard Austin Dwyer, Frank Belknap Long, Jr., and
HPL to DAW] [ANS][1]

[Postmarked Kingston, N.Y.,
13 May 1929]

Transplanted as you see from the wild domed hills I nevertheless find the old
Roman town of Caermaen fascinating. Grandpa and I had a great jaunt yesterday, having a delightful conversation with a library attendant who was the
very embodiment of old Colonial courtesy. Ask him about it. I hope to see
you before the summer is out. Kingston isn't so far.

Bernie

Greetings from one of a trio of Weird Tailors. A great reunion—The Man
from Genoa

Hail, ex-Melmoth, from the reigning Melmothick champion! This surely is a
great reunion! Wish I could drag the other two guys along to Athol when I
go! Yr obt Νεκρόφιλος

Notes

1. *Front:* Kingston, N.Y., Old Senate House by Night. Built 1676.

[122] [HPL and Bernard Austin Dwyer to DAW] [ANS][1]

[Postmarked Kingston, N.Y.,
13 May 1929]

Well—now I've made my pilgrimage to the Ulster County shrine of the Muses! Wish I could see the wild domed hills of Shokan as you did, but at least I
have a marvellous colonial town to wander in. Surely glad to see Bernardus
Artifex in person at last—your description did not err! Sorry I couldn't see
you whilst passing through N Y en route north, but the Longs gave me a motor lift to Kingston the very morning after I hit the big burg. Shall see Cook
in Athol next week.

Yr obt Πάππος Νεκρόφιλος

Dear Don—Wish you were here with us in this enchanted grove—recalled to
20th century reality only by the passing of an occasional aeroplane. We are in a

back country lane just back from the city, by the ruined wall of a former estate. Truly it is enough to make one dream of ice cream and root beer—wish I had some! Springtime is now definitely located in Kingston.

Bernie

Notes

1. *Front:* Old Captain Tappan House, now owned by Daughters of American Revolution, Kingston, N. Y.

[123] [HPL, W. Paul Cook, H. Warner Munn to DAW] [ANS][1]

[Postmarked Athol, Mass.,
16? May 1929]

Greetings from soil familiar to you as well as to me! Had a great time with Dwyer in Kingston—he's a splendid chap, with one of the most delicately fantastic imaginations I have ever encountered. After Kingston I explored the ancient villages of Hurley & New Paltz with their famous stone houses, & have now ascended the Hudson & cut across the Berkshires to good old New England—my native soil! Glad to see Athol, home of Ponkert's werewolf & the Recluse Press! Cook & I will go to Prov. en masse at the end of the week—great homecoming after a great trip!

Yr obt Πάππος Νεκρόφιλος

Here we are again! Are you going to see us this summer? Cook

Greetings from Wladislow Brenryk. With the help of God, the Master Has Been Defeated!![2]

Notes

1. *Front:* New Arch Bridge, Main Street, Athol, Mass.
2. I.e., H. Warner Munn. HPL and RHB alluded to Munn using this name in "The Battle That Ended the Century" (1934). "Master" refers to Munn's series of "Master" stories, which started with "The Return of the Master" (*WT*, July 1927).

[124] [HPL to DAW] [ANS][1]

[Postmarked Providence, R.I.,
18 May 1929]

HOME!!!!

ΠΑΠΠΟΣ
ΝΕΚΡΟΦΙΛΟΣ

Notes

1. *Front:* Water Front Showing Sky Scrapers by Night. Providence, R. I.

[125] [HPL and James F. Morton to DAW] [ANS][1]
[Postmarked East Greenwich, R.I.,
18 June 1929]

Alas that our expeditionary force today doesn't include its young misanthrope of the 1927 period. We must eat at Jake's in memory of the days that were! Drop in & see good old Mac some day—he's now at the U.S. Naval Hospital in Brooklyn. Are you back from your St. Paul trip?

Yr obt Πάππος Νεϰϱόφιλος

Greetings in memory of our former glad adventure and in hope of an early reunion.

J. F. M.

Notes

1 *Front:* Kent County Court House, East Greenwich, R. I.

[126] [HPL and Frank Belknap Long, Jr. to DAW] [ANS][1]
[Postmarked Onset, Mass.,
14 August 1929]

Adventure & the sea! Doesn't this call to your jaded soul? Belknap will tell you about Old New Bedford & the whaler we explored. We're seriously considering going to sea!

Greetings from the haunts of The White Whale. New Bedford is as splendid as Marblehead.

F B L Jr.

Notes

1. *Front:* Sperm Whaling, "The Capture."

[127] [DAW to HPL] [ALS]

14 Morningside Ave.,
New York City
Sept. 9, 1929

Dear H P L:

Returned to the fold! I finally became so disgusted with advertising that I resigned to write, and am now working on a story of age-old horror.[1] The past year I consider pretty much wasted.

What have you been writing? If I can make arrangements, I'd like to take another trip to Providence. New York City is no place to write, or live, for that matter. I regretted I was not along on the occasion of Belknap's visit.

There is one bit of information you may be able to supply me for my story. Would the correct Latin for "Devil's Highway" and "God's Highway" be Via Diabolus: via Deus, or via Diabola: via Dea, or via Diaboli: via Dei? It's a small point as far as the story is concerned but I'm a believer in accuracy. If you can straighten me out on this I would appreciate it.

You probably have seen "Beware After Dark!" by now, for you were put down for two or three copies. I think myself it is a good collection—what is your opinion? It ought to have a fair circulation.

What news from Cook, Munn, Dwyer, Smith? I have been shamefully lax in correspondence. But I trust my materialistic aberrations are now ended.

Melmoth

[Written on stationery of E. P. Dutton & Co., Inc.]

Notes

1. I.e., *Dead Titans, Waken!* (published in revised form as *The Web of Easter Island*).

[128] [HPL to DAW] [ALS]

10 Barnes St.,
Providence, R.I.,
Septr. 12, 1929

Dear Melmoth:—

Welcome home! I thought the Perfect Babbitt period couldn't be of indefinite duration, though I'd hoped you could in some way divide your time (not your creative imagination) betwixt literary matters & salaried endeavour, so that you would not have to worry about cash the way I have to! It has always been my hope that I might get some sort of a job which would give me a small dependable income without drawing too heavily on the energy which ought to go into my writing. So far I've never succeeded—

though I am still receptive to any miraculous chance which the future years may offer. And thus I thought it might be with you—that you could hang on to some lucrative job with your left hand, as it were, whilst keeping your brain & right hand free for original & spontaneous creation. So indeed it may be— but I fancy this Dutton job was rather too important an affair for purely mechanical & left-handed performance. Probably it required the presence of all your energies & faculties, & left nothing but exhaustion as a residue; so that you were wise in chucking it over. I doubt if I could have hung on to anything so exacting for even a small fraction of the time that you did. Congratulations on your liberation, & good luck to the blasphemous chronicle of age-old horror!

Providence is the very place to get your masterpiece under way, so don't let anything interfere with your coming! You can get your old room at 10 Barnes just as in 1927, & the longer you can make your stay, the more keenly the old town will feel honoured! The woods of Quinsnicket, atop whose great rocks you have reclined & reflected in days agone, still wave an autumnal invitation with green banners soon to turn to scarlet & gold in your honour; whilst down by the Great Bridge Jake's still dispenses its wholesome & copious fare for a pittance—not much patronised by me of late, though I should certainly resume my 1927 patronage if given the incentive of a guest's brilliant company! You will see changes here & there, but only in details. Steady & conservative through all the years the slow Georgian pulse of the quiet old town beats picturesquely on; its ancient domes & steeples limned immutably against the sky, & its mellow old brick sidewalks—soon to know the crisp swishing of fallen leaves & the acrid aroma of autumnal bonfires—still lined with fanlighted doorways & double flights of steps, all drowsing beneath the arching boughs of the great elms. Old Providence! Where broods a lovelier haven of the Muse? There are rustic spots near by which you have not yet seen, & old, curious villages in the hills & on the shores whose charms you have yet to sample. But your programme would be your own; so that if you preferred to spend all your time in your room or on Quinsnicket's rocks weaving tales of age-old horror, you would not be urged into unwished wanderings. You would probably, though, want to go to New Bedford & clamber over that reincarnation of the old *Lagoda* in the whaling museum whereof Belknap & I told you on our card. I recall your penchant for things maritime. So try to fix up your programme to include a Providential sojourn, & let me know ahead in time to see that your poet's garret is all engaged & prepared for you. There isn't a better place you could pick for your fall work—for as I told you aeons ago, New York is no place for a white man!

Incidentally—last Sunday I received a pleasant & unexpected call from Kirk & his wife, who had been on a long motor tour through New England. I took them to the quaint village of Pawtuxet, down the bay, (did I shew you that?) & guided them out of the tangled traffic on the road toward Manhattan. As I watched their car out of sight, I did not envy them their destination!

About your Latin question—there is no dispute at all but that *Via Diaboli* & *Via Dei* are the forms you want. Nouns in the genitive case are the only possible things to use—you know the analogy of *Via crucis* &c. The suggestions inherent in these dark scraps of mediaeval Latin washed up on the shores of modernity are very alluring indeed; & I am eager to sample the subterrene & archaic terrors of which they are symbols.

Yes—I have received three copies of the Harré anthology, one of which I gave to Belknap. I was sorry Harré left out Belknap's tale—especially after I took so many pains to persuade Belknap to let him have the particular one he wanted. But perhaps the publishers exercised some kind of a supercensorship. In general, I agree with you that the anthology is an excellent one; & I hope it may meet with general approval & a good circulation. I was surprised at the number of first-rate authors represented, & found only one or two tales (notably "The Quest of the Tropic Bird")[1] so dull that I could well wish them absent. Perhaps my greatest sorrow—for which, however, I believe you prepared me—was the omission of Shiel's "House of Sounds." Another thing—it seems to me that Harré might have given you some credit in his preface for all the aid you furnished him in his selective task. He wrote me that he was extremely indebted to you for various suggestions & recommendations. But anyway, it's a good collection.

As for 'what I've been writing'—that's all too easily answered: not a damn thing! Too much revision on hand to give me a chance to think—& even now I don't believe I'll get any free time till well into winter. But I'll get it then, or explode! I'll stage a sort of revolution like yours—in fact, I'm doing it now to the extent of refusing new revision for an indefinite period. But I *must* get the accumulated old jobs done up. The main one just now is, oddly enough, one which I *like*—the first to answer that description in all the history of my revisory activities. It is the preparation for publication of a text book by my good old friend Maurice W. Moe of Milwaukee—one of the old "amateur journalist" crowd & now an English teacher in West Division High School. This book, "Doorways to Poetry",[2] is without exception the best & clearest exposition of the inner essence of poetry that I've ever seen—& virtually the *only* work which comes anywhere near the miracle of making novices able to distinguish good verse from cheap & specious hokum. The method is absolutely original with Moe, & involves the insertion of many columns of parallel specimens of verse of varying badness & excellence, together with a key containing critical & elucidative comment. The answers in the key will be largely my work, since Moe thinks I can express subtle differences between degrees of merit better than he can. I am also preparing specimen bits of verse for illustrative use in the body of the text—unusual metres, stanzaic forms, Italian & Shakespearian sonnets,[3] & so on. This is really going to be a great book, & for once I am really interested in a revisory job! I shall use the volume, after its publication, in connexion with my own revision—

compelling certain types of clients to study it. It ought to be a hit in the schools, also—for which it is primarily intended. Moe is going to try it on the Macmillan Co. first; & then, if rejected, on the American Book Co. If again rejected, he will let a local firm handle it—the Kenyon Pub. Co. of Wauwatosa, Wis.—so that its printing in some form or other is absolutely assured. But unless the Macmillans are utter asses, they'll snap it up & be glad to get it; for it certainly forms the greatest single aid to the recognition & comprehension of real literature that I've ever seen compressed within a brief 150 pages!

As for news of your neglected friends—Cook & Munn were down here on the 22nd of June in Munn's new Graham-Paige car, but I haven't been able to extract a word from either of them since! I guess they're all right, though. Munn has the same explosive-truck job, but has given up his position in the fire department. He has also given up his room in the fire station, & has taken a flat with his father—who has moved in from the farm at Partridgeville. This flat—451 Main St.—is in the same building where Cook lived over a decade ago, when I first knew him. Cook himself is still—or was last June—on the farm he bought last autumn, though he can't live there in winter, & is very anxious to sell it. It's really a pity to let it go, though, for the place is an ancient & picturesque one—on a typical New England hilltop with magnificent vistas & exquisite landscape details on every hand. I stayed there several days in the spring, as you no doubt learned from my card.

As for Dwyer—here again postcard bulletins have told you of how I met him in person at last, how captivated I was by his hearty, agreeable, & imaginatively sensitive personality, & how I spent many delightful days exploring his ancient city of Kingston & its almost equally ancient environs, Hurley & New Paltz. I have written up all my spring travels in a long descriptive essay,[4] which I'll shew you when Belknap returns it—& therein have given the Kingston region quite an historic survey. Dwyer—boarding in a quiet house near the most ancient section—was an ideal host; & we discussed everything on the earth & off it . . . . mostly off it. He has one of the most fertile, dream-filled, & Machen-like fancies that I have ever seen in a mortal being. He is still working in a factory, but does not let that labour hinder his imaginative life. Now & then he does a bit of painting, or tries his hand tentatively at something literary. He hopes to get some commercial poster jobs this summer. Since my visit he has moved, & is now to be addressed at *292 Fair St., Kingston, N.Y.*

Klarkash-Ton, Emperor of Dreams, still reigns in wonted state; turning more & more to French poetry, in which he exhibits an uncanny Baudelairian skill. He seems to be writing more than he paints just now. Both he & Dwyer would vastly appreciate hearing from you—better add epistolary conscientiousness to your list of reforms!

My antiquarianism goes on as usual—as far as cash & time allow. Cards told you of my spring trip to Phila., Wash'n, Fredericksburg, Richmond, Williamsburg, Yorktown, & Jamestown, cradle of our civilisation on this continent—& of the homecoming through Kingston, Albany, & Athol. Morton visited here in June, & we went the rounds of colonial villages pretty well, & in July the young amateur Victor E. Bacon stopped off here for some sightseeing that included Newport. Early in August I took a motor tour to the ancient Fairbanks house in Dedham—built in 1636, & oldest house in New England—& to the celebrated "Wayside Inn" in Sudbury—seeing both of these for the first time.[5] Then came the week in Onset with the Longs—during which we did the lower part of Cape Cod pretty well, & toward the close of which I took my first ride in an aëroplane. Since then my principal trip has been to Foster—my maternally ancestral country in Western Rhode Island—with my younger aunt; visiting ancient family homesteads & copying ancestral epitaphs in the family burying-grounds. A great scenic region—I'd like to shew it to you! ¶ Well—here's wishing you luck with the age-old horror, & hoping I'll see you soon at the door of #10 Barnes!

Υr obt Πάππος Νεκρόφιλος

P.S. You ought to see the splendid bookplate our friend Talman is designing me! Colonial doorway motif—finely conceived & executed. I had proofs some time ago; but Talman's press broke down, so there will be delay about the bulk of the edition. Talman is certainly a decorative artist of sorts. ¶ My "Pickman's Model" will appear in a new volume of the British "Not at Night" anthology.

[*Enclosure:* "One of the Bed Rooms / Dedham, Mass. Fairbanks House, Built 1636." *On back:*] The Fairbanks house is perhaps the most impressive structure I have ever seen—the closest of all links with the dark Puritan age when New England was an infant colony trembling between the inhospitable sea & the edge of the black unknown woods. Built in 1636—when Boston was only 6 years old & Providence was just being established—it has undergone relatively little alteration, yet remains in singularly good condition. Wings were added in 1642 & 1648, so that the edifice is vague & rambling, & presents an ineffably quaint & sagging roof line as seen from the road. Within are sagging floors, massive, blackened woodwork, & all the earmarks of fearsome & immemorial age.

The house was built by Jonathan Fayerbanke of Sowersby, near Halifax, England—the ancestor of every Fairbanks in America. It is now owned by a society of Fairbanks descendants, & is open as a public museum. You ought to see this place—it would stimulate your imagination! It is in Dedham—between here & Boston. We passed through the town in the 'bus a couple of years ago.

[*Enclosure:* "The Parlor—Longfellow's Wayside Inn, South Sudbury, Mass." *On back:*] The old Red Horse Tavern in Sudbury, famous as the "Wayside Inn" of Longfellow's poetic collection,[6] was built in 1686—probably as a private mansion. In 1714 it became a tavern, kept by one Howe; & a tavern it has been ever since—long kept by successive generations of Howes, & now maintained by Henry Ford. It has been kept in the best of condition, & is now fully restored to its colonial state—with ancient tap-room, panelled dining-room, quaint kitchen, & everything else to match. The old parlour has been equipped precisely as in the Longfellow verses—every original piece of furniture & decoration having been traced, repurchased, & reinstalled.

The grounds have been landscaped, & the main highway relocated in order to divert heavy traffic. Not far away Ford has erected an old stone water mill from elsewhere in Massachusetts, while still nearer is an 18th century school house moved from Sterling & famous as the scene of the anecdote which evoked the doggerel "Mary's Lamb." The barns of the inn are stocked with horses, sheep, oxen, & ancient vehicles—so that all told, there are few better concentrated reproductions of the early America.

[On envelope:] [P.P.S.] Just had a line from Belknap saying that poor old Mac is in pretty bad shape. Too bad—wish you could persuade him to return to some hospital for observation! Better pay him a cheering-up call anyway.

Notes

1. John Fleming Wilson (1877–1922), "The Quest of the Tropic Bird," in Wilson's *Somewhere at Sea and Other Tales* (New York: E. P. Dutton, 1910), 426–53.
2. Never published, though its contents may have been used in highly truncated form in *Imagery Aids* (Wauwatosa, WI: Kenyon Press, 1931).
3. HPL's "Sonnet Study" (*AT* 197–98), comprising a Shakespearean sonnet and a Petrarchan sonnet, was prepared for this work.
4 "Travels in the Provinces of America" (*CE* 4.32–61).
5. Chronicled in "An Account of a Trip to the Antient Fairbanks House, in Dedham, and to the Red Horse Tavern in Sudbury, in the Province of the Massachusetts-Bay" (*CE* 4.62–66).
6. *Tales of a Wayside Inn* (1863).

[129] [HPL and Wilfred B. and Charlotte Talman to DAW] [ANS][1]
[Postmarked Providence, R.I.,
10 October 1929]
Welcome home, O Melmoth! Sorry to be missing your Providential sojourn, but I guess home is the best place after all! Meanwhile see what our friend Talman has been doing! Married—& bearing up nobly. Been seeing old Providence, including the exterior of Jake's. ¶ Mac is going to Tacoma, Wash. on Oct. 20 to rest at his sister's. Write him a good sendoff before he goes! Yr obt Νεκρόφιλος

Charlotte and Tal

Notes

1. *Front:* Greetings from Providence, R. I.

[130] [HPL to DAW] [ANS]

[Postmarked Providence, R.I.,
18 December 1929]

[Wishing you
all happiness at Christmas
and throughout the New Year]
To Melmoth from
Πάππος Νεκρόφιλος
—1929

[On envelope:] P.S. Just at this last moment melancholy news comes from South Tacoma—our good old friend Mac passed away on Saturday, Dec. 14. It's hard to get used to the idea—though of course we all realised he was gravely ill. I had a Christmas card all stamped & addressed to him—alas! no destination now.[1]

Notes

1. Toward year's end, HPL wrote a sonnet for *Fungi from Yuggoth*—"The Pigeon-Flyers"—inspired by recollections of Everett McNeil and Hell's Kitchen. (The provisional title of the sonnet was "Hell's Kitchen.")

1930

[131] [HPL to DAW] [ANS][1]

[Postmarked Charleston, S.C.,
29 April 1930]

Well—this indeed is wandering! Getting my first taste of a really subtropical milieu. Splendid climate—& Charleston is the quaintest & most unique city I have ever seen—bar none. I am at the Y M C A & shall stay as long as the requisite daily dollars hold out.

Regards—
Melmoth III

Notes

1. *Front:* Goose Creek Church, Near Charleston, S. C.

[132] [HPL to DAW] [ANS][1]

[Postmarked Richmond, Va.,
10 May 1930]

Melmoth the 3d wandering north again—though it's like pulling a tooth to do it! I miss the subtropical palmettos & live-oaks of South-Carolina—for Va. is exactly like New England in scenery & vegetation. Richmond seems disconcertingly metropolitan & Yankeefied after Charleston, but it's a great old place for all that. Poe's home town. I've just been looking up sites & buildings connected with Poe's youth & with his later editorship of the Southern Literary Messenger. Hope to stay here 3 or 4 days more—then some more reluctant northward edging. Shall spend a week in N Y confabulating with the gang, & then up the Hudson to Kingston to see Bernard Dwyer. After that across to Athol to see Cook. It will be a delightful & record-breaking trip for me—& the warm weather braces me up tremendously. Finished a new 58-page novelette at Charleston.[2] Best regards—when shall you visit the decadent East again?

Πάππος Νεϰρόφιλος

Notes

1. *Front:* Oldest Masonic Building in U. S., Richmond, Va. Franklin Street, Between Eighteenth and Nineteenth.
2. I.e., "The Whisperer in Darkness." But see letter 143n3.

[133] [HPL to DAW] [ANS][1]

[Postmarked Richmond, Va.,
17 May 1930]

Behold, O Melmoth II, the earthly paradise upon which Melmoth III hath stumbled! This series of gardens fairly takes my breath away—I don't believe there's another such thing open to the public in the U.S.! It is Poe's "Domain of Arnheim" & "Island of the Fay" all rolled into one. I can't believe I'm awake! As you know, to me the quality of *utter, perfect beauty* assumes *two* supreme forms or adumbrations: one, a mass of mystical city roofs & spires against a sunset, glimpsed from a distant height; the other, the experience of walking through ethereal & enchanted gardens of exotic delicacy & opulence, with carved stone bridges, labyrinthine paths, marble fountains, terraces, & staircases, strange pagodas, hillside grottos, curious statues, termini, sundials, benches, basins, & lanthorns, lilied pools of swans & streams with tiers of water-falls, spreading gingko-trees & drooping, feathery willows, & flowers of a wild, bizarre, Klarkash-Tonic pattern never beheld on land or beneath the sea . . . . Well, Sir, this garden almost *wholly fulfils* ideal or adumbration #2!! ¶ Hate like hell to move northward, but fear I must do it tomorrow. Regards—hope you're prospering.

Yr obt

Πάππος Νεκρο

Notes

1. *Front:* Japanese Garden in Maymont Park, Richmond, Va.

[134] [HPL and Bernard Austin Dwyer to DAW] [ANS][1]

[Postmarked Kingston, N.Y.,
4 June 1930]

Hail, Melmoth! Having spent 2 wks. with the gang in N Y, I am up in ancient Wiltwyck again conferring with your host of 1927—the gifted art-brother of Klarkash-Ton. My next move is across the Mohawk trail to Athol to see another ex-host of yours. Hope all is well in the academic groves of St Paul.

Yr obt Πάππος Νεκρόφιλος

Why the Hell—if you will pardon me—don't you write occasionally? You should have been with us today—we had a fine lunch, and tonight for dinner we had supper.

Bernie 292 Fair St Kingston

Notes

1. *Front:* Old Senate House, Built 1767. Kingston, N. Y.

[135] [HPL and Bernard Austin Dwyer to DAW] [ANS][1]

[Postmarked Athol, Mass.,
12 June 1930]

Over the hills to Athol to confabulate with another of your one-time hosts. Had a great ride on the Mohawk Trail, & am damn glad to be back in my native New England! Cook is pulling very slowly out of his winter breakdown. Today he is ill & away from the office, but his general health shews an upward curve. I am staying with Munn—who is just about to move to larger quarters on the edge of the village. Weather has been doubtful, but Munn has taken me to a number of scenic spots in his car. Tonight, if it doesn't rain, we're going to see some strange & exotic woodland waterfall quite a distance from town. Shall be home in Providence Sat. or Sun. ¶ When are you going to get around these parts again? All your old hosts will be delighted to see you! Regards to all the hellish cosmic brains of outer space.

Yr obt Servt

Melmoth III.

Notes

1. *Front:* Between the Mountains, Mohawk Trail, Mass.

[136] [HPL and James F. Morton to DAW] [ANS][1]

[Postmarked Newport, R.I.,
25 June 1930]

Hail, Melmoth! Would that the old 1927 Newport trio could be complete again!

Yr obt

Πάππος Νεκρόφιλος

A humble member of the deplorable human species ventures to slither to your feet with a presumptuous word of greeting.

James F. Morton.

Humans are poor stuff, for a fact! I never did have much use for 'em

H P L

Notes

1. *Front:* Sayer House, Gen. Prescott's Headquarters, Newport, R. I.

[137] [DAW to HPL] [ALS]

1152 Portland Ave.,
St. Paul, Minn.

June 26, 1930

Dear Νεκρόφιλος:

With a feeling almost of criminal laxity, I commence a letter that ought to have been written months ago. I have increasingly become an uncertain correspondent, and a much greater amount of university work than I had anticipated did still more to occupy my time. Now, school is out till fall; and for once even if only once (may the Gods let it be more!) I can regather lost threads; lost from this end, that is, for I followed with delight and envious best wishes your spring tour through approximate earthly Paradises, as outlined by post-cards.

It has been a full year for me. The university courses required the writing of eleven papers, from three to eighteen thousand words each, out of which effort I acquired much greater facility in writing, and a small assistantship in the English department for next year. I also wrote a considerable amount of poetry—as much as I had in all the years previous. Lately I have completed one long weird tale, which is now in the hands of Wright for consideration.[1] At present I am hard at work on a novel, tentatively entitled "Dead Titans Waken: A Mystery of Time and Spirit". As the title probably suggests, it is a romance of terror and horror, commencing near the locale of Stonehenge and concluding on Easter Island. This is the novel which I began in New York last summer, and which I mentioned to you at the time. The novel has great possibilities, if I can successfully achieve a rather stupendous feat in handling so long a work. I have many incentives to keep me at it—the sheer pleasure of creating, my father's failing health, necessity of improving my financial condition, and the interest of some three publishers who express their willingness to consider the novel when completed. With time, energy, and a little luck, I may be able to complete it by the early part of August.

What of your own activities, literary and otherwise? It is much too long between your short stories; but I suspect from their regrettable infrequency that you are occupied with revision and other duties. Have you completed any narratives recently, or does Weird Tales possess any of your stories for publication in the near future? I note from recent issues that Belknap is still producing occasional yarns; and Clark Ashton writes me that W.T. took some six or seven of his poetic tales. Someone in the "gang" constantly succeeds in keeping the Gothic note alive via Wright!

If my finances are in such shape as to warrant the expense, I hope to bring out another volume of verse next fall, with illustrations by my brother. If the project is completed, the work will probably appear as "Dark Odyssey."

How were Cook and Munn when you visited Athol, and what has he done on the book of yours which he intended to issue a year ago? And did you see any of the New York group during your trip? I hope to do some touring myself after the novel is written; but the New York fever is all out of my blood, as it has been since I left that scabrous blob.

I'm learning how to drive my brother's Ford runabout. Perhaps I may roll into Providence on my next visit; or perhaps I may roll myself into the hereafter if I commence day-dreaming when I am on the highway!

Temporarily paused,
Melmoth II

Notes

1. Possibly "Something from Above."

[138] [HPL to DAW] [ALS]

Banks of the Seekonk
—Sunset—
June 30, 1930

Dear Melmoth:—

Glad to hear at last that you are alive & conscious! Your additional scholastic pursuits sound very auspicious, & I surely hope you get the instructorship next year. That is the kind of thing for you—not the raucous & cheaply meaningless arena of trade & finance. I am anxious to see your new literary material both prose & verse, & hope that a good amount of it may get into W.T. The novel project seems alluring, & I certainly wish you the best of luck. I have thought of attempting something of that length myself, but latterly have ground out nothing but some odd verses & one longish story which will need re-casting before it can be considered in presentable shape. Revision & travelling, between them, have not conduced toward creative leisure! Wright has nothing of mine on hand save some verses called "Fungi from Yuggoth", which will appear in a series like your "Sonnets of the Midnight Hours." I am told that they will have a heading by Rankin.[1] Did I shew you the bits of publicity I received from the literary editor & columnist of the Prov. Journal last autumn?[2] If not, I will. He gave special notice to "Cthulhu", as appearing in the Harré anthology. Belknap has just finished a short novelette of age-old terror,[3] & the versatile Klarkash-Ton has become a veritable fountain of bizarre prose. Munn likewise remains prolific—having carried his Werewolf & Master series to elaborate lengths, with episodes at various periods of history. And young Derleth, as usual, is a never-failing Niagara of fiction.

I enjoyed my Athol sojourn immensely, though sorry to note Cook's poor health. The death of his wife last January, after a long illness, precipitated him into a severe nervous breakdown, from which he is recovering only slowly. Added to this is his chronic appendicitis, which gave him a great deal of trouble this month. He ought to have his appendix out, but refrains because of a morbid dread of the surgeon's knife. He is now boarding with one of the printers at his office—who lives on a farm about 2 miles from the village. The place is rather squalid & depressing, but Cook does not seem to mind such things. "The Shunned House", which at last reports was printed but not bound, is now at a bindery in Boston. Nothing definite can be said of its appearance, however, since further steps depend on Cook's uncertain health. I am led to assume that the little volume will be uniform with "The

Man from Genoa" & "The Hermaphrodite". Could Cook, if recovered, handle your "Dark Odyssey"? I am anxious to see that projected volume, & am sure your brother can ably back you up pictorially. Cook did finely, I think, with "Ecstasy."

Yes—I saw all the gang in N Y, & attended two meetings, one at Talman's (he is married & living on the top floor of the same place where he boarded—277 Henry St. Bklyn.) & the other at Belknap's. I stayed at Belknap's—getting a room in one of the upstairs apartments—for 2 weeks, & saw all the museums &c. The new Roerich museum at Riverside Drive & 103d St. has exotic paintings of Thibetan scenes which could not fail to stimulate your interest.[4] Roerich is a sort of mature Klarkash-Ton in many ways—but perhaps you know all about him. Another interesting thing is the new American Wing of the Brooklyn Museum, which in some respects surpasses its celebrated counterpart at the Metropolitan. Among the contents is a panelled room from the Joseph Russell house (1770) in *Providence*—which is regarded as perhaps the finest (though not the largest) interior in the museum. Another room from this house is said to have gone all the way to your region, at present adorning some museum in *Minneapolis*. (Have you seen it?) Meanwhile the house itself still stands here in N. Main St.[5]—an old brick mansion now raised above a row of shops in the slums, & housing the local district nursing association.

My visit with Dwyer in ancient Kingston was extremely delightful. Every clear day we fared forth to the wild and beautiful countryside, & I enjoyed the conversation of one who is in many respects the most spontaneous & Blackwood-like fantaisiste I know. He is eating as heavily as ever, & getting badly overweight—231 at present—hence is considering the adoption of a course of austere training; either boxing or a fling at a lumberjack's life. In order to secure advice on the latter career, he has made some inquiries of the well-known poet-professor Lew Sarett,[6] who was at one period in a lumber camp.

In Athol I stopped with Munn—Cook having no quarters for a visitor at present. Munn was married last January, & is now moving from the flat he has occupied for the past year into an excellently situated house on a scenic hillside just out of the thick of the village. His father continues to live with him. He is again—after a period of discontinuance in which he vainly tried to subsist by literary effort alone—driving the old nitroglycerine truck; but has resigned from the fire department. He looks about the same as when you saw him last.

I reached home June 14, & from then on have been wrestling with accumulated work. A pleasing diversion was Morton's visit last week, of which our joint Newport postcard doubtless apprised you. We visited several mineral sites & walked over the new Mt. Hope Bridge between the Bristol peninsula & the island on which Newport is situate—the 7th longest suspension bridge in the world. Whilst in Newport we went out to the Hanging Rocks—Berkeley's favourite haunt[7]—which you doubtless recall from 1927.

Later this week I may possibly attend the Boston convention of the Natl. Amateur Press Association, to which Morton is urging me. He is in Boston now, at an Esperanto convention which precedes the amateur event. I may, though, pass this up in favour of a cheap *Quebec* excursion which is just now advertised by the B & M. I want desperately to see Quebec—since the Melmoth element works strongly in my aged blood.

I am extremely sorry to hear that your father is in poor health, & hope he may get stronger as the summer advances. My elder aunt is now having another acute spell of her spinal neuritis, but not nearly so severe an attack as those of 1926, 1928, & 1929.

I certainly hope you will get around this way in the Ford runabout—I can steer you to many a place unpolluted by the presence of mankind! And Jake's still seems to be functioning gloriously, although I'll confess I have not been a patron of late. These warm aestival days I enjoy the open air as much as possible, taking my work along in ablack enamel-cloth bag to some appropriate rural spot. Yesterday I was at Quinsnicket—where one July afternoon you dozed perilously near the brink of a rock precipice—& today I am in my earliest childhood haunt, the wooded bluff beside the broad Seekonk.

My trip—as postcards have probably apprised you—was a tremendous success. I first went directly down to Charleston by motor-coach, travelling day & night to save time & hotel fare. I didn't find the Piedmont district of the Carolinas—Winston-Salem, Greensboro, Charlotte, &c—very distinctive, since recent industrial progress has Yankeefied it considerably; but when the coach descended into the region of Camden & Columbia, S.C., I knew I was in the midst of a rare & ancient civilisation. At Columbia—a city with the atmosphere of the 1850's about it—I saw my first *palmettos*. Later—on the road to Charleston—came the subtropical forests of pine & live-oak hung with Spanish moss. And then Charleston itself! . . . . . . Honestly, it is the most fascinating & most truly civilised city I have ever seen. I am not sure but that it is the *only* really civilised city I have ever seen—for nowhere else does there seem to be a perfectly integrated collective life with roots sunk deep in history. Charleston's linkage with the main stream of our civilisation is unbroken. The Revolution & Civil War alike passed over it without damaging its fabric or atmosphere; & so far it has been harmed equally little by the blight of commercialism & machinery. It is a city of quality & individualism—& is governed & peopled by the unmixed descendants of its founders, following the same impulses & cherishing the same time-tried values. If I can ever bring myself to leave Providence—as the severity of the Northern winter may some day force me to do—it is in Charleston that I shall live. God save His Majesty's Province of South-Carolina! After 11 days in Charleston, Richmond seemed northern & bustling; but I enjoyed it just the same. I stayed 8 days, looking up all the Poe sites & enjoying the exotic loveliness of the incomparable Maymont Gardens. I also went to Williamsburg, Petersburg, & Fredericksburg. Virginia is a great place—second only to S.C., & still thoroughly American & civilised. Then came the reluctant northward move—a few days in Philadelphia, & afterward a disgusted plunge into the mongrel cesspool of N.Y. Faugh! But Kingston & Athol took the taste out of my mouth very nicely.

I've been hearing lately from a chap at the U. of N.C.—named Bailey—who wants data on early pseudo-scientific fiction. Since I haven't much to give him, I'm referring him to such diligent bibliographers as you & Munn—& I trust you two can help him a bit. His work is really a very commendable one—a history of "scientifiction".[8]

Best wishes

—Yr most obt

Νεκρόφιλος

P.S. Have I shewn you my new bookplate designed by our friend Talman? If not, here's a sample. It suits me exactly—a Providence Georgian doorway. We decided on it after long & careful discussion.

[On envelope:] P.S. Belknap has given Felis away—an act for which Morton & I can hardly forgive him!

Notes

1. Of the 35 sonnets then constituting *Fungi from Yuggoth*, FW selected ten for publication (five had been published in the *Providence Journal*). They appeared as a series in *WT* between September 1930 and April–May 1931 with a heading designed by Hugh Rankin. The numbered headings (1–10) did not correspond with HPL's own numbering in the overall sonnet sequence.

2. Bertrand K. Hart (1892–1941) mentioned HPL in several of his columns, entitled "The Sideshow," in the *Providence Journal* in November and December 1929. See "H. P. Lovecraft in 'The Sideshow,'" *Lovecraft Annual* No. 11 (2017): 51–66.

3. *The Horror from the Hills.*

4. Nicholas Roerich (1874–1947), Russian painter who converted to Buddhism and spent much time in Tibet. His paintings of Himalayan mountain vistas partially inspired the Antarctic setting of HPL's *At the Mountains of Madness*. The Nicholas Roerich Museum is now at 319 West 107th Street.

5. The John and William Russell House (1772) at 118 North Main Street. One of the first large, grand houses built in Providence during the mercantile era. By the early twentieth century, it was a rooming house, and it was stripped of its interiors, now found in museums across the country. The room HPL refers to is at the Minneapolis Institute of Art.

6. Lew Sarett (1888–1954), a professor at Northwestern University, was the author of *Many Many Moons* (1920), *The Box of God* (1922), *Slow Smoke* (1925), and *Wings against the Moon* (1932).

7. The British philosopher George Berkeley (1685–1753) spent the years 1728–32 in or around Newport, R.I.

8. Of the correspondence between J[ames] O[sler] Bailey (1903–1979) and HPL, only Bailey's letter of 16 June 1930 to HPL survives (ms., JHL). Bailey eventually published *Pilgrims through Space and Time* (1947), the first academic treatise on science fiction; it contains a brief discussion of HPL's work.

[139] [HPL to DAW] [ANS][1]

> [Postmarked Newport, R.I.,
> 23 July 1930]

Hail, Melmoth! Once more in Georgian Newport, & on the same cliffs which we frequented in 1927, gazing on the wine-dark sea. Am guiding the brilliant young official editor of the Natl. Amateur Press Association[2]—& have just given him the first steamboat ride in his 21 years of existence! Wish you could get around to another Novanglian trip. Remember that New York isn't representative of the east by any means! ¶ How's the novel of ultimate horror coming on?

> Regards—yr obt
> Πάππος Νεκρόφιλος

Notes

1. *Front:* Old Frigate "Constellation" and the U. S. S. Boxer Naval Training Station, Newport, R. I.

2. Helm C. Spink, Official Editor of the NAPA.

[140] [HPL to DAW] [ANS][1]

> [Postmarked Quebec, Canada,
> 1 September 1930]

Behold where an aged Melmoth is wandering! This place eclipses everything I've ever seen before—a dream of archaic city walls, castellated cliffs, silver spires, pointed roofs, narrow, zigzag & precipitous streets, & the leisurely civilisation of an elder world. Only here on a cheap & brief excursion, but am working fast to absorb colour. You must see this place & die—as indeed Wolfe did! I am writing this on the Plains of Abraham where the immortal encounter took place at just about this season in 1759.

Regards—

> Πάππος Νεκρόφιλος

Notes

1. *Front:* Montcalm's House. Quebec, Canada—Maison de Montcalm. Quebec.

[141] [HPL and FBL to DAW] [ANS]¹
[Postmark partially obliterated; prob. Onset, Mass.,
3 September 1930]
In the Cape Cod region sharing the last phase of the Longs' aestival tour!
Stopping at Onset, but have been on trip to Falmouth, Cotuit, Hyannis, &c.
Back in Providence tomorrow—whilst Belknap's party keeps on toward the
decadent miasmata of Manhattan. Have had an excellent time despite the fre-
quent rains. Hope all is flourishing in the twin cities, & that the novel of ulti-
mate cosmic horror is coming along well.
Yr obt Πάππος Νεκρόφιλος

Greetings and best wishes from Cape Cod!
Belknap.

Notes

1. *Front:* An Early Cape Cod House.

[142] [DAW to HPL] [ALS]
1152 Portland Ave.,
St. Paul, Minn.
Oct. 27, 1930
Dear Νεκρόφιλος:
From the precincts of this ulterior citadel comes at last
news of the thrice mystically imprisoned Melmoth: thrice, for the ways of
Morgana, working above the sun, and runing beneath the moon; for the ways
of imposed design which the kingdom of thoughtful scrutiny thinketh best for
it; and for the ways of earth, than whose invisible fetters of blood and fire are
none stronger nor greater. In the name of him whom we worship, these things
being so, in the cacophony of Cthulhu and the hierarchy of Trismegistus, the
powers of darkness attending and the spirits of light overshadowed, hail!
Were I possessed of a dozen hands and equal pens, I could scarcely, I believe, within the space of a day encroach upon all those myriad actual and
speculative preserves which have been my companions the two months latest
gone. By this time you must know of the traveller from Wisconsin who arrived two or three weeks ago. You may remember that, because of the suggestion of Harre, I was offered a position as co-editor of Fawcett's lousy new
Mystic Magazine. This offer I declined; but made mention of to Derleth; who
expressed considerable interest; whereupon I recommended him and arranged an interview with Smalley, the general editor, as a consequence of
which young Derleth holds forth in the editorial holy of holies.¹
Derleth is an interesting, rather dynamic, socially unadjusted young writer

of great promise. He writes with a remarkable rapidity and facility which may require curbing before his style can be perfected. But I believe he has the potentialities in him. Physically, it would be hard to imagine a more uncharacteristic author of *The Early Years*[2]—he is heavy-set and looks more like a member of some football squad. He is a mixture of extreme sensitivity and almost callous brutality in speech and in his relations with people. I shall take great interest in watching his development, and I hope that you yourself may meet him before very long. He and I are attending the symphony series here for the season; occasionally I see him oftener than once a week, but the part of Minneapolis in which he lives is some ten miles from my home.

My novel was completely halted, first by my father's serious operation, then by two minor operations on my throat, then by reopening of University where I am spending the second of three years in quest of two degrees: M.A. and Ph.D. Nevertheless, the novel is more than three-quarters done, and shall be completed either during my Christmas vacation, or at the end of the school year. In the meantime, a chapter from it, slightly changed, appears as "Something from Above" in the forthcoming W.T.[3] I may add that the entire last two sections, comprising about one-half the story, were added on because Wright wanted a more definite ending. If you omit these, you will see the story much more as it was intended to be. Incidentally, my brother has two weird drawings in the Exhibit of the Work of Twin Cities' Artists at the Minneapolis Art Institute this month.

Derleth tells me you have completed a long story. If you have a carbon, I will be delighted to see it; and promise to let all my other work slide until I have perused it. Again, in the name of Cthulhu, greetings!

Melmoth II

Notes

1. *Mystic Magazine* was a short-lived pulp magazine (Fawcett Publications, 5 issues, November 1930–April 1931 [final issue titled *True Mystic Crimes*]) published in Minneapolis, MN, edited by Capt. W. H. Fawcett, and focusing on articles about the occult. DAW refers to Jack Smalley, an editor at Fawcett.

2. An early version of the novel that became *Evening in Spring* (1941).

3. There is nothing in the extant version of *Dead Titans, Waken!* that bears any resemblance to "Something from Above."

[143] [HPL to DAW] [ALS]

10 Barnes St.,
Providence, R.I.,
Novr. 2, 1930

Dear Melmoth:—

Your welcome communication reached me on the morning after the hellish Sabbat-eve, while I was still shuddering from the things I saw on Goat Mountain under the gibbous moon. God—those shapes of malign, half-vegetable vitality[1] that oozed out of the crevices of the great lightning-blasted rocks, & that monstrous, purposeful stream of translucent ethereal globules that drifted out of the sky when Orion cleared the far-off peaks of Black Ridge!!! But I must not think of these things, else I shall not have the courage to make The Dark Journey next May-Eve, as I promised The Vague Shape amidst the Standing Stones.

Yes—young Derleth told me how deeply he is indebted to you for his new professional opening, & I can assure you that no one could be more profoundly appreciative than he. I feel sure that he will make a success of it; for he has a sharp, workable intelligence apart from his aesthetic endowments, & seems much better able to meet the varied tests of practical life than most members of our somewhat cloud-dwelling circle. Derleth impressed me tremendously favourably from the moment I began to hear from him personally. I saw that he had a prodigious fund of activity & reserve mental energy, & that it would only be a question of time before he began to correlate it to real aesthetic advantage. There was a bit of callow egotism also—but that was only to be expected; & indeed, a boy of his age would scarcely have been normal if he hadn't had it. And surely enough, as the years passed, I saw that the kid was truly growing. The delicate reminiscent sketches begun a couple of years ago were the final proof—for there, indeed, he had reached what was unmistakably sincere & serious self-expression of a high order. Nor did it take long to see that this was the real stuff, & not any mere flash in the pan. He kept it up—naturally, spontaneously, & without effort—& the various fragments began to fit splendidly into a larger organic unity. There was no disputing that he *really had something to say*—which is true of woefully few prolific & often cultivated aspirants—& that he was trying to say it honestly & effectively, with a minimum of the jaunty hack devices & stylistic tricks which went into his printed pot-boiling material. Undeniably, a writer of substance was in the making—& I have since had every reason to confirm & reiterate that dictum. Even his hack work is shewing the difference—though Wright persistently favours his poorest things, & accepts the better items only after a campaign of attrition on Derleth's part. As you say, his tendency toward mass production is hardly a good thing for his style; & Derleth shews the right idea in his reminiscent pieces when he seeks utter simplicity of language, & places accuracy & significance of mood & impression above everything else. He will be worth watching in the years to come, for very few of us have as clearly-defined & serious a mass of impressions demanding an outlet. With his sensitiveness to shades of experience, we can well picture the effect of added years & wider life on his imaginative background & creative faculty. I doubt if he will be primarily a weird writer—though he will probably always retain an interest in the bizarre & the macabre. He actually believes in the supernatural—

a circumstance which will tend to counteract any drift away from weird interests that realistic experience & the prose of life might otherwise bring. I surely hope to see him some day—perhaps when he takes that eastern trip he has so long been planning. When he does, I wish you could come along with him & renew the impressions of 1927. What inroads the two of you could make on the voluminous cuisine at Jake's!!

I am indeed sorry to hear that your father has had such serious illness—& that your own throat has needed surgical attention. Let us hope that he is now out of all danger, & you out of all discomfort! When you get your two degrees you will be the most learned of all the old crowd—for even the august Mortonius is a mere M.A. Ph.D's are quite unknown so far in our humble & illiterate ranks! I assume that English instructorship & professorships form your ultimate goal—a very good goal for an author & poet whose aesthetic work offers scant economic rewards. References to your novel arouse my keenest expectations, & I shall be eager to peruse the specimen fragment in W.T. despite the additions dictated by our prosaic friend Farnsworth. In reading the chapter I will draw a mental line before the two final sections, thus gaining a truer impression of your artistic intent. I wish your brother could have illustrated the tale—as he certainly ought to illustrate your novel in its entirety. Some day I must see specimens of his weird work. Yes—I managed to finish a 69-page novelette with a Vermont setting, called "The Whisperer in Darkness", which Wright has accepted with commendable promptness at a price of $350.00—my largest return, so far, for any one story. It will appear as a 2-part serial next June & July.[2] Meanwhile I am putting the carbon in circulation—it being now in Auburn with our friend Klarkash-Ton, High-Priest of Tsathoggua, & next scheduled to reach young Derleth, whom I have expressly authorised to lend it to you. You can return it to me at your leisure. I read it (in a rough form differing somewhat from the present) to Belknap & Dwyer last spring, & they both seemed to think well of it.[3] I hope it may not bore you too badly. By the way—Klarkash-Ton is getting to be a marvellously fecund story-writer! I don't see how he can turn out so much. Have you seen his "Satampra Zeiros" & "Rendezvous in Averoigne"?[4]

Talman has left the Times & is editing trade papers for the Texas Oil Co. Cook has left Athol for good amidst a general nervous, physical, & financial breakdown, & now intends to live with Orton at Clarendon, Vt., where the two of them (housed in a rural ex-parsonage) will found a publishing venture to be known as "The Parsonage Press."[5] Loveman is back at Dauber & Pine's—which he ought never to have left in the first place. And the rest of the gang is much as usual.

Best wishes & good luck—
　　　　　Yr obt
　　　　　　Πάππος Νεϰϱόφιλος

Notes

1. Cf. the half-vegetable Old Ones of *At the Mountains of Madness*, which HPL began writing about two months later.
2. The story appeared complete in the August 1931 issue.
3. Actually, both suggested revisions to the story, which HPL appears to have incorporated. See Steven J. Mariconda, "Tightening the Coil: The Revision of 'The Whisperer in Darkness,'" *H. P. Lovecraft: Art, Artifact, and Reality* (New York: Hippocampus Press, 2013): 190–200.
4. CAS, "The Tale of Satampra Zeiros" (*WT*, November 1931); "A Rendezvous in Averoigne" (*WT*, April–May 1931).
5. This venture came to nothing.

[144] [DAW to HPL] [ALS]

1152 Portland Ave.

St. Paul, Minn.

Nov. 4, 1930

Dear Πάππος Νεκρόφιλος:

Inclosed herewith I am returning your "Whisperer in Darkness" which Derleth passed on to me two days ago. It is, I feel, one of your finest tales, with a power all its own. It may be called realistic—but good God, what realism! Somehow you achieve an infinite super-mundane terror based on physical horror, and transform the world we know into the world we fear. The last scene, the last paragraph, left a deep and vivid impression which I shall never forget; and this despite the fact that you prepared the reader to feel what was coming. I am especially pleased that Wright has taken the story, for I want it in permanent form; and I look forward to the reading of it again, and following it through once more, step by mephitic step.

I have a deep respect and a profound admiration for your abilities as a critic and as a "Maker"; and if my weird novel is completed, as I expect it to be by next summer, and if you then have time enough, I should like you to examine it and suggest improvements, at your regular fee. But of this more later when I have written "finis est".[1] The novel at present has the first half completed, with parts of, and one or two entire, later chapters.

The chill days are upon us, once again; though this morning provided a magnificent Indian Summer. I have been hoping for another day of red atmosphere and vast conflagrations beyond the clouds, such as I witnessed years ago; but I suppose the phenomenon comes only once a lifetime; nor can I reasonably expect another red snowfall. But the Aurora has sent its weird radiance across the northern sky with unnatural frequence and brilliance all this year, and no less than a dozen nights I have gone abroad to scrutinize the mysterious mystically lovely displays.

I have written almost no poetry in two or three months; but I am contemplating and germinating a rather longish, Element-al work tentatively called "The Druid-Bride",[2] set in the great oak forests of the days before the Legionnaires penetrated to the North. Yet if one create not temporarily, he may nourish his being with sonnets of Yuggoth.

As ever,

Melmoth II

Notes

1. Bad Latin for "it is finished" (DAW should have written *finitum est*).
2. Apparently no such work was completed.

[145] [HPL to DAW] [ALS]

10 Barnes St.,
Providence, R.I.,
Novr. 7, 1930

Dear Melmoth:—

I am indeed glad to hear that you liked "The Whisperer". It was written piecemeal between snatches of revisory work; & because of this lack of continuous composition, never gave me the impression of perfect unity which I meant to achieve. My idea was to have the idea of *tightening coils* of horror, reaching out & gradually dragging the narrator in. Derleth felt the same lack that I did myself, but Klarkash-Ton was very favourable. I surely hope that I can get at some more tales before the winter is over.

And I want tremendously to see your own novel when it is done. Actually, despite the myriads who write weird & horrible tales, there are very few authors who have any effective or poignant sense of the *cosmic*. Dunsany & Blackwood have—but what other well-known writers? And in our gang, you & Klarkash-Ton have the field to yourselves—unless I have been able to give some of my own moods real expression. You have the cosmic perspective & atmosphere to a superlative degree, & one longs to see more of your extraterrene conceptions on paper. That goes for verse as well as prose—hence I hope you will give me a look at "The Druid Bride" whenever it is in final shape. I think I told you that *vast deep woods*, with enormous-boled oaks & low-interlacing, gnarled boughs, form to me one of the most haunting & fascinating of all impressions. The picture has recurred to me since infancy, always with vague sensations of terror mixed with strange, expectant wonder.[1] I have never seen anything like it in the objective world—I *can't* have, since there is nothing like it in America—yet the "memory" is so vivid that sometimes I can scarcely believe it is not founded upon an actual sight of some objective reality.[2] In truth, I suppose the thing is a compound of pictures seen, & stories told me, at an exceedingly early date. I recall having the memory at the age of 3. Thus you see I am very well equipped to be an appreciative reader of your new poem!

Alas! The chill days are upon Providentium's ancient hill, & upon Goat Rock in the ancient Quinsnicket Woods, as well as upon the cosmic-skied heights of St. Paul; though probably ours are less severe than yours. My period of hibernation is about to set in, & I only wish I had the cash to transfer headquarters to Charleston until next May! Meanwhile let us trust that some of your cryptical sky effects will help to diversity the subarctic winter. I envy you your sight of the aurora—a phenomenon which has visited Providence at rare intervals, but which I have never had the luck to see with my own eyes. A very few degrees of latitude seem to make quite a bit of difference in auroral perception. You are only about 3° north of here, yet you seem to have auroras with a frequency beyond all Rhode Island standards.

Just had a letter from our W.T. colleague Henry S. Whitehead, who is an ineffably genial & affable person. He wishes, as we all do, that there could be a weird magazine of better grade to take care of such stories as Wright rejects. He is getting to be quite a correspondent of Dwyer's, & wants to hear from others in the gang—being a veritable "fan" over Klarkash-Ton's work. I fancy he will develop into quite a congenial member of the crowd. According to his snapshot he is a chap of early middle age—clean-shaven, trim of figure, & rather bald as to frontal cranial areas. His erudition & knowledge of weird literature are gratifyingly ample.

Derleth speaks of a recent trip home—which must have been welcome after so long an absence in the Great City. He has just sent his "Early Years" to C A S for a critical opinion. You ought to shew him some of Klarkash-Ton's poems & drawings.

Well—good luck, & speedy progress on novel & poem!
Yrs for brighter auroras & more cryptic skies
—Πάππος Νεκρόφιλος

Notes

1. Cf. *CB* 97: "Blind fear of a certain woodland hollow where streams writhe among crooked roots, & where on a buried altar terrible sacrifices have occur'd—Phosphorescence of dead trees. Ground bubbles." *CB* 134: "Witches' Hollow novel? Man hired as teacher in private school misses road on first trip—encounters dark hollow with unnaturally swollen trees & small cottage (light in window?). Reaches school & hears that boys are forbidden to visit hollow. One boy is strange—teacher sees him visit hollow—odd doings—mysterious disappearance or hideous fate." *CB* 213: "Ancient winter woods—moss—great boles—twisted branches—dark—ribbed roots—always dripping. . . ."
2. This impression of "pseudo-memory" is in part the basis of "The Shadow out of Time."

[146]　[DAW to HPL]　[ALS]

1152 Portland Ave.

St. Paul, Minn.

Nov. 23, 1930

Dear Νεκρόφιλος:

What you say about your memory of unseen vast woods is of peculiar interest to me, for I too since early childhood have been subject to a similar spell. I feel that the recollection of pictures and stories does not entirely explain the vividness and psychic, even cosmic, terror involved in this memory. Can it be a hereditary avatar—a surviving image carried across abysses of time to the present, retained in dim recesses of consciousness, from those remote dawn-ages of man when the forests he faced were vaster, filled with fear and horror, and in themselves of stranger and more alien frondage than ours? Many years ago, I put down two of these memories; so soon as I find them from their now forgotten place in a pile of manuscripts, I will copy them for you. Meanwhile, I dream of the Druid—and sooner or later you will see the finished work. One or two interpolated hymns and lyrics are done, but they barely touch on the setting which interests me most. I should like to complete the novel first—of which the part in *Weird Tales* will give a completely erroneous conception—before concentrating on the Druid theme which I hope to make into an impressive—for me—performance.

At present, I am damned annoyed by Weird Tales. I have received no check for my poem in the last issue, or for my story in the current issue.[1] In all, during the last six weeks, I have sent Wright two mss. and written four letters of inquiry; and not one word have I been able to get out of him in return.

Do you know where Cook and Orton can be addressed? I have written to both in recent months, but my letters evidently went astray. Do you know Munn's address also? And Whitehead's?

At present, I am planning to issue another small book of verse, with illustrations by my brother, about February or March. I have not made the selection yet, or gotten bids. I will probably have the work done here where I can keep a closer watch on it and have prompter action than would be the case elsewhere. There is not much chance of failing to break even on the venture—and that is all I care to do, or rather, all to be expected from a book of poems. This venture in any case is as much for the sake of the drawings as it is for my doggerel.

I wonder sometimes if your failure—and mine during the period I spent in New York—to observe the Northern Lights may not have been a result of unfavorable atmospheric conditions. The air is much damper along the seaboard, much drier and clearer here. In the east, I never saw a sky with nearly the brilliance and distinctness that are characteristic of less muggy inland regions.

Derleth thinks that the Twin Cities are highly sophisticated, and my friends embryo Peter Whiffles or Dorian Grays.[2] Well, well, well. Thus was it ever. I wonder what he would think of New York. For that matter, if Derleth considers us sophisticated, and I consider New York as Sodom, what possible hell of corruption can there be that New Yorkers would consider decadent?

May your hibernation be short—and your stories numerous.

Y^r ob't. and faithful Νεκροφιλίσκος

Melmoth II

D.W.

Notes

1. "The Cypress-Bog" and "Something from Above."
2. Peter Whiffle is the protagonist of the novel *Peter Whiffle* (1922) by Carl Van Vechten (1880–1964). He is an urban sophisticate, like Dorian Gray in Oscar Wilde's *The Picture of Dorian Gray* (1891).

[147] [HPL and Wilfred B. Talman to DAW] [ANS][1]

[Postmarked Providence, R.I.,
26 November 1930]

Hail, Melmoth! Here's an old-time reunion in an old-time place—& we had dinner at *Jake's* . . . . . first time either of us had been there since Sept. 1927. Not a thing changed, except that swarthy Domingo is not there. Perhaps some recent revolution has made him prime-minister of Portugal! ¶ Talman is connected with the Texas Co. now, & is gathering local data to print in the publication of his puissant corporation; but his main purpose in coming to Providence was to help me pack Morton's minerals for shipment—I'd been delaying four months; & it needed young blood to wake the old man up. Too bad you can't be on hand to make this a regular Kalem meeting.

Regards to Derleth—Yr obt
Πάππος Νεκρόφιλος

Greetings from one who never forgets old Kalemites—and young Kalemites

Talman

Notes

1. *Front:* Campus, Brown University, Providence, R. I.

[148] [HPL to DAW] [ALS]

10 Barnes St.,
Providence, R.I.,
Decr. 1, 1930

Dear Melmoth:—

As an index of the present paying schedule of W.T., I might

mention that I have just received a cheque for "Antarktos"—but nothing for anything later. With this cheque came the sad news that W.T. is to retrench & become a bi-monthly, thus cutting our potential market area in half. Probably Wright thinks he can hold a larger public by issuing a weird magazine one month & an Oriental the next than by confining himself to a monthly in any one field. I hope this curtailment is not merely a prelude to the total abandonment of the magazine. *Strange Stories,* the proposed third magazine, is (so Wright tells Robert E. Howard) held up through a legal dispute with the Macfadden firm over the right to use the title.[1]

You can address both Cook & Orton at plain *Clarendon, Vt.,* where Orton has just purchased (or leased, I don't know which) a house. The idea is for the two of them to found "The Parsonage Press" there, but Orton is so slow in getting the plan under way that Cook may not settle down until a press is actually purchased. At the moment I think Cook is visiting his sister at Lake Sunapee, N.H., but by the time a letter could reach him he will have moved on—either to Clarendon or to Walter J. Coates's at North Montpelier, Vt. Amidst all this uncertainty, Clarendon is the best permanent forwarding address to use. If Cook & Orton get together in this new press venture, they could do your coming book full justice typographically—for as you doubtless realise, Orton is more of a connoisseur of the aesthetic side of printing than Cook. Even now, Orton's present firm (The Tuttle Co., Rutland Vt.)[2] could turn you out a fine job; though probably not as cheaply as a firm of his own & Cook's could. However, I dare say local work would be a great deal more convenient for you—& not so much more expensive in the end. I am certainly anxious to see this Wandrei family venture!

Possibly the coastal nature of Providence & New York City explain the lesser prevalence of auroras in this region, though I think the latitude has something to do with it. There have been some fine displays hereabouts, but it has always been my ill fortune to miss them—tantalisingly hearing about them the next day. In the country, where there are no electric lights to dazzle, they are noticed more frequently; & in Northern New England they are said to be fairly common. Rhode Island is rather free from vivid natural extremes of any sort, be they heat, cold, auroras, earthquakes, hurricanes, floods, or tidal waves. If I am ever driven southward by the chill of the New England winter I shall have to get used to the hurricanes which come up from the tropics each autumn, & are very marked even at places as comparatively northerly as Charleston.

Munn's address is *168 Bliss St., Athol, Mass.* Whitehead's is *1159 Broadway, Dunedin, Florida.* Great authors' addresses seem to run in the 1150's! Whitehead is quite a chap—I have been hearing from him very fully & pleasantly of late.

It is interesting to learn that you share my vague, unplaceable memory of vast-boled, low-branching palaeogean forests, & am inclined to think that the sources are not so dissimilar as you imagine. It is doubtful to the point of impossibility whether any such thing as true hereditary memory exists, for acquired characteristics seem not to be transmissible under any recognised circumstances. Environment moulds a race not by implanting any new attributes, but simply by killing off those individuals unfitted for it, & thus causing the once casual types which it suits to become the dominant types through normal inheritance from a specially selected group of ancestors. In all this process there is nothing which would cause any specific visual impressions to be fixed in the heritable cell-structure of the race; hence it seems certain that all those cloudy memory-glimpses which we cannot identify, & which therefore suggest fragments of earlier lives in primordial worlds, are in reality nothing more than chance syntheses of infancy-gained impressions. These impressions, drawn from all possible sources, lie dormant in the subconscious until called up by some random association. Then, if the circumstances of revival be sufficiently striking, the new picture becomes still more firmly fixed in the subconscious & sometimes in the conscious mind—its fascination & persistence all the greater because of the tantalising mystery of its origin. There is plenty of opportunity for it to establish overtones of extreme cosmic terror—indeed, two of my own most terrifying memory-phantoms are traceable to an actual landscape & an illustration in "Robinson Crusoe", respectively. We cannot gauge the source of an emotion by its present intensity, for nothing is more deceptive & delusive than our inward feelings & impressions. Pictures of great enchanted forests—as well as vivid descriptions—are exceedingly frequent in the type of books (largely fairy tales, historic sketches, & old ballads) with which children are surrounded from birth, & it is easy to see how a highly sensitive mind might draw upon them heavily as a pseudo-mnemonic background. I certainly hope you will use your old notes in writing the Druidic poem, & am keenly eager to see the latter upon its completion. The interpolation of hymns & lyrics will undoubtedly help the atmosphere. Meanwhile I hope to see the novel—for which the early part of "Something from Above" whets my appetite.

You & young Derleth present interesting stages of relative sophistication. He thinks your world artificial & Baudelairian, whilst I am such a naive old gentleman that even he & Sauk City are blasé & fin de siècle by comparison! Then at the other end, you find Manhattan far gone in diabolism, Manhattan takes hints from a cryptical Paris, Paris shudders at Constantinople, Constantinople looks back to Imperial Rome & Alexandria & Antioch, they look back to Babylon, Babylon looks back to Irem, the City of Pillars, Irem looks back to sunken R'lyeh, & R'lyeh fears to mention the hellish N'gha-G'un, on that dark star whence the people of R'lyeh came to earth.

Yr obt Grandsire
ΝΕΚΡΟΦΙΛΟΣ

P.S. Trust you recd. the joint card from Talman & me. He stayed 3 days, & took a vast number of photographs of Old Providence. I am still dieting & reducing after that meal at Jake's!

Notes

1. FW edited *Oriental Stories* (later *Magic Carpet Magazine*) from November 1930 to Summer 1932 (14 issues). The Popular Fiction Publishing Co. published no magazine entitled *Strange Stories*, but a magazine entitled *Strange Tales of Mystery and Terror* was published by Clayton Magazines and edited by Harry Bates. It lasted for only 7 issues (September 1931–January 1933).
2. The Charles E. Tuttle Company is a well known American publisher and distributor of Japanese books.

[149] [HPL to DAW] [ANS]

[Postmarked Providence, R.I.,
17 December 1930]

[MERRY CHRISTMAS!
Wishing you the
Merriest kind of a
Christmas
and the Happiest kind
of
A Happy New Year!]

Πάππος
Νεκρόφιλος
—MDCCCCXXX

[150] [HPL to DAW] [ANS]¹

[Postmarked Providence, R.I.,
27 December 1930]

Hail, Melmoth!

Your brother certainly *is* an artist of the very first order—& with a rare touch of the mystical & fantastic about his technique. I enthusiastically congratulate you on having him as illustrator for your future literary works. The Wandrei team ought to go far in synchronised aesthetics! I can imagine how he would handle themes like the Druid Wood!

Providence had a very scenically appropriate Christmas, with roofs, spires, & boughs lavishly decked with snow. No doubt your sub-Arctic region is that way a good part of the year!

Regards— Νεκρόφιλος

Notes

1. *Front:* Pawtuxet Square, Pawtuxet, R. I.

1931

[151] [HPL to DAW] [TLS]

Castle Tenbarnz on the Heights
April 12, 1931.

Dear Melmoth:—

I must not lose a second in thanking you effusively and admiringly for the exquisite artistic trinity—poetry, drawing, and bookmaking—which reached me yesterday morning, and which I have read from cover to cover with the most profound appreciation. Truly, it is a marvel of balanced beauty—and my aunt concurs with me in enthusiastic praise of the poetry and its setting alike. Your poetry, I think, has substantially matured since "Ecstasy" days—excellent though that earlier output was. Any choices of mine would display merely personal caprice—and might be merely temporary even with me. As it is, I think a first reading has left me with strongest impressions of the title-poem—"Dark Odyssey"—"Look Homeward, Angel", "Morning Song", "The Whispering Knoll", "The Night Wind", "Chaos Resolv'd" . . . . . but if I don't look out I shall have the whole table of contents transcribed here! Your brother does marvellous pen and ink work—really, he is such a natural fantaisiste in his medium that you must look well to your supremacy within the Clan Wandrei! His "Night Wind" and "Whispering Knoll" drawings are veritable knockouts—though with him, as with you, it is hard to make choices. And the format of the book is utterly exquisite. Really, my poor bookplate has a distinctly shoddy and tawdry effect when pasted on the immaculate Japanese vellum of the inside cover. To do Talman credit I ought to get the next edition of those plates printed on better stock. You were surely lucky in unearthing the right sort of a publisher—and in the good old home town, too! I hope you have remembered the high lights of the gang in mailing complimentary copies—Belknap, Klarkash-Ton, and good old Cook . . . . the latter to be addressed ℅ Walter J. Coates, North Montpelier, Vermont. Poor Cook's physical and financial collapse has left him in sad need of cheering up, and a word from you would do much to brighten his horizon. His inability to find industrial openings in New England has caused him to look westward; so that in the summer he may migrate to Oklahoma, where an old-time amateur friend (Paul J. Campbell) has oil connexions and may be able to place him professionally. Among the minor implications of the Recluse disaster is the probable loss of my small "Shunned House" book. The whole edition, with introduction by Belknap, is printed and lying at a Boston binder's in loose sheet form; but nobody has the cash to go ahead with the binding. I have suggested to Cook that he try to get the sheets again, even if they can't be bound. I'll store them under the chairs and tables of my lowly cubicle, and perhaps have a few copies bound up cheaply to distribute to members of the gang. Possibly, however, the situation is such that the binders won't yield up the sheets—but will keep them to kindle furnace fires with.

Another matter with a possible though not probable publishing sequel is the interesting correspondence I have been having with Winfield Shiras, book editor of G. P. Putnam's Sons. He has looked me up through Weird Tales, and asked me to submit as many as possible of my MSS. for possible consideration as a published collection. After some further inquiries, I have sent some 30 tales out of the 38 I am willing to acknowledge. These represent the loose MSS. on hand—but I shan't go to the work of copying stuff from my magazine files unless I have a real assurance of strong acceptance-chances. In my opinion, nothing will come of the business—since all these publishers probably want is to size up the available MS. supply now and then— ascertaining what is or isn't suitable for their use, and taking care not to overlook any good bets. In a fortnight or so I shall probably get my junk back, together with a politely non-committal letter. If, however, a miracle did occur, I would naturally be more than glad to strut around as the author of a book with the solid and ancient Putnam imprint. Even so, however, I'll wager the book wouldn't be any such artistic unit as this new triumph of yours!

I haven't yet broken hibernation, though vernal signs are becoming increasingly apparent in the air and on the trees. Meanwhile I am dunning all revision clients for whatever they owe me, in a desperate attempt to scrape together enough cash for a little southward Melmothing. I have a delightful invitation from our fellow-weirdster Whitehead to visit him in Dunedin, Florida—but the $70.00 round trip on the 'bus is nothing to glide over as irrelevant! Whitehead is in poor health, and may have to come north for an operation in a month or so; but his health is nothing that interferes with his hospitality. In preparation for possible hibernation-breaking I've been toiling for three days on a task of singularly exhausting yet discouragingly inconspicuous nature—viz., the room-cleaning and file-sorting which I've been dodging for years. There were heaps and piles under certain chairs and tables which hadn't been classified since the winter after the summer you were here . . . . and the time had come when order had to make a slight inroad on the universal reigning chaos. It has left me about "all in", and doesn't show greatly on the surface; but upon recapitulation I think it was eminently worth the trouble. At last I have some vague idea of where to find things when I want them. Meanwhile my cursed left eye has been giving me some bother—so much that I am driven to depend a good deal on this hateful Remington relique, and may have to return to the full-time wearing of glasses . . . . which irritate my ears and nose-bridge abominably.

Last month I wrote a long tale—the longest yet, except those two things you tried to wade through in the original cacography—and which are yet untyped and unread by others than yourself. This new blasphemy runs to 80 pages of my crabbed script, which probably means damn near 100 of double spaced typing—30,000 or 32,000 words. It is entitled "At the Mountains of Madness", and has an antarctic locale. Monstrous things sleep and brood in and under the eternal ice of the austral pole—and you can imagine what kind of a layout would be turned up by an expedition from Miskatonic University in Arkham! The thing has 12 chapters, and a central organic division justifying 2-part publication. It will be devilish hard to land anywhere, though I shall peddle it considerably if I ever get it typed.[1]

I trust your new book is a typical index of all your contemporary activity, and that work on the new novel progresses apace. When will you get around these parts again? I have thought of you every time I have passed a bakery with its aromatic emanations, so dearly beloved of your olfactory sense—and also when my aunt and I commenced patronising the wagon of the Lonsdale Bakery last autumn . . . . the very bakery whose savour you remarked in Saylesville, just after our emergence from the haunted wood of titan rocks!

Well—again I congratulate you on the book, and thank you profoundly for the copy which now takes its honoured place in my shelves. I shall give it many a re-reading—for this is the kind of thing which sets my imagination off on its strangest and most picturesque paths. And what luck to have a brother who can back you up so well!

With good and grateful wishes, and trusting you will wander eastward in the course of your next few incarnations, I remain

Yr most obdt hble Servt,

Πάππος Νεκρόφιλος

Notes

1. *At the Mountains of Madness* is in fact almost 41,000. HPL's remarks suggest that he envisioned it as being potentially suitable for magazine serialization. He did not "peddle" the novel further following its rejection by *WT*.

[152] [DAW to HPL] [TLS]

The Sorcerers Warehouse
April 20, 1931

Dear Πάππος Νεκρόφιλος:

How fortunate for me that your letter arrived

upon the celebration of my two hundred and thirtieth birthday! I have spent a goodly time pondering upon its manifold and diverse contents; speculating as to whether I could have had a part in the production of a certain book which apparently pleased you; feeling grateful for appreciative comment; wishing that the first combined fruits of our efforts had been more imposing; and wondering when the oh so long promised and delayed book of your own is to appear. Naturally I am pleased that you like "Dark Odyssey". I hoped you would, for many poems in it and many which are not are the final products of that first dark Odyssey of mine in the summer of 1927. I enjoyed greatly the preparation of the book. I can truthfully say that from cover to cover, with the exception of my brother's talented drawings, it is a product of my fancy. Even the jacket, the color scheme, the type, the paper, the size, the reproduction method, were my choice. And I can assure you I wellnigh stood over the printers with bludgeons to see that it was done as I wanted! At that, they slipped up on a couple of minor details—one of the poems was left misspaced when it should have been corrected, etc. At the time I selected that group of poems, I made the choice for two other books also, one of which is now being illustrated by a gifted young artist of my acquaintance, Audrey Johnson, and the other of which will be provided with illustrations later this year by Barbara Craigie, another talented artist whom I know. These I plan to publish within a year or two.[1] My novel, "Dead Titans Awaken", should be completed by July or so of this year, and will be illustrated by Howard. I have not worked on it since last fall, because my duties at school for which I receive slightly more than bread and butter have occupied all my time, but there is not a great deal left to be written on it. Within the next couple of years I intend also to publish a large and splendid quarto of my brother's best drawings, of which there are some two dozen that loot the farthest flung outposts of the cosmos. After these volumes are out of the way—I know not what. I am writing a potboiler now for Astounding Stories[2] which pays two cents per word. I expect to write a half dozen more this summer to replenish my exchequer. The pedantic life is wearing me out, and I have virtually decided to break away before I dry up and to plunge, whatever the hardships, into creative writing. Lately I have had a violent case of cacoethes scribendi.[3] When my immediate interest in writing and finishing various weird or imaginative beginnings I have made is satisfied, I believe I will turn my attention to a satiric novel which has been germinating for some time, thence to a play of curious implications, thence to another novel, of a more familiar world and people, thence back to the "million colored sun of secret worlds incredible",[4] with such lyric interludes as the muses provide, and after that—oh well, I ought to have at least a few new ideas in the course of the five years or so which my program entails!

I am indeed sorry to hear about the wreckage of Cook's affairs. I shall write him at the address you give, and send him a copy of "Dark Odyssey".

And the news of "The Shunned House" is catastrophic. Will you find out whether the sheets can be possessed or whether there is still a claim against them? Goodness knows I have parted company with the $ sign but perhaps I can work out some sort of solution. I for one would gladly appreciate the simple sheets and bind them as I think they should be. As for your correspondence with Putnam's—I sincerely hope that, by the time this letter reaches you, editorial mania and myopia will for once have failed to such an extent that a collection so eminently extraordinary as your narratives will finally receive recognition and publication. Or publication and recognition, as the case may be. My opinion of Putnam's will certainly be doubly favorable if they accept the volume.

Meanwhile, what of Belknap, Loveman, Kirk, and Talman? I have not heard from or about any of them in much more than a year. Is Belknap's address still 230 W. 97th? And does Loveman hold forth at Dauber & Pine's? And is Kirk's Bookstore extant even now? And where hieth Talman, mainstay of the Times?

Derleth, as you no doubt know, has retreated to the hub of the universe, i.e., Sauk City, where he hibernated momentarily before wending onward to Madison where he at present is an associate editor of the Midwest Conference Magazine, a collegiate monthly of possibilities but rather ephemeral value. I wish young Derleth would devote himself to writing and drop much of his hack-work. With his prodigious energy and ability to write sensitively when he takes a little time, he could, I believe, establish an important name for himself within a few years. Are your own duties of revision still occupying so inordinate a part of your hours? May they lessen, if they are, and may your annual trip materialize in fullness! I have hopes of wandering again this year, uncrystallized hopes as yet, but nevertheless goals to work for. I feel the inner need of change for spiritual revitalization and contrast. Always, I think, I will return to Minnesota—one of the three symbols of "Look Homeward, Angel" was the expression of quiet and release that I felt when I returned from the frenzy of New York in the fall of 1929—but my occasional escapades furnish a certain nourishment that unbroken existence here does not provide. Nearly half of "Ecstasy" was written, for example, during or just after my first hegira under the direct response to new experiences. And I feel that the responses are becoming maturer, deeper; so far as my intelligence permits me to be impersonal in so personal a matter, I believe that "Dark Odyssey" represents a considerable stride forward in many ways; though there is less of spontaneous lyricism in it, there is more thought and an attempt to mould experience rather than to repeat it.

There was another strange phenomenon here last week that I know would have impressed you as it impressed me. It was in the afternoon of a day smoky with vast clouds of dust and an underlying heat, like a day of cosmic fires that I described to you two or three years ago. One could scarcely see a block distant, and the sky was obscured with the driving pall whipped by a desert wind. But in late afternoon, the sun crept vaguely out of the wild swirl and shone first with a dull-gray tone that gradually became a *strange, dusty green*.[5] Only the red snowfall has so powerfully affected me, among natural phenomena, as that green sun. I think that the weird natural mysteries which seem to appear here at least once a year must be one of the reasons why I find much spiritual sustenance in Minnesota.

I am tremendously eager to see "The Mountains of Madness" in any shape. If my novel is placed, I shall fulfill an old threat of mine and type later this summer the two long stories of yours that I have read in manuscript. Remember me to that charming aunt of yours whom I have not forgotten. And be very careful of your eyes. I hope that the difficulty is only temporary, for few things are so precious as vision. Greetings and best wishes, as ever, from the western

Melmoth

Notes

1. Except for *Poems for Midnight*, a compilation of his collected and uncollected poems, DAW published no other collections of poetry.
2. The story evidently was rejected (see letter 157). The first story DAW published in *Astounding Stories* was "Raiders of the Universes" (September 1932).
3. "The itch for writing," from Juvenal, *Satires* 7.52.
4. From CAS, *The Hashish-Eater; or, The Apocalypse of Evil*, ll. 2–3.
5. A "blue sun" is witnessed in *Invisible Sun* (Chapter 27).

[153] [HPL to DAW] [TLS]

[Postmarked Providence, R.I.,
27 April 1931]
Crypt of Yuggoth-Ninh
Saturn's Night. [25 April]

Dear Melmoth:—

Glad to hear the news, and to learn further details concerning the evolution of "Dark Odyssey". Both of my aunts are as fascinated with it as I am, and send you their especial regards and remembrances. The arrival of my epistle on your 230th birthday was highly opportune. I had not known the date was so near Belknap's, which comes on the 27th of this selfsame month. He, young imp, will be only 2900—just starting out on a cosmick career.

But your book is certainly a triumph, and I note with interest your dominant personal share in the format as well as contents. Surely you are entitled to take rank among the connoisseurs of art typography! These other books you mention will undoubtedly owe much to your supervision—indeed, you seem to be quite well equipped to start a choice publishing house for special

editions and esoteric aesthetic items. Glad that your novel will have the benefit of your brother's art work. You two surely make a team! And a book of his
drawings ought to be an event indeed. Would that it were within commercial
possibility for you to found and maintain a select publishing house devoted
exclusively to the issuance of strange and cosmic things in prose, verse, and
picture alike. How one would welcome, for example, a book of Klarkash-
Ton's nameless entities and Antarean vegetation reproduced in full colour!

I hope most certainly that you will be able to follow out your programme
of creative writing, and trust that you can arrange some sort of Black Pilgrimage[1] to precede and inspire it. I can well understand the yearning for nightmare Khorazin and the Vale of Pnath[2] which overtakes one after too long a
bondage to the usual and the expected. In arranging such a pilgrimage, pray
don't forget that one of the most hellish gates to the Abyss is hidden in the
Black Woods of Quinsnicket near Providence. God! the Shapes that fly up in
the night and make the cottagers draw close shutters over their ancient small-
paned windows!

It is certainly too cursedly bad about Cook, and I wish he could get a
fresh start toward mental contentment and financial solvency. I know he will
be keenly appreciative of "Dark Odyssey"—he has always maintained, with a
fine disregard of his auditors' egoes, that you come the nearest to the ideal
genius type of anybody he has ever seen. I have been hoping to see him
around here, but fancy I may not do so till I am back from my southerly
melmothing. As for "The Shunned House"—I am asking Cook what can be
done toward at least partial salvage, though without any especial hope that
much can be done. After all, even if the edition were saved, there would really
be nothing to do with so many copies. What I would like, would be a dozen or
so to bind and give the various members of the gang. Regarding Putnam's, I
have no particular hopes. They will come to their own conclusions in their own
way, and their sole criterion will be saleability. But I surely would appreciate the
imprint of such a solid old firm in case they decided to be favourable.

The gang seems to flourish much as usual. Belknap still holds forth at the
accustomed stand, and is busy writing some sort of a psychological or aesthetic novel with us—or thinly veiled representations of us—as characters.[3] I
don't know how much luck he'll have in marketing it, but at least its composition seems to afford him infinite satisfaction. Talman has left the Times, and
is now editing a group of trade magazines for the Texas oil company, with
offices in the new Chrysler Bldg. He has moved to Flatbush, and is now to be
addressed at 2215 Newkirk Ave., Brooklyn, N.Y. Loveman is still at Dauber
& Pine's, but hasn't written his old Grandpa Theobald since last summer!
Kirk still has his shop, but is still more delinquent in keeping in touch with
provincial old gentlemen. James Ferdinand Morton continues to uphold the
cultural life of Paterson, and to make long semi-official trips contributing
equally to his pure recreation and sense of importance. And Kleiner still radi-

ates urban sophistication as of yore. Good old Arthur Leeds, a gang member before your time, is back in the metropolis—connected, amusingly enough, with some sort of freak exhibition at Coney Island.[4]

Yes—young Derleth has kept me apprised of his return—which is undoubtedly best for him, just as my return to Providence was best for me, and yours to St. Paul for you. We all flourish best on our respective native soils—for it is from the soil that all true art is drawn, and one can't do much drawing without deep roots. Too bad the Mystic failed as a source of revenue, but for real aesthetic growth it is the best thing that could have happened. That kid has solid and remarkable stuff in him—it is very rare to see one of his age able to shake off the shell of commercial hokum and produce delicate and authentic fragments of impression and sensation like his "Early Years" cycle. His degree of energy is positively dizzying and incredible, and will undoubtedly lead to substantial things when it is thoroughly coördinated and embarked in a settled direction under its own full momentum.

Undoubtedly your new book shews great strides in maturity of thought and expression, and one may well believe that your future volumes will reveal no abatement in the tendency. A firm Minnesota background, plus adventurous excursions into the cosmic void outside, would seem to be an ideal programme for imaginative replenishment; and I hope you will be able ultimately to manage a steady policy of alternate wayfaring and home creation. Your account of the hazy and mystical green sun interested me extremely, and I hope you will be able to utilise the sensations you derived from it. By the way—have you noticed how much more attention the fantastic and picturesque Charles Fort is receiving of late, since the publication of his "Lo!"? I must get a look at that book, though I scarcely imagine it differs radically from the two earlier ones.

I'll let you see "At the Mountains of Madness" if I ever get the nerve to type it. I've just bought a new ribbon for this machine, but doubt if it will see much wear before my embarkation on the new dark odyssey. Those older things you read are pretty hopeless. I haven't glanced at them for years, and might want to make changes and contractions in them in the light of my present tastes. My style has changed somewhat, I hope—cast off a bit of its crudity and extravagance, though I am too old to be helped much. But bless my soul, you mustn't bother about typing endless tomes like these! Aedepol! But the very thought of such a favour is stupefying! It's bad enough to think of doing a job like that for oneself—but for another . . . . well, imagination can produce no adequate image!

Spring is half here, and I have broken hibernation to the extent of a few outdoor trips with my work; but one can't depend on genial warmth at this season. I hope to get off for a rigidly economical southern trip within a week now—putting everything into coach fare, and limiting my food programme to sweet chocolate. I shall probably get as far as St. Augustine—the oldest town in the nation, and potentially the source of much imaginative stimulation. On the way back I shall try to pause at my beloved Charleston, as well as paying visits to the gang in Manhattan and to Bernard Dwyer amidst the wild domed hills of the Esopus Valley. Dwyer is without industrial connexions just now, but an easy-going temperament saves him from the abyss of melancholy. He weighs about 250 pounds, some of which I shall try to walk off him in exploratory rambles when I get around his way.

And so it goes.

Good luck and regards from the Gulph of Eastern Senescence—

Πάππος Νεκρόφιλος

Notes

1. HPL refers to M. R. James's story "Count Magnus."
2. Khorazin (or Chorazin) is one of the places mentioned in the Bible as the birthplace of the Antichrist. It, too, is cited in "Count Magnus." The Vale of Pnath is from HPL's *The Dream-Quest of Unknown Kadath*.
3. Little is known about this work, but it apparently was never completed and does not now survive.
4. Arthur Leeds had been affiliated with Hubert's Museum and Flea Circus (208 W. 42nd Street in New York), which also had exhibited freaks.

[154] [HPL to DAW] [ANS][1]

[Postmarked Saint Augustine, Fla.,
8 May 1931]

Melmothing de luxe! Hey for the heart of the tropics & the oldest city on this continent north of Mexico . . . . . a place that Sir Francis Drake has sacked in his day! This climate peps the old man up marvellously—I hate to think of returning north!

Yr obt
Πάππος Νεκρόφιλος

Notes

1. *Front:* Entrance to St. Augustine, Fla.

[155] [HPL to DAW] [ANS]

[Souvenir Folder of Scenic Florida. Postmarked Saint Augustine, Fla., 16 May 1931]

[From]
Πάππος Νεκρόφιλος

[156] [HPL and Henry S. Whitehead to DAW] [ANS][1]

[Postmarked Dunedin, Fla.,
25 May 1931]

Sunset & the mystic gulf . . . . what lies beyond? That, O Melmoth, is what this tropic conference of nameless entities is seeking to learn from the mouldering Pnakotic Manuscripts spread out before us. Last night we evoked Something from the white crescent moon as it made a glistening path to the lonely coral key whereon we stood—but what It told us was not quite complete. ¶ Just read Klarkash-Ton's "Hunters" as kindly forwarded by you. Isn't it great? ¶ Watch *Adventure* for a marvellous weird tale—"The Black Beast"—by my genial present host.[2] ¶ You mustn't miss Florida on your next Eastern hike. Great place—has taken ten years off the old man! ¶ Yrs—Πάππος Νεκρόφιλος.

G. Canevin[3] also salutes you, dear Sir & Bro:—I'm going to keep H.P.L. here if I have to conjure a Jumbee to aid me! He is the genuine, original, Perfect Egg of the Universe.

Best—Whitehead

Notes

1. *Front:* Sunset / Dunedin Fla.
2. CAS, "The Hunters from Beyond" (*ST*, October 1932); HSW, "The Black Beast" (*Adventure*, 15 July 1931).
3. Gerald Canevin was a recurring character in the fiction of Henry S. Whitehead. HPL and his cronies referred to Whitehead as "Canevin" in their correspondence.

[157] [HPL to DAW] [ALS]

Nether Crypts—
Lammas-Eve
[31 July 1931]

Dear Melmoth:—

I am gratified to hear that the monstrous antarctic chronicle did not bore you, & hope that no adverse fate has overtaken its journey to the subterrene lair of Klarkash-Ton—insomuch as the latter mysteriarch, writing as recently as July 12, reports its non-receipt. When I consider the prostrating labour I put into those *115* pages of typing, I am reluctant that any part of it should be lost—even a carbon copy. Wright promptly rejected this tale on the ground that it is too long, not readily divisible, uninteresting, unconvincing, or something of the sort.

I must surely see your novel when it is done, & hope that it may gain advantageous placement. Putnam's has returned those stories of mine with polite hedgings & talk of rearrangement & postponement which virtually means a turndown. Sorry *Astounding* rejected your pot-boiler, & hope *Argosy* will have better sense. Let me know when anything of yours appears anywhere—or lend me the MS. of anything which isn't scheduled for publication. I'd like to see the new lyrics & sonnets you mention.

My recent trip, as postcards have doubtless apprised you, was a record-breaker in length & duration. I added two states to my list, & can now say that I have been in (a) every Atlantic coast state, & (b) each of the original 13 colonies. Also, I have been on former Spanish soil—thus (in connexion with home & Quebec) establishing contact with all three of the great colonial civilisations—English, French, and Spanish. St Augustine was a marvellous & glamourous place—where I saw houses built in the 1500's, 50 to 65 years older than any edifices I had seen before. The old fort, too, was marvellously attractive. I then crossed over to Dunedin, where I spent 2½ weeks with our fellow-weirdster Henry S. Whitehead—who is also an Episcopal clergyman. Whitehead is a prince of good fellows, & made my stay uniformly enjoyable. From Dunedin I proceeded down to Miami & out the Keys to Key Wet—southernmost point in the U.S., & part of the West Indies in all but name. Here I obtained my first taste of the real tropics—which I like tremendously. Florida as a whole gave me the most continuous comfort I have ever experienced—that is surely the climate for me. Finally I edged northward along the east coast, stopping again at St. Augustine & later at Savannah & my beloved Charleston. After that came Richmond & Philadelphia—& last of all New York, where I was detained three weeks by the hospitality of Belknap & Talman, whom I visited successively. I saw all the gang—including Arthur Leeds, who has returned from Chicago. Morton left for a Nova Scotia trip shortly after my arrival—obtaining many minerals & some long-sought ancestral data.

I reached home July 20, & the very next day welcomed Morton on his way back from the maritime provinces. We visited the old Manton Ave. quarry, but didn't find a single rock to suit the visitor! We also tanked up with 50 or 75 varieties of ice cream at Maxfield's in Warren. Yes—& ate a robust meal at Jake's in memory of the days that were.

Since then I have been desperately striving to catch up with unread papers, old correspondence, & the like—though I still owe 17 letters. It's a great life—but the trip was worth it.

Enclosed is a writeup of our bookselling friend Eddy. Morton & I were there, of course, last week.

With best wishes, & hoping to see some of your new worth shortly, I remain

Yr ob[t] h[ble] Servt

Πάππος Νεκρόφιλος

[*Enclosure:* Article from the *Providence Journal:* "Man Is Taxed for $200,000, But Dickers For 10-Cent Cut in Price of 25-Cent Book" by Elizabeth A. Williams.]

[158] [HPL to DAW] [ANS][1]

[Postmarked Providence, R.I.,

9 August 1931]

Have just read "The Lives of Alfred Kramer", & congratulate you on its malign vividness. That disintegrative ending is a winner! By the way, though, no witches were ever *burnt* in the American colonies. Whenever convicted, they were *hanged.* Nor was there, so far as I know, any Salem trial in 1638. The big witch year was 1692. Incidentally—wouldn't it strengthen the story to *omit the framework*—i.e. the confinement & suicide of Forbes? Why not have Forbes simply tell of his railway encounter, ending with the monstrous disintegration? I surely hope this tale lands professionally. Am sending it along to Klarkash-Ton in this mail. ¶ Went to Newport with my aunt last Tuesday, & thought of our trip in 1927. Today am going down to the waterfront to see the 44-gun frigate *Constitution,* here on exhibition for three days.

Best wishes—

Πάππος Νεκρόφιλος

Notes

1. *Front:* Campus, Brown University, Providence, R. I.

[159] [HPL and George Kirk to DAW] [ANS][1]

[Postmarked Providence, R.I.,

15 August 1931]

Ahoy, Melmoth! Get the . . . . conclave! Would that you were here to organise a dinner party at Jake's! ¶ The new Dashiell Hammett anthology[2] is going to use my "Erich Zann". ¶ G K has just surveyed "Dark Odyssey" with appreciation.

Yr obt Πάππος Νεκρόφιλος

Howareya? Donald, and where and why? Wherefor not N.Y.C.? Though I will admit it's been hot *this* summer. Just saw your book and like it much, both the writing & the makeup are superb. Congratulations to you & to your brother. Very best wishes

George

Notes

1. *Front:* Sunken Gardens, Roger Williams Park, Providence, R.I.
2. *Creeps by Night* (1931).

[160] [HPL to DAW] [ANS]¹

[Postmarked Plymouth, Mass.,
24 August 1931]

Melmothing around the oldest town in New England—& discovering quaint sections I never saw before!

Great stuff!

Yr obt

ΠΑΠΠΟΣ ΝΕΚΡΟΦΙΛΟΣ

Notes

1. *Front:* Old Harlow House, Built 1677 from Timber of Old Fort, Plymouth, Mass.

[161] [HPL to DAW] [ALS]

Septr 25, 1931

Dear Melmoth:—

This is a season of treats—for in the same mail with Yoh-Vombis came the enclosed delectable yarn through Dwyer! Both are splendid; & I must congratulate you on the novel & original cosmic thrills, & the extremely effective climax, of The Tree-Men. I surely hope this has found—or will find—favour with the editorial fraternity.

Klarkash-Ton's tale is great, too—replete with the musty, tenebrous, & menacing atmosphere of alien & unholy arcana.¹ I have not heard of its professional fate, but am certainly hoping for the best. Belknap has written a great tale lately—"The Brain-Eaters"—but that ass Bates (of Strange Tales) has rejected it on the ground that it is 'too horrible & depressing'!² Easy to see I can never land anything with that bird!

Did I tell you that W. Paul Cook had secured a position near Boston, & that he is now to be addressed at 17 Chambers St. (in the lee of old Beacon Hill) in that city? He is coming here tomorrow to stay over night & through Sunday, & will have your old room upstairs. I shall be glad to see him—haven't laid eyes on him since July 1930.

Hate to see the autumn come, but am still taking my work out to the woods & fields on the warmer days. This place is all upset by the installation of steam heat—hence indoor work is performed under a handicap. Hope all is flourishing in St Paul—& that the cosmic novel is progressing steadily.

Best wishes—

Πάππος Νεκρόφιλος

Notes

1. CAS, "The Vaults of Yoh-Vombis" (*WT,* May 1932).
2. FBL, "The Brain-Eaters" (*WT,* June 1932).

[162] [HPL and W. Paul Cook to DAW] [ANS][1]

[Postmarked Providence, R.I.,
27 September 1931]

Hail, Melmoth! Here is one distinguished guest of the 1927 days repeating—would that our Western delegate might do likewise! We've explored colonial streets & Eddy's shelves, & are about to do a little more of the latter this afternoon. Next Sunday I hope to get to Boston for the first time in 1931. Wish I'd saved the Tree Men for W P C to read—but he'll get it in print. Regards—Πάππος Νεκρόφιλος

I did not write you from Montpelier of my change of locale, inasmuch as the call came suddenly. Even my Boston address is subject to change without notice, but in all probability will remain at 17 Chambers St. for the winter. Luck to you!

Cook

Notes

1. *Front:* Dyer Memorial, Roger Williams Park, Providence, R. I.

[163] [HPL and Charles W. Smith to DAW] [ANS][1]

[Postmarked Haverhill, Mass.,
4 October 1931]

Hail, Melmoth! Amateur conclave at Haverhill—Tryout & Recluse meet for the first time in person with Grandpa as a benign spectator. Yesterday W P C & I saw the south shore, with Hingham's Old Ship Church (1681), & now we're going to ancient Newburyport. Congrats on having "The Red Brain" in the new Hammett anthology. Regards—

Πάππος Νεκρόφιλος

Tryout

Notes

1. *Front:* Kenoza Lake from State Highway, Haverhill, Mass.

[164] [HPL to DAW] [ALS]

Saturday
[24 October 1931]

Dear Melmoth:—

Well—since the joint Culinario-Nekrophilic card from Boston, I have had still further travel—painfully followed, however, by a fortnight of hard labour. When I got home from Boston I found a telegram from Orton asking me to meet him in Hartford, Conn. to discuss a book-revision job for the press which he is running in Brattleboro Vt. Glad of the excuse to visit central Connecticut—which I had never seen before—I went; & found the scenery even finer than I had imagined. Hartford is not an ugly town, but not nearly as picturesque as Providence. Didn't you pass through it on your hike of 1927? On my return trip I took a different route—bending south through Norwich & Plainfield—& found the landscape even better than along the direct course previously traversed. Great hills—spreading valleys—crystal lakes—breath-taking vistas—altogether, it is astonishing that such a magnificent scenic region could exist so close to me without my having previously visited it. Norwich is a fascinating old town—built on the steep terraces that rise above a bend in the river Thames. Near it is some famously rugged scenery, a bit of which appears on the accompanying card.

The book job, though, was hellishly exacting. It consisted of the revision & proofreading of the text of a long official history of Dartmouth College[1] by one of the professors therein—so full of errors that I fear my awe of the academic brotherhood (present company excepted) is permanently impaired. I've finally got it done & sent off—& am not sure whether I'll have to go to Brattleboro for a final conference. If the job turns out well, I may get more of the same kind of work from Orton's press.[2] I much prefer it to the revision of utterly crude MSS—or to hack fictioneering for the pulp magazines.

I certainly hope your European trip—to say nothing of a possible circuit of the globe—will turn out successfully. I'd like to do that very thing myself, but doubt if my dismal finances will ever be able to stand the strain. You are fortunate in having particular advantages in the matter of travel expense. I hope you won't neglect the East, & that 10 Barnes may once again have the honour of sheltering a cosmic wanderer. We have steam heat now—even on the 3d floor where the hot air furnace didn't use to reach—so you can be sure of genial temperatures at any season & on any level.

Glad to hear of the acceptance of "M'bwa" & "Kramer", & shall keep a lookout for them in W.T. Derleth lately made a fresh copy of my old rejected

"In the Vault" & persuaded me to send it in—& Wright surprised me by accepting it for $55.00. Hope to see "Raiders" & "Fire Creatures" eventually—in manuscript even if not in print. And I trust you'll manage to snatch some spare moments for the novel before long.

"Creeps"—& my XXV—came the other day, though I haven't had time to read the former yet. It is an imposing tome of over 500 pages, with a formidable list of eminent contributors apart from the W.T. element. I was glad to see "The Red Brain" justly honoured by inclusion.

Thanks for the good word about "Mts of Madness", but I guess Brother Farnsworth is adamant on that. He has conventional notions of proportioning the stuff in his magazine, & never breaks rules except for such favourites as Seabury Quinn & Otis Adelbert Kline.

I thought I told you that the Putnam thing all blew up as I expected it would. After tearing & mussing my MSS. without offering to make fresh copies, the book editor gave an adverse decision which boils down to two points—one utterly puerile & the other sadly reasonable. First—& most fatuously—the damn fool thought my stuff was too uniformly sombre. He wanted some sort of light relief material interspersed betwixt the real hell-raisers! To this my only reply is 'bah!' Secondly, however, he complained that my tales are lacking in subtlety—too explanatory—not vaguely suggestive enough—& all that. Here, curse him, he is really correct—for despite my efforts to avoid the devices of cheap fiction, the repeated demands of Wright for simpler & less mystical material seems to have had a kind of subconscious effect upon me. One wants one extreme, the other wants the other—so poor Grandpa falls betwixt two stools! No—I don't think I'll peddle my stuff around to the John Day Co.[3] or anywhere else. A good deal of it is undoubtedly too poor for publication between cloth covers, & it won't hurt the rest to wait.

I haven't had the heart to tackle Cook about that "Shunned House" matter—for I don't like to bring up topics reminding him of his ill-fortune. If the whole thing goes up in smoke, the loss will not be beyond the world's limit of endurance. Cook, by the way, has just changed his lodgings & is now situate at *7 Hancock St.*—on the farther slope of ancient Beacon Hill. His physical improvement over last year is astonishing, & I think he is close to getting back on his feet in every way—unless swamped by handicaps.

Belknap is busy writing. He lately produced an excellent thing—"The Brain-Eaters"—which I hope Wright has had the ordinary sense to accept. Whitehead's health has taken a turn for the worse, & he is now about to undergo a stomach operation. He has a new address, by the way—Box 414, Dunedin Isles, Dunedin, Fla.

There has been some delightful warm weather of late, but my book job has kept me from enjoying much of it. Hope I can get a breath or two of the woods & fields before the autumn foliage has vanished. Trust your work isn't too arduous—even though it interferes with fictional production. You will surely have earned that vacation next year!

Watched the sunset on Prospect Terrace (which you doubtless recall) last night. Many houses to the northward have recently been torn down, & I believe the terrace is to be enlarged into quite a sizeable little hillside park. All very well—though I hate to see any of the quaint, village-like houses go. There has been other colonial devastation elsewhere in the city, too—yet it will take longer than my few remaining years to ruin Providence's quaintness altogether.

Well—best wishes, & hope to see you next year!

Yrs most cadaverously,

Πάππος Νεϰϱόφιλος

[*Enclosure:* Postcard. *Front:* Indian Leap and Pale Face Maiden, Norwich, Conn.; no writing on back.]

Notes

1. Leon Burr Richardson (1878–1951), *History of Dartmouth College* (Hanover, NH: Dartmouth College Publications, 1932; 2 vols.).

2. Orton's Stephen Daye Press offered no more revision work to HPL.

3. The publisher of *Creeps by Night.*

[165] [HPL and W. Paul Cook to DAW] [ANS][1]

[Postmarked Boston, Mass.,
1 November 1931]

Hail, Melmoth! We're Melmothing, too—ancient Portsmouth & timeless Newburyport . . . . . . parts of New England which you have yet to see.

Best wishes—

Πάππος Νεϰϱόφιλος

You did not care a great deal for Deerfield, so you would care even less for Portsmouth & Newburyport, especially the latter, with its complete and unrestored, but run down ancient buildings and warehouses. In the former, much restoration has been done.

W. Paul Cook

Notes

1. *Front:* Governor Langdon House, Portsmouth, N. H.

[166] [HPL to DAW] [ALS]

[Postmarked Providence, R.I.,
27 November 1931]
Friday

Dear Melmoth:—

Wggrrh . . . nggrrr . . . . . . *that scratching* . . . . . *the rending woodwork* . . . help! help! . . . . shall I ever sleep again?

Klarkash-Ton has certainly done well, & I don't think the conclusion is really much of a letdown. I've just sent it on to B'na-Dwi-Y'hah, who I am sure will revel in it.

Congratulations on the completion of your novel—& shall be anxious to see it, postage or no postage. I surely hope it will land ultimately with a publisher, though these are said to be difficult days for book placement.

I have not finished anything new myself, having been veritably swamped by revisory activities. I have, however, done some experimenting in the hope of improving my style somewhat, & the result of such practice may soon take form as a kind of story called "The Shadow over Innsmouth". The experimenting consisted of writing out the same plot in different manners, but is ending rather negatively—with four versions torn up & the fifth taking form in about the same way that it would have if I hadn't experimented at all. My stuff does not satisfy me, & the Putnam verdict convinces me that it falls between two stools—being not cheap enough for the pulp market, yet not good enough for real magazines or book publication. I require more & more space to convey what I am trying to convey, & as a result many (like W. Paul Cook) who once liked my work like it no longer. Possibly another period of swearing off from fiction (like that of 1908–1917) would be a good thing for me to start.

Up to Wednesday the weather here remained astonishingly aestival, with temperatures of 71° & thereabouts. I was out very often in the woods & fields. Now, however, wintry conditions are suddenly setting in. Yesterday I succeeded in persuading my elder aunt into going out for a Thanksgiving dinner—her first trip except to the doctor's since last Christmas. My younger aunt is visiting in Washington D.C., & I often go over to her vacant flat[1] to read & write.

Belknap is busying himself grinding out pot-boilers with a view to Clayton-Bates acceptance, but so far the returns have not been auspicious. Whitehead's health has taken a less unfavourable turn, so that he believes he can escape the threatened operation. Dwyer is still back in West Shokan, though harbouring vague hopes that he may be able to spend at least part of the winter in ancient Kingston. Cook is now at Sunapee N.H., visiting with his sister, & will make a flying trip to Vermont to see Coates before returning to Boston. Munn, after a long period of unemployment, has started a bakery route with the aid of an old automobile rigged up with a decrepit bureau in the rear, & is actually making a moderate amount of cash.

Well—best wishes, & don't fail to let me see the nameless horror.

Yr obt Servt

Πάππος Νεϰϱόφιλος

[Enclosure? Postcard. *Front:* "Doorway," Old Lafayette House, Marblehead, Mass. On back:] Good stuff! You have certainly beaten Edmond Hamilton at his own game. Of course, something of the conventional interplanetary "scientifiction" plot & setting exists—the sketchy "action" style &c—but where Hamilton & his congeners have nothing new to add, you have introduced many strikingly original conceptions & efforts. I surely hope this will meet with professional success—as it seems to me quite likely to do.

¶ Had a great trip to antiquarian scenes, as postcards have doubtless apprised you. Cook accompanied me to Portsmouth & Newburyport, but I went alone to Salem & Marblehead. Weather was just about as cool as I can readily endure—so I fancy this ends my 1931 travel season.

Best wishes—

Πάππος Νεϰϱόφιλος

Notes

1. At 61 Slater Avenue.

[167] [HPL to DAW] [ALS]

[Postmarked Providence, R.I.,
3 December 1931]
Thursday

Dear Melmoth:—

Klarkash-Ton certainly holds the record for quantity production—& the odd thing is that so many of his tales are really splendid! This one has a very distinct charm of its own—leaning toward the Dunsanian in its conception.[1]

I pity you anent the ordeal of novel-typing. The principal reason I don't try a novel is that I could never face the job of typing it. But I hope you'll get it finished soon, so that your creative instinct may again get into play. And as I said before, I surely want to see the novel when it goes on its rounds.

I haven't heard about "The Sphinx" in a long while, & didn't even know it was scheduled for Novr. 1. I'm sure it can't be out, else Loveman would have sent me a copy. But anyhow, I have its complete text, for last July he gave me a carbon of the MS. I'd like to see it published in suitable style, & hope those issuing it will try to achieve a format in some way worthy of the work.

Indian summer is over now, & the long night of hibernation sets in. Wish I had the cash to start Melmothing around the West Indies! But at that, I suppose Providence never even approaches the rigours of St. Paul. We are virtually never below zero.

Best wishes—

Yr most obt

Πάππος Νεκρόφιλος

Notes

1. CAS, "A Vintage from Atlantis" (*WT*, September 1933).

[168] [HPL to DAW] [ANS]

[Postmarked Providence, R.I.,
17 December 1931]

[To greet you at
Christmas
and
To wish you good cheer
in the New Year]
Πάππος Νεκρόφιλος
1931.

[*On envelope:*] Here is Klarkash-Ton's latest—quite Dunsanian, especially at the conclusion.[1] How does he keep it up?

Best holiday wishes—

Πάππος Νεκρόφιλος

Notes

1. CAS, "The Weird of Avoosl Wuthoqquan" (*WT*, June 1932).

1932

[169] [HPL and W. Paul Cook to DAW] [ANS][1]

[Postmarked Boston, Mass.,
2 January 1932]

Hail, Melmoth! Improving the warm New Year's by getting around to old Bostonium for another Culinary week end. This is a 100% museum session. Today the Cambridge Group—Germanic, Semitic, Peabody, Agassiz, &

Fogg—& tomorrow the old Fine Arts (remember that, the thunderstorm, the Y, & the Excellent Lunch?) & the Gardner palace in the Fenway. ¶ They're tearing down the ancient Clough (1695) & Vernon (1698) houses in the Pickman's Model district. Remember them? They were still there in 1927, though the actual scene of the story had just been demolished. ¶ We were glad to see the Tree Men of M'bwa in the new W.T. ¶ Robert E. Howard has just expressed great interest in your work. You may hear from him before long. Regards—

Πάππος Νεκρόφιλος

W. Paul Cook

Notes

1. *Front:* Lowell House, Harvard University, Cambridge, Mass.

[170] [DAW to HPL] [ALS]

Jan. 6—1932

Dear H p l—

At long last! The novel was done a week ago. I thought I'd correct the thousand or so typographical errors but it took me two days to correct the original copy & I haven't the energy to go through the two carbons. My apologies, but you can—I think—get most of the story, even "as is". I shall wait with the greatest interest any comment, criticism, or suggestions you care to offer. I know there are at least two major weak spots, but I'm so exhausted from the job that I'm packing it off to publishers without more ado.

As ever,

Melmoth II

[Comments by HPL on verso of letter 170:]

This novel really strikes its finest stride with Chap. VI—the descent into the earth—though of course the earlier "Fragment of a Dream" is of equal power.[1]

Is there an indefinable disharmony in tone betwixt the popular "action" style of the first half & the tense cosmicism of the second half?

verbal errors
innumerous should be *innumerable*
ephemeris   "   "   *ephemera*
giantism   "   "   *gigantism*

Could you hint more clearly at the nature & function of the green eikon—&
especially suggest with greater concreteness & convincingness the reason for
Graham's instant intuition that it had gone to Easter Island?

Is it possible that the whole prologue connected with the Grants ought to be
made briefer, more mystically vague, & more subordinate?

Beginning too abrupt—i.e., horrors introduced without adequate emotional
preparation?

p. 18—abnormality of stone image introduced too casually—without adequate emotions of strangeness & incredulity? Or rather, with these elements
too locally grouped after the description of what was found? It seems to me a
greater preparation—a tenser atmosphere of strangeness—ought to cling
round the first mention of this thing.

p. 20 Is there enough gradualness & subtle restraint in the description of
Graham's finds & emotions?

Chap III—The adapted "Fragment of A Dream" is exceedingly effective.

Chaps II & IV—you use *American* railway terms in a British scene. Change
words as follows—track = *line;* rails = *metals;* car = *carriage;* engineer = *engine-
man;* railroad = *railway.*

pp 48–9 how about the psychology of Graham's expecting the image to be
miraculously returned? Also—ought it to take G *hours* to re-remove the earth
which he had put back in *less than 3/4 of an hour?*

Chap VI—well & skulls tremendously effective.

Chap VII—odours of corruption ought not to permeate a crypt where everything is ancient & skeletal.

¶ dimensional abnormality splendidly suggested.

Chap VIII—reaction to news of Alton's death inadequate

Chap X et seq. Graham's diary attains vast & poetic power, though mo-
nogamic "love interest" is a trifle naive & derivatively Poesque.

Chap XII—Easter Isl. atmosphere magnificent—though perhaps the monstrous prints should have been *suggested* more vaguely & darkly.

Should the abnormalities preceding the final cataclysm be slightly subtilised or
etherealised?

Chap XIII—are not chronological concepts transmitted from rescuer to Graham too easily in view of the lack of a common fund of knowledge? ¶ Ending
might be made a trifle more vivid—use of formulae &c suggested.

cause of rope fraying is tremendously clever

Notes

1. DAW slightly rewrote "Fragment of a Dream" as Chapter III of *Dead Titans, Wak-
en!* (later transferred to Chapter XII of *The Web of Easter Island*).

[171] [HPL to DAW] [ANS][1]

[Postmarked Providence, R.I.,
12 January 1932]

Congratulations & commiserations! I should think you'd be dead after all that typing! Certainly, I'll be abundantly charitable toward all errors in the text, & will correct any I see. Thanks immensely for sending it—I shall begin reading the moment I can arrange for a long continuous period, for I don't want the perusal to be broken. At a hasty glance, it looks about as alluring as anything I've seen in a long while. To whom shall I send it when I have finished it? ¶ I've written a tale of 68 script pages & can't get the energy to type it. ¶ Providence is now under a heavy snowfall—the first of the season—but it is warm, & the snow is fast melting. ¶ Everyone agrees that "Mbwa" is the best story in the current W.T.

Best wishes—

Πάππος Νεκρόφιλος

Notes

1. *Front:* First Baptist Church, Providence, R. I.

[172] [HPL to DAW] [ALS]

Jany. 16, 1932

Dear Melmoth:—

Well—I still survive in approximately my right mind (though inclined to look nervously over my shoulder in the dark, & to listen apprehensively for certain sounds from overhead) despite my perusal last night of your potently cataclysmic chef d'oeuvre!

Rrrrh . . . nghaaa . . . . gyyyh . . . . . .

Bless me, Son, but you certainly have caught the majesty & terror of the outer spaces, & the charnel necromancy of inner earth! It gave me the biggest genuine kick I have had in ages—& I certainly hope it will land in print sooner or later. If the low state of the market prevents immediate book publication, try it as a serial on the magazines . . . . . which reminds me that one *Carl Swanson, Washburn, North Dakota* is about to start a new weird magazine—worth investigating, even though its rate of remuneration is not likely to be high.[1]

I will despatch the MS. to Augustus Derletus as soon as I can get to the express office, & am sure that both he & Klarkash-Ton will echo my own shuddering admiration of your achievement.

As for comment—as I read the story I began jotting certain observations idly down on the back of your note; & now that I come to read them over I think I'll send 'em along just as they are. I don't know just what you picked as the two "weak spots", but my own prime criticism would be that the first half—antecedent to the descent into the earth—makes rather too many concessions to the atmosphere & ideals of the popular "action" story; thus contrasting somewhat sharply with the admirably poignant latter half. I would be inclined to wonder whether the beginning is not slightly too abrupt—whether it would not be well to let the initial horrors develop more subtly & slowly out of the familiar setting of the normal world. I have probably mentioned before that in my opinion a fictional unreality can be made convincing only by the most adroit & complete emotional preparation—the reader must be gradually & insidiously brought to a point where he is ready to believe anything for the time being. What might be done is to compress the preliminary parts a bit—the tragedy of the Grants & the flight of Farrell—giving them the aspect of fragments darkly reaching Graham in various ways. You could have the Grant affair seem vaguely & terrifyingly through village reports & hints, (letting Graham imply what could not be publicly known) & police reports might establish that Farrell had seized the valise, stolen a car, & embarked on the ill-fated aëroplane. But of course all these are minor points—as are also the others I have jotted casually down. The story is all right as it is, & you can use your own judgment about making changes. On the whole it's a great piece of work, & its cosmic scope & horror reach the level of genuine poetry again & again. I hope most strongly that it may sooner or later achieve the medium of print. You have my sympathy anent the job of typing those 200 pages. I've corrected any errors which I could detect, so that I hope Derleth & Klarkash-Ton will have fairly smooth sailing.

I hope St Paul has had a share of the merciful winter mildness which has postponed my hibernation this season. Wednesday, Thursday, & Friday the temperatures were respectively 58°, 63°, & 54°—& today is not much worse, although a swift lapse to frigidity is predicted for tonight. Let us hope there is nothing sinister or portentous about this abnormal juxtaposition of weather . . . . . though similar phenomena are said to presage millennial manifestations of The Others from Outside! ¶ With sincerest congratulations & bet wishes—

Πάππος Νεκρόφιλος

[On envelope:] P.S. Some of your onomatopoetic words describing manifestations of the Titans are tremendously vivid.

Notes

1. 1. See letter 173n2.

[173] [HPL to DAW] [ANS]

[Postmarked Providence, R.I.,
22 January 1932]

Here's a splendid tale by Klarkash-Ton which I hope will gain acceptance somewhere or other.[1] Derleth also likes it. As soon as I can get down to the express office I shall despatch "Dead Titans" to A W—together with a new 72-page attempt of mine about which I am very uncertain. If A W thinks it's any good he'll put it on the circulation route—C A S—D W—Dwyer—H P L

[On envelope:] Just recd. your note—& by this time you've recd. my appreciative estimate of "Dead Titans". Yes—I found that transmission schedule on the cover when I removed the MS. from its envelope the second time. The first time, that initial sheet stuck in the envelope & wasn't missed because the next one had the beginning of the story. Hope my remarks on the tale don't sound too unintelligent. As for corrections—I always correct carbons at the same time that I correct the original copy—making each change in duplicate. It isn't much harder than correcting one copy, for when you spot an error in the original, you don't have to hunt again in the carbon. Better try it next time. ¶ On second thought, if my "Shadow over Innsmouth" comes to you, you'd better return it directly to me instead of sending it to Dwyer as suggested within. I think I'll start the other copy in Eastern circulation, for I don't intend to try it professionally. Incidentally—Dwyer's new address is 48 Main St. Kingston, N.Y. ¶ Just heard from Swanson—of the new magazine. He is accepting both " Nameless City" & "Beyond the Wall of Sleep."[2]

Notes

1. "The Empire of the Necromancers" (*WT,* September 1932).
2. Neither story was published, as Swanson's *Galaxy* never saw print.

[174] [HPL to DAW] [ANS]

[Postmarked Providence, R.I.,
18 February 1932]

Well—here's another from Klarkash-Ton. Great stuff! How does he keep it up? ¶ You'll receive my "Innsmouth" shortly. Hope you won't think it too hopelessly rotten. When you're through with it, young Auguste-Guillaume, Comte d'Erlette, wants to see it again. ¶ A correspondent of mine—a W.T. fan from Pennsylvania named Harry Brobst—has just moved to Providence to take an hospital job, & I'm shewing him the antiquities of the town. He is a bright young fellow—& is very fond of your work.

Best wishes—
Πάππος Νεκρόφιλος

[175] [HPL to DAW] [ALS]

8 March 1932

Dear Melmoth:—

"A Sea Change" is great! It gave me a tremendous kick, & I feel sure it will land the very first time it is tried on an editor. The atmosphere of gathering horror & abnormality is ineffably potent, & the mounting, insidious strain begins the moment that peculiar & unidentifiable cargo is mentioned on p. 6 .... greenish powder, gummy, malodorous substance, packages of seeds .... All the incidents are extremely well knit & motivated, & the whole thing ought to "go over big." If any criticism is called for, it relates only to the minor point of the manuscript's doubtful archaism. Though an 18th century date is indicated, the language in several places assumes forms unmistakably modern; while some of the scientific reflections—chemical & biological—display a vocabulary & point of view which could not well antedate the latter half of the 19th century. But of course no average reader—& probably no editor—would ever stop to think twice on this point. I shall presently send the tale along to Auguste-Guillaume, Comte d'Erlette, & feel sure that he will reflect my own really enthusiastic opinion of it. If I didn't feel sure of getting it in print before long, I'd hate to let the MS. go.

Glad my remarks on "Dead Titans Waken" proved helpful. I can appreciate your reluctance to start extensive changes—this being my own feeling under similar circumstances. The novel as a whole is a great piece of work, & Klarkash-Ton echoed my praise when it reached him—so, for that matter, did Augustulus Gulielmus. I certainly hope it will find a market in time, whether in approximately its present form or in the ultimately remodelled shape you contemplate. You are right in thinking the composition of such a novel good practice in developing your technique. There's no training better than actual performance. That, if you'll remember, was my object in hammering out the two still untyped novelettes whose illegible rough draughts you waded through in 1927. Your second novel, I presume, is that which will include the first half of the short story published as "Something from Outside."[1] I am eager to see it when it's done.

I am indeed glad you liked "Innsmouth"—whose locale you can in some measure visualise after having seen Newport & Marblehead, although Newburyport is more particularly my model. Glad, too, that your father enjoyed it. In the matter of alterations, the vote now stands a perfect tie—with you & Dwyer against change, & Derleth & Klarkash-Ton advising me to hint at the hero's taint & fate earlier in the story.[2] I don't think I'll touch the thing—it is, even in its present form, the result of much experiment, revision, & re-revision; & I feel sadly sure that if I tried to make it any better I'd merely make a general mess of it. A young artist friend of Derleth's[33]—whom he has commissioned to illustrate one of his own stories for W.T. (& Wright has accepted the drawings)—has drawn two gruesomely excellent sketches for "Innsmouth" in case it is ever published. One is of the *things* on the reef & swimming in the adjacent waters, & the other is of the narrator in the railway cut watching the nameless procession pass. But as for magazine submission—I'm holding off for a while, since the number of rebuffs & rejections I've been getting lately—Wright's turndown of "Mts. of Madness", stuff shot back by Bates, the Putnam fizzle, Cook's poor opinion of my recent things, &c—has begun to act on my nerves & induce in me a sort of tongue-tied or pen-tied condition. Occasionally I fancy I'm petering out as much better men than I are doing (where's Blackwood now? look at Dunsany's late stuff! Machen & James say they will write no more weird things, &c . . .)—& at any rate, I think the best thing for me to do is to lay off the editorial sieges for a spell; letting MSS. pile up as they did in the old pre-1923 days. Later on I'll be over my nervous depression—& anyway, it is less annoying to take rejection-chances on stuff written some time before. I can write much better if I don't feel immediate editorial bludgeons over my head. Thus I'm afraid I can't well take advantage of your extremely generous & poignantly appreciated offer to say a word to Bates in my favour. Let me thank you none the less, though, for your idea & intention. I really don't think that anything of mine could ever land with a Clayton publication, for the whole contents of S. T. & As. S. seems to be overrun with a peculiarly pervasive & tantalisingly indefinable kind of atmospheric philistinism inherent in the Clayton standard & far beyond my power or inclination to attain or approach.

Swanson's magazine—to be called *The Galaxy*—has yet to appear. It will be 10¢ per copy & $1.00 per year—& I don't know how well it will be distributed on the stands. Klarkash-Ton, d'Erlette, & I are subscribing for a year—letting Yᶜ Ed deduct the dollar from our first cheques. Wright seems to fear the coming magazine as a rival, & frowns on the use of reprints from W.T. He implied that he would resent my exercise of second serial rights in selling reprints to Swanson; but I politely told him, in effect, to go to hell & sit on a red-hot tack—for it was certainly damn nervy of him to expect me to grant him favours after the things of mine he's rejected, & after his failure to issue the book promised 5 years ago! I can afford to take the upper hand with him at this juncture, since I'm not sending him any more material. Belknap, however, is rather alarmed at the possible threats inherent in Wright's attitude; & is scuttling out of Swanson reprint arrangements like a frightened rabbit! Have you sold many things to Swanson as yet?

I can't get a word out of Loveman about "The Sphinx", though he writes most interestingly & enthusiastically about the new Egyptian statuette which he picked up for 15 bucks—probably a young royal prince of the Saite period, circa 600 B.C. But of course this silence implies that the book *isn't* out, for he promised me a copy as soon as it came off the press in any form. In these days there's many a slip betwixt cup & lip, & I fancy the Times notice was mournfully premature.

So *you've* been mugged lately! So has Derleth—by the same young fellow who has done those "Innsmouth" designs. A W says the result is good except that it flatters him. There would seem to be an element of mystery in the refusal of all three artists to shew you their results—do you suppose their uncanny insight glimpsed some unsuspected indwelling daemon whose lurking presence creeps out insidiously in the painted features? It would be well to probe this mystery!

Providence now has the nucleus of a "gang", for one of the W.T. Eyrie fans—a young Pennsylvania German from Allentown named Harry Brobst—has recently come hither to serve as student nurse in a celebrated local hospital for mental & nervous diseases. Brobst is of the old stock which settled in the Lehigh Valley around 1700, & has an Indian great-great-grandmother. His ancestral region is a truly remarkable backwater where primitive customs & superstitions survive—the "hex" country where witches are taken as a matter of course—& he is well versed in its history & antiquities. I have shewn him the antiquities of Providence, & he seems highly appreciative. Last Saturday we "did" both Bristol & Warren, dining at Maxfield's on 12 varieties of ice cream—all they have in winter. A fellow said that our triangular visit with Morton in 1927 is well remembered—our signed statement of having sampled all 28 varieties being often shown to travellers from near & far! They lost it, though, last summer. Now I must introduce Brobst to Jake's!

The gang meets next Friday at Talman's. Wish you & I could drop in! ¶ Best wishes—

Yr obt

Πάππος Νεκρόφιλος

P.S. Talman has just been nominated a Trustee of the austere & important Holland Society—a rare honour for a young man. He is also to be editor of the Society's official quarterly publication, De Halve Maen.[4] He will move back to Spring Valley in May—having fixed up an unused stable on the old estate as a sort of Dutch cottage.

Notes

1. HPL means "Something from Above." Neither of DAW's novels included anything resembling the story, although *Invisible Sun* makes brief mention of red rain as in that tale (see letter 19n3).

2. The letter in which CAS gave HPL his first reactions to "The Shadow over Innsmouth" does not survive. But see CAS to AWD, 16 February 1932: "I liked it greatly, especially in its rendering of a decadent atmosphere, and of course urged H. P. to submit it to Wright. I did, however, make what seemed to me a rather obvious suggestion about the addition of a new chapter, which could be worked in next to the last with very little verbal alteration of the story as it stands. This chapter would be made of the narrator's broken, nightmare-like memories of being captured by the rout of monsters, who take him back to Innsmouth, but do him no vulgar harm, since they recognize his latent kinship to themselves. Without his guessing the reason at the time, they subject him to some horrible rite that is calculated to accelerate the development of the alien strain in his blood, and then let him go. I fear, though, that he won't care for the suggestion" (*Selected Letters* 168–69). See also CAS to AWD, 24

February 1932 (ms., WHS): "[T]there should be more emphasis on the development of the taint, which, as it stands, has more the effect of an afterthought than an integral part of the story. Something very tremendous could be made of it."

3. Frank Utpatel (1905–1980) of Mazomanie, WI, whose woodcuts and pen-and-ink drawings decorated many of AWD's later books.

4. HPL's essay "Some Dutch Footprints in New England" appeared in the 18 October 1933 issue of *De Halve Maen*.

[176] [HPL to DAW] [ANS]

> [Postmarked Providence, R.I.,
> 26 March 1932]

Here's a magnificent thing of Klarkash-Ton's—full of vivid colour & creeping menace, & with an atmosphere worthy of E. A. P.

¶ Have you heard of the failure of the new Swanson magazine venture? He may experiment with a *mimeographed* magazine or series of booklets, but that doesn't sound very impressive.

¶ Vanguard Press lately asked to see some of my stuff, but there's not much chance that anything will come of it.

> Best wishes—
> H P L

[177] [HPL, W. Paul Cook, and H. Warner Munn to DAW] [ANS][1]

> [Postmarked Boston, Mass.,
> 21 April 1932]

Behold! The old 1927 gang in session again! Doesn't it make you 'homesick' for good old New England? We've just been over the North End, where I *tried* to shew you the sinister scene of "Pickman's Model", only to find that the archaic, tottering houses were torn down.

> Regards—Πάππος Νεκρόφιλος

If you were here, we could attempt a midnight meeting in Copps Hill burying with the slab over Increase Mather to sit on, instead of Poe's lounging place in Providence.

> W. P. Cook

We plan to break into Copp's Hill shortly & unearth the remains of poor Pickman—H. W. Munn

Notes

1. *Front:* Esplanade along Charles River, Showing West Boston Bridge, Boston, Mass.

[178] [HPL to DAW] [ANS][1]

[Postmarked New Orleans, La.,
6 June 1932]

Aiming at Melmoth records again! This is a great trip. Stopped a week in N Y with Belknap & then hopped off for the real voyage. The Shenandoah Valley was magnificent. At Chattanooga I was fascinated by Lookout Mt.—the views therefrom & the marvellous caverns inside. All Tennessee is exquisitely beautiful—especially the Cumberlands & the bluffs along the Tenn. River. At Memphis I saw your own Mississippi River for the first time. Then the cotton country—Vicksburg & Natchez. The latter is a vivid relic of old times, with the finest subtropical scenery I have ever beheld. ¶ New Orleans is of course a modern metropolis, but the picturesque old quarter is not a disappointment. Exotic charm is as prevalent as in Charleston & Quebec. I'm here for over a week devouring as much of the past as I can. My return trip will be gradual, with stops at interesting old places like Mobile. Very faint hope of getting to Charleston. Best wishes—Πάππος Νεκρόφιλος

Notes

1. *Front:* Royal Street, New Orleans, La.

[179] [HPL and E. Hoffmann Price to DAW] [ANS][1]

[Postmarked New Orleans, La.,
15 June 1932]

Peace with thee, Melmoth! Look at this convocation of necromancers! A 25½ hour session was the result of our first contact.

Yr obt
Πάππος Νεκρόφιλος

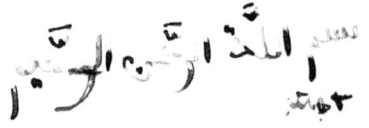 and after, Greetings & the Peace—
E Hoffmann Price

Notes

1. *Front:* Fan Window in Governor Claiborne Home, New Orleans, La.

[180] [HPL and James F. Morton to DAW] [ANS]

[Postmarked Newport, R.I.,
5 August 1932]

Hail, Melmoth! Here are two of the 1927 triad, but where is our young Tertius Quis? Yesterday we had quite a '27-ish day—Maxfield's at noon, & Jake's in the evening. When is that eastern trip of yours coming?

Yrs for the Elder Sign—
Πάππος Νεκρόφιλος

Salutations from the least of the erstwhile pilgrims to the Berkeleyan shrine. If you are acquainted with one Howard Wandrei, pray convey to him my gratulations on his admirable production.

J. F. M.

[P.S. by HPL:] A man in Los Angeles wants to set 2 of my Yuggothian fungi to music.[1]

Notes

1. Harold S. Farnese set "Mirage" and "The Elder Pharos" (*WT*, February–March 1931) from *Fungi from Yuggoth*, to music, but HPL neither heard nor saw the finished work. Now printed in *Fungi from Yuggoth: An Annotated Edition*.

[181] [HPL to DAW] [ALS]

10 Barnes St.,
Providence, R.I.,
Aug. 18, 1932

Dear Melmoth II:—

Welcome to the East! M. le Comte d'Erlette informed me that you were headed this way, & I have since been on the lookout for bulletins. Glad you have seen Kirk & Loveman, & hope you'll be in touch shortly with Belknap & James Ferdinand. The latter, as our Newport card may have informed you, has been in the Providence zone recently; & we spoke much of you & the old days at Maxfield's in Warren, assimilated hamburg & onions at Jake's, & discussed the cosmos with Dean Berkeley's shade on the rugged cliffs of Newport. You certainly must get around here—& for as long a time as possible—at the earliest possible date. Despite the melancholy changes wrought by time—& I thank you sincerely for your words of sympathy concerning my bereavement[1]—you will find plenty of landmarks remaining from 1927; & I feel sure that they will awaken pleasant recollections. My aunt Mrs. Gamwell will be delighted to see you once more. If possible, try to arrange for a side-trip to Boston, where Cook is now dwelling. He would be greatly disappointed if he did not see you.

I hope you have not renounced academic shades so definitely that you can't turn to them again if need presses. Parnassus, unfortunately, offers few financial rewards; & most strugglers on its slopes find themselves condemned to a degrading sort of hack-work & mob-catering far more undesirable than any amount of pedagogical routine. It is pitiful to see a finely-endowed chap like E. Hoffmann Price, for instance, turning all his energies to the cold concoction of catchpenny trash to suit the whims of philistine editors. I think I told you that I met Price & saw a good deal of him in New Orleans. I have also come into touch with the weird writer Hugh B. Cave—a fellow Rhode-Islander, though he is now spending the summer at Poultney, Vermont. As for the American Fiction Guild—here is a circular which came to me not long ago, & which will give you some idea of it. I'm not joining, because I am virtually out of the magazine field now. Wright rejected my best story, Bates has rejected all I've sent, & it is clear that I can never land anything more unless I cater to the debased pulp ideal—which I shall never do. Cave is New England manager of the Guild. He urged me to join, but I soon convinced him that I am not the right sort of material. Still—I think the venture is a good move for those interested in that sort of thing. I wish it luck, & would join except for the yearly $10.00. You might return the circulars some time—since the thing is of mild interest even though I don't find it suited to me.

Sorry you can't manage the European trip, but hope you can get to Baja-California or some subtropical equivalent for the winter. If you go there, you ought to plan a route through Alta-California & stop to see Klarkash-Ton, High-Priest of Tsathoggua & Consul-General for Atlantis & Saturn! My recommendation for winter-quarters, though, would be *Florida*. Old St. Augustine is delightful beyond words—& if you got over to Dunedin on the west coast Whitehead would be overjoyed to welcome you.

Cook & I expect to get north to Boston—say Newburyport or Portsmouth—to see the total eclipse. Septr. 2–5 I hope to take advantage of an incredibly cheap rail excursion ($12.00) to Montreal & Quebec advertised by the B. & M.

Did I mention that a composer named Farnese is about to set two of my "Fungi from Yuggoth" to music? Another faintly pleasing incident is the appearance in the July *American Author* of an article on fiction-writing in which Klarkash-Ton, Edmond Hamilton (de gustibus, &c) & I are selected for praise & quotation.[2]

Wishing you an uniformly pleasant season of wandering, & hoping to get a generous glimpse of you not far hence, I am ever

Yr obt Grandsire
Melmoth III.

Notes

1. HPL's aunt Lillian D. Clark died 3 July 1932.
2. J. Randle Luten, "What Makes a Story Click," *American Author* 4, No. 4 (July 1932): 11–13; rpt. in Joshi, *Weird Writer* 56–62.

[182] [HPL to DAW] [ALS]

Aug. 23[, 1932]

Dear #2:—

Good luck with your work in both hack & serious lines—& may you share the uncanny ability of Comte d'Erlette to keep the real stuff untainted by the pot-boilers. I dare say that much university work can be as monotonous & uninspired as literary hacking, though it seems to me it could scarcely have all the detestable insincerity of the latter process. Glad, anyway, that the return road is open—& I fancy the interruption will do you no harm. By the way—Robert E. Howard is tremendously fond of your work in W.T., especially those truly vivid verses "The Little Gods Wait." Possibly he has dropped you a line or so of congratulation—he asked for your address some time ago.

As for my stuff—what Bates probably meant was that the MSS. I sent were not new ones. The reason I hesitate to try new work on him is that he won't promise not to mutilate it. I can't have a garbled version of my things floating around—perhaps to be copied, unknown to me, in some anthology like the "Not at Nights." He'll never get any serious MSS. until he abandons his high-handed insistence on the *jus mutilandi.*[1] But I don't think he'd consider anything whatever of mine, for the existing contents of the magazine indicates a policy hostile to actual originality.

On the whole, I am getting very dissatisfied with my own work, & don't know how much longer I'll try to continue writing. My later things have elicited an unusually large number of unfavourable opinions from those to whom I have lent them, & the earlier things—with certain exceptions—look hideously crude & immature to me. Of course, I still do experimenting—but if I can't succeed in expressing myself better than heretofore I fancy I shall lapse into a dignified silence. So far, I don't believe I've produced more than two really good tales in all my years of effort—these exceptions being "The Colour Out of Space" & "Erich Zann." My most serious work was put into the "Mountains of Madness"—a thing which about ¾ of those who have seen it (including Cook) have disliked.

I surely hope to see you in Providence next month. While here you will meet an interesting young man who has a high opinion of your work—one Harry Brobst of Allentown, Pa., who came here last February to take a post in a local hospital.

Yesterday I received a complimentary copy of the new British edition of the Hammett anthology—which is quite prepossessing in appearance. You no doubt have one awaiting you at home.

Cook & I have decided to view the eclipse from Newburyport—or Portsmouth if we can find cheap 'bus connexions. We shall stop in Haverhill & see our 80-year-old friend C. W. Smith, & if possible will add him to our party as a guest. Then—on Septr. 2—I shall leave Boston for Montreal & Quebec. May great Tsathoggua grant me decent weather for both events!

Have you seen Morton & Belknap yet? They'll surely be overjoyed to revive old times. You'll find Talman at the offices of the Texas Co. on the 18th floor of the Chrysler Bldg.—his office telephone is MUrray Hill 2-7701, Extension 492. His home address is Spring Valley, N.Y., for this spring he fitted up the old disused stable on his paternal estate as a house for his own occupancy—deciding to become a commuter. He always did hate urbanism.

Well—best wishes, & hope to be taking you around to Jake's & Maxfield's & Eddy's Book Shop & Newport &c. before long.

> Yr obt Grandsire
> Melmoth #3.

Notes

1. HPL's coinage meaning "the law [or right] of mutilation," parallel to such legal phrases as *jus gentium* (the law of nations).

[183] [HPL and W. Paul Cook to DAW] [ANS][1]

> [Postmarked Newburyport, Mass.,
> 1 September 1932]

Hail, Melmoth! Eclipse expedition a success—& now some loafing in ancient Newburyport. Friday I start for Montreal & Quebec. The totality was longer than we expected, & the scene was darkened more deeply than in 1925. We both hope to see you in New England next month.

> Yr obt Melmoth III.

I shall most certainly plan to spend a day with you and Lovecraft in Providence if you get as far as that. Would that we could also induce Munn to come down and repeat our graveyard meeting of some years ago.

> P. Cook

Notes

1. *Front:* Dr. Peter Toppan House. Built 1697. Newburyport, Mass.

[184] [HPL to DAW] [ANS][1]

> [Postmarked Montreal, Canada,
> 3 September 1932]

. . . . And the Melmothing goes on! Montreal is all right—very fascinating in a way—but has not the rich antiquarian background of old Quebec. Shall be in Q. tomorrow after an all-night ride. Home Thursday—hope to see you soon.

Regards—
Πάππος

Notes

1. *Front:* Chateau de Raezay, Montreal.

[185] [HPL to DAW] [ANS][1]

[Postmarked Providence, R.I.,
8 September 1932]

Home again & digesting both your messages. Welcome! I'll be watching for you Saturday or Sunday morning. You'll probably meet another bright young poet with a book to his credit—Carl F. Strauch,[2] who is in town confabulating with Brobst (his closest friend in Allentown) & me. Strauch expects to leave around the 15th. ¶ Yes—space in good old #10 still awaits you; & if you want to get your old room, you can at least have its equivalent. They're installing a new 3d. floor bathroom—though probably too early for you to use. ¶ Did Marblehead yesterday, to make the letdown from old Quebec a bit easier. Cook is very anxious to see you, & I'm keeping him posted concerning your whereabouts in a series of up-to-date postcard bulletins. I surely hope that sunburn will clear up in time for you to enjoy your visit! Have you looked up *Morton* yet? He wants to see you. Until Sat—or Sun.—

Yr obt Servt
Melmoth III

Glad you can stay longer than you expected.

Notes

1. *Front:* Escaliers, Rue Petit Champlain, Quebec, Canada.
2. *Twenty-nine Poems* (Boston: Bruce Humphries, [1932]).

[186] [HPL to DAW] [ANS][1]

[Postmarked Providence, R.I.,
10 September 1932]

Damnation! Just got your special. Hope the doc will give you some quick-healing salve calculated to ensure your arrival on Tuesday at least! The dark entities of the nether crypts are impatient! I've notified Cook of the regrettable postponement. ¶ Strauch turned out to be a prodigiously bright & likeable young fellow—sorry you couldn't have met him. I took him to see the famous Harris Collection of Am. poetry at the Brown library—a thing I had never before inspected myself. The curator said that your two books would be very welcome if you'd send them in. At Maxfield's Brobst gave out after

the 3d double order, while Strauch was stalled in the midst of the 4th. I finished the 4th & wished I could afford more! Morton & I remain the undisputed champions! ¶ Well—don't fail to be here Tuesday the 11th. Awaiting the day—
Melmoth III

Notes

1. *Front:* Old State House, Boston, Mass.

Wandrei visited Lovecraft in Providence from 13 to 20 September 1932.

[187] [HPL to DAW] [ANS][1]

[Postmarked Providence, R.I.,
26 September 1932]

Welcome to your new address! Trust you had a pleasant trip back, & wish it could have been at a later date. I haven't done anything lately except try to get caught up on work. Still using Congo Black ink, but am going to do some more experimenting with exchanges of my fountain pen. I simply can't seem to get anything that will write smoothly & rapidly nowadays. ¶ Beastly cold yesterday, but today isn't so bad. Am getting my winter suits put in order by the tailor—brrrr . . . . . . ¶ Hope your new quarters are pleasant. I fancy you must be in the northern part of Greenwich Village, not so far from the Hudson River, if my memory for Metropolitan addresses remains sound.[2] Hope to hear from you soon.
          Best wishes—
                    Grandpa

Notes

1. *Front:* University Hall and Manning Hall, Brown University.
2. DAW had settled with his brother Howard at 84 Horatio Street in Greenwich Village.

[188] [HPL to DAW] [ALS]

Oct[r] 19, 1932

Hail, Melmoth!:—

Glad to hear that you find your new quarters comfortable, but sorry that a cold was piled on top of your sunburn. Trust you'll be careful to keep clear of ills from now onward!

A week ago Sunday I made the rounds of Salem & Marblehead as a sort of farewell to the season—the day was exquisitely warm & sunny, & the half-turned autumn foliage made a haunting landscape. Since then has come a cold spell, followed by a spell of summerlike warmth unfortunately vitiated with rain. A steady downpour of 2 days seems ambitious to rival the cloudburst which marked your recent visit! Incidentally, I hope you can get here again before you return to the West. Brobst inquired about you & sent his regards the other day. His feverish spell last month was not of long duration.

I surely hope Loveman can get here next week, & that he'll allow a decent amount of time for sightseeing. He ought to go over the Harris Collection of Poetry (in which he is represented) as well as taking in Newport (which he's never seen), Boston, & other points. Sorry our card didn't reach Georgius Circus.[1] But let that prove a lesson in legible addressing!

Commiserations on the rejection of "Dead Titans". Hope it can find a typographical haven in time. The long retentions prove that it was not looked upon with utter disfavour. I'll be interested to see the revised "Lives of Alfred Kramer", & am glad it is achieving publication. When I get a chance I must read the last two issues of W.T.—set aside at present for lack of an available moment. And your novel will command my interest whenever I receive the promised extracts. Hope that Bates-Clayton will take your time-travelling tale for *Astounding*.[2]

I must get this new *Strange Tales* of which you speak so highly, & which I didn't know was out. Possibly you have learned (as I did last week from E. Hoffmann Price) that the present issue is the last, the inexorable Clayton having ordered its discontinuance. This will be quite a blow for those who, like Whitehead, Klarkash-Ton, Cave, Little Augie, Howard, &c., had secured a regular entrée [*sic*] to its pages. By the way—Price has moved back to New Orleans from Bay St. Louis, & is now to be addressed at 1416 Josephine St.—which is in the old American section south of the Vieux Carré. He is urging me to collaborate on a sequel to "The Silver Key"—or perhaps I mentioned this before.[3]

Since my aestival truancies I've been trying to catch up with work & correspondence—but so far in vain. An additional difficulty is getting a fountain pen to suit me. My regular one wasn't smooth enough for the stack of work I had to do—hence a series of experiments not yet concluded. I'm about ready to give up & go back to the steel pen. I need something both highly flexible & unusually free of flow—something which will write without any bearing-on. At present I've gone back to blue-black ink because it flows a trifle better than Congo Black.

Have got my dinners at home a good deal lately—out of cans—but when I do go out I tend to favour our old reliable Plymouth.

Belknap read my "Shadow Over Innsmouth" & thought it shewed a decline in the old man's powers. Between that opinion & Comte d'Erlette's annihilation of "Witch House", I'm about ready to fade from the map. Incidentally—my present ghosting job amounts virtually to the writing of an original story.[4]

Well—be good.

> Yr most obt Grandsire
> —Melmoth III.

[*Enclosure:* Clipping from *Providence Evening Bulletin* (?): "A Severe Case of Sunburn North of the Arctic Circle: A School of Walrus . . ."] You Arctic denizens—it runs in the blood!

[On envelope:] Just got a fine set of rattlesnake rattles from Robert E. Howard. His letter accompanying them is a veritable prose-poem with the uncon-
querable serpent as its theme. I'll shew it to you.[5]

Notes

1. I.e., George W. Kirk.
2. Possibly "A Race through Time."
3. "Through the Gates of the Silver Key."
4. "The Horror in the Museum," written for Hazel Heald.
5. Published as "With a Set of Rattlesnake Rattles," *Leaves* 1 (Summer 1937): 24. In *A
Means to Freedom.*

[189] [HPL to DAW] [ANS]

> [Postmarked Providence, R.I.,
> 20 December 1932]

> [With Hearty Christmas Greetings]
> Melmoth to Melmoth—1932

[190] [HPL, Wilfred B. Talman, and FBL to DAW] [ANS][1]

> [Postmarked New York, N.Y.,
> 27? December 1932]

All hail, Melmoth! Another Melmoth has unexpectedly taken to the road, & is
the guest of our sophisticated young friend Belknap. Meeting of the gang at
230 W. 97th St. on FRIDAY, DEC. 30, 1932, at 8 P.M.—& it will not be
complete without your presence . . . if you're still in this decadent cosmopolis.
We may try to call on you before you get this, but we drop the line in case we
don't find you. How is the literary work getting along? Suppose you've heard
the depressing news of Whitehead's death.[2] Do you think you can get to
Prov. again this winter? Well—hope to see you—Grandpa

Long time no see! Why not drop in at Room 1830, Chrysler Bldg?

> Talman

Greetings! I sincerely hope you will be able to join us—Belknap

Notes

1. *Front:* Cathedral of St. John the Divine—New York City.
2. Whitehead had died 23 November.

1933

[191] [HPL to DAW] [ALS]

Tenbarnes Manor
—Feby. 4, 1933

Dear Melmoth:—

Note the delicate pen-stroke—my eternal troubles continue! At last I've got a device that feeds freely enough—but it has this microscopic point which isn't good for much except writing the Lord's Prayer on the head of a pin, or something of that sort. Back to the shop again tomorrow for Grandpa. This ink is what they gave me at the shop—I guess it's Sheaffer's. I fear I'll have to come around to the more expensive brands sooner or later, for they certainly have a free-flowing thinness which Waterman's & Carter's Kongo Black can't boast. But *damn* this pen-point! The oaf at the shop said it would spread & limber up with a bit of use—yet look at it! May Tsathoggua grind it to atoms with his fangs!

I shall be on the lookout for your novel, & shan't let the verdict of M. le Comte d'Erlette prejudice me.[1] But even if it isn't an uniformly perfect masterpiece, you have no reason to be discouraged. What do you expect from a *first attempt* in the serious non-weird field? Even if it falls short of your goal, it has been a potent aid toward your literary development—& you can always return to it with revisory touches. Yet on the other hand it may be quite all right as it is—for of course Comte d'Erlette represents only one critical point of view. Incidentally—I won't mention it to anyone save M. le Comte . . . . although Little Belknap would revel in it if it's really shocking! I'll endeavour not to suffer too great a shock at its more gamey parts—in these days of old age I'm rather unshockable, looking at the world from a distance, & treating all that happens on it as mere objective phenomena without preferential values. I'll tell you after I read it whether I think you need to employ a pseudonym. Authors can boldly get by with a lot in these latter days.

I was sorry not to see you on the final day of my sojourn in Antioch, & hope you'll get to old Providentium again before you quit this general part of the world. No doubt Jonckheer Wilfredus has apprised you of the arrival of David Frederic Talman, heir to the dignities of Rockland County Squireship. Sonny Belknap has had a bad attack of influenza since our get-together (temp. up to 105°), but is now well out of the woods. Hope you'll get around his way again. But what you *must* do is to pay a call on our good old pal James Ferdinand—who feels quite desolate at the desertion of a young friend. He is tremblingly awaiting the descent of the municipal axe upon museum appropriations, but does not believe his job will vanish entirely. Glad you had a good chat with Quinn—whom I haven't had a chance to see since 1931. Incidentally—I rather suspected that his reprint payments are due to reserved rights. I've been reserving all but first rights since May, 1926—but I had so much published *before* then that Satrap Pharnabazus can keep on reprinting me for years without coughing up anything.

Hope you'll take a good rest now that the novel is done. A full-length play sounds very interesting—but oughtn't you to practice considerably in the technique of the drama before attempting such an ambitious performance in an unfamiliar medium? Or perhaps you *have* done such practicing.

No—I haven't written anything lately. Other tasks have pressed, & I am more & more dissatisfied with my products. The somewhat discouraging criticisms & rejections of the last two years have tended to shake my confidence in the junk I grind out.

Quite an interesting series of poetry readings is being given in Prov. this winter. Last week, Robert Hillyer, tomorrow, Leonard Bacon, & Feby. 19 the one & only *T. S. Eliot*.[2] ¶ Awaiting the novel, & meanwhile exuding all the favourable wishes in Pegāna, I remain

> Yr most obt Servt
> Melmoth II.

P.S. Dwyer has a wistful little story on which he wishes the opinions of all of us. He is circulating it around, & you will soon get it from Belknap. After perusal please send it to Robert E. Howard.

Notes

1. *Invisible Sun.* For HPL's discussion of the novel with AWD, see *ES* 552–53.
2. HPL refers to the American poets Robert Hillyer (1895–1961), Leonard Bacon (1887–1954), and T. S. Eliot (1888–1965). He attended all three readings.

[192] [HPL to DAW] [ANS][1]

> [Postmarked Providence, R.I.,
> 17 February 1933]

NOTICE: Fra Bernardus asks me to ask you to insert one more name on the circulation list of the story which is coming or has come to you from Sonny

Belknap. Put it next your own, & before Two-Gun Bob's—
                        E. HOFFMANN PRICE,
                      1416 JOSEPHINE ST.,
                          NEW ORLEANS, LA.

Comte d'Erlette has not yet sent me your story, but will soon. Meanwhile the young imp shewed Wright my "Dreams in the Witch House", so that Satrap Pharnabazus is buying it at $140.00! I can surely use the cash! ¶ Price has lately come upon some *genuine* folklore closely resembling my pre-terrestrial Yog-Sothoth stuff—he promises particulars later.[2]
Best wishes—Grandpa

Notes

1. *Front:* Main Foyer, Looking Toward Front Door, Crane National Exhibit, Boardwalk, Atlantic City, N. J.
2. Price had mentioned the following books for HPL's consideration: Annie Besant (1847–1933), *The Pedigree of Man* (London: Theosophical Publishing Society, 1904); Helena Petrovana Blavatsky (1831–1891), *The Secret Doctrine* (London: Theosophical Publishing Co., 1888); C. W. Leadbeater (1847–1934), *The Inner Life* (Chicago: Rajput Press, 1911–12; 2 vols.); W. Scott-Elliot (1849–1919), *The Story of Atlantis and the Lost Lemuria* (London: Theosophical Publishing Society, 1925); and A. P. Sinnett (1840–1921), *Esoteric Buddhism* (Boston: Houghton, Mifflin, 1898).

[193] [HPL to DAW] [ALS]
                                    10 Barnes St.,
                                        Providence, R.I.,
                                            Feby. 21, 1933.
Dear Melmoth:—
              It's all right about Bnādvai-Aā's story. I've dropped a line to Klarkash-Ton which ought to deflect it toward the Peacock Throne in New Orleans—& even if it doesn't, the postage isn't so great that Bernardus can't sent it out again on an independent southward journey. My opinion of "Flash" seems to coincide with yours. Much in Dwyer's style is immature & naive—as is natural in one so largely a recluse—but for all that he has as delicate & sensitive a response to the subtle overtones of perception & existence as anyone I've ever encountered. If his energies could be properly centralised on a rigorous course of training, he could produce remarkable stuff. Indeed, I believe he *will* produce good material later on, training or no training—for he is slowly acquiring an experience & background which will serve him in good stead. I did not realise till lately how few weird classics he has read. He never approached *Blackwood* till this winter.
    About the novel—M. le Comte got ahead of your admonition & sent it on to Grandpa, so here it is before me. So far I've only dipped tentatively into

it—& mindful of what you say about the superseded nature of the present text, I shan't read it as thoroughly & critically as I otherwise would. Sorry it will require rewriting—but after all, it would be remarkable if it did not, since it is a first effort in its particular vein. What I have seen of it looks to me exceedingly mature & promising. I certainly think you are catching hold of the spirit & technique of serious general fiction—so that you'll be close on d'Erlette's heels in the climb toward actual literary achievement & recognition. I'll add a few more comments after skimming through the whole MS.— & will return the latter safely by express. Trust your hack activities won't keep you too exhausted to admit of the zestful tackling of the revision later on.

Comte d'Erlette was kinder to me than to Wright in negotiating the "Witch House" sale, since he does not like the story himself. No—I don't think Satrap Pharnabazus' attitude is greatly changed, since only recently he said he was in the market only for material under 10,000 words—which most emphatically lets "Innsmouth" out.[1] If I were you I'd send him more stuff. Even if the pay comes a year later it's better to have it then than not at all—& the sooner you get anything accepted, the sooner you *will* be paid. There's no longer any chance of placing a weird MS. anywhere except with Wright.

I certainly hope you can get a regular position of some sort. I'd give my eye-teeth for one, since I can't make revision & occasional writing yield any sort of adequate revenue. In a few years I shall have to bump myself off with gas, pistol, or anything else handy! Only last week my aunt & I had a desperate colloquy on family finances, & we virtually decided that I'll have to give up my quarters at #10 before long unless some fortunate miracle intervenes. Probably the two households will have to double up in one cheap flat— though I hope we can manage to keep in a good neighbourhood. I certainly wish that I knew how to get hold of some kind of regular job—though naturally the present period is about the worst conceivable time to look for such a thing. Ars longa, pecunia brevis![2]

Best wishes—& I'll be sending the MS. on before long.

Yr oblig'd & ob^t Servt

—Grandpa Melmoth III.

P.S. Heard an interesting reading by the erudite & chaotic T. S. Eliot last Sunday. He included the first & last parts of the now-classic "Waste Land."

Notes

1. Unknown to HPL, AWD had recently submitted "The Shadow over Innsmouth" to *WT*, but FW rejected the story because it was too long to publish in one installment and could not be published in two parts without disrupting the mood (see FW to AWD, 17 January 1933; ms., WHS).

2. "Art is long, money is short," a play on a Latin axiom, *ars longa, vita brevis* (art is long, life is short).

[194] [HPL to DAW] [ALS]

Monday [27 February 1933]

Dear Melmoth:—

Well—I've just finished going over "Invisible Sun", & must hasten to record an opinion *much more favourable* than that of the lofty young Comte d'Erlette. It is possible that an expert on the novel (which I most decidedly am not) could suggest useful reproportionings here & there; but to me the thing stands as a very effective unit—a consistent study of a definite, unique type in a distinctive artificial environment, with the significance of the early incidents well brought out in the final portions & denouement. Derleth thinks the violent ending immature—but I don't. Look at the multitudes of accounts of such tragedies in the newspapers! Nature & reality are often naively melodramatic. D'Erlette also objects to the flashy & artificial conversation, but I think that is essential in reproducing the artificial atmosphere. My own chief objection would concern the Greek-Chorus Fool, who seems to me rather mechanically theatrical. Eugene O'Neill employs such obviously symbolic devices, but I do not think they add to the strength & naturalness of his plays. Also—I am inclined to question the convincingness of the eleventh-hour diabolus ex machina effect furnished by Pudge—the sudden & complete success of his machinations. He has things too much his own way, it seems to me, for the *average* of real life, even though such an outcome might occur in an individual case. As for trifles—I think you have your *dates* a little vague. You place 1926 (the perfect Christmas) & 1930 (death of parents) too close together. It couldn't be more than 1928, I judge by the flow of the action, when Mr. & Mrs. Gordon were killed. You use the expression "flu" before that slang abbreviation was coined (1918) & have a Gandhi impersonation before the Mahatma became a wildly popular subject of jest. There may be other similar points which I missed in my cursory survey—but of course they are minor trifles. Look to your spelling, also—there are occasional slips.

But the whole thing is damned powerful—tragedy in the paramount sense which is independent of all transient values; i.e., the destruction, by deeply seated & inevitable forces, of a character having the highest innate potentialities. I think you have developed & modulated this tragic sweep magnificently, & would not advise any substantial change in the order of parts in any subsequent revision. And there is some splendid poetry in the early portions. The character-drawing seems on the whole excellent. If we at first wonder how a boy reared in such a wholesome home & with such cosmic tastes could so readily condone a decadent circle of companions, we have only, alas, to turn to real life in order to find that such cases actually exist.

Regarding the repulsiveness of the latter scenes—to which, amusingly enough, the otherwise none too squeamish Comte d'Erlette is inclined to object—I do not think that they form any breach of artistry. It is the business of the artist to relate whatever is significant in reality; & if this rottenness truly typifies an important stratum of contemporary youth, it is certainly of grave significance as a social tendency. Nothing is gained by whitewashing or sentimentalising. What is essentially bestial & inartistic in life must be bestially & harshly shewn. Blame life, not the artist. The loathsome lives of the swine portrayed in this novel, if they are indeed a widespread & characteristic phenomenon, are logical results of the so-called "new morality" which proceeds from the abandonment of harmonic patterns & aesthetic values in the art of living. Our younger generation now glorify fornication, adultery, & sodomy. Next will come a worship of incest—with brothers & sisters, parents & children, glorying in a warmer tie now despised by "old-fashioned prejudice"— the frenzied maenad & the goat of the Sabbat. A beautiful world, with beautiful trends, is that world of anti-Puritanism which our young friend Belknap exalts so passionately! You have shewn it as it deserves to be shewn!

Deep snow on the ground—damnation! Here's to its early melting. And again, congratulations on your achievement.

> Yr obt grandsire—
> Melmoth III.

P.S. Am returning the MS. by express.

[On envelope:] [P.]P.S. I think the *length* of the novel is just about right. If shortened at all, I think it ought to be by the compression of conversations, mental soliloquies, & single episodes, rather than by the omission of any chapter or element (except The Fool) as a whole. Don't let a few adverse verdicts shake your confidence in it. It's really great stuff! ¶ I suppose Klarkash-Ton has mentioned his design of having a booklet printed—containing six of his best tales, all rejected by Wright—"Double Shadow", "Malneant", &c.[1]

Notes

1. *The Double Shadow and Other Fantasies* (1933) contains "The Voyage of King Euvoran"; "The Maze of the Enchanter"; "The Double Shadow"; "A Night in Malnéant"; "The Devotee of Evil"; and "The Willow Landscape."

[195] [HPL to DAW] [ALS]
Note well for reference   66 COLLEGE ST.,
                                           Providence, R.I.,
                                           May 31, 1933.
Dear Melmoth:—

Here's just a line to apprise you of my changed address. I think I told you that economic pressure was forcing me to double up with my surviving aunt in an inexpensive flat—but I have yet to tell you of the marvellous bargain we found . . . . a bargain which makes our move *down* look like a move *up*, & which at last—after 40 years—places me for the first time in a *real colonial house.*

You no doubt remember our visit to the marble John Hay Library with its Harris Collection—& our taste of such worthies as Frederick Tuckerman & Park Barnitz.[1] At that time it is just possible that I pointed out to you a yellow colonial house behind the library—at the back of a rather quaint rustic court leading off from the steep slope of College St.—mentioning that a friend of my aunt's lived in the lower half of it. Well—your Grandpa Melmoth lives in the upper half of it now! My aunt's friend—a high-school teacher of German[2]—had long wanted her to move in above her if ever the flat should be vacant. On May 1st it *did* become vacant, & my aunt was duly informed. We looked it over, found it would be ideal for both, & at once clinched the bargain. You can imagine how I felt at the prospect of living in a real colonial house! Our respective quarters will be wholly separate except for dining room, &c.—& yet the general effect will be that of a complete & homogeneous home—my study corresponding to the library & my aunt's living-room to the parlour. The place looks ineffably homelike with my belongings—& since I have 2 rooms of my own, I don't have to crowd the furniture as I did at 10 Barnes. My colonial mantel is the focal point of the study—on it are old candlesticks, vases, & clock, & above it is that marine painting of my mother's, now framed in a manner suited to the Georgian atmosphere. My aunt has not moved in yet, but will begin tomorrow. I am wholly settled. Arranging my books & files was a hellish job—I had to get 4 new cases & a cabinet for pamphlets—but it is done at last. The house—as you may possibly remember from my having pointed it out—is a square wooden edifice of the 1800 period. The fine colonial doorway is like my bookplate come to life, though of a slightly later period with side lights & fan carving instead of a fanlight. In the rear is a picturesque, village-like garden at a higher level than the front of the house. The upper flat we have taken contains 5 rooms besides bath & kitchenette nook on the main (2nd) floor, plus 2 attic  storerooms—one of which is so attractive that I wish I could have it for an extra den! My quarters (see sketch map)—a large study & a small adjoining bedroom—are on the south side, with my working desk under a west window affording a splendid view of the lower town's outspread roofs & of the mystical sunsets that flame behind them. The interior is as fascinating as the exterior—with colonial fireplaces, mantels, & chimney cupboards, curving Georgian staircase, wide floor-boards, old-fashioned latches, small-paned windows, six-panel doors, rear wing with floor at a different level (3 steps

down), quaint attic stairs, &c.—just like the old houses open as museums. After admiring such all my life, I find something magical & dreamlike in the experience of actually *living in one* . . . . . I keep half-expecting a museum guard to come around & kick me out at 5 o'clock closing time! And yet the whole thing costs only what I've been paying for one room & alcove at #10. The house is owned by the university, & steam heat & hot water are piped in from the adjacent John Hay. Little did I think, when we were there last summer on the trail of Barnitz & Tuckerman, that from that classic building would come my daily supply of caloric! Since I now have so much space, I have picked up a folding camp cot to enable me to accomodate an occasional guest. Thus the next time you're here—which I hope will be during the present season—you need not worry about hotel bills. What lodging could be more appropriate for you than one next to Barnitz & Tuckerman, & just up the hill from Jake's? Brobst has seen the place both before & after the moving, & agrees that it's a pretty homelike dump.

I trust all goes well at #84. Have you been to see James Ferdinand at the museum yet? Cook has found the unbound edition of my "Shunned House", & it is about to be bound & marketed by Coates of *Driftwind*. I'll see that you get a copy. By the way—I presume you've seen Klarkash-Ton's circular describing his forthcoming brochure of tales.

Moving has made me miss all the spring weather, & I doubt if I can take a southern trip this year. But Cook & I may get to N.Y. early in July for the N.A.P.A. convention.

Best wishes—& don't forget the new address.

Yr obt Grandsire—Melmoth III.

[On envelope:] [P.S.] As arranged, my weird books fill over 17 feet of shelfage!

[P.P.S.] Pardon the envelope. Nobody's dead, but I found some of these in looking over my things & want to get rid of 'em. Fairly appropriate, though, for a necrophagous old ghoul!

Notes

1. Frederick Tuckerman (1821–1873), American poet, lawyer, and scientist; David Park Barnitz (1878–1901), American poet.
2. Alice Sheppard.

[196] [HPL to DAW] [ALS]

June 10, 1933

Dear II:—

        Breaking in the new stationery with which my aunt surprised me this morning. She is now getting settled here, & the place is beginning to have an exceedingly homelike atmosphere. Many things from the old home, long in storage from lack of space, are now exhumed & displayed—so that I am often carried back in fancy to pre-1904 days. Over the staircase is a huge painting (Rocks at Narragansett Pier) by my late elder aunt. For 29 years there has been no place large enough to hang it—I wish she could have survived to see it reinstated in visible dignity! I certainly hope you can get around here before long. As I told you, I have obtained a camp cot for occasional guests, so that no hotel responsibilities will be involved. Incidentally—Cook & I may see you in N.Y. next month, for we have a vague idea of attending the N.A.P.A. Convention July 3–4–5.

        I've just written Culinarius asking if he can get you an unbound set of Shunned House sheets. If he can't, you can have my set after I get a bound copy. It certainly flatters me to hear that you deem my humble yarn worth preserving in more than average elegance! I haven't the remotest notion of what the price & manner of distribution will be. Coates of Driftwind has taken over the whole business—& I suppose he will try to market it just as he does the books he prints himself—however that is. By the way—Coates's new Driftwind anthology is just out (containing my Yuggothian fungus "The Canal"),[1] & presents a very neat appearance. As for the circular of Klarkash-Ton's booklet—here it is. You've probably read most of the tales, but you'll want them in this form. They are among his choicest items—rejected, of course, by the hard-headed Satrap Pharnabazus. The brochure ought to be ready within a month—though the tardiness of the Auburn Journal's job press is without limits. I've offered to distribute about 50 of the circulars among my correspondents if C A S will send them to me. I shall look for your "prose-poem" in W.T.[2]—& hope that the remuneration therefor may not be too long delayed.

        Sorry there has been so much financial stringency at #84, & hope you'll be able to float along somehow. This, however, is an unprecedentedly unfavourable time to try to make a living by the pen! Wish you could get a position remunerative enough to keep you going, yet easy enough to give you leisure for creative work. You certainly have an ambitious enough programme, once you get the opportunity to put it into effect.

This is my kind of weather—with the thermometer getting close to 90°. Have taken almost daily exploring trips in a delightful rural region north of the town & west of my favourite Quinsnicket woods—a region which for some reason or other I never penetrated before. It contains some exquisite landscapes—rocky hills, winding roads, mystical woods, ancient farmsteads, & blue lakelets—yet is surprisingly near the urban fringe. I've averaged about 12 miles per day of walking.

Best wishes for all your endeavours—& hope to see you soon.

With a grandsire's blessing—

Melmoth III

P.S. The enclosed cutting will cause you regret—but the establishment carries on.

[Enclosures: Flyer for *The Double Shadow and Other Fantasies* by Clark Ashton Smith. Clipping from *Providence Evening Bulletin* (?): "Mrs. Julia Maxfield Dead in 78th Year."]

Notes

1. Walter John Coates (1880–1941), ed., *Harvest: A Sheaf of Poems from* Driftwind (North Montpelier, VT: Driftwind Press, May 1933; *LL* 186).
2. Possibly "The Lady in Grey."

[197] [HPL and Helen V. Sully to DAW] [ANS][1]

[Postmarked Newport, R.I.,

20 July 1933]

Oy, you shood see it how ve got into dees place dees efternoon a'ready! Remember how we cut the cord of the shutter & peered in in good old '27? This is my first sight of the interior under favourable conditions. Too bad you can't be along—if you were, we'd let the boat go & make an extra trip to the Hanging Rocks where you & Mortonius licked me in the poetry contest. Try to work in a Providence trip before long. Hope I haven't bored Klarkash-Ton's gifted emissary with colonial sights. We tried a new boat today—a rival to the old Sagamore. Yr obt Grandsire

Melmoth III

and Helen

Notes

1. *Front:* Old Jewish Synagogue, Newport, R.I.

[198] [HPL and FBL to DAW] [ANS][1]

[Postmarked Onset, Mass.,
25 July 1933]

Hail, Melmoth! Old M. III manages to keep up his migratory reputation despite service at home as an amateur nurse.[2] Spending 2½ days with the Soviet expedition which is investigating the economic & revolutionary potentialities of Onset. ¶ Your late guest—the High-Priestess of Tsathoggua—departed safely for Gloucester Friday despite the ghouls of the hidden churchyard[3] & the cuisine at Jake's. ¶ My aunt's plaster cast was reduced in area Friday night, & she may be up on crutches by the end of this week. ¶ I expect Mortonius (whom you have so basely neglected!) on the ancient hill shortly—about August 1st. Wish you could come along & renew the antient triad of 1927! ¶ May Yog-Sothoth bless thee—

Yr obt Grandsire
Melmoth III

Greetings, O Donaldus! Parting from our gracious guest was bitter-sweet sorrow. She is a divine person, really. I shall drop in for a chat when I return
Regards
Belknap

Notes

1. *Front:* The Old Discarded Mill, Cape Cod, Mass.

2. HPL's aunt Annie Gamwell broke her ankle shortly after taking up residence at 66 College Street.

3. See Helen V. Sully, "Memories of Lovecraft: II": "After dinner, he took me into a graveyard associated with Poe. . . . it was dark, and he began to tell me strange, weird stories in a sepulchral tone and, despite the fact that I am a very matter-of-fact person, something about his manner, the darkness, and a sort of eerie light that seemed to hover over the gravestones got me so wrought up that I began to run out of the cemetery with him close at my heels, with the one thought that I must get up to the street before he, or whatever it was, grabbed me. I reached a street lamp, trembling, panting, and almost in tears, and he had the strangest look on his face, almost of triumph. Nothing was said" (*LR* 278).

[199] [HPL and James F. Morton to DAW] [ANS][1]

[Postmarked Providence, R.I.,
1 August 1933]

Greetings, O Melmoth! Have just been gorging at Jake's—which is more than we got around to doing last September! The old place looks much the same—except that Talman's favourite waiter Domingo is there no more. Bet-

ter come along here on your next vacation to renew old associations & see Grandpa's new Georgian headquarters. ¶ Yr obt Servt
Melmoth III

Hail, Master of the Red Brain! I have vainly waited in Paterson for word, sign or presence. Are we not to get together in days not too remote? I shall be on deck after Labor Day. Just now, H.P.L. and I are busily decoding the ciphers of the cosmos.

Mortonius

We're going to have an ice-cream championship bout at Maxfield's tomorrow noon. Since each of us has eliminated all other opponents, it's up to us to decide the supremacy betwixt ourselves. Wish the management would appreciate our advertising value & furnish the materials!

Notes

1. *Front:* Providence River Looking Toward Narragansett Bay, Providence, R. I.

[200] [HPL and James F. Morton to DAW] [ANS][1]

[Postmarked Newport, R.I.,
2 August 1933]

Hail, O Hater of the Stigmata of mankind! Why aren't you here as in good old 1927 to revel in the primal wastes of rugged rock & boundless billows? We're emulating old Dean Berkeley & evolving philosophick reflections from beneath the shelter of an overhanging cliff. No verses so far[2]—but if the old trio were complete, I'm sure the Muses would start up with inspiration. Good day except for one brief shower (so far)

Thine for the Elder Rite—Melmoth III

May the aforesaid trio again foregather at no too distant day, amid these scenes of changeless beauty.

J. F. M.

Notes

1. *Front:* Surf and Rocks along Cliff Walk, Newport, R. I.
2. When DAW had visited HPL in 1927, they had made a trip to Newport in the company of James F. Morton. There the three sat in a sheltered spot favored by Bishop Berkeley, known as Hanging Rocks, and composed memorial poems in Berkeley's honor. See DAW, "Lovecraft in Providence" (LR 306–7).

[201] [HPL to DAW] [ALS]

#66—

August 19, 1933

Dear Melmoth:—

Congratulations on your dual sources of revenue! I'd feel damn lucky if I could get & hold either one of these life-saving props—or anything which would assure me 10 fish per week, the minimum to which I have managed to whittle down my expenses. I had heard of the first job, but the second is fresh news. Again, congratulations!

Thanks tremendously for mentioning me to *Astounding*. Hall[1] sent me a form letter a week ago, & I replied—stating that I could not supply the essentially conventional material his specifications seemed to indicate. He came back at once with a personal response in which he said that the rubber-stamp stuff was not by any means necessary, & that his policy would include many stories of an individual, non-orthodox type if well-written. This sounds distinctly encouraging; & I really think that if I can get around to writing some more tales, I shall send them to *Astounding* first of all. At present I have nothing within the prescribed space-limits which seems to me good enough for submission. However—it may be that my type of tale will not "click" with Hall after all; for I notice that he lays stress on *characterisation*, whereas my efforts deal primarily with *phenomena & moods*—the characters being purely incidental. I am delighted to hear that you have already landed a tale, & hope the new venture may become a regular gang rendezvous. As soon as I heard from Hall I passed the tip on to Sonny Belknap, Comte d'Erlette, Klarkash-Ton, & Jonckheer Wilfredus.

But speaking of tips—as M. Auguste-Guillaume told you about two other new markets for weird stuff? They are: Rogers Terrill, Popular Publications, 205 E. 42nd St. N.Y.C. (1¢ per word promptly on publication) & Jay Publishing Co., 125 W. 45th St., N.Y.C. (½¢ per word tardily after publication).[2] The Jay, adds Comte Auguste, is rather a fly-by-night concern not very satisfactory to deal with. And there is the new but non-paying *Fantasy Fan* (vide enc.), of which Klarkash-Ton may have told you. This is a good medium upon which to unload hopelessly unsalable MSS. for the purpose of getting extra copies for lending. C A S & I have stocked it up with old stuff, & I may let it print my weird fiction article as a serial. It will henceforward specialise in weird material, since the editor (Charles D. Hornig) has just been hired as managing editor of *Wonder Stories* & does not wish to duplicate his scientifictional activities.

Incidentally—our friend Samuelus has lately been extolling my products to an acquaintance of his in the Knopf firm—one Allan G. Ullman—with the result that the latter has written asking me to send along some MSS. to be considered for possible book publication.[3] *Possible* is good! After the Putnam & Vanguard fiascos I know how little such a request really means—though I have shot Ullman a batch of stuff in order not to let Loveman down. It'll come back soon enough! These fellows are merely trying to make sure that they aren't missing anything. Oh—by the way—did Little Belknap tell you that he has sold a sensational 'confession' yarn to Macfadden for $100.00? It will, needless to say, appear pseudonymously. It would be amusing if the child had found a lucrative medium at last in this none too palatable underworld of letters!

I liked Miss Sully exceedingly—as, evidently, did all the several hosts along her route. She certainly does combine intelligence & prepossessing charm to a remarkable degree—& she appeared to appreciate the venerable antiquities of Providence & Newport more than is common with members of her iconoclastic generation. It was highly interesting to hear at first-hand of Klarkash-Ton (the only previous personal link being Kirk, whose visit to Auburn is a dozen years or more in the past)—who would appear to be struggling against environmental handicaps which make his achievements seem all the more phenomenal. By the way—has C A S told you of the rattlesnake which he killed after it had almost crept up to the outdoor table where he sat writing?

No doubt you received the Onset card from Young Stalin & his grandpa, & the sundry echoes of 1927 scenes from James Ferdinand & his aged host. At Onset we had rotten weather conditions, though congenial & combative discourse palliated the leaden & chilly dampness. Sonny—whilst passing through Providence—thought the Old Gentleman's new Georgian quarters quite appropriate, though proletarian ideology forbade him to exude enthusiasm. The Mortonian visit was blessed with fine hot weather, so that many outdoor events were included. In making a pedestrian trip through the western part of the state we came upon a picturesque old well-sweep in active use, as well as a drowsy village where the atmosphere of 1820 still lingers. Of course we patronised Jake's, & made our usual pilgrimage to Maxfield's (though good old Aunt Julia died last spring)—where your absence was sincerely regretted. Each had six flavours of the Warren product—mine being grape, chocolate chip, macaroon, banana, cherry, & orange-pineapple. Only lack of cash prevented us from exhausting the list more thoroughly. Later we walked to Bristol & returned to Providence by train—& in the evening went to ancient Pawtuxet, where I watched Mortonius surround a couple of shore dinners. On the last day came the Newport trip—& the sojourn on the cliffs at which our 1927 colleague & fellow-rhymer was keenly missed! Morton is now in New Hampshire, after having climbed Camel's Hump in Vermont.

My aunt's cast has been off a fortnight, but the doctor is still slow about getting her up on crutches. Nurse still here—& I am closely chained to the house as substitute during her afternoon absences. I see Brobst quite often, & he always enquires cordially after you. He goes to Boston for a year in October—hope you can get around here before that time!

Well—congratulations once more, & renewed thanks for the kind words with Hall. Shoot along bulletins whenever you get a chance!

Yr obt grandsire

Melmoth III.

P.S. I was sorry as hell to miss the July convention,[4] when so many sages—including Culinarius—were congenially assembled. My one compensation was the visit from E. Hoffmann Price—who had his 1928 Ford Juggernaut along, & helped me to explore historic but inaccessible parts of R.I. which I had never seen before. He may get to see you before he quits the North for Florida—whence he will winter. His fictional success is astounding!

Notes

1. Desmond Hall (1909–1992), associate editor of *Astounding Stories*.

2. The first magazine was *Dime Mystery Magazine* (December 1932–September 1938), edited by Rogers Terrill (Popular Publications), which began as a mystery magazine but switched focus to weird menace stories with the October 1933 issue. The other magazine proposed by Jay Publishing Co. never appeared.

3. HPL sent two submittals to Allan G. Ullman (1908–1982) of Knopf on 3 and 16 August 1933.

4. I.e., the annual convention of the NAPA, held in New York.

[202] [HPL and W. Paul Cook to DAW] [ANS][1]

[Postmarked Boston, Mass.,

2 September 1933]

Hail, Melmoth! I couldn't wind up the summer without a little Melmothing of my own, so have broken loose for a week—others will stay with my aunt afternoons. Bound for QUEBEC—but pausing at the Recluse's cave. Trust all flourishes at Rue d'Horace. Sonny Belknap has just sold a detective story to Street & Smith.[2] You boys surely are getting ahead! ¶ Now for a bite at the Waldorf & a dash for the train.

Pax vobiscum—

Grandpa

That train must be caught and so my greetings must be short. Don't forget your promise to visit Boston.

Culinarius

Notes

1. *Front:* Business Section of Boston.
2. "Medicine for Three," *Street and Smith's Detective Story Magazine* 144, No. 1 (25 January 1934): 112–21.

[203] [HPL to DAW] [ANS][1]

[Postmarked Quebec, Canada,
3 September 1933]

Some Melmothing! Having a glorious time—weather hot & sunny so far. No place like La Vielle Québec! Trust you got the Culinary joint card. I shall see good old W P C again on the return trip—& may take in Salem & Marblehead. ¶ Have found a near-Jake in Quebec! A Chinaman with a counter joint who caters to hard-boiled English-speakers—not as tough as Jake's bunch, tho'. When do you hit the road again?

Blessings—
Grandpa

Notes

1. *Front:* St. Louis Gate, La Porte Saint-Louis, Quebec, Canada.

[204] [HPL to DAW] [ANS]

[Postmarked Providence, R.I.,
18 December 1933]

[A Cargo of Good Wishes
for Christmas and
The New Year]
To Melmoth II
from
Grandpa Melmoth III.

1934

[205] [HPL to DAW] [ALS]

Jany. 16, 1934

Dear Melmoth:—

I must hasten to acknowledge the photographic records of our recent conference—which arrived yesterday. Really, the portraits are excellent in a vivid, Rembrandt-like fashion—but curse the luck which caused the lens to catch me with my mouth slightly open . . . . thus increasing that expression of grave vacuity with which Nature has so unkindly endowed me. Belknap certainly looks cynical & middle-aged enough—in a shadow-mantled way—to suit even his own Baudelairian tastes; whilst you maintain the same debonair jauntiness as of yore. Too bad your poetic locks didn't get swept back from your classic brow in the group picture as they did—by request—in the solo portrait.[1] But why carp at trifles? Really, the results were splendid, & I congratulate you upon an artistic proficiency in the camera's use which I am never likely to attain!

My homeward journey was uneventful—but God! what a maelstrom of work & correspondence awaited me! I'm still floundering futilely. It seems that lots of my important mail wasn't forwarded because it was in large manila envelopes which my aunt didn't recognise as first class. But this hair-trigger pen has been a vast aid in helping me dispose of the postal accumulation. The flow is none too free—now that I'm getting used to its effortless gliding I resent the less liberal feed of the Parker which previously represented the ultimate word in Niagaran copiousness!

I was infernally sorry not to see more of you in Manhattan—& it surely is ironic that your present week should be so unfilled. You'll undoubtedly hear from Merritt, for his genial conscientiousness is such (if I'm any judge) as to make neglect of obligations impossible. He was obviously deeply interested in you & your work, & in what I said of your brother's marvellous drawings. Incidentally—I'll be tremendously your debtor for any even half-way decipherable photographs of some of those aforementioned drawings!

Glad you've had an opportunity to start your third novel, & hope it may continue to develop powerfully & successfully.[2] There's nothing like actual experiment to shew you your natural metier & give you momentum in the chosen direction. Objective work is always harder than subjective—it is said that everybody has *one* novel in him . . . . his own story . . . . but that the real test of one's creative powers comes when one gets beyond himself. To create a character distinct from oneself—who truly talks, thinks, & acts consistently with the alien conception & not like oneself in a false beard & moustache—is a full-sized job which only a minority can suitably put over. Go to it—& may your Moll Flanders be truly modern & emancipated in her depths of decadent & inartistic disgustingness!

Among the piled-up stuff at home was a copy of the Crossman opus[3]—plus two joint cards from Cook & Coates (mailed during the cold week) whose temperature bulletins congealed my blood & paralysed my imagination. As compared with North Montpelier figures, Byrd & Ellsworth are in the subtropics![4] It was 50 below one night when the alcohol retreated into the bulk of the thermometer & left the rest to speculation!

Remember me to Belknap & anybody else I know when you see 'em. Hope the gang can get together more frequently than it has been doing. Don't fail to get to Paterson & see James Ferdinand's museum . . . . . which reminds me, I heard the old boy over the radio last night as he discoursed of dinosaurs & other little pets of the mesozoic world. He speaks on some phase of organic evolution on the 3d Monday of each month at 7:45 P.M. Station WOOA.

No time to finish the Roman Britain book,[5] but what I've seen of it is enthralling. Enclosed is a *Fantasy Fan* which just came—one of several duplicates. You can keep it or throw it away. I suppose you've read Klarkash-Ton's "Ghoul" in MS. form.[6]

With renewed thanks & congratulations about the pictures—

Yr most ob^t h^{ble} Servt

Melmoth III.

[*Enclosure: FF* 1, No. 5 (January 1934).]

Notes

1. Presumably a set of photographs taken at a gang meeting in New York during HPL's visit in late December and early January The group photo appears in *SL* 2, facing p. 329; the portrait of Wandrei appears in *SL* 3, facing p. 407.

2. So far as is known, DAW did not start another novel; at any rate, it does not survive.

3. Willis T. Crossman [pseud. of W. Paul Cook], *It Happened at Dunbar* (North Montpelier, VT: Driftwind Press, 193-).

4. Admiral Richard E. Byrd (1888–1957) and Lincoln Ellsworth (1880–1951) were conducting separate explorations of Antarctica at the time. In 1935 Ellsworth became the first human being to fly across the continent.

5. Arthur Weigall (1880–1934), *Wanderings in Roman Britain* (London: T. Butterworth, [1926]; *LL* 933).

6. "The Ghoul," *FF* 1, No. 5 (January 1934): 69–72.

[206] [HPL to DAW] [ALS]

The Ancient Hill
March 28, 1934

Dear Melmoth:—

Thanks an infinity of times for those prints of your brother's drawings! Despite what you say of their inadequacy—& of course no photograph could ever catch all the nuances of work as complex as this—they seem to me marvellous in their sinister cosmic power. Even the fine detail counts heavily in many—especially under varying degrees of magnification. That large Sabbat scene comes out surprisingly well. The *least* distinct print, perhaps, is the dancing Siva. I shall, naturally, be delighted to see any better reproductions which your photographic ingenuity may devise—as well as any additional subjects on which you may experiment. Naturally, I appreciate these all the more for having seen the originals. Your brother's artistic power is certainly tremendous & enviable, & I feel sure that he will eventually become recognised as one of the long line of fantastic pictorial geniuses along with Beardsley, Sime, Segrelles, Harry Clarke, Angarola,[1] & all the rest. As I said before, I wish his work could be brought to the attention of some publisher issuing bizarre books—for he would be the most admirable of illustrators in this field. I can imagine "The Great God Pan" or "The White People" with designs by Howard Wandrei!

Of late I have been seeing quite a bit of art, for the local museum has harboured an unusual number of special loan exhibits with excellent accompanying lectures. Etruscan & Egyptian tomb paintings, & now a quite memorable assemblage of modern Spanish paintings—rivalling, while it lasts, the treasures of the Hispanic Museum!

Glad to hear that you have had some profitable sales—though if I were you I would not refuse a regular position when it comes along. It is always well to have some steady anchorage when such is possible, so that one will not be forced to turn out an endless stream of mechanical—& in the end aesthetically stultifying—hack work. E. Hoffmann Price is realising this at last, & has accepted a partnership in a garage business in Pawhuska, Okla. as a steadying standby. Sounds prosaic—but his mechanical genius & the engineering knowledge acquired at West Point make it easy for him. However—much depends on one's facility & luck with hack work. If, like Graf August-Wilhelm von Derleth, one can grind it out effortlessly & market it easily—all without injury to one's own style & imagination—it would naturally pay to go ahead with it. Each writer must decide for himself, as his own luck & nature dictate. Outside advice can be no more than tentative suggestion.

Glad you are getting your poetry polished & coördinated, & hope you will have luck in marketing your complete metrical works. Just as well to go easy on the novel till you are sure what you want to say. No work is first-class except the spontaneous work which *has* to be written. If dramas call, go ahead with them—& return to the novel when that demands attention. Nothing but experiment will truly reveal the natural direction or directions of one's capacities. Here's hoping you find prose, poetry, and the drama equally fruitful in the end! Meanwhile your brother is certainly lucky to succeed so well in fiction in addition to his drawing. His "In the Triangle"[2] certainly revealed a narrative imagination of keen strength & originality, & I was glad to note its laudatory reception by the readers. Virtually all my correspondents singled it out for praise.

As for the "Shunned House"—I guess I told you that the Coates plan of binding & issuance fell through. Cook is now having the sheets sent to the young bibliophile, embryonic fantaisiste, & would-be publisher R. H. Barlow of De Land, Florida, who hopes after a while to be able to bind & issue them gradually, as orders warrant. I think it will be easier to get an unbound set out of Barlow then it was to extort such from Cook, & I shall certainly exert all my efforts on your behalf. It is possible that I can get down to Florida to visit Barlow this spring—he has invited me for May 1st—& if so I will surely annex a few copies of the ill-fated opus—by force if necessary!

Regarding recent work—I have produced nothing new of an original nature; having become thoroughly dissatisfied with my products, & being by no means certain that it is of any use to continue further with fiction. However, I have continued in the intensive re-reading of weird classics, & the close analysis of fictional methods, of which I recently spoke—so that I may be prepared to make a fresh fictional start, profiting by former mistakes, if I think it feasible.[3] Such pauses & stock-takings are common with me. As I once mentioned, I took a 9-year vacation from fiction between 1908 & 1917. One thing I did lately was to construct a *map of Arkham,* so that allusions in any future tale I write may be consistent.[4] As Arkham stories multiply, the various geographical allusions become harder & harder to keep track of without some guide. I have an unformed idea for another possible Arkham story—a tale of a strange old house inherited by a man, & of the tree-overgrown graveyard on a distantly-visible hill which played upon that man's imagination till he was moved to disturb the huge boulder covering an oddly hieroglyphed grave dug in 1708.

Give my regards to the urbane Hall when you see him. I must look up a copy of his magazine. Which reminds me that Belknap sent me your "Colossus"—duly explaining that the conventional preliminary moon-trip was an editorially demanded excrescence. The story proper has some magnificently cosmic passages—a fine sense of space & magnitude. If I had any criticism to make, it would be of the astronomical accuracy of some of the sights & conditions on leaving earth, of the too-human aspect, interests, & instruments of the macrocosmic beings, & of the conventionality & lack of climax in the final voyage—the routine beauteous damsel & all that. But aside from these details, I'd say you've surely rung the bell! It is hard to get away from what Belknap would call the "ideology" of the pulp tradition. Merritt is half-engulfed in it—I've just read his "Metal Monster"[5] . . . . magnificent—almost unparalleled—presentation of the *utterly alien & non-human,* but human characters lifeless & puerile. By the way—I've also just read Machen's new weird item—"The Green Round"—lent me by C A S. It has much of the old magic, though tending a bit to tameness. Well worth reading. I've also read the famed "Anthony Adverse"—took 5 days to do it.[6] Good picture of late 18th & early 19th centuries, but marred by obtrusive coincidences, overdone mysticism & symbolism, heavy philosophising, & a general letdown during the final third. Bernard Dwyer lent it to me. My correspondence is now under control—except for a 22-page (closely typed) argumentative epistle from Two-Gun Bob, the Terror of the Plains. ¶ As for *weather*—I fancy St. Paul has lost all its distinction! On Feby. 9 all records for Prov. were broken with **-17°**. Snows till a week ago. There have, however, been brief respites. On March 5th I sloshed over the melting hills & brook-flooded woods of the countryside, & on the 18th my aunt & I were treated to a motor ride toward Worcester—temperature 66°.

    And so it goes. Grandpaternal blessings!
        Yr obt Servt
          Melmoth III.

[P.S.] And again thanks for those pictures!

[P.]P.S. I presume you've heard of the marriage on March 5 at the Unitarian parsonage in Ridgewood, N.J., of one Pearl K. Merritt (aet circa 45—plain, quietly humorous spinster whom you may have met) of Brooklyn & JAMES FERDINAND MORTON, ESQ., of Paterson, N.J. After a 9-years' engagement the young people ought to know what they want! Hope the venture will prove lasting & felicitous.

[P.P.P.S.] Cook is planning to return to Boston

[P.P.P.P.S. on enclosed slip of paper?] P.S. Brobst may drop in on you next week. He's developed a tonsil trouble & must have the offending members out April 6th—meanwhile enjoying a vacation at home in Allentown. When he returns to New England for the operation it is possible that he will pause a day in Manhattan to look up members of the gang. If you want to drop him a line of special invitation, address
        Harry Brobst,
         1321 Gordon St.,
          Allentown, Pa.

[*Enclosure:* Advertisement for "Printed Personal Stationery" from The Hampshire Press, 14 Hutchins St., W. Concord, N. H.]

Notes

1. HPL refers to the weird artists Aubrey Beardsley (British; 1872–1898), Sidney H. Sime (British; 1867–1941), José Segrelles (Spanish; 1885–1969), Harry Clarke (British; 1890–1931), and Anthony Angarola (American; 1893–1929). For Beardsley see letter 1n9; for Clarke, letter 65n1.
2. Howard Wandrei, "In the Triangle" (*WT*, January 1934).
3. This re-reading resulted in "Weird Story Plots," "A List of Certain Basic Underlying Horrors Effectively Used in Weird Fiction," "List of Primary Ideas Motivating

Possible Weird Tales," and "Suggestions for Writing Story" (revised as "Notes on Writing Weird Fiction"). All items are in *CE* 2.

4. HPL included such a map in his letter to F. Lee Baldwin of 19 April 1934, apparently "Map of the Principal Parts of Arkham, Massachusetts" (AMS, JHL), copied by an unknown hand in the *Acolyte* 1, No. 1 (Fall 1942): 26 (as "Map of Arkham"). Other maps of Arkham are reproduced in *Marginalia* (Sauk City, WI: Arkham House, 1944), preceding p. 279, and *Letters to Robert Bloch* (West Warwick, RI: Necronomicon Press, 1993), frontispiece.

5. Serialized in *Argosy-Allstory Weekly* (7 August–25 September 1920).

6. A bestselling novel by Hervey Allen.

[207] [HPL to DAW] [ANS][1]

[Postmarked Charleston, S.C.,
26 April 1934]

Hail, Melmoth! Reached Washington an hour ahead of time, & spent 4 hours exploring the ancient Georgetown section. Amazing lot of 18th century material left. Richmond in the afternoon, & Raleigh, N.C. in the evening. Hit Charleston at dawn Tuesday. Stopping at the Y & doing the venerable town as usual. A great place—& with a climate that gives me funds of energy unknown in the north. Full summer here—rich green vegetation, hot days, & all. In Washington & Richmond it is merely springlike—with delicate young foliage. There's a big kick in passing from winter to summer in a few hours. I'm going hatless & vestless, & picking up a good coat of tan on the Battery. On to Savannah May 1st, & in De Land May 2, unless plans change. But I hate to leave old Charleston. There's absolutely no other place like it—an earthly paradise if there ever was one! Don't miss it in the course of your coming Melmothing. New Orleans is pale in comparison. Regards to your brother—hope his cold is all over now.

Patriarchal benedictions—
Melmoth III

Notes

1. *Front:* St. Philips Gateway, Charleston, S.C.

[208] [HPL and RHB to DAW] [ANS/TNS][1]

[Postmarked De Land, Fla.,
7? May 1934]

Hail, Melmoth! Grandpa is in the tropics at last, & having a great time. Feel 50 years younger than usual . . . . almost as spry as you boys! My host is a gifted artist, fantaisiste, & bibliophile, & has a marvellous collection in the crypt which he calls the Vaults of Yoh-Vombis.[2] Delightful region here—& such an array of felidae . . . . & opossums! A blue lakelet (which we call the Moon Pool)[3] stretches behind the house, & on its glassy surface we row each evening. You'd have liked this place in your misanthropic 1927 period—it's out of sight of any other human habitation. Hope all prospers in the arctic! Regards to Sonny & the gang.

> Yr obt Grandsire—Melmoth III.

Might I add great appreciation for the manuscript you sent, which enters into Yoh-Vombis with due interment.[4] I'm behaving as should anyone who had not seen a strictly human being for fourteen months!

> R. H. Barlow 𝕽𝕭

Explored Savannah 8½ hrs. on trip south. Great place!

Notes

1. *Front:* A beautiful Southern Sunset Scene. N.B.: RHB's part of the letter is typed.
2. After CAS's story.
3. After A. Merritt's celebrated story.
4. Unknown, but probably the ms. entitled "Poems from *Broken Mirrors*" (typescript, JHL; deposited there by RHB). RHB had been unsuccessful in obtaining a copy of *Broken Mirrors*, which contained DAW's work. There is also a typescript at JHL (also deposited by RHB) entitled "Poems from *Weird Tales*." RHB referred to the closet where he stored his weird fiction collection as the "Vaults of Yoh-Vombis," after CAS's story; see letter 211.

[209] [HPL to DAW] [ALS]

> % Barlow, Box 88,
> De Land, Fla.,
> May 17, 1934.

Hail, Melmoth!

Does this succeed in catching you before your hop-off on the long trek? To perpetuate an Hibernianism, the best part of this letter isn't in it, but will be found under separate cover . . . . . this being nothing less than the long-promised copy of "The Shunned House", which I believe you desire for fancy binding or something of the sort . . . . a waste of good effort on a bum object. This is the best set of sheets we can assemble out of the 115 copies—just arrived from Cook—which have survived from an original edition of 250. Not much of a story, but a pretty fair piece of printing. Barlow plans to issue the thing gradually—a "limited signed edition", a "general trade edition", & all that. Youth loves its pomposities! The volume of Whitehead letters[1] will probably be delayed till after Barlow's trip north next autumn in search of ocular relief. His eyes are in no shape for work at present. You'll probably see him when he is in N Y—for I believe you plan to return to decadent megalopolitan shades by that time. I think you will find him very likeable. His versatility is astonishing—you ought to see the bas-relief of Cthulhu he has just made!

His most recent proposition concerns your gifted artist-brother—one or more of whose marvellous drawings he wants to issue in the form of 11 × 14 photographic reproductions done by an expert professional & sold at cost . . . . simply to spread the creator's fame without financial profit to anyone. This ambition has arisen from Barlow's study of the photographs you so kindly made & sent to me, & which have since been going on a course of select rounds. They recently reached me from Rimel & Baldwin, (who were enthusiastic), & no sooner did young Barlow see them than he went into ecstasies, pestering all the photographers in town with enquiries about large reproductions of the originals. It appears that pretty good pictures can be secured with proper filters & processes, hence I hope ardently that the plan will prosper. Barlow has written your brother, & I trust you will use your influence in a favourable way. Incidentally, my youthful host has a vast idolatry for yourself; & you will probably hear from him shortly on the subject of MSS. & reliques. I hope you can help to satisfy his hero-worship!

Heard from H E[2] a week ago, & learned of his transfer to Cape Cod. I trust he'll pause at least a moment in ancient Providence on his way back in the autumn. Meanwhile I fancy your own extensive swing around the circle will be as memorable an event as the Melmothing of 1927.

I'm having a great time. Visited a ruined Franciscan mission of 1696 at New Smyrna last week, & am enjoying the genial climate to the limit. Don't know just when I'll move on—my hosts veto all suggestions of immediate migration. I intend to spend a week in St. Augustine, & may possibly visit an old-time amateur journalist in Macon, Ga. If I'm not broke when I get north, I may visit Bernard Dwyer in West Shokan—who, by the way, is now having *mumps* for the first time at 37! That beats my measles at 19 & chicken-pox at 25! At such a rate, I may have whooping-cough at 98.

Well—I hope the old Shunned House doesn't seem too badly disappointing after your long wait. The edition has no fly-leaves, but I suppose the paper can be matched without excessive trouble. I wonder whether the bulk of it will ever be issued? Barlow is confident that it will . . . . . . but then, so was Cook!

With appropriate benedictions, I remain
　　　　　Yr obedient grandsire,
　　　　　　　　Melmoth III.

P.S. E. Hoffmann Price & Klarkash-Ton had their long-awaited get-together at last. It seems to have been a tremendously festive occasion!

[*Enclosure:* Letter by R. H. Barlow to Donald Wandrei, May 19, 1934.]

[*Enclosure:* Postcard (*Front:* Blue Springs, Near De Land, Fla.); no writing on back.]

Notes

1. RHB had long planned an edition of Henry S. Whitehead's letters, to be titled *Caneviniana,* but the project came to naught.
2. I.e., Howard Wandrei.

[210] [DAW to HPL] [ALS]

84 Horatio St., N.Y.C.
May 21, 1934

Dear Melmoth—

At once I hasten to record my deep appreciation of the sheets of "The Shunned House" which just arrived. I had really given up hope of ever seeing them, but now they come, ready for a fitting and unique binding. I will gladly reimburse you for them, and I want to purchase at least one more copy when the edition is bound. What has young Barlow done about the sheets? Is there any certainty of the time when they are likely to be between covers?

After June 1, my address will again be 1152 Portland Ave., St. Paul, Minnesota. If you should pass through New York City before June 10, telephone Mr. Andrew Overby,[1] Irving Trust Co., Digby 4-3500. There is a possibility that I may be here or at another address until June 10; Andrew will know where I am, and naturally I would be delighted to have one more session before I commence my wanderings, which may not bring me back until late autumn.

My year looks as if it would be fairly prosperous. Street & Smith this week purchased "Advertised For Death", almost 16,000 words, the first of a planned series of detective novelettes to run in "Clues".[2] They are ready to take six to ten more if I can write them between now and next February. Also, it is unquestionable that "Colossus Eternal" will be bought at $210. "Astounding Stories" changes its body type with the August issue, increasing the contents by 25,000 words per number, thus expanding the market by that degree. In other words, I have a good market for two stories or novelettes a month, and can earn a nice income by devoting only two weeks a month to pot-boilers, and assigning the other two weeks to my serious work. I shall spend this time on plays, for I have the eagerness to write them and the producer-acquaintances to consider them. Incidentally, S. & S. believe that the movie and book rights to my detective series may prove valuable, but I am much less optimistic.

Inclosed is the print of Belknap. I have been too busy to do much developing recently, and may not be able to send you more prints until after I return to Minnesota. I expect to acquire an enlarging camera this summer; among other projects, I plan a small edition of a photographic book of large size, covering my brother's work, both pen-and-inks and batiks.

I sincerely hope that your travels are proving idyllic, and that you can make an extended stay under hot suns. Again, let me express my truly boundless gratitude for the sheets of "The Shunned House". Convey my regards to Barlow.

As ever,

Donald Wandrei Melmoth II

P.S. If here after June 1, my address will still be 84 Horatio. Just had a talk with the landlord. But I will be on my way before June 10th.

D.W.

P.P.S. Copy of "Fantasy Magazine" arrived, containing interview with me. Schwartz & Weisinger garbled a remark I made about "The Call of Cthulhu" into an anecdote that is discreditable to both you and me.[3] I have already taken them to task, and I herewith extend apologies for my unfortunate part in the incident. I knew nothing of their action until the interview appeared, and the quotations are flatly not mine.

D.

Notes

1. See HW10n3.

2. Published as "Frost." DAW's stories in the series are gathered in *Frost* (2000).

3. "Donald Wandrei," interviewed by Julius Schwartz and Mort Weisinger, *Fantasy Magazine* 3, No. 3 (May 1934): 10–11, 32 (quotation from p. 11): "When I met Lovecraft I chanced to comment on his excellent story, 'Call of Cthulhu,' and I pronounced the word as it was spelt. Lovecraft enlightened me on its correct pronunciation, which sounds like a series of witches' whistles. I asked Lovecraft how he could possibly pronounce the name different from my version of it, which was correct phonetically. He then said to me, 'Look here, I ought to know how to say it, don't you think?'"

[211] [HPL to DAW] [ALS]

[Postmarked De Land, Fla.,
26 May 1934]

Dear Melmoth:—

I am surely glad to learn that "The Shunned House" reached you safely at last—after all the years of delay. I had almost given up hope myself, but once in a while a pleasant disappointment occurs. It further develops that the edition is not as depleted as we thought. Cook writes that there is another box of the sheets stowed somewhere in his sister's cellar at

Sunapee, although there is no immediate prospect of getting at them. Perhaps they'll never come to light—but anyhow, 115 copies are assured! As for reimbursement—don't make Grandpa laugh! No such thing as *sale* is to be thought of in connexion with the gang. All that is for outsiders . . . . . . the good old group will be supplied with my compliments! Regarding the bulk of accessible copies—Barlow has them safely stowed on his shelves in the windowless crypt (called The Vaults of Yoh-Vombis) housing his collection. He plans to bind & issue them gradually, as the demand warrants . . . . first a "limited signed" edition & then a "general trade edition". The little imp is trying to make me promise never to sign any copies except those of the "limited edition"—in which your sheets will be technically included. It amuses me to see so much bibliophilic nonsense woven about a worthless trifle! I don't know what the kid's time-schedule is—he probably won't do anything till next winter, after his ocular siege in the north. You'll undoubtedly see Barlow in the autumn, & I fancy you'll find him very likeable & interesting. He is certainly enormously gifted & versatile. Right now he is modelling in wax a hellish poison flower of which he dreamed last night, & the effect is really marvellously potent.

I wish you luck with your travels, & trust the stay at good old 1152 will be pleasant. Perhaps you won't want to return to the Manhattanese vortex after getting a fresh taste of home! It hardly looks, at present, as if I'd be repassing through New York as early as June 10th—but if I do, I'll certainly look you up. Delighted to hear of your fresh successes in commercial fiction. Is "Colossus Eternal" a sequel to "Colossus"? You seem to have mastered the pulp formula as cleverly as E. Hoffmann Price, & I surely hope there will be no break in the market. Glad that your standby *Astounding* is presenting enlarged purchasing opportunities. If this keeps up—the combination of profits & leisure—you will actually have Price licked—for he keeps afloat only through the most incessant & nerve-racking tripe-scribbling, which leaves him with scarce a moment to call his own. Hope the serious writing programme will go through with flying colours. Have you definitely decided, for the nonce, that the drama is your natural medium of expression? Incidentally, it would be a marvellous piece of luck if your magazine material could be resold for book & cinema use.

Thanks vastly for the snap of Sonny. Can you let Barlow have one—also of yourself? The little fat dandy! But where is the promised shot of yourself? No hurry, though—I know how crowded one's programme becomes in times of transition. Barlow was vastly disappointed at the veto of his plan for the issuance of your brother's work—a plan which of course included ample copyright protection. However, your own design is more ambitious still—& with the aptitude which you show in your small-camera work I have no doubt but that you can equal the professionals in such matters as size, detail, colour values, & the like as soon as you have the proper equipment & a reasonable time for practice. Put me down for an early copy whenever the edition is out!

I'm sorry I can't get the early 11 × 14 print which Barlow had promised . . . . the professional photographer here[1] was confident he could do an eminently satisfactory job. By the way—hasn't your brother gone to Provincetown?

As for your *Fantasy* interview—I haven't seen the magazine yet, but will make due allowances for misquotation when I do see it. Leedle Shoolie[2] can be pardoned for careless reporting, considering the wide territory he covers!

I am still lingering in the tropick solitudes of De Land—thanks to the super-hospitality of the Barlovii, who veto all suggestions of moving along. Soon, however, I shall be pulling up stakes & edging toward ancient San Agustin. Hopes of Havana have virtually vanished. I may pay a visit in Macon, Ga., & shall certainly stop in Richmond & Washington—so as you see, I shan't be likely to tread northern soil before the middle or end of June. But I hope to see you sooner or later!

Blessings—
Melmoth III.

P.S. Barlow wants to know what C A S paintings or drawings you own—how many & what they're like. He plans a sort of catalogue of Klarkash-Tonic art.

[On envelope:] [P.]P.S. Barlow wants to know whether you can lend him, after you get home & at your files, (a) The early series of cosmic tales, which I read with such admiration in 1927 & of which "The Red Brain" is a part, & (b) "Dead Titans Waken". He will defray all postal expenses both ways. ¶ And incidentally, You ought to let Hornig or Schwartz or Crawford publish these cosmic tales. They're really magnificent—I've never forgotten them despite the 7 intervening years.
[*Enclosure:* Letter by R. H. Barlow to Donald Wandrei, May 26, 1934.]

[*Enclosure:* Postcard (*Front:* A Cocoanut Tree, Florida); no writing on back.]

Notes

1. Lucius Beecher Truesdell (1873–1974) took the familiar studio portrait of HPL, of which there are three different poses, at about the time RHB took his own famous snapshot (16 June 1934).
2. I.e., Julius Schwartz.

[212] [HPL to DAW] [ANS][1]

[Postmarked Saint Augustine, Fla.,
23 June 1934]

Well—Old Melmoth as well as young Melmoth is on the road again! Terminated a 7-week visit last Thursday, when the Barlows brought me up to ancient San Agustin in their car. It is certainly a relief to be amongst old houses

again .... & America has none older than St. Augustine's. Dwellings two
generations old when Providence was founded are a common sight. You
must stop here if you ever make that Southern trip you were talking about.
I'm staying a week—at the same place I stopped at in 1931. Have a fine tower
room with running water—& a magnificent view—for $4.00 per wk. ¶ A
fortnight ago I visited a marvellous place—Silver Springs, 6 miles N.W. of De
Land. There's a chain of placid lagoons there whose floor is riddled with vast
pits 30 to 80 feet deep & covered with strange marine vegetation. In some of
the pits are the huge bones of prehistoric animals. I saw these things from a
glass-bottomed boat. Out of the lagoons flows the Silver River—as typical a
tropical stream as the Congo or Amazon. Palms, cypresses, & trailing moss &
vines on the banks, & alligators, turtles, & snakes everywhere. I took a 10-
mile launch trip on it. ¶ Trust your trip was pleasant—Wright mentioned a
call from you. I'll bet you're glad to be at good old 1152!
     Regards—
Melmoth III

Notes

1. *Front:* Old Watch Tower, Fort Marion, St. Augustine, Florida.

[213] [HPL and James F. Morton to DAW] [ANS][1]
                                    [Postmarked Buttonwoods, R.I.,
                                              4 August 1934]
Hail, Melmoth! Lookit the convention you're missing? Yesterday we cleaned
up Maxfield's & Jake's, & the guy at the former place (who waited on us in
'27) enquired particularly about you. Today Roger Williams Park, Pawtuxet, &
the tranquil shore of old Buttonwoods. Tomorrow—the gods shall decide.
Meanwhile Mortonius has dug me up a line of progenitors extending back to
1300! ¶ Got home July 10 after 2 d. in Charleston, 1 in Richmond, 2 in
Washn, & 1 in Phila. Saw newly opened Poe cottage in latter place. In N Y
had no time to look up gang—broke. Home July 10, & neck deep in accumulated work. This is my first period of relaxation—& with what a noble excuse!
¶ Hope your travel plans are panning out satisfactorily. ¶ Blessings—
Grandpa Melmoth III.

_____

Only a line left to express greetings, hearty good-will and best wishes.—
J. F. M.

Notes

1. *Front:* Benefit Temple of Music, Roger Williams Park, Providence, R. I.

[214] [HPL and W. Paul Cook to DAW] [ANS][1]

[Postmarked Salem, Mass.,
24 August 1934]

Greetings in the name of old 1927 days, O Melmoth! The elders are in council, & recalling things that are no more. Going to Haverhill today, & later on I expect to make ancient Nantucket—of which more anon. Recd. your letter as I left Prov.—will reply soon. Blessings—

Melmoth III

I did not receive that letter you did not write. Please give Barlow what he asks for.[2]

Cook

Notes

1. *Front:* Bunker Hill, Monument, Charlestown. / Boston, Mass.
2. RHB was attempting to create a file of the contents of the second issue of Cook's magazine, the *Recluse,* some items of which had been printed as proofs before the project was aborted. In particular, RHB desired DAW's tale "The Face at the Window" and his article on M. G. Lewis.

[215] [HPL to DAW] [ALS]

Ancient Marblehead
—August 25, 1934

Hail, O Melmoth!

By this time you have the card from Culinarius & me telling of my present season-ending trip. Today I am in my favourite of all towns with my genial host—Edward H. Cole—& his car. I guess I mentioned that both Cole & Cook are coming to Providence with me tomorrow to look the old burg over, & that I have strong hopes of persuading Cook to stay over & accompany me to ancient & isolated *Nantucket*—of which more later. Cook isn't permanently leaving Vermont after all, but is in Boston only on dental business (how you can sympathise!) & to do some errands for Coates. He won't leave Vermont, probably, till next spring—when he plans to try his luck in New York. We had a good call on old Tryout Smithy yesterday afternoon, though the near-loss of my black bag brought the shadow of tragedy close. Tonight I shall attend a get-together with several of the old amateur journalistic crowd—& then Providence . . . . & Nantucket! Nantucket is said to be more purely colonial than any other place in America.

As you say, cards have kept you posted anent the details of my vast spring trip—& of the Morton visit with its Maxfield & Jake nourishment contests & its trip to familiar scenes in Newport. I'm glad to hear that you have also been immersed in vacational relaxations—boons which will make your work all the fresher when you return intensively to it. The camping must have been delightful to one of your wilderness-&-solitude-loving temperament—& I am glad you have such congenial companions available. I recall the Overbys very well. Glad you have come through all the hazards safely (at least I assume you will have by the time you get this!), & hope you have enough vivid new impressions to motivate a whole new series of tales.

I can't get at all enthusiastic about that Silver Key sequel—indeed, I am resolved never to attempt another collaboration. I mean to lie fallow a while, & see whether any new period of spontaneously-motivated fertility dawns— as in 1919–20. Glad you can still count on remuneration here & there. When you buckle down to steady production, you certainly ought to put into effect the programme of quiet seaport retirement which you suggest—& I hope you'll consider Providence small & placid enough for your purpose.

Anyhow, you must get around to visiting Providence sooner or later, for the old familiar scenes fairly demand your presence. Have discovered a joint where one can get a *good & ample course dinner* for *25¢* complete—soup, meat, potato, vegetables, bread & butter, & dessert! And of course Jake's is always running when you want something of a wholesale nature. If such scenes don't pep up your creative work, I'll eat my hat! If this Nantucket trip turns out any good I might take it again when you're here—*there* would be a retreat for you!

Back in Boston—or rather,
Wollaston, at Cole's House

Well, we had quite a day, & in the evening called on some old-time amateurs[1] in Cambridge. The son of the family—an infant of 6 when I saw him last in 1923—has grown up to be a marvellously brilliant, scholarly youth . . . . who, oddly enough, admires the past almost as much as I do, although his specialty is the 1840–1860 period instead of my 18th century. He has bought a costume of the 1850 age & sometimes wears it even on the street—especially after dark. I tried it on & it fitted me exactly—& was vastly more becoming than my ordinary costume. This boy curiously illustrates the occasional cases of reaction or ultra-conservatism which recur in the younger generation—as with young Randolph Churchill, son of Winston. He is naively religious—interested in the Buchman movement[2] & a deep admirer of the popish, orthodox Greek, & other churches out of the common Protestant rut. The Greek church with its Byzantine ritual is just about his idea of a faith. And in politics he is an extreme conservative—I'd like to pit him against Little Belknap! His name is Peter Myers, & his father is secretary of the World Peace Foundation.

One of my fountain pens has gone bad, & I fear I'm getting too sleepy to write legibly. Tomorrow we all hit the trail for Providence. ¶ Loveman, quite broken down nervously, is in Cleveland at his mother's for a 3-weeks' vacation. ¶ Cook is also in rotten health. He was due to accompany us this evening, but had to beg off on account of some attack. Hope he'll be all right tomorrow!

And so it goes. Trust I'll see you before very long. ¶ Have you discovered the weird author William Hope Hodgson? I'm incorporating a note about him in the reprint of my article.[3]

Be good—

Melmoth III.

[*Enclosure:* Postcard (*Front:* Christ Church [Old North], Boston, Mass.); no writing on back.]

Notes

1. Mr. and Mrs. Denys P. Myers.

2. Frank Buchman (1878–1961) was a former Lutheran minister who in the 1920s began an evangelist movement calling for individuals to take command in the spiritual transformation of society.

3. *FF* ceased publication before SHL with the note on Hodgson could appear. Instead, a separate article was published—"The Weird Work of William Hope Hodgson," *Phantagraph* 5, No. 5 (February 1937): 5–7.

[216] [HPL to DAW] [ANS][1]

[Postmarked Nantucket, Mass.,
28 August 1934]

Hail, Melmoth! Cook had a sort of nervous collapse & hastened back to Vermont, so only the Coles accompanied me to Providence. My aunt & I took them down to Maxfield's—but we skipped Jake's. The chap at Maxfield's who served us in 1927 asked after you. ¶ I merely stopped at home over night & set out again in the morning for Nantucket. Fine day & good sailing. Cold, though, on the water, so that I had to stay inside the cabin the latter part of the sail. I embarked at ancient New Bedford. ¶ Nantucket is positively the most fascinating old town in existence—its quaintness is not overrated. I wish I lived here—it is absolutely the world of 100 to 150 years ago! Don't know yet how long I can stay, but it won't be over a week at most. Hope your more strenuous outing has been not less pleasant than mine is proving!

Blessings—
Melmoth III

Notes

1. *Front:* Sand Dunes, South Shore, Nantucket, Mass.

[217] [CAS and DAW to HPL] [ANS, in private hands]
[Postmarked Auburn, Cal.,
21 November 1934]

Dear E'ch-Pi-El:

Melmoth and I are holding a session among my wizard towers! Wish you were here to utter the third incantation!

Klarkash-Ton

Written from the heart of the cryptical dwelling-place of the Elder God Klark-Ash Ton: Greetings! I would that you were here in abysmal & hyper-cosmic conclave, roaming with us the enigmatic regions beyond time, & after space.

Melmoth II

[218] [DAW and Helen V. Sully to HPL] [ANS, in private hands]
[Postmarked Auburn, Cal.,
21 November 1934]

Dear HPL—This is where my charming young hostess daily disappears—you must eventually include Auburn in your own Neo-Classical Odysseys. These ancient hills hold mysteries & riddles not lightly to be spoken of, and never to be fathomed. And the climate is of that magnificent variety which sedulously avoids dropping below the freezing-point. Now westward & southward my wanderings continue.

Melmoth II

But, he's coming back again next week, which he neglects to mention. The California climate has been exceedingly temperamental and *barely* avoids the freezing point. We all wish that you were here also.

H. V. S.

[P.S.] 6 P.M. His train just left 21st Nov. H. V. S.

[219] [HPL and W. Paul Cook to DAW and CAS][1]
[Postmarked Boston, Mass.,
25 November 1934]

Greetings, O Klarkash-Ton & Young Melmoth, who I understand are—or recently have been—assembled in joint conventinon! If the young visitor is still there, I hereby authorise his host to chastise him for not including Providence in his late Eastern itinerary! ¶ Culinarius is down in ancient Bostonium for a week, & will later spend some time with his sister in Sunapee, N.H. He has a lot of old family papers with him, including letters from a soldier at the front in the war of 1812, Civil War letters, & some from forty-niners—including a rare, rich, & racy specimen (written in 1853) in which *Auburn* is mentioned. We're going to lend this to Klarkash-Ton very shortly. ¶ Visited the old Royall mansion in Medford yesterday—built in 1737. Splendid specimen of early Georgian. ¶ Warm spell ended yesterday—it is now as cold as hell. Grandpa's outdoor season is just about over! ¶ Last night we called where there are three fine cats & they send greetings to Mother Simaetha, & pray that Genl. Tabasco may yet turn up somewhere. ¶ Shall be home again tonight. ¶ Patriarchal blessings to all. ¶ Yrs for the Crescent of Black Stars—E'ch-Pi-El.

This Wanderer is certainly having one of the spells that give him his nickname. Lucky devil. Of course you won't be able to read this, so it doesn't matter what I say.

W. P. Cook

[*Note on front:*] Built 1676 on the site of the Rev. Increase Mather's parsonage, where Cotton Mather was born. In the 'Pickman's Model' district—as Young Melmoth may remember.

Notes

1. *Front:* Paul Revere Home, Boston, Mass.

[220]   [HPL to DAW]   [ANS]

[Postmarked Providence, R.I.,
17 December 1934]

[With every good wish for Christmas and
your happiness throughout
the coming Year]

Grandpa Melmoth
—MDCCCCXXXIV

1935

[221] [HPL to DAW and HW] [ANS][1]

[No postmark;
c. July 1935]

Greetings from a second-season visitor at Barlow Manor! Left Prov. June 5 & shot straight down to Fredericksburg, Va. Only other stop Charleston. In De Land June 9, & have been having a great time ever since. Programme much the same as last year, except that Bob's father—a retired colonel—is home. Bob's brother Wayne—a fine chap of 26—has been here on a furlough from Ft. Sam Houston, Texas, but has now returned to his 2nd Lieutenanting. ¶ Bob has built a cabin in an oak grove across the lake from the house, & is busy there with various printing projects—of some of which you'll hear later on. ¶ I am now feeling splendidly—3 or 5 times stronger than ever in the north. Summer or winter, this is the climate for me! ¶ Last month we explored a marvellous tropical river near the Barlow place. It is called Black Water Creek, & is lined on both sides by a cypress jungle with festoons of Spanish moss. Twisted roots claw at the water's edge, & palms lean precariously on every hand. Vines & creepers—sunken logs—snakes & alligators—all the colour of the Congo or Amazon. ¶ Don't know how long I'll be here . . . super-hospitable hosts urge an indefinite sojourn. ¶ Hope all is flourishing in the arctic regions, & that the fiction business prospers. Any new drawings? ¶ C A S has taken up *sculptural carving* in stone, dinosaur bone [deposits of which exist in the vicinity of Averoigne], & other congenial media. Specimens sent to Barlow & me are tremendously impressive. ¶ All good wishes to both—

Yr obt Servt
Ech-Pi-El

Notes

1. *Front:* [Photograph of trees and lake; no caption.]

[222] [HPL to DAW] [ALS]

℅ Barlow, Box 88,
De Land, Florida
Aug. 14, 1935.

Dear Melmoth:—

Congratulations on the success of the fiction-mill! Belknap would seem to be quite outdistanced, while Price must look to his laurels.

And even Comte d'Erlette will have to rely on his serious work as a basis for claims to distinction! The present excess of markets over producing capacity sounds like the materialisation of every pulpist's dream—& I rejoice that young Albrecht Dürer[1] shares your good fortune. Long may such conditions prevail! Apparently those who can master the prevailing pulp formulae are in luck, even amidst the ravages of worldwide depression! Sorry W T has become such a bad market—though 6-to-9-month payment is better than Gernsback's policy of no payment at all! As for my sending things to pulp markets—I doubt greatly if any products of mine would be wanted. Everything I do is in a vein directly opposed to the tastes & ideals of cheap editors—& the better I succeed in *my* way, the more unacceptable my stuff would be to the lords of the commercial hierarchy. I unfortunately lack that clever adaptability & dualism whereby some persons can turn out pulp material with one hand while they produce serious literary attempts with the other hand. As for new efforts—I have done no more than finish the story on which I was working last January.[2] I sent the MS. to Comte d'Erlette, but his slowness in reading it (I recalled it after 5 months, & he had not finished perusal) shews how lacking in merit it must be. Probably I shall destroy it. I shall continue to experiment, but may never exhibit another product of my striving.

Meanwhile I hope your serious playwriting is going ahead despite your present commercial activities. By the way—I wish I could see once more that complete series of cosmic studies which you shewed me in 1927, of which "The Red Brain" is a part. That was really a splendid performance—ending with the dissolution of all entity to celestial dust. It is a pity it has never been published as a unit. No doubt it is now in St. Paul, but I wish you would shoot it along to 66 the next time you are home. Safe return, of course, abundantly guaranteed.

Well—I have had a great summer down here. My super-hospitable hosts urge me to remain all winter—not returning till May—but I could not be absent from my library & files long enough for that. I cannot do serious writing away from my books & familiar setting. Hence I shall be starting for home almost any time now—endeavouring to pause briefly at St. Augustine & Charleston en route, despite an appalling state of brokeness. This factor of brokeness may prevent my pausing in New York, though I certainly hope most sincerely I can do so. If there is any prospect of such a stop on my part, I shall send due notification. Meanwhile I pray to Yog-Sothoth & Cthulhu for some unexpected cheque from somewhere!

My visit surely has been a pleasant & extended one. Side trips to notable scenic spots have varied the monotony, & I have become quite a specialist in gardening . . . . helping the Barlovii keep the lawn in good condition. Outdoor activity in this genial climate forms a marvellous tonic for me—I feel infinitely better than I ever do in the north, & dread the thought of returning to subarctic conditions. I have likewise coöperated in young Bob's ventures. He has constructed a cabin across the lake, in which he is gradually assembling a complete printing & binding equipment—so that within a year he will be able to inaugurate the somewhat ambitious publishing programme which has so long been a favourite dream of his. His binding work is infinitely & impressively clever.

Recent W T issues are certainly discouraging in quality. Too bad also that *The Fantasy Fan* expired. Did I mention having a call from Hornig last May—before I set out on my Bright Odyssey? Not a bad chap in his way.

All good wishes—& hoping to see you—

Yrs for the Pnakotic Seal—

E'ch-Pi-El

[P.S.] Regards to Young Dürer!

[P.]P.S. Last minute news from home (financial) raises my hope of stopping in N.Y. ¶ Bob has just copied my "Shadow out of Time", so that I may be able to shew it to you.[3]

[*Enclosure:* Postcard (*Front:* Sunset Scene in Florida); no writing on back.]

Notes

1. HPL's epithet for Howard Wandrei.
2. "The Shadow out of Time."
3. HPL means that RHB had typed the story from HPL's AMS.

[223] [HPL to DAW] [ANS][1]

[Postmarked Saint Augustine, Fla.,
21 August 1935]

Melmothing northward at last! Accompanied the Barlows to Daytona, where they are spending a fortnight, & then took a diligencia for ancient San Agustin. Good to see centuried gables & facades & balconies & garden walls—& hear the sound of tinkling fountains at twilight, & of cathedral chimes cast in 1682—after 2 mo. & 9[d] amidst rural modernity! Am revelling in the atmosphere of a 370-year old city—a city founded when Shakespeare was a year old, & still containing houses which had 50 years behind them when the Pilgrims landed on Plymouth Rock. ¶ Am staying a week at the usual cheap but cleanly place—the Rio Vista on the bay front. Got a good basement (but above ground) room with bath & kitchenette for only *$3.50.* Eating on 20 to 25¢ per day, with canned beans as a heavy staple. Spent most of my time absorbing ancient vistas, & writing atop the venerable fort. Moving along Aug. 25—& will get a few hours in Savannah before striking ancient Charleston. Too broke to plan any stops N. of Charleston, & don't even know how long I can stay there. N.Y. stop again doubtful—but I hope some 11ᵗʰ hour cheque will render it possible. If so, I'll hope to see you. Meanwhile I pray fervently to Cthulhu & Yog-Sothoth. ¶ Trust all goes well in Manhattan.

Regards—
E'ch-Pi-El

Notes

1. *Front:* Oldest House in America, 54 St. George Street, St. Augustine, Fla.

[224] [HPL to DAW] [ALS]

La Ciudad Vieja de San Agustin
—24 de agusto, 1935.

O Generous Melmoth:—

Both of your cards duly reached me, since forwarding arrangements from De Land exist. Let me say at the outset how keenly I appreciate your magnanimous suggestion of housing the old man during his passage through the metropolis—a suggestion upon which I shall most gratefully, appreciatively, & delightfully act if (as is probable) the date of my Manhattan transit coincides to any extent with the vacancy at #155. My keenest regret is that this opportunity involves the absence of Young Albrecht Dürer. Possibly—if by any chance I find a slight amelioration of my destitution in my mail at Belknap's—I shall be able to lodge myself for a day or two after H E's return, so that I may greet him in person. For a long time I've been meaning to investigate the Y M C A hotel in N Y—Wm. Sloan House, at 34ᵗʰ St. & 10ᵗʰ Ave. Moe stopped there last July, & informs me it is marvellously cheap. If it looks favourable, I may let it form my independent headquarters in the metropolis at times when I don't want to bother my friends. But meanwhile let me express my profound appreciation of your invitation!

I shall—according to my most abridged schedule—leave here tomorrow at midnight—reaching Savannah at 4:50 A.M. Aug. 26. I shall explore there for 5 hours, taking the 10:30 coach for Charleston & arriving there at 2:10 P.M. This is the place where I'd *like* to make my longest stop—but it isn't as cheap as St. Augustine. At present it looks as if I'd spend 3 nights in Charleston—at the Y M C A—giving me 3 full days besides the afternoon of the 26ᵗʰ. Then on Aug. 29 I shall take the 8:45 for old Richmond, getting in just 12 hours later. Full day in Richmond, (Aug 30) & stop over night. Then next day to Washington (Aug. 31)—lighting out on the midnight coach for Philadelphia. Ancient Phila. in the grey dawn—& coach for Manhattan in the afternoon (Sun., Sept. 1). Now here comes the rub. Sept. 1st. is the Sunday before an holiday, so that everybody may be out of town on this or that week-end trip. I cannot be *sure* enough of my own programme to ask anybody to change plans on my account, but if I don't find anybody around after preliminary telephoning—&

can't collect my mail—there will be no alternative but to keep on to 66 College & do my visiting on the next trip. You can see how it is—while I'm in the South it would be foolish & suicidal to cut out any time I can get . . . . . yet I probably haven't cash enough to hold out till Sept. 3d. Of course, I *might* thus hold out—in which case my sojourn at 155 would be rather brief in case H E returns on the 5th. But we shall see. In any case, don't alter any plans you may have made . . . & I, on my part, will keep you fully advised by postcard as to my movements. By Friday the 30th Richmond I will be so far north that my final card will reach you in 1 day—on Sat. the 31st. By that time I'll know what's what. And in any case, superabundant thanks for the idea!

Sorry you're so rushed with pulpy responsibilities, but trust we'll have time for at least a chat! If by any chance Belknap will be away Sept. 1–2 & you won't, I'll ask him to get my mail to you somehow. I'm writing him now. And incidentally—if either of you wants to slip another word to me before my arrival, you can probably catch me with a return-mail card ℅ *Y M C A, George St., Charleston, S.C.* This note ought to reach you on the 27th, & a card mailed then would make Charleston on my (probable) last day there—the 29th.

Well—anyhow, we'll hope for the best. Trust you got my card from here. I'm still having a great time. Yesterday I had a surprise visit from little Bobby Barlow—up for the day from Daytona to give Grandpa a second farewell. I shewed him a number of San Augustinian sights which he'd never seen before—including the largest known live-oak in the world, & the newly-discovered (April 1934) Indian burying ground north of the town (on the site of the original Indian village of Seloy, later called Nombre de Dios by the Spaniards), where the disinterred skeletons lie *in situ*—preserved in cement & roofed over.

And so it goes. Thanks again for the invitation—& I surely hope to see you. Barlow typed my new story, which you can read if you have time & patience.

Regards & all that—
   Yrs for The Elder Sign
    —Melmoth III.

[*Enclosure:* Postcard (*Front:* Post Office and Custom House, St. Augustine, Florida); no writing on back.]

[225] [HPL to DAW] [ANS][1]

          [Postmarked Richmond, Va.,
            30 August 1935]

Almost knocked out by the *cold*, but on my way! The essentially northern landscape of Virginia seems really bleak & strange after so long a time in the live-oak region. Yesterday I was coatless & comfortable & full of energy—today I am shivering in coat & vest, & without the strength of a wet rag. So

numbed with the cold that I can hardly write. Drizzly day after a cold night ride. Am dodging showers & circulating among the Poe vestigia. Just now on a bench in Capitol Park with a squirrel virtually climbing over me. Rain seems about over—but no heat in sight. ¶ Washington tomorrow—Phila. Sunday morning—& hope to see you Sunday evening. Now I'll have to get up & begin walking to keep warm! Only politically & culturally can Richmond be called "southern" . . . . to an old Charlestonian like Grandpa it sure is plumb north! ¶ Yrs between tooth-chatters—
Melmoth III

Notes

1. *Front:* The Old Stone House and Enchanted Garden, Edgar Allen [corrected in pen by HPL to "Allan"] Poe Shrine, Richmond, Va.

[226] [HPL to DAW] [ANS][1]

[Postmarked Providence, R.I.,
13 September 1935]

Hail, O Melmoth! Had a good call on Kleiner, but nearly froze on the home-bound coach. Arrived to find my room piled ceiling-high with mail . . . amidst which I am still hopelessly floundering. Even the bugbears of the remote past arise to harass me . . . . a revision order from that ass *D. V. Bush*,[2] who has been silent for a decade! ¶ Local felidae all cordial—one of them is now purring in the chair beside me. Aunt also well, & sends regards. ¶ Bad news—*JAKE'S HAS FAILED.* Found only "For Rent" signs in empty windows. After all these years . . . . . sic transit gloria mundi! ¶ Lower College St. all torn up for new building—I hate to look at the scene of desolation! ¶ Can scarcely say how grateful I am for your hospitality of the past fortnight. Again, my sincerest & most appreciative thanks! Regards to young Albrecht Dürer when he returns! ¶ I may be briefly on the move again next week-end—visiting Edward H. Cole in the Boston zone & taking a trip to Wilbraham, Mass. with him. The good old Melmothic tradition must be maintained! Cook may *possibly* be in on the trip. ¶ And so it goes. Don't forget to get around here when you can—& good luck with the prospective house-hunt!
      Yr obt Servt
Melmoth III.

Notes

1. *Front:* The Carrie Tower, Hope, Manning and University Halls at Left. / Brown University, Providence, R. I.
2. David Van Bush (1882–1959), "psychological lecturer" and longtime revision client of HPL.

[227] [HPL to DAW] [ALS]

Home for a while, at least!
—Septr. 24, 1935

Hail, Melmoth:—

Off & back again! Left Friday, met Cole in Boston, did Nahant & Marblehead, & planned for the descent on "Dunwich". Saturday the party sallied forth to the haunted hills which I had not seen since 1928, found the region unchanged, & performed the melancholy rites for which we had come—scattering the ashes of a deceased old lady upon her native soil.[1] Magnificent scenery & views—would that I might sojourn there at greater length some summer! Sunday I accompanied the Cole household on a picnic to Cape Cod—taking in all the villages, lunching at S. Yarmouth, & loafing on the sands at Chatham—with only the blue Atlantic betwixt us & Spain. Monday Cole & I made the rounds of Swampscott—& that evening (last night) I again returned to these classic shades to wrestle with my unmanageable stacks of correspondence, reading, &c. &c. Had good hot weather until yesterday— so that it was really a great little outing. This ample & varied dose of New England scenery was especially welcome after my long absence from my native land. It is barely possible that I shall have one more such outing this year—overcoated, & in Cole's well-heated Chevrolet—exploring the Mohawk Trail & certain adjacent parts of Southern Vermont. 1935 sure seems to be a ground-covering year!

Congratulations on H E on his matrimonial venture—may it prove felicitous & permanent![2] Despite drawbacks there is in the long run no better state than the married one—provided, of course, a partner of the right degree of basic congeniality can be found. It would pay those with the requisite youth, attractiveness, & financial competence to look about for a suitable wife before they are too old to capture the attention of the nubile fair.

Pleased to hear that you are back in the ancient retreat—& that you now have the added advantage of a garden view. Let us hope that this recapture of seclusion & quiet may facilitate both your literary & commercial writing, & prove a restful influence in general. I see you have a different number this time—88 instead of 84—but presume this is a mere matter of doorways.

And so I have missed "Dr. Caligari" *again!*[3] And by so tantalisingly narrow a margin! Curses & damnation! I presume it will be shewn in Providence the very day after my death!

About "The Shadow Out of Time"—here's a circulation list including those whom I recall to have expressed a wish to see it. In order to save postage, I'm grouping all the N.Y. readers first—you can just hand it on to Koenig, & he can give it to Leedle Meestah Stoiling[4] on one of the all-too-numerous occasions when that bright little divvle drops in at the Elec. Testing Lab. In listing the other names, I've followed a sort of roughly geographical plan in case anybody uses express (where distance counts) instead of 1st class mail. I regret the heaviness of the paper—which was Bobby Barlow's choice. Hope nothing happens to the thing, for it is the only legible copy existing! In passing on the MS., you can simply include the circulation list in the envelope with it.

Well—I presume you have received the sombre news from Averoigne . . . . of the passing of Klarkash-Ton's mother.[5] I suppose it is really best in the long run, though the shock to C A S is no lighter on that account. He had been expecting the blow ever since March, when Mrs. Smith sustained a stroke affecting both her speech & memory. This must be a rather bad jolt for C A S's father—whose own health is bad enough—& it will probably hasten his own departure.[6] One wonders how C A S will react to the circumstance of being alone in the world—whether he will remain an hermit of the hills, or seek some less isolated environment. I surely wish he would visit the East!

Cook is once more contemplating the westward plunge. We tried to get in touch with him & have him meet us in Wilbraham, but Cole's message arrived too late.

Have all the Providence papers read up to date, but no N.Y. Times's since Aug. 4! It will take weeks to get my programme back to normal. Steam heat, thank Yuggoth, is on at last—but only in the daytime as yet, so that the old oil stove remains in commission.

Rumours come of impending changes in the "fan magazine" field, but everything seems hazy as yet. Meestah Vollheim shoost esk me haff I seen hiss *Fentygreff* a'ready—to which I had to reply that I haven't.[7] If Hill-Billy Crawford was given the responsibility of mailing, he sure fell down on the job! Skimmed through W T & found it lousy except for "Vulthoom".[8]

And so it goes. Again, congrats to H E. The eternal elementals . . . birth, marriage, death. Searight has a new son,[9] H E a wife, & C A S has lost a mother.

With best of wishes, & pleasantest of memories of my recent visit, I am, Sir, ever

Yr most oblig'd,

most ob^t Servt—

Melmoth III.

[*Enclosure:*]

The Shadow Out of Time

Circulation List[10]

H. C. Koenig, 540 East 80th St., N.Y. City.
Kenneth Sterling, 240 West 73^d St., N.Y. City.
Robert E. Howard, Lock Box 313, Cross Plains, Texas.
E. Hoffmann Price, Route 2, Box 100-U-5, Redwood City, California.
Clark Ashton Smith, Box 385, Auburn, California.
Duane W. Rimel, Box 100, Asotin, Washington.

Emil Petaja, Box 85, Milltown, Montana.

Miss Margaret Sylvester, 2714 Java Court, Denver, Colorado.

Mrs. Natalie H. Wooley, 20 N. Early St., Rosedale, Kansas.

Robert Bloch, 620 East Knapp St., Milwaukee, Wisconsin.

R. F. Searight, 19946 Derby Ave., Detroit, Michigan.

Miss C. L. Moore, 2547 Brookside Parkway, S. Drive, Indianapolis, Indiana.

William Lumley, 742 William St., Buffalo, N.Y.

H. P. Lovecraft, 66 College St., Providence, R.I.

Notes

1. Jennie E. T. Dowe (1841–1919), amateur journalist and mother of Edith Miniter. HPL wrote a poem about her: "In Memoriam: J. E. T. D.," *Tryout* 5, No. 3 (March 1919): [6].

2. Howard Wandrei's marriage to Connie Comstock proved anything but "felicitous." See D. H. Olson's introduction to Howard Wandrei's *Time Burial.*

3. *The Cabinet of Dr. Caligari* (German, 1921), directed by Robert Wiene; starring Werner Krauss, Conrad Veidt, and Lil Dagover.

4. I.e., Kenneth Sterling.

5. CAS's mother, Fanny (Gaylord) Smith, died 9 September 1935 at the age of 85.

6. CAS's father, Timeus Smith, died 26 December 1937 at the age of 82.

7. Donald A. Wollheim was editor of the *Phantagraph.*

8. CAS, "Vulthoom" (*WT*, September 1935).

9. Franklyn Searight, the son of HPL's colleague Richard F. Searight (1902–1975), was born 5 August 1935.

10. DAW did not fulfill his duty, but instead took the story to *Argosy* (which rejected it), and then to *Astounding Stories.*

[228] [HPL and Samuel Loveman to DAW] [ANS][1]

[Postmarked Boston, Mass.,
17 October 1935]

Behold, O Melmoth II, a Bostonese Kalem gathering involving our Aonian colleague Es-El, & the ceaselessly circulating dotard Melmoth III! Es-El arrived in ancient Providentium yesterday at 6 A.M., & we later proceeded to the Hub to investigate books, museums, & antiquities. Passed by the Excellent Lunch (where we took refuge from a thunderstorm in 1927) on our way to the art museum. We're now in Ashburton Place atop Beacon Hill. Back to Prov. tomorrow night, when Es-El returns to your decadent cosmopolis. ¶ Last week my aunt & I had a ride to New Haven. Fine autumnal Connecticut scenery. Town not as colonial as Providence, but fascinating withal. I had 7½ hours for exploration, & used them all. Saw all the ancient houses & churches, toured 3 museums & 2 botanic gardens, & absorbed atmosphere generally.

The premier attraction is the labyrinth of new Yale quadrangles all in perfect Gothic or Georgian style—spires, oriels, arches, colonnades, walks, gardens—little enchanted worlds of the past. Like entering bodily into a region of dream. ¶ Trust you're getting used to Horatio St. again. ¶ Regards to H E, Sonny, or anybody you see.
Yrs by the sign of Nug
Melmoth III

Well, Donald—I've worked hard here but the recompense has been—Howard.

Sam Loveman

Notes

1. *Front:* Old South Church, Boston, Mass.

[229] [HPL to DAW] [ANS][1]

[Postmarked Providence, R.I.,
3? November 1935]

Hail, Melmoth! What's this I hear about philanthropic agenting activities behind Grandpa's back? A couple of days ago certain rumours began to filter in from Sonny & little Meestah Stoiling—& this morning a $280 cheque from S & S confirmed the most extreme reports. Yuggoth, what a stroke! Hope you took out a good commission—if you didn't, Grandpa'll have to send you one![2] ¶ No doubt you heard that Leedle Shoolie managed to sell the "Mts. of Madness" to S & S for a sum which nets me $315.[3] The coincidence of *two* such stories successfully landing is almost unbelievable, since neither has anything in common with the policy & formulae of *Astounding*. I thought they had not the slightest shadow of a chance with Tremaine.[4] The combined sum—595—comes as a crisis-postponing life-saver at this juncture . . . & I certainly wish such marketing could keep up! But I have no illusions in that direction. Two swallows don't make a summer. However, the whole pair of incidents is ineffably encouraging, & strengthens my determination to get some more stories written. If I could be sure of making $550 per year, I could keep afloat indefinitely. ¶ It is hardly possible to formulate my thanks in fitting language—but pray accept the spirit for the phrase! ¶ Suppose Sonny told you of the death of his aunt—instantly killed in a motor accident near Miami Oct. 20.[5] I was tremendously sorry to hear it. ¶ And has he shewed you "The Goblin Tower", which Barlow & I printed last summer?[4] ¶ Trust your good luck continues in the fiction field—& once more, my profoundest & sincerest gratitude!
Yr obt Grandsire
Melmoth III

Notes

1. *Front:* New Providence County Court House, Providence, R. I.

2. HPL refers to DAW's selling of "The Shadow out of Time" to *Astounding Stories.* DAW took no commission. HPL did not know that DAW had first surreptitiously submitted the story to the *Argosy,* which rejected it.

3. Julius Schwartz, acting as HPL's agent, sold *At the Mountains of Madness* to *Astounding* for $350, from which he took his 10% commission.

4. F. Orlin Tremaine (1899–1956), editor of *Astounding.* He apparently accepted both stories without reading them.

5. FBL, *The Goblin Tower* (1935) was a small collection of poetry published by RHB. HPL helped set the type when he visited RHB in the summer of 1935.

[230] [HPL to DAW] [ALS]

Acropolis of Leng—
Nov. 10, 1935.

O Mighty Melmoth:—

Yea, verily, the results in the case of the "Shadow" submission certainly reduce to absurdity any ethical quibbling to which the principle involved might give rise! Gratitude & gratification are the only emotions for which any room could possibly remain. Coming directly on top of the "Mountains" acceptance, you can imagine the effect of the phenomenon upon a dizzily astonished old man! Two in a row! Ædepol, & they rule coincidence out of realistic fiction! Well—there's no use expecting such things to keep up. It's good luck while it lasts (a decade ago Wright was taking my things month after month . . . . eheu fugaces!), but lucky streaks always break. Incidentally—the recent week seems to have been quite a gang festival at S & S's . . . with 3 novelettes of Sonny's, two of young Dürer's, two of Grandpa's, & one of yours all received within the glittering gate! Congrats to all my fellow-beneficiaries—whose luck, something tells me, will last longer than the old gentleman's! In view of all I had heard of Tremaine—whose philistinism as compared with Desmond Hall's had been impressed upon me from several sources—I cannot but be amazed at the acceptance of the "Mountains" & the "Shadow". No two items could possibly be further than these from the pulpish norm. It leads one to speculate as to whether Belknap & others are not making *unnecessary* concessions to the popular formula in their efforts to please the capricious tyrants of pulpdom—though on the other hand I suppose that all these concessions increase the chances of steady placement. A serious story *might* land—but it would be against heavy odds; whereas a carefully concocted bit of pulp mechanism by the proper craftsman would be *virtually certain* to land. That, I believe, is Price's experience. No serious & independent writer could place his products at the *rate* that the Peacock

Sultan places his. He has virtually *no* final rejections now. As to the matter of *commission*—while of course I understand & appreciate your generous attitude (indeed, I wouldn't accept a commission myself unless I were in some stern & definitely predetermined deal), I hated to think of your receiving so little return for a type of service which had just netted our pushing little friend Shoolie t'oity-five bucks a'ready! It surely was easy money for The Listener (to give him a Blackwoodian title based on his recent unabashed procedure at S & S's), but of course he technically earned it fairly enough. The fact that the MS. he was handling landed at the first shot was simply his good luck. In another case an agent might have to tramp around interminably & waste postage on something which would never yield any return. It is on a preponderance of good "breaks" over losses that the ability of an agent to carry on his business depends. I would never have given Leedle Shoolie the "Mountains" MS. if I had had the least idea of its acceptability at S & S's. I thought it had not a ghost of a chance there, & frankly told Shoolie as much. I didn't think the venture was worth wasting postage on, although I did have a vague notion (imbibed from Leedle Meestah Stoiling) of trying the thing on the moribund *Amazing* if Hill-Billy Crawford decided not to make a booklet of it. When Shoolie insisted, I told him to get the thing from Hill-Billy at his own risk— but that I thought he'd be wasting his time. I assumed he would try it vainly on *Astounding*, then (probably vainly) on *Amazing*—& then shoot it back to Crawford or to me. I merely wished no stone to be left technically unturned. Later I meant to let him do the same with the "Shadow"—but it seems that a more enterprising young gentleman got ahead of him! Well—such strokes of luck can't last. Now Hill-Billy wants to try "Innsmouth" on Tremaine, & I may let him—although warning him (a) that the pitcher generally goes to the well once too often, & (b) that "Innsmouth" is vastly more removed from the science fiction field than is either of the two other things.[1] However, as I've said, such temporary incidents surely are encouraging while they are fresh. On the strength of this one I've just finished a new tale—"The Haunter of the Dark"—which may or may not be worth typing. It is a straight weird effort, with no possible market save the non-receptive Brother Farny. Taking the suggestion of a writer in the Eyrie, I've dedicated it to young Bloch, who lately killed Grandpa off in "The Shambler from the Stars".[2] In this yarn I've left Bloch dead—of fright—in an ancient Providence house by no means dissimilar to #66. Well—I'd like to see old Farny's face (tho' perhaps the Parkinson's disease would hide his emotion) when he reads of the publication of the "Mountains" as a two-parter. "Oh, no," said he 4 years ago, "such a long MS. couldn't possibly be published in less than 3 parts . . . ."[3] W T's financial policy seems to be getting pretty much like Hugo the Rat's.[4] A few April contributors are beginning to be paid—Searight for one. I presume H E's half-cheque is for the "O'Mecca".[5] Commiserations on the *Argosy's* title-monkeying—though perhaps the counterbalancing advantage of having landed such a market makes congratulations really in order.[6] Financially, I believe the house of Munsey is especially advantageous to deal with, is it not?

Well—I'm certainly glad to hear of young Albrecht Dürer's success in the matrimonial field, & hope he'll find the felicity permanent. There are, of course, persons difficult to adjust to any sort of marriage; but so far as the vast majority are concerned, I believe that a well-chosen & highly discriminating entry into that state (mostly possible, I suppose, only after one or more unsatisfying trials & divorces) affords a greater promise of reasonable felicity, & a larger quota of high-grade emotional values, than any other arrangement which can be envisaged. Certainly, it does not provide an ideal happiness— but then, nothing else does, either! Still, it approaches so much more closely to tolerableness than any other condition (always assuming that the right sort of partner has, through a combination of luck, intelligence, & persistence, been secured), that I would not advise its dismissal from the plans of any man young & attractive enough to command the interest of gentlewomen of suitable youth, beauty, & mental & temperamental endowments. Pray convey my sincerest congratulations & good wishes to Young Dürer & his spouse! Which reminds me—did I mention that our energetic young friend Harry Brobst is likewise enrolled in the husbandly ranks? He is swinging a large programme these days—setting up light housekeeping with his bride, acting as a nurse at the Charles V. Chapin Hospital (where he secured a position after graduating at Butler), & taking a course at Brown University with the object of an ultimate degree. He has taken an apartment at 73 Brown St., only about 2 squares from #66. Little did I think, in his Allentown days, that he would some time be a near neighbor of mine!

Glad you've seen the edition de luxe of "The Goblin Tower"—which is more than I've done! It seems to have taken Belknap completely by surprise—& I fancy he is properly grateful to little Bobby. I helped to print the thing last summer—& the typography sadly attests the fact that it was a first job both for me & for my youthful host! What we *do* think is that there isn't a single misprint—unless you call our stupid neglect of connected fi's, fl's, ffi's, ff's, and ffl's at the beginning of the text misprints. Later we learned to watch out & always use those combinations—or rather, *I* did, for I see in the new *Dragon-Fly* (Bob's N.A.P.A. paper—a marvellously select thing of its kind) that my colleague has done considerable backsliding. But on the whole, he's getting better & better impressions—so that by the time he tackles C A S's "Incantations"[7] he'll be able to turn out something really creditable. I shall probably read proof on that, so that there won't be any flagrant breach of accuracy in the text. As a binder, Bob is hard to beat. He fixed me up a magnificent "Shunned House",[8] & his own "Star-Treader" is a work of art. I can imagine what this new "Goblin Tower" achievement is like. You'll receive a copy of the G.T. in course of time, & I doubt whether the young publisher would accept any cash in return. I'm certainly glad to see Sonny's poems so compactly collated, & hope this edition will inspire the little rascal to forget his bolshevism & money-making now & then, & turn out some new Aonian offerings for a future collection. The young imp certainly *can* write when he puts all extraneous matters out of his head. Oh, for another "Man from Genoa" or "White People"![9]

Cook is doing pretty well out west. The paper he is on has improved 200% since his advent, & he has a bungalow all to himself—with a separate press shed in the back yard, & a view of the prehistoric Cahokia Indian mounds in the background! But the most marvellous news is that the inexplicably silent *Munn* has been heard from! It took a complete stranger to break through his baffling isolation, but the young weird fan Emil Petaja (of Milltown, Montana) has turned the trick. The Werewolf is still in Athol, though he had a job as a life-guard somewhere last summer. (Hope it took off some of his excess weight) And he is still writing stories in the hope of publication. Dwyer is still in the C.C.C., but is beginning (after a year & a half) to get a bit homesick. He will probably go home, job or no job, after the expiration of his third enlistment in April. I suppose little Augie sent you his new detective novel—which to me seems as good as any he's produced so far. He kept me guessing much longer than ever before.[10] It appears almost certain that his serious work (regional novels of Wisconsin from 1830 onward) will be handled by Scribners from now on. Price is en route back from Mexico City, where he revelled among Aztec temples & pyramids. At one point he was halted by a landslide & forced to live on primitive native fare for 3 days—then, on a rocky detour, he punched a hole in his gas tank & had to mend it with chewing-gum! From all accounts he had a great time—even though he had to do some pulp writing (about the inevitable Pawang Ali) whilst on the road. He stopped to see W. K. Mashburn, & I trust he'll manage to have a session with Two-Gun Bob at Cross Plains before he finally returns to the grove-circled mosque atop the Horrible Kaf. Hope the cats—Nimrod & Battle Axe—have fared well in his absence. He left them at the old homestead in Oakland.

I surely hope you'll be able to make that homeward trip at Yuletide, even though it means a 40,000-word grind. If you do, I hope you won't forget to ransack 1152's cobwebbed attic or nitre-encrusted vaults for that missing series of early cosmic tales! I wanted to see that once more before I die!

Samuelus's book business seems to be coming on. Has he given you his new business address? Bodley Bookshop, 104 Fifth Ave., Room 1709. Tel. ALgonquin 4-9762. He has moved his residence to a smaller flat in the same apartment-house—17 Middagh St. Bklyn. The other day I looked up some prices for him at the Dana Rice shop in Providence—so perhaps business will induce him to honour these ancient shores again ere long. And as the months progress, I trust that you can yourself do the aforementioned shores a kindred honour. I have discovered that the *slum* branch of *Jake's* is still open; so that if the call of old times is sufficiently strong, we can plunge down South Main St. & tank up with the familiar overdoses in a hardy waterfront section where the sparrows chirp in bass & the policemen go in carbine-bearing squads! I wonder, incidentally, whether Talman & James Ferdinand will think enough of Jake's to make this pilgrimage in its honour! I'll confess I haven't done so myself—my glimpse of the Wickenden St. sign having been secured only fleetingly, as I went down to the N.Y. boat to welcome Samuelus. Incidentally—*don't* patronise the *Colonial Line* when you come. It has gone all to hell since the revived Providence Line drew off its better patronage, & Loveman found the boat an intolerable babel of bums. Never again for him! Morton now uses the Providence exclusively—it's a N Y N H & H subsidiary.[11]

As I probably said on my card, this has been a record-breakingly mild autumn for Providence (80° on Oct. 29), so that I have prolonged my outdoor sessions beyond all accustomed limits. But I suppose the time of hibernation has come at last. I hope to get quite a programme of reading & writing accomplished during the winter—though it never does to count on plans. Just now I'm slowly absorbing the monumental Wells-Huxley "Science of Life"—one could never do the volume (over 1200 pp) justice within the time-limits imposed by a public library.

Oct. W T rather above the average, with 3 stories exclusive of reprint worth reading. "The Way Home", by Paul Frederick Stern, is great stuff. Never heard of the author before, but he's certainly a guy to keep an eye on. Two-Gun & Sultan Malik also appear to advantage—indeed, I like Malik's "Hand of Wrath" better than any other recent thing of his I've seen.[12]

Well—thanks again for your benevolent high-handedness! Since Barlow's typing of the MS. was also a surprise, this venture is certainly quite an adventure in grateful astonishment for me! Here's hoping the two tales won't be mis-titled, hashed up, & panned in the end by the yelping circle of juvenile "scientifans"! ¶ Benedictions—

Yr obt Grandsire

Melmoth III.

Notes

1. It is not clear whether William L. Crawford actually submitted "The Shadow over Innsmouth" to *Astounding*. If he did so, it was rejected.

2. In the November 1935 *WT*, B. M. Reynolds suggested in "The Eyrie" that "Robert Bloch deserves plenty of praise for *The Shambler from the Stars*. Now why doesn't Mr. Lovecraft return the compliment, and dedicate a story to the author?" (p. 652). "The Haunter of the Dark" is "Dedicated to Robert Bloch."

3. *At the Mountains of Madness* was in fact published in three parts in *Astounding Stories*.

4. I.e., Hugo Gernsback.

5. Howard Wandrei, "The Hand of the O'Mecca" (*WT*, April 1935).

6. Evidently a reference to "The Monster from Nowhere," which perhaps was not DAW's title. He never restored the putative original title in subsequent reprints.

7. No typescript of *Incantations* is known to exist, although a table of contents for it is among CAS's papers at JHL. *Incantations* was never issued as a book, but there is a section in *Selected Poems* titled "Incantations."

8. RHB's presentation copy of *The Shunned House*, inscribed "For H P L—Who only wrote it—With the compliments of the binder. R. H. B. June 9, 1935. On the occasion of his second visit," was bound in full leather, and hand tooled with raised bands.

9. The reference is to FBL's poem "The White People" (in *A Man from Genoa*, his first book), presumably inspired by the Arthur Machen story of that title.

10. AWD, *Sign of Fear: A Judge Peck Mystery* (New York, Loring & Mussey, [1935]; *LL* 236)

11. New York, Hew Haven, and Hartford, a railway line.

12. *WT* (November 1935): Paul Ernst [as "Paul Frederick Stern"], "The Way Home"; Robert E. Howard, "Shadows in Zamboula"; and E. Hoffmann Price, "The Hand of Wrath."

[231] [HPL to DAW] [ALS]

Friday
[6 December 1935]

Dear Melmoth:—

The new "Haunter" is due to reach you very soon from old Bill Lumley, & I wonder if you'd mind substituting the enclosed new circulation list—with 3 new names—for the old one? Thanks in advance. Hope the thing won't form too bad a disappointment. It is a disappointment to me, for the more I reflect upon it the more trivial & commonplace it seems to me. I certainly cannot successfully write anything as *short* as that nowadays.

Trust all goes well in the metropolis. Koenig spoke of a pleasant meeting up at Sonny's with you & H E present. Give my regards to such of the gang as you meet. No events whatever hereabouts—hibernation begun at last. Just saw Dec. W T—nothing of any merit in it except Klarkash-ton's "Chain of Aforgomon"—that is, nothing short. Two-Gun's serial may be good, but I never read serials until I have all the parts.[1] Also recd. the *Fantasy* issue with the composite tales.[2] You continued the scientifiction one very cleverly— right in the spirit of such things! My instalment is puzzlingly misprinted in places. It amused me to see how quickly Two-Gun made a rip-roaring san-guinary Conan out of the mild & scholarly George Campbell, & how Sonny worked in his romantic illusion that all human beings are repressed savages! All the boys true to form!

Yrs for the Black Avatar of Azathoth—
—Melmoth III.

[*Enclosure:*]

The Haunter of the Dark

Revised Circulation List

F. B. Long, 230 W. 97th St., New York, N.Y.
H. C. Koenig, 540 East 80th St., New York, N.Y.
Kenneth Sterling, 240 W. 73d St., New York, N.Y.
Mrs. Natalie H. Wooley, 20 N. Early St., Rosedale, Kansas.

Richard E. Morse, 40 Princeton Ave., Princeton, N.J.

Bernard Dwyer, C.C.C. Camp 25, Peekskill, N.Y.

H. P. Lovecraft, 66 College St., Providence, R.I.

Notes

1. *WT* (December 1935): CAS, "The Chain of Aforgomon"; Robert E. Howard, "The Hour of the Dragon" (1 of 5).
2. "The Challenge from Beyond," *Fantasy Magazine* 5, No. 4 (September 1935): weird story by C. L. Moore, A. Merritt, HPL, Robert E. Howard, and FBL; science fiction story by Stanley G. Weinbaum, DAW, Edward E. Smith, Harl Vincent, and Murray Leinster. Both stories were reprinted by Necronomicon Press (1990).

[232] [HPL to DAW] [ANS]

[Postmarked Providence, R.I.,
19 December 1935]

[May the joy
that comes at
CHRISTMASTIME
linger with you
all the Year.]

Melmoth III
—1935

1936

[233] [HPL to DAW] [ALS]

66 College St.,
Providence, R.I.,
May 14, 1936.

Mighty Melmoth:—

Commiserations to you & Belknap upon the vicissitudes you have suffered! Let us trust that better times lie ahead. And if misery loves company, attend the ensuing tale of woe from your aged Grandpa!

For verily, the old man can boast a prostrating maximum of afflictions—being in truth one "whom unmerciful disaster follows fast & follows faster".[1] No sooner was I back from my New-Year trip than I became utterly swamped by a mountain of tasks & epistles—a load with which I could not possibly cope. Next, I came down with grippe & was flat for a week. And *then*—just as I was able to stagger around again—the *real* trouble began! My aunt was seized with a grippe attack vastly worse than mine,[2] & from mid-February on I was enslaved as a sort of combined nurse, butler, secretary, market-man, & errand-boy. All my own affairs went absolutely to hell—letters unanswered, borrowed books piled up unread, N.A.P.A. duties shifted to good old Kleiner, revision jobs returned unperformed, story-writing a by-gone memory . . . . .

"With ruin upon ruin, rout on rout—
Confusion worse confounded."[3]

But it was a damn sight worse on my aunt than on me! Complications set in, & in mid-March she had to go to the hospital. This changed—without much lessening—my responsibilities. The patient improved slowly, & on April 7 migrated to a convalescent home—finally returning to 66 April 21. She is now up & about—taking walks on good afternoons—though requiring considerable coöperation in household tasks. My own programme is totally shot to pieces, & I am about on the edge of a nervous breakdown. I have so little power of concentration that it takes me about an hour to do what I can ordinarily do in five minutes—& my eyesight is acting like the devil. But warmer weather & outdoor activities will be giving me a little more energy later on.

The goddam weather in itself was enough to leave me limp. After a little deceptive warmth in March—followed by the memorable floods—there came a chilly April which about wore me out. Not till the 28th was there a really warm day. Since then I have been able to take my work out to Prospect Terrace several times—& on April 30 my aunt & I were treated to a delightful motor ride through the awakening countryside to Westport Point, Mass. The landscape is now a captivating spectacle with its new verdure & abundant blossoms, & I hope to find time for some rural walks ere long. Barlow has invited me down to De Land again, but I greatly doubt my ability to accept. This, I fear, will be no travel year for Grandpa!

I've heard some pretty good lectures during recent months—at the college a block over the hill & at the School of Design a block down the hill. Subjects pleasantly varied—Plato's Republic, modern painting, Chinese influences on western culture, philosophy & poetry, Mayan ruins, & the Michelson-Morley experiment. No excuse for being ignorant in this neighbourhood!

On May 4th the R.I. Tercentenary observances began with a costumed parade which started at the college gate—just a stone's throw from here. Later there was a mock-session of the rebel legislature of May 4, 1776—held in costume in the selfsame room of the ancient colony-house (1761—you've seen the exterior) where the original session was held. In this, each old-time deputy was impersonated by a lineal descendant. Both acting & costumes were so convincing that one might easily fancy the bygone period returned—with the intervening 160 years merely a bad dream. I was one of the few spectators lucky enough to get into the colony-house & witness the proceedings. In the afternoon—in a ceremony at the State House which I did not attend—Gov. Curley of Mass. presented to Gov. Green of R.I. a copy of the recent resolutions of the Mass. Genl. Court, rescinding the banishment imposed on Roger Williams in Oct. 1635. After 300½ years, Mr. Williams no doubt highly appreciates this delicate mark of consideration!

The Mar. & Apr. W T struck me as not quite as bad as usual—tales by Binder, Klarkash-Ton, Hamilton (!!), Kuttner, Jacobi, Derleth, & Bloch[4] having marked points of merit. I have the May issue, but have had no time to read it. Too bad "The Red Brain" couldn't have appeared in proper shape, but the readers will be glad to see it again in *any* condition! As for the financial side—probably you sent the story before you learned the trick of reserving all but first rights—hence Pirate Farny can reprint it all he likes without pay. That's the way with all the tales of mine which he has reprinted—he invariably chooses things prior to April '26, when I began to reserve rights. Something for nothing whenever possible is the old boy's motto. I liked the "Mts. of Madness" illustrations in *Astounding*, & hope the "Shadow out of Time" will be treated as well. No—Hill-Billy Crawford is still dawdling over "Innsmouth" with no issuance in sight—though he has secured 4 excellent Utpatel illustrations. And Barlow has been so laid up with throat trouble that "Incantations" must be regarded as a *future* item.

Hope the other Wandreis will have enjoyable St. Paul vacations—pray give them my best regards! Do you expect to get home during the summer?

Glad your new acquaintance—Morton the inventor-to-order—likes my tales. As an electrical guy he ought to prove congenial to our friend Koenig.

Have you seen the loan-exhibit of Klarkash-Ton's sculpture now in Loveman's custody? If not, better get in touch with S L. It will later be sent successively to me & to Barlow. While in N.Y. it ought to be seen by all members of the group there. By the way—Barlow may get to N.Y. during the summer, though his plans depend largely on his health.

Stumbled on an interesting genealogical discovery recently—which I wish I had made before we visited the Hayden Planetarium 4 months ago. In brief—I learned for the first time that I am a great-great-great-great-great-great-great-great-great-grandson of the Elizabethan *astronomer* who introduced the Copernican theory into England! Ordinarily I'm not much of a genealogist—being content to take whatever existing charts tell me & let it go at that. The other day I ran into some callers of my aunt's—venerable sisters related to us in the *Field* & *Wilcox* lines—& one of them remarked how proud I ought to be of our common forbear, *the astronomer John Field*. That rather floored me, since our charts carried the Field line back only to the original Prov. settler John F., who died in 1686, & I knew *he* was no star-gazer! Well, it soon turned out that the ancestry of this settler has been known to genealogists for ages, though I had no inkling of it. The 16th cent. astronomer John Field (whose Ephemeris, published in 1557, contained the first Eng. account of the Cop. system, & who has been called "The Proto-Copernican of England") was the Prov. John's *own grandfather*—hence my 9-times-great-grandfather. It surely gave me a kick to get a real man of science in my pedigree—which as a general thing is lousy with clergymen* but short on straight thinkers. Later I looked up the standard Field genealogy at the library & found out all about the line. It comes from Sir Hubertus de la Feld, a follower of Wm. the Conqueror who took lands in Lancashire in 1069; the Prov. stock springing from the Yorkshire branch centreing around Sowerby, Ardsley, & Thruscoe. I've copied a lot of notes & now have my Field lineage straight back—in just 20 generations—to one Roger de la Feld of Sowerby, born in 1240. But it's the *astronomer* who interests me. I have more than an average amount of Field blood, being descended from 3 of the Prov. settler's grandchildren.

And so it goes. Hope you can get to Prov. before long & check up on your intuition regarding #66 & its interior! Trust your tales continue successful—I hear you're becoming quite an *Argosy* bulwark these days! And I hope that the slowly increasing warmth of the season may shortly banish all traces of indisposition. ¶ Yrs. by the Black Trilithon—Ech-Pi-El

---

*& damn me if this new find hasn't added *one more* divine to the bunch—for it seems that the Providence colonist's maternal grandfather was the Rev. John Sotwell, Vicar of Peniston, Yorkshire!

[P.S.] Robert Bloch says of "The Red Brain", "I wish I could do something like that!" ¶ When am I going to see other surviving parts of the cosmic series?

[P.]P.S. Hope you received the copy of *Causerie* with Edkins' review of "The Goblin Tower."⁵ E A E didn't quite do justice to the *massed effect* of the poems, since he is unfortunately impervious to weird influences. ¶ The little Sterling kid has been desperately ill with abscess of lower colon—operation, blood-transfusion, intra-venous nourishment, &c. Now nearly well, & plugging up with tutors to see whether he can make Harvard in the autumn after all.

Notes

1. ". . . whom unmerciful Disaster / Followed fast and followed faster . . ." Poe, "The Raven," ll. 63–64.
2. Actually, Annie Gamwell was hospitalized at this time for breast cancer.
3. John Milton, *Paradise Lost* 2.995–96.
4. *WT* (March 1936): "Eando" Binder, "The Crystal Curse"; CAS, "The Black Abbot of Puthuum"; Edmond Hamilton, "In the World's Dusk"; Henry Kuttner, "The Graveyard Rats." *WT* (April 1936): Carl Jacobi, "The Face in the Wind"; AWD and Marc Shorer, "They Shall Rise"; Robert Bloch, "The Druidic Doom"; DAW, "The Red Brain" (orig. October 1927).
5. [Ernest A. Edkins], *"The Goblin Tower," Causerie* (February 1936): 2–4.

[234] [HPL to DAW] [ALS]

66 College St.,
Providence, R.I.,
June 24, 1936

Dear Melmoth:—

Glad to hear that the Klarkash-Ton loan exhibit is safe in your lair. Samuelus' long silence regarding it had C A S rather worried. I am surely eager to behold this collection of horrors from beyond Yaddith, but believe that on the whole you had better retain it until Young Dürer & all the rest of the metropolitan group shall have had a chance to inspect & assimilate it fully—thus avoiding extra packings & shipments. My orders are to ship it directly to De Land—after which it is to go straight back to its creator in Averoigne. It is possible that little Ar-E'ch-Bei will be in the north during the late summer, but I think he will want the collection at his home none the less, in order to photograph its bizarre components at leisure.

As for my whereabouts—I am still on the ancient hill, with little likelihood of being elsewhere during the hoodoo year of 1936! My aunt continues to improve, but I am about 'all in'—on the verge of some sort of nervous collapse, & with the worst digestive trouble since the autumn of 1934. The persistence of cold weather has drained me of every particle of energy—

though my faithful oil heater manages to keep me alive. My programme clears up with extreme slowness, but is less utterly sunk than when I last wrote. I had a stupendous file-cleaning ordeal a month ago, during which I must have discarded a couple of tons of old papers, letters, &c. Now I am once more able to find things when I look for them!

I am extremely sorry to hear of your sister-in-law's accident, & trust her recovery may be rapid & complete. It is fortunate that she was well insured (a precaution I never take . . . nor have I ever been in an accident), & I hope she may recover suitable damages from the company.

A more tragic & less remediable blow is one which has just hit weird fictiondom in a very vital spot—a disaster which I can hardly bring myself to believe. It reaches me (without particulars) in the form of card from Miss Moore, who says she received the dire news directly from Texas—& is nothing less sad than the announcement that Robert E. Howard . . . good old Two-Gun Bob . . . . has committed suicide.[1] It still sounds incredible to me— for I had a long, normal letter from Two-Gun written May 13. He was worried about his mother's health, but otherwise seemed perfectly all right. If the news is indeed true, it forms weird fiction's worst blow since the passing of good old Whitehead in 1932. What a year is 1936! Scarcely anybody else in the gang had quite the driving zest & spontaneity of tough old Conan. It is hard to say just what made his yarns stand out so, but the real secret is that *he was in every one of them.* Even when he made outward concessions to commercial critics & mammon-guided editors he had an inner force & sincerity which broke through the surface & put the imprint of his personality on everything he wrote. By Crom, how he could surround primal megalithic cities with an aura of aeon-old fear & necromancy! His latest tale—"Black Canaan"[2]—is likewise magnificent in a more realistic way; reflecting a genuine regional background & giving a clutchingly powerful picture of the horror that stalks through the moss-hung, shadow-cursed, serpent-ridden swamps of the farther South. I can't understand the tragedy, for although R E H had a moody side expressed in his resentment against civilisation (the basis of our perennial & voluminous epistolary debate), I always thought that this was a more or less *impersonal* sentiment—like Belknap's rage against the injustices of a capitalistic world. He himself seemed pretty well adjusted to his environment. Well—weird fiction certainly has occasion to mourn! It is probable that Two-Gun never read my last letter to him—a 32-page affair mailed about a week before the bad news reached me. Some time, if you like, I'll lend you R E H's last picture—a snap taken this spring, & now lent to Dwyer. He had changed much since his better-known pictures—getting stout & round-faced, & growing a large moustache which (in conjunction with his ten-gallon hat) made him look quite like a western cinema sheriff. Eheu, fugaces! A great guy, who will not soon be forgotten!

Glad you received the Feb. *Causerie,* & that my old (1930) lines struck you favourably.[3] Poor Edkins is having a frightful time with repeated kidney operations—another black mark for '36! The second *Causerie* has just appeared, with an excellent review of Loveman's Herm—& I'm making efforts to get you a copy.[4] Also—Barlow's second *Dragon-Fly* should reach you soon.

Leedle Meestah Stoiling is recovering finely from his operation, & is hoping that special tutoring will get him into Harvard next autumn despite the interruption. He is now in Sharon, Mass., & may get around here for a call before long.

Hope your health is now back to par, & that you'll be thinking of Novanglian explorations in the not too remote future. Two of the ancient mansions of Providence (whose exteriors you saw in '27 & perhaps in '32) are now open as museums, & I explored both of them yesterday.[5] ¶ Well—use your judgment about the C A S exhibit, but I fancy it would be wisest to keep it in N.Y. till everyone there has absorbed it to the full. ¶ Regards to all—& sincere sympathy to your sister-in-law. ¶ Yr obt Grandsire—Ech-Pi-El

[*Enclosure:* Booklet for "Historic John Brown House: Built 1786."]

Notes

1. Howard had committed suicide on 11 June.

2. *WT,* June 1936.

3. HPL, "Continuity" (from *Fungi from Yuggoth*).

4. Ernest A. Edkins reviewed Samuel Loveman's *Hermaphrodite and Other Poems* in *Causerie* (June 1936): 2–4.

5. One was the John Brown House (1786–88), 52 Power Street; now one of the museums of the Rhode Island Historical Society. The other was the Edward Carrington House (1810; 1812), 66 Williams Street.

[235] [HPL to DAW] [ALS]

The Ancient Hill
Aug. 29, 1936.

Honour'd Melmoth:—

It surely was a reminder of the good old days to receive a letter from 1152—though I'm sorry a threatening illness was the cause of the return. Glad to hear that your father is better—& that your stay at home is to be prolonged. As I've always said, there's no place like one's native soil—no region out of which one may draw more authentic literary & aesthetic material, or to which one can feel a really stable & harmonious adjustment. A rootless cosmopolitan centre like New York is merely a museum & menagerie—very well for rare visits & research periods, but no place for a white man to live.

I'm surely sorry to hear that your sister-in-law's injury still lingers, & that it is likely to have disastrous economic consequences. 1936 is certainly a year of uncannily bad luck all along the line—its latest distinct event being a tangle in the Barlow household over the De Land estate, which will probably transplant Bob to Kansas & in any case keep him from his beloved printing-press & bookbinding paraphernalia. Meanwhile the restless young author-publisher has been paying Grandpa a visit on the ancient hill—absorbing the sights (& books) of Providence, tracing his genealogy* at the libraries, & otherwise trying to keep himself busy. On Aug. 15 we had an enjoyable sail to ancient Newport, & on the 20th (my 46th birthday) we visited Salem & Marblehead in the company of Leetle Meestah Stoiling, who is now recovering from his operation & preparing to enter Harvard in September. Barlow has grown a fierce set of moustachios & side-whiskers, & I can't induce the young rascal to shave them off. He is staying at the boarding-house across the back garden.

I may have spoken of the pleasant visit of Moe & his son July 18–19. Another social event was the sojourn of old Adolphe Danziger de Castro early in August. You've probably heard me speak of old Dolph—the semi-charlatanic chap whose biography of Bierce Belknap adorned with a preface, & whose stories I used to doctor up. He was here for 5 days at the Hotel Dreyfus—on his way back to N.Y. from Boston, where he had been to scatter his late wife's ashes on the sea in accordance with her last wishes. Old Dolph vainly tried to saddle me with some wholly unprofitable revision work, & is now pestering Kleiner about the same stuff. On one occasion we all—he, Barlow, & I—sat on a tomb in the hidden hillside churchyard & wrote rhymed acrostics on the name of Edgar Allan Poe—who 90 years ago used to roam that selfsame necropolis when on visits to Providence.[1]

Yes—the Klarkash-Ton material arrived almost simultaneously with Barlow, & we have been admiring it off & on ever since. I wish I had the cash to annex one or two of the pieces—& I'll welcome a glimpse, in photographic form, of the pieces which have been purchased & removed. I must send the material back to Averoigne before long, though I hate to let it go.

Congratulations on the *Esquire* sale & puff—may it be only a prelude to greater successes among the "slicks"! I must see this "Eye & Finger" sooner or later. Meanwhile I hope the fiction mill is duly producing a lucrative diurnal grist.

No—Hill-Billy aint ben set rightly to git the Innsmouth Shadder out yit-a-while. *Fanciful Tales* will appear shortly, with "The Nameless City". The Barlow-printed "Incantations" is of course held up by the general Barlovian upheaval. As for *Astounding*—I've heard of the unfavourable reception of my material, but doubt whether I'd have contributed any more anyhow.[2] When I

---

*he & I find we are 6th cousins, by virtue of a common descent from one John Rathbone, born in 1658.

saw how utterly the text of "Mts. of Madness" was ruined—especially toward the end—I simply threw up my hands & ceased to think about Street & Smith as a living force. By dint of hard labour, I corrected 3 copies of the printed text—joining up ruined paragraphs, rectifying the boners of an insane style-sheet, & reinstating long important passages toward the end. "The Shadow Out of Time" did not fare so badly.[3] Incidentally—two more things of mine are scheduled for W T.[4] Whenever I can get the time & leisure to write anything more, I can't say. I'm simply driven to the wall with other tasks, & my nerves are shot to pieces. In spite of the occasional hot spells which have saved me from a breakdown, the absence of any real trip this year has left me in a wretched state. ¶ All good wishes—

E'ch-Pi-El.

Notes

1. For the three acrostic poems, and others by M. W. Moe and Henry Kuttner, see David E. Schultz, "In a Sequester'd Churchyard," *Crypt of Cthulhu* No. 57 (St. John's Eve 1988): 26–29.

2. Both *At the Mountains of Madness* and, to a lesser degree, "The Shadow out of Time" received generally negative comments in *Astounding*'s readers' column.

3. In fact, as the AMS of "The Shadow out of Time" establishes, this story also suffered editorial tampering in *Astounding*, chiefly in the matter of paragraphing. See *The Shadow out of Time*, ed. S. T. Joshi and David E. Schultz (New York: Hippocampus Press, 2001).

4. "The Haunter of the Dark" and "The Thing on the Doorstep."

[236] [HPL, James F. Morton, and Harry Brobst to DAW] [ANS][1]

[Postmarked Providence, R.I.,
13 September 1936]

Hail, Melmoth! Mortonius & I have just been down to Warren & surrounded 4 double orders of ice cream apiece at Maxfield's. We would that you had been on hand to redeem your defeat of 1927. The folks around the place still recall our classic struggle with the 28 flavours! ¶ *Jake's* Wickenden St. joint has *reopened*, but not the central Market Square one. I haven't eaten there yet. ¶ It's raining like hell (like the day we splashed down from 10 Barnes to the [*illegible*] Lunch), & Westminster St. is flooded.

—Yrs by The Black Sign—Ech-Pi-El

Receive hearty greetings from the wandering spirit, now briefly tarrying in the ancient city.—J. F. M.

Morton & Lovecraft are here! We all send our hearty greetings.

Brobst

Notes

1. *Front:* Campus, Brown University, Providence, R. I.

[237] [HPL to DAW] [ANS][1]

[Postmarked Providence, R.I.,

9 October 1936]

Just recd. the forwarded letter—which surely did go on a long set of rounds! I used to admire old Fritz Leiber's work immensely 25 or 30 years ago when he was a young fellow in Robert Mantell's company. Didn't know he had a son. I'll be glad to lend them any tales they haven't read—but of course have none to spare permanently. ¶ Hope all is flourishing in the Twin Cities! I didn't get on any trips this year. Barlow visited me from Jul. 28 to Sept. 1, & later stopped in N.Y.—as Young Albrecht Dürer has doubtless written you. He is now situated in Kansas City, Mo. (810 W. 57th St. Terrace). Had a pleasant visit from Morton in September—as you know from our card. Cold weather has put a stop to my outdoor reading & writing, but I still take walks of exploration in the countryside on warm days. Have discovered some excellent woodland regions nearby which I never knew in youth. ¶ Have come in touch recently with young Finlay, the new W T illustrator. An extremely brilliant youth—poet as well as artist. ¶ Had a good glimpse of Pres. Roosevelt the other day when he was in town. Here's hoping he wins by a real landslide! I'm trying to do a bit of reading on economics—damn dry, but necessary in these days for an understanding of history.[2]

Yrs by the Dark Monolith

—Melmoth III

Notes

1. *Front:* Brown University, Van Wickle Gate and University Hall, Providence, R. I.
2. H. G. Wells, *The Wealth and Happiness of Mankind* (1931).

[238] [HPL to DAW] [ALS]

The Ancient Hill

—Nov. 8, 1936.

Dear Melmoth:—

Damn the luck regarding "The Shunned House"! The only loose sheets I have are those of my single lending copy—& gawd only knows where the bulk of the ill-fated edition is stored! Barlow alone can supply the key . . . but even so, he may not be able to get at the supply for an indefinite time. He'll undoubtedly tell you what, if anything, he can do. He *may* have one or two sets of the sheets with him in Kansas City, & if so, he'll surely be glad to supply them. If not—& if there's no prospect of early access to the edition—I'll let you have the desired "signature" from my lending copy— copying the pages involved on sheets of the same size in order to retain a complete text for circulation. I believe the copy is still in fair condition—it's away on a loan now. Let me know (unless Barlow himself does first) how you make out, & if you can't get the "signature" elsewhere I'll send you mine. I have, of course, one complete copy carefully bound in leather by the youthful craftsman. The bad luck which has pursued this story from its rejection by Wright in 1924 to the present moment is almost enough to make a strong man superstitious. Cook prepares to publish it—& goes to pieces. Barlow takes over the edition—& his home busts up. And even the salvaged copies have to be defective! Well, in your care there's no need to worry, for you'll certainly get the missing pages either from me or from Little Bobby. Incidentally, he made me up a rather crude bound copy to send to Dr. Howard for the Robert E. Howard Memorial Collection.

Meanwhile Hill-Billy Crawford is actually finishing up "The Shadow Over Innsmouth". In spite of my most careful proofreading 32 bad errors remain, & Hill-Billy is printing a list of errata for insertion in the volume. I had the proof of this list last week—& it was itself so misprinted that it wouldn't have done much good in its original form! I've now read & returned the proof, & have told Hill-Billy to send me another. I fear the volume won't be very impressive, though the Utpatel illustrations form a saving spot. A sort of hoodoo seems to hang over all my book ventures!

I recalled your experience with "The Red Brain" when cursing over *Astounding*'s treatment of "The Mountains of Madness". I am now lending corrected copies to as many readers as possible. Minor misprints can be excused, but the wholesale slaughter of text by commercial editors devoid of a stylistic sense is utterly outrageous.

Congratulations upon your new avuncular honours! I doubt whether the distinction will add seriously to your burden of years—for does not young Talman still remain hale, hearty, & well-preserved despite the even greater responsibility of repeated paternity? And look at good old Leeds—ever young despite the existence of *grown* children somewhere in the dim Chicago background!

Yes—now is the time of year when congratulations on your homecoming have to be tempered with a sympathy based on climatic considerations! Thirty days of -6 to -35 . . . . . Yuggoth, but that sounds like the plateau beyond the Mountains of Madness! And here in Providence we call +10° or so damn cold! Here's hoping your furnace is in good shape!

The autumn here was not of the most extreme severity, & my occasional outings extended over the line into November. As I possibly mentioned on my card, I succeeded in discovering several splendid rural regions within a 3-mile radius of here which I had never seen before. One is a wooded hill—Neutaconkanut—on the western rim of the town, whence a series of marvellous views of the outspread city & adjacent countryside may be obtained. I had often ascended it before, but the exquisitely mystical sylvan scenery beyond the crest—curious mounds, hummocked pastures, & hushed, hidden valleys—was wholly new to me. Oct. 20 & 21 were phenomenally warm, & I utilised them in exploring another hitherto untapped region down the east shore of the bay—finding a highly fascinating forest called the Squantum Woods, where there are great oaks & birches, steep slopes & rock ledges, & marvellous vistas beyond the trees. Our autumn, though, was notably lacking in visual splendour. Half the trees were swept bare by heavy rains as soon as they began to turn, while the other half remained green for an anomalous length of time—the leaves then falling almost as soon as they did turn. From Comte d'Erlette's reports, I judge that the west fared better.

Well—good luck with all your ventures, & let me know if Barlow can't supply the missing sheets.

Yrs by the Eye in the Tower—

E'ch-Pi-El

[239] [HPL to DAW] [ANS]

[Postmarked Providence, R.I.,
17 December 1936]

[The wish
This carries
Right to your
Door
Is bigger
And better
Than ever
Before!]

—E'ch-Pi-El

MDCCCCXXXVI.

[240] [HPL to DAW] [ALS]

The Ancient Hill
—Dec. 20, 1936.

Dear Melmoth:—

Glad that Barlow thinks he can fix you up regarding "The Shunned House" sheets—but as he just reminded me, the responsibility is more mine than I had suspected! It seems that I was in De Land, & presumably coöperating in the shipments, when he sent the unbound sets to you & Loveman. Anyhow—my offer is still open in case anything prevents Ar-E'ch-Bei from getting hold of the missing signature. The poor old "Shunned House" surely has seen vicissitudes—if I could, I'd like to get hold of the whole damned edition & distribute sets to the gang once & for all!

I'm interested to hear of your recent magazine appearances, & shall watch for "Uneasy Lie the Drowned." The title sounds distinctly promising! "Black Fog" likewise has an alluring sound. But most of all, I am eager to hear of the completion of your drama. You had long ago spoken of future experiments in this field, & I am pleased to see them materialising. The drama is without question a great field of expression—especially where delineations of human character & psychology are concerned—& calls for an even greater range of qualities than does narrative fiction. The principal reason I have never tried it is that what I have to say seldom deals so much with human traits as with *phenomena* & *scenes*. That even the weird can be finely exploited in dramatic form is amply proved by the plays of Dunsany—"The Gods of the Mountain", "A Night at an Inn", &c. I hope to see your play some time. You surely have run the gamut of forms pretty thoroughly—though after you've finished your cinema scenario you might try epic poetry, history, travel books, critical studies, stream-of-consciousness novels, scientific treatises, & so on. Or how about imagist poetry, & verbal repetition in the manner of Gertrude Stein? Don't despair—the range of literature is wide!

Glad you liked the "Haunter" & "Doorstep", Finlay's illustration to the latter is remarkably good. In the "Haunter" I fancy you can recognise the authentic touches of Providence geography . . . . even though your acquaintance with #66 is still an occult or dreamlike one. I'm wondering what other local readers (of whom there must be some, since copies eventually vanish from the stands) think of it—especially on Federal Hill! By the way—I'm extremely glad that your father likes my sombre efforts. Pray give him my regards, & tell him how much I appreciate his favourable opinion.

Your meteorological reports send me into a sort of combined teeth-chattering & paralysis! Holy Yuggoth, but if St. Paul has been down to -16° *this* early, what will Jany. & Feby. bring? Bad as this burg is, your data make me feel that I am living in the subtropics . . . even though our "subtropical" lows of +20°, +15°, +10°, & so on keep me imprisoned pretty effectually when they appear. We seldom get down to zero—perhaps 3 or 4 times in the course of a winter—& ultra (or I should say *infra*) lows like -12° (Dec. 30, 1917) & -17° (Feby. 9, 1934) are matters of shuddersome historic record. *Interior* New England, however, is worse—& I fancy New Hampshire & Vermont could compare notes with the Twin Cities without any marked disparity. Well—you have my sympathy . . . & I hope the furnace at 1152 is a damn good one! This year we had early snows—Nov. 24 & 28—but both melted off quickly. Dec. 10–12 was a record-breaking rainy season—tears for abdicating King Edward, perhaps—which would have caused serious flood trouble had it not come to a close when it did.

As for news—I probably told you of Goodenough's death,[1] & of the collapse of Cook's neighbourhood newspaper venture. This time the salient item is more cheerful. Cook has found a job in E. St. Louis, & is now to be addressed at 1305 Missouri Ave., E. St. Louis, Illinois. I'm going to send him an Old Farmer's Almanack for 1937 just to keep him in touch with his ancient New England background! Hard to realise that it's *7 years* since he was an Athol fixture.

Yule approaches, & we expect to have a tree as in '34 & '35. I'm filling my clothespress with sundry surprises for my aunt to arrange around it on Christmas Eve. ¶ Best holiday wishes—

Yrs by the Black Eidolon—
E'ch-Pi-El

Notes

1. Arthur Goodenough had died 15 September at the age of 65.

1937

[241] [DAW to HPL] [TLS]

1152 Portland Ave.,
St. Paul, Minn.
March 17, 1937

Dear HPL:

St. Patrick's Day furnishes as good a reason as any for me to drop other activities and tackle the accumulated mass of correspondence which I have totally neglected for three months. First I must report that Barlow sent me, some time ago, the missing sheets of "The Shunned House", so that now at long last I finally possess a complete copy. The book is worth its weight in diamond dust, considering the time and persistence that seem essential to the assembling of a set of the sheets.

Of much more importance to me is the fact that I completed, some ten days since, my first full-length drama. I had thought to write it in a month— fantastic optimism! It actually required three solid months of my concentrated energy, to the exclusion of all else; which is the reason why my correspondence and other interests suffered an acute drought. The play itself can by no stretch of lenient indulgence be called a contribution to either the interpretation of life or the theater, and yet I am highly delighted. My satisfaction derives mainly from the mere fact that I actually have completed a full-length play, and that I feel that I have mastered the principles of a new medium as a basis for future development. The mastery may not show in the first play, but it is there just the same, a tangible profit from both successes and mistakes within the structure. Of the two dramas that I had in mind, I purposely chose the lesser for first development, and I am convinced now that I will thereby achieve much greater results with the second than would have been possible had I done it first.

This first drama, if you are interested, has been sent to my agent under the title "Love To Murder", and has a dozen alternative titles among which I favor "It's Later Than You Think". It's a mystery drama, in three acts, outdoing the classic unities—all the action takes place in the same place and setting within a period of about twelve hours—with an ending in poetic justice. It has many features of a melodrama, but could more properly be called a tragedy, save for the caustic and often satiric treatment of the central theme.

I have no copy of the play in my possession right now. Three sets went to the agent, one for copyright, and the fifth is in the hands of a stenographer for preparing additional copies. They should be ready in a week or so, at which time I will keep one for myself and one for circulation.

Some time this spring I expect to visit New York to see editors, agents, friends, and make an intensive survey of current theatrical production. But I'm damned if I'll swelter through another summer of that metropolis's sticky inferno. I intend to retire to a secluded spot in the mountains or on the seashore to complete the second and vastly more ambitious, more important drama, which will, I hope, not only express my philosophy of living but also be a significant contribution to contemporary drama, life, and thought. Well, that sounds like a whale of an undertaking. It is.

I have managed to come through the winter in far better shape than I expected. My health not only has recovered from the hoodoo year 1935–36, but seems to have improved to finer condition than ever before. There were perhaps a dozen or fifteen days when the thermometer touched -15, but the winter has on the whole been moderate and tolerable.

Aside from writing the play, and a new Ivy Frost novelette immediately thereafter to replenish depleted funds, I have done little else. I haven't had time. However, for essential relaxation I attended a series of film programs at fortnightly intervals under the auspices of the Museum of Modern Art; among which were "The Cabinet of Dr. Caligari," one reel of "The Golem", "Hands", and a number of minor pieces from the pre-war cinema.[11] You will undoubtedly find an opportunity to see the first two in their entirety, since the programs are now available to groups throughout the entire country; or perhaps you too saw them this winter, in Providence.

I have also made at least a half-dozen trips to the new St. Paul City Hall and Courthouse, where reposes Carl Milles's[2] "Indian War God", truly one of the most magnificently impressive and majestically executed works of inspired sculpture in modern art, and I am tempted to add, of all time. There is a sculpture that has captivated my esthetic spirit as deeply as that splendid Roman in the Metropolitan Museum in new York impressed itself upon yours.

What of your own winter? Did you make a holiday visit to Belknap, or indulge in explorations farther south? Have you written, or are you writing, any new tales?

With best wishes for a successful and benign spring,

Yours, by the wig and false face

of the Daimon Thespis,

Melmoth II

Notes

1. *The Golem* (*Der Golem* Universum Film [German], 1920), directed by Carl Böse and Paul Wegener; starring Paul Wegener, Albert Steinrück, and Lyda Salmonova. *Hands* may refer to *The Hands of Orlac* (Pan-Film, 1924), directed by Robert Wiene; starring Conrad Veidt, Alexandra Sorina, and Fritz Kortner. For *The Cabinet of Dr. Caligari* see letter 227n3.

2. Carl Milles (1875–1955), Swedish sculptor.

Howard Wandrei

Letters of H. P. Lovecraft and Howard Wandrei

[1]   [HW to HPL]   [TLS]

156 Waverly Place, NYC, April 30, 1934

Dear H. P.,

Very much tickled to hear from you, and I agree that I ought to be far-ther south. I hate winter and I hate cold, reasons why I ventured to New York last year. My disappointment is measureless. The cold, grippe, whatever it was, has been felled almost to the point of satisfaction, largely through heavy pill consumption and lying in bed, which is another thing I hate. I look upon all colds and sicknesses as upon personal enemies. I, also, do much bet-ter work in the hottest weather, look forward to a sometime permanent resi-dence in the south or far west. I envy your coasting from old city to old city.

As to the drawings and batiks, I imagine the pleasure was more mine than yours. I may have run into a rare person before this who appreciated those things of mine as much as you did, but I have never run into anyone so well equipped to show that appreciation, as my stricken idiocy at the time may have indicated.

Sorry to have departed so suddenly the last evening. The cold was in good form that night, a valid argument for absenting oneself anywhere, but I suppose you were aware of the senseless, petty difference among brothers which pre-ceded departure. I apologize for that. Don in for dinner yesterday with life fixed up, telling me I missed another session of the gang by going. Too bad.

Sold another story to Astounding Stories,[1] not such a good one, I feel. They had a hole in the makeup that wanted plugging. Otherwise life goes on. Best regards to you.

H E Wandrei

Notes

1. Probably "Guns of Eternal Day," *Astounding Stories* 13, No. 5 (July 1934): 123–33 [as by Howard W. Graham, Ph.D., a thinly disguised variant of his own name].

[2]   [TLS] [HW to HPL]   [TLS]

156 Waverly Place, NYC, May 7, 1934

Dear HPL,

Good to hear from you again, and so soon. The character of the south-ern country appeals to me just as much as the climate, which I suppose is a foolish thing to say, the climate producing the character. Here the weather

365

has undergone a startling change. It is very warm, uncomfortably so. That delights me, but the dirt that has come with it is unbearable. The wind is pretty strong, and a long walk through the streets will cost you your eyesight. The windows here at 156 stay open or we'll suffocate, but if we open them the dirt comes through by the pound. None of us has enough energy to see about cleaning the place up before we move, which makes us pretty bad tenants. We are moving out on the 11th.

A letter from Augie D. today, commenting on your commenting. Again thanks. I hope that eventual recognition is something more than a sweet dream; indeed, little things continue to happen which persuade one to keep up the fight yet a little longer. That abominable store, Macy's, has taken eight drawings to show in their art department as advertising, tacitly, materials which they sell there. This thing will go on for about two weeks, I think. What I wanted most to do, however, seems slowly to be coming about, and is something I mentioned to Augie, whom I have just written. Wright at last found something in a story I sent him, called THE HAND OF THE O'MECCA.[1] Werewolf base. He disliked the ending, and returned it, saying that, and that the story was vague. He wrote again yesterday, requesting me to change the ending and return it, which I am going to do. Frankly, now that I re-read the story, parts of it are pretty cheesy, and were really the faults he objected to. The thing is being re-written; I expect to send it off to him tomorrow with an illustration. Bearing in mind his mortal detestation of detail, the sketch will be fairly broad, and I do not see why he cannot take both the ms. and the deco. If he takes both I shall feel that I have taken one decided step forward. I should like you to read the O'MECCA if, as, and when it appears, and receive your comment on it. essentially I feel that it is first-rate material.

How about your own writing? Don was in yesterday, and we spoke of you. He said something of your revising material, was vague. I don't recall seeing anything of yours for some time, yet you stand in every WT Eyrie as a mark to shoot at.

As for myself, I have been grinding out attempts in the detective story line, one of which I expect will sell eventually. The editor who wanted detective pornographica got his, and I think it was a good one if eccentric in his direction. I sent it under a pseudonym, do not expect to hear from him for some time. This month I have made almost a living wage, with two checks totaling seventy-five dollars.

As I said, were are moving, and I am going up to the cape to live with a friend of mine remarkable in the way of silversmithing. I am going to try selling batiks and small things of various kinds to the summer trade up there, if there is any, keeping up the writing as well. if things turn out badly, I shall return, but somehow I don't feel that they will. This is as much a move of economy as anything else, but I shall gain by a new setting, by a continual view of the bay and sometimes the Atlantic, perhaps lose by the presence of a fleet of sailors. I am looking forward to it a great deal, and do not see how I can lose much by such a venture.

I shall be interested to hear from young "Barlow himself", he being from your description, of that species which is rapidly becoming extinct. My address in Provincetown will be: *% Alvin Von Hinzmann*,[2] *543 Commercial Street, Provincetown, Mass.* I understand the mail service there is lousy, and that paradoxically the government is establishing an air field and port, the point of the cape possessing strategic value. My best regard,

Yours most sincerely,
H E

Notes

1. HPL once remarked (to RHB), "O-Mecca? It sounds like an Irish Arab" (*OFF* 403).
2. A European-trained goldsmith.

[3]   [TLS] [HW to HPL]   [TLS]

320 West 11th Street, NYC, May 23, 1934

Dear HPL,

Your letter forwarded down to Don's and my final receipt of it. The Provincetown venture has been sidetracked here, as you see, and I will probably not get up there after all till late in June. What happened is rather difficult to explain, but had the earmarks of what is commonly known as a chisel, with myself as the object of it. but I will probably go there later, and visit Provincetown.

Barlow's proposition, as far as I can see, has everything to recom[m]end it, but I don't see just what I can do about it now for many reasons. Chief among which is the fact that the drawings are not at hand! The Macy show has been receiving a great deal of attention, and I have been twice asked to send up more work, which I have done. I don't know how long they intend to keep the thing going, but I suppose it will be as long as the drawings sell materials for them. This morning Miss Colestock,[1] the red-haired girl we call Connie, told me her superior had ordered a larger and more imposing announcement card for the show. Then, in moving from Waverly Place, some of the drawings were loaned to friends for safe keeping, since I simply had too much material to handle by myself. Connie did that for me, and I have yet to find out how many drawings were loaned, which ones were loaned, and to whom. These were framed pieces, of course. I have not told Don about this, for fear he would lose his mind. Otherwise, I have only a few negligible works on hand, and am more than ever reminded of the fact that I have done no important drawing for much too long a time. However, when the drawings are assembled, something should be done about them. Donald has long planned to get an enlarging apparatus and photograph the entire collection of drawings and batiks, and said something about doing it at last this summer. He has taken snaps of many of them. But if they were sent to Mr. Barlow[2] I think it might be a good idea to unframe the lot. Have had a lot of breakage, and one drawing scored by glass. Do you imagine we could wait yet a little longer? I feel that some good may come of the Macy exhibit, so long as it does attract attention. Barlow must be commended for his energy, to be sure. It is flattering to come upon such appreciation.

It may interest you to know that Wright has taken THE HAND OF THE O'MECCA. He seems to have knocked five dollars off the price, which I think is his usual practice. He rejected the illustration, which, for your amusement, I enclose. I can only say damnation. His excuse was the same as before,—it would not reproduce. Nevertheless, I feel that he didn't care for it a great deal. I admit I have done better work, but think the illustration should have gone with the story. The O'Mecca has a werewolf base, by the way. I think the story is first rate, but people have disagreed with me before. I am quite sorry that I cannot take advantage of Mr. Barlow's eagerness at the moment besides this meager offering, which will of course not be of great interest to either of you.

The weather here holds fair during the day, but it has rained heavily three nights running, with what I think is called chain ligh[t]ning. Broad violet bolts that melt into rows of balls. Perhaps it's ball and chain lightning. Today it is sunny and cool, clear, making ideal weather.

My detective story man wrote me a long letter, inviting me to write for both of his magazines, which of course I will do. His prices run to better than a penny a word, and I need desperately to get a little ahead of the game. The cramped feelings of dependence on the next small check makes life unsatisfactory; I should have managed to enlarge and field of my activities long before this.

I am glad you are enjoying yourself. The 'tenfold energy' the sun gives you is unmistakable as it shows in your letters. My own output is at least twofold. Yesterday I finished a batik commission for Gil Southwick[3] in half the time it would have ordinarily taken me. When I have money and leisure at last, I shall most certainly junket through the south, since I have had my eye on it for so long. Winters are vile. I have always thought America's ideal climate existed only in Florida or lower California, and that life was scarcely worth living anywhere else. Perhaps if all goes well I shall get south sometime later in the year. Minnesota is impossible, and New York none too satisfactory.

I have so much work to do that I must close now. Let me say, though, that Mr. Barlow's plan seems to me a most admirable one, and that I shall be glad to send down drawings when I can. And since you have having so good a time, why not stay in the climate you enjoy so much as long as you can? I wish I were down there.

Yours cordially, as always,

H E

Notes

1. Connie Colestock, whom HW married in 1936.

2. RHB made photographs of three batiks and five other pieces of artwork, but nothing came of his attempt to publish a folio of HW's artwork.

3. The Wandreis were friends with Gil Southwick and his wife Lloyd.

[4]   [TLS] [HW to HPL]   [TLS]

320 West 11th Street, NYC, May June 15, 1934

Dear HP,

I have been so swamped with what I call work that very little time has been left over for my personal pleasures, pleasures like this. Today I am free all afternoon by my own choosing, and I begin the afternoon with an apology to you for an unforgivable delay in writing.

I have sent a short note back to Minnesota, and await hearing from the owner of NIGHT, DEATH, AND THE DEVIL,[1] but God knows whether I ever shall. I have a tiny snapshot of that picture somewhere, taken with a group, but it would never enlarge. Otherwise the drawing may be lost for good. That woman. I am co-operating, anyhow, as far as I can. The Macy show still goes on apace. Connie Colestock arranged the show so beautifully that her work is being used as a model up there, which explains, I suppose, why the display has not been taken down long before this. As far as Macy's are concerned, the pictures are serving a double purpose, now complicated with a third. In their art contest, which closed recently, my clay model, LAUGHING ARCHER, took first place in sculpture, which represents me twice on the floor, the opinion of a dozen judges in the award being sufficient to carry on specimens in another medium yet a little longer. Hoick. I think you would enjoy the little model. I have taken pictures of it, fearing that it would be mishandled up there, which it was. But newsmen took shots of it also, before the mishandling, so I have not taken my films out to be developed yet. Professional work is so much better, and I have been waiting to get copies of the 'official' pictures. May not be able too, but if I do I'll send them down.

I have a letter from my father expressing a desire to see such illustrations for my own stories as editors have turned down, in order to compare them with professional work that has been used instead. Wright will probably not use the O'MECCA for some time, but when he does I wish you would return the sketch so that I can send it to Minnesota. Only keep this in mind; Wright may not use an illustration at all. Otherwise the drawing, such as it is, is as safe in your keeping as in the Bank of England. I still do not know what *two* pictures disappeared into the household down the street, have been trying to get them back but haven't managed it yet.

Life goes on here as usual, otherwise. I am at the point of being anxious about the check from Macy's, which has to pay my rent, now due. Yesterday and the day before went into a story for AS. Including interruptions, I find that it takes thirty hours to clean, press, and sew the buttons on a six thousand word manuscript. First draft, rewrite, typing, correcting, taking it up there to S&S. No sleep, of course, so last night I felt something like a cuckoo clock when I finally got to bed. Sincerely hope Hall takes one of the three stories of mine he is now holding, for I need the money like the mischief. No delusions here about grandeur in science fiction. This latest 'vehicle' is called TIME HAVEN, is a pointed take-off on time travel yarns that have been appearing on all sides. It is rather literary and for other reasons may default any acceptance of Hall's. I have been sending out a number of little stories, also, which I supposed were rather good. Most editors will comment if you pester them long enough; my pestering generally elicits a comment of awkward length. It always surprises me to find a publication turning down a manuscript for length alone, too short or too long. A good story loses much when it is taken out of its natural course. So this morning, on a story of 1800 words which Action Stories refused. The comments I have collected so far make amusing reading.

A letter from Augie, who missed Don on his way back to Minnesota. I have not heard from Don myself; he has been gone for two weeks now. Hope he gets along well in Minnesota, but I don't suppose he will. Augie, as you probably know, is quite excited over the good quality of his latest book, name of which I have forgotten at the moment.[2] My best regards; sending a note to Mr. Barlow along with this.

Yours,

H E

Notes

1. Apparently some sort of parody of "Knight, Death, and the Devil" (1513) by Albrecht Dürer (1471–1528), and the reason HPL referred to HW by the epithet "Albrecht Dürer." The whereabouts of HW's drawing is unknown.

2. Probably *Murder Stalks the Wakely Family: A Judge Peck Mystery* (New York: Loring & Mussey, 1934).

[5]   [ALS] [HPL to HW]   [ALS]

De Land—
June 19, 1934

Dear H E:—

I surely hope that "Night, Death, & the Devil", as well as any other straying pieces, can eventually be recovered. This matter of dispersed &

possible loss is the eternal tragedy of the artist whose medium does not involve duplication. In future I surely hope you will partly offset this necessary evil by keeping good-sized photographs of everything you have to part with. That is one of the reasons Barlow is so anxious to have your choicest specimens preserved by professional camera reproduction.

Congratulations on the success of the Macy exhibit—& especially on your capture of the sculpture prize. I trust I may eventually see the winning object, manhandled though it is; & am also eager to inspect the pictures of it in the undamaged condition. What a pity it had to be injured! Later on I'll shew you photographs of Barlow's sculptural attempts—a bas-relief of the mythical monster Cthulhu, & a statuette of an elephant-god something like the one on Belknap's mantel.

I'll see that you get the O'Mecca drawing in good condition—either by mail or through personal delivery. At the moment Barlow is anxious to photograph it with a 5×7 camera he has just purchased. This contraption seems to be rather a good one, and he has used it to photograph some of Clark Ashton Smith's drawings—belonging to me and down here for the nonce. Hope the O'Mecca appears soon. No matter what the drawing is, it isn't likely to be even approximately as good as the one so foolishly turned down by Wright.

I sincerely hope that a maximum of your short stories will land—including the new 6000-worder. The capricious & arbitrary requirements of cheap magazine editors are wholly beyond my fathoming—so that when anything of mine finds a home it is purely a matter of luck. I can't shorten or lengthen stories at will, for with me the material itself dictates the space it needs to occupy in order to be effectively developed. Once I have written a thing, it has to stay at about the same length. Hence the rejection of so many of my long later things—such as the 115-page antarctic novelette "At the Mountains of Madness."

Too bad Donald missed Comte d'Erlette at Sauk City—I supposed his passing through coincided with M. le Comte's pilgrimage to Prairie du Chien. Trust the Wanderer may find the atmosphere of good old 1152 a welcome change after his long sojourn on alien shores. Give him my regards when you write. The energetic August-Guillaume surely is making quite a splash in the book field!

Well—I certainly didn't expect to be in De Land so long, but the hospitality of the Barlow household is of an almost unprecedentedly cordial & insistent sort . . . so that every suggestion of moving along is sunk in some plan for another week's activities. this week, however, I simply must be getting in motion. I shall pause in ancient St. Augustine a bit, & thereafter drag myself north by easy stages—seeing you, I trust, when I pass through the metropolitan zone. A fortnight ago I visited a most impressive place—Silver Springs, some 60 miles N.W. of De Land. Here is found a series of placid lagoons whose floor is riddled with vast pits 30 to 80 feet deep, & covered with curious marine vegetation. In many spots divers have exhumed the huge bones of prehistoric animals. I saw these varied wonders from a glass-bottomed boat.

Out of the lagoons flows the Silver River; as typical a tropic steam as the Congo or Amazon, with tall palms, trailing vines, & moss, & bending cypresses along the swampy banks. Alligators, turtles, & snakes abound, & on either side the jungle stretches away uninterruptedly for miles. It is here that the cinema of "Tarzan" was photographed.[1] I took a 10-mile launch trip on the river, & could easily have imagined myself in the heart of Africa.

Every good wish, & hope to see you soon.

Yrs most sincerely——H P.

Notes

1. *Tarzan the Ape Man* (MGM, 1932), directed by W. S. Van Dyke; starring Johnny Weissmuller, Neil Hamilton, and Maureen O'Sullivan. Based on the novel by Edgar Rice Burroughs.

[6]   [TLS] [HW to HPL]   [TLS]

320 West 11th Street, NYC, May June 25th, 1934

Dear HPL,

I am always delighted to hear from you, though I may not seem to show it with my lazy replies. This may not reach you before you are back in NY again. I hope it does, since I'd like to see you again, the which may prove an inconvenience for you. This apartment of mine is abominable in many respects, and it is impossible or nearly so for me to receive anyone here. There is frequently no one here to take messages, and I can not hear the single bell in my room if I am at home. There is no individual bell.

I suppose it would be best if you could find time to drop a short note letting me know where I can reach you. In the evenings you can get me by telephone by calling the number of Wyman Fitz at this address and asking for me. He is the landlord and a very good fellow, usually home evenings. He will be glad to take any calls for me. One reason, I suppose, why there is a dearth of bells is the fact that I am the sole tenant in this building, which was formerly a longshoreman's boarding house.

I would enjoy another session such as came into occasional being when you were last here,—see Belknap again, whom I liked very much. If that is agreeable to you, may I invite myself herewith? There might be some conversation with the sold accessible partner in the Barlow plot. Concerning which, the Macy exhibit closes this week and my pictures are to be returned. Apparently Barlow did not want the illustration I suggested to him, one here now called "Fool! Fool!"—illustration for one of Don's poems. Still no word from Minnesota on the missing drawing. Probably gone for good, the fault entirely mine. But I needed money badly then.

I have word from Don, saying that he enjoys the Minnesota change enormously, that that [*sic*] the Minnesota geographical and intellectual waste (what structure!) is downright falsehood. He is meeting his old gang there and being wined, dined, generally feted, I suppose. He turns thumbs down on my new appearance in AS, for which I don't blame him a great deal. The story was hastily written to fill a gap in the makeup, was done in a matter of five hours. Last Friday, however, they took my new TIME HAVEN, which I think is a superior story.

I had an amusing experience with my det story editor, whom I sent a story of awkward length. 7700 words. He emphasizes the love element, and with that in mind I gave him a yarn that I thought boiled with passion. Saturday I received it marked up in pencil and a long note with it, a request to 'sex up' the penciled passages! I feel like apologizing for this, as it is not the type of market I care to get mixed up in. However, I am writing under a pseudonym, and this gentleman pays on acceptance. Just how much I don't know. His scale starts at ½¢ as I understand it, but if he pays me bottom rates I can scarcely afford to do business there. I think my work is worth more than that. (Wright has been knocking dollars off his checks, though, so that 1¢ begins to look like a first-class rate!)

Have been writing all day, and am very hungry now. My best regards, then, with the hope that I see you again when you come through.

Yours most sincerely,

H E

[7]   [TLS] [HW to HPL]   [TLS]

320 West 11th Street, NYC, May July 23, 1934

Dear H.P.,

First, I am intensely sorry to have missed you on the return journey, when I might have gotten the flavor of the South at least at second hand. Next best to going there is to hear of it, but perhaps I shall have better luck in the future, as you say.

Then, as to the Astounding stories containing my work, I accept the flattery by warning you that not much of the 'flavor' you expect is likely to be present. Friend Augie, in fact, gave me a round panning on one of the things, did not mention the last one at all. He liked the first a great deal, one called THE GOD BOX. A new one will appear next month called TIME HAVEN, and you might have some fun in reading these two, especially the latter. However, science fiction is written in such narrow latitudes that the shape of the beast is militantly against its interest. I hate to write science fiction, largely because one has to follow childish, exact rules. Though I think I got by with something in TIME HAVEN.

Yes, I collected my stock of pictures at Macy's, unframed two that Barlow requested especially and sent them down. That was over a week ago, and

I have not heard from him since. Also there is a piece of news that pleases me a great deal, and which arrived this morning. I receive a fat letter from the Minnesota school teacher. My letters caught up with her in Onamia, Minnesota, which is in the northern section. She advises me that the drawing in question hangs in a bedroom of hers in Milaca, wherever that is, and that when she can get over there or get in touch with someone who can do it for her, she will have the picture packed and sent on forthwith. I want a record of that drawing particularly, as it is the best by far, and has passed out of my possession. Perhaps I'll see it in a month or two, at least I hope so.

I have not had much further luck here in writing, apparently cannot compete with my indefatigable brother in his first love! Wright will publish my VINE TERROR in September, otherwise I can see no money coming in. Wish I did not have to worry about the lucrative end of the game. No word on the detective stories.

I have begun to do some drawing again, thanks to your interest and Barlow's I have sent out a manuscript with an illustration or two, and last week finished a watercolor which I sent to Esquire.[1] So I now chase two hares, without being positive of winging either. The rewards are solely in the preoccupation thus far, but editors seem to be interested in contributors who do both, if that means anything. It's a slow game. I have been trying to get a leg up over the pulp fiction market, and by only success so far has been encouraging letters from the same Esquire.

My eroto-detective editor seems to be Price's, as I find his name in the two magazines in question. The editor is Frank Armer.[2] He has not taken any action on three stories of mine that he has held a month. I believe he will take at least one of them in the end. I am using the pseudonym of H. W. Guernsey, which, oddly enough, is one that Donald was using at the same time.[3] Since I had several stories out under that name, he very kindly consented to withdraw from that particular competition.

Donald seems to be having a high life at the moment, gone into a total regeneration as a result of his trip west. Advantages in both places. Just now the Midwest seems to be cooked with everlasting heat. One spot out there has had a temperature of more than a hundred degrees for thirty-five consecutive days. Terrible. A temperature of a hundred and fourteen for three days running. You have more information than I on his continuing westward. I understand that it may be just as likely that he will return to NY with my mother and sister sometime in late August. If my affairs here have not improved before that time, it is just as likely that I will return to Minnesota in the Plymouth. I hope not for many reasons, though I would like to see Minnesota this year, and friends back there. But Don's first meeting with Clark Ashton Smith should indeed be memorable.[4]

Nothing would please me more than to visit New England this summer, and I may do it yet if all goes well. It's good of you to offer me the camp cot, and I shall most certainly let you know about any journeys of mine in the direction of College Street. Just now I am watching all incoming mail like a hawk over the barnyard, and writing fourteen hours a day.

If there is anything in Charles Fort and mass thought influence, one of these days Wright will take a drawing of mine. I have a good story in mind which I think he may take, and intend to illustrate it, bearing in mind all the characteristics which have no place in commercial technique. So far I have been directing all my energies toward those editorial sancta which pay on acceptance, with the exception of the O'Mecca, of course. I hope to find more time to do what I want hereafter. I think Wright allows one a fairly free hand. Save in art.

Not long ago I finished an immensely detailed drawing for an Esquire short. It would reproduce well on the tile paper they use, but the story unfortunately is not much. Not including a private item or two, I have sold just one commercial drawing. That was an advertising border to Dutton's when Donald was advertising manager years ago. Six years of pen and ink have brought twelve dollars and fifty cents into the coffer. Phooey.

Word from Augie, and you both tell of the mountain correspondence which you are disposing of inchmeal. Don't feel compelled to answer this note until such time as you have leisure.

Yours cordially,
H E

P.S. I have seen the new Weird Tales, but can not afford to buy it. Your story with Price[5] has the name of a foregone masterpiece, which of course it must be. I will not let it go by, hope to have the magazine sometime this week.

Notes

1. HW's only sale to *Esquire* was "The Eerie Mr. Murphy" (November 1937).
2. Frank Armer (1895–1965), editor of *Spicy Mystery, Spicy Detective, Spicy Western,* and analogous magazines.
3. As with the Graham pseudonym, the H. W. is meant to cloak HW's own name. Guernsey was the maiden name of the Wandrei brothers' mother. DAW published nothing with the pseudonym.
4. The meeting occurred in November.
5. "Through the Gates of the Silver Key."

[8]   [ALS] [HPL to HW]   [ALS]

66 College St.,
Providence, R.I.
July 29, 1934

Dear H E:—

   Haven't yet got hold of the A.S., but will make due allowances in reading "The God Box" & "Time Haven". I can understand your aversion to the conventional science fiction—it is all a matter of elementary formula, though real literature in the given field *could* be written. I shall look for "Vine Terror."

Glad the pictures have gone to Barlow—he'll be overwhelmed with delight & you'll undoubtedly hear from him shortly. A slight delay in his replies to letters does not mean inattention—since there is no free delivery in his section & the family go to town only about three times a week. A letter might be lying in the P. O. a day or two before he could get at it, and it might be a day or two before he could mail his reply. Alas it takes mail 2 to 3 days to go from NY to De Land & vice versa. Immensely glad to hear that the picture bought by the Minnesota schoolmarm can be located, & hope you'll have it in your hands—& in Barlow's—before long. According to the cartography of Messrs. Rand & McNally, *Milaca* is a railway junction town between St. Cloud & Duluth—perhaps 60 or 70 miles, as the crow flies, from the Twin Cities.

I am certainly delighted to hear that you are producing some more pictures, & hope that some of the illustrated stories will land. A combined author–artist is always a fortunate individual, for he can be sure that the illustrations mean precisely what he is trying to say. Hope the water-colour will please *Esquire*—they certainly ought to be classed as a hopeful market if they write encouraging letters. So you & Donald are going to share a pseudonym in the literary underworld! Quite an idea—& so tailored-to-order does that stuff have to be, that I fancy few will pause to note stylistic differences!

Wright is undoubtedly less hide-bound in fiction than in drawing—his bad taste seeming to reach its maximum in the latter field. Fancy a person turning down the O'Mecca sketch, & yet using the incredible crudities of bunglers like Olinick & Doak, as he did a few years ago! Today he employs a succession of utterly uninspired hacks—Wilcox, Hammond, &c—who ought to be drawing Kollegian-Kast-Klothing advertisements—& reduces to a minimum the work of Rankin,[1] yourself, & others who really possess imaginative vision.

Hope the *Esquire* drawing will be able to put over the story, even if the latter is slight. Once one acquires a foothold in these pretentious magazines, all editors seem to become more hospitable.

I'd hardly call the current W T worth wasting cash on—it is provokingly mediocre, & my collaborated tale is extremely disappointing. I like it even less in print than I did in MS. last year. By the way—have you any use for . . . or even interest in . . . . the little semi-amateur weird magazines? I enquire because I have several duplicates of the first *Marvel Tales* & of many issues of the Fantasy Fan. If you care for any of these, they are yours.

I'm surely glad to hear that Donald is flourishing so actively, & hope he won't have to forego the far western trip. I hope, too, that you won't have to leave Manhattan before you are ready to do so. The midwest surely has been enjoying some sizzling temperatures—curious how inland places run to extremes. In R.I. it is never over 99° or so in summer, & *almost* never below zero (despite the shattered records of the last terrible winter, when the mercury hit 17 below) in winter. Incidentally, I hope you'll be able to get to R.I. before you leave the east.

You will probably hear before long from a young friend of mine named Richard E. Morse—of Princeton, N.J.—who recently asked your address.[2] He may try to call on you—with suitable advance heralding—during some week-end in N.Y. He is quite a connoisseur & collector of weird art in an amateur way, & has been vastly interested by what I have said of your work. The set of photographs of your drawings is just reaching him in the course of its long round; & if I'm not mistaken, the sight will redouble his anxiety to beard you in your lair!

Price is visiting Clark Ashton Smith again, & I can imagine how congenial the occasion must be. I fancy the Peacock Sultan will get some photo[s] from the mining operations & traditions of Auburn.

Hoping that the 11 × 14 reproduction process will soon be in operation—I remain

Yr most h^ble & ob^dt Servt

H P L

P.S. I note that Comte d'Erlette is qualifying as an unofficial Sidewalk Inspector! No doubt he's sent you a copy of his broadside of protest.

[P.P.S] I expect James F. Morton here Aug. 2–3–4. I think you've met him at some of the N.Y. gatherings.

[P.P.P.S., on envelope] Last moment—have just found a copy of A S with "The God Box." Really very effective—a great idea, & full of tense moments. The brief tale by Donald[3] is good—I think I read it—or its prototype—in MS. long ago. ¶ I hear rumours of a new magazine—*Terror Tales*—issued by the publishers of *Dime Mystery*. Have you heard of this?

Notes

1. HPL refers to the *WT* artists G. O. Olinick (1888–1957), James Milton Wilcox (1895–1958), H. R. Hammond, and Hugh Rankin (1878–1956) Doak is a pseudonym of Hugh Doak Rankin).
2. Richard Ely Morse (1909–1986), a librarian at Princeton University and author of a poetry volume, *Winter Garden* (1931), owned by HPL (*LL* 687).
3. "The Atom Smasher."

[9]   [HPL and James F. Morton to HW]   [ANS postcard][1]

[Postmarked Buttonwoods, R.I.,
4 August 1934]

Hail, Spawner of Daemons! Am harbouring a guest of honour with whom I believe you are not unacquainted. Have just produced an ice-cream famine at Maxfield's, & a general famine at Jakes (has Donald told you about these famous centres of refection?) & are now absorbing scenic impressions. Now by the shore at Buttonwoods. Hope you'll get over to these parts before you float away toward the sunset

        Regards—H P

Greetings out of the dark from the unknown, but not malefic, James F. Morton.

Notes

1. *Front:* New Providence County Court House, Providence, R. I.

[10]   [HW to HPL]   [transcription by RHB][1]

                                       August 7, 1934

Dear HP—

    Delay—I have been drawing pictures, so am doubly in your debt for card and letter. In reality, this is my first writing in weeks. The picture is done now; before I start the next I must do a little writing. I do not chose to starve in 1934!

    Glad you enjoyed God Box. The others are not much save for Time Haven, which should appear this month. Yes, Terror Tales is on the way, but I do not think it will compete strongly with WT. Esquire rejected my cartoon, or, as they put it, "your art work." I have had no luck with that outfit; they do not choose to consider either my illustrations or other work as contributions. I wish I could make them sorry (!) because I feel rather peeved at wasting so much time on them. My detective story editor Armer is silent as of old. You might enjoy seeing a small batch of drawings I have done in NY. When I receive them back from St. Paul I shall be delighted to send them to you if I cannot avail myself of your hospitality.

    I heard from Barlow by card, and am promised a letter. I heard from Donald also, who is taking the car and friends north to Rutledge, Minn. to visit Clara Mairs and Clement Haupers, artists.[2] I believe Milaca is accessible on the march, but since Don hates the woman who has the drawing I will probably miss this opportunity of entering Barlow's folio. Don dampens the project anyhow, and would refuse to cooperate. His good times do greatly [?] carry on apace, with many parties, discussions, affairs of every nature, from which he emerges [___?] with some plot ideas that he can well handle. (My own muse has been practically strangled to a finish lately: I think I am suffering from some kind of chronic [___?]). The Overbys[3] here, Andrew and An[n]ette, waft westward this week and take my brother north with them on a canoe binge of a solid week through the Rainy Lake regions. He, Don, enjoys canoeing enormously, as do I, and will enjoy [the] basics of outdoor fun in congenial company.

What you say of Esquire is quite correct. A man named Louis Paul had his first story published there this year, turned round and sold them another, and two to Woman's Home Companion at first class rates.[4] But I note with sorrow that these bugled "new writers" never get more than $50 for first takes. [At] pulp paper rates! Armer is the same. If he takes either of the stories of mine which he has held for so long, I will not get more than ½ to ¾¢ a word. This "new writer" idea is a vicious "gag", one way for an editor to increase circulation and cut expenses at the same time. No matter how many tales I sell in one market. I remain a "new writer" in a new market.

Thank you for the offer of duplicate magazines. If you have a copy of the Fantasy Fan containing [*sic*] the editorially garbled account of DONALD WANDREI,[5] I would appreciate having it if it is among the duplicates. Hail and farewell, with regards to your malefic friend James Morton. They seem somewhat rare. I hope I can see Rhode Island, too, before I go on, and now back to the machine.

Yours cordially and faithfully,

HE, ⊕ or The Spawner of Daemons.

Notes

1. The card does not survive. HPL refers to it in his letter to RHB of 22 August 1934: "As for your naked-eye perusal of H E's card—I simply gasp in astonishment. And *you're* the guy supposed to have trouble with his eyes!" (*OFF* 166). The blanks are the result of the editors' inability to read the transcription on microfilm. Presumably the card, much like No. 11 following, was written in a nearly microscopic hand. RHB transcribed the card fully.

2. RHB had written "Harbers." Clara Mairs (1878–1963), painter, printmaker, and decorative artist, and Clement Bernard Haupers (1900–1982), painter, printmaker, arts administrator, and arts educator, were both from St. Paul. Their relationship raised eyebrows, because of the difference in their ages and because they lived together unmarried. Haupers painted the portrait of DAW shown in part on the jacket flap of *DD*.

3. Andrew N. (1909–1984) and Annette (1901/02–1988) Overby were friends of the Wandreis. Both had attended the University of Minnesota. Andrew was a prominent banker and served as Assistant Secretary of the Treasury in the Eisenhower administration. Annette was a practicing psychologist. Marion Overby [relation not determined] had artwork published in *Minnesota Quarterly* (Winter 1930), which also included DAW's "Dead Fruit of the Fugitive Years: Ten Sonnets."

4. Pseudonym of Leroi Placet (1901–1970), American short story writer and novelist. His work appeared in *American Mercury* and *Esquire*. His earliest story in *Esquire* appears to be "A Cup of Coffee" (January 1935).

5. The account, an interview of DAW, in *Fantasy Magazine*, has numerous typographical errors, but does not appear to be "garbled." HW may be referring to the fact that DAW considered himself to be badly misquoted in the rendering of his anecdote about HPL correcting his mispronunciation of *Cthulhu*.

[11]   [HW to HPL]   [ANS, mutilated; upper left corner missing][1]
                                   [postmarked New York City? 25 August 1934]
                                                                  8/24/34

[. . .] the drop on me, but I die fighting. Upon [. . .] [dis]tinguished all micrographic honors and the relinquishment [. . .] have again been wasting my time
drawing. This writing is [. . .] on for the worst. Not as to detail, which is
[vol?]___en in itself, but in study [. . .] is the same drawing, All The Silences.
When I have finished this piece I [. . .] in mind, then the job of illustrating the
Hound of Heaven in full I [imagine it wi]ll take me a year, but it will be worth
the trouble easily. I have some hope [of selling] these illustrations, but will not
be particularly disappointed if things do not [turn] out that way. Incidentally, I
received copyright notice for one of my drawings via Barlow, so that business is
under way, though I am not yet in receipt of the product of any of his labor. Also incidentally, I uncover Donald's noncooperation is a consequence of an experience of his own—he loaned a number of items from his library to a man
who was preparing an anthology. The items were valuable, and he never got
them back. They are in storage here, & the anthologist is unwilling or unable to
pay accumulated charges. This looks like dirty work to me. Is this man's name
Harré? . . . I looked at a copy of Terror Tales, but could see no reason for buying a copy. Old friends seem to have sent out tentacles from the W. T. strong-
hold. I don't feel like making an effort in that direction myself. Esquire has held
a story of mine for four weeks, which, while unusual, means nothing, however good the story may be. . . . . I think Time Haven is all right, though it could
have been made more exciting. Yesterday I got a check for a new one, The
Other. I was greatly and pleasantly surprised, for there was not much science
in it. This money put me a little ahead, but will not do by itself, of course. I
believe I have other work in the process of being sold, and will shortly be able
to stir ahead from my cave. I hope to visit you in Sept. Perhaps Donald will be
home by that time, and there will be trips by car. Just now Don is canoeing in
northern Minnesota. If there is to be any eastern trip, he would do much of the
driving, of course. . . . I have a note from "Little Augie," who has slacked considerably in his literary output by virtue of taking a job in the local canning factory to balance the purchase of stories. I had no idea he would think of
accepting such a job. . . . Have here some thirty-odd magazines, through
which I seem to have exhausted the det. story field. All I can say about them
is that editors buy crap. Bilge. We are breeding a cheap, unconvincing, smart-
aleck school of writers. After this bit of I corroborate the statement of my
agent in turning down two of my pulps—"I have stories [of what?] is wanted
in this field." Will send you the drawings when they arrive.

                                        Yrs. faithfully & sincerely
                                                    H E

Notes

1. *Front:* New York Stock Exchange.

[12] [HPL to HW]   [AHT]
Nantucket, Mass.
30 August 1934

Greetings from the quaintest spot in N. America! Only 90 m. from Providence—& to think I never saw it before! Had a pleasant time in Boston last week, then for New Bedford & the Nantucket boat. Nantucket is an utterly marvellous place—you must see it or perish in the attempt! Whole tangles of cobblestoned streets with nothing but colonial houses on either side—narrow lanes—ancient belfries—picturesque waterfront—nothing is lacking! Am seeing the whole thing in a week's sojourn. Have a 3d story room with splendid view of town, harbour, & sea. Have explored old houses, windmill, Hist. Soc., whaling museum, Maria Mitchell observatory, &c. Also took sightseeing 'bus trip over entire island, with a stop permitting a good stroll through the flower-garden lanes of ancient Siasconset—a fishing village now forming a summer resort. Shall be home again Sept. 3—just in time to see my aunt off for a fortnight in Ogunquit, Maine.

Trust all your plans are maturing well, & hope you get to N. E.
Regards—
H P

[13] [HPL to HW]   [AHT]
66 College St.
Sept. 7, 1934

Dear H. E.:—
[. . .]

As for commercial, tailored-to-order fiction such as that which Price & Belknap & Kline are now grinding out—I simply could not even begin to write it. I have not the cleverness to study herd & editorial caprices & deliberately suit them in a cold-blooded way despite the repulsiveness of the process. Even if I conquered my nausea & attempted it, the result would be lifeless & unacceptable. The very editors who demand the sacrifice of artistic integrity would be the first to object to the stiltedness of the result. Literature & pulp writing can't mix—& only an exceptional person (like Auguste-Guillaume, Comte D'Erlette, for example) can successfully prosecute both at the same time. I, alas, am far from exceptional! I need the cash desperately enough, but don't see how I could possibly get it that way. If I could ever be sure of $15.00 per week—or even $10.00 per week—through some honest employment outside the writing field, I'd never think again of the commercial side of authorship. The really lucky guy is the one whose natural mode of expression happens—through pure chance—to coincide with some form of writing in popular demand. Robert E. Howard is the best example of this I can think of at the moment—his stories sell, but they have a zest & naturalness which at once distinguish them from the listless, synthetic pap of Hamilton, Quinn, Kline, & all the rest of the hacks. Of course, a really gifted writer has an ultimate chance of making the better grade of magazines—but even then there are limitations. At present the "quality group" subscribe to so rigid a tradition of realism & conventionality that I doubt whether any highly original or imaginative author could have much of a chance with them. It's a great world!

[. . .]

Yrs most cordially & sincerely—
H P L

[14]   [HPL to HW]   [AHT]

66 College St.
Providence, R. I.
Dec. 27, 1934

Dear H E:—

I surely hope you'll be able to get to N Y again if that's where you want to be (it's about the last place in the U.S. I'd ever wish to inhabit permanently!)—& I can abundantly sympathise with your attitude toward the Minnesota winter! You can probably appreciate the sentiment behind one of the stanzas of a juvenile "poetic" effusion of mine:

It was in the cold season
It* dawn'd on my gaze;
The mad time of unreason,
The brain-numbing days
When Winter, white-sheeted & ghastly, stalks onward to torture and craze.[1]

As you may see, the abysmal period was never exactly popular with me, even in my youth! And the long decades have done nothing toward reconciling me to it. Providence has just about as bad a climate as I can endure at all. Even here I have to hibernate closely all winter—& one shade more of cold would form the final straw. I may yet have to light out for the South—but sheer attachment to my native landscape & architecture has so far held me here. Key West is the town I could choose for climate—though antiquarian interests would probably cause me to compromise on St. Augustine or Charleston. But if I ever broke loose from Rhode Island, I would certainly live no farther north than Charleston.

---

*A sinister, unknown city of dream.

All good wishes—& hopes for a mild winter.

Yrs most sincerely—

HPL

Notes

1. "The City" (1919), ll. 6–10 (the first line should read "I remember the season" [*AT* 65]).

[15]   [HPL to HW]   [Christmas card][1]

[Postmarked Providence, R.I.,

19 December 1935]

[With every good wish for a
Merry Christmas and happiness
in the New Year]

H.P.L.

—1935.

Notes

1. *Front:* House of Seven Gables.

[16]   [HPL to HW]   [AHT]

66 College St.

Providence, R. I.

Nov. 7, 1936

Dear H E:—

Here is something by Comte d'Erlette[1] which I am supposed to forward to you in the course of general circulation, & which seems to me a pretty good piece of work. There are those who might find a touch of preciosity in prose as close to poetry as this; but I believe it forms a legitimate genre in itself—& one which M. le Comte handles with peculiar aptitude. The tale is delicate, but powerful & sincere, & leaves a residue of convincing emotion. I recall the parallel episode in "Evening in Spring" & believe the present version displays distinct improvement. Assuredly, Little Augie is headed somewhere!

All good wishes—& with the guess that your opinion of the enclosed will not differ great[ly?] from my own—

Yours most sincerely—

HPL

Notes

1. Evidently "Goodbye, Margery," incorporated into *Evening in Spring,* but also published separately.

Emil Petaja, Montana, 1930s

Letters to Emil Petaja

[1]   [ALS, mutilated]

66 College St.,
Providence, R.I.,
Novr. 7, 1934.

Dear Mr. Petaja:—

You quite overwhelm me with your more than kindly estimates of my fictional efforts—for I am only too well aware of the crudities & shortcomings of the latter. Really, you ought not to harbour the idea that any of the writers for cheap pulp magazines are figures of any standing in the world of general literature. Most of this popular magazine stuff is tawdry & artificial—written around a hackneyed formulate & wholly without artistic sincerity. I *try* to escape this stereotyped conventionality; but even so, do not get very far. The older I grow, the more dissatisfied I become with everything I have written. And in any case, don't imagine for a second that my stuff enters the real literature class along with the work of Machen, Poe, Blackwood, Dunsany, & other standard writers. The gap between these actual literary creators & the commonplace world of magazine fiction is too great for any bridging. I used to think I might work up into the Blackwood class some day, but I don't entertain that consoling illusion any more. However, I endeavour to write as well as I can, hence am always glad when anybody finds my products acceptable.

I feel greatly flattered when someone considers an autograph of mine worth saving—so am glad to send along any sort of signature you may prefer. I don't know just what the form of your collection or album is, but presume a scrawl on a small piece of paper will be the easiest kind of thing to file. Wherefore one of the accompanying items. As for a 'scrap dealing with my writings'—I don't know exactly what would best answer to that description, but am herewith enclosing a MS. of one of my early tales (of which I have duplicates—hence my ability to spare it) which may be at least partly suitable, even though hard to file in your scrapbook. I trust it does not fall too wide of the mark. This story appeared in W T during the magazine's first year, so that you have probably never seen it before unless you are a collector of old magazines. Hope it won't prove too great a disappointment—there are many weak spots which I might be able to avoid today.

I am greatly interested to hear of your own weird writing activities, & shall look for "Syzygy" in the F F. That little periodical, by the way, forms an admirably encouraging influence for beginners & others interested in the weird—& I strongly hope it may survive & prosper despite its present financial troubles. Sometimes its misprints rather exasperate me—my serial article is an especial sufferer from that defect—but in all probability it could not be printed so cheaply if a higher standard of proofreading were demanded. So I am quite content to accept it as it is, & to be thankful for its existence in any form.

Weird literature seems to be getting a slightly better 'break' than it had when I was young. Rumours of new weird magazines continue to appear—the most interesting one being the mention of a *high-grade* periodical published in England & featuring Blackwood, Wells, &c. You possibly noticed the item in the latest F F.[1] I must learn more about this. So far, no really high-grade weird magazine has ever been thought practicable—though I have often wished that such might be ventured. Perhaps this new experiment contains mostly reprint material—but even so, it will be eminently acceptable.

Well—here are the signatures &c. [I] hope they are in approximately the form you wish. Not of much value as literary reliques, but given for what they are worth!

With all good wishes, & looking forward to the perusal of your story, I am

> Yours most cordially & sincerely,
> H. P. Lovecraft

Notes

1. Julius Schwartz and Mort Weisinger, "Weird Whisperings," *FF* 2, No. 3 (November 1934): 40, announcing the publication of *Tales of the Uncanny*, edited by H. Norman Evans in September 1934. The issue contained "The Willows" by Algernon Blackwood, and stories by W. Somerset Maugham, John Buchan, H. R. Wakefield, Oliver Onions, and other writers of spectral fiction. The magazine did not seem to continue with contributors equally stellar.

[2] [ALS, mutilated]

> 66 College St.,
> Providence, R.I.,
> Nov. 21, 1934.

Dear Mr. Petaja:—

Yours of the 12th duly arrived, & [I'm] glad to hear that the "Dagon" manuscript proved acceptable. If you'd care to see other old stories of mine, I'd be glad to *lend* any of which I have available copies—in MS. or otherwise. I am herewith enclosing a list of all the stories of mine which I have not destroyed or repudiated. If you'll check off (faintly, in pencil, so that the list can be similarly used again) the items which you haven't seen, I'll send you all that I find lying around here upon the list's return. These tales vary greatly in merit, & some are so poor that I shall probably destroy them eventually. Meanwhile, as per request, I am sending a MS. (to be returned) with all the "Fungi from Yuggoth" except two—which I'll try to dig up later.[1] You can copy any you think worth it . . . . & I'm also sending for your permanent retention a few odd copies of cuttings & proofs which will reduce the extent of the copying. Hope you won't find the whole series a disappointment. What you say of the musical possibilities of some of them reminds me that "Mirage" & "The Elder Pharos" have been set to music by a composer of some minor distinction—Harold S. Farnese of the Los Angeles Inst. of Musical Education, who has specialised in weird compositions. He is a native of Monaco, educated in Paris, & winner of the 1911 Prize at the Paris Conservatory. I have not seen the musical scores of the two "Fungi",[2] but am told that they are highly effective . . . . more so than the verses, no doubt.!

Regarding the status of my work—I fear that you'll gradually discover, in the course of time, the dull-grey truth of my not over-flattering [es]timate! The whole question of artistic merit is [a c]omplex one, & as a critic I can easily see where [my] stuff fails to make the grade. Machen & Blackwood have written much poor stuff—for all writers are uneven—but their best products have a magic that I can never hope to duplicate. What is more, no weird writer can really be regarded as competing with the masters of general literature—whose comprehension & reflection of the human scene are so much fuller & better-proportioned. The weird artist is dealing only with a very small subdivision of human mood, whereas the general writer copes with a field a thousandfold wider & more complex. Even Poe & Blackwood are pygmies beside Shakespeare or Balzac. Of course, to a person especially interested in the weird, Poe & Blackwood may indeed be much more *interesting* than Shakespeare or Balzac. It is so, I freely confess, with me! But that does not mean that those who claim our chief interest are equal or greater. Artistic value is an intrinsic, objective thing which has nothing to do with the personal preferences of any individual. However, I don't agree with those who attempt to rule the weird out of serious literature. On the contrary, I believe that this element expresses something genuinely basic & permanent in human nature—certain symbolising & associative processes, plus the instinctive revolt of consciousness against the galling limitations of time, space, & natural law. Therefore I say that real literature *can* be founded on the spectral & fantastic, although it must necessarily be a narrow & minor form.

I shall be very glad to see an advance copy of "Syzygy" if you have one to lend. Some of the tales in the small magazines do get atrociously postponed. It is interesting to know that you are a violin student. I studied the violin between the ages of 7 & 9, but experienced a reaction against good music & gave it up. Today I've even forgotten how to read music! My imagination seems to be exclusively *visual*—but I realise most profoundly what a tremendous medium of expression music is for those capable of appreciating & using it. One of my friends—Alfred Galpin of Appleton, Wis.—has studied music in Paris under the late Vincent d'Indy & others, & has great ambitions as a composer. I certainly wish you all possible luck in your musical career!

I'm about ¾ through a new story, which I'll probably call "The Shadow out of Time". It will probably run to about 50 pages, & (alas!) is of the sort which Wright will be almost certain to reject. I may not even type it—for I have a nervous loathing of the task of typing.[3]

Again thanking you for your kind opinion of my stuff—I remain

Yrs most cordially—

H P Lovecraft

Notes

1. Although *Fungi from Yuggoth*, including "Evening Star" and "Continuity," was completed in January 1930, HPL had not typed the two poems he wanted to reserve for the conclusion in the event that he might add more sonnets to the sequence.
2. These are now reproduced in *Fungi from Yuggoth: An Annotated Edition*. A compact disk of *Fungi from Yuggoth* (Fedogan & Bremer, 2015) includes renditions of the pieces for the first time (piano solo and piano and voice).
3. In fact, R. H. Barlow secretly typed the story during HPL's visit to DeLand the following summer.

[3]   [ALS, mutilated]

66 College St.,

Providence, R.I.,

Dec. 1, 1934

Dear Mr. Petaja:—

Let me hasten to thank you for the [copy] of the delightful sonnet addressed to the mighty Klarkash-Ton & myself! It is really splendidly written, & no one would ever suggest that it is a first effort. It has a genuine & pervasive grace, & a series of eminently powerful & appropriate images. Work of this grade really ought to be published, & I trust you may in the course of time prepare a series of "Echoes from the Ebon Isles" for one of the magazines.[1] CAS & I surely ought to feel complimented—I trust he has a copy. If not, I must lend him this one.[2] The crayon sketch is delectably clever, & excites my mixed admiration & envy. I've always wished I could draw, but am abominably inept at anything pictorial. The younger generation seems to be naturally artistic—possibly you know that your fellow-weird-fans Barlow, Dwyer, & Bloch are likewise skilled with pencil & crayon. Your design is full of a pleasing glamour—one wonders *who* inhabits that turreted castle, & *what* inhabits that tenebrous cliffside cavern!

The address of H. Warner Munn is Route 1, Athol, Massachusetts—but if you can extract a communication from him these days you will be accomplishing a feat of major surgery beyond anything achieved by your baffled contemporaries! For some reason or reasons unknown, the young Werewolf of Ponkert[3] has shut up like a clam during the last year & a half, & no one can elicit any response from his moated citadel—even though many have important literary & bibliophilic matters to discuss with him. But go to it—& good luck!

Just received the booklet from *Marvel Tales* [con]taining Klarkash-Ton's "White Sibyl" & Dr. Keller's "Men of Avalon." Smith's fantasy is magnificent, though the Keller opus tends toward mediocrity. And yet Keller's story in the recent M T was broodingly powerful.[4] All writers have their high & low spots.

Again thanking you most sincerely for the tuneful sonnet & poignant sketch—

Yrs most cordially,

H P Lovecraft

Notes

1. Apparently EP intended to write sonnets in honor of various authors, including (besides HPL and Clark Ashton Smith), C. L. Moore, Duane Rimel, and H. Warner Munn. His sonnet to Robert E. Howard was "The Warrior."
2. The title of the poem is unknown, and it appears not to have been published.
3. HPL's epithet for Munn, derived from Munn's story of that title.
4. "The Golden Bough" (Winter 1934).

[4]   [ALS]

66 College St.,
Providence, R.I.,
Dec. 4, 1934

Dear Mr. Petaja:—

Let me thank you sincerely for the copy of "Syzygy" with which you have so kindly presented me. It is a delightfully haunting little sketch, with all sorts of suggestions of bizarre wonders & lurking outside mystery. It reminds me of the shorter work of Barry Pain, & certainly indicates a gratifying & enviable degree of talent on your part. I assume—in the absence of contrary evidence—that the "old Russian song" serving as a motto is actually a product of your own fertile imagination, just as many of the "ancient & exotic verses" prefixed to Robert E. Howard's tales are really his own. The coloured sketch forming the heading is infinitely clever & graceful, & I regret that it cannot be used in the F F. You are certainly fortunate in having three aesthetic outlets—music, literature, & drawing.

Glad you were not bored by the "Fungi from Yuggoth". I've never seen the music which goes with "Mirage" & "The Elder Pharos", but you might find out something about it by writing the composer—Harold Farnese, 4001 S. Harvard Blvd., Los Angles, California. I have not heard from him in a long while.

Enclosed & under separate cover I am sending all the old stories of mine which you have marked & which are available at the present moment. As soon as certain others are returned by the borrowers I'll send them along.

This stuff is very uneven in merit, & some of it is undeniably rotten. "He" & "Red Hook", for example, are detestably poor—while "The White Ship", "The Tree", & others are stilted & mawkish. On the other hand, I rather like a few. Still others would be made fairly good if I would take the trouble to doctor them up a bit . . . . which I probably never will. No hurry at all about [rea]ding & returning these things, so long as they come [bac]k safely in the end. Sooner or later these old [co]pies will fall to pieces—but in most cases I have duplicates. I'm certainly glad you hold such a high opinion of my efforts— rather a contrast to the fellow in the recent Eyrie who says my stuff isn't realistic & plainly-diagrammed enough.[1] My own criticism is not based on these grounds—indeed, in my opinion no weird story should be other than dreamlike & indefinite in many places.

No—my stuff is very unpopular with the editors. Bates of *Strange Tales* never accepted anything of mine, & I doubt if Hall of *Astounding* would, either. The pulp magazines have a whole set of standards & requirements which I despise & abominate to the last degree, & I could not cater to them even if [I] were willing to. They want conventional, oversimplified formula-stories involving artificially pleasant & breezy stock characters & incessant "action"—whereas to my mind such stories are unrelievedly trivial & worthless. Seabury Quinn—whose longer tales I simply cannot wade through—is the perfect popular ideal—those who differ from him have just so much less chance of suiting cheap editors. My goals & models are utterly antipodal to anything which these magazines really want—hence it is only occasionally & by chance that they take anything of mine. Of course, in latter years I don't send things around as often as I used to do. The experience becomes rather discouraging, & actually forms a handicap to good work. It freezes one into silence.

That was a mistake about my being a Shakespearian authority—the writer in the Eyrie confused me with someone of roughly similar surname (Samuel Loveman of New York, formerly of Cleveland) who is. Actually, I have only a layman's casual—albeit appreciative—knowledge of the plays & poems.[2] You are right in calling attention to the large amount of fantasy & supernaturalism in Shakespeare—something also found in virtually all the other Elizabethans. However—these writers used it in a slightly different spirit from the moderns; since they actually believed in the possibility & occurrence of supernatural manifestations. Regarding the Baconian theory—your teacher is certainly right in considering it arrant nonsense. There is absolutely nothing to be said for it— indeed, the plays themselves contain all sorts of evidences that nobody like Bacon could possibly have written them. For example—Shakespeare abounds in bad scholarship & careless anachronisms, whereas Bacon, had he written plays, would surely have been as accurate as Ben Jonson.

Well—let me thank you again for "Syzygy", & express the hope that it may be well-received on publication. Meanwhile I trust you will evolve more fantasies of kindred sort . . . . duly illustrated by your clever pen.

With all good wishes & appreciation—
Yrs most cordially—
H P Lovecraft

Notes

1. Ernest H. Ormsbee, *WT* 24, No. 6 (December 1934): 780: "Lovecraft puts beauty into some of his creations. He has a charm of wording that produces pleasurable tingles in the reader's mind, but several of his later stories have approached the phantasmics of the hashish dreamer; the creeping, creaking, billowing, bubbling excrescences of the slimy places. You may call them weird, perhaps they are, but they do not conform to my idea of the weird. They are shadows, disappearing things that can not be clearly seen by the human eye, or comprehended by the human brain. Several times you, or some one of your readers, has made the statement that the truly weird was the thing suggested, not the thing described. I will go along with this view to a certain point but I can't subscribe to it after it has reached this certain point. To be charming, a story must contain something of the known and knowable, something of our own workaday world. [. . .] I would examine a Lovecraft book before I purchased it. I would buy a Quinn or Howard book 'on faith', feeling that I was going to get my money's worth in pure enjoyment when I got around to the reading of it."

2. Alexander Ostrow (*WT*, October 1933) had written: "Your readers might be interested in knowing that not only is Lovecraft a master of weird fiction, but that he is also an authority on Shakespeare" (Joshi, *Weird Writer* 76).

[5]   [TLS]

66 College St.,
Providence, R.I.,
December 15, 1934.

Dear Mr. Petaja:—

Let me hasten to correct, and in a more legible medium than my own deplorably careless handwriting, any misapprehensions which my former letter may have excited. You speak of "half-hidden suggestions" of some opinion of your work other than that which I expressed in my text, whereas in truth no such suggestions even remotely existed in my mind. I liked your work very much, and said so—and nothing could have been further from my thoughts than any reserved contrary opinion, or any secondary meaning in what I wrote.

Obviously the whole trouble lies in my hasty and careless script, which you evidently have trouble in deciphering. I can't recall my exact wording, but in commenting on your sonnet I said either one of two things: "no one would ever suspect that it is a first effort" or "one would never suspect, etc". At any rate, my meaning was that and only that. I meant that it was good, and that it did NOT seem like a first effort. That was all that I had in mind. I am not in the habit of hinting and insinuating things. I always speak with much directness, and never resort to the double entendre. Another thing—I certainly did *not* apply the word "tearful" to your sonnet. Such an adjective could not be applicable in any sense. I can't remember what I did say, but it certainly wasn't that. I may have written "tasteful", "colourful", or something like that . . . give the text another look or send it back to me. I didn't realise my writing is so bad, because my older correspondents have become used to it and seem to get its purport. "Poignant sketch" is correct—but what is uncomplimentary in that? By "poignant" I meant exactly what the word means—acute; sharp and genuine in its emotional appeal—and what but a compliment is that? The idea of any hidden slur behind the expression is ridiculous. I repeat—I liked your work and plainly said so. And I *never* conceal adverse opinions behind favourable expressions. The "slur" is a rhetorical form entirely outside my range of writing and speaking. When I dislike a piece of work yet don't wish to offend the author I simply refrain from offering any criticism at all. I *thank* him for his courtesy in submitting it without telling him what I think of it—and usually manage to work in a few recommendations for helpful reading and study. Now as you can see, that was not what I did in your case. Your poem and story really are good—with a sense of colour and fantasy which many a writer may well envy—so I felt free to say that they are.

But I certainly am sorry that my bad writing led to misapprehensions. I ought to use the machine, but hate typing so badly that I never do unless driven to it. I still wonder what it was you interpreted as "tearful"!

Regarding my criticisms of my own stuff—I don't think they are excessively severe. My stuff wouldn't be bad for a beginner; but when one reflects that I've been dabbling with fiction ever since I was seven years old, it will be seen that I ought to write a lot better than I do. It means nothing to do better than the gang of listless, tongue-in-cheek commercial writers who flood the pulp magazines. They aren't even trying to do their best—cash being their goal. But I *am* trying to do my best—yet don't make the Blackwood–Machen–Poe–Bierce grade. There's no modesty in admitting limitations when one chooses so high a criterion. Anybody—or almost anybody—writing *seriously* could beat the dollar-chasing pulp crowd; but it takes a titan to rival the few admitted masters of fantastic literature. I don't merely say that *I* fail to make the grade. The fact is, not a single regular contributor to the cheap magazines has produced anything equal to the best of Blackwood or James or Machen or Dunsany. Smith comes the nearest to it. and more—I didn't call *all* my things "detestably poor". I applied that term only to certain pieces ("The Hound", "He", etc) whose cheapness, extravagance, and overcolouring stand out with a grotesque plainness after a lapse of years. And likewise, it is only to certain pseudo-Dunsanian pieces of the 1919–23 period that I apply the terms "stilted and mawkish." I distinctly like such things as "Erich Zann" and "The Colour out of Space". I try to be a realist in estimating my own as well as others' work. The items are very unequal in merit, and when something is rotten I make no bones about calling it so. Many things are so bad I've ceased to list or acknowledge them.

Well—I'm glad you're enjoying the batch which I sent. Don't hurry with them . . . . . there's no waiting list! I like the "Rats" and "Pickman" pretty well myself, although "The White Ship" is distinctly mawkish and mechanical. Compare it with work of the same kind by Dunsany and you'll see what I mean. That was never my natural medium of expression, but represented my excessively admiring reaction to Dunsany when I first discovered him in 1919. I dropped it altogether after doing the "Strange High House" in 1926—or rather, I worked it out of my system in a long novelette of 1926–7, which I have since repudiated.[1] The urban setting in "Pickman's Model" is taken from real life— such a district having existed in Boston prior to 1927. In that year Wandrei first visited the east, and I set out to show him the Pickman locale. Imagine my rage and humiliation at finding the whole tangle of old houses freshly torn down, with only the line of the crooked alley, outlined amidst gaping cellar walls, to prove that it had ever existed! Since then the old North End has suffered still further denudations—a couple of years ago two houses dating respectively 1695 and 1698 were demolished to make way for a broad new street.

Hope you have good luck with your various stories—let me see some more some time. Also verses. I'll be interested to see whether your sonnet to Munn serves to loosen up the dense silence now hanging over Athol! If you get a reply from the young rascal, W. Paul Cook and I will feel like clubbing together and buying you a gold medal!

I wish you had the power to issue that thin black volume of Lovecraft stuff with daemoniac illustrations! As artist, I'd nominate Donald Wandrei's younger brother Howard, whose accomplishments in the weird drawing line amount positively to genius. I really think this chap does better and mature work in his line than any of the rest of us do in our literary line. He belongs to the school of Sime, Beardsley, and Harry Clarke.[2] I think I'll enclose some photographic reproductions of his work (taken by his brother) to give you an idea of its subject-matter and general nature. But don't think for a minute that the camera can do even approximate justice to the technique and real effect. Much of the original material is in colour. Please return these prints some time—but no hurry.

Good luck with your bibliography. If you'll send me the list you have, I'll make all the additions I can think of. *Joris-Karl Huysmans* (born 1848; died some time around 1900), a Frenchman of Dutch ancestry, was indeed a real author, and perhaps the crowning development of the decadent school. *Francisco Goya y Lucientes* (1746–1829) was not a writer, but was one of the greatest painters in the history of the world—a Spaniard, whose fantastic and hideously sardonic drawings *Los Caprichios*[3] depict nightmare shapes, Witches' Sabbaths, and the like. Look him up in any good encyclopaedia or history of painting. Some of the hellish books mentioned in the tales of Smith, Howard, and myself are imaginary—of these the Necronomicon, Pnakotic MSS., Book of Eibon, &

Unaussprechlichen Kulten[4] are all I can recall at the moment. Several books mentioned in Poe, Bierce, and Machen are also imaginary. Send me your list and I'll strike off all the imaginary items which I can recognise as such. Incidentally, I'll gladly lend any books I have which you can't get hold of in Milltown.

All good wishes—

Yrs most sincerely,

H P Lovecraft

P.S.—That musician's name is FARNESE. Again, my bad handwriting led to a misreading!

Notes

1. I.e., *The Dream-Quest of Unknown Kadath*. HPL never typed the novel.
2. See DAW 206n1.
3. *Los Caprichos* is a set of 80 aquatint prints made by the Spanish artist Francisco Goya in 1797 and 1798, published as an album in 1799.
4. HPL devised the first two titles, Clark Ashton Smith the third, and Robert E. Howard the last.

[6]   [ALS, water damaged]

66 College St.,

Providence, R.I.,

Dec. 29, 1934

Dear Mr. Petaja:—

Thanks for the first kind words [ever bestowed] upon my Waterman rooster-scratchings since I was 12 years old! But you may yet regret your generous encouragement of a lapse into [such] hieroglyphs. I seem to get worse & worse all the time, as the need for speed increases, & nothing—apparently—can be done about it!

I was very glad to see your verse & story. Both are really very good. The poem has melody & haunting imagery, & leaves a dream-like, ethereal picture on the imagination. There are only a few changes—two of which you have yourself indicated in the text—which I would suggest. In the first stanza you use *whence* (= *from* which) in a place where *whither* (= *to* which) should be used. I would recommend the following alternative line:

"And whence they come, & whither go"

In the second stanza you have *cypress* spelled wrong. And finally, I think the poem's last line could be strengthened a bit. There is quite an art of ending a short poem powerfully & effectively, so as to avoid a letdown; & in this case I feel strongly that the note of *questioning* ought not to be reversed. Such a reversal would be effective only if the final assertion were distinctly a *revelation* of something with a previous & sufficiently important meaning for the reader. In this case, the assertion does not fulfil such conditions—being instead a presentation of other fictitious names like those used in the questionings. This causes a distinct sense of letdown which would not be present if the note of questioning were continued to the end. Also—it is well to avoid interjections possibly suggestive of sentimentality (such as ah!, oh!, &c.), as well as "poetic" contractions like *'twill, 'twas,* &c. Still further—I think it would be more effective not to depart from the rhyming scheme in this concluding [line?]. Therefore—considering all those things—I propose for your approval the following alternative final line—

"Or crystal-templed Barracrith?"[1]

But it's a delightful piece of work anyhow, and I trust it may find an appropriate haven in print.

I like the story very much, too. The few emendations I have suggested in pencil are all minor ones—& largely, I trust, self-explanatory. If any seem obscure, let me know, & I'll endeavour to explain them. I put in suggestions of *locality* which I don't think can be wrong. Though I've never [be]en to London, I've looked over quite a few maps & descriptive books; & am virtually certain of the shabby & potentially mysterious character of the small streets in Southwark just back of the Bankside waterfront. Of course, no reference to locality is really necessary—I merely stuck it in as an added bit of colour. I trust the tale may meet with good fortune on its editorial rounds. I'm sure the F F or *Marvel Tales* ought to welcome it even if it doesn't land in any of the remunerative magazines. You certainly shew a great fluency & facility in story-construction, & will doubtless be turning out better & better specimens as your experience & reading increase. Keep it up constantly—the more practice the better. Without question, your style is much maturer than mine was when I was your age. It took me a devilish long time to shake off certain weak points—indeed, I haven't shaken some of them off yet.

Now about your list of weird authors. I can't offer as many additions as you probably expect, but here's the best I can do. Enclosed are two sources—a catalogue of the weird part of my library, from which you can copy names, & a random list of others, which you can keep. One can't sit down and think of every one at a given moment—but this makes at least a start. I've also added a note or two to your list. You can't expect to list every human being who has ever written as much as one weird tale. There must be some limit of classification, however elastic. For one thing, you'd better cut out all writers below a certain qualitative grade—indeed, I've listed pulp names separately. Absolute duds like some of the W T small fry had better be left out altogether. There's no point at all in mentioning such. Then again—among real authors, there's no need of listing non-weird authors who at times merely *approach* the weird, or who use the weird in an incidental or conventional way. Thus I'd never include Shakespeare—or even Webster and other "terrible" Elizabethans. In the case of general authors who have produced a little weird material, one has to use one's own judgment. I would, in such cases, ask (a) how typical of the author is his weird stuff, & (b) all apart from this, how *important* is this weird material? On this basis, Kipling and F. Marion Crawford come definitely in; for their few weird tales are both typical & important. I'd admit Mrs. Gilman for her *one* weird tale—"The Yellow Wall Paper"—because of its great importance, though it is wholly non-typical of her. But I'd tend to exclude Ellen Glasgow & Michael Arlen because of the relative insignificance of their weird material. Of poets, Coleridge gets in easily for "Christabel" and "The Ancient Mariner"; but I don't think "Lamia" would properly let Keats in. As you can see, accurate classification is damned difficult—& you have to use your own judgment in the long run. Some would admit Cabell, but I don't consider his pale-pink irony as weird or fantastic in the truest sense. Some of the weird names you list are of writers I never heard of. Regarding them, naturally, I must reserve judgment.

Regarding loans: if you're feeling in an energetic mood, you might copy my catalogue for reference before returning it. Anything listed there is at your disposal for borrowing. Some books you'll recognise as things you've always wanted to read. Others will be doubtful. In such cases I'll take it upon myself to veto any suggestions which I know will turn out disappointingly . . . substituting really interesting items instead. You'd better send me a list of all the weird books—at least, all in this library—you've read; so that I can pick items for you without duplication. Another & more valuable source of loans is our fellow-fan *H. C. Koenig, 540 East 80th St., New York City.* He has a weird library much better than mine, & like me is willing to lend any item in it. At present certain books of his are going the rounds among an appreciative circle of borrowers. He'd be glad to add your name to the circulation list. This batch includes the remarkable work of William Hope Hodgson, recently discussed in the F F. Tell Koenig or me if you'd like to sample Hodgson, & the books will be switched your way . . . . though considerable time will elapse before your receipt of them. Koenig has all the famous old witchcraft books of the Middle Ages—like the "Malleus Maleficarum", which I'm now borrowing from him. In weird reading, I'd advise you to concentrate at first upon the masters—Blackwood, Machen, Dunsany, James, Bierce, Poe, Hodgson, &c. Read all you can of the best, but don't minutely copy any. Each of them has his typical faults as well as virtues. Hodgson in particular has notable weaknesses. By the way—I didn't find any fabulous authors on your list—although you had one name—*Mrs. Amworth*—which is that of a character in E. F. Benson's short story of the same name in the collection "Visible and Invisible."

Glad my yarns proved interesting—though I _____ your praise of "The White Ship" & "The Hound." Nor would I place any of them above Clark Ashton Smith's best. Have you seen his collection "The Double Shadow & Other Fantasies"? This contains items considerable [*sic*] better than most of the things published in W T.

Regarding settings for tales—I try to be as realistic as possible. The [cr]umbling old towns with winding alleys & houses 100 to 250 or more years old are realities on the New England coast. Providence has any number of houses dating back to 1750 & thereabouts—the one I live in was built 130 years ago. Boston's oldest house dates from 1676; Haverhill has one built in 1640, & so on. My fabulous "Kingsport" is a sort of idealised version of Marblehead, Mass.—while my "Arkham" is more or less derived from Salem—though Salem has no college. "Innsmouth" is a considerably twisted version of Newburyport, Mass. I hope you can see some of these old towns some time—they are my principal hobby. All up and down the Atlantic & Gulf coast from Quebec on the north to St. Augustine & New Orleans on the south & west there are venerable, picturesque old cities full of the houses & atmosphere and traditions of other days. I try to get around to as many as possible, but have not cash enough to go very often. The best, as I view them in retrospect, are Quebec (founded 1608), Portsmouth, N.H. (1623), Newburyport, Mass. (1647), Gloucester (1623), Salem (1626), Marblehead (1639), Plymouth (1620), Nantucket (1720) (on an island 30 miles out at sea), Newport, R.I. (1639), Providence, (1636), Wickford, Farmington, Conn. (1635—up in the Conn. Valley near Hartford), Deerfield, Mass. (still farther up the Conn. River), Kingston, N.Y. (up the Hudson—1658) with old Dutch houses, Philadelphia— & its suburb Germantown (stone houses of early German origin), Annapolis, Md., Georgetown, D.C., Alexandria & Fredricksburg, Va., Chattanooga, Tenn., Charleston, S.C. (next to Quebec, the most interesting city north of Mexico), St. Augustine, Fla. (with houses as old as 1565 or 1570—of Spanish construction) New Orleans, La., & Natchez, Miss. Key West is fascinating, though dating only from 1822. It is virtually a West Indian town. All of those places have different kinds of architecture & atmosphere, & I never tire of visiting them. But my journeyings have never extended beyond this narrow strip. I have never seen the Old World, though I'd give anything if I could. Here we think a building 300 years old is incredibly [an]cient—whereas in Europe the 2000-year-old vestiges of Roman occupation are common sights, while Egypt boasts reliques 4000 & 5000 years old. The oldest building I have ever seen— in St. Francis Street, St. Augustine—is 365 to 370 years old. The oldest in New England—in Dedham, between Providence and Boston—is 298 or 299 years old. Providence is quite rich in houses & public buildings of the late 18th & early 19th centuries—we have a 1761 court house, a 1770 college edifice, a 1773 market house, churches of 1775, 1808, 1809, 1816, & later, a huge tavern of 1783, & any number of private houses from 1742 onward. The steep hill section near the college—where I live—is the oldest part of the city. Its almost precipitous contour has prevented the spread of business over it & tended to keep it in its original condition. We have quaint old colonial doorways with fanlights & railed double flights of steps—things so typical of the atmosphere that I love, that I have selected one of them as a design for my bookplate. I enclose a sample, which you can keep if you wish.

I thought you'd find the Wandrei stuff notable. As a *writer*, Howard is not up to Donald's best as yet; but as a *pictorial artist* I think he represents almost the maturest development of any of "the gang". His work is miles ahead of any of the pictorial junk in W T—the only ones at all comparable with him being Utpatel (a friend of Derleth's who has had a few designs in W T) & Rankin. Your own pictorial work is really excellent. Of course it is not as far as advanced as Wandrei's, but it has all the solid foundations which I so utterly lack. As for colour—I don't think I agree with CAS that your design for the Ebon Isle Echo should have been in black [&] white. In the copy you sent me, the colours seemed decided assets. At least, they struck me that way. Yes—CAS is a bizarre artist of undoubted power. Some day, if you like, I'll lend you an envelope full of his smaller work—things he has given me from time to time. Many of his larger & more ambitious paintings are unbelievably impressive. Your young nephew must be gifted indeed, & I trust he will have the persistence & opportunities to develop his talent. About Goya—you could find something about him in almost any encyclopaedia or compendium of art. The Britannica's latest edition reproduces some of his pictures, if I recall aright. Unfortunately the ones generally favoured for reproduction are not the weird series. The best Goya exhibit I ever saw—of the grotesque *Caprichios,* that is—was a temporary display a decade ago in the Boston Museum of Fine Arts. The best permanent exhibit is probably that in the Hispanic Museum in New York. By the way—no hurry at all about returning the Wandrei material. Keep & examine the prints as long as you like.

As for my library—it is by no means a notable one, as such things are reckoned. I am not a bibliophile at all in the accepted sense—that is, I care nothing whatever about "first editions" & such. I cherish books simply for what is *in* them, & one good printed text is just the same as another to me. However, I love *old* books just as I love all ancient objects, & I likewise cherish volumes which have been long in my family, or which I have myself had since childhood. My oldest book is a copy of Ovid's Epistles printed in 1567—when Shakespeare was 3 years old. The next oldest is an Italian Geography printed in 1605.[2] Then comes a curious work on astronomy printed in 1681,[3] after which is a play of Dryden's published in 1694. That completes my 17th century items, but I have scores of books published in the 18th century—beginning with the original edition (1702) of Cotton Mather's "Magnalia Christi Americana". I am an enthusiast regarding the 18th century, & have been overwhelmingly influenced by its literature, art, philosophy, & general atmosphere. Roughly, the part of my library not in storage consists of about 2000 volumes—slightly over half inherited; the rest personally acquired. As I have said, it is *not* a bibliophile's library. Just books that I like or need—in any old editions. Greek & Roman classics are fairly well represented, & there is a tolerable batch of standard English literature—especially 18th century material. History & the various sciences have a good representation, & there are minor sections devoted to art, rhetoric, geography, travel, &c. A few translated classics of modern foreign literature—& the *weird* section of which I am enclosing a catalogue. A great many of my books are in frightfully poor shape, though I can't afford to have them re-bound. I also collect old almanacks—especially Thomas's "Old Farmer's" established in 1792. ¶ Best wishes—Yrs most sincerely—H P L

P. S. Tomorrow night I am going [to New York] _____
shall also see Barlow & Donald Wandrei, both of _____ metropolis.
Likewise I shall see Koenig, Talman, & _____
you've heard. ¶ Had an excellent Christmas—with _____
a boy.[4] Trust you enjoyed the holiday, & that you'll have a _____.

Notes

1. An elephant in Edward Lucas White's "The Elephant's Ear," is named Barranith, but EP refers here to a place.
2. It is difficult to say what this may have been. Possibly Giovanni Botero and Agostino Angelieri, *Le Relationi Universali di Giovanni Botero: Divise in Qvattro Parti . . ., Nuovamente ristampate & corrette* (Venice: Appresso Agostino Angelieri, 1605), although there are others.
3. By Robert Wittie.
4. HPL had received *Tales of Mystery,* ed. George Saintsbury, as a gift from Frank Belknap Long.

[*Enclosure:* TMs]
Alphabetical List of Fantasy Authors

Aiken, Miss
Ainskallas,
Ainsworth, Harrison
Alarcon, :Pedro de
Ames, Joseph P.
~~Amworth, Mrs.~~ *a character in one of E. F. Bensons' tales*
Andreyev, Leonid
? Atkey, Bertram

Balzac, H.
Barham, Richard
? Bedford-Jones, H.
? Beerboh*n*m, Max

Emil Petaja, Milltown, Mont.

Benson, E. F.
Beresford, J. D
Beangrand, H.
Bierce, Ambrose
? Birch, A. G.
Benson, Father
Bowen, Marjorie
Blackwood, Algernon
Bland, Mrs. E.
Bulwer-Lytton
Burrage, A. M.
* Burroughs, Edgar Rice
? Butler, Ellis Parker
Brevior, Thomas

Braddon, Miss
Bronte, Emily
? Broun, Heywood
Brown, C. B.

Calmet, Don Augustine
Collins, Charles
   "   , Wilkie
Chambers, Robert W.
Chekov, A. P.
? Crane, Stephen
Crawford, F. Marion
Cristmas, Grace
Crookenden, Isaac
Crowe, Mrs.

* De Castro, adophe
Defoe, Daniel
De la Mare, Walter
   "   , Colin (ed.)
Dickens, Charles
Doyle, A. Conan
? Deu Maurier
Dumas, Alexandre *(fils)*
Dunsany, Lord

Edwards, Amelia B.
Ewers, Hanns Heinz

? Finger, C. J.
Ford, Ford Madox
Foque, Baron de la Motte
French, *Joseph Lewis (ed.)*
Freeman, Mary E. Wilkins

Gautier, Theophile
Glanvil, Joseph *author of a book*
  on witchcraft—not fiction
? Gibbs, Sir Philip
† Goethe
Guinan, John

Harper, Charles G. *not fiction*
Harvery, W. F.
Hawthorne, Nathaniel

Hein-Karl, Fredrich *misprint /*
  Friedrich Heinrich Karl, Baron de
  la Motte-Foque
Heron, E. and H.
Hervey, Harry
? Hichens, Robert
Hodgson, *William Hope*
Hogg, James
Horsley-Curtiss, T. J.
Hunt, Violet

* Ibsen, Henrik
Ingram, *John H. (not fiction)*
Irving, Washington

Jacobs, W. W.
James, G. P. R.
James, Henry
James, Dr. M. R.
? Jerome, Herome K.
John, Jasper

Kompert, Leopold
Komroff, Manuel
Kipling, Rudyard
* Kline, Otis Adelbert

Landon, Percival
Lavater, Ludwig
Lee, Vernon
Lee, Dr. F. G.
Le Fanu, J. Sheridan
Le Loyer, Pierre
Lewis, Matthew Gregory
Loring, F. G.
Lovecraft, H. P.

MacDonald, George
Machen, Arthur
Mason, Eugene not
† Matthews, Brandoner
Marryat, Fredrick
Mather, Cotton *not fiction*
Mather, Increase *not fiction*
Maturin, Charles

Maupassant, Guy de
? Melville, Herman
Merritt, A.
Metcalfe, John
McSpadden, J. E. (ed.)
Middleton, Jesse Adelaide
† Middleton, Richard
Moreton, Andrew
Morrow, W. C.

Nashe, Thomas
Nesbit, E.
Northcote, Amyas

O'Brien, Fitz-James
O'Donnell, Elliot
Oliphant, Mrs.
† Onions, Oiver
O'Sullivan, Vincent
Owen, Frank

Pain, Barry
Pater, Roger ?
Philipotts, Eden
Poe, Edgar Allean
Priestley, J. B.
Prest, Thomas Preskett
Proby, W. C.
Pushkin, Alexander

Quiller-Couch, Sir Arthur

Radcliffe, Ann
? Reeve, Arthur B.
Reeve, Clara
Reynolds, G. W. M.
Roberts, Morley
Rohmer, Sax
Roman, Victor
Royde-Sith, Naomi
* Russell, Bertram

"Saki" (H. H. Munro)
Scott, Sir Walter

Sayers, Dorothy L. (ed.)
Scarborough, Dorothy (ed.) *no fiction*
Seabrook, W B.
† Shakespeare, William
Shelley, Mary, W.
Sinclair, May
Smith, Clark Ashton
Spicer, Henry
Stenbock, Count Eric
Stevenson, Robert L.
Stringer, Arthur
Stoker, Brram

Verne, Jules

Walpole, Horace
Walpole, Hugh
Wells, H. G.
White, Edward Lucas
White, S.
Wickwar, J. H.
Wilde, Oscar
Williams, Charles
Wright, S. Fowler
Wylie, Philip

"X. L."

(a great many of these I have only read or heard **of,** so probably many aren't really fantasy authors—also some have written only *one* or two fantasies.—E.)

Better leave mere editors *out of a list of* authors.

* *doubtful because of poor quality*

†*Doubtful because of the very small & insignificant amount of fantasy produced—or because work does not form real fantasy in the fullest sense.*

[N.B. HPL's insertions are in italic; strikeouts as indicated. ED.]

[7]   [ALS, mutilated]

66 College St.,
Providence, R.I.,
Jany. 17, 1935.

Dear Mr. Petaja:—

All the returned tales duly arrived—both MSS. & printed copies. Don't worry about the wear & [tea]r—that is inevitable. I'll have to find a way to get new [copie]s of some of my things sooner or later. Glad my [an]notations on your recent story & poem proved of assistance. Yes—I'd surely be delighted to see a copy of the poem decorated in your clever fashion.

Regarding sales—it is never wise to expect too much at first. Remunerative magazines are very odd & arbitrary in their requirements, so that beginners seldom succeed in placing material with them except after 2 or 3 years of continuous practice. Of course, different individuals have different luck. Young Bloch of Milwaukee has landed two stories with W.T. after about a year—or a year & a half—of practice writing. On the other hand Bernard Dwyer of N.Y. State has been dabbling in weird fiction for almost a decade off & on, without professionally placing anything except a single poem ("Ol' Black Sarah"). One never can tell. It is wise to keep on trying out various magazines, but unwise to entertain too high hopes. If we expect too much, we shall be disappointed & perhaps discouraged—that is, we should erroneously feel that our work isn't as good as it ought to be, whereas in truth we may be making excellent progress. Experience & observation prove that very few writers ever land a story during the first 2 or 3 years of their apprenticeship to the art—so when our own work is rejected we ought not to feel any discouragement. Still—I certainly hope that as many of your things as possible can land. I can sympathise concerning financial trouble—my own economic future being alarming in the worst degree—& trust that you may eventually be able to make the current markets without too much sacrifice of [ar]tistic quality.

I note the list of weird books you have read, & shall very shortly choose a sample of the unread volumes to send you. I'll also place your name on the circulation list of the Hodgson books—owned by Koenig. Regarding your list of weird authors—it's just as well that I didn't cross out the names I had never heard of, since I have undoubtedly missed dozens of top-notchers. Take W. H. Hodgson, for example. I never heard of him till 1931, & never read anything of his till 1934. Yet I find he is one of the most notable of all weird writers, & have prepared a whole page of material about him for insertion in my serial F F article. Many of the unknown names on your list may represent authors just as important as Hodgson. As for the writers I designated with a question-mark—remember that I meant no more than such a mark implies. I wasn't ruling them out, but merely recommending that their cases be examined individually. I haven't read Ibsen in 30 years, so ought not to be dogmatic about him. I ought to brush up a bit in his direction. It was merely a vague impression of mine that the touches of weirdness in him were connected largely with allegory & social criticism. It is very hard to draw the line in many cases. There is a werewolf incident in Petronius, for instance—& yet the net effect of the Satyricon certainly is not weird. On the other hand, a single tale like "The Monkey's Paw" is sufficient to admit the humorist Jacobs to the weird category. Molnar[1] us a typical borderline case . . . & so is Capek, originator of the "robot".[2] One must decide for oneself in such cases how much the element of fantasy is subordinated to some ulterior motive such as humour, social criticism, &c.

I recall your articles on fantasy fiction, but am not enough of a bibliographer to pick any flaws in them.[3] Koenig is certainly wrong about "Wolves of God". I've really forgotten just how much of the collection Blackwood wrote.[4]

I'll be glad to see the new piece—or part of it—on which you are now working. Wish I could get time to do something myself—but press[ure] of immediate tasks has tied me up completely. I can never write unless I have something approaching complete leisure.

During the New Year period I visited Frank B. Long in N Y, & saw most of the weird-literature crowd, old & new. Young Barlow was up from Washington, & the two Wandrei brothers had just blown in, so that the event had something of the aspect of a convention. At one gathering 15 were present—including Long, Barlow, Talman, the Wandreis, Koenig, Leeds, & others[5] whom you might not recall so readily. This was Barlow's first visit [to] N Y since infancy, & Belknap & I shewed him all [the] museums, galleries, bookshops, &c. He picked up a number of bargains, including a fine old copy of George W. M. Reynolds' "Wagner the Wehr-Wolf" for 15¢. I secured an excellent copy (modern) of Lewis's "Monk" for a dollar—one more item to add to the catalogue. The Wandrei boys have taken a joint apartment at 155 W. 10th St. in Greenwich Village, & hope to keep afloat through hack writing for Street & Smith. On one occasion, at the home of Samuel Loveman (a poet & lover of bizarre literature), we were shewn from 300 to 400 of Clark Ashton Smith's weird drawings . . . probably the greatest collection of them outside Auburn. I had seen these in 1922, but they were absolutely new to Long, Barlow, & the Wandreis. The weather during this trip was, on the whole, distinctly favourable—only 2 days being so cold as to give me great inconvenience. I can't stand any temperature under -20°, & am at my best over 80°. The sessions began to break up Jany. 7—when Barlow returned to Washington on the 10:30 a.m. coach. I left for Providence the following midnight—arriving home at 6:30 a.m. Naturally I found a frightful accumulation of work awaiting me—amidst which I am still hopelessly foundering.

Well—I trust all your projects may develop favorably. I shall be sending along a couple of books presently—perhaps Machen's "House of Souls" (with "The White People" & "The Great God Pan") & one of M. R. James's volumes. Which stories of James (beside "The Tractate Middoth", which you mentioned) have you read?

    With all good wishes—

        Yrs most cordially,

            H P Lovecraft

Later—Find that H. of S. is already lent. Am sending 3 volumes—1 of Chambers containing "The Yellow Sign",[6] Shiel's memorable "Purple Cloud", & the first & best of the James collections.[7]

Notes

1. Ferenc Molnár (1878–1952, anglicized as Franz Molnar), Hungarian-born author, stage-director, dramatist, and poet regarded as Hungary's most celebrated and controversial playwright.

2. Karel Čapek (1890–1938), Czech playwright, dramatist, essayist, and reviewer. His science fiction play *R.U.R.* [Rossumovi Univerzální Roboti, or Rossum's Universal Robots] (1920) introduced the word *robot* to the English language and to science fiction as a whole.

3. HPL refers to EP's "Famous Fantasy Fiction" in *FF*.

4. "Again he [EP] mentions 'Wolves of Darkness' [*sic*] by Algernon Blackwood. If memory serves me correctly, I believe the only story in the book written by Blackwood was the title story, 'Wolves of Darkness.' All the others were written by Wilford [*sic*] Wilson." Koenig, letter to the editor, *FF* 2, No. 2 (October 1934): 18. Koenig refers to *The Wolves of God and Other Fey Stories* (1921), co-written by Blackwood and Wilfred Wilson. The stories in *The Wolves of God* had appeared earlier in magazines with only Blackwood's byline. Koenig means that only "'Vengeance Is Mine'" is credited to Blackwood alone in the first British edition (London: Cassell, 1921).

5. Others included attendees at the annual gathering included James F. Morton, Samuel Loveman, Rheinhart Kleiner, George Kirk, and Dean P. Phillips and his unnamed friend. The fifteenth person is unknown.

6. *The King in Yellow.*

7. *Ghost-Stories of an Antiquary.*

[8]   [ALS]

                       66 College St.,

                       Providence, R.I.,

                       Feby. 8, 1935.

Dear Mr. Petaja:—

        I read yours of Jany. 23, with its two really delightful enclosures, & was vastly interested in all the items. You certainly have a very keen sense of atmosphere & dramatic values, & a natural grace & force in the use of language—so that there is every reason to expect increasing success for your prose & verse alike. Don't let yourself get discouraged from reading the work of experienced writers. Probably very few of them did as well at your age as you are now doing! As for rejections—everybody has to be prepared for those. Some of Clark Ashton Smith's best things have been turned down—only the other day Wright refused his magnificent "Chain of Aforgomon."[1] Regarding the wide & frequent submission of material—it probably is a good idea unless the phenomenon of rejection is especially discouraging. Naturally, the more things sent, the greater the chances for an acceptance now & then. It depends largely in the writer's particular temperament. But of course one should not usually send around material which is frankly minor or experimental. It is not well to have editors associate one's name with trivial material. Yes—it is always advisable to put the inscription "First North American Serial Rights Only" in the upper right-hand corner of all MSS., prose or verse. This means that you will have to be paid again for any subsequent reprinting—either in the same magazine or elsewhere. If I had known enough to jot this down on my earlier tales, I'd be getting second pay for all the reprints which Wright so blithely & unremuneratively uses. I began to reserve rights in May 1926—& when any of my subsequent work is reprinted, I get the cash. There's nothing at all conceited about reserving rights—for reprinting really is quite common. Fully a fourth of my junk has been reprinted somewhere or other—& "Erich Zann" has seen six printings. Most of our weird gang have had things reprinted in the "Not At Night" series of annual anthologies published by Selwyn & Blount of London.[2]

Glad you like the books—when they come back, I'll send more. I noticed Koenig's correction of the Blackwood matter in the F F.[3] As for M. R. James—I guess I'll send you all his books, since each volume would include much you haven't read. He is a fantaisiste whose methods are worth studying. As for Howard Wandrei—"Vine Terror" is *not* his best work. It would be fairer to judge him by "In the Triangle". Still—his great distinction is as a pictorial artist. Utpatel certainly is splendid—so good that Mrs. Brundage has plagiarised two of his motifs for cover designs! I don't know his address, but Derleth (whose address is simply *Sauk City, Wis.*) could give it to you. Talman's address is *Spring Valley, N.Y.* You would probably get replies from both Derleth & Talman. Barlow & Long are both notoriously poor correspondents, while Munn—as I mentioned before—has become a widely-discussed sphinx & enigma. I'll be glad to see part of that novel of yours—& to hear what the plan of the whole is. My own stuff tends more & more to attain novel—or at least novelette—length as I grow older. "At the Mountains of Madness", for example, runs to 115 typed pages. Yes—I think your coloured drawings are delightful, & hope to see more of them. You will certainly do splendid work when you get to the university art school. By the way—I think Rimel has made a splendid linoleum block cut for your "Echoes from the Ebon Isles". He is marvellously gifted in that medium. Drawing is an accomplishment I've always vainly wished I possessed. My mother, elder aunt, grandmother, &

great-aunt were all accomplished amateur painters, but I have an utter lack of the first rudiments of talent in that field.

It certainly is rather difficult to determine just who shall & who shall not go into a list of weird writers. Ibsen was, without question, first of all a critic of human nature & society who used symbolism as a means of illustrating psychological, ethereal, & social situations. Whether, in any play such as "Peer Gynt", this symbolism sufficiently approaches sheer independent fantasy to stand out distinctively in that field, only a fresh reading could decide. Unfortunately I haven't read P. G. in 30 years, & haven't a copy at hand—although, ironically enough, most of Ibsen's *other* plays are indeed on my shelves. If my memory is any good, Peer Gynt is a sort of ethical (rather than *religious*) allegory in which the mythical & fantastic lore of Norway (the plastic entity called the "Boig",[4] & sundry grotesque adventures) is used to illustrate the salient qualities of mankind—vanity, egotism, &c. It is my impression that the central figure—Peer Gynt himself—is a folklore character older than Ibsen's time—a typical picaresque rogue of the sly parasitic type like the German Tyl Eulenspiegel. Such characters are themselves basically allegorical—embodying on a small & homely scale the essential craftiness, indolence, bombast, callousness, & hypocrisy of all humanity. As for Ibsen in general—no, I do *not* think that he is in any sense local. His plays reflect far more than their outward Norwegian setting—embodying the profoundest & most universal situations of mankind. If they have any limitations, it is matter of 19th century perspective. Possibly Ibsen laid too much stress on the ideas & conventions of his age as permanent forces—but his pictures of human nature in relation to those forces were generally flawless. He was, I think, best in his middle period ("Doll's House", "Ghosts", "Wild Duck"), when he kept his exuberant symbolizing tendency most under control.

And now let me congratulate you most sincerely on the poem & story enclosed. "Witch's Berceuse" is extremely vivid & well-written, & I think the last line amply conveys the desired climactic effect. There's no change I could suggest—unless you'd like to have a name for the daemonic father which is a little less suggestive of "Dracula". Hellish-sounding disyllables are very easy to coin . . . . you could use Rimel's pet devil *Sotho*, or concoct such name as *Yabon, Nagoth, Zathu*,[5] &c. But of course the existing name is quite all right, since many will not take the resemblance amiss. I hope to see this excellent piece of work in print before long.

"Silia" is a splendid tale—full of the atmosphere of real folklore, & admirably vital & convincing as a pensive pastoral idyl. It certainly reflects its background with notable power & beauty, & I think your opinion of its merit in relation to earlier work is well-justified. The development is especially good—each event being approached with suitable emotional preparation instead of just casually jotted doom in the manner of cheap pulp fiction. It is convincing—for the reader is thoroughly initiated into the folklore spirit before the marvels are unfolded. And when the unfolding comes, it is of the right sort to harmonise with the initiation. The few & trivial changes I have made are wholly verbal—& no doubt largely self-evident. Be on guard against certain characteristic misspellings—& always verify the precise definitions of uncommon words. I surely hope this story will land somewhere—it certainly ought to. It weaves just the right kind of a glamour to carry the action along—& evokes the mystical northern scene with gratifying realism. It is interesting to know that you have so close a connexion with the magic-touched, aurora-litten land of the "Kalevala"—a really great country despite its limited area. I have always heard of the potent & mystical legendry of Finland—& perhaps you know that one of the finest of all studies in weird literature—"The Haunted Castle", an analysis of the Gothic novel & all its sources—is by the Finnish professor Eino Railo, whose first name I am inclined to think is another sp[elling] of the name of your central character "Aoino". If, by the way, you [have not] read "The Haunted Castle", you certainly ought to do so. I don't o[wn a copy,] but am constantly on the lookout for one. Finland has certainly p[roduced?] a tremendous amount of intellectual & aesthetic activity—which, when its size & location are considered, forms a marvelous testimonial to the innate quality of its race-stock. I was reminded of this only the other day by a friend of mine who is engaged to marry a young lady of Finnish descent in Detroit. He had been visiting her family, & was impressed by the superior intellectual tone of their ordinary household conversation—as distinguished from the banalities & personal gossip so lamentably predominant in ordinary American chatter. The brother of his fiancee [*sic*] is—or lately has been . . . I forget which—American consul at Helsingfors;[6] so chosen because of his ancestral understanding of the Finnish cultural background. My friend gave me a couple of Finland travel folders—one of Helsingfors & one of Kuopio—which made me wish I could visit that fascinating land during its brief & lovely summer. It is difficult to realise that the latitude of Kuopio is the same as that of southern Greenland & Baffin Land & Central Alaska in this hemisphere . . . . yet Hammerfest, Norway, is above the 70th parallel—corresponding to central Greenland & (almost) Point Barrow, Alaska! I fancy that the region of "Silia" must be, in general, that of Kuopio—the lake country. Incidentally—for the benefit of the lay reader, had you not better specify that *Suomi* means Finland?

Regarding the semi-pseudonym *E. Theodore Pine*—it is surely a pleasant & appropriate enough signature if you care to adopt it. It is very hard to give advice on the pseudonym question. In my old days in the United Amateur Press Association I used to write under a dozen different names, but latterly I have thought the practice unnecessary & rather unmotivated. It all depends on the specific case. In instances where pseudonyms [are] chosen purely for affectation or fancied distinction, I'm dead against them. Thus I'm trying very hard to dissuade a young man named John D. Adams[7] from signing his verses with the ostentatious & meaningless Scandinavianised title (he isn't Scandinavian at all) *"Jon Adams"*. There is *no reason* for that—*John Adams* was a good enough name for a president, & it ought to be for a poet! When a writer bears a name of different linguistic origin from the public he addresses, the most sensible course is to let individual circumstances govern his procedure. If his own name sounds harsh or "jaw braking" in the language of his public, a modification is surely justified. Thus it was wise for Josef Conrad Korzenewski (or something like that) to become Joseph Conrad.[8] On the other hand, when the name possesses reasonable euphony in the language used, there is no need of changing. Thus, although Paul Dreiser chose to become Paul *Dresser*,[9] I think his infinitely greater brother Theodore did just as well to stay the way he was. You'll also notice that Joris-Karl Huysmans, whom we mentioned before, retained his original name of Dutch form despite being a French writer. In his case it was the *pronunciation* that suffered. *Huysmans* (as long famous through Joris-Karl's collateral ancestor, the painter Cornelis Huysmans) is pronounced in Dutch something like *Hice'manz*, whereas in France Joris-Karl pronounced his name in a Gallic way—something like *Weece'maw*. Your own name is certainly not a harsh jawbreaker in any sense— indeed, it is really very simple & harmonious & pleasing. There is surely no intrinsic need of pseudonymity, for the age is long past when non-English names looked strange when signed to English text. (Which reminds me that Railo's book is written directly in English, the author having lived & taught for long periods in England, & his work [since it centres in Radcliffe, Lewis, & Maturin] being aimed at English readers.) So it is really all a matter of choice with you. If you dislike the idea of having your name mispronounced by unknown readers [I'll admit I called it *Pat-ah'jah*, though thought it *might* be *Pat-ah'yah* . . . . I wouldn't be sure what language it came from, hence was uncertain what sort of rules to apply.], you might well adopt a translated form . . . . though of course there are just as many habitually mispronounced English name. The question of odd name-pronunciations is a highly interesting one. Probably the most *misleading* cases in America are those of certain old Huguenot names in South Carolina. Would you believe that *Huger* is pronounced *You-jee'*, and *Legare*, *Le-gree*? Incidentally—our friend *Rimel* (whose name is of Dutch origin) had me stumped for a while. I thought it was *Ri-mell'*, whereas it is actually *Rye'-mel*. Another puzzle was the name of our generous colleague *Koenig*. I carelessly called it *Coin'ig*, while Long (the *k* in whose *Belknap*, by the way, is silent) called it *Kō'-nig*. Later a person familiar with German corrected us & told us it ought to be *Kĕr'-nig* . . . . but when I called him up with that pronunciation the people at the office didn't know at first whom I was looking for. Finally, a secretary exclaimed—"Oh, you mean Mr. *Kay'-nig*"! And so it was! Yet others have since told me that this is not a good German pronunciation. Koenig is quite far removed from Germany, & had to learn the language in school.

No—I hardly fancied that Montana possessed a subtropical climate! Providence has been down to -17° just once in the history of its weather bureau (Feb. 9 last year); the next two recorded lows being -12° on Dec. 30, 1917, & -9° on Jan. 24, 1907. Ordinarily we are seldom below zero; & indeed, temperatures below +20° seldom occur save in occasional spells of from 1 to 4 days. But this & the preceding winter have been atrocious. Jany 23–4 we had a record-breaking snowstorm (see enclosed cutting—which you needn't return) which tied up traffic & has remained persistently on the ground owing to a subsequent cold spell. For days the mercury has been below +20°, often sinking near zero, & once getting down to -5° . . . . the lowest since that all-time low of last February. And yet R.I. is easily the warmest of the New England states. Northern New England—Vermont & New Hampshire—probably resemble your region in its extremes. If I weren't so intensely attached to the scenes of my youth, I'd go south. I am never really comfortable under 75°, & can't safely endure anything under +20°[.] I simply have to stay indoors when the thermometer sinks below that +20° safety–line. Southern Florida or the West Indies has the sort of weather I like. I literally don't know what it is to be too hot. 90° braces me up! Different people, of course, differ in their ability to stand the cold. Donald Wandrei can weather a St. Paul winter without trouble—but it weakens & enervates his artist-brother. In your own state I presume the western part gets just a trace of Pacific-Coast mildness. Baldwin & Rimel speak of winters apparently far warmer than Rhode Island's—& they are in Asotin, which is nearer to you than it is to the ocean.

Lately I've been trying to snatch opportunities to finish my new story, but progress is slow at best. However, I've gone ahead some 10 pages. The thing is turning into a novelette in spite of me! Another thing I'm trying to do is to get my extensive files of cuttings, MSS., pamphlets, &c. in shape. To this end I've just acquired a couple of dark walnut chests of drawers which—piled up to form a single vertical cabinet—will help to reduce the prevailing litter considerably.

Well—again let me congratulate you upon your recent good work, & thank you for the permanent copy of "Witch's Berceuse".

All good wishes—

Yrs most sincerely

H. P. Lovecraft

Notes

1. But *WT* ultimately published the story in December.

2. The gang would include HPL, Frank Belknap Long, Clark Ashton Smith, Robert E. Howard, Seabury Quinn, H. Warner Munn, Henry S. Whitehead, and August Derleth. Zealia Bishop was not in the "gang," but a story by her had been revised by HPL.

3. See H. C. Koenig, "Mr. Koenig Corrects": "The book was written by Blackwood and Wilson [. . .] I find, however, that the only story credited directly to Blackwood

was the last story in the book entitled 'Vengeance Is Mine' and *not* the title story. . . . it may be well that Blackwood had a hand in the other stories." *FF* 2, No. 5 (January 1935): 66.

4. Also referred to as the "Great Bøyg of Etnedal," a troll in Scandinavian folklore.

5. EP employed the name "Zathu" in his poem.

6. The Swedish name for Helsinki.

7. John D. Adams, amateur journalist from Oklahoma, editor of the *Literati,* and member of the Coryciani round-robin letter group.

8. Joseph Conrad (born Józef Teodor Konrad Korzeniowski; 1857–1924), Polish-British writer regarded as one of the greatest novelists to write in the English language.

9. Paul Dresser (born Johann Paul Dreiser, Jr.; 1857–1906), American singer, song-writer, and comedic actor of the late 19th and early 20th centuries.

[9]   [AHT; ALS]

66 College St.,

Providence, R.I.,

March 6, 1935.

Dear Petaja:—

Glad you enjoyed the various volumes—& will be pleased to send more whenever you say the word. Shiel's "Purple Cloud" is certainly a masterpiece of its kind. Last-man stories are not uncommon, but I don't know of any other with the power, scope, & convincingness of this one. It somewhat falls down in the second half—but the early part is as nearly perfect as a fantasy could be. Regarding the matter of religion—while a story is of course no place to air philosophic views, I must say that I myself do not believe in any form of the supernatural. While religion was a perfectly natural thing for mankind in early ages, when nothing definite was known about the constitution of matter & the causes of natural phenomena; there is really no basis for its existence in the light of what we know about the universe, & about our own mental & emotional processes, today. We now realise that the varied happenings of the universe, & the phenomena of life & consciousness, are all parts of are all parts of a general pattern of force-&-matter mutations whose perpetual flux of alternate building-up & breaking down does not even remotely suggest such a thing as conscious direction or purpose. While there is no positive *disproof* of a cosmic consciousness, there is *no reason to assume* that any such thing exists. It is just as if I were to say that a man named Smith lives in a brick house in a city called Nuth on the 3d. satellite of Jupiter. There is no way of *disproving* what I say—but who would believe anything so gratuitous & improbable? And when we come to analyse supernaturalism, we find that it forms an assumption no less gratuitous & improbable. What really disposes of supernatural belief is our modern understanding of *the reason it has existed.* Psychology & anthropology have now shewn us how & why the concepts of "spirit", "deity", "immortality", "right & wrong" (as distinguished from the sound values based on aesthetic & utilitarian ethics), "worship", "sin", &c. &c. came into existence among primitive races trying to explain the unknown tangle of the external world & their own emotions, & have made it overwhelmingly clear that the growth of these concepts is an inevitable concomitant of primitive ignorance—in no way implying any truth behind them. The same sciences also make it manifest why these concepts have come to exert so great a sway over the emotions of the majority, & why they have survived so persistently in the face of the increased knowledge which has virtually disproved them. Thus it is no longer possible to argue that the intense *wish* or profound emotional *belief* of the majority in all ages forms any indication of the truth of the "deity" or "immortality" concepts. We know today, through psychology, that *any* belief or emotional bias, no matter how untrue or absurd, can be implanted in the brain & nervous system of a human being with tremendous force & firmness if the victim be inoculated with it in infancy. A person thus subjected to indoctrination with some special idea at an age under seven will always have a deeper instinctive predisposition toward that idea—but this has nothing to do with the truth of the idea. There is no natural leaning toward religion. Originally, it merely attempts to explain the unknown through poetic symbolism & crude personification; today it survives among the less analytical majority merely because they lack scientific information, & because their emotional apparatus has been permanently biassed or crippled by religious propaganda hammered into them in childhood, before their mind & emotions had developed beyond the infantile state of helpless & uncritical receptivity. It is really a crime against a child to attempt to influence his intellectual belief in any way. Anything like bias or indoctrination should be confined to such broad concepts as have been universally found expedient & harmonious through racial experience—concepts like honesty, order, non-encroachment, &c., which relate to practical conduct & not to matters of *opinion*. So far as points of theory & belief are concerned, the only decent & honourable thing to do with a child is to teach him *strict open-mindedness* & *intellectual integrity*—urging him to accept nothing through mere hearsay or blind tradition, but *to judge everything honestly himself on the basis of existing evidence*. If religion is true, he will then sooner or later accept it. If it is not true, he will then be free from a degrading mental slavery which cannot honestly be called *belief*. The fact is, a *real* friend of religion would not *wish* anyone to accept it if he did not do so through an honest & open-minded appraisal of the evidence offered by the phenomena around & within him. All attempts to mould belief on emotional, non-rational grounds are to be condemned without qualification as unworthy of any organism as highly evolved as man. This applies to non-religious & anti-religious propaganda as much as to religious propaganda. The Russian soviets are just as reprehensible in warping popular emotions in the direction of Marxism, as the orthodox churches are warping popular emotions in favour of religion. What really ought to be taught people is *how to think*. Nine-tenths of the people in the world *never really think* on any topic of large scope. The *imagine* they have "opinions"—but these "opinions" are so completely the product of irrational emotion, blind heritage, & sheer mental indolence, as to be unworthy of the name. And this applies to most atheists as well as to most religious people. We would be a lot better off if our preceptors would stop trying to teach us *special attitudes*, & buckle down to the vital business of teaching us *accurate thought & strict intellectual honesty*.

In view of what we know today about the universe and ourselves, there is very little likelihood that the old concepts of dualism ("spirit"), immortality, & cosmic consciousness & purpose can have any truth in them. But this need not disturb us in the least. Actual[ly,] the supposed longing for such things is merely an artificial emotional condition determined by our [past] environment. As soon as we put such ideas out [of] our head, we shall cease to feel any sorrow at the[ir] untruth. There are plenty of bases for a fruitful, orderly, & harmonious life without any assumption [of] the supernatural. Although life & mankind are on[ly] trivial accidents or incidents in the universe, they are none the less important to themselves. [Man] has a well-defined set of instincts & emotions; & [the] planning of a way of life which shall satisfy these with the least possible conflict & disharmony & encroachment, & with the greatest possible opportunities for the growth & expression of the species' most highly-evolved attributes, is a full-time job of which no philosopher or leader or ethical teacher need feel ashamed. This task of ethical leadership, based on sound principles of aesthetics & sociology, is the one now awaiting the sort of man who in earlier ages formed a religious leader. I do not advocate the forcible extirpation of religion, but I think it is [wise to] transfer energies to something which has a foundation in reality. The conditions of life are growing mor[e &] more different from what they were in the ages when the various religions took form; hence one can no longer expect any religion-based ethics to be at all times as useful as an ethics based on reality. What is more, religion is rapidly losing its emotional & ethical hold over all classes— even those who consciously believe it. The wide gap between what it teaches & what we now know to be real is too vast a thing to conceal & gloss over. People realise it subconsciously even then they are blind to it with their conscious minds. Religion *as a practical force in life* is dead—& if we expect to rally the emotions of the people to anything today as those emotions were rallied to religion in the past, we must provide something in which they can *really believe* . . . with their subconscious as well as conscious minds. The Russians have got something of the sort in their new way of life based on social adjustment. If we want anything as powerful, we must also devise some ideal of human adjustment *which has a real chance of working* & of offering the people an actually bearable set of living conditions. Religion always promises, but has no power to perform. It is simply a sort of emotional intoxication—as helpless as whiskey to make real the grandiose visions it holds forth. The race is too disillusioned & realistic at this stage of the game to follow any such phantom. If we want to rally everybody to a single purpose, we must formulate a goal which has a demonstrable chance of giving the whole of mankind *better conditions in the only life it is certain of having*. I don't think the soviet ideology embraces the best possible goal, & would hate to see it established in the western world. But at least it is a *real goal*—something to which men can be intelligently loyal. At the moment, the western world possesses no such thing—even though the Nazi movement thinks it has found one. We live in an era of unmistakable decadence—the last phase of a way of life founded on conditions & beliefs forever vanished so far as this cycle of civilisation is concerned. Shall we ever find a substitute—a practicable social order which may at once solve the economic & political problems of the present, & preserve (as the soviet system fails to do) what is still sound & infinite[ly] valuable in the cultural heritage of the past? I don't know—but if we do, we shall have something around which our children can rally as our fathers rallied around the ideals of the past. The chances are about even whether such a thing can come to pass, or whether there will be a long period of decay under some ruthless fascist system . . . or a plunge into a bolshevism for which the western world is certainly not fitted.

But pardon the digression. Regarding M. R. James—his style fits him, although it is only a matter of chance how well that style would fit another. It is never well to copy anybody else, except in the early stages of practice work when one is still uncertain about the best [sort] of style to adopt. At first, one must experiment co[nstantly]—but later on one's own personality will assimilate all the various models studied, & dictate a wholly individual & spontaneous manner embodying what is useful in the styles of others but moulding & proportioning everything according to its individual nature & needs. As a rule, I don't think that a comic or flippant style—or one with much satire—mixes well with the *weird*. Dunsany has lost power through giving over too extensively to humour, & Cabell's weird touches are pallid for the same reason. Among our crowd, Long is much the loser through his addiction to "sophistication". M. R. James joins the brisk, the light, & the commonplace to the weird about as well as anyone could do it—but if another tried the same method, the chances would be 10 to 1 against him. The most valuable element in him—as a model—is his way of weaving a horror into the every-day fabric of life & history—having it grow naturally out of the myriad conditions of an ordinary environment. Certainly, he is the best possible master to study if one wishes to mix the casual with the spectral or the macabre. About the hellish volume—"The King in Yellow"—supposed to lurk behind those early tales of Chambers—it is indeed a virtual equivalent of the imaginary "Necronomicon", except that it is supposed to be *modern* instead of mediaeval. It is represented as a *play*—presumably in the decadent manner of the 1890's . . . . Beardsley, Huysmans, Wilde, &c. . . . . but embodying certain scraps of a hideous secret lore trickling down from the past. In the 1890's the fashionable decadents liked to pretend that they belonged to all sorts of diabolic Black Mass cults, & possessed all sorts of frightful occult information. The only specimen of this group still active is the rather over-advertised Aleister Crowley[1] .... who, by the way, is undoubtedly the original of the villainous character to H. R. Wakefield's "He Cometh & He Passeth By". The monstrous elder world—atavistic glimpses of which sometimes flash into the memories of modern persons—conjured up by Chambers is founded on one or two chance allusions in the stories of Ambrose Bierce . . . "Hastur", "Lake of Hali", &c. Chambers borrowed Bierce's artificial mythology just as Clark Ashton Smith & I allude to each other's artificial mythologies in our respective tales.

About Wright and his reprinting—he's doing no more than any editor would . . . . indeed, he is *more* generous than most, since he has never attempted to annex the small sums brought in from the anthological re-sale of stories to which (through my inadvertence) he has the technical rights. The only time he ever shewed any commercial smallness was when I planned to let a magazine of reprints (planned by Swanson of N.D., but never published) use some of the tales to which I *do* retain the rights. He then asked me, as a favour, not to do so—in reply to which I directed him to a warmer and more sulphureous clime in about the frankest letter ever despatched toward N. Michigan Ave.! No—I've collected on all the "Erich Zann" reprints except the one in *Weird Tales*. About "The Mountains of Madness"—it is *not* a new story, but was written—& rejected by Wright—in 1931. I forgot that I hadn't sent it to you, but have now found the list I made of things sent & not sent. Before long, I'll try to dig it up & shoot it along. It is the longest thing of mine which I have not repudiated . . . coming to 115 typed pages. My new story—finished Feby. 24—is called "The Shadow out of Time", but I am so uncertain about its merit that I may destroy it. My work dissatisfies me extremely, & of late I have destroyed much more than I have saved.

Regarding the Dilbeck efforts in the F F—I must say that it looks to me pretty immature. In the first place it hasn't any metre, & in the second place it is full of mis-spellings like "bourne" for *borne,* & "gristly" for gri.ily.[2] Thirdly, it misuses the word *ghoul* (which means a special being that lives on corpses, but is not a corpse itself), & perilously strains the word *parade* (who ever heard of a *parade* of one?). Fourthly, it is full of weak, flat, expressions & stock phrases. Fifthly, it has a false rhyme . . . two, in fact . . . *roam–moan* & *qui´-et–fright.* Sixthly, all the images are trite & hackneyed & unoriginal. Outside of these points it may be all right—but I'd scarcely call Master Dilbeck a critic competent to wield lofty judgments concerning the work & weaknesses of others! You can certainly afford to laugh away faultfindings of his concerning your work.

About "Dracula"—while I doubt the value of Dilbeck's comments, I must say that I really think the novel is considerably overrated. It has some magnificent high spots—the castle scenes, & the coming of Dracula to Whitby—but as a whole it drags woefully toward the end, & is here & there pervaded by a certain mawkishness. Stoker was a queer bird—absolutely devoid of literary ability yet full of splendid ideas & images. _____ his work _____ the pitifully ludicrous "Lair of the White Worm" was revised by others. As co-incidence would have it, I knew an old lady (Mrs. Miniter of Wilbraham, Mass. [the original of "Dunwich"], who died a year ago) who saw the the *original* [MS]. version of "Dracula" in 1893, when a newspaper woman in Boston. Stoker was then in the U.S. as a manager of Sir Henry Irving's company, & was submitting his MS. to various revisers. He offered the job to Mrs. Miniter, but she found it too difficult work to accept at the offered price. She read the MS., & always said it was one of the poorest & most rambling pieces of writing she ever saw. Whatever merits of form the published book may have are due not to Stoker but to whatever unknown person did the revision. The same, of course, is true of his other better products—"The Jewel of Seven Stars", &c.

By the way—while on the subject of *Dracula* and *dracus*—I didn't mean to imply that *you* got the latter word from the novel, but merely that the *average reader* would think you did. Of course I know all about the *drac*- root, which in one form or other goes all the way back to the Sanscrit. (Eng. *dragon*, Lat. *draco*, Gr. δράκων, &c.) I think the source of the word in the Carpathians must be Slavonic, Greek or (through Romanism) Latin, since it is obviously Aryan whereas Hungarian is a Turanian language. The word in its varying meanings as *serpent*, *dragon*, & *devil* probably came from some verb like the Greek δέρκομαι (of which one form is δρακεῖν) meaning *to look sharply* or *to flash fire from the eyes*. The Sanscrit root is *dric*.

Regarding Howard Wandrei—his best stories are good but not nearly as good as his *drawings*. As a writer he is simply *among* the better grade fantaisistes, but as a pen & ink artist he is really important & distinguished. I think his drawings represent a higher level of effect than the work of any of the rest of our crowd. As for the second Brundage steal from Utpatel—it was an end-piece representing a woman clasping a skull . . . which Mrs. B. adopted as a cover design in Nov. '33. Derleth & I don't recall ever seeing the original end-piece, but Donald Wandrei thinks it was published some time in '32. Yes, Barlow is still in Washington, & will probably remain there till June. As for his deficiencies as a correspondent—I'll let him tell his own story by quoting from his latest letter:

> "It grows, for unknown reason, increasingly difficult for me to write letters. I shirk; I evade; in a word, I loathe the process. What shall do, when I like so much to receive them? I seem to have practically everybody angry at me, so I'm not getting any, anyway, at present."

I can't understand that curious inhibition against letter-writing which he & Long & Loveman & others see[m to] possess. These chaps are fluent enough in oral conversation—so why does a pen & paper dry up the founts of their discourse? I'm telling Barlow to cease regarding correspondence as a formal process—to imagine that he's sitting just across the table from the other fellow, & set down words just as he would *speak* them! His eyes are distinctly better, but his general health is poor. His acutely nervous condition saps his strength & acts badly on his digestive system. As for Munn—he is a major enigma to us all. Cook & I try to devise all sorts of explanations for his persistent & deliberately stubborn silence in the face of repeated enquiries & (in Cook's case) actual property obligations, but speculation gets us nowhere. At first we fancied we two might have personally offended him—for both had to refuse his invitation to Athol for Christmas '32. That was the last either of us heard, except when he sent the cutting about his father's death last summer. But now that we have found he ignores *others* as completely as he ignores us, we are obliged to look for a wider explanation. Some condition of complete nervous exhaustion may account for the silence. He is highly neurotic (although [yo]u'd never guess it to look at him—he's a great, husky [sec]ond Hercules who can lift prodigious weights & who [dr]ives a car like a speed-demon) & may have formed [some] freakish desire to shut off the outside world [alto]gether. His nervousness caused him to react [again]st the darker types of weird literature some [time] ago—so that his own work (in grotesque [contra]st to his early products) became either namby-[pamby] sentimentality or straight adventure stuff. [Cook?] has a notion that he may wish to avoid contact [with] anything *weird* these days—either stories or [peop]le who write them. Which, if true, (& I must [say I] rather doubt it) would be grimly ironic enough, [sin]ce he has what is without doubt the best weird [lib]rary—not excepting Koenig's—of any member of [the] group . . . . a collection partly of his own gathering, & partly given him by Cook when the latter broke up his residence & disposed of all his effects in 1930. The whole thing certainly is a mystery!

Don't hurry with your novel. As I say to everyone, *forced* writing is never advisable. Short pieces are really best for experimental work; since they allow one to try all sorts of different styles, whereas in a novel one has to keep on with the same style until the end. I'll be glad to see the specimen chapters—as well as the new shorts you mention. Regarding the changed title of your recent excellent tale—on the whole, I think the new one *is* the better; since after all, it is the pipers who form the unique central feature. "The Pipers of Kallinen" sounds very alluring—& I surely hope the public may have a chance to see the name on a printed table of contents! It is really a fine story, & ought to be generally appreciated.

Yes—you ought to get hold of a copy of Railo's "Haunted Castle". This somewhat unusual title was chosen because most of the old gothic tales had just such an edifice for their principal setting. It is really curious how—even to this day—weird tales tend to cling around vast & ancient buildings. I myself can scarcely keep from putting *great stone ruins* into all my stories . . . . I've done it in the new effort. Yes—I thought *Eino & Aino* must be really the same. It is certainly tragic that your brother should have met with a fatal accident—& ironic that such should follow a successfully weathered period of military service. As for the Petaja vs. Pine question—there is certainly no need of resorting to any change, since the original form is extremely harmonious. Opinions on such matters differ curiously. Only the other day I was reading that the French government is considering a measure to compel all candidates for naturalization to give their names a Gallic form—but to me this seems wholly needless & often absurd. It might be easy enough for a Smith (who would become M. Forgeron or M. Fabricateur), a Jones (M. de Jean), or a Brown (M. Labrun)—but what kind of a deal would I get? The *Love-* half of my name would probably become some form of *aimer* or *cherir*—but the rest would depend on how one interpreted the *-craft*. As a matter of fact, the original pre-Elizabethan form of the name is *Lovecroft*—implying a lover of his *croft* or allotted field. This would give some form like *Cherchamp* or *Champamant*. But if the authorities insisted on a literal translation of the modern form borne for the last 400 years, they will have to decide among themselves just what the *-craft* meant . . . whether the *quality of craftiness* (*artifice*) or a profession (*metier*). Amusingly, my branch in the 16th century chose the former interpretation, & assumed a coat-of-arms representing 3 foxes' heads on a green field. Possible _____ _____ *Aimmetier* or *Cherartifice* or something like that. On the whole, if I lived in France I guess I'd [stick with my] old handle & refrain (assuming a proposed law passes) from getting naturalised!

Yes—Rimel said his cut for your "Ebon Isles" was based on your own drawing. He is tremendously clever at that kind of thing. I hope you & he & Baldwin can all [get] together some time when travelling conditions are fa[vourable], since you're really only about as far from Asotin as I [am] from New York. It surely will be a festive event when you are all rounded up. The other day the boys sent me a fine copy of Merritt's "Creep, Shadow"—the original *Argosy* instalments bound & decorated by themselves.

I hope you can see New England some time. Despite the decay & mechanisation of some parts of it, it is still as beautiful as ever in the remoter sections. Of all parts of America, it most resembles the Old World—with ancient dwellings that perfectly fit the landscape. I love Hawthorne's "Seven Gables" & Whittier's "Snow Bound"—& have seen most of the houses associated with both authors. I'm not so great an Alcott fan, but have seen the Alcott home (now a museum) in Concord. Concord is very little changed since the days of Emerson, Hawthorne, Thoreau, & the Alcotts—or since colonial times, for that matter.

Thanks enormously for the illuminated version of "Partings"—a splendid piece of work, & one which excites my envy. Hades, how I wish I could draw! The poem is surely graceful enough in its new form—& I'm highly grateful for the text, since there's no telling what Brother Ruppert[3] will do to it in the free-&-easy press room of the F F!

The other day I had a letter from Loring & Mussey of N.Y.—young Derleth's publishers—asking to see some of my MSS. with a view to collected book publication. Since this is the 5*th* time (WT 1926, Putnam 1931, Vanguard 1932, Knopf 1933) I have been so approached, with no tangible results thus far, I am not as naively excited about the matter as I might otherwise be. However, I sent along some junk . . . which will undoubtedly come back sooner or later. It never does to leave any stone unturned. I haven't sent anything to magazines of late, so that nothing of mine is scheduled to appe[ar] anywhere save in the semi-amateur sheets. W[hen I] get some more things written—as I hope to do d[uring] the spring—I'll possibly begin submitting again, although editors seem very hostile toward the type of work I've recently been doing.

Well—the books safely arrived—& don't fail to let me know when you're ready for some more. Weather has been milder lately—spring can't come any too quickly for me! Best wishes—Yrs most cordially—H P L

Notes

1. Aleister Crowley (1875–1947), English occultist, ceremonial magician, poet, and mountaineer, known in the press as "the wickedest man in the world."
2. Lionel E[dgar] Dilbeck (1917–1977), a member of the Wichita Science Fiction League whose poetry appeared in *FF* and *Supramundane Stories.* HPL refers to his poem "The Ghoul's Parade" in the January 1935 issue of *FF.*
3. Conrad Ruppert (1912–1997), printer of the *FF* (1933–35).

[10] [ALS, water damaged]

66 College St.,
Providence, R.I.,
April 5, 1935.

My dear Petaja:—

Glad to hear the news! I sent a copy of "At the Mountains of Madness" immediately upon receipt of your letter, & hope it will not prove a disappointment. The *antarctic* has fascinated me ever since I was ten years old. Fancy a *whole continent* upon which *no human being ever set foot until the year 1895,* & which today is no better known than America in the time of Columbus! This story represents my reaction to the whole subject—but readers don't seem to like it. Wright ruthlessly turned it down. It is barely possible that Crawford of *Marvel Tales* may some day print it as a booklet—but I'm not counting on that. No hurry about returning the MS.—but don't lose it, since no other perfect copy exists. Good luck, by the way, with your own story— the non-weird adventure juvenile.

As for the subject of the supernatural—I had the usual Sunday-School experience, but such precepts simply didn't "take". The teachers couldn't or wouldn't answer any questions pertaining to fundamentals, nor could they give any reason why the especial religion which they expected me to believe was any truer than the other religions which are taught with equal zeal elsewhere. Merely *emotional* appeals get nowhere with me. I think on a pure *is-or-isn't* basis, & consider nothing but genuine facts. My family had the usual stereotyped beliefs—in fact, my aunt still attends the old First Baptist Church—although they weren't excessively & ostentatiously pious. But what other people thought didn't affect what I thought. I knew there were plenty of people—including the greatest creative minds of the age—Huxley, Haeckel, Spencer, &c.—who *didn't* believe in the supernatural, & I rather fa[ncied] they were right. Then when I came to survey the vario[us] sciences for myself, I felt pretty darned sure they were right.

I can't see the point of finding it difficult to reconcile the highest levels of beauty & art with a "mere animal origin". The fact is, the tendency to despise & belittle a natural organic source is a purely fallacious convention based on blind tradition & primitive [de]lusion. *Why shouldn't* the process of biology be the means of building up the most complex & delicate perceptions & creations of harmony & rhythm? Analyse the situation & you will see that the prejudice against the relationship between simple & highly evolved manifestations is completely groundless. An infinitely delicate watch & a common crowbar are both made of iron—but do we have to doubt that the watch *is* made of iron merely because it is vastly finer than a simple crowbar? That kind of doubting is supremely illogical, since it ignores the stupendous differences inherent in *degree* irrespective of *kind*. The idea that one must presuppose some fantastic "spiritual" world to account for everything that seems at all removed from obvious simplicity is an essentially childish one—natural enough when the race was young, but more & more obsolete today. Incidentally—it is not strictly correct to regard the higher phenomena of biological action as just "happening". The natural process of atomic & molecular building-up which we call *life* is obviously a basic & well-defined property of matter under certain conditions—of which the life-forms on this insignificant planet are only one negligible example. The tendency to develop these complex forms is clearly inherent in the cosmos (vegetation on Mars is virtually proved), so that the idea of *accident* is scarcely correct. Of course, it is only a matter of chance whether or not a given line of biological evolution will ever have opportunities to reach a high stage—but that is another matter. That does not mean that high organisms are the result of fortuitously thrown-together molecules. In the endless cycles of the cosmos, highly-evolved life must have occurred again & again—in many cases leaving even the highest life-forms of our terrestrial dust-grain far behind. On the other hand, highly evolved life is probably not a very common phenomenon, since it demands (or at present appears to demand) certain celestial conditions (planets with cooling crust) which are not often produced. At a guess, one might say that at any given moment the universe may possess about half a dozen habitable solar systems. Whenever the crust of a planet with carbon, hydrogen, & nitrogen cools in a certain way, life is almost undoubtedly produced. In that life are all the *potentialities* of complex evolution . . . . Sometimes they get a chance to work extensively, & sometimes they don't. On this especial sand-particle called "the earth" they got (so far as we have any standard of judgment) a fairly good break from nature. I'm sorry that any of the arguments in my former letter seemed obscure—if you'll let me know what fails to be clear, I'll try to elucidate. Read Ernst Haeckel's "Riddle of the Universe" as a general elementary introduction to what I'm talking about. Though written in 1902 or so, the main parts are still valid.

As for crude & visible "supernatural" manifestations—no, I've never had any experience even remotely suggesting a "spiritual world", or ever heard of one which did not, on analysis, resolve itself into natural factors or sheer intentional deception. Most reports come from egocentric neurotics whose evidence is [no]t to be trusted. Man's capacity for self-delusion is infinite, & anthropologists understand how typical supernatural legends are built up. When a person believes in the possibility of certain kinds of impossible phenomena, he often imagines he has witnessed actual manifestations—& will go to any length to convince others. Some of the stuff in Flammarion & Chevreuil is pathetic![1] As for the actual beliefs of celebrated weird writers—I fancy they are divided. Blackwood & Machen seem to have lingering supernatural ideas, but Dunsany, Poe, Bierce, James, Shiel, & Ewers do not. Of the cheap magazine weirdists, the only orthodox religionist I know of is the peculiar H. Warner Munn. Derleth believes in natural telepathy but not in the supernatural. Donald Wandrei believes in undiscovered natural laws, but not in immortality, deity, or anything religious. Clark Ashton Smith, Barlow, Cook, Long, Koenig, Francis Flagg, Howard Wandrei, & I have no beliefs outside recognised natural science. R. E. Howard & some others are undecided agnostics—suspending all belief till further proof is available. Most of the science-fiction writers—Hamilton, Williamson, Keller, &c.—believe as little as I do.

Regarding the Black Mass & its devotees—it is really even more repulsive than fascinating. The whole thing is described minutely in Joris-Karl Huysmans' "La Bas"—which was posthumously translated into English in 1923 & promptly suppressed. The Black Mass consisted in general of a malevolent & incredibly obscene parody on the Catholic Mass—involving public actions & natural substances almost impossible to describe in print. It originated in the Middle Ages, & has [ev]er since been secretly celebrated by groups of half-crazed, psychologically degenerate sensation-seekers—largely in the great metropolitan centres. Paris, Berlin, London, & New York are probably its greatest centres today. It seems to draw its devotees almost equally from the decadent artist class & from the general run of over-sophisticated psychopathic personalities. Aleister Crowley is a now-elderly Englishman who has dabbled in this sort of thing since his Oxford days. He is really, of course, a sort of maniac or degenerate despite his tremendous mystical scholarship. He has organised secret groups of repulsive Satanic & phallic worship in many places in Europe & Asia, & has been quietly kicked out of a dozen countries. Sooner or later the U.S. (he is now [in] N.Y.) will probably deport him—which will be bad luck for him, since England will probably put him in jail when he is sent home. T. Everett Harré—whom I have met & whom Long knows well—has seen quite a bit of Crowley, & thinks he is about the most loathsome & sinister skunk at large. And when a Rabelaisian soul like Harré (who is never sober!) thinks that of anybody, the person must be a pretty bad egg indeed! Crowley is the compiler of the fairly well-known "Oxford Book of Mystical Verse",[2] & a standard writer on occult subjects. The story of Wakefield's which brings him in (under another name, of course) is in the collection "They Return at Evening",[3] which I'll lend you if you like. You've probably seen some of the tales in anthologies.

As for Munn & his silences—I give it up! I've no explanation! No—Athol doesn't lie on any of the routes ordinarily traversed by our group, though it's only 60 miles from here. Cook intends to go back there some time & see just what the matter is, but he has been busy & far from well recently, so that the raid would form rather a tax on his nervous strength.

Good luck with "The Pipers of Kallinen"—& I'll be glad to see some of your more recent products in course of time. As to forced writing—it depends a good deal on the *kind* of writing involved, & on the individual concerned. Curwood[4] was more or less of an objective, mechanical writer, & I can well imag[ine] that he would be one to succeed with a daily st[ory.] But what worked with him wouldn't work with others—especially in cases where genuinely artistic self-expression is involved. Most writers can sit & write a whole day without producing anything but the most lifeless & wooden material conceivable—material which they ultimately find too poor to use at all. Then at other times they can reel off in a propitious hour more & better stuff than they could ordinarily produce in a week. It would clearly be foolish for them to adopt a Curwood-like programme of factory-like production. There is enough *else* to do on the "off" days—polishing, revision, typing, &c.—so that the effective days can be devoted to creative writing. Of course—the pulp [ha]cks who grind out cheap commercial junk work on a strict quantity basis—so many words per day or week. That is what Price is now getting to do.

Too bad no neighbouring library contains Railo's "Haunted Castle". If I ever succeed in acquiring it, you shall certainly be first on the waiting-list.

Yes—that proposed official name-changing in France is certainly a cumbrous & confusing process—but is part of the wave of fanatical hyper-nationalism engulfing the western world today. Countries everywhere are changing place-names, expelling allegedly foreign words from their languages (as in Turkey Mustapha Kumal is trying to eliminate the Arabic vocabulary), & so on. The latest instance comes from Italy—where there is a movement to make the Austrians of the Italian Tyrol (ceded to Italy at Versailles) adopt the Italian equivalents (when such can be found) of their German names.

I surely hope that you, Baldwin, & Rimel can arrange that triangular meeting. Baldwin has just informed me that he is moving to Lewiston, Idaho—his mother having decided to go south. If Rimel & yourself both attend Montana U., [times?] will surely be delightful all around! He spoke of collaborating with you, though he did not mention the name of the story. As you describe it, it sounds interesting—& I trust its professional reception may be favourable. Hope the longer tale will pan out well.

About "Partings"—I think I'd try it on Crawford's *Marvel Tales,* of which the March–April issue came some time ago. This current number has two pieces of verse,[5] & its general appearance is gratifyingly improved. Have you seen it? In contents it is mediocre—nothing very good, nothing very bad. The best item, I think, is John Beynon Harris's "The Cathedral Crypt." Hope Crawford will put all his energies into M T & not scatter them through trying to float another magazine, as he may do.

No [word?] from Loring & Mussey—& I greatly doubt whether any book of my stuff will ever appear. I'll surely let you know whenever a new thing of mine comes out (the old "Sarnath" yarn is in M T). "The Shadow out of Time" is finished, but I'm so uncertain of its value that I may destroy it & begin all over. I certainly mourn the passing of the F F—& hope that all of Rimel's linoleum block cuts can be used eventually in F M [or] M T. F M will take over many F F features (not, [I] think, my serial article), though it will doubtless continue to subordinate weird to science fiction.

About the snapshots taken by Talman at that N.Y. meeting—that of me was so poor that I tore it up.[6] Two others (of Wandrei & Loveman) are lent to Baldwin, & you're welcome to see them after he's through with them. Regarding Howard Wandrei—he is a slim, 6-foot young man 25 years of age, with light complexion, light brown hair, & a faint light-brown moustache. Wears rimless glasses & is very fastidious in dress. Graduate of U. of Minn. 2 years younger & 2 inches shorter than his brother Donald. Had very little formal instruction in art—first drew merely to illustrate Donald's weird conceptions. Style resembles Sime & Harry Clark [*sic*], but recognises no model save for John Austen.[7] Wrote brief prose sketches while in college, & is doing more & more writing—largely of a cheap hack nature at present. Has had his pictures exhibited, but they do not sell well. Born & reared in St. Paul, Minn. Now shares an apartment with his brother at 155 W. 10th St., N.Y. City—in the Greenwich Village section. Is very quiet, modest, & unassertive. What he needs, in order to be recognised, is a commission to illustrate some important fantastic book. One such, & I prophesy he'll be "made". I think he is farther ahead in his art, than any of the rest of us are in our writing.

Spring has tended to be decently early here[abouts.] There have been days up to 65°, 71°, &c.—& I [have] taken several walks of considerable length—up to 12 miles. Yet much cool weather lies ahead, & I wish I could get down to Charleston!

With all good wishes—

Yrs most cordially & sincerely

H P L

Notes

1. Camille Flammarion (1842–1925) and Léon Chevreuil (1852–1939) were proponents of spiritualism and other pseudo-science.
2. HPL refers to *The Oxford Book of English Mystical Verse,* compiled by D. H. S. Nicholson and A. H. E. Lee (Oxford: Clarendon Press, 1917). The book contains three poems by Crowley.
3. The character Apuleius Charlton in "'He Cometh & He Passeth By'" is based on Crowley.
4. James Oliver Curwood (1878–1927), American action-adventure writer and conservationist. *Publishers' Weekly* ranked his books among top-ten best sellers in the U.S. in the early 1920s. At the time of his death, he was the highest paid (per word) author in the world.
5. "Sanctuary" by Natalie H. Wooley and "Haunted House" by Lovell Hart. EP's "Witch's Berceuse" appeared in the following issue.
6. Of the photograph, HPL wrote [15 January 1935], "The young rascal caught me as I was looking upward & saying something which put my mouth in an utterly comic position . . . as if I were going to whistle or expectorate!" (*OFF* 202).
7. John Archibald Austen (1886–1948), English book illustrator whose early works were Beardsleyesque in style, but after 1925 influenced by the Art Deco movement.

[11] [ALS]

66 College St.,

Providence, R.I.,

April 24, 1935.

Dear Petaja:—

As to the expression in my earlier letter—"glad to hear the news"—I fancy I meant merely 'the news' in general . . . . all the news of recent events in your part of the globe—rather than any specific piece of news. No—you had not mentioned the placing of "Antiqua" & "Witch's Berceuse"—& I am now pleased to learn that they are on their way to print. Hope I may in time hear a similar report regarding the "Pipers". Also—I shall be glad to see the fragment from ["D]r. Crowe's Assistant"—concerning the title of which I can speak more intelligently [af]ter reading it. By the way—I'm tremendously sorry to hear that [yo]u've been ill, & hope you're fully recovered by now.

Meanwhile I am indeed glad to learn that you liked "At the Mountains of Madness"—which, as I have said, is one of my favourites among my own products. Whether it will ever see print, I'm sure I don't know. I certainly hope so, for this copy won't survive an indefinite number of mailings. Hope Searight will like it—he tends to share my interest in the antarctic, & read W. Clarke Russell's "Frozen Pirate" with great zest when a boy. No—school curricula don't have much to say regarding the antarctic—or at least they didn't when I was young. In these days—with great expeditions active & knowledge rapidly increasing—it seems as if the subject ought to receive some kind of mention. When I was eleven I fixed up a series of little books on the antarctic—typing them & binding them quite elaborately. One was about Ross's explorations (1839–43), another dealt with the U.S. Naval Expedition under Wilkes (1847), while a third was an atlas covering the parts of the antarctic then known.[1] I still have these booklets—quaint samples of juvenile composition & workmanship.

Concerning the supernatural—the only thing to do is to observe the actual phenomena around us, disregard legends & attitudes blindly inherited from the primitive past, & examine scientifically the various psychological concepts & impulses commonly held in this field. That such a sensible procedure makes it impossible to accept the naive myths of the popular religions is well shewn by Prof. James F. Leuba's survey of the present beliefs of representative American men of science. He found that 95% of all eminent thinkers in the sciences most concerned with the question are disbelievers in the myths of a conscious deity & immortality. An interesting article of his occurs in *Harpers* for August, 1934.[2] As to the quotation you give: "I have never been able to see how such common, base animal processes as birth & death can be links with eternity. At the same time I have always been inclined to the belief that time is not a sequence as it appears, that it is a complete, static whole . . . ."—All this is, of course, simply obvious sentimentality. The words "base", "common", & "animal" applied to birth & death are a dead give-away. *By what standard* does the speaker or writer call any natural cosmic process "base" or "common", or attach overtones of derogation to the concept "animal"? Palpably, this is merely a [ca]se of primitive mythological comparison & loose thinking. The idea of trying [to] separate cosmic processes into "base" & "non-base" ones is simply silly. [Cl]early, some process are infinitely more *complex* than others. The movement of a watch is more complex than a simple lever, & the evolution, birth, & death of a man involve more adjustments than the evolution, birth, & death of a jellyfish or the precipitation of a salt crystal. But anyone with even half a brain ought to be able to see that *the difference in degree of complexity* is in itself such a *tremendous, overwhelmingly vast form of differentiation,* that *no other form of differentiation is needed* to explain the difference between such dissimilar phenomena as the life-cycle of Sir Isaac Newton & the life-cycle of a marine crinoid. The idea that some other sort of differentiation is required is a plainly primitive & childish concept. That is, it is childish **today,** when we know that the only differences between *any* phenomena—or even between force & matter themselves—are such as arise from the different arrangements & motions of electrical energy-units. The whole mental process of inventing an hypothetical secondary world of phenomena (i.e.—a "spiritual" world) apart from the actual world & its phenomena is a needless & primitive device without a shred of justification. There is no reason whatever for such an assumption—although there once was, in the ages of early ignorance when man could discover no rational clues to the causes of surrounding events. But I think you can easily see what a limited outlook, & poverty of comprehensive imagination, are implied in the popular unwillingness to recognise that differences in nature & *complexity of organisation* can easily account for all the observed differences between such phenomena as human life & lower-animal life, or life as a whole to the processes roughly grouped as inorganic. Behind this unwillingness there lies simply a mass of irrational sentiment fostered by the false basic concepts of things which have grown out of blindly-transmitted primitive mythology. As for the matter of *time* as a static whole rather than as a sequence—that is simply a question of *mathematical interpretation*, & really irrelevant to the point at issue. Whatever time *is*, the relation of a single organic life to it is the same. If time is a *stream*, then each separate animal or vegetable lifetime is a dot in the course of that stream. If, on the other hand, time is a fixed dimension, then each separate animal or vegetable lifetime is a dot on the static expanse of that dimension. The two hypothetical conditions mean exactly the same thing. Whatever "time" [only a *name* for a non-understood relationship, after all] may be, we know that no individual animal or vegetable life is coextensive with it. I think you'll enjoy "The Riddle of the Universe". The more recent books of Bertrand Russell are also extremely informative in cognate fields.

Now as to the distribution of organic life in the cosmos—there are many factors to be considered. First—what is it? Is it an unique principle transmitted through space in the form of spores, as Arrhenius believed, or is it a form of electrical energy separately produced whenever a plastic mass containing carbon, hydrogen, & nitrogen cools into solidity? Can it exist under conditions widely different from those of the earth? What seem to be its requirements? Well—the dominant belief is that life is separately produced when a plastic mass cools on a large scale under certain conditions of mechanical equilibrium. Probably it could not exist except on a cool solid body, & under certain specific conditions like the presence of oxygen & water. Primitive organic energy, as first generated from inorganic matter & energy, must necessarily operate in unicellular matter-units. One of the basic properties of these units is to build up into more & more complex forms when stimulated by changes in their environment—but what especial forms will be produced, depends wholly on what these changes may happen to be. Relatively slight environmental changes are found to give rise to tremendous differentiations of organic form even on *this* planet—hence it is inconceivable that any of the higher organic species we know can be duplicated or even closely resembled on any *other* planet. The chances of the existence of some other planet *just* like the earth, revolving under *just* the same conditions around some sun *just* like ours, are so slight as to be virtually negligible. It is not, then, to be expected that anything even remotely resembling *human* life or *human* thoughts & feelings can exist anywhere in the cosmos save on the earth. It is the constant mistake of cheap science-fiction writers to depict the denizens of other worlds (whatever their *physical* shape) as having mental & emotional processes (modes of reasoning & communicating; values, desires, motivations, objectives) either like ours or at least comprehensible to us. The absurdity of this is self-evident—since of *all* human attributes, the *psychological* ones are the *most* unstable, local, & accidental. Even within the human species the accidents of differing environment give rise to wholly alien modes of thought & feeling & valuation. What, then, can be expected of the organic life of differing worlds? Of the *degree* of complexity of evolution on different worlds we can set no arbitrary limits. Many planets have doubtless failed to produce life-forms as complex as the earth's highest products (= Caucasian-Mongolian man), while many others have doubtless surpassed these forms to a substantial degree. The extent of possible development would seem to be determined both by chance & by the life-span of the given planet. No planet lasts for ever. Its sun expires sooner or later, & eventually the very material substance of its system—& galaxy—& universe—disintegrates into its constituent electrons & leaves only an "empty" field of force [out of which another universe is later born]. We have no means of predicting what the future of organic life on the earth will be— whether the human race can find a way to resume the evolution which slowed up about 100,000 years ago, whether it will remain dominant at its present level, or whether it will be superseded in its dominance by another form of life—probably of the insect order, which shews signs of [be]ing better adapted than the mammalia to the varying conditions of this [pl]anet.

Now as to the distribution of life in the cosmos—it is plain that just one thing determines how widely living protoplasm can occur: i.e., the number of *cool, solid planets* throughout space. We can no longer dispute the independent existence of protoplasm on different worlds, since *vegetation* on Mars has been well authenticated by direct visual & photographic evidence. The question then boils down to this: how many cool, solid worlds are likely to exist at any one time in the cosmos? Up to a decade or a decade & a half ago it was commonly thought that such worlds are virtually unlimited—i.e., that a large number of stars possess planetary systems like the sun's. Recently, however, the mathematical calculations of Jeans & Eddington have very gravely challenged that concept, & have tended to indicate that a planet-system represents a kind of celestial accident of relatively rare occurrence. The number of planets existing at any one time, then, is perhaps very limited. Furthermore— of these planets, only a few are likely to possess the special conditions needed to sustain life & raise it to any substantial degree of evolution. There must be heat—a temperature between certain maxima & minima; there must be oxygen in certain proportions; there must be carbon in assimilable forms; there must be water or water-vapour; there must be an atmosphere of adequate density & without gases antagonistic to life; & so on. This brings down still further the possible number of life-bearing planets at any one time. I think Eddington has ventured the guess that (granting the finite Einsteinian space-time continuum) the cosmos may possess about *six* worlds with highly-developed life at any one time. In our solar system, no planet but the earth is likely to possess complexly-evolved organisms at the present moment. But of course, counting the "dimension" of *time*, the number of inhabited worlds in the cosmos becomes infinite. It may be added that the Jeans–Eddington doctrine of the scarcity of planetary systems is not *universally* accepted—[th]ough it is certainly the *prevailing* present belief. One of its chief [op]ponents is Prof. Dinsmore Alter[3] of the U. of Kansas, who has a very ingenious [al]ternative theory of planetary formation. In any case we may hold it extremely unlikely that highly-developed life is anything peculiar to the earth.

About your idea of interpenetrating dimensions or regions of existence whose constituent units may have internal motions (= vibrations) of a frequency different from that of material electrons, & of the possibility of catching glimpses of such dimensions or regions through the abnormal stimulation of the human brain or senses to the alien "vibration-frequency"; I would say that it forms a splendid basis for a science-fiction story, but that it is, so far as actuality is concerned, at a great extreme of improbability. The existence of other levels of entity coincident with ours is *theoretically possible*, but tremendously improbable. Certain interference-phenomena connected with atomic physics would probably lie within the range of detection if such levels were truly present. Nor is there any presumable reason why, according to what we know of cosmic architecture, they should be present. Furthermore—the glimpsing of such levels by the human senses, if they existed, would be inconceivable. The vibration-frequency of atoms & electrons, whereby their position in the scale of matter is determined, has nothing further to do with the properties of any of the more complex forms of matter built up through combinations of those atoms & electrons, save in the case of radio-active substances. It is a totally false thing to associate these intra-atomic motions or pulsations (indeed, they probably aren't *vibrations* at all in any strict sense) with the mechanical vibrating properties of definite masses of matter—properties depending on size, weight in proportion to size, manner of suspension, degree of tension [cf. laws of pendulum, strings, &c. &c.], & similar conditions. As will be seen on close inspection, the so-called "vibration-rate" or "vibration-frequency" of an object does not imply that the object in question is *vibrating* collectively at all. It refers simply to the way it *will* vibrate *when* (& not unless) external force is applied. There is not a shred of connexion between—for example—the *vibration-rate* of a suspension bridge, & the pulsation-frequencies (different in each case) of the different elemental atoms involved in its chemical composition. Only in *radio-active* substances do we have any overt & tangible evidence of the intra-atomic pulsations of matter. Thus it is simply impossible to speak of the "vibration-rate" of a *person*. There is *no such thing* in the sense implied by pseudo-scientists. You realise, of course, that the pompously pseudo-scientific mystics who talk of "your vibrations" & "vibrations of good & evil" & all such crap are simply charlatans.

The explanation of apparently supernatural phenomena is very largely to be found in anthropology & psychology—whereby we see (a) how events which never occurred come to be reported as facts, (b) how the details & order of occurrence of events come to be unconsciously altered or transposed, (c) how artificial emotional backgrounds influence our perceptions & predispositions to belief, & (d) how large a part hallucination & uncertainty play in even the commonest of our unverified perceptions. No first-rate man of science believes in the commonly reported forms of supernaturalism. At the same time you are right in maintaining that *if* one believes in "immortality" or a conscious deity or deities, there is no logical reason in the world why he should not also accept the less official myths of popular folklore & believe in all the fanciful imaginings of mankind from ghosts to werewolves, "karma" to leprechauns, ghouls to jumbee, & reincarnation to the Pipers of Kallinen!

Regarding the loathsome cults now represented by Satanism & the Black Mass—it is not strictly fair to regard them, in essence, as mere *conscious* cloaks to cover degenerate practices . . . . even though they are undoubtedly just that to a large proportion of their own members. Their origin was without question as spontaneous & sincere as that of any mythus-cult from Judaism to Mormonism, Zoroastrianism to Christianity, Hindooism to Holy-Rollerism. The first people who adhered to them believed they were genuinely in touch with superphysical cosmic forces, & a good many of their present adherents no doubt believe the same. That systems scarcely less repulsive exist as official regions in many parts of the world—& are sincerely & honestly adhered to by millions—you are already aware through perusal of "The Last Home of Mystery"[4]—which I read some years ago.

Well—I trust you've duly received "They Return at Evening" & "John Silence" (the best Blackwood volume which I own). No hurry about either. You will have seen a good many of the Wakefield stories in various anthologies, but others will probably be new to you. Of the Blackwood episodes, the first & the last are least powerful as weird literature. I have a personal fondness, though, for the first—because of the delightful & sympathetic portrayal of a *cat* . . . of whose species I am intensely fond. Hope Dwyer & Derleth will start Koenig's loan-books on their way before long. Their delay is really inexcusable. As for "Jane Eyre"—did I mention *that* in my article on weird fiction? I don't see why, for it certainly fails to fall within the category. Are you sure you didn't get sidetracked by the name of Bron[të?] What I did allude to was "Wuthering Heights", by *Emily* Brontë—sis[ter] of Charlotte. But J. E. is a first-rate piece of literature, so that you needn't consider your time as lost. Hope you can land "The Haunted Castle."

I surely hope that Rimel can get to Missoula—though he says he fears it may not be financially possible. He seems very anxious to get there if he can. There seems little doubt but that you & he would prove highly congenial, & that you could discuss—& perhaps collaborate—to great advantage. Baldwin also seems to be extremely likeable.

In time Crawford may be able to settle down to one magazine & make something of it. It is too bad his literary taste is not a little more mature, for he certainly could choose MSS. for books a lot more wisely. By the way—did I mention that his ex-partner Lloyd A. Eshbach has founded a very artistic & high-grade little [m]agazine of general scope called *The Galleon?* It has just occurred to me that [s]ince weird subjects are not debarred—you might send "The Pipers" to Eshbach. [Tr]y it—the address is 1337 Good St., Reading Pa. He has just taken an old fantasy of mine, & two of the Fungi from Yuggoth.[5] As for *Fantasy*—I doubt gravely whether it will wish to continue my article. The April number is far from bad—but of course science-fiction will always remain the dominant policy. April W T rather mediocre—though Bernal's story (which embodies an idea I had meant to use!) is clever in a light way. H. Wandrei's "Hand of the O'Mecca" has genuine weird atmosphere, but "Shadows of Blood" is full of historical boners. The Romans never heard of the Huns till more than 300 years after Caligula's time. Klarkash-Ton's "Last Hieroglyph" is excellent. "Out of the Æons" is a piece of my own ghostwriting—the alleged author's share being only the vague idea of an ancient mummy discovered to have a living brain. "The Aztec Ring" & "The Man Who Could Not Go Home" are routine stuff. Best of everything in the issue is the reprinted "Canal"—one of the weirdest & most truly sinister things the magazine has ever printed.[6]

The apparent early spring in March proved a false alarm. A beastly cold spell followed—& there was a snow-flurry as late as April 17. But at least the buds & early flowers are out, so that my resumed hibernation is more or less over. I expect a guest with a car the coming week-end, & we may do some antiquarian exploring as far as old Newport. The week-end after that I shall probably visit a friend in the Boston zone, incidentally taking side-trips to such ancient places as Salem & Marblehead. Still later—in June, probably— W. Paul Cook & I may tour Vermont in his sister's car . . . but that remains to be seen. And in July, a Wisconsin friend may get east & have me shew him around this historic region. Not such a bad programme—but I wish just the same that I could get to Charleston.

Speaking of Charleston—& thence of New Orleans—I certainly *have* been to the latter place (that's where I first met E. Hoffmann Price in person

[in] 1932), & can heartily endorse your interest in it. A fascinating old [tow]n—& in some ways more thoroughly European than any other place I've [visi]ted—not excluding Quebec. Hope you enjoyed the pictorial matter & [ma]p which I chucked in with the books. I enclose another folder. If your interest is really profound—so that you'd like to refresh your memory continually anent the Crescent City—you can keep this material for your collection. I have one duplicate set. If, on the other hand, it seems slated for the waste-basket, you might eventually shoot it back for further loaning instead of consigning it to the indifferent depths of that yawning repository. New Orleans was founded in 1715 by the French, transferred to Spain in 1763 (though it never exchanged its French population for a Spanish one), & sold to the U.S. in 1803 after a momentary re-transfer to France. All this, of course, along with the whole vast territory of Louisiana—of which most of Montana (though *not* your especial western end of it) was once a part. The ancient section comprises a rectangle on the Mississippi River f[ront?], S.W. of which the enormous American metropolis has grown. The descendants of the French—now all English-speaking—have tended to spread north & east. The old quarter or *Vieux Carré* once sank to the state of a slum, but has been to some extent reclaimed. It is largely a section of antique shops & studios—on the Greenwich Village idea—though ordinary commerce has tended to penetrate it from the American side. A very broad thoroughfare—Canal St.—divides the American section & the Vieux Carré. The old quarter's houses are largely of the 1780 or 1790 period—earlier wooden structures having been swept away by fire. They tend to be of brick & stucco, with inner courtyard & delicate wrought-iron galleries. Since they were built during the period of Spanish rule, with the assistance of military engineers from Spain, their French architecture is peculiarly blended with unmistakably Hispanic lines. Thus the patio or courtyard—& the long arched passage from the street—are essentially Spanish. On the whole, these houses make one think more often of St. Augustine (Sp.) than of Quebec (Fr.). The Vieux Carré is now fully appreciated by the townsfolk, & every effort is made to preserve it in its pristine condition. Instead of ordinary electric light poles, the street lights are bulbs placed in small iron lamp-posts of antique design. New Orleans is so low-lying that levees are required to protect it from the river in front & Lake Pontchartrain (an inlet from the sea) in the rear. Cellars have to be pumped free of water, & the whole surface is drained by an elaborate canal system . . . once open in the Dutch or Venetian fashion, but now covered over & made into streets. The climate is excellent, though (to my mind) not as mild as that of Charleston . . . even though it is substantially farther south. Luxuriant live-oaks are found here & there, & great palms (all originally imported) flourish everywhere. The city has spread greatly, & now covers a vast area on both sides of the river. Nearby are many once-imposing but now declining sugar-plantations—with ancient houses both of the high-basemented French type of the 18th century, & of the classi-

cally pillared Greek type introduced by the Americans in the early 19th century. A great place—I'd like to get there again. Price lived in Royal St. in the Vieux Carré. The reason I prefer Charleston is that that ancient city is *all* a "vieux carré" .... there isn't any modern metropolis to hem it in, & much more of the continuous life & social fabric of the 18th century persist. Another town I'm tremendously fond of is ancient *Natchez*, on the Mississippi river-bluffs some 200 m. N. of New Orleans. I shall probably live in the south some day—I can't stand this accursed subarctic climate, much as I love the atmosphere & colour of old New England.

So you resemble Howard Wandrei as described? Let's see a snapshot of you some day. Which reminds me—since you'd probably be interested in knowing what some of "the gang" look like, I'm enclosing a set of snap[s] covering 14 of them. Please return these eventually, though there's no hurry about the matter. I wonder whether most of the subjects confirm or contradict your previous impressions? You may, of course, have seen some of these from other sources.

I've lately read Meyrink's "The Golem"—a magnificently subtle weird novel lent by Barlow, Merritt's "Creep Shadow" (rather pulpish), & Hugh Walpole's study in brooding sadism, "Portrait of a Man with Red Hair".

With every good wish, & trusting that the spring mildness will reach Milltown before long, I remain

Most cordially yrs

H P L

Notes

1. These items, no longer extant, were "Wilkes's Explorations" (1902), "Voyages of Capt. Ross, R.N." (1902), and "Antarctic Atlas" (1903).

2 James H. Leuba, "Religious Beliefs of American Scientists," *Harper's* 169, No. 3 (August 1934): 291–300.

3. Dinsmore Alter (1888–1968), American astronomer and meteorologist, and director of the Griffith Observatory in Los Angeles.

4. By E. Alexander Powell.

5. Eshbach published "The Quest of Iranon" and "Background," but his magazine folded before it could publish "Homecoming."

6. Arthur William Bernal, "The Man Who Was Two Men"; Howard Wandrei, "The Hand of the O'Mecca"; Eando Binder, "Shadows of Blood"; Clark Ashton Smith, "The Last Hieroglyph"; Hazel Heald (revised by HPL), "Out of the Aeons"; John Flanders, "The Aztec Ring"; L. E. Frailey, "The Man Who Could Not Go Home"; Everil Worrell, "The Canal" (December 1927).

[12]   [ALS, water damaged]

> 66 College St.,
> Providence, R.I.,
> May 31, 1935.

Dear Petaja:—

I fear I shan't be able to do justice to yours of May 6, since I am in rather a rush—getting things in order before attempting another visit with Barlow in De Land. He himself gets home June 3, & if all goes well I shall follow shortly thereafter. It may seem odd to be going to Florida in summer—but this is more of a visit than a climatic quest. And anyhow—there isn't any time of year that I don't prefer the Florida climate. This has been a beastly cold spring hereabouts—so much so that I've had very few outings. Don't hurry about the section of "Dr. Crowe's Assistant"—leisurely work is better than hurried—but I'll be glad to read it whenever it's ready.

Congratulations on the coming appearance of "Partings" & "Evening Star"! I like the latter very much, & believe it ought to be swell received. It has unusual charm & imagination. In looking over the text I seemed to find the following slight changes advisable:

l. 5 for *a million*	read	*countless* (improves metre)
l. 11 for *stirs*	read	*stir* (refers to dreams)
l. 12 for *majic*	read	*magic* (spelling)

I've mentioned these points in a note to Crawford, & hope you'll authorise their incorporation. Thanks abundantly for the typed copy. I also like "The Viking" immensely, & cannot see why it was rejected. To me it seems full of the true spirit of weirdness, & with the dark suspense which adds so much to a tale of its kind. The only changes which seem at all necessary to me are very minor ones—largely mere matters of spelling. This certainly ought to land somewhere some time, & I hope you will keep the MS. carefully in expectation of such an occasion. Meanwhile I hope "The Pipers of Kallinen" will land with *The Galleon*. They profess to have a limit of 3000 words—but I think they are willing to stretch it when necessary. I don't recall the precise length of the Pipers. Yes—I noticed Rimel's "Charlotte" in U.S. It was, I think, the best tale in the issue. The opening story—"Waning Moon"—was one of the most ridiculously poor things I've ever seen in print.[1]

_____ Hill-Billy Crawford may use my "Mts. of Madness" _____ either as a serial or as a book—_____ in any case of lending-copies. Glad you intend to make bound booklets of your MSS. Those juvenile brochures of mine are pretty crude, but they help[?] to remind me of my youth.

Glad your health is better. I'm feeling rather better now that there have been a few warm days. Florida will quite set me on my feet. The coming trip was wholly unexpected, for I hadn't thought Barlow would leave Washington so soon. Details are still uncertain, but it looks as if everything might be all right.

Regarding legends of the supernatural, & the various "miracles" mentioned in folklore—there is no reason to think that any specific things corresponding to the latter ever really occurred. These mythological wonders are repeated in connexion with virtually all magical & religious systems—each system takes a few out of the common stock of floating myth & weaves it around the central figure of that particular system. Thus with the myths of the New Testament—these "miracle" stories were all old legends, & were simply woven by the promulgators of the Christus-legend around their especial hero or demigod. Most religions are built up out of these common circulating tales. The events never happened, although the various *types* of stories were moulded through various processes of myth-building from natural happenings or characteristic phenomena or dreams or wishes. But this moulding occurred thousands of years ago—before the birth of any known civilisation. All that the newer systems do is to repeat the tales with variations, & give them local settings.

Yes—human emotions are certainly limited to our species & planet. I don't recall any tale which has definitely emphasised the non-human character of the thoughts & feelings of other-planetary denizens, although a few have tried to suggest it. Generally, writers don't go far enough in that direction. As for the matter of secret cults—there really isn't any one work dealing with them that I know of. The facts about the Black Mass are incorporated into J. K. Huysmans' "La Bas"—& are essentially correct despite the fictional guise. The *witch* cult is exhaustively treated in the classic work of Prof. Margaret Alice Murray—"The Witch Cult in Western Europe". Much information (though written in a biassed spirit by one who actually believes in such things) can be found in the various books of the Rev. Montague Summers on vampires & witchcraft. Koenig could lend you most of these. Keep the review of the O'Donnell book—& here's another from the Times. I'd like to see the Crowley one again—though there's no hurry. Your "Haunted Book" must be quite an institution. I keep a rather disorderly box of cuttings touching on weird events—& if you'd care to look the contents over I'll be glad to lend it to you. Regarding Roger Bacon & Cagliostro—I really don't know of any recent books about them, although I think there are some. I'll try to find out later. You might ask at a library—of the college, for instance—or you might look at the end of the Bacon & Cagliostro articles in the latest Britannica (which I haven't). The only books on Bacon that I know of are in French & German: "Roger Bacon, Sa Vie, Ses Ouvrages, ses Doctrines d'apres des textes inédites"—by E. Charles, 1861 . . . . . & "Roger Bacon, Eine Monographie", by Schneider 1873. Then there is a study in English by J. K. Ingram (1858)—"On the Opus Majus of Bacon". But you'd better read a modern work if you can find one. I think there is a modern study of Cagliostro, but know nothing about it. A good deal about him will be found in the magical works of Arthur Edward Waite (any of which you'd find interesting)—especially "Lives of the Alchemists." A good

German work (translated) is "Cagliostro & Co.", by Franz Funck-Brentano. The latest one which I know of is marred by a rather naive attempt to take Cagliostro seriously—to whitewash him & make it appear as if he were not (as he undoubtedly *was*) the Italian Giuseppe Balsamo.[2] This is "Cagliostro", by W. R. H. Trowbridge (1910). Old Balsamo was certainly a charlatan de luxe—one of the greatest fakers in history.

Regarding vampirism & witchcraft—while there is not the slightest spark of truth in either, it is a fact (cf. the Murray book previously mentioned) that up to some 200 years ago an organised secret cult of people who called themselves *witches* existed. They were, despite certain notable exceptions, ignorant & degraded creatures, & held furtive meetings at which the most repulsive rites occurred. This much of fact lies behind the curiously similar reports brought out at witchcraft trials. Cult-members probably believed seriously in their supernatural powers—& often employed poison & something like hypnotic influence in their malevolent operations. Whether any branch of the cult really obtained a foothold in New England cannot be told with certainty. Perhaps one did—but it would be equally easy for the *folklore only* (& not the excitant cause) to cross the Atlantic. A vast number of popular tales concern things which never happened *on the spots mentioned,* but which are derived through vague & erroneous accounts of things which happened *elsewhere*—& perhaps far in the past. The abhorred & prohibited rites commonly known as "witchcraft" probably represent the furtively surviving remnants of some primitive fertility-religion which preceded the Druidic, Teutonic, Graeco-Roman, & Christian religions in western Europe. It was probably a pastoral religion—indeed, the great Sabbat-festivals (May-Eve & Hallowe'en) fall at the traditional breeding-seasons of the flocks & herds. Regarding *vampirism*—a legend whose source is clearly in southeastern or Balkan Europe (Greece, Turkey, Bulgaria, Hungary, &c.)—there is no basis at all for it, but it probably arose as a means of accounting for *wasting* diseases—which seemed very mysterious & significant to primitive man. These phenomena, linked with the aeon-old fear of ghosts (a belief with a complex but known history—cf. Frazer's "Golden Bough"), & with the observed cases of parasitic sucking of blood (bat, leach), finally gave rise to the concept of the sanguinary un-dead. Kindred myths—some homely & frequently observed—are those related to minor cases of vitality-sucking—like the old New England belief [that] cats *suck the breath* (whatever that means) of children. The belief in *were-animals* probably arose from the many lower-animal resemblances in man, & from certain types of homicidal mania wherein animal impersonations are indulged in. Other common beliefs involve the poetic personification of the forces of Nature.

Regarding popular myths & supernatural reports in general—there is certainly no reason to believe in any parallel order of existence apart from that whose tentatively recognised units we call electrons, protons, neurons, &c.— while the notion of *consciousness or personality* apart from the infinitely complex material structure of which such qualities are a delicate specialised product is simply grotesque & infantile. There is really no evidence whatever to the contrary—since religious tradition is obviously a blind emotional heritage from ages of ignorance & fantastic speculation, while the marvels claimed by spiritualists & kindred dupes & fakers constitute folklore syntheses of a type pretty well accounted for by anthropologists & psychologists—men who study & analyse (a) the multiform & surprising capacities of the human mind for hallucination & (intentional or unintentional) self-delusion; (b) the apparently fixed mania of certain mental types for spreading supernatural belief & inventing (often consciously & elaborately) supposed evidences of it; & (c) the universal phenomenon of myth-making & myth-diffusion through the multiple repetition (with distortions, accretions, & re-colourings at each stage) of some fragment of observation or narration either real or false. In accounting for persistent popular myths—& occult "evidences" as investigated & set forth by men like Flammarion & Chevreuil—one can reckon several varieties of types according to different principles of classification. Division into understood or solved examples & baffling & unsolved examples means little, since we know from past experience that even the most baffling mysteries always turn out—when finally solved—to involve only the material, non-dualistic physical principles with which we are familiar. However—judging from the vast number of solved examples we can attempt a fairly significant classification which undoubtedly applies to both solved & unsolved examples. Thus of all the incredible marvels reported in folklore, oral anecdotes, religious writings, press reports, scientific studies, &c. &c., virtually every one would probably turn out to belong in one (or *more*, since there are curious compounds & mixtures in legendry) of the following categories: (a) actual event produced by unknown natural principle or principles [rare]; (b) erroneous or magnified account of some actual event; (c) hallucination or other psychological source, either total or based on some objective nucleus; (d) intentional deception; (e) psychopathic deception; (f) folklore synthesis whereby an "event" *which never happened* becomes accepted as reality & embroidered by repetition, or whereby some trifling circumstance, allegory, or personification of natural forces or phenomena set off a train of typical folklore accretions. [variant of (b) except that in this case the accretions are likely to be of a standardised type based on popular mythology. There are certain *standard stories* invented before the dawn of history or later, which endless generations whisper about, repeat in new settings, & fasten to contemporary events. When one comes upon such a stock story (man changed to animal, disease miraculously cured, poltergeist effects, food indefinitely multiplied, rapping on table, man snatched up to paradise, apparition of distant dying relative, virgin birth, vampire, dead man moving, ghost, premonitory warning of death, &c. &c.), one can be sure that the report containing it is merely a repetition of old lore.]; & (g) repetition of some work of fiction as supposed fact (cf. Machen's

"The Bowmen" . . . angels of Mons.) In 1924–6 I did a good deal of revisory work for the late magician & exposer of spiritual fakes—Houdini—& he had tremendously interesting & important things to say about the origin of certain typical myths from *absolute fiction*.[3] Take the well-known tales of Hindoo fakirs—the man who throws a rope up straight into the sky & has a boy climb up & out of sight on it, or the one who puts a boy in a wicker basket, has spectators run swords through it, & then has the boy clamber out unhurt. Up to recent times these things were attributed to the *collective hypnotism* of the crowd by the magician. There were frequent stories of people who smuggled cameras to such demonstrations, obtained pictures of the magician in which none of the apparent phenomena shewed—even though the visual effect on the living audience was perfect. Well—Houdini went into this matter pretty exhaustively, *& found that no first-hand report of such a performance could ever be secured.* Dozens of people "had it straight from an eye-witness"—*but no real eye-witness could ever, during a long course of years, be located.* The inference is obvious. These extreme feats of the fakirs *have never been performed.* They constitute a well-defined type of folk myth—something everybody believes has occurred, but which has in truth never occurred. Even to this day one can find serious statements of the old "mass hypnotism" theory—but the investigations of Houdini tell their own story. Incidentally—the growth of the *camera* myth, as above outlined, is an even more vivid specimen of synthetic folklore without base—doubly vivid because of its conspicuous *recency*.

Assorted marvels like those in the eccentric books of Charles Fort[4] are not hard to account for. Fort scraped up all sorts of press anecdotes of a certain type—which in turn were typical misstatements, misinterpretations, exaggerations, & distortions of actually observed things, or else hallucinations or fabrications. Track down any one of them to its reported place of occurrence, & the marvel evaporates. Unusual atmospheric effects, natural phenomena like the "fairy crosses" of western Virginia, optical & chemical properties of dust storms & kindred things—these are the real sources of much of the Fort data. Another fruitful source is conscious press sensationalism—the kind of hokum peddled by the flamboyant "American Weekly" (of which A. Merritt is Asso. Ed.!) of the Hearst rags. It ought to be significant that no genuine man of science has ever taken Fort seriously.

The group of reported phenomena involving the *telepathic* principle deserves a somewhat separate study, since certain vague quasi-electrical distance-effects of human cerebration (though not, of course, the projection of speech or visual images in the manner of old wives' tales) are not outside the realm of possibility. Even so, however, the best authorities (except for a very recent change of opinion on the part of Dr. Freud) doubt any such thing—while it is of course plain that *most* of the reported instances of telepathy are well-defined cases of the usual myth-building process.

Glad you're enjoying the books. No I've read nothing by Thorne Smith,[5] though Barlow likes him. I don't care for humour in fantasy. Neither have I read anything by the redoubtable Aleister Crowley. Yes—I think the earlier parts of Blackwood's "Ancient Sorceries" are best. You won't be let down by "Wuthering Heights", even though the weirdness is subordinated to dark & tempestuous human emotions. Hope you can eventually get "The Haunted Castle".

_____ to see my young friend _____ save for a white shirt _____y. A great boy! By this time you have _____ heard from Rimel of Crom's melancholy disappearance. There is some adverse influence at work—for within a half-year Barlow's Doodlebug & Clark Ashton Smith's General Tabasco have likewise vanished! It's up to the Priests of Bast & Sekhmet to investigate! Incidentally—I gave Crom his name . . . which is that of the oft-mentioned Cimmerian deity in Bob Howard's Conan stories. Hope you & Rimel (& Baldwin, too) can get together for the Pony Express celebration at Missoula.

About those Heald stories—bless my soul, but there's no theft involved![6] Mrs. Heald is one of my revision clients, & I've been paid for every one of them. They are really my own stories—"ghost-written", as the phrase goes. I put in all that artificial mythology myself—since Smith & Howard & I like to have our synthetic demons popularised by wide use. Such use tends to give them a convincing air of actual mythological standing. I've also put Yog-Sothoth & Tsathoggua[7] in yarns ghost-written for Adolphe de Castro, & have encouraged other writers (Derleth, Long, Bloch, Wandrei, &c.) to use them. Smith constantly mentions my gods & I constantly mention his.

"The Canal" is one of the most powerful tales W.T. ever printed—but I didn't like "Light Echoes", which to me suggested the namby-pamby. "The Bird of Space" wasn't bad[8] I understand from Wright that Everil Worrell is a woman. He once thought of hiring her as assistant editor, but later decided not to. I don't know her address, but fancy W T would gladly forward a letter addressed to her in its care. She ought to be glad to furnish an autograph to one who appreciates her work. "The Golem" is great stuff—better get Rimel to sublend it to you while he has it. Hope Derleth & Dwyer can be induced to get the Hodgson books in motion soon. I also wished that the suspense in the "Man with Red Hair" hadn't petered out in mere physico-psychological sadism & insanity. Such a build-up really deserved a cosmic horror as a climactic finale!

Glad you found the print _____. Of course, one can't always judge how anybody really looks from any single likeness. The view of _____ which really resembles him is the square _____ view taken by Wandrei. Talman looks very much like his pictures. As for a shot of me to retain permanently—keep the large head-&-shoulders view if you like. Barlow has the negative & can get me more. Whitehead certainly was a great chap—one of the most gifted, pleasant, learned, & versatile persons I have ever encountered. The picture looks very much as he did. Barlow started printing that collection of his letters, became dissatisfied with the typography of the sheets & stopped work. I don't know when he will resume the project. Hope to see a snap of you when you get one. If you're really anxious to see what the cryptical H. Warner Munn looks like, I'll send you a large-size cabinet photograph taken in 1927. He's grown prodigiously fat since then—but that will shew how he looked when he wrote his best work. A really handsome cuss!

Well—my guest[9] of April 27–8 duly came in his car, & we put in a strenuous 2 days of historic sight-seeing. Saturday we visited ancient Newport—seeing 2 old windmills; a flock of sheep with small lambs; the home of Bishop Berkeley (1729—the guy who wrote "Westward the course of Empire takes its way"); the Hanging Rocks where Berkeley wrote his famous "Alciphron"; the lofty cliffs; a strange rock cleft called Purgatory, where the sea pounds thunderously in; & the venerable town itself . . . with 1698 Quaker meeting-house, 1726 Anglican church, 1739 colony-house, 1749 library, 1760 market-house, 1763 Jews' synagogue, & private dwellings as old as 1675. Glorious hot day—82° in Providence, though not quite so good in Newport. Sunday we went to ancient New Bedford, the quondam whaling centre—& thence to the Round Hills estate of Col. E. H. R. Green (son of the famous miser Hetty Green) in S. Dartmouth, where the old whaling barque *Charles W. Morgan* (built 1841) is preserved at a wharf—solidly embedded in concrete as a permanent exhibit. We went all over the vessel—which is tremendously fascinating. _____ ancient windmill moved _____ explored a region—where S. Mass. _____ S.E. Rhode Island—which I had never seen before in my life. Splendid unspoiled countryside with idyllic villagers of the old New England type. Then back home—after which I regretfully guided the guest on his route out of town.

May 3–4–5 I visited a friend in the Boston zone, but sight-seeing was hampered by cold grey weather. We took in Marblehead—whose charm is never-failing. By the way—Marbleheaders hate Whittier for that poem about Skipper Ireson,[10] alleging that their womenfolk were never such viragoes as to ride a citizen out of town in the manner represented. To this day the issue is a live & bitter one with the older generation. Actually—as Whittier later acknowledged—the poem is founded on an error. Poor Ireson's real story is tragic. He was really innocent—his men having forced him against his will to ignore the distressed ship. Then, to cover their own shame, they accused him. The incident wrecked his career as a sea-captain, even though the truth finally came out. He was never ridden out of town, but after years was lost at sea in a dory. I've seen his house in Circle St. Poor old boy!

Yes—Nouvelle-Orleans is a great old town. Mashburn[11] used to live there, but had moved to Texas before my visit (1932)—hence I've never met him. A very nice chap, according to Price—who knows him well. As for the climate—it's hard to account for such paradoxes. Prevailing winds—warm currents—topographical features . . . Do you realise that London is in the latitude of Labrador? Well—if all goes well I shall be seeing Charleston & St. Augustine before long. I'll send you cards.

On May 25 I had an interesting visit from young Hornig—erstwhile publisher of the F F. He's a very pleasant & intelligent youth—reminding me slightly of Donald Wandrei, though with a vaguely quasi-Semitic cast of features. He seemed to appreciate quite keenly the charm of old Providence—which is not unlike his own Elizabeth, N.J. I showed him most of the historic high spots, including the hidden churchyard on the ancient hill.

With all good wishes—

Yrs most cordially & sincerely—

H P L

Notes

1. *Unusual Stories* 1, No. 1 (May–June 1935): Duane W. Rimel, "The Jewels of Charlotte"; Robert A. Wait, "Waning Moon."

2. Count Alessandro di Cagliostro (1743–1795), Italian adventurer and self-styled magician, and glamorous figure associated with the royal courts of Europe. His reputation deteriorated as he came to be regarded as a charlatan and impostor. Thomas Carlyle pronounced him the "Prince of Quacks."

3. Harry Houdini (stage name of Ehrich Weiss, 1874–1926), celebrated escape artist and opponent of spiritualism for whom HPL ghostwrote the story "Under the Pyramids" (1924; published as "Imprisoned with the Pharaohs") and for whom he did other revisory work in 1926, just prior to Houdini's death.

4. See HW 7n3.

5. James Thorne Smith, Jr. (1892–1934), American writer of humorous supernatural fantasy fiction under the byline Thorne Smith, best known today for his two *Topper* novels.

6. HPL revised or ghostwrote five stories for Heald.

7. Inventions of HPL and Clark Ashton Smith, respectively

8. Everill Worrell (1893–1969) was the author of "The Canal" (*WT,* December 1927), "The Bird of Space" (*WT,* September 1926); "Light-Echoes" (*WT,* May 1930).

9. Robert E. Moe.

10. John Greenleaf Whittier, "Skipper Ireson's Ride" (1857). Benjamin Ireson (1775?–after 1808), 19th-century American sailor, captain of the schooner *Betsy*. In 1808, during a gale, the *Betsy,* heading to home port (Marblehead), discovered the ship, the *Active,* wrecked and taking on water. Ireson tried to rescue the *Active's* crew, but his own men insisted upon giving up the attempt because of the danger. On return to Marblehead, when the crew found itself blamed for the loss of life, it placed responsibility upon Ireson. The outraged people of Marblehead tarred and feathered him and dragged him out of town in a cart.

11. Science fiction writer W. Kirk Mashburn, Jr. (1900–1968).

[13] [TLS]

% R. H. Barlow,
Box 88 De Land, Fla.
[after 17 June 1935]

Dear Petaja:—

Well—Florida would have been the right address, but your letter was promptly forwarded from home. I left June 5, and shot straight down here with stops only at Fredericksburg, Va. and my beloved Charleston. I dropped you some pictorial matter from Charleston, and hope you ultimately received it safely. You will note that I am using Barlow's typewriter—for which, in spite of the mistakes incident to a strange machine, my correspondents will doubtless be abundantly thankful. The reason, however, is not altruistic—but is merely a result of a curious writers' cramp or fatigue . . . probably picked up from having to write dozens of long letters while on tour—in odd moments and in unfamiliar positions. My writing has become absolutely unreadable—even to myself—although it will probably straighten out as soon as I have some settled leisure. All returned material arrived safely. Thanks endlessly for the two attractive photographs, both of which I will gratefully keep for my archives with your permission. Some time, after I get home, I'll send you the view of Munn which I mentioned. No hurry with Dr. Crowe—perfection is more important than speed.

Glad the "Evening Star" corrections proved useful. Crawford says he will adopt them. I'm interested to hear of the circumstances of "The Viking's" composition. I feel sure that Crawford ought to be glad to print the entire "Echoes" series. Hope *The Galleon* will keep "The Pipers"—long retention is a favourable sign. Yes—that quatrain on chlorine certainly beats little Effjay's scientipoetical effort in Crawford's paper. I read Rimel's "Organ" and thought it splendid. He certainly ought to be able to place it somewhere. Glad you like "The Outsider", though I am not especially fond of it. It was rather a mechanical thing, and has a somewhat cheap jack-in-the-box ending. I noticed the Eyrie fan who connected it with the Kaspar Hauser incident,[1] but in truth I never thought of this celebrated case when writing the tale. My real object was merely to amplify the churchyard-dweller idea which I brought up in "Randolph Carter". The story, however, has proved rather a favourite with others.

Your idea of cosmic waves or pools in various parts of space which alter basic human emotions is extremely clever, and I trust you will sooner or later employ it in a tale. Of course, the probable emotions of non-human beings on other planets would probably have no relation at all to human emotions—but the idea of modified human emotion is none the less fictionally fruitful. Go to it!

Yes—I read (and owned) "La Bas". I don't think it is very rare now—the censorship (I think) having been withdrawn. You might easily find a copy. Yes—the erotic side of witchcraft is necessarily minimised by popular writers—that is, in proportion to its original prominence. However, it is only in a few of the earth's superstitions that sex has so dominantly figured. You can get a vast number of valuable loans of folklore books from Koenig—and sooner or later I hope you can get a whack at Railo's "Haunted Castle". Your idea of a coma mistaken for vampirism is excellent, and I trust you will use it eventually. Frazer's "Golden Bough" belongs to Koenig—or part of it does. As coincidence would have it, it is down here now—not in Barlow's possession, but lent to another chap in the neighborhood—Charles B. Johnson. I'll see if I can't get Johnson to return it and have it ready for re-lending. You certainly must see "The Golem". As for Houdini—my work was largely ghost-writing stories (see "Imprisoned with the Pharaohs" in the large midsummer 1924 WT) and exposes [*sic*] of occultist fakes. I had nothing to do with the book you mention—for H. used other ghost-writers . . . including a fellow-resident of Providence. C. M. Eddy, Jr. Charles Fort was a curious nut—probably sincere, but infinitely gullible. He believed all the fake anecdotes of impossible happenings which appeared in the papers, and thought the ordinary ideas of space and time and nature were all wrong. His books are interesting as a source of weird ideas, but have no other value. Yes—Abe Merritt is Asst. Ed. of the American Weekly. Most of the stuff therein printed is pure or partial fake. I never heard of the castle mentioned.

Your mention of tamed animals is highly interesting. Cats are my chief delight. Down here I have a fine family to contemplate—3 ordinary felidae and 2 Persians. No news from Crom—but appropriate gods must be invoked!

About the Heald junk—all of it is virtually written by myself. No—I can't see what kick these people get out of having their stuff written by others—but that's their own funeral so long as they'll pay for it. Other tripe I've ghost-written is the Houdini tale just mentioned, old Adolph deCastro's [*sic*] "Last Test" and "Electric Executioner". Zealia Brown Reed's "Curse of Yig" (which was copied in an anthology),[2] etc. No—I didn't know Arlton Eadie. After all, there are more WT writers whom I don't know, than writers whom I do know.[3]

Eventually I hope that you can visit some of the remote and exotic places which you see in dreams—especially the lakes and rivers and oceans which so fascinate you. The old towns of Europe and eastern America would likewise give you an endless store of ideas and pleasing impressions.

Glad you enjoyed the photographs—and thanks again for yours. I'll later send some views—illustrating my antiquarian trip of last April and showing the hidden churchyard on Providence's ancient hill—which I fancy you haven't seen before, and which I'll ask you to return eventually . . . though there's no hurry about the matter. I herewith send you some typical Florida views—postcard—which you can retain permanently.

Regarding nomenclature—there would surely be no harm in using the signature E. Theodore Pine—it's all a matter of choice. Half the writers for WT use pseudonyms . . . "Murray Leinster" is named Jenkins, etc.

Thanks exceedingly for the attractively illustrated lines "Dawn". One or two points require attention. For instance—there is no such word as "enrapted", which you use in the second line. Better say "wrapped". In the second stanza you use ";lush" [*sic*] as a noun, whereas it's an adjective. Better have the line go; "And springtime warm and lush". Later in the stanza it would be well to avoid the subtly trite word "entrancing"—though I'm not actually cutting it out. Still later, be sure of the correct spelling of "sprightly". On the whole, an admirable appealing poem—and I surely hope that it may meet with appropriate publication.

I am surely having a great time down here—the climate puts new life into me. My sleep actually rests me—which almost never happens in the north. In short, I am feeling *well* for the first time im [*sic*] 1935. The improvement began as soon as I hit the Carolina low country around Charleston—but possibly I mentioned that on the envelope of cards. Reached De Land June 9, and found things much as they were last year, except that Barlow's father—a retired army colonel—is home. His elder brother—a lieutenant from Ft. Sam Houston, Texas—has been here on a furlough and has formed a delightful companion, but recently his leave expired and he left for the west. We read, write letters, classify books, set type on sundry ventures, explore the country, and in general follow the programme of last year's visit. Bob has built a cabin across the lake to which—for the sake of seclusion—he transferred his press, desk, and various accessories as soon as it was ready for occupancy. On June 17 we visited a fascinating thing—Black Water Creek, a tropical river whose lush scenery suggests the Congo, Amazon, and other exotic streams famed in history and legend. It winds through a steaming jungle of tall moss-draped cypresses, whose grotesque, twisted roots writhe curiously at the water's edge. Palms lean precariously over the brink, and vines and creepers strow the black, dank earth of the bordering forest aisles. Sinister sunken logs loom up at various points, and in the forest pallid flowers and leprous fungi gleam whitely through the perpetual twilight. It is much like the river at Silver Springs (where the Weissmuller cinemas of Tarzan were photographed) which I saw last year, though I enjoyed it more because of the more leisurely observing conditions. Then I was whizzed ahead in a launch; this time we (Bob, his brother and I) went along slowly in a rowboat. Each bend of the tortuous stream brought to light some unexpected vista of tropical luxuriance, and we absorbed the spectacle to the full. Snakes and alligators were somewhat in evidence—though none came near our boat. I hope for more trips of this kind.

   With every good wish—
      Yours most cordially   HPL

Don't know how long I'll stay—the Barlows urge an indefinite sojourn.

P.S. Clark Ashton Smith has lately taken to sculptural carving in *dinosaur bone* [a deposit of which exists near Auburn] & other local substances. Some grotesque heads which he has just sent to RHB & me are marvellously impressive.

[P.P.S.] Also recd. your note of the 16th[.] Glad the cards proved interesting. Rimel's design for your letterhead is admirable!

[P.P.P.S.] Speaking of linoleum art—what do you think of Barlow's cryptic designs as used on the envelope of this epistle?

Notes

1. Charles H. Bert pointed out in "The Eyrie" (*WT*, June 1935) that HPL's "The Outsider" bore some resemblance to the story of Kaspar Hauser (1812?–1833), a German youth who claimed to have grown up in the total isolation of a darkened cell.
2. In *Switch On the Light.*
3. Leopold Leonard Eady (b. 1886), who published under the name Arlton Eadie, had died on 20 March 1935. Petaja had a letter regarding Eadie published in *WT*, September 1934.

[14]   [ALS]

℅ Barlow, Box 88,
De Land, Florida,
July 31, 1935.

Dear Petaja:—

Your interesting letter of July 12, with various piquant enclosures, duly received & appreciated. Let me congratulate you most heartily on your art work—both wash drawings & linoleum cuts. I didn't know you did any work in linoleum—hence my erroneous attribution of the earlier cut to Rimel. Pray pardon this attribution, & accept for yourself the very sincere compliments I mistakenly extended to him. Anyhow—cut & drawing alike were creditable in the highest degree. You & Rimel both do the best linoleum work I've so far seen . . . . there must be something in the air of the northwest which brings out talent! That "Partings" design is superb.

No hurry about the "Crowe" chapter—& meanwhile let me congratulate you on your excellent current verse. I don't wonder that Two-Gun Bob thought you had ideally captured the half-savage, half-sullen, but always unbroken "Conan" spirit. The picture that goes with this sonnet is delightful—& if Hill-Billy Crawford doesn't accept the contribution he's an utter ass. Four of the lines seemed to call for a bit of metrical improvement—as here suggested—& in writing Crawford I have again taken the liberty of making the same suggestions to him. The following substitute lines[1] seem to me to be just a trifle smoother than their respective originals:

‿ — ‿ — ‿ — ‿ — ‿ — ‿ —
(1) From an/cient dark / Cim-mer-i-a / he came

‿ — ‿ — ‿ — ‿ — ‿ —
(4) And still / triump/hant spurn / eter/nal fame

‿ — ‿ — ‿ — ‿ — ‿ —
(9) I saw / him then, / & still / I see / him now,

— ‿ — ‿ ‿ — ‿ — ‿ —
(10) Cryptic / & si/lent—on / a lone / hill's brow;

The sonnet to our mysterious young friend Munn is extremely fine—quite a weird masterpiece in itself. Did you send a copy to the baffling & unresponsive subject? Your earliest weird poem—"Night Noises"—certainly forms an interesting study in evolution. While extremely vivid & clever, it is obviously less sure & effective in technique than your later products in the same line. The use of a homely semi-dialect hurts rather than helps the atmosphere, while the rhyme of *fool* & *O'Toole* (a name obviously used for rhyming purposes) conveys a distinctly forced effect. The climax is vivid & excellent . . . full of the stark horror of the unexpressed. In short, the poem is good of its kind, though obviously a bit immature as compared with your later verses. Young Dilbeck certainly had no justification at all for tearing it to pieces. Wright prints infinitely poorer things in W T every month.

About "La Bas"—I believe you'll have a chance to borrow a copy in the very near future. W. Paul Cook—who is giving most of his choice books to Barlow—is about to send his copy down here; & when he does, my genial young host will be very glad to lend it to you. You'll find it disgusting but historically important. Not only does it give (under the guise of fiction—"Durtal" being Huysmans himself) authentic data concerning the Black Mass, but it relates in accurate detail the loathsome & hideous career of the infamous Gilles de Retz (or de Rais), about whom so much apocryphal legendry is woven. When this book was published its account of de Retz was the only correct & scholarly one in print. Huysmans was a profound student of all this kind of thing. Yes—Koenig can lend you all the famous mediaeval & renaissance books about witchcraft. Indeed, he has about the best weird library of anybody in the bunch. About "The Horror from the Hills"[2]—the only connexion with it I have is authorship of the Roman (or Hispano-Roman) dream given in the second part. That was an *actual* dream of mine—experienced some time in 1927—& when I wrote about it to Belknap he put it into his story with no changes of wording. I was quite surprised to find it blending so well with the major narrative!

Sorry the "Pipers" didn't land with *The Galleon*—but you might try something else on them. How about the Viking tale? I'll be glad to see "Rene Passes through the Veil" whenever you wish to send it along.

Glad the Florida cards proved interesting. Here are a couple more—& when I get to St. Augustine I'll send you some shots of that fascinating place . . . a city founded in 1565, when Shakespeare was a year old, & which still has houses that were standing when Sir Francis Drake looted it in 1586!

About returning the books—better send them to *Providence*. My aunt receives & takes care of all my things. When I get home I'll shoot along some more volumes.

And now let me express my delight at the prospect of a fantasy magazine from you & Rimel! No better editorial team could be found—& if you can get hold of a press you'll be avoiding the heaviest drain (printer's expenses) which Hornig had to meet. You can undoubtedly make the magazine of much higher grade than the F F—seeking better material & eliminating the frivolous & inferior. Virtually all of the old contributors would be at your disposal—& a fairsized clientele would be assured at the outset. Of the two titles you suggest, I'd be inclined to favour the one which (judging from your attractive circular design) you yourselves favour—"The F's Mirror". At the same time let me urge you to verify carefully the nature & spelling of the word forming the bulk of the title. In my opinion, the word you really mean to use is the French one indicating a creator of fantasies—*FANTAISISTE* . . . pronounced Fahntay-*seest*. This term has been gradually working itself into the English language since 1916, when Ernest Boyd published his small critical brochure called *"Lord Dunsany—Fantaisiste"*[.] Be sure to get the spelling accurate in both the circular & the paper. With cuts by yourself & Rimel, & articles by all the old gang, it ought to form an ideal successor to the F F. Don't hesitate to call on me for any service I can render—advice or contributions. I'd be delighted to have you go on with my "Supernatural Horror in Literature", & to let you have weird stories from time to time. Would you like, for your first issue, my "Nameless City"? If so, let me know, & I'll either send it as soon as I get home, or have my aunt haul it up & send it to you in case I don't return till later. Hope Rimel can get to Missoula in 1936 & coöperate at close range. Some of your novel & original ideas would undoubtedly be highly advantageous—although a mystical editorial style ought not to be carried to extravagant extremes. I'll keep the matter a secret, as you wish, until I receive permission to disseminate it. I told Barlow, but he will let it go no further.

Meanwhile you may have a bit of competition in the form of *The Phantagraph* (or something like that), official organ of a band called "The Terrestrial Fantascience League".[3] This organisation—headed by one Wilson Shepherd of Alabama—has appointed a new editor, Donald A. Wollheim of N.Y., & is resolved to duplicate the glories of the old F F if it possibly can. I wish it luck—but doubt if it will get very far. This venture is likely to be received with considerable coolness by Hornig, since the Fantascience League conflicts in certain ways with The Science Fiction League of which he is an official . . . . & to which I believe you & Rimel (or perhaps only D W R) belong.

Possibly your own venture—in which no possibilities of infringement exist—will receive the perhaps substantial benefit of Hornig's endorsement. Now that the F F has gone, all sorts of talk about a successor become prevalent. Hill-Billy Crawford, & Smith & Anger of the San Francisco zone—have at various times dreamed ineffectively of resumption. So, too, did little Kenneth Sterling—who was in Providence earlier this year & whose address is now 26 Burling Ave., White Plains, N.Y.

July W T doesn't amount to much, though the Moore item has its moments.[4] Recently received *Marvel Tales*—which certainly is getting to be quantitatively ambitious despite its low qualitative level. But all the pulps are pretty poor, & I have less & less patience in wading through them.

My Florida visit continues to be delightful, & the super-hospitality of my hosts makes the date of its conclusion more & more a matter of doubt. This climate gives me new reserves of health—I certainly must live down here some day. Barlow's printing ventures proceed apace—& before long he expects to try his hand at the *binding* business. He also has an idea of printing an amateur paper—connected with the National Amateur Press Association,[5] to which Rimel now belongs. I've aided in the typesetting—a sort of activity rather unfamiliar to me, since I haven't set type before since the days of my own childish printing-presses.[6] You'll hear before long of some of Barlow's projects—& incidentally, you'll find him an enthusiastic well-wisher for your own magazine venture.

I've recently read a highly impressive book—belonging to Barlow. "The Last & First Men", by W. Olaf Stapledon, published in 1930. It deals with the future of the human race from the present to a period 5,000,000,000 years ahead—during which time the stock has migrated successively to Venus & Neptune. Of all books dealing with cosmic cycles & other planets this is the only one since Wells[7] which can be regarded as in any way serious. This, indeed, has the mature philosophic perspective so utterly wanting in hack interplanetary junk—& involves a really disciplined imagination. You really ought to read it—I'm sure Barlow would be glad to lend it if you'd like. Speaking of loans—hope you'll like "The Golem". When you're through with it, please send to the next person on the lending list—*R. F. Searight, 19946 Derby Ave., Detroit, Michigan.*

With every good wish, congratulating you again on your excellent art work, & hoping to hear of your success in founding The Fantaisiste, I remain

Yrs most cordially & sincerely—

Ech-Pi-El

P.S. Just had word of death of Robert Nelson, author of "Lost Excerpts" &c—on July 23. Too bad. Do you want any posthumous things of his for the new paper? I think Barlow has some. (He may use them himself in a memorial leaflet.)[8] Also—Wollheim's Phantagraph wants some.

Notes

1. For EP's poem "The Warrior." EP adopted ll. 9 and 10, 4 in part, and 1 not at all.

2. By Frank Belknap Long.

3. *Phantagraph* had been known as *Bulletin of the Terrestrial Fantascience Guild* and before that as *The International Science Fiction Guild's Bulletin.*

4. C. L. Moore, "Jirel Meets Magic."

5. This became the *Dragon-Fly.* Barlow had acquired the printed sheets of HPL's *The Shunned House* but bound only a few copies, and also various personal items (such as his set of *Amazing Stories*).

6. In youth, HPL printed by hectograph, whereas R. H. Barlow had a letterpress, on which HPL set type by hand.

7. Referring to *The Time Machine* (1895).

8. Robert Nelson (1912–1935). Surviving parts of his "Lost Excerpts" are gathered in *Letters to Robert Bloch and Others;* also in *Sable Revery: Poems, Sketches and Letters* (2012).

[15]   [ALS]

St. Augustine, Florida,
August 19, 1935.

Dear Petaja:—

       Your new stationery is very attractive—beating Derleth at his own game![1] Don't do your linoleum work injustice—it is really extremely good. Sorry *Fantasy* has pirated the design for the "Echoes" series. You ought to recall it for use in M T. unless Rimel makes you a much better specimen for the purpose. By the way—I hope you won't withhold the "Partings" cut from Crawford. What he really means by "high type" is *type-high* . . . . that is, he wants you to be sure that the thickness of the linoleum & of the block on which it is mounted make the whole thing *just the same as a piece of standard type in height,* so that it can be used without alteration on the press in connexion with regular type. That is not difficult to arrange—for all linoleum block material on the market is made to conform to the standard height.

       Regarding your professional ambitions—I wish you luck, though of course you realise that almost no writers make frequent remunerative placements until they have been in the game for years. If you do want to place your material in the pulps, there is certainly no agent more competent, conscientious, & genuinely helpful than Kline. He takes a personal interest in his clients, & gives free advice of immense value in "making" the cheap markets. Long, Price, & R. E. Howard swear by him, & vow that he has helped them more than any other person. He won't handle a story unless he believes it has a good chance of acceptance. The only trouble with writing for the cheap magazines is that such a practice tends to hurt one's literary style unless one builds up a very determined resistance. What the pulp editors want is not *good* material, but simply material modelled to suit a certain artificial, non-life-like, & genuinely tawdry formula which their circle of low-grade readers like. When one becomes a fluent & accomplished pulp hack like Price or Wandrei or Long, one tends to lose the art of really graceful & sincere expression. All that is *really excellent* in a story—truth to life or human nature, absence of artificial "plot", leisurely unfolding, &c. &c.—is violently opposed by pulp editors & those who teach the art of suiting them. Conversely—everything that these editors & teachers recommend or insist upon is *very bad* from an artistic point of view. Most writers who cater to this demand find themselves ruined for serious work, since they unconsciously adopt the methods & point of view of inferior composition. But of course it helps a great deal to be on guard.

As for my giving professional revision—the main trouble is that I have nothing to do with the hack pulp methods demanded by commercial fiction. I don't know the ropes—the tricks & idioms & odd devices called for by cheap editors. I always revise with *intrinsic excellence* as a goal—so that what I would do to a story might *injure* its prospects in the professional market instead of *helping* them. Of course in some cases stories by clients of mine *have* sold professionally where they would not sell before—but this is not a general rule. However—if at any stage of your career you think my professional criticism or revision would help you, I'd be glad to have you outline your needs when the time comes. My rates, of course, vary according to the *difficulty* of each separate job—I'll send you a table of prices covering typical cases. Remember, though, that revision for pulp markets is *not* my specialty. By the way—I'm very sorry to hear that your industrial standby has vanished, & hope you may soon find its equivalent as an aid to financing your college term.

About the sonnets Hill-Billy Crawford has—you'll recall that I sent corrections both to you & to him of one of the *earlier* ones as well as of the one to Two-Gun Bob. He has now *lost* my corrections to your *earlier* sonnet (or verse—was it a sonnet?), & wants to know what to do. Since I can't remember what the poem was, I've had to refer him to you—trus[t]ing that you have remembered the corrections & incorporated them into your reference copy. I hope you can supply him again with the corrected text, so that the lines can appear in the most advantageous possible way. I'll be interested in seeing the sonnet you dedicate to Miss Moore—embodying, no doubt, some of the characteristics of her work. About the power of *suggesting* rather than *describing* horror—of course, there are limits to the extent to which non-expression can be carried. It is not enough to say that one saw "something" & forthwith went mad with fright. Naturally, there must be some *suggestion of what was seen.* The art is to *conceal* this suggestion in the general body of the text; so that by the time the supreme climax is reached, the reader will *tend to know what sort of a horror is impending* . . . . even though he cannot be *sure,* & though he *will not know why he has the dark suspicion he has.*

Barlow hasn't yet received "La Bas"—but "The Golem" is gradually getting toward you in the course of circulation. I think Rimel has it now. Glad "The Nameless City" reached you safely—& hope it may find lodgment in a publication of yours. Hope *The Galleon* will take "The Viking"—though they are rejecting some excellent material of late because of an excess on hand. Only a few weeks ago Eshbach turned down a splendid thing of Barlow's. Trust the Roman dream interpolated into Belknap's story won't bore you. It sounds like my style, though it seems to blend curiously well with Belknap's surrounding text. Yes—the plot of that Chaugnar story came from a suggestion of mine.

Glad the cards were of interest—I'll try to find some more along my homeward route . . . embracing more historic material than the De Land region afforded. I've accumulated an enormous collection of such material—& Robert E. Howard also has quite a file.

Regarding the magazine—of course Koenig is right in pointing out difficulties. The fact is, Hornig's circulation was only about *60* at most. Your advantage lies in the fact that there will be no printers' bills to meet. Naturally, one cannot take Hornig's experience as an absolute precedent. You might—with favourable "breaks" do much better than he did . . . attracting a clientele from sources which he did not adequately exploit. About the *title*—I still incline toward *The Fantaisiste's Mirror*, though of course there must be better ones . . . . if they could only be discovered. I really can't think of any good title to compete with your suggestion. The derivation of *The Raven's Plume* is extremely clever—but I can't help thinking the other title is a trifle apter in the long run. As for various possible other names—*The Dark Tower*, *The Sabbat*, *The Haunted Chamber*, *Shadows*, or anything of that sort might be considered. Better ask all the members of the gang for suggestions—somebody might shew a stroke of genius in hitting on something. Of *The Phantagraph* I have seen not a sign & heard not a word since writing you. On the whole, I doubt whether it will constitute any very formidable rival to your projected enterprise. I don't know much about these various Shepherds—except that Barlow has corresponded with Wilson & doesn't like him very well.[2] The L. C. Smith project for a similar magazine has definitely fallen through. Smith means to issue a mimeographed transcript of all the tables of contents of W T from the first issue to June 1935—but has abandoned the idea of printing my "Fungi from Yuggoth".[3] Barlow intends to issue the latter in book form. You're welcome to any that you wish, except those previously published in W T & certain other places. Barlow's book won't appear for ages. You can also have first choice of the Nelson material. Poor chap . . . he was still crude & extravagant, but had definite promise. Barlow would probably be glad to contribute various fantasies later on. And I would take pleasure in reading & commenting on your prospectus before it is issued.

Yes—I've now seen the August W T & noted the Eyrie. Thanks for the puff! Hope Wright will heed it—but I doubt it. The issue as a whole is rather mediocre.

Barlow is rapidly assembling a full-fledged bindery, so that he can handle bookmaking in every phase from idea to dust-jacket. He is now printing a paper to circulate in the National Amateur Press Association.

On the 14th of August, at 8 p.m., we saw a very extraordinary phenomenon—something which no one present had ever seen before—a *lunar rainbow*. It was a faint but perfect bow in the northwest—cast by the full moon as it rose above the grotesque pines beyond the lake. The moon is a marvellous spectacle in Florida—the scenery making an especially fine foreground for it.

Well—I'm under way at last . . . northward bound, though I dread the thought of the cold days ahead. My stops along the route will be conditioned by my very shaky purse. The Barlows are also away—spending a fortnight at Daytona Beach. I am now in venerable St. Augustine for a week—the most ancient town in the U.S. . . . which was 42 years old when Jamestown was settled, & 55 years old when the first Pilgrims landed on Plymouth Rock. The original narrow streets still remain, & there are old Spanish houses built as early as 1570 or 1580. The ancient fort & entry gates—built of coquina stone—still stand. Many of the old Spanish families survive, though English has been universally spoken for a century. Here are some views. ¶ All good wishes & appreciation—

Yrs most sincerely—

H P L

Notes

1. August Derleth had new stationary printed for each new season.
2. See "Correspondence between R. H. Barlow and Wilson Shepherd . . ."
3. Louis C. Smith and William Frederick Anger (1921–1982) had in June 1935 proposed a mimeographed edition of HPL's *Fungi from Yuggoth*, but that venture, and also a proposed "index" to *WT*, came to nothing.

[16] [ALS]

66 College St.,

Providence, R.I.,

Septr. 19, 1935

My dear Petaja:—

Your letter & card (with Rimel) duly received, & I am surely glad to hear of the delightful outing you are having. Meeting Rhi-Mhel must have been a tremendous pleasure—while the various family reunions were doubtless equally felicitous. Curious that *you* should have an elder brother named *Wayne*—so has Barlow! I think I spoke of Wayne Barlow (a Lieutenant in the army) in one of my recent letters. Quite a coincidence! Many thanks for the attractive postcards. Evidently the noble red man has not vanished as completely from the northwest as from my part of the country. The only place I ever saw Indians in their native haunts was in southern Florida in 1931. The Seminoles still maintain their tribal organisation there.

Glad to hear you are in touch with Utpatel—who is really a splendid artist, probably destined for more than amateur recognition. He may be able to give hints of real assistance in developing your own undeniable talents. I was sorry when a change of publishers' plans prevented him from illustrating Derleth's "Place of Hawks". He & Howard Wandrei both need to get some important illustrating assignment in order to come to public notice.

Regarding the sale of fiction—as I said, it is notoriously uphill work. Sorry Kline returned your fatefully titled story—but remember that *his* grounds of rejection have nothing to do with actual merit, but pertain only to commercial saleability. I'll be glad to look over "I Will Return" whenever you care to send it along—although, as I said before, my criticisms in the popular-fiction field must not be considered authoritative. Glad that Rimel's "Organ" seems to have a favourable reception, & hope it will land with Wright. I hope, too, that your "Rene" may find a haven with W.T. As for revision on my part—when I see your recent fiction I'll see whether I think any tinkering of mine would increase its marketability. In general, I do not profess to be expert in pulp requirements—& doubt whether I could write a story myself that would land with the average conventional pulp editor. The stock formulae & devices of such tales are both unfamiliar & repugnant to me.

You didn't enclose the new poems you spoke of enclosing, but I'll be glad to see them at any time. Too bad you don't recall the first piece Crawford took. I'll have to ask him to send me the text . . . . unless it happens to be among the items you send, or unless you find the corrections in my letter of last winter or spring. The list of corrections alone will be sufficient, since Crawford has the text. Don't hurry about your Moore sonnet—better late & good than early & careless. Sorry the Munn one didn't land—but you can send it to Schwartz or use it yourself later on.

Good luck with the magazine when you get around to it. That, likewise, can well afford to wait for an auspicious opportunity. No hurry about deciding on a name—indeed, it might be well to solicit more opinions before making the matter conclusive.

No—I don't know the particulars of Nelson's death. I was not well acquainted with him, & probably never wrote him more than 4 or 5 letters in all. The only one I know who ever met him in person was Charles D. Hornig. He was a neurotic, ill-adjusted type, & often had considerable friction with his parents. Barlow will send you his posthumous "Lost Excerpts" whenever you are in a position to use them.

Well—I certainly had a great trip. Hope you received the envelopes of cards I sent from St. Augustine & Charleston. I paused in both of these ancient towns, as well as in Poe's home town of Richmond—views of which I enclose herewith. Of all these places I find Charleston the most fascinating—

a perfectly preserved city of the 18th century. But of course St. Augustine—a Spanish outpost with surviving houses built in the 1500's—has a charm all its own. I also paused briefly in Washington & Philadelphia. In N.Y. City I spent a fortnight as guest of Donald Wandrei—Howard being away. I saw all the group—Long, Koenig, Hornig, Schwartz, Talman, Leeds, &c. &c., & the young son of Otis Adelbert Kline. Got home Saturday, & have since been lost amid the mountains of piled-up work awaiting me. It will be weeks before my programme gets back to normal. May take a brief trip into Massachusetts before the winter closes in on me—though this is problematical.

All good wishes—& hoping your trip will end as pleasantly as it began—
Yrs most cordially & sincerely—
H P L

[17] [ALS]

Home—Septr. 29[, 1935]
Dear Petaja:—

By this time you have doubtless received the letter I sent after my arrival home. Meanwhile yours of the 19th with interesting MSS. has arrived, & I have perused both the story & the poem with keen interest. In the verses there are only two changes which I would deem imperative. Stanza IV, l. 4 speaks of a man *wearing* a gun, which is hardly idiomatic. Change *wearing* to *Bearing* & you're all right. in the last line of the next stanza the metre is crowded—too many syllables. Better cut out the *away* & let the line read:

And snatched him from the dead.

As a whole the poem is very vivid & excellent—& surely merits publication somewhere. Regarding Whitman—I must say that personally I don't find him very interesting. He occasionally produces images which form genuine poetry, but this genuine strain is hopelessly intermixed with a sort of shrill egotism, neurotic bombast, & prosy preaching & cataloguing which tends to kill my enthusiasm for the "good grey poet".[1] There are many violent Whitman fans—my friend James F. Morton is one of them—but can't say that I'm one of them. The old fellow slops over so often—& so often lets a sort of messy emotionalism replace his sense of beauty—that I get bored before I have a chance to admire. I can't see the point of those who couple him with Poe in America's apex of poetic utterance. Walt was a curious cuss—probably an unstable, highly neurotic type with a twisted psychology that tried to find compensation in hyper-assertive, bombastic eloquence. He indubitably hit the mark at times—but all the same I've never bothered to go across the bridge to Camden & visit his home on any of my Philadelphia trips.

Regarding "Dorian Gray"—I haven't read it since 1920 or so, but somehow I feel that it wouldn't impress me so much now as it did then. It is without question clever, & the weird element is considerable; but as I recall it there was a smartness & affectation which detracted considerably from its force. Of course it is primarily an *allegory* rather than a true weird tale—its spirit & motivation differing widely from those of Machen or Blackwood work.

I read "Rene" with much pleasure, & must congratulate you upon its fluency, animation, & dramatic force. Some might, of course, consider it a trifle too much inclined toward the sentimental; but that is to a certain extent a matter of taste. I'm sorry it has not yet landed in print, & hope it may do so later on. In looking it over I have made a few trivial corrections in spelling, wording, &c., which may enhance the smoothness a bit. One thing I'd suggest is that you avoid the use of *parenthesis* whenever possible. This device seriously mars the flow of fictional prose, & always excite adverse criticism.

Well, as I said before, I'm extremely glad you've managed to meet Rimel at last, & can imagine what a congenial session you must have had in Spokane. Sooner or later, I trust that your joint plans for *The Fantaisiste's Mirror* may successfully bear fruit. Meanwhile let me congratulate you upon your coming university studies—which will certainly reward you amply in the end, even though they may crowd your programme a bit just now. Don't hurry on the science-fiction story—better leisurely & good than rapid & unconvincing.

Glad the cards from Charleston duly arrived—& trust the Richmond specimens may also be interesting. Richmond, however, cannot compare with Charleston in charm & picturesqueness. Hope "The Golem" & the Hodgson material may reach you soon, & that you will not be disappointed by any of it. I've suggested to Rimel that he disregard the circulation list & give you a look at Hodgson after himself. Then the stuff is to go to Crawford. "The Golem" goes to R. F. Searight. "La Bas" may not get into circulation, for its owner has gone westward without sending it to Barlow.

Sept. 20–23 inclusive I was in Massachusetts visiting my friend E. H. Cole & taking a number of rural trips with him in his car. We went to Nahant & ancient Marblehead, to the brooding "Dunwich" country among the Connecticut Valley hills, & to the gentle seaside landscapes of Cape Cod—giving me an unusually welcome & comprehensive glimpse of New England scenery after my long absence amidst palms, live-oaks, & Spanish moss. It is just possible that I shall have a still further glimpse before winter sets in—for I may accompany Cole over the Mohawk Trail & up into Vermont when the autumn foliage is at its height. This, however, is highly tentative.

Meanwhile my programme-congestion continues. 3 large revision jobs unperformed, magazines since July to read up, correspondence in unanswered heaps—& general chaos everywhere. Steam heat is on now—for which I am profoundly thankful. Oct. W T ought to be out any time now, but in view of recent issues I don't expect much of it.

Once more congratulating you on our recent week, & wishing you luck in all your enterprises, I remain

Yrs most cordially—HPL

Notes

1. See HPL's "Fragment on Whitman."

[18]   [ALS]

66 College St.,
Providence, R.I.,
Octr. 9, 1935.

Dear Petaja:—

A letter from *Munn!* Yuggoth, what an event! And a manuscript, too! Is the world coming to an end? You stand unique in your ability to elicit a message from this chief of sphinxes! I must tell Cook—who has now gone to St. Louis.

Glad your college course has begun—though sorry your house is so inconveniently situated with respect to the university. Your course sounds tremendously interesting—especially that "humanities" item. As for languages—while French may possibly have a greater cultural importance than German, there is no question but that the latter stands high among the tongues which ought to be known. I regret my own ignorance of it. Sorry you dislike biology—I find it intensely interesting so far as I know it, but within its compass comes everything which determines the nature of life & mankind. Have you ever read any popular books on the subject? I recently borrowed the new Wells–Huxley "Science of Life", though I have not yet had a chance to read it.

With your heavy programme, I don't wonder that you won't have time for any new fiction. I surely wish Rimel luck. By this time, no doubt, you have received my letter returning "Rene" & expressing my liking for it. Glad you've sent something for *The Phantagraph*. I've received a copy—after some delay—& will be glad to lend it to you if you don't receive one. It is really commendable effort to carry on the old F F tradition, & contains some items (especially an article on the weakness & puerility of pulp science-fiction) distinctly worth reading.[1] Let me know if yours fails to come.

And now let me thank you exceedingly for the Missoula cards. The region would seem to be one of considerable beauty—& your college certainly has an interesting mountain background. The Bitter Root region contains vistas of profound impressiveness.

Yesterday my aunt & I had a ride to New Haven through magnificent Connecticut scenery. My aunt visited a friend, while I had 7½ hours free for exploration. The town is intensely interesting, though by no means as full of colonial architecture as Providence or Charleston. The oldest college building—where Nathan Hale once roamed—dates from 1752. I explored Centre Church (1812) & saw the graves in the crypt. Also the ancient Pierpont house (1767)—a good example of Connecticut-Valley architecture, now serving as the Yale Faculty Club. Visited historical, art, & natural history museums—all notable. But the most impressive things in New Haven are the *new* Yale quadrangles—all faithful imitations of old-time architecture. They are magical little worlds in themselves—taking one backward through time, & across to Old England. The Gothic specimens look just like pictures of Oxford & other mediaeval colleges, while the colonial ones are just as perfect in their way. New Haven is, on the whole, a very beautiful town—full of great elms & gardens & mansions about a century old. I visited two fine botanic gardens, from one of which (on a hill) there was a splendid view of the rest of the town. The day was ideally sunny, though not as warm as I wished it might be. We were only 2½ hours getting there (a matter of 95 miles), & 3 hours coming back after dark.

Well—here's wishing you luck in your new course! Oct. W.T. not as bad as Sept. Flanders & Moore stories good, & Machen reprint (minor but wholly new to me) very welcome.[2]

Best regards—

HPL

Notes

1. C. W. Lonsdell, "Is Science Fiction in a Rut? [Part 1]," *Phantagraph* 4, No. 1 (July–August [1935]): [7]–8; [Part 2] 4, No. 3 ([June?] 1936): 13–14.
2. *WT* (October 1935): C. L. Moore, "The Cold Gray God"; John Flanders, "The Mystery of the Last Guest"; Arthur Machen, "The Lost Club" (1890).

[19]   [ALS, water damaged]

66 College St.,

Providence, R.I.,

Nov. 7, 1935.

Dear Petaja:—

Glad the remarks on "Rene" proved helpful, & hope to see the tale in print eventually. Don't underestimate this, or the poem—& don't let down in your defiance of commercial taste. Let your only criteria be truth, mood, & human nature as you understand it. As your education advances, you will see new phases of truth, suffer modifications of mood through new perspectives on familiar things, & arrive at new interpretations of human nature. Therefore the tone & method of your fiction may well change with it. But don't let the basic motivation be altered. Continue to hold truth (whatever changed aspect it may bear), mood (however difficult from your present moods), & human nature (however different from your present ideas you may discover its workings to be) as your only criteria. For directness & sincerity are the most important elements in any form of creative art.

Glad the studies are going well, & that the merits of biology are gradually becoming apparent. Don't bother about writing when it interferes with your regular studies. Just now the curriculum is of prime importance—there will be plenty of opportunities for literary practice when the scholastic tension is a bit less. Regarding the value of collegiate studies—I don't think there is any doubt of their extreme usefulness. A good instructor can help his pupils master a book—with all the invaluable explanations & testings—much better than the average pupil could master it himself. A determined person can somehow get an education without such instruction—but he usually spends much more energy in the process than he would if enrolled in a well-taught course. And if the instructor is especially keen & thorough, a systematic course usually gives a firmer & wider grasp of a subject than could ordinarily be obtained through unaided reading. I think almost every serious student is the better for college training, although my poor health in youth prevented me from enjoying this advantage. My knowledge in many fields would be more thorough & workable if I had been through an university. Indeed, if you plan a career of teaching, it will be *absolutely necessary* for you to have a college degree; since school boards are increasingly particular about the formal academic standing of teachers. I certainly think the career of an English instructor is very much to be desired. Despite the routine side, it does unmistakably involve a very congenial field, & offer abundant opportunities for the exercise the services of literary taste. It has none of nagging, ignominious atmosphere which clings around most of the phases of commercialism, & occasionally gives one a chance to accomplish important things in the domain of character moulding the discovery of talent & genius. I would surely advise you to keep this goal in view—though never hesitating to alter or modify it if anything better suited to your temperament develops. It is true that most teachers are able to study & pursue literary work while engaged in the practice of their professions. So I back up the opinion of your brothers & hope you'll feel inclined to plan accordingly.

Glad you've received *The Phantagraph,* & hope we shall see more issues of that ambitious & well-intentioned journal. It is crude, of course, but the best thing that can be expected under the circumstances. Congratulations on the cut for "The Two Doors". It is really extremely vivid & tasteful, & ought to put the reader in a very receptive mood.

Your success in reaching the inaccessible Munn is surely a record-breaking achievement—akin to that of the few white men who succeed in entering the forbidden city of Lhasa! Cook & I—old friends of Munn, at that—are away behind you! Interested to hear of the Werewolf's recent fortunes, & hope the life-guarding (a vocation he plied years ago) has helped to cut down the excess weight which he had in '32, when I last saw him. Hope he'll have good luck with his new fiction[.] Wright seemed at one time to be rather coolly disposed toward his work—as toward mine. As for that cabinet photograph of Munn—by this time I trust you have duly received it. No hurry about return—& I hope your nephew can make you a good copy. You *could* get it *photographed*—Barlow has a photographic copy made from a picture of good old Whitehead in my possession. Remember, however, that it is not a contemporary likeness. It was taken back in 1927, when Munn was slim & tremendously handsome. By 1932 you couldn't have recognised him by it— he was so fat that he had almost ceased to have a neck! There is, though, just the barest possibility that in the 3½ years since I have seen him he has knocked off a bit of poundage & got back closer to the old-time norm. It can be done—I've done it myself. I grew alarmingly fat in the early 1920's through systematic & unconscious overeating, but took matters in hand in 1925 & ditched 50 lbs. in 5 months. Never had any tendency to gain since— so that today I weigh only 145 (height 5 ft 11 in.) & have a waistline of 31.

Regarding the ethics or "morals" of the Hellenic world—while on the one hand the Greeks really laid the foundations of *all* rational ethics, removing the matter from the field of superstition & supernatural belief & identifying good conduct with *knowledge* & *beauty*, it must be admitted on the other hand that the *practical ethical average* of Hellas does not compare favourably with that of early Rome & of the Nordic world. Greece produced the greatest teachers, but not the most consistent, instinctive, & habitual practicers, of socially & aesthetically harmonious conduct. In practice, the average Greek was inclined to be tricky, callous, & rudely or messily self-indulgent. He was deficient in courage & stamina except when worked up by some particular enthusiasm, & had a sort of capriciousness & lack of responsibility which exasperated the Roman mind—hence the term of contempt, "Graeculus". In domestic organisation & sex ethics he shewed an astonishing lack of taste— tolerating to a disgusting degree the unnatural Oriental pederasty picked up from the Persians. All told, the Greek's contribution to western civilisation's ethical stream must be accounted a purely theoretical one. He gave us the *principles* which must serve to motivate conduct & social organisation now that supernatural illusions are dead; but it is from other cultural sources— Roman, Nordic, & Semitic—that the tradition of exact & conscientious behaviour as an instinctive & practical habit is primarily derived.

I've never read "The Well of Loneliness",[1] although I recall seeing it reviewed in the press some years ago. I rather fancy that much of its popularity comes from its subject-matter as distinguished from intrinsic merit—at least I don't think that anything else by Miss Hall has attained more than passing notice. It is probably a fact that in recent years homosexual vices have reached their greatest prevalence since the 16th century, though I doubt if they will ever attain the maximum reached in the ancient world. Today there is no deeply seated tradition in their favour, so that they are not likely to spread far beyond the persons of actually diseased psychology—who certainly do not form more than ¹/₆₀ th of the population. In Persia & Greece, on the other hand, pederasty was an accepted *custom*, so that it was casually followed by ordinary persons who had no innate inclination toward it. That condition is not likely to recur, since any attitude so basically unnatural & repugnant to the healthy members of the species would be very difficult to foist on a race with traditions of its own. It is, indeed, rather curious that the Greeks picked it up when they did. Possibly the dark Dorian or Mediterranean half of the race acquired it gradually through their eastern contacts, but there was not a trace of it in the blond Achaians of the Homeric period. It did not spread to Rome until the decadent later-republican period, & was nauseatingly repulsive to the real old Romans of the Punic War days. Sir Richard Burton, the great Orientalist, had a theory of the transmission of this custom along certain geographical lines, & mapped out what he called the "Sotadic Zone",[2] within which it has generally been tolerated. This zone does not include any Nordics, although at present Germany is said to suffer from such perverted attitudes. Whether this degeneracy has invaded CCC camps in America to any *universal* extent I would tend to doubt. I haven't studied the matter, but from casual reports I'd infer that the looseness of CCC boys is largely of the normal sort—involving visits to the shady ladies of the nearby towns. This is disgusting enough to a person of fastidious tastes, but it is perhaps not quite as repugnant as a return to unnatural Graeco-Persian attitudes would be. However, I dare say the extent of perversion is indeed greater today than in the last few centuries. To the non-student this would seem indicated by the changed nature of obscene *graffiti* in public places. But the subject is a narrowly specialised one, & really does not need to be bothered about except by legal & medical specialists. A much larger problem for the sociologist is that afforded by changing concepts of *normal* sex ethics—the growing vogue of complete promiscuity among the younger generation. While of course only the most profound biological & anthropological research can qualify one for intelligent opinions on such a subject, I am inclined to deplore the present trend. To my mind—so far as I can understand & interpret the evidence—certain very valuable emotional elements can be preserved only through the restriction of erotic activity to selected & socially recognised channels; hence I am old-fashioned enough to deplore all extra-matrimonial sex-relations. I would make divorce reasonably easy in order to accomodate changing emotions & to rectify mistakes, but I would discourage furtive, unsanctioned, & carelessly regarded relations as far as possible. Just what the permanent trend will be, no one can yet say. I fear the outlook isn't any too bright for my conservative side, because—as a matter of hard fact—the conditions which established monogamy & its resultant emotions were largely *accidental*, & based on economic factors not likely to be present in the society of the future. However, one can't tell—even the Russian bolsheviks are now encouraging family life!

Yes—I know that Wollheim & Schwartz haven't much use for each other. It is part of a general feud which Wollheim has with the Gernsback magazines & all who favour them. The same feud is what causes Hornig to be cool toward *The Phantagraph*. These quarrels really don't mean much, & one side hasn't much advantage over the other. Schwartz may have his sharp characteristics, but I've found him honest enough. *The Phantagraph* is distinctly worth encouraging, & I shall contribute anything I may happen to have on hand. If you & Rimel haven't any specific use for "The Nameless City" at present you might send it to Wollheim—although you of course have first choice. By the way—another feud which may cause *The Phantagraph* a bit of awkwardness is that between Barlow & Wilson Shepherd, which arose out of an old magazine deal that left both parties feeling aggrieved. Too bad there was confusion about "Two Doors". Keep the cut, though, for there may be a chance of reprinting some time. The design is surely apt & clever indeed.

Too bad you haven't local museum facilities. Hasn't the college any art exhibits at all—plaster casts or such? Providence is really well provided with museums, although we have nothing as extensive as those in Boston & N.Y. The principal art museum—that of the Rhode Island School of Design—is only a block down the hill from here—I can see its glass roof from my window. I have haunted the place ever since I was 7 years old. It has a good collection of classical casts, & an increasing number of original works of art. One of the features is a great Grecian amphora of exquisite workmanship which has put Providence on the aesthetic map in a very literal way. It is the work of an unknown craftsman, but a very *characteristic* artist whose technique can be recognised in thousands of vase-fragments dug up near Athens. Nobody knows his name, but the same touch of workmanship is instantly obvious whenever a sample is found. Now there are hundreds of cases like this—of unknown makers of Greek vases identifiable only through their work—so that a few years ago the artistic & archaeological leaders of the world, under the aegis of the British Museum, decided to devise an *artificial nomenclature* covering such instances. This group, having carefully catalogued *all* the Greek vases in the world's museums, decided to name each unknown artist *after the city or museum where the choicest known specimen of his work happened to be at the time of the cataloguing.* Thus if an unknown craftsman's best piece was in the Berlin New Museum, he would be listed as "The Berlin Painter"; if in the Paris Louvre, as "The Louvre Painter", &c. If two unknown artists had their best pieces in the *same* museum, they would be known as (for example) "Boston Painter No. 1", & "Boston Painter #2". Well—it so happens that the great amphora in our local museum was decided upon as the *best* known sample of its unknown maker's work— hence the international catalogue listed that maker as *"The Providence Painter".*[3] Work of this artist can be found in most of the world's larger museums; & I have great fun when, in taking someone through the Metropolitan in New York or the Fine Arts in Boston, I lead the way up to certain cases & point out vases labelled "By the Providence Painter". I tell such persons that Providence has always been at the front in art matters—even in the days of antique Hellas!

I shall be glad to see the section of "Dr. Crowe" when it is ready. The novel requires a technique & type of planning rather different from those of the short story, but many succeed equally well in both forms. In recent years I have gravitated naturally to longer & longer tales (against the protests of those who like the short ones), until today I find it really difficult to write anything short. This is a great handicap professionally, since novels & novelettes are always difficult to place.

Glad the earthquake didn't disorganise your section of the country. I saw pictures of the Helena damage in several rotogravure sections, but Montana papers may have been more detailed. Thanks for suggesting the loan of cuttings—if you have a ready batch, I wouldn't mind a look.

Autumn continues to average warmish, though we had a 5″ snowfall Nov. 23—earliest in the history of the local weather bureau. Several good lectures recently—W. B. Savery of the U. of Wash. on modern American philosophers, Sir Normal Angell on the muddled international situation, &c. &c.[4] I missed a fine lecture last night—on the latest discoveries in the Athenian agora—because of the cold. It was down to +20°—just my deadline—& I didn't feel quite equal to breasting it. That is the autumn's coldest so far. Not so bad today, so I'll do some shopping.

Best wishes—Yrs most cordially—HPL

[P.S.] Tragic news—Long's aunt[5] was killed instantly in a motor accident near Miami Oct. 20. Barlow has just sent to FBL the surprise volume of the latter's poems which were printed last summer.

[P.P.S.] Holy Yuggoth! Last moment news. *Astounding* has accepted my "Shadow Out of Time" (for $280), which Wandrei submitted to it!

Notes

1. A pioneering novel of lesbianism by Radclyffe Hall.
2. Which Burton derived from Sotades, a 3rd-century B.C.E. Greek poet who was the chief representative of a group of writers of obscene, and sometimes pederastic, satirical poetry.
3. Sir John Beazley, a famous British vase scholar, dubbed the anonymous painter (active in Athens from 480 to 450 B.C.E.) of a large red-figure amphora in the collection of the Rhode Island School of Design Museum in Providence, showing Apollo with a lyre, the "Providence Painter."
4. William Briggs Savery (1875–1945), professor of philosophy at the University of Washington (1902–45) and a follower of George Santayana, William James, and John Dewey. Sir Ralph Norman Angell (1872–1967), British lecturer, journalist, author, and Member of Parliament for the Labour Party. He served on the Council of the Royal Institute of International Affairs, was knighted in 1931, and awarded the Nobel Peace Prize in 1933.
5. Mrs. Cassie Doty Symmes (1872–1935). HPL ghostwrote the preface to her book, *Old World Footprints,* for Frank Belknap Long.

[20] [ALS]

66 College St.,
Providence, R.I.,
Dec. 5, 1935.

Dear Petaja:—

Glad to hear that my previous letter contained matter of interest. That placement of my stuff was surely encouraging, & may possibly start me on a new streak of writing. I believe I mentioned that I've written one new thing—"The Haunter of the Dark"—which will reach you in the course of its circulation. I have two carbons going the rounds.

Commiserations on the cold! I've had hell-raisers in my day, though nowadays they seem to have dissolved into a permanent sinus trouble—which vanishes when I get down to Charleston or Florida. Hope you're all right again by this time.

"The Last Devil" is on its way to you. No hurry about its return. As you will see by the biographical note in the book, Signe Toksvig is the wife of the well-known critic & biographer Francis Hackett.[1] The book is very vivid, although it has its sentimental & amateurish spots. As history, it is not so hot. The witch-cult was an infinitely more sordid & degraded thing than the secret world envisaged by this romancer!

Glad biology seems more interesting as your course advances—& congratulations on your high marks in the Humanities. It is fortunate that you have an instructor really interested in his subject, who teaches classical thought as a living thing rather than according to some desiccated academic tradition.

As to the Homeric poems—I don't think their merit is at all overestimated in common opinion. They really do possess a freshness, vitality, & truth to human nature which entitles them to the front rank in literature. Their use of language is magnificent, & the illustrative images would be hard to improve upon. I prefer the Odyssey to the Iliad, & have always done so. Its story, in simplified juvenile form, was one of the first things I ever read—& was probably what turned my interest away from the Arabian Nights toward the classical world. The origin of the poems is still a puzzle—that is, just how far they can be considered the work of a single author or editor. As you doubtless know, they are the only survivors of a once-ample cycle of epic poetry revolving round the Trojan War.

Regarding the dramatists—though their forms seem artificial & conventional to us, & though their ideas of fate, justice, & the like seem quaint to the modern biologist or psychologist who really understands the mechanical basis of human life & motivation, it is nevertheless impossible to deny their masterly aesthetic power & poignant emotional appeal. They knew the surface of life & action as they saw it, & interpreted it in the manner of their time. The moment one comprehends their perspective, their really majestic qualities become apparent. Of the three, I probably enjoy the grandiose & frankly mythological Æschylus the most. Euripides—the more or less sentimental & almost mawkish pathos-vendor—I like least. Old Sophocles, I believe, was really the greatest of all. But they are all titans, & probably head the world's dramatists with the possible exception of the greatest Elizabethans.

Regarding Socrates—we really know very little about him, since it is only through Plato (whose own philosophy is put into his mouth) that we have any systematic presentation of his ideas. However, by checking Plato with Xenophon's Memorabilia, the quips in Aristophanes, & other ancient references, we can form a general notion of his personality & method. His chief value is as a *clarifier of ideas*—one who made thinkers examine & test the validity of their own mental processes. He was the first to apply systematically the questions: "how do you know this?" & "why do you think so?" His contribution to *accuracy in thinking* was probably very great indeed, although the Sophists (who soon lapsed into ponderous theoretical emptiness, & deserved the lambasting they got in "The Clouds") had begun the epistemological movement which he harnessed & made practically available. As a contributor to the *body of knowledge* he was not great. Indeed, he displayed an annoying indifference toward the higher love of truth for its own sake. He was less a scientific philosopher than an ethical teacher (not that ethical teachers aren't valuable & necessary in their place), & almost despised disinterested enquiry. Modern science, with its instrumental research, would not have appealed to him—indeed, he once rather foolishly ridiculed those who sought for truth [']'with pieces of wood & stone & metal & string such as little boys use in fishing". I have always cared less for Socrates than for the really scientific physical & atomic philosophers of Ionia & their long line of successors—Thales of Miletus, Anaximander, Anaximenes (who vaguely anticipated atomism), Xenophanes, Diogenes of Apollonia (not the later & more famous cynic), Heraclitus, Leucippus & Democritus (the great atomists), Epicurus, &c—who through Lucretius transmitted the tradition of rational materialism & sound investigation & analysis to the modern world. It is the old atomists who stand behind the sound opinions of Santayana & Russell & Dewey today.

Glad Koenig has continued to lend vital books on the shadowy borderlands of folklore. Old Monty Summers[2] is a curious case—an exasperating mediaeval survival with the most childlike credulity ever met with in a man of such undisputed scholarship. Of course one must take every *interpretation* of his not merely with a grain of salt but with a whole ton of salt. Whenever it comes to belief in ultimate causes or things depending on ultimate causes he's absolutely cockeyed—just plain nuts! But his strong points are profound erudition & absolute sincerity, & once you get the hang of his foibles you can sift out the basic data from the horsefeathers & do your own rational deducing from the facts. For the blessed old boob is so utterly honest that he always publishes opposing opinions—as footnotes or otherwise—even when they obviously make his own wild claims look feeble & silly. He gives them, of course, with contempt & hostility—as "damnable materialistic heresies"—but we don't have to mind that. The footnoted theory of the rival whom he damns the loudest is in many cases the plain & logical explanation with which our common sense makes us agree. Some boy, Monty!

Now about the actual anthropological realities underlying the phenomena of systematical witchcraft—let's take one thing at a time. Curious, but I thought we had discussed this before. The anthropologist whom Summers so bitterly attacks, but who is probably about 85% right despite such minor slips as the confusion of *Roodmas* with *May-Eve* (a thing about which Summers makes an absurdly disproportionate fuss), is Miss Margaret Alice Murray of the University of London, a leading student of Egyptology & general anthropology who ranks with the foremost scientific authorities of the day. Her book "The Witch Cult in Western Europe", published in 1921, is the recognised classic in its field. I wish you could get hold of it, but it is infernally hard to find. I read it a decade ago. Briefly, Miss Murray shows that a furtive organisation of low-grade secret worshippers really did exist throughout antiquity, the middle ages, & the early modern period, & that their rites, meetings, & malevolent deeds (poisoning, cattle-stealing, intimidation, psychological influencing, &c.) form the basis of the traditional accounts of witchcraft. This fact Miss Murray believes to be established through the similarity of the evidence given in hundreds of minutely reported witch trials throughout Europe. She furthermore believes, from the *nature* & *season* of the reported rites & practices as correlated with the vast data of comparative mythology, (see some such book as Frazer's "Golden Bough"—of which Koenig can lend you 3 odd volumes) that this evil organisation was not connected with any known sect of historic times (i.e., Druidic, Gnostic, Manichaean, Dionysiac, &c.); but was instead of vast & incalculable antiquity, antedating the settlement of the Aryan tribes in Europe & probably originally forming the dominant fertility-religion of a Mongol population whose last survivors are the Lapps of northern Scandinavia. The great festivals of such a religion would almost certainly be at the breeding-seasons of the flocks & herds—& surely enough, the two great "witch-sabbats" (April 30 & Oct. 31) fall at such dates, while the orgiastic rites follow closely the pattern immemorially found in known fertility-cults. This was doubtless an openly practiced & unchallenged religion around 30,000 B.C. or so, when the Lapps covered western Europe. Then the Aryans came, & an eternal struggle between their polytheistic pantheism & the Mongol fertility rites began. When the Aryans became all-powerful, they doubtless suppressed the older rites very drastically—for to the Aryan mind these latter were not only hideously repulsive but profoundly evil. Thus the ancient fertility religion was driven underground (like Jewish worship in Spain under the Inquisition), to be secretly practiced in increasingly corrupt form by people who stole forth at night unknown to their neighbours. In time, certain lawless, shiftless, abnormal, & oppressed individuals among the conquering Aryans filtered into the secret religious cult, for it offered them an escape from accustomed restrictions & repressions. And of course, after thousands of years the comparatively few surviving Lapps (except in the north, whither the majority fled) were absorbed & lost in the Aryan population, so that there was no longer any racial difference between the renegades & degenerates who carried on the underground faith, & the dominant majority who tried to stamp that faith out. Modern anthropologists call this faith a *Dianic* cult because its central essence helped to mould the conception of that primitive earth-&-moon goddess to whom the name *Diana* (before that name became transferred to the Greek virgin huntress moon goddess Artemis) was applied in Italy. It is curious to note that when the Roman fused their mythology with Greece's, they chose to purify the concept of their moon-goddess & identify her with Artemis, whereas the *old* native Italian *Diana* was really much closer to the Greek *Hecaté*. Traces of the old & horrible Diana can be found in the ritual of the famous Temple at Aricia, by the Lacus Nemorensis. Well—what happened was simply the gradual transformation of the suppressed faith from a true religion to a mere clique of degeneracy, bestiality, malevolence, & orgiastic escape from austere Aryan group-codes. It was crushed & trodden down by Druids, Graeco-Romans, & Christians alike, yet survived somehow (in all probability) till a period about 200 years ago.

Of the *existence* of the cult very few thoughtful students are now sceptical. Where opinion is divided, is on the question of just *what* it was. Old Doc Summers thinks it was a cult of heretics or opponents of orthodox (Catholic) Christianity—whether real seceders, or groups influenced by Gnosticism & Manichaeism. He thus repudiates the idea of its Mongol origin & vast antiquity. Oddly enough, the rigid rationalist & agnostic writer Joseph McCabe[3] agrees with him—although he thinks the cult was originally a *justified* reaction or revolt against the repressiveness of Christianity. McCabe has a curious sympathy with the cult, & seems to overlook its utterly degenerate features. His actively bitter prejudice against Christian beliefs & ethics gives him as bad an emotional bias as Summers! I myself—a rank layman, of course—am inclined to lean largely toward the Murray theory of a very ancient Dianic cult. Miss Murray may be wrong on details—we can't, for example, be sure just *who* the founders of the fertility-religion were . . . whether Lapps, Cro-Magnards, Grimaldi men,[4] or any of the other races who scattered & fought their way over western Europe between the heyday of the Neanderthals & the coming of the Aryan. I agree with Miss M. that the ritual of the cult comes too close to very primitive forms to admit of any origin as recent as Christian times.

Now as to the MANICHEES or MANICHÆANS whose names (together with the names of such derivative sects as the Paulicians, Albigenses, Lollards, &c) are frequently brought into this matter. To begin with, I don't think they had a damn thing to do with the witch cult. They were simply the members of an ancient religio-philosophic sect or line of tradition originally non-Christian but eventually mixed with unorthodox Christian sects & regarded as a "heresy" from Catholicism rather than as a separate religion. This line of philosophy was subtle, ethereal, maturely cultivated, & highly moral & ascetic—the product of learned & civilised Oriental sources as opposed to savage sources. Its adherents were usually people of purer lives than those of orthodox Christians—the sect being a sort of ancient form of Puritanism. There may have been a degeneration toward the last, just as all sects (cf. Buddhism in Thibet, Brahmanism in India, &c.) degenerate under certain conditions; but without question all the persecution inflicted by the mediaeval church was caused by theological prejudice alone. We cannot compare the savage attacks on the Albigenses in the early 13ᵗʰ century—a vicious slaughter of innocent & virtuous people—with the justified pressure exerted alike by church & state against the bestial degenerates of the furtive witch cult.

As for the origin of the Manichaean type of thought & faith—it goes away back to Alexandrian times . . . approximately the same period when Christianity arose. It was an obscure & mystical sect which sprang up in the near East under the name of GNOSTICISM (the word derived from the Greek verb meaning *to know*), & which drew its various elements from Hindoo, Persian, Egyptian, Jewish, Babylonian & primitive Christian sources—mixing them with liberal doses of conventional astrology & magic. The earliest exponent of this doctrine was the shadowy Simon Magus, mentioned in the New Testament (Acts VIII).⁵ Gnosticism involved cabalistic rites, talismans, & images, & laid great stress on the supposed duality of the universe—good & evil, light & darkness—an idea clearly taken from Persian sources (Ahura-Mazda, Alvimanos, &c.). It exalted a god called *Abraxas*—the Cthulhu or Yog-Sothoth of his day—who looked like a sort of tripartite cross between a rooster, a man, & a pair of snakes. However, there were factions with far less gross beliefs; & in the 3d century A.D. the sect got a tremendous boost through the influence of a bird called *Mani*—a Persian of the new Sassanian Empire who proclaimed himself a prophet in 241 A.D. & founded a system (drawn from Gnostic sources) with which he hoped to supplant the old Persian religion. Henceforward, after him, the main stream of this kind of mystical thought was called *Manichaeism*. In the late imperial period, when declining culture & advancing Orientalism undermined all the older faiths & philosophies, the three leading systems of belief were *neo-Platonism*, which formed a sort of etherealised projection of Greek thought; *Christianity*, which joined Hellenistic cult-elements to a Jewish foundation; & the *Gnostic-Manichaean* type of faith (to which the extremely popular Persian cult of Mithras was closely allied). Around 300 A.D. it was about an even toss-up which of these three would become the dominant & official faith of the empire. One was about as good as the other, so that it merely became a question of relative popularity. Christianity won through pure chance—because the shrewd & unscrupulous emperor Constantinus thought he could best use it as an instrument of policy. Once this religion became official, it turned at once against its rivals & began to persecute them just as it had itself been persecuted by the older State religion. Nevertheless both Neoplatonism & Manichaeism continued to flourish side by side with the lucky winner—so that the forcible suppression of both was attempted. In 529 A.D. the eastern emperor Justinianus cracked down on both—indeed making the profession of Manichaean faith a capital offence. It is curious that the Gnostic-Manichaean strain persisted more tenaciously than the Neoplatonic—cropping out, as we have seen, in the Paulicians, Albigenses, &c. Amusingly enough, in recent years Neoplatonism has been used as the foundation of one of those cheap sucker-catching fake cults (Rosicrucian, &c.) which hold forth in Southern California & advertise in the low-grade magazines. Before long, there'll probably be some mystical branch of the Gnostics advertising in *Weird Tales* & telling how to conquer the Powers of Darkness on the style of Mani or Simon Magus!

Well—I trust I've helped to clear up the question of the witch-cult just a bit. I wish you would get hold of the Murray book, but am damned if I know how you can. I'd give a lot to own a copy. Too bad about La Bas. Some day I may try to get a copy to replace the lost one.

Bits of good luck to report. Young Schwartz, to whom, as a literary agent, I languidly & sceptically entrusted the "Mts. of Madness" MS. at his earnest solicitation, has actually sold the tale to *Astounding Stories!* The event really astounds me, for I can't imagine anything *less* fitted to the magazine's policy than this frankly un-pulpish yarn. Got a cheque for $315.00 (350 less Schwartz's 10% commission) a few days ago. Not so bad—wish I could depend on A S as a steady market, though I know damn well I can't! The publication of this item—so contemptuously rejected by Wright, who will use nothing *long* of mine—is certainly an encouraging incident. Maybe the psychic influence of your note in the August Eyrie had its subtle & ethereal effect!

Did I mention my delightful trip to New Haven Oct. 8, when the pseudo-archaic Yale quadrangles so intensely fascinated me? Oct 16–18 I was in Boston—with the poet Samuel Loveman, who came in from N.Y. We absorbed bookstalls, museums, & general antiquities—spending a good deal of the time in the Greek & Egyptian departments of the Museum of Fine Arts. Later we scoured the bookstalls of Providence quite thoroughly. The autumn has been phenomenally warm—an almost record-breaking October in that respect—so that I've been able to postpone hibernation to a surprising extent. Out to the woods & fields day after day. From what I hear of Montana temperatures (Hope the Helena 'quakes haven't been rocking you!), you haven't been having quite as good luck. ¶ Excellent lecture course on art going on at the college. I lately heard Prof. H. A. Overstreet (whose books I have read) speak on the future of American art as affected by economics.[6]

All good wishes—

Yrs most cordially—

H P L

Notes

1. Francis Hackett (1883–1962), Irish writer most famous for a detailed book about Henry VIII but also a noted critic and author of nonfiction or biographies. Danish writer Signe Toksvig (1891–1983) also wrote a biography of Hans Christian Andersen.

2. Montague Summers (1880–1948), British editor, ecclesiastic, and occult scholar; author of *The Geography of Witchcraft* (1927), *The Vampire: His Kith and Kin* (1928), *The Vampire in Europe* (1929), *A Gothic Bibliography* (1938), and others.

3. Joseph McCabe (1867–1955), well-known philosopher, historian, and freethinker, author of such works as *The Evolution of Mind* (1910) and *The Story of Evolution* (1912). He also translated Ernst Haeckel's *The Riddle of the Universe* (1900).

4. The name formerly given to two human skeletons of the Upper Paleolithic discovered in Italy in 1901.

5. See Acts 8:9–24 for the confrontation of Simon the Sorcerer with Peter. *Simony*, or paying for position and influence in the church, is named after Simon.

6. H[arry] A[llen] Overstreet (1875–1970), chairman of the department of philosophy and psychology at City College of New York (1911–36) and author of *The Enduring Quest: A Search for a Philosophy of Life* (1931) and other works.

[21]   [ALS]

66 College St.,
Providence, R.I.,
Feby. 6, 1936.

Dear Petaja:—

No need to apologise for slow writing—for as you see, my own correspondence is wholly beyond control. I visited Long in N.Y. around New Year's, & when I got back I found a hopeless accumulation of tasks awaiting me. My programme was completely disrupted, & I still have almost 30 letters—some of them postmarked as far back as Dec. 30. Nor is daylight yet in sight. Last week I was down with the grippe, & lost 5 or 6 days completely—& even now my strength is not sufficient to let me work long at a time.

I am extremely sorry to hear of your mother's illness, & trust she is by this time wholly well again. Your late autumn & Christmas season was surely a strenuous one, & I hope you have at least a little more leisure now. Very glad to learn of your excellent examination marks. You are certainly getting the most out of your courses—& are evidently the kind of student whom instructors ought to appreciate. That "A" in the Humanities course is surely something to be proud of.

Glad you enjoyed "The Last Devil"—which certainly is an absorbing story despite its obvious limitations. No hurry about its return. The author once had a story in W.T.[1]—which was not nearly as good as this. I don't know of any recent work of hers. No hurry about the Munn portrait, either. By the

way—I actually had a note from Munn this Christmas—first in about 3 yrs.—
& imagine that your letters to him were instrumental in stirring him up. Now
I hope he'll write W. Paul Cook & settle up the various book matters calling
for discussion!

Hope both "Viking" & "Pipers of Kallinen" will appear in print soon. By
this time you have doubtless seen the second issue of *The Phantagraph*—which
is, it must be admitted, a rather poor piece of printing. Typography is evidently
something new to Shepherd, so that one can excuse the crudities of this first
issue, but one hopes he will improve shortly. Some of the misprints—such as
that of *MEMNON*, which is repeated—are rather hard to forgive. Some of the
linoleum cuts came out very well, & we may heartily congratulate Rimel on his
work as art editor. I've forgotten whether *all* the cuts are his, or whether some of
them are yours. Anyhow, they are all good. Perhaps some of the copies printed
better than others. Wollheim still has hopes for the new fiction magazine—
though these things always take shape slowly. You might send W. "The Nameless City" some time if you have it around—though I presume there's no hurry.

I was rather pleased with the appearance of "Mts. of Madness" in
Astounding—the illustrations are good, & the artist[2] represented the Nameless
Entities perfectly though he had only a written description to go by. "Innsmouth" will not appear in the magazine, but will be printed by Crawford—
both in *Marvel Tales* & as an separate booklet. I am reading proofs now. I
don't know when "The Shadow out of Time" will appear. The Jan. W T had
a reprint of "Dagon", & I am told that something else of mine is reprinted
this month[3]—though I haven't secured a copy of the latest issue. Haven't had
a chance to read anything whatever in over a month, anyhow!

I'm surely glad you are enjoying your Humanities course. I myself don't
care as much for the Middle Ages as for Roman antiquity, but everyone has
his own tastes. A year ago I wrote rather a long article on Roman architecture
& how it petered out in the mediaeval period, but unfortunately it seems to
have been lost by the friend to whom it was sent.[4] I note with interest your
mention of "The Kalevala", which I have for years been meaning to read.
Last year I noticed many references to the centenary of its first collected publication—the edition of Dr. Elias Lonnrot. I must look up a good translation
somewhere—for the material is obviously of the sort to interest me greatly. I
must, too, become familiar with the work of Sibelius. It is very remarkable
that your instructor had *never heard* of the Kalevala, for the epic has been fairly
well known in England & America since the publication of Lonnrot's edition.
Indeed, as you probably know, Longfellow knew it well & chose its curiously
haunting metre for his own "Hiawatha". But certainly, all too few have really
read it—which reminds me that there is a vast body of mediaeval & renaissance literature about which everybody knows, but which the average layman
has seldom actually read. How many ordinary persons, for example, have *read*
Tasso's "Jerusalem Delivered", (I have a copy of Fairfax's translation) Ario-

sto's "Orlando Furioso", &c.? "Beowulf" is read in schools because it is directly ancestral to English literature—the historical as well as the literary element entering in. I own a copy of it.[5] Another vivid relique of northern antiquity is provided by the Eddas & Sagas, of which better & more unified translations ought to exist. I have read only fragments of these—but much in northern mythology fascinates me extremely. The lore of Finland, I imagine, differs considerably from that of the rest of the Scandinavia because of the unique Turanian element behind the culture & language. It would probably have links with the lore of Hungary, & other regions where the Finno-Ugorian or Ural-Altaic languages & cultures are dominant. Like the Teutonic mythologies, it doubtless personifies the forces of nature—but probably in a different way. I suppose the Kalevala itself is about the best summing-up of the mythology which one could secure.

Koenig has been in N.Y. except for a short trip to an electrical engineers' convention at Boca Raton, Fla. (on his return from which he explored old Charleston, following an itinerary I prepared for him), but has been so busy that I imagine his correspondence has suffered. He couldn't get to our general group meeting at Long's last month, & I didn't have a chance to see him during my brief sojourn in N.Y.

Glad to hear that your college has a few typical art objects—even if they are not of the most perfect or pretentious sort. A small & primitive collection is often very useful if supplemented with good photographic views of masterpieces. Congratulations on the new building & the various travelling exhibits & performances it accomodated. I wonder if you'll get the migratory exhibit of contemporary British painting which was here last autumn. The dance exhibition & lecture were doubtless notable—though choreography is an art which I can appreciate even less than music. Glad the school orchestra is good, & that you have visits from its illustrious Seattle contemporary.[6] I surely hope you can secure a place in this organization next year.

Don't hurry about your story, though I'll be glad to see it when it is ready. And don't worry about the lost earthquake cuttings—many of which, including the most vivid & typical[,] were probably duplicated in the eastern papers I have seen. Hope you'll collaborate with Rimel on the weird music article. Why not try to get in touch with the weird composer who set two of my Fungi to music? He is Harold Farnese, 4001 S. Harvard Blvd., Los Angeles, Cal.

Some very cold weather during the past few weeks—snow on the ground, & temperature once as low as +5° . . . . which is pretty low for Providence. I've been out of the house only twice since my return from N.Y.

My visit, though only of a week's duration, was very enjoyable. I saw the old group—Long, the two Wandreis, Morton, Loveman, Leeds, Kleiner, Talman, Kirk, &c.—& met several new figures (Arthur J. Burks, Otto Binder, Donald Wollheim, &c.) for the first time. At a dinner of the Am. Fiction Guild I saw good old Seabury Quinn for the first time since 1931. On two occasions I visited the new Hayden Planetarium & found it extremely fascinating. It is a complete & well-equipped centre of popular astronomical instruction, & draws crowds of surprising size. I never realised that astronomy was getting to be so popular, but I suppose the spectacular discoveries of the past 30 years—plus the increased hold of all science on the public mind—have aroused the majority to a new & unprecedented interest in it. The planetarium has one hall shewing the motions of the solar system, & another (up under the great dome) shewing the sidereal heavens. There are also on display astronomical books, instruments, & reliques of every kind. Lectures—a different one each month—are given several times each day. I wish some such thing had existed when I was young—although I ought not to complain, since I had the run of a real observatory. There are now many such planeteria in Europe. In America, besides the N.Y. one, there are specimens in Philadelphia, Chicago, & Los Angeles. At this N.Y one small planispheres—charts revolving in frames to shew the sky as seen at any hour on any day of the year—are sold for 25¢— the cheapest I ever encountered. I got one apiece for Belknap & Wandrei, so that they'll make fewer mistakes about the constellations in future stories!

Rimel tells me that he has at last sold a story to W.T.[7] Good stuff! I always like to see a new writer get a start. I knew he'd land something sooner or later—& before long you'll be doing the same. He employed Otis Adelbert Klein [*sic*] (whose son in N.Y. I saw again last month) as agent.

All good wishes, & hope you can excuse this sadly inadequate scrawl. Yrs most sincerely—HPL

[P.S.] Hornig made a trip to New Orleans around New Year's, & had a good time despite rather bad weather.

[P.P.S.] Here's a circular of a new book by my friend Loveman—published not so far from your region![8]

Notes

1. Signe Toksvig, "The Devil's Martyr" (*WT*, June 1928).
2. Howard V. Brown (1878–1945) illustrated both *At the Mountains of Madness* and "The Shadow out of Time."
3. "The Temple."
4. "A Living Heritage: Roman Architecture in Today's America." HPL's friend Maurice W. Moe had lost the article but later found it among his papers.
5. *LL* 1078; specific edition unknown.
6. HPL may be referring to his correspondent Helen V. Sully, a violinist, who took classes in Seattle in 1936.
7. "The Disinterment" (1935) did not appear until January 1937.
8. The Caxton Printers of Caldwell, ID, were located more than 350 miles from Milltown.

[22]   [ALS]

66 College St.,
Providence, R.I.,
April 1, 1936

Dear Petaja:—

This will be more of a stop-gap than a real epistle—for such is the chaos around me that coherent & leisurely writing is impossible. I thought my schedule was badly awry before—but now it has simply exploded! For no sooner was my own grippe attack well over, than my aunt suffered a far severer attack of the same trouble; a thing which demanded all my time as nurse, market-man, errand-boy, & what not. Complications set in, & now my aunt is at the hospital—through at last recovering steadily.[1] All my own affairs are hopelessly sunk. Letters remain neglected, unread books pile up, & revision jobs have to be returned unperformed. Heaven knows when I'll ever get straightened out—though naturally, my aunt is a much worse sufferer than I!

Glad your college work progresses well. No haste at all about the Munn picture & Toksvig book. Glad Rimel is illustrating "The Nameless City"—I had not expected any pictorial embellishments! Hope you've seen a copy of *The Phantagraph* by this time. Some of the linoleum cuts came out well despite the execrably bad typography. You surely make a valuable addition to the illustrating staff!

I've now seen all three instalments of "Mts of Madness"—good illustrations throughout. Utpatel is illustrating the edition of "Innsmouth" which Crawford intends to publish. Hope your tale & poem land with W T. That weird musical article sounds highly promising. Hope I can get hold of that "Devil is not Dead" article.[2] The portraits would be very welcome—I've never seen one of Stoker.

Yes—I believe it is agreed more & more nearly unanimously that Sibelius is the greatest living composer. I must try to hear some of his greater works, even though my musical knowledge & taste approach zero. I'm sure it is erroneous to assume that the field of music is too exhausted to produce any new first-rate composer. As with the other arts, there are always fresh emphases & recombinations which express the artistic emotion & incorporate authentic symbols of his personality.

The Middle Ages are certainly not without their fascination—even if one does not care for their intellectual outlook or customs. After all, any period which produced the Gothic cathedral can't be dismissed without a hearing!

It interests me vastly to hear that Longfellow adopted more than the metre from the "Kalevala". I had thought that Indian legends, plus original embellishments, formed the entire substance of "Hiawatha". I must get hold of the K. sooner or later . . . . & meanwhile I hope to read your folklore article in *The Phantagraph*. I own a copy of "Beowulf."

By the way—have any W. H. Hodgson books (belonging to Koenig) reached you on their circulation rounds? There is some confusion as to the volumes forwarded by Dwyer. I'm swamped with borrowed books which I haven't time to read.

Jan. & Feb. W T issues very poor—saved only by Moore stories.[3] March unusually good—the tales by Binder, C A S, Hamilton, & Kuttner being above the average.[4] Kuttner is a California youth who has copied certain features of my prose style.

Price expects to make an eastern trip in May, at which time I hope to see him. He has a new Hudson car with almost unlimited speed.

Spring is here at last—but floods (as if to match your Montanan earthquakes) have come with it. Providence—like most seaports—has escaped the engulfing waters.

Again let me apologise for this inadequate scrawl. Hope to do better when my programme is straightened out.

Yrs most sincerely & appreciatively—

HPL

Notes

1. In fact, Annie Gamwell was diagnosed with breast cancer and underwent a mastectomy.

2. Basil Davenport, "The Devil Is Not Dead," *Saturday Review of Literature* 13, No. 16 (15 February 1936): 3–4. It mentions Arthur Machen.

3. "The Dark Land" (January 1936) and "Yvala" (February 1936).

4. Eando Binder, "The Crystal Curse"; Clark Ashton Smith, "The Black Abbot of Puthuum" Edmond Hamilton "The Creaking House"; Henry Kuttner, "The Graveyard Rats."

[23] [ALS]

66 College St.,
Providence, R.I.
May 19, 1936.

Dear Petaja:—

Chaos still reigns here in the form of a crowded programme & enfeebled energies, but my aunt is now well on the road to recovery. She returned home April 21, & is now constantly up & about—taking walks each sunny afternoon, though still needing considerable help around the house. I shall feel stronger when continuous warm weather comes. April was vilely cold—no decent day till the 28th. Since then I've been able to take my work out to Prospect Terrace several times—& on April 30 my aunt & I were treated to a delightful ride through the awakening countryside to Westport Point, Mass. The landscape is now a captivating spectacle with its new verdure & abundant blossoms, & I hope to find time for some rural walks ere long. Barlow has invited me down to De Land again, but I greatly doubt my ability to accept.

Your art work is certainly splendid—indeed, you & Rimel are the artistic salvation of *The Phantagraph*. No recent progress on the "Innsmouth" book—though Utpatel's illustrations are now made into cuts. Sorry to hear that your MSS. have not yet landed.

Congratulations on the praise of Professors Clark & Merriam! Hope you can arrange for a scholarship—& glad you have meanwhile landed a tutoring job. Your athlete must form quite a problem—like some of the alleged authors who expect me to help them write stories! I wish you luck in your pedagogical debut! Meanwhile your own course—Faust, modern music, &c.— seems to be admirably interesting.

Glad you safely have the Hodgson & other books. "The Night Land" has great stuff in it, but is wretchedly bad in many ways—a hideously inept & inaccurate attempt at archaic prose, sickening sentimentality, verboseness, &c. &c. It is, in the long run, very much worth wading through. Of these, all *except "The Golem"* are to go to Rimel. "The Golem" is a wholly different proposition—Barlow's, not Koenig's book, & circulating in another direction. Rimel has read it, & it is to go from you (but no hurry at all) to R. F. SEARIGHT, 19946 DERBY AVE., DETROIT, MICH., & from him back to the owner—R. H. BARLOW, BOX 88, DE LAND, FLORIDA. You'll find "The Golem" a very subtle, haunting, & unusual novel. Superior from an artistic standpoint to anything of Hodgson's. Meyrink is a living German author,[1] but "The Golem" was written 30 or 40 years ago.

Haven't had time to read the May W T as yet, but fear it won't equal Mar. & April issues. I suppose the June *Astounding* with my "Shadow Out of Time" is now on the stands, but I've had no opportunity to get it.

Don't know how Munn fared amidst the floods—but I saw some pictures of the Millers River on the rampage. 1936 seems to be a bad year for many—both of Long's parents having been ill, Wandrei being in miserable health, Barlow half laid up, Clark Ashton Smith nearly driven to the wall with the care of his place & of his increasingly feeble father, & Robert E. Howard gravely worried about his mother's health.

I was very glad to see your two new poems—both of which are really extremely good. You surely have the true poetic instinct—knowledge of what to say & how to say it—& I hope each of the enclosed may find publication in a suitable medium. "Asphodel" could be good for the *weird* magazines—why not try it successively on W T, *Marvel*, & *The Phantagraph*? [By the way, there's a new fan magazine called *The Planeteer* (pub. by Wm. Miller Jr. 69 Halsted St, E. Orange, N.J.)[2] which seems to be looking for bizarre bits.] Well—I've taken the liberty of suggesting a change or two in the recent specimens (explained in margins) which I hope you'll find useful.

R.I. Tercentenary observances are beginning. A fortnight ago there was a costumed parade which started almost at our door—followed by a mock-session of the legislature of May 4, 1776 in the same room in the ancient colony house, where the real session was held 160 years ago.[3]

All good wishes—

Yrs most sincerely—

H P L

Notes

1. Actually, Gustav Meyrink had died in 1932.
2. James Blish (1921–1975) and William Miller, Jr. (1921–1979?) published several issues of a mimeographed fanzine entitled the *Planeteer*.
3. HPL attended this event. See p. 349.

[24] [ALS]

66 College St.,
Providence, R.I.,
July 9, 1936

Dear Petaja:—

Very glad to hear the news, & to learn that your studies are progressing so brilliantly. I surely hope you win the scholarship—& that next year you will duplicate your fine current record. The new studies of the present summer quarter sound very attractive, & I'm sure you'll do them justice. It is indeed fortunate that you have an instructor as capable & well-grounded as Prof. Curry. He undoubtedly appreciates your ability & serious application—a happy contrast to the perfunctory listlessness of the average student. Glad you managed to squeeze your footballer through on one subject, & hope the winter-quarter repetition will prove equally successful. All this certainly forms splendid pedagogical experience—& success under the eyes of your teachers will count you in good stead as you pursue your career. Glad you have found a congenial associate in the professor's son whom you mention.

My own recent annals are very uneventful. My aunt continues to improve, but my own health has been very indifferent—nervous exhaustion & bad digestion being supplemented by the effect of persistent cold weather. Warm days are rare—whereas it would take a solid week or two of 90° temperatures to set me on my feet. Work is still in chaos—though a titanic file-cleaning early in June (I worked steadily for 4 days, including 2 nights of sacrificed slumber) has helped to clarify things a bit. I must have thrown away a couple of tons of junk.

My story in the June *Astounding* is rather badly printed but not seriously mangled. When I tried to correct the magazine version of the "Mts. of Madness" I was utterly sickened by the wholesale mutilation. To all intents & purposes, the "Mts" is still unpublished!

Glad you've sent *The Planeteer* a good item. I've never seen the magazine, & am rather curious to know just what it looks like. I note your disclaimer of the "Goblin Tower" review. It is provoking to have other people's material attributed to one! If you'd like to see "The Goblin Tower" I'll lend you my rather poor copy—the only one I have, though Barlow promised me another. I've no idea when Crawford will finish "Innsmouth"—he & Barlow are just about tied for the tardiness championship! Recently I saw some advance pages from the future *Fanciful Tales* of Wollheim & Shepherd, & believe the magazine won't be quite as crude as I had feared. I also received the recent *Fantasy Magazine*—which seems to be retrograding.

Yes—this has been a singularly unlucky year for everybody. Miss Moore's fiancé was instantly killed last February in a hunting accident. But the really paralysing blow is one which I have only recently heard—& which I wish I could see denied as a hoax. I refer to the report that Robert E. Howard committed suicide. It seems incredible—for I had a long normal letter from him as recently as May 13. He was worried about his mother's health, but otherwise seemed perfectly all right. I can't understand the tragedy, for although R E H had a moody side (as expressed in his hatred of civilisation), he seemed personally very well adjusted to his environment. If this is true, weird fiction has suffered its worst loss since good old Whitehead's death in '32. There was nobody else quite like Two-Gun Bob—for his tales had a sincerity & vitality achieved by no other popular fantaisiste. He was in every one of them himself. I'll let you know anything further which I hear about this melancholy matter. And just to add to 1936's bad record—I lately learned of the deaths of Montague Rhodes James at the age of 73, & of George Allan England at the age of 59.

One of the items in my attempted conquest of chaos has been a reading-up of recent W T issues. Poor old Two-Gun plainly dominates them with his splendid serial & short story. How he could surround primal megalithic cities with an aura of aeon-old fear & necromancy! His "Black Canaan"[1] is potent in a more realistic way—reflecting a genuine regional backgro[und &] giving a clutchingly powerful picture of the horror that st[alks] through the moss-hung, shadow-cursed, serpent-ridden swamps of the far south. Bloch is doing well—& Kuttner is up & coming, though still imitative & experimental. I didn't think much of Quinn's opus[2]—an obvious bid for cheap sensational interest. It spoke of Petersburg & Alexandria before those towns existed, & I think the science was a bit askew in spots. Comte D'Erlette's yarn wasn't bad, & Burks just missed creating something powerful. M. J. Bardine's "Harbour of Ghosts" has promise & atmosphere, as has Shane's "Lethe". In the long run, though, R E H's stuff is the only first rate material. Yuggoth, what a loss!

Glad you've been seeing some Providence material. Recently two of the most famous colonial mansions on the ancient hill—somewhat south of here—were thrown open as public museums. Enclosed is a folder about one of them. This Brown house is really unsurpassed in classic elegance—John

Quincy Adams was right![3] The other place—the Edward Carrington house—is of later date (1809), & of a less classical interior arrangement. I believe I told you of my visit in May to Rhode-Island's oldest house—built in 1654.[4] ¶ *Later*—just had word from Two-Gun's father. Sad report is all too true. R E H shot himself when he learned his mother's illness was fatal. Double funeral. Shock to poor old Dr. Howard must be unbearable—wife & splendid only child gone at one blow. R E H's melancholy streak must have gone deeper than we thought—for most can take the inevitable loss of the elder generation more philosophically. ¶ Best wishes—H P L

Notes

1. *WT,* June 1936. It also contained Bloch's "The Grinning Ghoul," Kuttner's "Ballad of the Wolf," Bardine's "Harbor of Ghosts," Harold G. Shane's "Lethe," and August Derleth's "The Telephone in the Library."

2. "Strange Interval" (*WT,* May 1936). The story describes the capture and flogging of Colonel Willoughby Moncure Munro by pirates. When a beautiful woman captive of the pirates refuses the advances of the skipper and shows favor to Willoughby, the pirates stage a mock wedding, castrate Willoughby (whose voice laughably becomes high and feminine), cut his beard, pierce his ears for women's earrings, comb his hair in women's fashion, dress him in women's attire, and force him to watch the rape of the woman, Carmelita. Willoughby assumes a new life as "Joaquina" having become nearly thoroughly "feminized," and his relationship with Carmelita takes on a lesbianlike turn.

3. HPL refers to the John Brown House (1786–88), 52 Power Street; now home of the Rhode Island Historical Society. John Quincy Adams stated in his diary that it was "the most magnificent and elegant private mansion that I have ever seen on this continent."

4. John Corliss built the original two-story part of the Edward Carrington House (1810; 1812), 66 Williams Street, in 1810. Margarethe Dwight (1871–1962), a descendant of Carrington, gave the house and many of its furnishings to the Museum of Art, Rhode Island School of Design as a museum showing the influence of the China trade in New England. It has been a private residence since 1931. The Thomas Clemence house outside Manton was built in 1654.

[25] [ALS]

66 College St.,
Providence, R.I.
Aug. 27, 1936.

Dear Petaja:—

R E H's suicide is surely the most tragic event to hit weird circles in recent years. Possibly you have heard the particulars by this time. He shot himself upon being told that his mother could not live more than 48 hours more—dying 8 hours later without regaining consciousness. 30 hours after that his mother died. The blow to poor old Dr. Howard must be terrific—wife & splendid only child gone at one stroke—but he is bearing up like a true Texas pioneer. He has given his son's books to the latter's alma mater—Howard Payne College in Brownwood—as the nucleus of a Robert E. Howard Memorial Collection. Mrs. Howard had been gravely ill with a pleural trouble for over a year, & I knew Two-Gun Bob was worried. I did not, however, think he would resort to so desperate an act. Most of us realise the grim inevitability of the elder generation's passing, hence accept these bereavements philosophically despite the keenest sorrow. Evidently R E H's moody streak—as manifest in his hatred of civilisation—ran deeper than we ever suspected. *Conan* would have shed a tear, performed the funeral rites, & moved on to new slayings. Obviously he was not quite autobiographical! But of course nobody is quite like the characters he depicts. Even the most virile-penned of authors is at bottom just an average guy like the banker, plumber, or soda clerk! As to suicide in general—it's foolish if one hasn't a real reason for it, but sensible when one has no possible chance of securing endurable living conditions. I shall probably take an overdose of something or other when my cash gives out & I can no longer hang on to my library & cherished family possessions. The mere cessation of consciousness is really nothing to get excited about. There will be many obituaries of Two-Gun published during the months to come.[1] Barlow has written a remarkably good elegiac sonnet which Wright has accepted for W T.[2] Too bad his first professional acceptance has to have so tragic a background. Your own sonnet is excellent indeed, & ought to achieve publication eventually. In its present form I notice some obscurity—doubtful syntax—early in the octave, & also a false rhyme (syllable rhymed with itself) toward the end. I wish I had time to suggest alternative passages—but anyhow, I return the text with annotations in the hope that you will be able to do the emendations without trouble.

I don't envy you your typing job! Hope the revision of "Rene" will prove satisfying, & that the final version will land professionally. The advice of your instructor will surely be helpful. I liked the music article in *The Phantagraph* very much, & only wish the full version could have been printed. That letter from Two-Gun about "Dream W[arrior?]" is surely worth preserving with pride.[3]

Had a pleasant call from young Sterling—now in Lynn, Mass. & about to enter Harvard in the autumn—June 30. Took an enjoyable Newport trip July 11—exploring the ancient town & doing considerable writing on the oceanward cliffs. July 18–19 I had a delightful visit from my old friend M. W. Moe of Milwaukee (poet-teacher) & his gifted son Robert (the latter the youth who was here with his car in the spring of '35), & we covered quite a bit of scenic & historic ground in the all-too-brief 2 days at our disposal. Weather favoured us greatly, for we had warmth & sun throughout—whereas the very next day was damp & cold, with myself heavily blanketed & shivering over an oil heater.

Had an interesting view of Peltier's comet on July 22 at the Ladd Observatory of Brown University—through a 12″ telescope. The object shewed a small disc with a hazy, fan-like tail. I could have seen it through my own small glass (3″) were the northern sky less obstructed in the vicinity of #66.

Later local news is pleasant—consisting of nothing less than *Barlow's* arrival in Providence for a stay which will end Sept. 1st. Some property adjustments about the De Land place are occurring, & R H B thought this would be a good time to pay me a visit & make his headquarters in ancient New England for a while. I surely was glad to see him—& I forgave him the fierce-looking moustache & sidewhiskers he has grown! He secured a room at the boarding-house across the garden from 66, & certainly formed a most congenial neighbour while he stays. He is full of literary plans—including the establishment of a high-grade mimeographed magazine of distinctive material.[4]

Speaking of guests—old Adolphe de Castro—one-time friend of Ambrose Bierce & creator of endless reams of fictional junk & learned charlatanry—blew into town Aug. 6 after a trip to Boston for the melancholy purpose of scattering his wife's ashes in the sea in accordance with her ante-mortem request. I shewed him about quite a bit, & he, Barlow & I wrote rhymed acrostics on Poe[5] while seated on a tomb in the hidden hillside churchyard just north of here—where long ago the bard of Nis & Aidenn used to roam when on visits to Providence.

On Aug. 15 Barlow & I visited ancient Newport. Aug. 20 we went the rounds of Salem & Marblehead in company with young Sterling, who is now recovering finely from his operation & about to enter Harvard. The old town seemed as fascinating as usual. Barlow will go from here to Kansas City (where his mother is), stopping en route at New York, Washington, & Indianapolis.

All good wishes—

Yrs most sincerely—

H P L

Notes

1. HPL himself published two: "In Memoriam: Robert Ervin Howard" and "Robert Ervin Howard: 1906–1936."

2. R. H. Barlow, "R. E. H.," *WT* 28, No. 3 (October 1936): 353.

3. This may be referring to "Echo from the Ebon Isles" (published as "The Warrior"). Regarding the poem, Howard had written "Thank you very much for the splendid sonnet, 'Echo From the Ebon Isles.' I feel deeply honored that a poem of such fine merit should be dedicated to me. You seem to grasp the motif of my stories, the compelling idea-force behind them which is the only excuse for their creation, more completely than any one I have yet encountered. This fine sonnet reveals your understanding of the abstractions I have tried to embody in these tales. [. . .] I foresee an enviable future for you as a poet and artist" (14 December 1934; *Collected Letters* 3.259–60).

4. *Leaves* (two issues) did not appear until after HPL's death.

5. See HPL to DAW 235n1.

[26]   [ALS]

> 66 College St.,
> Providence, R.I.
> Oct. 15, 1936.

Dear Petaja:—

      Howard's death was certainly a tragedy of the first water—& the vacancy in fantasy fiction can never be filled. Your sonnet is excellent, & I strongly hope you'll revise it at the points indicated. I strongly regretted my inability to get at it—my failure being due not to any lack of merit in the poem, but to my own feverishly overcrowded programme. I simply cannot cope with all the things which turn up—& now & then something has to suffer! Usually the thing that suffers is what requires most attention & judgment—such as the creation of apt rhymes or formulation of original plot details. Glad your [*sic*] writing more poetry, for the medium fits you very well. Let me see some more of it—I'll be glad to give comments & point out places needing revision even if I haven't the leisure to attempt the revision myself. Barlow's elegy on R E H was very good—indeed, R H B's literary skill both in prose & in verse has increased spectacularly during the past year. This is the first poem he ever sent W T.

      Glad Prof. Curry liked your revised René story. His change of career will be a loss to the university—though I presume his newer activities will suit him better. I'm interested to know that he will study at Harvard—only 45 miles from here. He *might* run across young Sterling, though Harvard is a vast institution, & the points of contact betwixt a raw freshman & graduate student doubtless few. By the way—in case you have occasion to write Sterling, his new address is Room A-11, Lionel Hall, Harvard College, Cambridge, Mass. Sorry you found the scholarship unavailable, but trust you'll be able to continue your brilliant regular record. That row of straight A's—even in the less congenial subjects—is something to be vastly proud of! Hope you can find good housing accomodations in Missoula this year.

      Good luck with your writing! I was very glad to see "Shadow of Fear", & enjoyed it immensely. It is truly excellent in atmosphere & events, & has a delightful touch at the end—where the sating of the hunger of both mechanical beasts is suggested. It seems to me that this tale ought to land professionally sooner or later—it even has the style most favoured by contemporary popular editors. In the enclosed copy I've made a few pencil emendations which you may find useful. All, I believe, are self-explanatory. Your "World of Sensation" sounds extremely clever, & ought to go well in one or another of the science-fiction magazines. If it doesn't land professionally, the ever-increasing horde of "fan" magazines is always waiting!

      Your recent visitors must have been interesting indeed—& I envy Taves[1] his contact with Shiel. Shiel's "House of Sounds" is without question one of the few *great* weird stories ever written. Woodard certainly has reason to feel proud of Parrish's praise, even though Parrish does fall a bit short of genius.[2]

Sorry you & Rimel couldn't get together during his Montana stay—& it was surely too bad that Shelby brought back D W R's rheumatic trouble.

Yes—"Haunter" & "Thing" are scheduled for W T. The new illustrator Finlay is doing the heading for H.—which pleases me exceedingly. Finlay is a young genius of 22 who lives in Rochester, N.Y. He seems to be a very picturesque & colourful figure, & is a remarkable poet as well as artist. It's only a question of time before he'll be heard from importantly. I've had several letters from him recently.

Very glad indeed to hear that you've joined the N.A.P.A.—you make the 5th or 6th of the weird fan element to get into the fold. I think you'll enjoy it, even though the institution isn't what it was 40 or 50 years ago. Yes—I was president in 1922–3. As for data & information—have I ever sent you sample papers? If not, let me know. Have you *both* issues of Edkins' *Causerie* & of Barlow's *Dragon-Fly*? Have you *any* issues of Bradofsky's *Californian*? I can supply some of these if you lack them—to give you a good start in amateurdom, as it were. Wish I had an extra copy of the official organ—*The National Amateur*—to send you, but I lack duplicates. However, you'll doubtless receive the current issue very shortly. Amateur journalism is a curious & unique institution—informal, slipshod, loosely organised, & full of cheap & irrelevant elements, yet for all that a peculiarly valuable influence in encouraging the literary aspirant whose professional foothold is as yet non-existent or insecure. It is, in brief, a miniature world of letters where amateur work is published in amateur papers & given the benefit of the same general reading (on a small scale) & reviewing (by amateur critics) which professionally published work receives in the outside world. You can easily see the advantage of this. Without the amateur press associations, a beginner has no place to air his work except in the rural press—where it is largely lost amidst a scattered & indifferent audience, & never singled out for comment or review. In amateurdom, however, one's work reaches a circle of 200 or 300 persons, all interested in writing, & in some cases genuinely & intelligently appreciative. It is really noticed & commented on, & the authors are criticised both officially in the columns of *The National Amateur* & unofficially in the various individual papers & by letter from sundry interested members. The beginner is placed at once in the midst of a literary circle, some part of which is bound to prove congenial to him. Letters are exchanged, controversies started, criticisms offered—in short, all the encouraging influences imaginable are provided. If one is isolated in a barren or unsympathetic environment, there is no quicker way of getting in touch with potential kindred spirits—indeed, there are many whose whole intellectual & social life centres around the epistolary contacts of amateurdom. The notice & criticism extended to one's work help to give one hints for improvement which might otherwise come very slowly. Amateurdom helps most young writers "find themselves"—& their polish & development are often greatly accelerated by it. Its aid to me has been tremendous—for when I first entered it my style was incredibly heavy & pedantic, while my ideas were naive in the extreme. It proved the greatest single broadener & civiliser that I ever encountered, & placed me in contact with those from whom my present circle of best friends—Morton, Long, Moe, Cook, Clark Ashton Smith, &c. &c.—largely grew. I knew Long & Smith through amateurdom long before the W T or fantasy group developed. Indeed—one may compare amateur journalism to the fantasy circle despite its less specialised province & more compact organisation. However—as I have said, amateurdom today isn't what it was. Literary standards have suffered with the years, & childish association politics & aimless sociability have usurped an undue place. Much mediocrity & puerility gets by nowadays despite our efforts to inaugurate a renaissance. Yet after all I think it would be hard to beat amateurdom as an encouraging influence for the isolated aspirant. The institution first grew out of the little papers printed by small boys. The N.A.P.A. was founded in 1876, & by another decade emphasis had begun to shift from publishing to good writing. The Golden Age of high literary standards was probably the decade from 1885 to 1895. Other associations than the N.A.P.A. exist & have existed—especially the United Amateur Press Assn. founded in 1895. This divided into two branches through a feud in 1912, & it was one of these branches (which unfortunately became abeyant in 1927) that served to introduce me to amateurdom in 1914. I was wholly a United man till 1922. Another United branch still survives. Amateur papers are of all kinds, & vary from extreme crudity to a high degree of proficiency. Indeed, the total democracy of amateurdom is a striking phenomenon. I feel sure you'll enjoy the National, & hope your contributions may achieve early publication. Send long stories to Hyman Bradofsky, 2315 W. Second St., Pomona, California—also poems. Poems also welcomed by Ralph W. Babcock, 58 Maple Drive, Great Neck, N.Y.—for *The Scarlet Cockerel.* You'll note other papers welcoming contributions as time passes. Send freely to any amateur journal you may receive. And call on me for any further information you may wish.

Barlow spent some time in N.Y. after leaving here—seeing Long, Sterling, Koenig, Howard Wandrei, &c. He also paused in Indianapolis to see Miss Moore. His new address is ℅ LANGWORTHY, 810 W. 57th STREET TERRACE, KANSAS CITY, MO. (a maternal aunt's). On Sept. 11–12–13 I had an enjoyable visit from James F. Morton, (amateur journalist—Curator of Paterson Museum) who later attended the Harvard Tercentenary.

All good wishes—
Yrs most sincerely—
H P L

Notes

1. Harold Taves of Seattle was a correspondent of Shiel's who worked with the poet

Edward Doro (1909–1987) to sell Shiel's novels to Hollywood. He later owned a bookstore in Seattle. With Petaja, he founded the Bokanalia Memorial Foundation in 1967, to promote the work of the artist Hannes Bok.

2. Wayne Francis Woodard (1914–1964), American artist and illustrator, known as Hannes Bok. Petaja had illustrations by Maxfield Parrish (1870–1966) in *Brief Candle*.

[27]   [ALS]

> 66 College St.,
> Providence, R.I.,
> Dec. 3, 1936.

Dear Petaja:—

Very glad to hear the current news, & to know that you are having such a congenial time at college this year. You are surely fortunate in having Dennis Murphy as an instructor, & I imagine the class in writing will prove highly valuable. Let us hope that you will eventually join the legion of Murphy pupils with published books to their credit! The Quill Club[1] sounds extremely helpful, & ought to furnish a great deal of stimulation & encouragement. Regarding your curriculum as a whole, I believe you are wise in concentrating on preferred subjects, & not seeking such extraordinary works in the various minor fields. Nowadays the field of knowledge is so bewilderingly vast that no one can hope to shine in everything—as the scholars of the Renaissance used to do. The only sensible policy today is to have a general outline-knowledge of all subjects—well correlated & proportioned—& confine detailed research & endeavours to a limited field based on one's own interests & aptitudes.

As I said, I liked "Shadow of Fear" very much—& I'm not sure I wouldn't have liked it better without the detective. I have no use for popular commercial standards—though of course one can't expect to see work extensively if one repudiates them. Young Kuttner certainly is coming along rapidly. He is phenomenally gifted, though he may spoil his style if he caters too systematically to cheap market requirements. He & Bloch can, when they choose, do wonders toward creating that elusive atmosphere of tension & utter horror which is the soul of a weird tale. Hope you have good luck with "The World of Sensation". Long retention by a magazine is said to be a good sign—a sign that the MS. has passed the reader & is receiving personal consideration from the editor.

Concerning M. P. Shiel—I think it would be going a long way to call him the "best living author", but he certainly has created at least two imperishable weird classics—"The House of Sounds" & "The Purple Cloud". He has also written much mediocre & downright poor material. A certain extravagance of conception & floridity of expression are his besetting weaknesses. He cannot easily get rid of the mannerisms of his early period—the '90s. I have not read "This Above All". What is it like?

December W T is about average. I liked the Finlay illustration to the

"Haunter", even though it belies the text a bit. As you'll see by careful reading, the skeleton in the tower was not intact nor articulated. St. John[2] is indeed a good cover artist—the best of the lot so far, though Finlay may best him when he gets going. No—not a single story of mine has received a cover in W T (although *both* of my *Astounding* contributions took the cover). I don't know why. Probably because my tales are primarily of atmosphere rather than of action, hence lend themselves less readily to definite visual tableaux. I don't regret the omission, since the "art" work in W T is for the most part simply a joke—a completely negligible factor. Finlay hasn't much competition! *The Phantagraph* comes with commendable regularity, & I was very glad to see your interesting folklore article in the October issue. You open some very fruitful territory, & the information conveyed is likely to prove broadening & enlightening to the bulk of the magazine clientele. I was once again reminded of my long-standing wish to read the Kalevala.

Glad you've joined the National, & hope the papers will begin to flow in before long. A certain slowness in assimilating new members is inevitable in a society as loosely organised as this, & every recruit needs to be patient during the first few months. There's no question, though, but that you'll find it tremendously helpful & encouraging once you become thoroughly adjusted to it. By this time you've no doubt digested the papers which I sent—& which were meant to give you a sort of start in the society. Yes—I indirectly encountered Klarkash-Ton through amateurdom, since he is a friend of our fellow-member Samuel Loveman. Reversing your quite natural assumption, it was Smith who first brought W T emphatically to my attention.

Crawford has finished "The Shadow Over Innsmouth" at last—with 34 misprints. Whether it will sell to any extent is another matter.

The season of my hibernation is now at hand—though I kept up my rural outings till a remarkably late date this year. One feature of these trips was the discovery of several fine woodland regions within a three-mile radius of here which I had never seen or known about before!

All good wishes—

Yrs most sincerely

H P L

[P.S.] *Fanciful Tales* just arrived. My "Nameless City" contains *59* misprints. On the other hand, *The Science-Fantasy Correspondent* is almost free from typographical errors.

Notes

1. A writers' group at Montana State University. See "Quill Club Started at the University," *Helena Independent* (27 November 1936).
2. J. Allen St. John (1872–1957), illustrator for *WT* and other pulp magazines.

[28]   [TLS][1]

66 College St.,
Providence, R.I.
[March? 1937]

Dear Petaja:—

Reduced to the hated machine by a spell of bad health (more or less allied to grippe, and involving swollen feet, intestinal disorders, and general weakness) which has rendered my script illegibly shaky in any substantial quantity.

That N.A.P.A material wasn't a mere loan—I didn't need it back at all. Such shipments can always be passed on to possible recruits or others if you haven't any use for it yourself. Glad various bundles of papers have begun to reach you. Did you get the splendid Winter CALIFORNIAN and the December Official Organ? Before long the MS. bureau will begin to show results regarding the placement of your material.

Congratulations on your congenial Seattle visit, which must surely have been a rare treat. Even in winter the scenery en route was doubtless tremendously impressive. That's the advantage of mountain regions—their charm and grandeur do not depend upon anything seasonal. Seattle alone, w[i]th bookshops and other facilities, was doubtless a delight in itself.

Sorry to hear of your influenza—about which, as you may see, I can sympathise very eloquently. Hope all traces are now worn off, and that you are rapidly repairing the scholastic damage. Glad you are increasing your Murphy courses. The results will undoubtedly be manifest in your literary products—and in the public's reception of them.

Glad you liked the "Haunter" and "Doorstep". Finlay belied the narrative a bit in illustrating the first, but his "Doorstep" drawing is a classic. Wright has given me the originals of these two sketches, and they far excel the reproductions in effect. Much is lost in even the best cuts. As for Utpatel's "Innsmouth" illustrations—I enclose (please return) the set. They really are excellent, even though the white-bearded nonagenarian does appear as smooth-faced. The book is out now, and is rather a damned mess in format, typography, and binding. Crawford's printed list of errata leaves many uncorrected, so that I am asking purchasers of the book to let me know and receive a supplementary list. Sorry your "World of Sensation" didn't quite land—but the next attempt may bring better luck. I was glad to see Rimel's "Disinterment" in print, and found it as powerful on a second reading as when I first saw it in MS. I've just seen another good story of Rimel's—"From the Sea"—which Wright ought to accept eventually.[2]

Glad you liked "The Purple Cloud". Yes—I've seen "Shapes in the Fire".[3] Isn't this the book which contains a powerful but florid and over-ornate take (I can't recall the title here used) about a tower of brass amidst the swirling water of the Norwegian coast? If so, you've read the crude prototype of one of the finest weird stories ever written—for about 1907, Shiel resur-rected and revised this opus and presented it (in "The Pale Ape and Other Stories") [*sic*] as that unforgettable classic, "The House of Sounds". I'm rather sorry that you won't have the chance good luck (as I had) to read the superior version first, and thus get the effect of the better craftsmanship combined with absolute freshness and unexpectedness. The resemblance to Poe's "House of Usher" is obvious, but not offensive. Shiel has not plagiarized, but re-created. "This Above All" sounds like a delicate and tragic character-study.

Hope you receive most of the small weird magazines—whose numer-ousness is quite bewildering. Did you know that the SFC is about to absorb FANTASY MAGAZINE?

Commiserations on the cold winter! Ours has proved very warm—seldom below 40—so that I've been able to get occasional bits of air and ex-ercise. A really cold winter would have finished me!

All good wishes—yrs most sincerely,

H P L

Later—This damn grippe has got me down at last! Doc has me taking 3 nos-trums at once, & I can't stay up very long at a time.

Notes

1. On the verso, Petaja wrote "Lovecraft's last letter to me. He died two weeks later."

2. The story was not published.

3. See DAW 5n7.

Donald Wandrei

Appendix

Donald Wandrei Interviewed

Julius Schwartz and Mortimer

When the editors of *Weird Tales* published Donald Wandrei's masterful story, "The Red Brain," back in their October, 1927 issue, they were not surprised at the sudden influx of letters from readers all over the country proclaiming the story to be one of the most outstanding weird tales of all time. As a matter of fact, they expected it. Nor were they surprised to learn that Dashiell Hammett had deemed the story so good that it merited reprinting in his anthology of weird tales, "Creeps by Night." And it seemed only natural for the story to appear in a collection of weird stories published in England.

Followers of fantastic literature were not surprised at all these manifestations of literary approval, we say, because they knew the story was destined to be a classic when they first read it. But, we venture to guess, not a single person of all the thousands who read the tale would have imagined the author to be a lanky lad of sixteen!

This story, extremely mature in expression, and which the author himself considers one of the best of his published output, was originally titled by him "The Twilight of Time." It was Farnsworth Wright, the editor, who gave the story its final caption, and Wandrei was satisfied with it.

Donald Wandrei was born April 20, 1908. He received his B. A. at the University of Minnesota. He put in two years of work towards his Ph. D. degree, but finally decided against it. Later, he taught English at this university for a period of two years. He is not married and emphatically asserts that he "never will be."

At the youthful age of twenty, Wandrei was advertising manager of the Dutton Publishing Company, where he held his position for two years. now he is a public relations man, and believes there is a great future in the field. His work employs so much of his time that he has little time left for writing. His mind is seething with an abundance of unusual plots which have not yet found an outlet, due to the aforesaid reason.

Wandrei has flocks of friends who are continually regaling him with plots, usually based on their dreams. Wandrei has [so] many of his own that their suggestions are politely, but firmly rejected.

Recently Wandrei completed a stupendous, super-science novel, titled "Dead Titans, Waken!" which attempts to explain the pyramids of Egypt, the statues of Easter Island and similar phenomena. Publishers have been fascinated by the idea behind this book, which Wandrei himself says "will drive readers crazy." Essentially, the theme is similar to "Colossus." Wandrei has optimistic hopes concerning this novel.

Unlike other authors, Wandrei does not dash off his stuff. He writes the story out in longhand, putting in about 1000 words a night. Each night he revised the work he wrote the night before. At times he becomes so enthused with a story that he writes it at white heat, and usually at one sitting. This happened with his "A Race Through Time" and "The Tree Men of M'Bwa." This latter story was suddenly inspired, and Wandrei thought it so good that he decided to write it up immediately. He finished the ms in five hours, and sent the story to *Weird Tales* the next day. Many of Wandrei's personal experiences furnish fodder for his stories. For example, he wandered one day into a friend's curio shop. There he saw a sealed bottle. He started thinking how long the bottle had been sealed, why it was sealed and what was in it. His answer to these questions appeared in "Spawn of the Sea."

On still another occasion, which takes us back to 1925, Wandrei tells of the time when he resided in Minneapolis where during the winter he was astounded to see a red snowfall. This phenomenon perplexed him to such an extent that he offered his own explanation in "Something from Above."

Wandrei has met many author-celebrities. He knows Seabury Quinn, H. P. Lovecraft, F. B. Long, Jr., Farnsworth Wright, Desmond Hall, and Hugh Rankin. Of Lovecraft he tells us the following anecdote:

"When I met Lovecraft I chanced to comment on his excellent story, 'Call of Cthulhu,' and I pronounced the word as it was spelt. Lovecraft enlightened me on its correct pronunciation, which sounds like a series of witches' whistles. I asked Lovecraft how he could possibly pronounce the name different from my version of it, which was correct phonetically. He then said to me, 'Look here, I ought to know how to say it, don't you think?'"

At one time Wandrei possessed a complete file of the rare *Black Cat Magazines,* which published copious amounts of fantastic literature. This magazine might still be existing, were it not for the fact that they once published a story, of such a gruesome nature that the circulation dropped to almost nothing. This story was called "The Pain Thermometer," and told about a scientist who perfected a thermometer which was able to record various degrees of pain. He vivisected dogs and cats and performed various operations on them in an effort to get the thermometer to rise. But his efforts succeeded in raising it only a few degrees. The scientist then decided to try it on a human being. He captured a man, strapped him to the operating table, and proceeded to flay him alive. after a very graphic description of the torture, the author goes on to show the thermometer bursting from the excessive amount of pain it registered. The story ends with the lifeless mass of the flayed man slowly making its way towards the scientist . . .*

---

*The editors are mistaken. "The Pain Thermometer" by H. G. Addison appeared in *Black Mask* 6, No. 23 (1 March 1924): 46–50. It was reprinted the following year in the UK edition of the magazine, 13, No. 9 (June 1935): 2–6.—ED.

Wandrei would like to do serious writing. He writes fantasy because he is interested in it, and modestly refers to his published work as "a pile of junk." However, our readers will dispute that. His greatest thrill in the writing occurred when he completed the framework for his "Dead Titans, Waken!" His greatest disappointment was the rejection of his series of short fantastic poems, "Post-Historian Legends," which he himself thought really good. His best stories are "The Red Brain," "The Tree Men of M'Bwa," and "The Lives of Alfred Kramer."

His brother, Howard Wandrei, is the author of "Over Time's Threshold" and "In the Triangle" which have appeared in *Weird Tales*. He is also an artist and is the illustrator of Wandrei's book of verse, "Dark Odyssey." He has also written another book of verse, "Ecstasy."

One of Wandrei's best stories, "The Fragment of a Dream," appeared in *The Recluse,* a now defunct periodical which also featured material by Lovecraft, C. A. Smith, and H. Warner Munn. He corresponds regularly with Smith, and thinks his stories much above the average weird tale.

He thinks W. Olaf Stapledon's "Last and First Men" is a masterpiece of science fiction. He enjoyed "The Invisible Man" so much that he saw it twice. He sees a great future in scientifilms. He thinks Hugh Rankin's stuff is much above the average pulp magazine artists['], and he calls him "my favorite illustrator." His favorite authors are Arthur Machen, C. A. Smith, Lovecraft, and the early H. G. Wells. He does not read his stories over after they are published, and does not save acceptance slips.

THE SHEPARD CAFETERIA, 122-124-126 MATHEWSON STREET, PROVIDENCE, R. I.

Picture postcard, with drawn figures added by Lovecraft.

Other Known Letters to Howard Wandrei

An unidentified book dealer's catalogue long ago listed various letters and postcards by Lovecraft to Howard Wandrei. Some are contained herein, but those listed below have not been found. The book dealer's descriptions of the items have been added to each entry.

ANS postcard, postmarked Charleston, S.C., 28 April 1934.

> Written from Charleston, where HPL is temporarily residing. He mentions plans to visit Robert H. Barlow in Florida for "a visit of some duration."

ALS, 2 pp., De Land, Fla., 5 May 1934.

> Lovecraft describes luxuriously tropical aspects of De Land, Florida, where he is visiting young, ardent fan R. H. Barlow, "a really remarkable infant prodigy . . . a book-collector and general aesthete of astonishing versatility for his age." Also remarks upon artwork H.W. has done, comparing it to that of John Vassos.

ALS, 2 pp., De land, Fla., 13 May 1934.

> Describes his host R. H. Barlow's admiration for H.W.'s artwork, and comments enthusiastically on Barlow's plan to publish, in photographically reproduced limited editions, portfolios of H.W.'s work, to be available at virtual cost to devotees of "Weird." Mentions salubrious climate, shooting snakes on the lake for book-binding material, and acquiring a "veritable Mediterranean cast of cuticular swarthiness" in contrast to his normal pallor. Notes that while staying with Barlow in Florida "I have tenfold the energy, mental & physical, that I have in the north," but admits later "I have written nothing lately, being dissatisfied with my style. . . ." Mentions visiting architectural ruins, a subject always dear to Lovecraft's heart.

ALS, 2 pp., De Land, Fla., 30 May 1934.

> Thanks H.W. for the drawing he sent, "arrived safely & uncreased, & which is just now exciting the envious interest of my young host. A Wandrei original is an item indeed, & will some day be duly known as such." H.P.L. encourages H.W. to proceed with Barlow's plan for reproduction of his art. Once again, extols the Florida climate. "I will probably get down here permanently in the end, although it will be hard to break away from the New England scenes to which I am accustomed. I have a strong sense—like my favourite feline species—of geographical attachments."

ANS postcard, postmarked Providence, R.I., 8 August 1934.

Writing in a very tiny hand (although begins by noting the need for optical assistance when reading Wandrei's letters), H.P.L. mentions that a correspondent of his ("young Robert Bloch of Milwaukee") has seen *Terror Tales,* "& says it is pretty bad." Included are further references to pulp publications, Donald Wandrei, etc.

ALS, 4 pp., 7 September 1934 (present herein only partially, from AHT).

Lovecraft begins, "Duly armed with the requisite optical assistance, I peruse your appreciated message of the 24th & humbly retire from the micrographic field in undisputed defeat," in recognition of Wandrei's minuscule handwriting. Discusses at some length Barlow's reproduction of Wandrei's drawings and advises Wandrei to be patient regarding return of art & prints. Mentions "vague rumours" of a magazine to compete with W.T., & notes that "Belknap is having marvellous luck placing things since he got hold of Otis Adelbert Kline as a coach & agent." Later, H.P.L. declares that "literature & pulp writing can't mix—& only an exceptional person (like Auguste-Guillaume Comte d'Erlette, for example) can successfully prosecute both at the same time. I, alas, am far from exceptional . . ."

ANS postcard, postmarked New York, N.Y., 7 November 1935.

Lovecraft is staying with Donald Wandrei in Howard's New York apartment, but claims he is "NOT patronising the barroom beneath," although Donald is, & said establishment (Julius' in "the heart of New York City") is the origin of the postcard. With greetings & short notes to Howard Wandrei from Donald Wandrei & Frank Belknap Long. Signed H.P.L., Don & Belknap.

ALS, 1 p., Providence, R.I., 7 November 1936 (presented herein only partially, from AHT).

Comments upon an accompanying 3-page article by August Derleth (the example actually present is a 1942 offprint of the article, "American Regional Literature"). Written during the last full year of Lovecaft's life, he notes that "1936 has been a rotten year for me. No trips, indifferent health, & a severe illness of my aunt in the spring which greatly disrupted things. I did, though, enjoy the visit from Barlow, as well as briefer visits from good old Morton & others."

Emil Petaja

Elemental

1
Sun,
Crimson fop,
seducer of stars,
arrives hastily by air.

Strides over still-slumbering hills
mopping dew from daffodils.
Bathing termites and men in ultra ultra-violet.

Braggadocio,
he swaggers across trembling sky
and kisses lachrymose maiden moon
mocking goodbye.

2

Wind,

Eon ancient harlot
flirting with sailors,
dances wild mazurkas,
singing abandonment of lust—
then, lies still
while they curse.

Creeps slyly behind men in the dark,
slaps their coat backs,
tipping toppers,
shrilling raucous love,
then tossing hoardocks about fingertrees
in toothless glees.

Throws smarting cinders
in the eyes of those
who deserve more,
or less.

3

Rain,
Sottish slave driver
lashes men to work and war.

Coaxing from flint earth
flecks of food,
so they may live in dearth
and kindly death
may not embrace then
erase their pain.

Clouds,

vortex of vampire mouths,
greedily sucking
earth men's tears.
Then
flinging them back
again, again, again,
till time escapes his bondage.

4

Earth.
Rock breasted sister of wind
holds its germ life in mock security.
At times
moves suddenly
to see them scat,
and grins.

Smoldering inwardly
with Jove for sun,
sister wind tears hair
in frenzy of hate,
sun smiles contemptuously at both
and plays with moon.
So whore wind lies with rain
in drunken marshes.

All wait for death.
The gibbering idiot
who in worlds without

who holds the cosmos globule in his hand
and picks off overripe life like grapes
drops it,
and it breaks . . .

Dream within a Dream Within

I think god
must be everything
and everything
must be god.

Good is no more good
than wickedness is good
or good is bad.
And all is god
and all of god is good.

He was some brief part
of god's mind,
Socrates . . .
who learned to know,
and knew how little can be known
by one infinitesimal part.

Shakespeare, I think
was an atom from god's eyes.
He saw beauty in lost life
and saw it kindly
and saw it gently
and brought it into life.

God's ears, in part,
was Wagner
who passioned
overtones of cosmos floating,
velvet silk and silver wildness,
valhalla heaven
otherwise only dreamt
in beautydeath.

Part of his hands
was one who held

a dying comrade in his
nightlong.

He who was love
and is love more
and died in love for loveless
(for lesser god)
was his heart.

Lost Dream

To H. P. Lovecraft

Exalted, whose far-off visions see
In memory's mist a land of whispered dreams
Where beings god-like move in shadowed schemes,
A silver city by a sapphire sea.
They work their spells, and plan when they will be
Among the mystic dancers, under beams
Of crystal crescent moons whose radiance seems
A light or necromantic sorcery.

I gaze enchanted while they pass me by;
Ascend the hill where crumbling ruins lie—
An eery sea-deep sound rings out the moor;
They pause before a rock which hides a door:
One fumbles in his scarlet cloak. I see
His slender fingers move—he turns a key.

Partings . . .

To Duane W. Rimel

All alone
I wander, where the ocean's spray
Wipes the tears from my eyes away . . .
And I see
In the dusky blue twilight air
Two phantom ships a'sailing there:
And whence they come, and whither go,
I dare to dream, but cannot know.

A shine
From far across the darkened sea
Melodiously sings to me . . .

And a wind
In the sad, somber cypress tree
Soothingly . . softly . . sighs to me,
And tells me so that we'll meet again,
But whispers not of where or when . . .

In azure Shamure! In ebon Yith?
Or crystal-templed Barracrith?

The Warrior

To Robert E. Howard

From ancient, fabled Cimmeria he came
With sword uplifted, on that bloody day,
To join the beaten forces in affray,
And all triumphant spurn eternal fame.
Men trembled at the mention of his name,
And humbly stepped aside to clear a way.
"You are our King," they said. He answered, "Nay,"
And left them wondering what could be his aim.

I saw him then, and still I see him now,
Cryptic and silent, on a lone hill's brow,
Watching with brooding eyes the scene below
Where flame the earth and sky in scarlet hands
He grasps his curious staff in mighty hands
And strides into the dusk, toward other lands.

Asphodel

Down where skies are always dark,
Where is ever heard the bark
Of monstrous ebon hounds of hell,
In a dreadful fearsome knell,
Never fading, ever bright,
With a weird and spectral light,
Blooms a flower of ancient days,
Shining in a crimson maze;
When the black bat shrilly screams
Asphodel, you haunt my dreams—
From the lands of distant death
Steals the perfume of your breath:
Some night soon the wind will blow

Saffron seeds to fall and grow
By my casement window, where,
Sleeps my loved one, still and fair;
Then, the night you are to bloom
I shall creep from out my room,
From your blossom by the wall
Shall I hear her dear voice call:
Mournfully the wind will cry,
And shadows cover all the sky—
My lips will touch the loved dead
When where you nod I lay my head. . . .

Marmok

Sleep that doth harbour a dream of dread,
Whence come the fingers that beckoned and led
My dream-stung soul from my canopied bed—
Whither dost take me, ere I am dead?
Beyond the skull-grinning mid-March moon
Over the phosphorous-lit lagoon
Out past the darkest pits of the night,
Fast thru the stars in this evil flight;
Lead thee me out past the rim of space,
Show me that ravenous, pain-black face,
Marmok, whose myrmidons ever are questing
For souls who wander at nite, unresting.
Then shall I know an ultimate bliss
Tasting the fury of that cosmic kiss,
Whilst my earth-cloak lies limply on the floor
To waken and gibber forevermore.

The Witch's Berceuse

Hush, my babe,
Thy wailing wild;
Black wings hover
O'er my child;
When midnight's crimson moon ins high,
Far from this dungeon cell we'll fly
Not to the stake to burn and die.

Hark! a sound
Rings in thine ear;
Though loud it screams,

Do not fear . . . .
This clanging of the daemon's bell
Bids us, with its awful knell,
To seek the depths of darkest Hell!

We, my son,
Have done *his* work . . . .
In this land we
Dare not lurk——
A night-black steed beats through these walls,
Mount—ride on—to the flaming halls;
Witch-brood, thy father—Zathu—calls!

Famous Fantasy Fiction

Perhaps the most interesting collection of mystery stories ever brought together under one cover is Dorothy L. Sayers' *Omnibus of Crime.* This is of special interest to weird story fans, as of its 1177 pages, over 400 are devoted exclusively to this type. It's authors include A. Conan Doyle, Bram Stoker, Arthur Machen, Ambrose Bierce, and many others whom Fantasy Fans are familiar with. Don't miss reading it.

Among other weird story collections are *Famous Modern Ghost Stories* and *Famous* [*sic*] *Humorous Ghost Stories,* both edited by Dorothy Scarborough. These books are filled with fascinating ghost stories, all by famous authors of all times.

Elliot O'Donnell, famous English author, has written many collections of true ghost stories. His two latest are *Haunted Houses of London.* You will find many of his stories and articles reprinted in various collections. He has also written for *Weird Tales.*

Some years ago, The Macauley Company published a collection under the title, *Beware After Dark.* It includes H. P. Lovecraft's "Call of Cthulhu" and Machen's "Novel of the White Powder," and others of note. A splendid addition to your book shelf.

The Modern Library's collection "Best Ghost Stories" is no doubt familiar to most of you, but it is certainly worth mentioning. It contains an introduction by Arthur B. Reeve, and stories by Algernon Blackwood, Dr. M. R. James and Rudyard Kipling.

————

The Supernatural Omnibus, edited by Montague Summers; Doubleday Doran Co. This remarkable collection contains thirty-six stories of the best fantasy fiction. It is of particular interest to American readers as most of its stories are taken from English magazines and out-of-print books which most of us would find difficult to obtain. The introduction is especially interesting.

A. Conan Doyle has written several books of a scientific and weird nature. Perhaps the best of these is "The Maracot Deep." In this story the scientific theme predominates, until the very last chapter, in which we find a typical Jules de Grandin finis. Among the other stories in this book, "When the Earth Screamed' is easily the best. This book can now be had in the 75 cent reprint list. *Famous Mystery Stories* and *Famous Ghost Stories*, both edited by J. W. McSpadden, contain many old favorites, such as O'Brien's "The Diamond Lens," Crawford's "The Upper Berth," and de Maupassant's "Horla." You can get these books at any public library.

Ghosts, Grim and Gentle, edited by L. C. French; Dodd, Mead & Co. Although many of the stories in this volume have been reprinted very often, it is well worth reading. One of its best is "The Tractate Middoth," by Dr. M. R. James; mentioned by Clark Ashton Smith in his article in the February *Fantasy Fan*.

Uncanny Stories, Macmillan Co. This splendid collection contains F. Marion Crawford's "For the Blood is the Life" (considered one of the best vampire stories ever written) and Sinclair's "Where their Fire is not Quenched." Other of its stories are equally interesting.*

Algernon Blackwood is well known to lovers of fantasy. Of the books containing his short stories "Wolves of God" and "The Dance of Death" are two of the best. "The Man Who Found Out" (in *Wolves of God*) I consider one of the best short stories I have ever read. Like Lovecraft, he merely hints at unmentionable things, leaving the reader with a vague sense of fear.

Visible and Invisible, E. F. Benson, Doubleday, Doran & Co. This is probably Benson's best work of fantasy. Readers of *Weird Tales* will remember some of his splendid stories that have appeared in his magazine.

Lord Dunsany's two delightful books, *A Dreamer's Tales* and *Book of Wonder* can now be had in the Modern Library list. After reading the dark takes of Lovecraft, Howard, etc., these are a refreshing change.

Some of the other good collections of stories of ghosts, vampires, ghouls, etc. are *Psychic Stories*, French; *The White Ghost Book, The Grey Ghost Book*, Middleton; *Sinister Stories*, Walker; *Stories of the Seen and Unseen*, Oliphant. Frank Owen's two fantasies *The Wind That Tramps the World* and *The Purple Sea*—and Birch's *The Moon Terror* should be mentioned. A rare treat is Clark Ashton Smith's booklet *The Double Shadow*. These tales range from the wild terror of Edgar Allan Poe, to the weird, imaginative beauty of Dunsany.

---

* Actually from two separate books by the authors named; see Bibliography.—ED.

The Mist[*]

David's pen slipped from his fingers, to fall and spatter blackness on the page he was writing. He brushed his hands over his face, and his lips quivered in an agony of mental upheaval.

"What's the use?" The question burned itself through his mind like a damnable, inextinguishable torch trail.

"Philip Croft," he thought, his agitated mind soothed a little, "What a wonderful author—and splendid man! He's so freely and unstintingly helped so many struggling authors like me!"

He picked up the top letter, dated February twenty-ninth.

"Reduced to the hated typewriter by a sudden spell of bad health . . . which has rendered my script illegibly shaky . . ." It began.

Later on, David read:

"When I received and read through the manuscript copy of *Behind the Veil,* I was struck by its genuineness and persuasive grace. It is really splendidly written and no one would ever suspect that it was your first effort. The second was even more sure and well-handled. I anticipate with much pleasure the perusal of your latest book upon its completion. Rest assured, David, that I desire intensely to aid you with your new volume and I promise you that I will do so, no matter how busy or far away I may be . . ."

David had counted on Philip Croft's appraisal and criti[ci]sms of his new effort. It *was* better than the first two; he knew it was. But it still lacked all the power and sweep of Croft's own great works. He knew that Croft's praises of the books were far in excess of their worth—that it was his kindly way of encouraging a young writer.

The letter concluded,

"Later: this damn grippe has got me down at last! Doc has me taking three nostrums at once and I can't stay up very long at a time."

Placing the letters carefully in a folder, and into a drawer for safe keeping, David muttered half-aloud, "He *can't* be dead. How can such a fine, generous master-artist die?"

He reflected in poignant reverie on the one occasion when he had actually met and talked with Philip Croft. He remembered vividly the quiet charm and impressive serenity of the man. They had strolled together over the cemetery hill above waves wildly surging up on the sand and rocks, and dark clouds scudding above in the wind. After that visit David had felt uplifted, certain that now he could write something fine, inspired by the long, intimate talk with the author he reverenced.

The failure of his first book had brought with it crushing disappointment. But he had plenty of courage in store, then. Even after the second,

---

[*]"'The Mist' is really a character study of HPL" (p. 2 of *Fantasmagoria*).

nearly two years of fruitless effort, he had been able, though sadly battered, to take up his pen and try again. But a *third!*

"I guess I'm no good," he told himself, in curiously calm despair. "Three strikes—*out!*"

Slowly he lifted to his feet, and walked with mechanical steps to the window. Then he went back, extinguished the desk light, & returned, and stood looking out into the rain.

A tracery of tears weaved itself over the many small panes. The night wind skirled in shrill ululations through cracks somewhere in the high attic walls, that quivered, flimsy boards clapping together.

Six stories below ran a squalid narrow street, through which incongruously ornate cars whizzed. Somewhere in the West Side Addition had been an important evening event, and traffic back to town was heavy.

"How like stars are the street lights—stars too large," mused David, watching through the diffusion of rain on the window. "And the carlight reflecting on the glossy pavement! There aren't any there . . ."

He looked upward at a sky that was covered with ugly clouds, like dark, dripping bags.

His eyes wandered off to the distant slumbering hills. They were unseen in the night, but he knew they brooded out there beyond the city.

"And that beautiful grey cloud of mist against them. How light it is! Strange, I can see it from so far."

He looked down again, and wondered vaguely how the wet asphalt would feel against his cheek.

His face was pale in the gloom, his black hair tousled. His fingers were smeared with ink. But he was quite calm.

Tap . . . tap . . . tap.

Cold rain fingers were striking on his window.

He grasped the knobs on the door-windows and pulled them open.

The curtains shook angrily. Icy drops struck his hot, white face.

He lifted a foot to the ledge . . .

The mist . . . in a formless phantasmic swirl of grey that shimmered as though the hidden moon's light was caressing it . . . was closer now, and it had been so far away, near the mountains. So close soon he could almost reach out into the night and touch it. it gathered and floated toward him in a sheen of silver. It was enveloping him, now, in a tingling cool veil that bathed his feverish body—that seeped into his skin, his nostrils, and halted that throbbing pain in his mind.

He stood poised on the ledge in ecstasy, while the vapour floated into the room . . .

Suddenly, sickeningly, he realized what he had been about to do—the wet pavement and the rushing cars . . . He murmured,

"My God!" and jumped into the room, and closed the window quickly.

Briskly he ran to the desk, snapped on the light, and took up his pen . . .

It was six weeks later that David stood again at the open window, dressed in a smart brown suit, his black hair immaculately brushed back. He held in his hand a letter.

His eyes passed rapidly over the dismal little room he was now leaving. It was quite bare; his belongings had already been moved to the new department early in the afternoon.

Now in late evening, he looked out at the bright sky stars, and thought of that other night. That April night when he had been in so desperate . . . how he had gone to the window . . . the coming of the mist . . . then, the mad rush of writing that had resuscitated his book completely. That had transformed it into something spiritually fine and great.

He looked down at the letter from the publishing company that was to print it.

"It is the most stupendous, yet simply and gently styled, book we have been privileged to read in many years. Although in some parts it is curiously reminiscent of the work of the late Philip Croft, it is above his finest, we believe. *Shadows in the Mist* seems, in some occult way, to go beyond mortal experience. It is as though the author had caught a brief glimpse into Eternity. . . ."

David's eyes were bright and brimming as he turned far into the night, to watch the sheen of mist that couched against the dim blue mountains.

"Philip Croft," he whispered, *"You are not dead."*

[Fragmentary Story]

youthful fancies I little dreamed that one day I was to meet this exotic charmer of men in the flesh—that I even—but wait, I'm getting ahead of my story.

"I, Elwin Osborn Emanuel Filbein, was born of humble but honest parents, right here in London. My father was himself an uneducated man<,> but, seeing in his infinite wisdom the numerous advantages of a high<er> education, <he> put me through the very best schools in all of England, thought [*sic*] it cost him much scraping and saving to do so. I had just finished my college career (my mother died when I was eight) and was looking about for a suitable position, when my dear pater died, leaving me a few hundred pounds with which to start life. Now, I had always had an intense craving, a great longing to visit that land of Mystery and Enchantment, Egypt; so I decided to use this money to quench this feeling—and, who knew what wonders might befall me in that land of lands!

"So I made this journey, and had the time of my young life. I saw the tombs of the Kings, the Sphinx, the beautiful Nile, and all the rest of it's <its> magic marvels. I spent weeks and months in little-visited parts of Egypt. I drank deep, and smelled deep of it's <its> many varied sights and odors, for I knew that all too soon I must leave. So Time passed, as Time does, and soon I found that my slim fortune was dwindling to a mere morsel, and I knew that soon I must tear myself away. Already I had long exceeded my stay, and would have nothing left when I returned to England, but I remained. Yes, I stayed. I couldn't bear the thought of leaving the land that had captured my heart and my whole being—yes, my very soul. at last came a day when I woke from my dreaming and found that I couldn't return to England ~~had I wanted to~~ <even if I wished>, for my money was practically gone—I no longer had even enough for steamship fare. What could I do? I had to admit to myself that I was a little glad that I *couldn't* return—but I had to live. I pondered and pondered over my dilemma, and at last the thought occurred to me—why couldn't I hire myself as a guide? I knew more about the places the tourists were wont to visit than the native dragomen themselves, could speak four European languages, and moreover I could recite the entire history of each point of interest as from a book.

"Well, that's what I did. I stayed on there for three years at this occupation. The salary was not munificent, as salaries go, but I supplemented it with various other earnings, and lived very nicely indeed. During the time when tourist trade was at a minimum, I found a posit<i>on at the British consul<ar offices>. I had learned the language so that I could speak it as well if not better than the natives; not only the scholar's ~~tongue~~ <Arabic> but the mongrel gibberish as well. Thus I lived in peaceful content and blissful happiness. Many adventures I had, too, but none that can hold a candle to the one I am about to relate to you.

"One day while out on a [*sic*] expedition with an American party that was doing some excavation work at the Sharaghut Tombs (Ever hear of the Sharaghut Tombs? No? I thought as much. Few people have.) I left the group and began to do a bit of exploring on my own. I went down underground to the original vault, and it so happened that there was no one there—and while I was poking about in the dark corners, something peculiar caught my attention. It looked extremely like a trap-door or something, so I dug around it and tugged and tugged at it, until I had it loosened. This huge stone was prodigiously heavy but, with the aid of an iron bar, I I [*sic*] managed to lift it up; and found to my unspeakable amazement and delight a passageway leading to a cellar even fu<a>rther down. You may be sure that I lost no time in going down, my electric torch in my hand. The steps of this new tomb ~~led to unfathomable depths and~~ seemed to descend endlessly; ~~and~~ <so that> I had to walk very carefully~~, for they~~ <They> were steep, and I feared I might tumble off and fall down to God ~~knew~~<knows> what depths. After some time I reached the bottom of the stairs, and flashed my light around to see what sort of a place I was in. The room was small, and appeared to have been carved out of solid rock. There ~~were~~ <was> no sarcophagus or <heap of> bones, or any <other> evidence of the room's having been used for burial purposes, and this fact surprised me not a little. The floor was thick with the dust of centuries, and I saw large tomb-spiders scuttle along the wall in the light of my flash-lamp. The only thing of any importance that I could discern, was a small niche carved into the wall at the fu<a>rther end. This seemed worth investigating, so I went over to it, and saw something on it that looked like a metal box. It wasn't heavy or large, so I lifted it off, and when I brushed the dust off of it I saw that there was writing on the cover. Perhaps I didn't tell you that in addition to learning the modern ~~language~~ <Arabic> of the Egyptians, I ~~also had~~ <had also> learned the ~~hieroglyphic picture writing used by the ancients~~ <ancient language of the hieroglyphics> so far as it had been deciphered at the time of which I speak. So, after puzzling over the strange drawings on this box for some time, I made out what, if it were written in our language, might sound something like this:

'*He who possesses the content<s> of this box is the Master of Time. The years will roll back, and he may vision again his former lives.*'

"I can tell you, that upon seeing these words, I became so excited that I nearly let the box fall out of my hands. ~~Naturally~~ <Incredulity never occurred to me, and> I became feverishly curious to behold the marvels on the side. But that took some time. Seated on the first stone step, I pried at the lid with my pocket knife for houres, it seemed, until finally the rust gave way. Why it was so difficult to open I can not understand, for the moment it did open, it fell entirely to pieces."

Here the little man began to stroke his chin in silence, a strange rapt look on his face, as though he were brooding over this curious fact. The story ~~intrigued~~ <fascinated> me, and I felt like screaming at him to go on, but forced myself to say, in a semi-bored tone: "Well, what was in the silly thing?"

"What was in it?—what was there? you ask; well, be patient and I will tell you. I must tell you the *whole* story just as it occurred to me, so that you will no longer think that I am insane," he repeated uselessly, "As I have said, after what seemed houre<s> I got the box open, and as it opened it broke into small pieces, leaving the contents ~~or content,~~ lying on my gloved hand. *It* was a large stone which cast off a dull, sinister green light—yet itself was not green, ~~nor~~ <or> any other color you could name, ~~nor~~ transparent <either>. ~~This~~ <The> light it shed didn't seem to come directly from the stone, in the way that most precious gems shine; in fact<,> it didn't *appear* to glow at all. Only the moment the box was opened the whole room brightened as though an incandescent lamp had been suddenly turned on. In size it was almost as large as a golf-ball. I gazed at it ~~a moment~~ in dumbstruck awe, for it assumed the properties of a gigantic eye of a hideous monster glaring at me madly, and *winking* loathsomely. But it was bewitching, and I shifted it to my other bare hand; then I dropped it as quickly as if it had been red-hot, which it certainly was not. Quite the opposite, in fact. It was *very* cold, like a piece of ice, only more so; it caused me to shiver all over. And it seemed to move in my hand. Besides all this, it left my hand feeling damp and creepy.

"There I sat, after I had plucked up courage enought to pick it up, gazing at it fearfully yet fascinated. It had an unholy power that made me want to keep staring at it for the rest of my life. My brain becae sluggish as I gazed, yet I was powerless to remove my eyes from the evil thing. I sat there, ~~becoming more dopy and drugged~~ <as if drugged, growing drowsier> all the time, until at last I must have gone to sleep altogether."

The aggravating narrator, at this point, got up and put more fuel on the fire, so slowly and deliberately that I could have wrung his neck. After satisfying himself that I would not die of cold, for he had begun to lament and battle over my sickly appearance, the imbecile continued his outrageous tale, after hinting that the bet was yet to come:

"I went to sleep, you remember—well, I was awakened by someone shaking me vigourously. I opened my eyes dully, but when I s<a>w where I was I rose up with a cry. I looked in amaze at the one who had been shaking me. Well I could, for it was *Cleopatra*. Yes, you can shake your head and laugh and murme<u>r that I'm feeble-minded, but I tell you, that I speak from pure facts. ~~It was *her*, all right.~~ <It was from my vivid, recurrent dreams that I recognised her; and there was never the least doubt in my mind that it was she.> She began to speak to me rapidly <in Greek>, and though I could but vaguely hear her and even more vaguely tell what her strange-sounding words meant, ~~in her entrancingly lovely dark eyes was written stark terror~~—<I could guess from the stark terror in her lovely dark eyes that she was telling me to get up and aid her in some way. Then my brain cleared<,> and as it did I remembered who I *really* was, and her ~~tongue~~ <speech> became at once wholly familiar. I was in her royal palace, and why not? I was her trusted slave, Rendema.

"'Quick, Rendema!' she cried, 'They are even now killing him—you must go at once!' She didn't seem to be overjoyed at fining [*sic*] me dozing at my post. 'To the Belvina Room. Here is the vase that contains my message to Antony—hurry, you must not stand so stupidly here, staring at me. Go—go!' I took the vase from her beautiful hands, and ran out of the room and up the long, sweeping stairway. Through the gorgeously appointed apartments I sped, and didn't seem surprised to see the<at> the hallways and rooms were all deserted. I knew, in my ancient mind, that the downfall had already come and that the Roman armies had already captured the Palace. Cleopatra, the goddess of Egypt, had fallen. I paused at the entrance to room [*sic*] spoken of by the Queen, for I heard voices within, and realized the [*sic*] Mark Antony was not alone.

"'Then you will allow me to drink this draught, rather than surrender myself to disgrace!' The strong, rich tones I knew to be Antony's.

"'That is your privilege.' [*sic*] was the mocking answer, in sneering tones. 'come men, we must leave the Egyptian *king* alone to sup his last goblet of wine.' The man appeared to find a great deal of humor in this statement<,> for they laughed loudly as they passed out of the room, and down the stairs. When the footsteps and voices of the Roman soldiers died away, I quickly entered the room, and saw Antony lifting the golden cup to his lips. I ran to him and hurriedly told him of the message from my Queen.

"'I need no message to tell me that she is untrue. She is a ———' From his voice I could tell that the <Latin> name was uncomplimentary, but I didn't understand it. His powerful fingers gripped the cup with a clasp that could have easily twisted the thick metal into a shapeless mass. His voice was thick, too, with passion and self-contempt as he said: 'Of all the fool ssince Time began, I—I, Mark Antony, am the greatest!'

"'Noble sire, I swear that she *is* true to you, and to you only. Will you not read the message?' I begged, as I held out the vase. He wrenched it from my hands, and unrolling it, read it. I was cognizant of it's <its> contents, knowing that according to the Queen's hastily laid plan—Antony was to slip out to a certain spot on the Nile where *she* awaited with the few faithful slaves that still remained. They were to steal up the river in her barge, to a spot which was known only to a very few and which the Romans could never find, and there to live in carefree abandon together, in the Eden of waving palms and luscious fruits.

"His bronze face changed as he read—and he grasped me by the arm in a grip that nearly broke it, as he exclaimed:

"'Then she *isn't* a serpent—my Goddess! You swear this is not a plot?'

"I swore by all the Gods that all was as the message had said.

"Then his face clouded. 'But there will no b time for us to get away.' Look—' He pointed out the large window, [*sic*] "They have a sentry posted across there on the wall, who can see into this room; when he sees tat I'm not here, they will come up and finding me gone, will suspect our plan, and—. If there was <were> some way—.' The Roman's face darkened in perplexity.

"'I have a plan, your majesty.' [*sic*] I began timidly.

"[']What is it?' He didn't seem to have much faith in my abilities.

[']'They are watching the window to see you drink the poison. They will probably allow you a little time before they come up. If you were to slip out now, sir, I will pace back and forth across the window, wearing your cloak. They cannot see very distinctly from where they are, so they will believe me to be you. You will have time to get away, thus.' I unfolded my plan.

[']'Then how will *you* escape—they're sure to slit your throat when they find out the trick we've played on them; and Cleopatra values you highly, Rendema.'

[']'Surely I will find some way, sire. Please go quickly—so there will be time.' [*sic*] I implored.

"With a hearty handclasp, and a Roman salute which embarrassed me very much, the great Mark Antony gave me his cloak and left. I paced back and forth across the window, showing the scarlet cloak to advantage but taking care to hide my own features. I believed that they would allow me some time to meditate, so I continued to go back and forth until I saw the sentry leave his post. I knew then that they were going to come up, so I went over to the massive ebony table and, lifting the cup of poisoned wine from it, drained it. My mind began to get sluggish again, and I soon found that my *two* souls were merging into one body. My ancient mind began to remember some of the same thoughts that my modern mind thinks. It was most peculiar—indescribable. My *modern* mind was terrified for fear I should die, while my ancient mind was exultant and happy that in dying, I should bring happiness to the two I loved above all else. As my thoughts became dimmer and my mind faded I once more assumed the ego of Elwin Filbein, the dragoman—in the ancient body that has long since rotted to dust. I remember wondering that it took so long to die—the seconds became hours, the moments years. In the midst of this wondering, or *wandering*, the absurd thought occurred to me: 'Why not take something back with me, to prove my story?' The first thing my eyes fell upon, as I reelingly glanced about me, was this vase—so I grabbed it, just as my mind passed into oblivion; *and here it is.*"

I shook my head, sadly. "Surely," I said, "surely you don't expect me to believe this bizarre tale you tell?" I wanted to know, "Where is the proof you speak so glibly of? Where is the Jewel of Time? What happened when you awoke? Why didn't you die if you drank the poison?"

He smiled on me paternally.

"Isn't this vase proof enough? As for the Jewel of Time, as you have so aptly and accurately named it—that has disappeared. I awoke in the tent outside the Sharaghut ruin which we were excavating. I had been missed and traced to this underground room by two of the Egyptian helpers. They had carried me out, and the doctor had tried to waken me, but had failed. He said that I had remained in this room for hours, and muttered constantly in my sleep in ~~an unknown~~ tongue <he could not understand>. Isn't that significant? The natives that found me undoubtedly hocked the stone, knowing it to be valuable. Dragomen in Egypt will take anything they can lay their hands on, even your false teeth. You ask: 'Why didn't I die?' I'm surprised at you! That is quite obvious. I *did* die in that incarnation—naturally, then resuming again my present self."

"But the story itself is wrong. History says—"

He waved that aside impatiently. "History can say anything it wants to. *That* is what really happened to Cleopatra and Antony. I *know. I was there, Sharley.*"

I made innumerable other objections. I raged about the small room rearing madly, but the child-like face of the successor to Munchausen retained ~~it's~~ <its> serene calm.

"The next time I came upon the Jewel was in Paris—this snuffbox I carry with me was presented to me by Louis XIV in gratitude for—" he began.

But I waited to hear no more. With a suppressed groan, I grabbed my coat and hat, and ran out of his accursed shop—into the fog and dismal rain of the London dusk—to be alone once more with my bereavement.

Glossary of Frequently Mentioned Names

Baird, Edwin (1886–1954), first editor of *Weird Tales* (1923–24), who accepted HPL's first submissions to the magazine. Also editor of *Real Detective Tales and Mystery Stories*.

Baldwin, F[ranklin] Lee (1913–1987), weird fiction fan and late associate of HPL. He wrote columns for the *Fantasy Fan* and wrote a biographical sketch of HPL for *Fantasy Magazine* (April 1935). For HPL's letters to him, see *Letters to F. Lee Baldwin, Duane W. Rimel, and Nils Frome*.

Barlow, Robert H[ayward] (1918–1951), author and collector. As a teenager he corresponded with HPL and acted as his host during two long visits in the summers of 1934 and 1935. In the 1930s he wrote several works of weird and fantasy fiction, some in collaboration with HPL. HPL appointed him his literary executor. He provided assistance to August Derleth and DAW in the preparation of the early HPL volumes for Arkham House. In the 1940s he went to Mexico and became a distinguished anthropologist. He died by suicide. For HPL's letters to him, see *O Fortunate Floridian*.

Bates, Harry (1900–1981), editor of *Strange Tales* and *Astounding Stories*.

Bierce, Ambrose (1842–1914?), distinguished American author of tales of horror and of the Civil War.

Blackwood, Algernon (1869–1951), prolific British author of weird and fantasy tales.

Bloch, Robert (1917–1994), author of weird and suspense fiction who came into correspondence with HPL in 1933. HPL tutored him in the craft of writing during their four-year association. For HPL's letters to him, see *Letters to Robert Bloch and Others* (2015).

Brobst, Harry K[ern] (b. 1909), late associate of HPL who moved to Providence in 1932 and saw HPL regularly thereafter.

Cave, Hugh B[arnett] (b. 1910), prolific author of stories for the pulp magazines.

Clark, Lillian D[elora] (1847–1932), HPL's elder aunt, with whom he lived at 10 Barnes Street (1926–32). For HPL's letters to her, see *Letters to Family and Family Friends*.

Coates, Walter J[ohn] (1880–1941), editor of *Driftwind* and sporadic correspondent of HPL.

Cole, Edward H[arold] (1892–1966), longtime amateur associate of HPL, living in the Boston area.

Cook, W. Paul (1881–1948), publisher of the *Monadnock Monthly*, the *Vagrant*, and other amateur journals. In 1927 he issued the *Recluse*, containing HPL's "Supernatural Horror in Literature" and works by DAW.

Crawford, William L[evy] (1911–1984), editor of *Marvel Tales* and *Unusual Stories* and publisher of the Visionary Publishing Co., which issued HPL's *The Shadow over Innsmouth* (1936).

de la Mare, Walter (1873–1956), British author and poet who wrote occasional weird tales.

de Castro (Danziger), Adolphe (1859–1959), author, co-translator with Ambrose Bierce of Richard Voss's *The Monk and the Hangman's Daughter*, and correspondent of HPL. HPL revised his "The Last Test" and "The Electric Executioner."

Derleth, August W[illiam] (1909–1971), author of weird tales and also a long series of regional and historical works set in his native Wisconsin. HPL introduced him to DAW by correspondence. After HPL's death, he and DAW founded the publishing firm of Arkham House to preserve HPL's work in book form. For HPL's letters to him, see *Essential Solitude*.

Dunsany, Lord (Edward John Moreton Drax Plunkett, 18th baron Dunsany, 1878–1957), Anglo-Irish writer of fantasy tales whose work notably influenced HPL after HPL read it in 1919.

Dwyer, Bernard Austin (1897–1943), weird fiction fan living in West Shokan, NY. He corresponded sporadically with HPL. For HPL's letters to him, see *Letters to Maurice W. Moe and Others*.

Farnese, Harold S. (1885–1945), musical composer and sporadic correspondent of HPL. It was he who provided AWD with the spurious "Black Magic" quotation attributed to HPL.

Finlay, Virgil (1914–1971), one of the great weird artists of his time and a prolific contributor of artwork to the pulps. He corresponded with HPL toward the end of the latter's life. He also produced the artwork for the cover of *The Outsider* when Howard Wandrei failed to do so.

Galpin, Alfred (1901–1983), composer, French scholar, and longtime friend and correspondent of HPL. For HPL's letters to him, see *Letters to Alfred Galpin* (2003).

Gamwell, Annie E[meline] P[hillips] (1866–1941), HPL's younger aunt, living with him at 66 College Street (1933–37). For HPL's letters to her, see *Letters to Family and Family Friends*.

Gernsback, Hugo (1884–1967), editor of *Amazing Stories*, *Wonder Stories*, and other pioneering science fiction pulp magazines.

Hodgson, William Hope (1877–1918), British author of weird fiction whose work had fallen into obscurity until it was rediscovered in the 1930s, largely through the efforts of H. C. Koenig.

Hornig, Charles D[erwin] (1916–1999), editor of the *Fantasy Fan* (1933–35) and managing editor for *Wonder Stories* from November 1933 to April 1936.

Howard, Robert E[rvin] (1906–1936), prolific Texas author of weird and adventure tales for *Weird Tales* and other pulp magazines; creator of the adventure hero Conan the Barbarian. He and HPL corresponded voluminously from 1930 to 1936. He committed suicide when he heard of his mother's impending death. For his joint correspondence with HPL, see *A Means to Freedom*.

Kirk, George [Willard] (1898–1962), member of the Kalem Club. He published *Twenty-one Letters of Ambrose Bierce* (1922) and ran the Chelsea Bookshop in New York.

Kleiner, Rheinhart (1892–1949), amateur poet and longtime friend and correspondent of HPL. For HPL's letters to him, see *Letters to Rheinhart Kleiner* (2005).

Kline, Otis Adlebert (1891–1946), prolific writer for *Weird Tales* and other pulp magazines; also a literary agent for Robert E. Howard and others.

Koenig, H[erman] C[harles] (1893–1959), late associate of HPL who spearheaded the rediscovery of the work of William Hope Hodgson.

Leeds, Arthur (1882–1952?), an associate of HPL in New York and member of the Kalem Club.

Leiber, Fritz, Jr. (1910–1992), late associate of HPL who became one of the leading figures in science fiction and fantasy. For HPL's letters to him, see *Letters to C. L. Moore and Others*.

Long, Frank Belknap (1901–1994), fiction writer and poet and one of HPL's closest friends and correspondents.

Loveman, Samuel E. (1887–1976), poet and longtime friend of HPL and DAW as well as of Ambrose Bierce, Hart Crane, and George Sterling. Author of *The Hermaphrodite* (1926) and other works. For HPL's letters to him, see *Letters to Maurice W. Moe and Others*.

Lumley, William (1880–1960), eccentric late associate of HPL for whom HPL ghostwrote "The Diary of Alonzo Typer" (1935).

Machen, Arthur (1863–1947), Welsh author of weird fiction much admired by both HPL and DAW.

McNeil, Everett (1862–1929), prolific author of historical and adventure novels for boys; member of the Kalem Club.

Moe, Maurice W[inter] (1882–1940), longtime amateur associate of HPL, residing in Wisconsin, where he taught in various high schools in Appleton and Milwaukee. For HPL's letters to him, see *Letters to Maurice W. Moe and Others*.

Moore, C[atherine] L[ucile] (1911–1987), late associate of HPL who later married Henry Kuttner and became a leading figure in science fiction and fantasy. Their joint correspondence has been published in *Letters to C. L. Moore and Others*.

Morton, James Ferdinand (1870–1941), amateur journalist, author of many tracts on race prejudice, free thought, and taxation, and longtime friend of HPL. For HPL's letters to him, see *Letters to James F. Morton*.

Munn, H[arold] Warner (1903–1981), prolific contributor to the pulp magazines, living near W. Paul Cook in Athol, MA.

Orton, Vrest (1897–1986), member of the Kalem Club. He was for a time an editor at the *Saturday Review* and later the founder of the Vermont Country Store.

Price, E[dgar] Hoffmann (1898–1988), prolific pulp writer of weird and adventure tales. HPL met him in New Orleans in 1932 and corresponded extensively with him thereafter.

Quinn, Seabury (1889–1969), prolific author of weird and detective tales to the pulps, notably a series of tales involving the psychic detective Jules de Grandin.

Rimel, Duane W[eldon] (1915–1996), weird fiction fan and late associate of HPL, who revised some of his early tales. For HPL's letters to him, see *Letters to F. Lee Baldwin, Duane W. Rimel, and Nils Frome*.

Schwartz, Julius (1916–2004), editor of *Fantasy Magazine* who acted as HPL's agent in marketing *At the Mountains of Madness* to *Astounding Stories*.

Shiel, M[atthew] P[hipps] (1865–1947), British author of weird fiction whose story "The House of Sounds" and novel *The Purple Cloud* (1901) were much admired by HPL.

Smith, Clark Ashton (1893–1961), prolific California poet and writer of fantasy tales. He received a "fan" letter from HPL in 1922 and continued to correspond with him until HPL's death. He corresponded with DAW from 1924 into the 1950s. For his joint correspondence with HPL, see *Dawnward Spire, Lonely Hill*.

Starrett, Vincent (1886–1974), American bookman best known for the treatise *Buried Caesars* (1923) and for a long-running column about books in the *Chicago Tribune*. He also published tales and poems in *Weird Tales*. He corresponded briefly with HPL in 1927–28. For HPL's correspondence with him, see *Letters to Maurice W. Moe and Others*.

Sterling, George (1869–1926), American poet and author of "cosmic" verse, notably in *The Testimony of the Suns* (1903) and *A Wine of Wizardry* (1909). Early mentor of CAS.

Sterling, Kenneth (1920–1995), science fiction fan and late associate of HPL. He collaborated with HPL on the story "In the Walls of Eryx" (1936). For HPL's letters to him, see *Letters to Robert Bloch and Others* (2015).

Strauch, Carl Ferdinand (1908–1989), friend of Harry Brobst and correspondent of HPL. He later became a distinguished professor and critic. For HPL's letters to him, see *Letters to J. Vernon Shea, Carl F. Strauch, and Lee McBride White*.

Sully, Helen V. (1904–1997), friend of CAS who visited HPL in Providence in 1933, then saw DAW and others in New York.

Talman, Wilfred Blanch (1904–1986), late member of the Kalem Club. He and HPL collaborated on the story "Two Black Bottles" (1926).

Whitehead, Henry S[t. Clair] (1882–1932), author of weird and adventure tales, many of them set in the Virgin Islands. HPL visited him in Florida in 1931.

Wollheim, Donald A[llen] (1914–1990), editor of the *Phantagraph* and *Fanciful Tales* and prolific author and editor in the science fiction field. For HPL's letters to him, see *Letters to Robert Bloch and Others*.

Wright, Farnsworth (1888–1940), editor of *Weird Tales* (1924–40).

Howard Wandrei

Bibliography

A. Works by H. P. Lovecraft

Books

The Ancient Track: Complete Poetical Works. Edited by S. T. Joshi. 2nd ed. New York: Hippocampus Press, 2013.

Charleston. [New York: H. C. Koenig, 1936.] In *CE* 4.

Collected Essays. Edited by S. T. Joshi. New York: Hippocampus Press, 2004–06. 5 vols.

Collected Fiction: A Variorum Edition. Edited by S. T. Joshi. New York: Hippocampus Press, 2015, 17. 4 vols.

Dawnward Spire, Lonely Hill: The Letters of H. P. Lovecraft and Clark Ashton Smith. Edited by David E. Schultz and S. T. Joshi. New York: Hippocampus Press, 2017.

Essential Solitude: The Letters of H. P. Lovecraft and August Derleth. Edited by David E. Schultz and S. T. Joshi. New York: Hippocampus Press, 2008. 2 vols. (numbered consecutively).

Fungi from Yuggoth: An Annotated Edition. Edited by David E. Schultz. New York: Hippocampus Press, 2017.

Letters to F. Lee Baldwin, Duane W. Rimel, and Nils Frome. Edited by David E. Schultz and S. T. Joshi. New York: Hippocampus Press, 2016.

Letters to Family and Family Friends. Edited by S. T. Joshi and David E. Schultz. New York: Hippocampus Press. 2 vols. (numbered consecutively). Forthcoming.

Letters to J. Vernon Shea, Carl F. Strauch, and Lee McBride White. Edited by David E. Schultz and S. T. Joshi. New York: Hippocampus Press, 2016.

Letters to James F. Morton. Edited by David E. Schultz and S. T. Joshi. New York: Hippocampus Press, 2011.

Letters to Maurice W. Moe and Others. Edited by David E. Schultz and S. T. Joshi. New York: Hippocampus Press, 2018.

The Materialist Today. North Montpelier, VT: Driftwind Press, 1926. In *CE* 5.

A Means to Freedom: The Letters of H. P. Lovecraft and Robert E. Howard. Edited by S. T. Joshi, David E. Schultz, and Rusty Burke. New York: Hippocampus Press, 2009. 2 vols. (numbered consecutively).

O Fortunate Floridian: H. P. Lovecraft's Letters to R. H. Barlow. Edited by S. T. Joshi and David E. Schultz. Tampa, FL: University of Tampa Press, 2007.

Selected Letters. Edited by August Derleth, Donald Wandrei, and James Turner. Sauk City, WI: Arkham House, 1965–76. 5 vols.

The Shunned House. Athol, MA: Recluse Press, 1928 (printed but not bound or distributed). In *CE* 1.

Uncollected Letters. Edited by S. T. Joshi. West Warwick, RI: Necronomicon Press, 1986.

Stories

"The Alchemist." *United Amateur* 16, No. 4 (November 1916): 53–57. In *CF* 1.

"Arthur Jermyn." See "Facts concerning the Late Arthur Jermyn and His Family."

At the Mountains of Madness. Astounding Stories 16, No. (February 1936): 8–32; 17, No. 1 (March 1936): 125–55; 17, No. 2 (April 1936): 132–50. In *CF* 3.

"The Beast in the Cave." *Vagrant* No. 7 (June 1918): 113–20. In *CF* 1.

"Beyond the Wall of Sleep." *Pine Cones* 1, No. 6 (October 1919): 2–10. *Fantasy Fan* 2, No. 2 (October 1934): 25–32. In *CF* 1.

"The Call of Cthulhu." *WT* 11, No. 2 (February 1928): 159–78, 287. In T. Everett Harré, ed. *Beware After Dark! The World's Most Stupendous Tales of Mystery, Horror, Thrills and Terror.* New York: Macauley, 1929. 223–59. In *CF* 2.

The Case of Charles Dexter Ward. In *CF* 2.

"Celephaïs." *Rainbow* No. 2 (May 1922): 10–12. *Marvel Tales* 1, No. 1 (May 1934): 26, 28–32. In *CF* 1.

"The Colour out of Space." *Amazing Stories* 2, No. 6 (September 1927): 557–67. In *CF* 2.

"Cool Air." *Tales of Magic and Mystery* 1, No. 4 (March 1928): 29–34. In *CF* 2.

"Dagon." *Vagrant* No. 11 (November 1919): 23–29. *WT* 2, No. 3 (October 1923): 23–25. In *CF* 1.

"The Doom That Came to Sarnath." *Scot* No. 44 (June 1920): 90–98. *Marvel Tales of Science and Fantasy* 1, No. 4 (March–April 1935): 157–63. In *CF* 1.

The Dream-Quest of Unknown Kadath. In *CF* 2.

"The Dunwich Horror." *WT* 13, No. 4 (April 1929): 481–508. In *CF* 2.

"Facts concerning the Late Arthur Jermyn and His Family." *Wolverine* No. 9 (March 1921): 3–11; No. 10 (June 1921): 6–11. *WT* 3, No. 4 (April 1924): 15–18 (as "The White Ape"). *WT* 25, No. 5 (May 1935): 642–48 (as "Arthur Jermyn"). In *CF* 1.

"The Festival." *WT* 5, No. 1 (January 1925): 169–74. *WT* 22, No. 4 (October 1933): 519–20, 522–28. In *CF* 1.

"From Beyond." *Fantasy Fan* 1, No. 10 (June 1934): 147–51, 160. In *CF* 1.

"The Haunter of the Dark." *WT* 28, No. 5 (December 1936): 538–53. In *CF* 3.

"He." *WT* 8, No. 3 (September 1926): 373–80. In *CF* 1.

"Herbert West—Reanimator." *Home Brew* 1, No. 1 (February 1922): 84–88; 1, No. 2 (March 1922): 45–50; 1, No. 3 (April 1922): 21–26; 1, No. 4 (May 1922): 53–58; 1, No. 5 (June 1922): 45–50; 1, No. 6 (July 1922): 57–62 (as "Grewsome Tales"). In *CF* 1.

"The Horror at Red Hook." *WT* 9, No. 1 (January 1927): 59–73. In Christine

Campbell Thomson, ed. *You'll Need a Night Light.* London: Selwyn & Blount, 1927. 228–54. In *CF* 1.

"The Hound." *WT* 3, No. 2 (February 1924): 50–52, 78. *WT* 14, No. 3 (September 1929): 421–25, 432. In *CF* 1.

"In the Vault." *Tryout* 10, No. 6 (November 1925): [3–17]. *WT*, 19, No. 4 (April 1932): 459–65. In *CF* 1.

"The Lurking Fear." *Home Brew* 2, No. 6 (January 1923): 4–10; 3, No. 1 (February 1923): 18–23; 3, No. 2 (March 1923): 31–37, 44, 48; 3, No. 3 (April 1923): 35–42. *WT*, 11, No. 6 (June 1928): 791–804. In *CF* 1.

"The Music of Erich Zann." *National Amateur* 44, No. 4 (March 1922): 38–40. *WT*, 5, No. 5 (May 1925): 219–34. *WT* 24, No. 5 (November 1934): 644–48, 655–56. In Dashiell Hammett, ed. *Creeps by Night: Chills and Thrills.* New York: John Day Co., 1931. 347–63. In Dashiell Hammett, ed. *Modern Tales of Horror.* London: Victor Gollancz, 1932. 301–17. In *CF* 1.

"The Mysterious Ship" [juvenilia]. In *CF* 3.

"The Nameless City." *Wolverine* No. 11 (November 1921): 3–15. *Fanciful Tales* 1, No. 1 (Fall 1936): 5–18. In *CF* 1.

"Nyarlathotep." *United Amateur* 20, No. 2 (November 1920): 19–21. *National Amateur* 43, No. 6 (July 1926): 53–54. In *CF* 1.

"The Outsider." *WT* 7, No. 4 (April 1926): 449–53. *WT* 17, No. 4 (June–July 1931): 566–71. In *CF* 1.

"Pickman's Model." *WT* 10, No. 4 (October 1927): 505–14. *WT* 28, No. 4 (November 1936): 495–505. In Christine Campbell Thomson, ed. *By Daylight Only.* London: Selwyn & Blount, 1929. 37–52. In Christine Campbell Thomson, ed. *The "Not at Night" Omnibus.* London: Selwyn & Blount, [1937]. 279–307. In *CF* 2.

"The Picture in the House." *National Amateur* 41, No. 6 (July 1919 [*sic*]): 246–49. *WT* 3, No. 1 (January 1924): 40–42. *WT*, 29, No. 3 (March 1937): 370–73. In *CF* 1.

"Polaris." *Philosopher* 1, No. 1 (December 1920): 3–5. *National Amateur* 48, No. 5 (May 1926): 48–49. *Fantasy Fan* 1, No. 6 (February 1934): 83–85. In *CF* 1.

"The Quest of Iranon." *Galleon* 1, No. 5 (July–August 1935): 12–20. In *CF* 1.

"The Rats in the Walls." *WT* 3, No. 3 (March 1924): 25–31. *WT* 15, No. 6 (June 1930: 841–53. In Christine Campbell Thomson, ed. *Switch On the Light.* London: Selwyn & Blount, 1931. 141–65. In *CF* 1.

"The Secret of the Grave" [juvenilia]. HPL's mistitling of "The Mystery of the Grave-Yard." In *CF* 3.

"The Shadow out of Time." *Astounding Stories* 17, No. 4 (June 1936): 110–54. In *CF* 3.

"The Silver Key." *WT* 13, No. 1 (January 1929): 41–49, 144. In *CF* 2.

"The Statement of Randolph Carter." *Vagrant* No. 13 (May 1920): 41–48. *WT* 5, No. 2 (February 1925): 149–53. In *CF* 1.

"Strange High House in the Mist." *WT* 18, No. 3 (October 1931): 394–400. In *CF* 2.

"The Temple." *WT* 6, No. 3 (September 1925): 329–36, 429, 431. *WT* 27, No. 2 (February 1936): 239–44, 246–49. In *CF* 1.

"The Thing on the Doorstep." *WT* 29, No. 1 (January 1937): 52–70. In *CF* 3.

"The Tree." *Tryout* 7, No. 7 (October 1921): [3–10]. In *CF* 1.

"The Whisperer in Darkness." *WT* 18, No. 1 (August 1931): 32–73. In *CF* 3.

"The White Ship." *United Amateur* 19, No. 2 (November 1919): 30–33. *WT* 9, No. 3 (March 1927): 386–89. In *CF* 1.

Revisions and Collaborations

Bishop, Zealia. "The Curse of Yig." *WT* 14, No. 5 (November 1929): 625–36. In Christine Campbell Thomson, ed. *Switch On the Light*. London: Selwyn & Blount, 1931. 9–31. In Christine Campbell Thomson, ed. *The "Not at Night" Omnibus*, London: Selwyn & Blount, [1937]. 13–29. In *CF* 4.

de Castro, Adolphe. "The Electric Executioner." [orig. "The Automatic Executioner"]. *WT* 16, No. 2 (August 1930): 223–36. In *CF* 4.

———. "The Last Test." *WT*, 12, No. 5 (November 1928): 625–56. In *CF* 4.

Heald, Hazel. "The Horror in the Museum." *WT* 22, No. 1 (July 1933): 49–68. In Christine Campbell Thomson, ed. *Terror by Night*. London: Selwyn & Blount, [1934]. 111–41. In Christine Campbell Thomson, ed. *The "Not at Night" Omnibus*. London: Selwyn & Blount, [1937]. 279–307. In *CF* 4.

Price, E. Hoffmann. "Through the Gates of the Silver Key." *WT*, 24, No. 1 (July 1934): 60–85. In *CF* 3.

Talman, Wilfred Blanch. "Two Black Bottles." *WT*, 10, No. 2 (August 1927): 251–58. In *CF* 4.

Essays

"Correspondence between R. H. Barlow and Wilson Shepherd of Oakman, Alabama—Sept.–Nov. 1932." In *CE* 5.

"In Memoriam: Robert Ervin Howard." *Fantasy Magazine* No. 38 (September 1936): 29–31. In *CE* 5.

"A Living Heritage: Roman Architecture in Today's America." *Californian* 3, No. 1 (Summer 1935): 23–28 (abridged; as "Heritage or Modernism: Common Sense in Art Forms"). In *CE* 5.

"Robert Ervin Howard: 1906–1936." *Phantagraph* 4, No. 5 (August 1936): 4–5. A condensed version of "In Memoriam: Robert Ervin Howard," appearing in print a month before the full version. In *CE* 5.

"Supernatural Horror in Literature." *Recluse* No. 1 (1927): 23–59. In *CE* 2.

"Vermont—A First Impression." *Driftwind*, 2, No. 5 (March 1928): [5–9]. In *CE* 4.

"The Weird Work of William Hope Hodgson." *Phantagraph* 5, No. 5 (February 1937): 5–7. [Incorporated into SHL.]

"The Work of Frank Belknap Long, Jr." *United Amateur* 23, No. 1 (May 1924): 1–4 (unsigned). In *CE* 1.

Poems [All poems are found in *AT.*]
"Ave atque Vale: To Jonathan E. Hoag, Esq.: February 10, 1831–October 17th, 1927." *Tryout,* 11, No. 10 (December 1927): [3–4].
"[Fragment on Whitman.]" In "In a Major Key." *Conservative* 1, No. 2 (July 1915): 9–11 In *CE* 1.
Fungi from Yuggoth.
> XXIII. "Mirage." *WT* 17, No. 2 (February–March 1931): 1975.
> XXVII. "The Elder Pharos." *WT* 17, No. 2 (February–March 1931): 175.
> XXXVI. "Continuity." *Causerie* (February 1936): 1.
"Nathicana." *Vagrant* [Spring 1927]: 61–64.
"The Poe-et's Nightmare." *Vagrant* No. 8 (July 1918): [13–23].
"Psychopompos: A Tale in Rhyme." *Vagrant* No. 10 (October 1919): 13–22.
"To Zara: Inscribed to Miss Sarah Longhurst—June 1829." As by "Edgar Allan Poe." Included in a letter by HPL to Maurice W. Moe, [August] 1922.

With Donald Wandrei
Mysteries of Time and Spirit: The Letters of H. P. Lovecraft and Donald Wandrei. Edited by S. T. Joshi and David E. Schultz. San Francisco: Night Shade Books, 2002.

B. Works by Donald Wandrei

Books
Broken Mirrors (with Francis Bosworth, Karl Litzenberg, Gordon Louis Roth, and Harrison Salisbury; illustrated by Leo Henkora). [St. Paul, MN:] Avon Press, 1928. [*BM*]
Colossus: The Collected Science Fiction of Donald Wandrei. Edited by Philip J. Rahman and Dennis E. Weiler. Minneapolis, MN: Fedogan & Bremer, 1989, 1999. [*C*]
Dark Odyssey. With Five Illustrations by Howard Wandrei. St. Paul, MN: Webb Publishing Co., [1931]. (*LL* 1009) [*DO*]
Dead Titans, Waken! and Invisible Sun. Edited by S. T. Joshi. Lakewood, CO: Centipede Press, 2011. Nampa, ID: Fedogan & Bremer, 2017. [*DT*]
Don't Dream: The Collected Horror and Fantasy Fiction of Donald Wandrei. Edited by Philip J. Rahman and Dennis E. Weiler. Minneapolis, MN: Fedogan & Bremer, 1997. [*DD*]
A Donald Wandrei Miscellany. Edited by D. H. Olson. St. Paul: Sidecar Preservation Society, 2001.
Ecstasy and Other Poems. Athol, MA: Recluse Press, 1928. (*LL* 1010) [*E*]

The Eye and the Finger. Sauk City, WI: Arkham House, 1944. [*EF*]

Frost. Edited by D. H. Olson. Minneapolis, MN: Fedogan & Bremer, 2000.

Poems for Midnight. Sauk City, WI: Arkham House, 1964. [*PM*]

Sanctity and Sin: The Collected Poems and Prose Poems of Donald Wandrei. Edited by S. T. Joshi. New York: Hippocampus Press, 2008.

Strange Harvest. Sauk City, WI: Arkham House, 1965. Cover by Howard Wandrei. [*SH*]

The Web of Easter Island. Sauk City, WI: Arkham House, 1948.

Stories and Prose-Poems

"Advertised for Death." See "Frost."

"The Atom Smasher" [formerly "The Decomposer," "The Decompositor," and "Schonheim"]. *Astounding Stories* 13, No. 2 (April 1934): 85–86. In *C.*

"Beyond the Milky Way." Nonextant. [= "The One Who Died"? RMB 82.]

"Black and Silver" [also "Ebony and Silver"]. Unpublished. "A short story about a man and his encounter with two different statues of Venus" (RMB 29).

"Black Fog." *Thrilling Wonder Stories* 9, No. 1 (February 1937): 33–41. In *EF, C.*

"The Black Pool." Nonextant.

"The Chuckler." *Fantasy Magazine* 4, No. 1 (September 1934): 26–27. In *SH, DD.*

"Colossus." *Astounding Stories* 12, No. 5 (January 1934): 41–72. In *C.*

"Colossus Eternal." *Astounding Stories* 14, No. 4 (December 1934): 50–87. In *C.*

Dead Titans, Waken! In *DT.*

"The Death of the Flowers." Unpublished. "A piece of straight fiction, dealing with an unsmiling, beautiful woman and her curious secret garden" (RMB 22). Originally "The Lost Moon."

"The Decomposer" [or "The Decompositor"]. See "The Atom Smasher."

"The Door to the Room." See "Nightmare."

"The Eye and the Finger." *Esquire* 6, No. 6 (December 1936): 70, 319–20. In *EF, DD.*

"The Fire Creatures." See "When the Fire Creatures Came."

"The Fire Vampires." *WT* 21, No. 2 (February 1933): 179–190. In *SH, DD.*

"Fragment of a Dream." *Minnesota Quarterly* 4, No. 2 (Winter 1926): 28–34. *Recluse* No. 1 (1927): 18–21. In *EF, DD.*

"Frost." *Clues Detective Stories* 32, No. 4 (September 1934): 6–34. In *Frost.*

"The Green Flame." *WT* 16, No. 1 (July 1930): 47–48. In *SH, DD.* Originally "Symphony in Green."

"In the Billionth Aeon." See "The Red Brain."

Invisible Sun. In *DT.*

"It Will Grow on You." In *EF, DD.*

"The Lady in Gray." *WT* 22, No. 6 (December 1933): 764–67. In *EF, DD.*

"The Lives of Alfred Kramer." *WT* 20, No. 6 (December 1932): 817–29. In *EF, DD.*

"The Lost Moon." See "The Death of the Flowers."

"The Messengers." *Minnesota Quarterly* 4, No. 1 (Fall 1926): 58–59. In *EF*, *DD*.

"The Monster from Nowhere." *Argosy* (23 November 1935). In *EF*, *DD*.

"Nightmare" [formerly "The Door to the Room"]. In *SH*, *DD*.

"The Purple Land." In *DD*.

"The Pursuers." *Minnesota Quarterly* 4, No. 1 (Fall 1926): 59. In *EF*, *DD*.

"A Race through Time." *Astounding Stories* 12, No. 2 (October 1933): 18–34. In *C*.

"Raiders of the Universes." *Astounding Stories* 11, No. 1 (September 1932): 63–77. In *C*.

"The Red Brain" [formerly "In the Billionth Aeon" and "The Twilight of Time"]. *WT* 10, No. 4 (October 1927): 531–37; rpt. 27, No. 5 (May 1936): 626–28, 630–33. In *EF*, *C*.

"A Sea Change." See "Uneasy Lie the Drowned."

"Schonheim." See "The Atom Smasher."

"The Shadow of a Nightmare." *WT* 13, No. 5 (May 1929): 619–24, 716. In *DD*.

"Something from Above." *WT* 16, No. 6 (December 1930): 763–78. In *SH*, *C*.

"The Tree-Men of M'Bwa." *WT* 19, No. 2 (February 1932): 220–27. In *EF*, *DD*.

"Uneasy Lie the Drowned." *WT* 30, No. 6 (December 1937): 740–44. In *SH*, *DD*. Originally "A Sea Change."

"Unto the End." Nonextant? (story? poem?).

"When the Fire Creatures Came." In *DD* (first appearance).

"The Woman at the Window." *Leaves* 2 (1938): 98–99. In *EF*, *DD*.

Poems [All poems are found in *SS*]

"Aftermath." In *BM*, *CP*, *SS*.

"The Challenger." *Minnesota Quarterly* 4, No. 3 (Spring 1927): 36.

"Chant to the Dead." *Minnesota Quarterly* 4, No. 3 (Spring 1927): 34.

"Chaos Resolved." In *DO*, *CP*, *SS*.

"The Corpse Speaks." See "In the Grave."

"Credo." In *BM*, *CP*, *SS*.

"The Cry of the Mad." Nonextant?

"The Cypress-Bog." *WT* 16, No. 5 (November 1930): 714. In *CP*, *SS*.

"Dark Odyssey." In *DO*, *CP*, *SS*.

"The Dead Mistress." In *BM*, *CP*, *SS*.

"Drink!" In *BM*, *CP*, *SS*.

"Fling Wide the Roses." In *BM*, *CP*, *SS*.

"In the Grave" [also "The Corpse Speaks"]. *Recluse* No. 1 (1927): 76. In *PM*, *CP*, *SS*.

"The Little Gods Wait." *WT* 20, 1 (July 1932): 116. In *CP*, *SS*.

"Look Homeward, Angel." In *DO*, *CP*, *SS*.

"Lost Atlantis." *Minnesota Quarterly* 4, No. 3 (Spring 1927): 34–35. In *DO, PM, CP, SS*.

"Morning Song." In *DO, CP, SS*.

"My Lady Hath Two Lovely Lips." In *BM, CP, SS*.

"Mystical Quest." Nonextant?

"The Night Wind." In *DO, CP, SS*.

"Old Fantasy." Nonextant?

"Red." In *E, CP, SS*.

"The Sleeper." In *BM, PM, CP, SS*.

"The Song of Autumn." *Minnesota Quarterly* 4, No. 1 (Fall 1926): 15. In *E, PM, CP, SS*. Awarded honorable mention in the Witter Bynner Undergraduate Poetry Prize for 1926.

"The Song of Oblivion." *Minnesota Quarterly* 4, No. 3 (Spring 1927): 33. In *E, PM, CP, SS*.

Sonnets of the Midnight Hours.

"1. The Hungry Flowers." *WT* 11, No. 5 (May 1928): 674. In *PM, CP, SS*.

"2. Dream Horror." *WT* 11, No. 5 (May 1928): 674. In *CP, SS*.

"3. Purple." *WT* 11, No. 6 (June 1928): 837. In *PM, CP, SS*.

"4. The Eye." *WT* 12, No. 1 (July 1928): 69. In *PM, CP, SS*.

"5. The Grip of Evil Dreams." *WT* 12, No. 2 (August 1928): 231. In *CP, SS*.

"6. As I Remember." *WT* 12, No. 3 (September 1928): 374. In *CP* and *SS* as "The Torturers."

"7. The Statues." *WT* 12, No. 4 (October 1928): 480. In *PM, CP, SS*.

"8. The Creatures." *WT* 12, No. 5 (November 1928): 624. In *CP, SS*.

"9. The Head." *WT* 12, No. 6 (December 1928): 815. In *PM, CP, SS*.

"10. The Red Specter." *WT* 13, No. 1 (January 1929): 110. In *CP, SS*.

"11. Doom." *WT* 13, No. 2 (February 1929): 254. In *CP, SS*.

"12. A Vision of the Future." *WT* 13, No. 3 (March 1929): 420. In *CP* and *SS* as "The Ultimate Vision."

"Strange Flowers." Nonextant?

"Ultimate Horror." Nonextant?

"Valerian." In *E, CP, SS*.

"The Whispering Knoll." In *DO, CP, SS*.

"Witches' Sabbath." In *PM, CP, SS*.

"The Woodland Pool." In *E, PM, CP, SS*.

Drama

Love to Murder [or *It's Later Than You Think*]. Unpublished. "A drama played out on the coast of the Yucatan" (RMB 69).

Essays

"Arthur Machen and *The Hill of Dreams*." *Minnesota Quarterly* 3, No. 3 (Spring 1926): 19–24. *Studies in Weird Fiction* No. 15 (Summer 1994): 27–30.

"The Dweller in Darkness: Lovecraft, 1927." In H. P. Lovecraft et al., *Marginalia*. Ed. August Derleth and Donald Wandrei. Sauk City, WI: Arkham House, 1944. 362–69.

"The Emperor of Dreams." *Overland Monthly* 84, No. 12 (December 1926): 380–81, 407, 409. *Klarkash-Ton: The Journal of Smith Studies* No. 1 (1988): 3–8, 25.

"The Lilies, Perfume Perfume-Bottles, and Some-Will-O'-the-Wisps." In *A Donald Wandrei Miscellany* 21–28.

"Lovecraft in Providence." In H. P. Lovecraft et al., *The Shuttered Room and Other Pieces*. Sauk City, WI: Arkham House, 1959. 124–40. In *Ave atque Vale: Reminiscences of H. P. Lovecraft*, ed. S. T. Joshi and David E. Schultz. West Warwick, RI: Necronomicon Press, 2018. 264–78.

"The Monk, the Monk, and the Monk" (unpublished?).

C. Works by Howard Wandrei

The Eerie Mr. Murphy: The Collected Fantasy Tales of Howard Wandrei. Edited by D. H. Olson. Minneapolis, MN: Fedogan & Bremer, 2003.

The Last Pin. Edited by D. H. Olson. Minneapolis, MN: Fedogan & Bremer, 1996.

Saith the Lord. Minneapolis, MN: Fedogan & Bremer Mystery, 1996.

Three Tales. Edited by D. H. Olson. Minneapolis, MN: Fedogan & Bremer, 1995.

Time Burial: The Collected Fantasy Tales of Howard Wandrei. Edited by D. H. Olson. Minneapolis, MN: Fedogan & Bremer, 1995.

"The Eerie Mr. Murphy." *Esquire* 8, No. 5 (November 1937): 59–63. In *EMM*.

"The God Box." *Astounding Stories* 13, No. 2 (April 1934): 74–84, as by Howard Von Drey.

"The Hand of the O'Mecca." *WT* 25, No. 4 (April 1935): 425–32. In *Three Tales, TB*.

"In the Triangle." *WT* 24, No. 4 (October 1934): 109–12. In *TB*.

"The Other." *Astounding Stories* 14, No. 4 (December 1934): 31–40 (as by "Howard W. Graham, Ph.D."). In *TB*.

"Over Time's Threshold." *WT* 20, No. 3 (September 1932): 104–10. In *TB*.

"Time Haven." *Astounding Stories* 14, No. 1 (September 1934): 42–52 (as by "Howard W. Graham, Ph.D."). In *EMM*.

"Vine Terror." *WT* 24, No. 3 (September 1934): 35–50. In *EMM*.

"In His Own Words: The Autobiographies of Howard Wandrei." In *Saith the Lord* 25–27.

D. Works by Emil Petaja

As Dream and Shadow. San Francisco, SISU, 1972.

Brief Candle. Self-published, 1936. A mimeographed brochure of Petaja's poems, made while he was attending Montana State University.

"Antiqua." Nonextant.

"Asphodel." *Futuria Fantasia* 1, No. 3 (Winter 1940): 11, as by E. T. Pine. The poem was to appear in *Phantagraph* 6, No,. 1 (May 1937), but the editor destroyed the botched printing.

"Dawn." Nonextant.

"Dr. Crowe's Assistant." Nonextant.

"Dream within a Dream Within." *Californian* 5, No. 1 (Summer 1937): 74.

"Echo from the Ebon Isles." See "The Warrior."

"Elemental." *Californian* 5, No. 1 (Summer 1937): 73.

"Enigma." *Acolyte* 1, No. 2 (Winter 1942): 5.

"Evening Star." Nonextant.

"Famous Fantasy Fiction." *FF* 1, No. 6 (February 1934): 95; 1, No. 11 (July 1934): 172; 1, No. 12 (August 1934): 180.

"I Will Return."

"The Intruder." *Futuria Fantasia* 1, No. 3 (Winter 1940): 8–10.

"Lost Dream." First appeared in *Brief Candle. Weird Tales* 31, No. 1 (January 1938): 96. In H. P. Lovecraft et al., *Marginalia.* Ed. August Derleth and Donald Wandrei. Sauk City, WI: Arkham House, 1944. 372.

"Marmok." *Futuria Fantasia* 1, No. 3 (Winter 1940): 11.

"The Mist." *Fantasmagoria* 1, No. 2 (July 1937): 10–15. *Diversifier* No. 21 (July 1977): 14–16.

"Night Noises." Nonextant.

"Partings . . ." Previously unpublished?

"Phantasies That You May Have Missed." *Phantagraph* 4, No. 3 (Spring 1936): 14–16.

"Phantasy in Folklore." *Phantagraph* 5, No. 1 (October 1936): 5–8. As by E. Theodore Pine.

"The Pipers of Kallinen." Nonextant.

"Rene Passes through the Veil." Nonextant.

"Shadow of Fear." Nonextant.

"Silia." Nonextant.

"The Sky Hermit." *Phantagraph* 4, No. 2 (November–December 1935): 8. Dedicated to H. Warner Munn.

"Syzygy." Unpublished, nonextant.

"The Two Doors." *Unusual Stories* 1, No 2 (Winter 1935): 92–97, as by E. Theodore Pine.

"The Viking." Nonextant.

"The Warrior." *WT* 33, No. 1 (January 1939): 60.

"Weird Music" (with Duane W. Rimel). *Phantagraph* 4, No. 4 (July 1936): 6–7. In Donald A. Wollheim, ed. *Operation Phantasy*. Rego Park, NY: Phantagraph Press, 1967. 24–26. In *Letters to F. Lee Baldwin, Duane W. Rimel, and Nils Frome* 374–75.

"Witch's Berceuse." *Marvel Tales* 1, No. 5 (Summer 1935): 273, as "Witch's Bercuese."

"The World of Sensation." Nonextant.

Letters

WT 19, No. 6 (June 1932): 860.

"A Campaign for Moving Pictures of Science Fiction Stories Suggested. Reprints." *Amazing Stories* 8, No. 1 (April 1933): 94.

Amazing Stories 8, No. 8 (December 1933): 136. As by Emil Pataja.

FF 1, No. 8 (April 1934): 114.

"Arlton Eadie's Stories." *WT* 24, No. 3 (September 1934): 396.

FF 2, No. 3 (November 1934): 35.

"An Admirer of Lovecraft." *WT* 26, No. 2 (August 1935): 270. Rpt. in *Lovecraft in "The Eyrie."* Edited by S. T. Joshi. West Warwick, RI: Necronomicon Press, 1979, 39–40. Extract in Joshi, *Weird Writer* 79–80.

WT 31, No. 4 (April 1938): 512.

E. Works by Others

Dates in angular brackets indicate dates of first publication.

Allen, Hervey (1889–1949). *Anthony Adverse*. New York: Farrar & Rinehart, 1933.

The Arabian Nights Entertainments. Ed. Andrew Lang (1844–1912). New York: Longmans, Green, 1898. (*LL* 49)

Asquith, Cynthia (1887–1960), ed. *The Ghost Book*. London: Hutchinson, 1927. New York: Scribner's, 1927.

Austen, Jane (1775–1817). *Northanger Abbey*. London: John Murray, 1818.

Barbey d'Aurevilly, Jules (1808–1889). *The Story without a Name*. Tr. Edgar Saltus. New York: Bedford & Co., 1891, *or* New York: Brentano's, 1919 (*LL* 74).

[Barnitz, Park] (1878–1901). *The Book of Jade*. New York: Doxey's, [1901]. Rpt. in *The Book of Jade: A New Critical Edition*. Ed. David E. Schultz and Michael J. Abolafia. New York: Hippocampus Press, 2015.

Barrett, Eaton Stannard. *The Heroine; or, Adventures of a Fair Romance Reader*. London: H. Colburn, 1813. 3 vols.

Baudelaire, Charles (1821–1867). *Les Fleurs du mal; Petits Poèmes en prose; Les Paradis artificiels*. Tr. Arthur Symons. London: Casanova Society, 1925.

Beckford, William (1759–1844). *The Episodes of Vathek.* Tr. from the French by Sir Frank T. Marzials. <1912> Boston: Small, Maynard & Co., [1922?] or [1924?]. (*LL* 83)

————. *The History of the Caliph Vathek.* Printed Verbatim from the First Edition, with the Original Prefaces and Notes by [Samuel] Henley <1786>. New York: W. L. Allinson, [1868?] or [188-?]. (*LL* 84)

Beddoes, Thomas Lovell (1803–1849). *Death's Jest Book; or, The Fool's Tragedy.* London: William Pickering, 1850.

Benoit, Pierre (1886–1962). *Atlantida.* Tr. Mary C. Tongue and Mary Ross. New York: Duffield, 1920.

Benson, E. F. (1867–1940). *Visible and Invisible.* New York, George H. Doran, 1923 or 1924. (*LL* 90)

————. *Two Masterly Ghost Stories.* Girard, KS: Haldeman-Julius, n.d. [Contains "The Man Who Went Too Far."] (*LL* 91)

Béraud, Henri (1885–1958). *Lazarus.* Tr. Eric Sutton. New York: Macmillan, 1925. (*LL* 92)

Bierce, Ambrose (1842–1914?). *Can Such Things Be?* <1893> New York: Boni & Liveright (Modern Library), 1918. (*LL* 98)

————. *Collected Works.* Washington, DC: Neale Publishing Co., 1909–12. 12 vols.

————. *In the Midst of Life: Tales of Soldiers and Civilians.* <1891> Introduction by George Sterling. New York: Modern Library, [1927]. (*LL* 99)

————, and Adolphe Danziger [de Castro] (1859–1959). *The Monk and the Hangman's Daughter; Fantastic Fables; [etc.].* <1892; 1899> New York: A. & C. Boni, 1925. (*LL* 100)

Birkhead, Edith (1889–1951). *The Tale of Terror: A Study of the Gothic Romance.* New York: E. P. Dutton, 1921. (*LL* 105)

Bishop, John Peale (1892–1944), and Edmund Wilson (1895–1972). *The Undertaker's Garland.* New York: Alfred A. Knopf, 1922.

Blackwood, Algernon (1869–1951). *The Bright Messenger.* London: Cassell, 1921; New York: Dutton, 1922.

————. *The Dance of Death and Other Tales.* London: Herbert Jenkins, 1927. New York: Lincoln MacVeagh/Dial Press, 1928.

————. *Day and Night Stories.* London: Cassell, 1917. New York: E. P. Dutton, 1917.

————. *The Empty House and Other Ghost Stories.* London: Eveleigh Nash, 1906. New York: Donald C. Vaughan, 1915. New York: Alfred A. Knopf, 1917.

————. *The Human Chord.* London: Macmillan, 1910. New York: Macmillan, 1911.

————. *Incredible Adventures.* London: Macmillan, 1914. New York: Macmillan, 1914.

————. *Jimbo: A Fantasy.* New York: Macmillan, 1909. (*LL* 106)

————. *John Silence: Physician Extraordinary.* London: Eveleigh Nash, 1908. Boston: John W. Luce, 1909. London: Macmillan, 1912. New York: Vaughan & Gomme, 1914. New York: Alfred A. Knopf, 1917. New York, E. P. Dutton, [1920]. Contains "Ancient Sorceries." (*LL* 107, 108)

————. *Julius LeVallon: An Episode.* London: Cassell, 1916. New York; E. P. Dutton, 1916. (*LL* 109)

————. *The Listener and Other Stories.* London: Eveleigh Nash, 1907. New York: Vaughan & Gomme, 1914. New York: Alfred A. Knopf, 1917. [Includes "The Willows."]

————. *Pan's Garden: A Volume of Nature Stories.* London: Macmillan, 1912. New York: Macmillan, 1912.

————. *The Promise of Air.* London: Macmillan, 1918. New York: E. P. Dutton, 1918.

————. *Ten Minute Stories.* London: John Murray, 1914. New York: E. P. Dutton, 1914.

————. *Tongues of Fire and Other Sketches.* London: Herbert Jenkins, 1924. New York: E. P. Dutton, 1925.

————. *The Wave: An Egyptian Aftermath.* London: Cassell, 1916. New York: E. P. Dutton, 1916.

————, and Wilfred Wilson. *The Wolves of God and Other Fey Stories.* London: Cassell, 1921. New York: E. P. Dutton, 1921.

Boyd, Ernest A. (1887–1946) "Lord Dunsany—Fantaisiste." In *Appreciations and Depreciations.* New York: John Lane, 1918; Freeport, NY: Books for Libraries Press, 1968. 71–100.

Bradshaw, William R. (1851–1927). *The Goddess of Atvatabar: Being the History of the Discovery of the Interior World and Conquest of Atvatabar.* New York: J. F. Douthitt, 1892.

Brontë, Emily (1818–1848). *Wuthering Heights.* London: Newby, 1847. (*LL* 666)

Brown, Charles Brockden (1771–1810). *Wieland.* <1798> Extract in Julian Hawthorne, ed. *The Lock and Key Library.* (*LL* 428)

Buchan, John (1875–1940). *The Runagates Club.* Boston: Houghton Mifflin, 1928. (*LL* 141)

————. *Witch Wood.* Boston: Houghton Mifflin, 1927.

Bullett, Gerald (1894–1958). *The Street of the Eye and Nine Other Tales.* London: Lohn Lane, 1923. New York: Boni & Liveright, 1923.

Bulwer-Lytton, Edward (1803–1873). *A Strange Story; The Haunted House [sic]; Zanoni.* <1862; 1859; 1842> Boston: Desmond Publishing Co., [18—?]. (*LL* 145). [The second story is "The Haunted and the Haunters; or, The House and the Brain."]

Burroughs, Edgar Rice (1875–1950). *Tarzan of the Apes.* Chicago: McClurg, 1914.

Cannon, Peter, ed. *Lovecraft Remembered.* Sauk City, WI: Arkham House, 1998.

Čapek, Karel (1890–1938). *Krakatit: An Atomic Fantasy*. Tr. Laurence Hyde. New York: Macmillan, 1925.

[Carver, Mrs.?] *The Horrors of Oakendale Abbey: A Romance*. New York: John Harrison, 1799. 3 vols.

Chambers, Robert W. (1865–1933). *In Search of the Unknown*. New York: Harper & Brothers, 1904. (*LL* 183)

———. *The King in Yellow*. New York: F. Tennyson Neely, 1895. (*LL* 184)

———. *The Slayer of Souls*. New York: George H. Doran, 1920.

Charles, Émile Auguste (1825–1897). *Roger Bacon: sa vie, ses ouvrages, ses doctrinces, d'après des textes inédits*. Bordeaux: Typ. G. Gounouilhou, 1861.

Cline, Leonard (1893–1929). *The Dark Chamber*. New York: Viking Press, 1927. (*LL* 198)

Crawford, F. Marion (1854–1909). *Wandering Ghosts*. New York: Macmillan, 1911. London: T. Fisher Unwin, 1911 (as *Uncanny Tales*).

Cummings, Ray (1887–1957). *The Girl in the Golden Atom*. <1919> New York: Harper & Brothers, 1923.

De Mille, James (1837–1880). *A Strange Manuscript Found in a Copper Cylinder*. <1888> New York: Harper & Brothers, 1900. (*LL* 245)

Defoe, Daniel (1660–1731). *The Life and Surprising Adventures of Robinson Crusoe, of York, Mariner, as Related by Himself*. <1719> With One Hundred and Twenty Original Illustrations by Walter Paget. New York: McLoughlin Brothers, [1895?]. (*LL* 242)

Derleth, August (1909–1961). *Evening in Spring*. New York: Charles Scribner's Sons, 1941.

———. *Place of Hawks*. Illustrated with wood engravings by George Barford. New York: Loring & Mussey, 1935. (*LL* 235).

Dickinson, Sidney (1859–1919). *True Tales of the Weird: A Record of Personal Experience of the Supernatural*. New York: Duffield, 1920.

Doyle, Sir Arthur Conan (1859–1930). *The Lost World: Being an Account of the Recent Amazing Adventures of Professor George E. Challenger, Lord John Roxton, Professor Summerlee, and Mr. E. D. Malone of* The Daily Gazette. <1912> London: George Newnes, 1921 or 1925. (*LL* 275)

———. *The Maracot Deep and Other Stories*. London: John Murray, 1929.

———. *The Poison Belt*. London: Hodder & Stoughton, 1913. New York: George H. Doran, 1913.

Dryden, John (1631–1700). *The Wild Gallant: A Comedy*. <1669> London: Printed by T. Warren for Henry Herringman, 1694. (*LL* 284)

Dunsany, Edward John Moreton Drax Plunkett, 18th baron (1878–1957). *The Blessing of Pan*. London: G. P. Putnam's Sons, 1927. (*LL* 287)

———. *The Book of Wonder* <1912> [and *Time and the Gods* <1906>]. New York: Boni & Liveright (Modern Library), [1918]. (*LL* 288)

———. *The Charwoman's Shadow*. New York: G. P. Putnam's Sons, 1926.

————. *Don Rodriguez: Chronicles of Shadow Valley.* New York: G. P. Putnam's Sons, 1922. (*LL* 289)

————. *A Dreamer's Tales and Other Stories.* <1910> New York: Boni & Liveright [Modern Library], [1917], [1919], or [1921]. [Also contains *The Sword of Welleran* (1908).] (*LL* 290)

————. *Fifty-one Tales.* <1915> (*LL* 291)

————. *Five Plays: The Gods of the Mountain; The Golden Doom; King Argimēnēs and the Unknown Warrior; The Glittering Gate; The Lost Silk Hat.* <1914> Boston: Little, Brown, 1923. (*LL* 292)

————. *The Gods of Pegāna.* <1905> (*LL* 293)

————. *The King of Elfland's Daughter.* London: G. P. Putnam's Sons, 1924. (*LL* 294)

————. *The Last Book of Wonder.* Boston: John W. Luce, 1916. (*LL* 295)

————. *Plays of Gods and Men.* Boston: John W. Luce, [1917]. (*LL* 296)

————. *Plays of Near and Far: The Compromise of the King of the Golden Isles; The Flight of the Queen; Cheezo; A Good Bargain; If Shakespeare Lived To-day; Fame and the Poet.* New York: G. P. Putnam's Sons, 1923. (*LL* 297)

————. *Tales of Three Hemispheres.* <1919> (*LL* 298)

————. *The Travel Tales of Mr. Joseph Jorkens.* London: G. P. Putnam's Sons, [1931]. (*LL* 299)

————. *Unhappy Far-off Things.* Boston: Little, Brown, 1919. (*LL* 300)

Eddison, E. R. (1882–1945). *The Worm Ouroboros: A Romance.* Illustrated by Keith Henderson. New York: A. & C. Boni, 1926. (*LL* 309)

Egbert, H. M. (pseud. of Victor Rousseau Emmanuel, 1879–1960). *The Sea Demons.* <1916> London: J. Long, 1924.

Everett, Mrs. H. D. *The Death Mask and Other Ghosts.* London: Philip Allan, 1920.

Ewers, Hanns Heinz (1871–1943). *The Sorcerer's Apprentice.* Tr. Ludwig Lewisohn. New York: John Day Co., 1927.

Ferenczy, Arpad (1877–?). *The Ants of Timothy Thümmel.* New York: Harcourt, Brace, 1924. London: Jonathan Cape, 1924.

Fish, Horace (1885–1929). *The Wrists on the Door: A Short Story.* New York: B. W. Huebsch, 1924.

Flammarion, Camille (1842–1925). *Haunted Houses.* London: T. Fisher Unwin, [1924]. (*LL* 340)

Flecker, James Elroy (1884–1915). *The Collected Poems of James Elroy Flecker.* London: Martin Secker, 1916.

Fort, Charles (1874–1932). *The Book of the Damned.* New York: Boni & Liveright, 1919.

————. *Lo!* New York: C. Kendell, 1931.

————. *New Lands.* New York: Boni & Liveright, 1923.

Fox, Richard A. *The People on Other Planets.* Los Angeles: Wetzel Publishing Co., 1930.

Frank, Waldo (1889–1967). *Chalk Face.* New York: Boni & Liveright, 1924.

Frazer, Sir James George (1854–1941). *The Golden Bough: A Study in Magic and Religion.* <1890–1915> New York: Macmillan, 1930.

French, Joseph Lewis (1858–1936), ed., *The Best Ghost Stories.* New York: Modern Library, 1919. Introduction by Arthur B. Reeve.

———, ed. *Ghosts, Grim and Gentle.* New York: Dodd, Mead, 1926.

French, Nora May (1881–1907). *Poems.* San Francisco: Strange Co., 1910. (*LL* 357)

Funck-Brentano, Frantz (1862–1947). *Cagliostro and Company: A Sequel to the Story of* The Diamond Necklace. New York: Brentano's, [191-?].

Gautier, Théophile (1811–1872), and Prosper Mérimée (1803–1870). *Tales Before Supper.* Told in English by Myndart Verelst [i.e., Edgar Saltus] and Delayed with a Poem by Edgar Saltus. New York: Brentano's, 1887. [Contains Gautier's "Avatar" and Mérimée's "The Venus of Ille."] (*LL* 368)

Gernsback, Hugo (1884–1967). *Ralph 124C41+.* Boston: Stratford, 1925.

Glasgow, Ellen (1874–1945). *The Shadowy Third and Other Stories.* New York: Doubleday, Page, 1923.

Godwin, William (1756–1836). *Things as They Are; or, The Adventures of Caleb Williams.* London: B. Crosby, 1794.

———. *St. Leon.* London: G. G. & J. Robinson, 1799.

Gorman, Herbert S. (1893–1954). *The Place Called Dagon.* New York: George H. Doran, 1927.

Greg, Percy (1836–1889). *Across the Zodiac: The Story of a Wrecked Record.* London: Trübner, 1880.

Haeckel, Ernst (1834–1919). *Die Welträthsel.* <1899> Tr. Joseph McCabe as *The Riddle of the Universe.* New York: Harper & Brothers, 1900.

Haggard, H. Rider (1856–1925). *She: A History of Adventure.* <1887> (*LL* 411)

———. *The Witch's Head.* London: Hurst & Blackett, 1885. London: Hodder & Stoughton, 1914.

———. *Wisdom's Daughter.* New York: Doubleday, Page, 1923.

———, and Andrew Lang (1844–1912). *The World's Desire.* London: Longmans, Green, 1890.

Hall, Radclyffe (1886–1943). *The Well of Loneliness.* London: Jonathan Cape, 1928.

Hammett, Dashiell (1894–1961), ed. *Creeps by Night: Chills and Thrills.* New York: John Day Co., 1931. [Contains HPL, "The Music of Erich Zann" (347–63); DAW, "The Red Brain" (423–40).] (*LL* 421)

———, ed. *Modern Tales of Horror.* London: Victor Gollancz, 1932. (*LL* 422)

Harré, T. Everett (1884–1948), ed. *Beware After Dark! The World's Most Stupendous Tales of Mystery, Horror, Thrills and Terror.* New York: Macaulay, 1929. [Contains HPL, "The Call of Cthulhu."] (*LL* 425)

Hastings, Milo (1884–1957). *City of Endless Night.* New York: Dodd, Mead, 1920.

Hawthorne, Julian (1846–1934), ed. *The Lock and Key Library: Classic Mystery and Detective Stories.* New York: Review of Reviews Co., 1909. 10 vols. (*LL* 428)

Hawthorne, Nathaniel (1804–1864). *The House of the Seven Gables, and The Snow-Image and Other Twice-Told Tales.* <1851; 1852> Boston: Houghton Mifflin, 1886. (*LL* 430)

———. *The Marble Faun; or, The Romance of Monte Beni.* <1860> Boston: Houghton Mifflin, 1887. (*LL* 432)

Hearn, Lafcadio (1850–1904). *Fantastics and Other Fancies.* Ed. Charles Woodward Hutson. Boston: Houghton Mifflin, 1914.

Huysmans, Joris-Karl (1848–1907). *Down There.* Translated by Keene Wallis. New York: Albert & Charles Boni, 1924. (*LL* 484)

Hodgson, William Hope (1877–1918). *The Night Land.* London: Eveleigh Nash, 1912.

Hogg, James (1770–1835). *The Private Memoirs and Confessions of a Justified Sinner.* <1824> London: A. M. Philpott, 1924.

Howard, Robert E. (1906–1936). *The Collected Letters of Robert E. Howard.* Volume 3. Plano, TX: Robert E. Howard Foundation Press, 2008.

Howells, William Dean (1837–1920), and Henry Mills Alden, ed. *Shapes That Haunt the Dusk.* New York: Harper & Brothers, 1907.

Ingram, John H. (1842–1916). *The Haunted Homes and Family Traditions of Great Britain.* London: Gibbings, 1897. (*LL* 489)

Ingram, John K. (1823–1907). *On the "Opus Majus" of Roger Bacon . . . From the Natural History Review and Quarterly Journal of Science,* vol. v. Dublin: University Press: Dublin, 1858.

Jacobs, W. W. (1863–1943). "The Monkey's Paw." In Dorothy L. Sayers (1893–1957), ed. *The Omnibus of Crime.* <1928> Garden City, NY: Garden City Publishing Co., 1931. (*LL* 830) In *Twin Spirits: The Complete Weird Stories of W. W. Jacobs.* Ed. S. T. Joshi. New York: Hippocampus Press, 2018.

James, M. R. (1862–1936). *The Collected Ghost Stories of M. R. James.* London: Edward Arnold, 1931.

———. *Ghost-Stories of an Antiquary.* London: Edward Arnold, 1904. (*LL* 499)

———. *More Ghost Stories of an Antiquary.* <1911> (*LL* 500)

———. *A Thin Ghost and Others.* <1919> London: Edward Arnold, 1925. (*LL* 501)

———. *A Warning to the Curious.* London: Edward Arnold, 1925. (*LL* 502)

Joshi, S. T. "The Poetry of Donald Wandrei." In Wandrei, *Sanctity and Sin,* 9–20 (as "Introduction"). In *The Development of the Weird Tale.* Seattle, WA: Sarnath Press, 2019. 134–44.

———, ed. *A Weird Writer in Our Midst: Early Criticism of H. P. Lovecraft.* New York: Hippocampus Press, 2010.

Joshi, S. T., with David E. Schultz. *Lovecraft's Library: A Catalogue.* 4th ed. New York: Hippocampus Press, 2017.

Killen, Alice M. *Le Roman "terrifiant"; ou, Roman "noir" de Walpole à Ann Radcliffe et son influence sur la littérature française jusqu'en 1840.* Paris: G. Crès, 1915; rev. ed. Paris: E. Champion, 1923.

Kitchell, Joseph Gray (1862–?). *The Earl of Hell.* New York: Century Co., 1924.

Knowles, Vernon (1899–1968). *Here and Otherwhere.* London: R. Holden, 1926.

———. *The Street of Queer Houses and Other Stories.* New York: Boullion-Biggs, 1924. London: W. Garder, Darton, 1925.

La Motte-Fouqué, Friedrich Heinrich Karl (1777–1843). *Undine and Sintram.* <1811; 1815> Boston: Estes & Lauriat, [18—]. (*LL* 549)

Leblanc, Maurice (1864–1941). *The Three Eyes.* Tr. Alexander Teixeira de Mattos. New York: Macaulay, 1921. New York: A. L. Burt, n.d.

Le Fanu, J. Sheridan (1814–1873). *All in the Dark.* <1866> London: Downey & Co., n.d.

———. *The House by the Churchyard.* <1863> London: Macmillan, 1899. (*LL* 559)

———, et al. *A Stable for Nightmares; or, Weird Tales.* New York: Amsterdam Book Co., 1896.

Level, Maurice (1875–1926). *Tales of Mystery and Horror.* Tr. Alys Eyre Macklin. New York: Robert M. McBride, 1920. (*LL* 565)

Lewis, Matthew Gregory (1775–1818). *The Monk: A Romance.* London: J. Bell, 1796. (*LL* 567)

Long, Frank Belknap (1901–1994). *The Goblin Tower.* Cassia, FL.: Dragon-Fly Press, 1935.

———. *The Horror from the Hills.* *WT* (January and February/March 1931). Sauk City, WI: Arkham House, 1963.

———. *The Man from Genoa.* Athol, MA: Recluse Press, 1926.

Lönnrot, Elias (1802–1884). *Kalevala taikka vanhoja Karjalan runoja Suomen kansan muinosista ajoista. 1 osa.* [s.n.]: Porvoo, 1835.

Loveman, Samuel (1889–1976). *The Hermaphrodite: A Poem.* Athol, MA: W. Paul Cook, 1926. (*LL* 593)

———. *The Hermaphrodite and Other Poems.* Caldwell, ID: Caxton Printers, 1936. (*LL* 594)

———. *The Sphinx: A Conversation.* [North Montpelier, VT: W. Paul Cook, 1944.]

Machen, Arthur (1863–1947). "The Bowmen." *Evening News* (London) (29 September 1914): 3. In *The Angels of Mons: The Bowmen and Other Legends of the War.* London: Simpkin, Marshall, Hamilton, Kent, 1915. New York: G. P. Putnam's Sons, 1915. London: Martin Secker, 1923.

———. *The Canning Wonder.* New York: Alfred A. Knopf, 1926. (*LL* 614)

———. "The Coming of the Terror." *Century Magazine* 94, No. 6 (October 1917): 801–25. [Abridged version of *The Terror.*] (*LL* 174)

———. *Far Off Things.* <1922> New York: Alfred A. Knopf, 1923. (*LL* 615)

————. *The Great God Pan and The Inmost Light*. London: John Lane; Boston: Roberts Brothers, 1894, 1895. London: Grant Richards, 1913.

————. *The Green Round*. London: Ernest Benn, 1933.

————. *Hieroglyphics: A Note upon Ecstasy in Literature*. <1902> (*LL* 616)

————. *The Hill of Dreams*. <1907> London: Martin Secker, [1922] (blue paper edition).

————. *The House of Souls*. <1906> New York: Alfred A. Knopf, 1923. (*LL* 618)

————. *The London Adventure: An Essay in Wandering*. New York: Alfred A. Knopf, 1924. (*LL* 619)

————. *The Secret Glory*. London: Martin Secker, 1922. New York: Alfred A. Knopf, 1922. (*LL* 620)

————. *The Shining Pyramid* [miscellany]. Ed. Vincent Starrett. Chicago: Covici-McGee, 1924.

————. *The Shining Pyramid* [short stories]. London: Martin Secker, 1925. New York: Alfred A. Knopf, 1925. (*LL* 621)

————. *The Terror*. New York: Robert M. McBride, 1917. London: Duckworth, 1917.

————. *Things Near and Far*. New York: Alfred A. Knopf, 1923. (*LL* 622)

————. *The Three Impostors*. <1895> New York: Alfred A. Knopf, 1930. (*LL* 623)

McNeil, Everett (1862–1929). *The Shadow of the Iroquois*. New York: E. P. Dutton, 1928.

————. *The Shores of Adventure*. New York: E. P. Dutton, 1929.

McSpadden, J. Walker (1874–1960), ed. *Famous Ghost Stories* New York: Thomas Y. Crowell Company, 1918.

————, ed. *Famous Mystery Stories*. New York: Thomas Y. Crowell Company, 1922.

Mather, Cotton (1663–1728). *Magnalia Christi Americana; or, The Ecclesiastical History of New-England, from Its First Planting in the Year 1620, unto the Year of Our Lord, 1698*. London: Printed for T. Parkhurst, 1702. 7 parts in 1. (*LL* 645)

Maturin, Charles Robert (1782?–1824). *Fatal Revenge; or, The Family of Montorio*. London: Longman, Hurst, Rees, & Orme, 1807.

————. *Melmoth the Wanderer*. <1820> London: Richard Bentley & Son, 1892. 3 vols. (*LL* 646)

Mérimée, Prosper (1803–1870). "The Venus of Ille." See Gautier, *Tales Before Supper*.

Merritt, A. (1882–1943). *Creep, Shadow! Argosy* (8 September–20 October 1934). Garden City, NY: Doubleday, 1934. (*LL* 51)

————. *The Moon Pool*. New York: G. P. Putman's Sons, 1919.

————. *Seven Footprints to Satan*. New York: Boni & Liveright, 1928.

Meyrink, Gustav (1868–1932). *Der Golem*. <1915> Tr. Madge Pemberton as *The Golem*. London: Gollancz, 1928. Boston: Houghton Mifflin, 1928.

Moore, Thomas (1779–1852). *The Epicurean: A Tale.* <1827> (*LL* 674)

Murray, Margaret A. (1863–1963). *The Witch-Cult in Western Europe.* Oxford: Clarendon Press, 1921.

Nichols, Robert (1893–1944). *Fantastica: Being the Smile of the Sphinx and Other Tales of Imagination.* London: Chatto & Windus, 1923.

O'Donnell, Elliott (1872–1965). *Haunted Houses of London.* London: Eveleigh Nash, 1909.

———. *More Haunted Houses of London.* London: Eveleigh Nash Co., 1920.

———. *The Sorcery Club.* London: W. Rider, 1912, 1923.

O'Neill, John (1869–?). *Souls in Hell: A Mystery of the Unseen.* New York: Nicholas L. Brown, 1924.

Ovid (P. Ovidius Naso) (43 B.C.E.–17 C.E.). *The Heroycall Epistles of the Learned Poet Publius Ouidius Naso, in English Verse.* Set Out and Translated by George Tuberuile. London: Henry Denham, 1567. (*LL* 725)

Parry, David MacLean (1852–1915). *The Scarlet Empire.* Indianapolis: Bobbs-Merrill, 1906.

Peacock, Thomas Love (1785–1866). *Nightmare Abbey.* London: T. Hookham, Jr., and Baldwin, Cradock & Joy, 1818.

Pemberton, Clive. *The Weird o' It.* London: Henry J. Drane, 1906.

Pepper & Stern Rare Books, et al. *Selections from the Archive of D. Wandrei: Manuscripts, Letters, Pirinted Ephemera, and Original Art.* Santa Barbara, CA: Pepper & Stern Rare Books, 1994.

Poe, Edgar Allan (1809–1849). *Tales of Mystery and Imagination.* <1855> Illustrated by Harry Clarke <1919>. New York: Tudor Publishing Co., 1933. (*LL* 768)

Plante, Louis. *The Shadow of the Astral: A Mystic Narrative.* Los Angeles: Austin Publishing Co., 1921.

Polidori, John William (1795–1821). *The Vampyre: A Tale.* London: Sherwood, Neely & Jones, 1819.

Powell, E. Alexander (1879–1957). *The Last Home of Mystery: Adventures in Nepal Together with Accounts of Ceylon, British India, the Native States, the Persian Gulf, the Overland Desert Mail and the Baghdad Railway.* New York, London, The Century Co., 1929.

Priestley, J. B. (1894–1984). *The Old Dark House.* New York: Harper & Brothers, 1928.

Radcliffe, Ann (1764–1823). *The Castles of Athlin and Dunbayne.* London: T. Hookham, 1789.

———. *Gaston de Blondeville.* London: H. Colburn, 1826.

———. *The Italian; or, The Confessional of the Black Penitents.* London: T. Cadell & W. Davies, 1797.

———. *The Mysteries of Udolpho.* London: G. G. & J. Robinson, 1794. (*LL* 787)

———. *The Romance of the Forest.* London: T. Hookham & J. Carpenter, 1791.

————. *A Sicilian Romance*. London: Hookham & Carpenter, 1790.

Railo, Eino (1884–1948). *The Haunted Castle: A Study of the Elements of English Romanticism*. New York: E. P. Dutton, 1927.

Ransome, Arthur (1884–1967). *The Elixir of Life*. London: Methuen, 1915. New York: Hippocampus Press, 2009.

Reeve, Arthur (1880–1936). See Joseph Lewis French, *Best Ghost Stories*.

Reeve, Clara (1729–1807). *Old English Baron: A Gothic Story*. London: Colchester, 1777 (as *The Champion of Virtue*). (*LL* 793)

Renard, Maurice (1875–1939). *New Bodies for Old*. New York: Macaulay Co., 1923.

Reynolds, George W. M. (1814–1879). *Faust: A Romance of the Secret Tribunals*. London: G. Vickers, 1847.

————. *Wagner the Wehr-Wolf*. London: J. Dicks, 1848, 1857, 1872.

Rhys, Ernest (1859–1946), and C. A. Dawson Scott (1865–1934), ed. *Twenty-three Stories by Twenty and Three Authors*. New York: D. Appleton, 1924.

Rodd, Sir Rennell (1858–1941). *Rose Leaf and Apple Leaf*. Philadelphia: J. M. Stoddart, 1882. Portland, ME: Thomas Bird Mosher, 1906.

Robbins, Tod (pseud. of Clarence Aaron Tod Robbins, 1888–1949). *Silent, White and Beautiful and Other Stories*. New York: Boni & Liveright, 1920.

Rohmer, Sax (pseud. of Arthur Sarsfield Ward, 1883–1959). *Brood of the Witch-Queen*. <1918> New York: A. L. Burt, 1926. (*LL* 811)

Rollins, Hyder Edward (1889–1958), ed. *The Pack of Autoycus*. Cambridge, MA: Harvard University Press, 1927.

Rosny, J. H. Aîné (1856–1940). *The Giant Cat; or, The Quest of Aoun and Zouhr*. Tr. Lady Whitehead. New York: Robert M. McBride, 1924.

Rousseau [Emmanuel], Victor (1879–1960). *The Messiah of the Cylinder*. Chicago: McClurg, 1917.

Rudwin, Maximilian J. (1885–1946), ed. *Devil Stories: An Anthology*. New York: Alfred A. Knopf, 1921. (*LL* 816)

Russell, W. Clark (1844–1911). *The Frozen Pirate*. London: Sampson, Low & Co., 1887. 2 vols. (*LL* 821)

Saintsbury, George (1843–1933), ed. *Tales of Mystery*. New York: Macmillan, 1891. [Contains extracts of Ann Radcliffe, *The Mysteries of Udolpho;* Matthew Gregory Lewis, *The Monk;* and Charles Robert Maturin, *Melmoth the Wanderer.*] (*LL* 824)

Saltus, Francis S. (1849–1899). *The Bayadere and Other Sonnets*. New York: Putnam's, 1894.

————. *Dreams After Sunset: Poems*. Buffalo: C. W. Moulton, 1892.

————. *Shadows and Ideals: Poems*. Buffalo: C. W. Moulton, 1890.

————. *The Witch of En-Dor and Other Poems*. Buffalo: C. W. Moulton, 1891.

Savile, Frank Mackenzie. *Beyond the Great South Wall: The Secret of the Antarctic*. <1899> New York: Grosset & Dunlap, 1901. (*LL* 828)

Sayers, Dorothy L. (1893–1957), ed. *The Omnibus of Crime.* <1928> Garden City, NY: Garden City Publishing Co., 1931. (*LL* 830)

Scarborough, Dorothy (1878–1935). *The Supernatural in Modern English Fiction.* New York: G. P. Putnam's Sons, 1917.

———, ed. *Famous Modern Ghost Stories.* New York & London: G. P. Putnam's Sons, 1921.

———, ed. *Humorous Ghost Stories.* New York & London: G.P. Putnam's Sons, 1921.

Schneider, Leonhard (d. 1874). *Roger Bacon, Ord. Min.: eine Monographie: als Beitrag zur Geschichte der Philosophie des dreizehnten Jahrhunderts.* Augsburg: Kranzfelder, 1873.

Schultz, David E. "Lovecraft and the *Argosy.*" *Lovecraft Annual* No. 11 (2017): 67–73.

Schwartz, Julius (1915–2004), and Mortimer Weisinger (1915–1978). "Donald Wandrei Interviewed." *Fantasy Magazine* 3, No. 3 (May 1934): 10–15.

Serviss, Garrett P. (1851–1929). *The Moon Metal.* New York: Harper & Brothers, 1900.

———. *The Second Deluge.* New York: McBride, Nast, 1912.

Shelley, Mary (1797–1851). *Frankenstein; or, The Modern Prometheus.* <1818> New-York: H. G. Daggers, 1845. (*LL* 864)

Shelley, Percy Bysshe (1792–1822). *St. Irvyne; or, The Rosicrucian.* London: J. J. Stockdale, 1811.

———. *Zastrozzi.* London: G. Wilkie & J. Robinson, 1810.

Shiel, M. P. (1865–1947). *The Lord of the Sea.* <1901> New York: Alfred A. Knopf, 1924. (*LL* 869)

———. *The Pale Ape and Other Pulses.* London: T. Werner Laurie, 1911. [Contains "The House of Sounds."]

———. *Prince Zaleski.* Boston: Roberts Brothers, 1895. (*LL* 870)

———. *The Purple Cloud.* <1901> New York: Vanguard Press, 1930. (*LL* 871) Rpt. New York: Hippocampus Press, 2005.

———. *Shapes in the Fire.* London: John Lane, 1896.

———. *This Above All.* New York: Vanguard Press, 1933.

Sinclair, May (1863–1946). *Uncanny Stories.* New York: Macmillan, 1923.

Smith, Clark Ashton (1893–1961). *Complete Poetry and Translations: Volume 3—The Flowers of Evil and Others.* Ed. S. T. Joshi and David E. Schultz. New York: Hippocampus Press, 2007.

———. *The Double Shadow and Other Fantasies.* Auburn, CA: Auburn Journal Press, 1933. (*LL* 880)

———. *Ebony and Crystal.* Introduction by George Sterling. Auburn, CA: [Auburn Journal,] 1922. (*LL* 881)

———. *Selected Letters of Clark Ashton Smith.* Ed. David E. Schultz and Scott Connors. Sauk City, WI: Arkham House, 2003.

————, and David H. Keller. *The White Sibyl and Men of Avalon.* Everett, PA: Fantasy Publications, 1934. (*LL* 885)

Snaith, J. C. (1876–1936). *Thus Far.* London: Hodder, 1925. New York: D. Appleton, 1925.

Stapledon, Olaf (1886–1950). *Last and First Men.* London: Methuen, 1930.

Starrett, Vincent (1886–1974). *Arthur Machen: A Novelist of Ecstasy and Sin.* Chicago: Hill, 1918. Also in *Buried Caesars.* Chicago: Covici-McGee, 1923. 1–31.

Stockton, Frank R. (1834–1902). *The Great Stone of Sardis.* New York: Harper & Brothers, 1898.

Stoker, Bram (1847–1912). *Dracula.* London: Constable, 1897. (*LL* 926)

————. *The Jewel of Seven Stars.* London: Heinemann, 1903.

————. *The Lair of the White Worm.* London: Rider, 1911.

————. *The Mystery of the Sea.* London: Heinemann, 1902.

Summers, Montague (1880–1948), ed. *The Supernatural Omnibus.* London: Victor Gollancz, 1931. Garden City, NY: Doubleday, Doran, 1932.

Tasso Torquato (1544–1595). *Godfrey of Bulloigne; or, The Recovery of Jerusalem.* <1580> Done into English Heroical Verse, from the Italian of Tasso, by Edward Fairfax <1624>. 1st American ed. from the 7th London ed. To Which Are Prefixed, an Introductory Essay, by Leigh Hunt, and the Lives of Tasso and Fairfax, by Charles Knight. New-York: Wiley & Putnam, 1845–46. 2 vols. in 1. (*LL* 947)

Thacher, James (1754–1844). *An Essay on Demonology, Ghosts and Apparitions, and Popular Superstitions.* Boston: Carter & Hendee, 1831.

Thomson, Christine Campbell (1897–1985), ed. *By Daylight Only.* London: Selwyn & Blount, 1929. [Contains HPL's "Pickman's Model."] (*LL* 960)

————. *You'll Need a Night Light.* London: Selwyn & Blount, 1927. [Contains HPL's "The Horror at Red Hook."] (*LL* 882)

Thomson, James ("B. V.") (1834–1882). *The City of Dreadful Night.* <1886>

Toksvig, Signe [Kristine] (1891–1983). *The Last Devil.* New York: John Day Co., 1927. (*LL* 973)

Train, Arthur (1875–1945), and R. W. Wood. *The Man Who Rocked the Earth.* New York: Doubleday, Page, 1915.

Trowbridge, W. R. H. (1866–1938). *Cagliostro.* New York: Brentano's, 1910.

Tyson, J. Aubrey. *The Barge of Haunted Lives.* New York: Macmillan, 1923. [First published in *All-Story Magazine,* August 1905 (as "The Harbor of Living Dead").]

Vaughan, Robert Alfred (1823–1857). *Hours with the Mystics: A Contribution to the History of Religious Opinion.* London: Gibbings, 1856.

Verne, Jules (1828–1905). *From the Earth to the Moon.* <1865> (*LL* 995)

————. *Journey to the Centre of the Earth.* <1864>

————. *20,000 Leagues under the Sea.* <1869> (*LL* 996)

Waite, Arthur Edward (1857–1942). *Lives of Alchemystical Philosophers Based on Materials Collected in 1815 and Supplemented by Recent Researches . . . to Which Is Added a Bibliography of Alchemical and Hermetic Philosophy.* London: George Redway, 1888.

Wakefield, H. Russell (1890–1964). *They Return at Evening.* New York: D. Appleton, 1928.

Walpole, Horace (1717–1797). *Jeffery's Edition of the Castle of Otranto, a Gothic Story.* <1764> London: Printed by W. Backader . . . for the Publisher [Edward Jeffery], 1800. (*LL* 1007)

Walpole, Hugh (1884–1941). *Portrait of a Man with Red Hair.* London: Macmillan, 1925.

Webster, J. Provand. *The Oracle of Baal: A Narrative of Some Curious Events in the Life of Professor Horatio Charmichael, M.A.* Philadelphia: J. B. Lippincott Co., 1896. (*LL* 1019)

Weird Tales: English [Scottish, Irish, American, German]. London: William Paterson, [1888]. 5 vols.

Wells, H. G. (1866–1946). *The Country of the Blind and Other Stories.* London: Nelson, 1911.

———. *The Food of the Gods.* London: Collins, 1923.

———. *The First Men in the Moon.* London: Newnes, 1901. (*LL* 1027)

———. *In the Days of the Comet.* New York: Doran, 1906.

———. *The Island of Dr. Moreau.* London: Heinemann, 1896. New York: Stone & Kimball, 1896. *Amazing Stories* (October & November 1926).

———. *Men Like Gods.* New York: Macmillan, 1923.

———. *The Sea Lady: A Tissue of Moonshine.* New York: D. Appleton, 1902.

———. *Tales of Space and Time.* London: Harper & Brothers, 1899.

———. *Thirty Strange Stories.* New York: Harper & Brothers, 1897.

———. *The Time Machine and Other Stories.* New York: Hold, 1895. London: William Heinemann, 1896.

———. *The War in the Air.* New York: Harper & Brothers, 1908.

———. *The War of the Worlds.* New York: Harper & Brothers, 1898.

———. *When the Sleeper Wakes.* New York: Harper & Brothers, 1899.

———. *The Wonderful Visit.* New York: E. P. Dutton, 1898.

———. *The World Set Free.* New York: E. P. Dutton, 1914.

Wells, H. G.; Huxley, Julian (1887–1975); and Wells, G. P. (1901–1985). *The Science of Life: A Summary of Contemporary Knowledge about Life and Its Possibilities.* London: Amalgamated Press, 1929–30. 3 vols.

Werfel, Franz (1890–1945). *Goat Song.* Tr. Ruth Langner. Garden City, NY: Doubleday, Page, 1928.

Whittier, John Greenleaf (1807–1892). *The Poetical Works of John Greenleaf Whittier.* Boston: Houghton Mifflin, 1887. (*LL* 1048)

Wilde, Oscar (1854–1900). *The Picture of Dorian Gray.* <1890> New York: Boni & Liveright (Modern Library), 1918. (*LL* 1049)

Williams, Harper (pseud. of Margery Williams Blanco, 1881–1944). *The Thing in the Woods*. <1913> New York: Robert M. McBride, 1924.

Wittie, Robert (1613?–1684). *ΟΥΡΟΝΟΣΚΟΠΙΑ; or, A Survey of the Heavens: A Plain Description of the Admirable Fabrick and Motions of the Heavenly Bodies. To Which Is Added the Gout-Raptures, Augmented & Improved. In Englishe, Latine, and Greek Lyrick Verse*. London: Printed by J. M. for the Author, 1681. (*LL* 1062)

Yardley, Edward. *The Supernatural in Romantic Fiction*. London: Longmans, Green, 1880.

Index

www.ingramcontent.com/pod-product-compliance
Lightning Source LLC
Chambersburg PA
CBHW070352030726
47504CB00001B/156